P9-BHS-087

THE ROUGH GUIDE TO
TAIWAN

WITHDRAWN

This fourth edition updated by
Thomas Bird, Simon Foster, Stephen Keeling and
Martin Zatko

**ROUGH
GUIDES**

Contents

Introduction to
Taiwan

Taiwan remains largely undiscovered and seriously underrated by Western travellers, but those that make it here are in for a real treat. Modern Taiwan – an eclectic mix of Chinese, Western, Japanese and indigenous cultural influences – has given us everything from Ang Lee, Jay Chou and Mandopop to Acer computers, Giant bikes, instant noodles, General Tsou's chicken and the global bubble tea phenomenon. Yet first-time visitors should expect some real surprises, beginning with mesmerizing scenery: though cities such as Taipei, Taichung and Kaoshiung are enticing cultural hubs, Taiwan is above all a land of mountains, tranquil forests, whitewater rapids and rustic hot-spring resorts.

Packed onto this small island are the mighty **central ranges**, the wild, beautiful **beaches** and gnarly surf breaks of the east coast, the giant **cypress trees** of Alishan and the plunging **waterfalls** of Shifen and Wufengchi. You can sample tasty snacks at Taipei's **night markets**, go **windsurfing** in Penghu, laze on Kenting's tropical **beaches**, soak in the saltwater **hot springs** of Green Island, **hike** up Taroko Gorge and explore the lavish Taoist **temples** of Tainan. Or you could plan a trip that takes in striking **Chinese and aboriginal celebrations**, from the Dajia Mazu Pilgrimage and Tsou Mayasvi Festival to the "beehive" fireworks of Yanshui and "heavenly lanterns" of Pingxi.

One of the island's most endearing qualities is the overwhelming **friendliness** of its people – Taiwan is one of the most welcoming countries in the world and you are bound to encounter numerous acts of generosity or kindness, whether it's a taxi driver rounding down a fare, a stranger helping with directions or a family providing a bed for the night. **Eating** in Taiwan comes a close second, with everything from Imperial-style Chinese banquets served in ornate restaurants to the oyster omelettes and sumptuous beef noodles cooked up quickly at street stalls. **Travelling** around the island is relatively straightforward, though the lack of English speakers can be a

ABOVE GOLDEN WISHING BELL

FACT FILE

- Taiwan's 23 million people enjoy the world's nineteenth largest **GDP** (PPP) per capita in the world, while only Brunei, Hong Kong, Singapore and Macau are higher in Asia.

- Despite the "Taiwan Miracle", **prices** are generally lower than in other developed nations.

- No country has more **7-Eleven** stores per person than Taiwan – over five thousand in total.

- Taiwan's national sport is **baseball**; it actually holds the most Little League World Series titles (seventeen as of 2014).

- At 222nd place, Taiwan has one of the lowest **birth rates** in the world (although Macau and Singapore are even lower).

- **Yuan T. Lee** is Taiwan's only **Nobel Prize winner** – he won the prize for chemistry in 1986.

- "Chinese Taipei" has won a total of 24 **Olympic medals** (including three golds).

- The best-known Taiwanese **celebrity** internationally is Oscar-winning director **Ang Lee**, though Mandopop singers such as Jolin Tsai and Jay Chou are wildly popular in Asia.

- **Yushan** (3952m), the highest peak in Taiwan, is also the highest mountain in the western Pacific region outside of the Kamchatka Peninsula. It is even higher than Japan's famous Mount Fuji (3776m).

- The most popular **surname** in Taiwan is **Chen** (陳), at around 12 percent of the population, followed by Lin (林) and Huang (黃).

challenge at times, particularly as most timetables tend to be displayed solely in Chinese – but the willingness to help from almost everyone you meet means it's practically impossible to get stuck.

Where to go

Most visits to Taiwan begin in **Taipei**, the capital and largest city, home to the Taipei 101 skyscraper, the National Palace Museum and some of the island's best restaurants, bars and night markets. It promises a host of worthy day-trips too, including the cable car to the teahouses of Maokong, the hot springs at **Beitou** and the volcanic peaks of **Yangmingshan National Park**. The storm-battered **North Coast and Guanyinshan National Scenic Area** is a short ride away, as is the picturesque **Pingxi Branch Line Railway**. Also nearby, the old mining towns of **Jinguashi** and **Jiufen** are deservedly popular for their historic streets and teahouses, while the **Northeast and Yilan Coast National Scenic Area** contains some of the most rugged coastline on the island. Southwest of Taipei, **Hsinchu** makes a fine base for trips to **Hakka country**, the primary home of Taiwan's small but influential Hakka minority, while **Shei-Pa National Park** provides an opportunity to tackle some of Taiwan's largest and most memorable peaks.

Central Taiwan is home to some spectacular scenery, though it pays to spend a couple of days in vibrant **Taichung**, renowned for its teahouses and lively nightlife. Not far from the city, **Changhua** is noted principally for its Great Buddha Statue, while atmospheric **Lugang** is celebrated for its craftsmen and classical architecture. East of Taichung, picture-perfect **Sun Moon Lake** makes a stunning introduction to Taiwan's mighty central ranges. Just outside Puli, to the north of the lake, **Chung Tai Chan Monastery** is a man-made wonder, a remarkable blend of modern architecture and Zen Buddhism. Heading south, **Chiayi** provides a

OPPOSITE FROM TOP RAOHE STREET NIGHT MARKET, TAIPEI; BASALT FISHING FENCE, PENGHU

BETEL NUT BEAUTY

Betel nut, the seed of the betel palm (*Areca catechu*), has almost iconic status in Taiwan, where chewing it is often viewed as stereotypically Hoklo or Taiwanese behaviour. It's also big business: some estimates claim the industry nets annual revenue of around **NT$20 billion**. In Taiwan, it's particularly popular with truck drivers, who prefer its stimulating effects to coffee: the nut is wrapped in *areca* leaf, topped with slaked lime paste and chewed without swallowing. The so-called "**betel nut beauties**" (bīnláng xīshī) are young women – often scantily clad – hired to sell the nuts from glass-encased booths on roadsides all over the island. Ominously, betel nut is a known **carcinogen**: Taiwan has one of the highest rates of mouth and throat cancer in Asia, primarily as a result of chewing the nut.

staging post for the cool valleys and Tsou villages of the **Alishan National Scenic Area**. Beyond this lies **Yushan National Park** and the scintillating hike up Taiwan's highest mountain, commanding awe-inspiring, cloud-capped vistas.

South Taiwan is the most traditional part of the island, with **Tainan** making the obvious introduction to the region, a modern city crammed with historic sights, particularly temples, complemented by superb food. **Kaohsiung** is Taiwan's second city and an earthy counterweight to Taipei, its smattering of sights enhanced by a growing number of parks, outdoor cafés and bars. Nearby is the elegant monastery at **Foguangshan**, while the dramatic **Southern Cross-Island Highway** heads east across the mountains to Taitung, slicing through the northern end of **Maolin National Scenic Area**, rich in Paiwan and Rukai culture. The southern tip of Taiwan is dominated by **Kenting National Park**, with its popular beaches and surf spots.

The **east coast** is a world apart and still home to the greatest concentration of Taiwan's indigenous tribes. Most visitors make for **Taroko National Park**, which has

OPPOSITE FORMOSAN ABORIGINAL CULTURAL VILLAGE

spectacular Taroko Gorge at its heart, with its incredibly narrow gaps between lofty walls of stone. **Hualien** is the largest settlement on the east coast and makes the ideal gateway to Taroko, with plenty of opportunities to sample its tasty dumplings and sweet-filled rice cakes. From here there are two routes south: the **East Rift Valley** is noted for its hot springs and rafting on the Xiuguluan River, while the **coastal road** twists past isolated beaches and Amis villages. Both end up at the laidback town of **Taitung**, location of the National Museum of Prehistory and base for trips to **Ludao** (Green Island) with its exceptional outdoor springs and the more remote Lanyu, celebrated for its indigenous Tao culture.

Taiwan's **offshore islands** have their own distinctive cultures and histories. **Penghu**, in the middle of the Taiwan Strait, is an archipelago of magnificent beaches, old temples, crumbling fishing villages and superb watersports, particularly windsurfing and, increasingly, kitesurfing. Just off the coast of China's Fujian province, the **Matsu Islands** provide a rare taster of traditional northern Fujian culture, as well as Taiwan's recent military history. The theme is continued on **Kinmen**, literally within sight of the now booming mainland city of Xiamen, and rapidly remodelling itself as an open-air museum.

HOT SPRINGS

With over 150 locations scattered all over the island, Taiwan has the world's second-highest concentration of **hot springs** after Japan – many were developed commercially during the Japanese occupation and offer the same quality, scenery and therapeutic effects at a fraction of the cost. Several of the most famous springs are piped directly into hotel rooms and spa pools, where you can sample the waters via **public baths** or private tubs, but there are still places, usually in the mountains, where springs gush naturally from rocks or rivers and can be experienced for free.

When to go

Taiwan has a subtropical monsoon **climate**, with wet, humid summers (May–Oct) and short winters (Dec–Feb) that are relatively mild (though it can snow on the highest peaks). The north tends to be several degrees colder, and a lot wetter, than the tropical south. The **northeast monsoon** lasts about six months, from October to late March, and brings wet weather to Keelung and the northeast side of the island. The **southwest monsoon** starts in May and ends in late September, primarily affecting the south. The latter part of this monsoon season is associated with **typhoons** that batter the east coast and central mountain range, with an average of two to three direct hits a year. That's not the end of the rain, however – the annual "**plum rain**" season (named for the fruit that appears at this time) can bring two months of rain any time between early spring and early summer, affecting the whole island.

In winter, the average monthly **temperature** ranges from 15°C to 20°C across the island, while mid-30s are common in the summer. Temperatures in the high mountains can be substantially lower than on the plains. In general, autumn and winter are the best times to visit, though early summer (May–July) can also be pleasant at higher elevations and in the north, and the high temperatures in midsummer make watersports and beaches far more tempting at this time.

AVERAGE DAILY TEMPERATURES AND MONTHLY RAINFALL

	Jan	Feb	Mar	Apr	May	Jun	Jul	Aug	Sep	Oct	Nov	Dec
TAIPEI												
Max/Min (°C)	19/13	19/14	22/15	26/19	29/22	32/24	34/26	34/26	31/24	28/22	24/19	21/15
rainfall (mm)	87	166	180	183	259	319	248	305	275	139	86	79
TAICHUNG												
Max/Min (°C)	22/12	22/13	25/16	28/19	30/22	32/24	33/25	32/25	32/24	30/21	27/18	24/14
rainfall (mm)	36	88	94	135	225	343	246	317	98	16	18	26
KAOHSIUNG												
Max/Min (°C)	23/15	24/16	27/19	28/22	30/24	32/26	32/26	32/26	31/25	30/24	27/20	25/17
rainfall (mm)	20	24	39	73	177	398	371	426	187	46	13	12
HUALIEN												
Max/Min (°C)	21/15	21/16	23/17	26/20	28/22	30/24	32/25	32/25	30/24	28/22	25/19	22/17
rainfall (mm)	72	100	87	96	195	220	177	261	344	367	171	68

Author picks

Our discerning authors have scoured every inch of the island to bring you some unique experiences: here is a sample of their personal favourites.

Street food Taiwanese "small eats" are justly famed; sample the squid at Keelung Night Market (p.133), fish ball soup in Jiufen (p.138), danzi noodles in Tainan (p.246) and "shrimp monkeys" in Lugang (p.196).

Lavish temples Gems include the gorgeous Tianhou temples in Lugang (p.193) and Magong (p.345); Confucius Temple, Tainan (p.239); and Donglong Temple, Donggang (p.270).

Indigenous Taiwan Meet the Tsou in the Alishan National Scenic Area (p.219), experience Amis culture in Duli (p.310), or learn about aborigine history at the Shung Ye Museum of Formosan Aborigines (p.73) and Taiwan Indigenous People's Culture Park (p.268).

Tip-top teahouses Superb options include Taipei's *Wistaria* (p.92); Maokong's *Yaoyue* (p.92); *Laughtear Chinese* in Taichung (p.187); *Little Six* in Beitou (p.101); and the *Jiufen Teahouse* (p.138).

Cycling the east coast Little-used roads, quality bike rental and an ever-expanding network of trails make cycling the spectacular Pacific coastline a real treat (box, p.308).

Best hikes Conquering mighty Yushan (p.227) comes high on many hikers' wish-lists, but there are countless other rewarding options: the Walami Trail (p.316) offers a glimpse of the little-visited southeastern corner of Yushan National Park, while further to the north, Taroko National Park (p.298) has over a dozen beautiful trails.

Fabulous festivals Traditional festivals are exhilarating and offer rich insights into Taiwan's unbroken cultural legacy. Two to prioritize include Pingxi's Lantern Festival (p.141) and the "beehive" fireworks festival in Yanshui (box, p.250), which both fall early in the Chinese New Year.

> Our author recommendations don't end here. We've flagged up our favourite places – a perfectly sited hotel, an atmospheric café, a special restaurant – throughout the Guide, highlighted with the ★ symbol.

FROM TOP TEAHOUSE, JIUFEN; HIKING IN YUSHAN NATIONAL PARK; TSOU FESTIVAL, ALISHAN

24

things not to miss

It's not possible to see everything Taiwan has to offer in a single trip – and we don't suggest you try. What follows is a selective taste of the island's highlights: vibrant temples and monasteries, exuberant festivals, mouthwatering cuisine and spectacular landscapes. All highlights are colour-coded by chapter and have a page reference to take you straight into the Guide, where you can find out more.

1 TAROKO NATIONAL PARK
Page 298

Taiwan's most visited national park is sliced in half by narrow, deep-cut Taroko Gorge, one of Asia's top natural wonders and an absolute must-see.

2 EAST COAST NATIONAL SCENIC AREA
Page 306

From the north's towering cliffs to the south's expansive beaches, the east coast is a feast for the eyes and a hotbed of aboriginal cultures.

3 HAKKA FOOD
Page 159 & 264

Beipu and Meinong are among the best places to sample Taiwan's Hakka cuisine, from delicious *bantiao* noodles to rich *leicha* ("cereal tea").

4 ABORIGINAL CULTURE
Page 399

Taiwan's indigenous peoples, divided into sixteen officially recognized tribes and several other distinct groups, have their own vibrant cultures quite separate from the Chinese majority.

5 KINMEN
Page 356
This remote island is an absorbing blend of former battlefields and imperial Chinese monuments.

6 HOT SPRINGS
Page 10
From the ultra-hip to the cheap and cheerful, a dip in one of Taiwan's 150 hot springs is a must.

7 KENTING NATIONAL PARK
Page 276
This resort-fringed national park covers Taiwan's southern tip and is a haven of snorkelling and diving.

8 FESTIVALS
Page 35
Take your pick: "beehive" fireworks, "heavenly lanterns", dragon boat races and Ghost Month parades.

9 CHUNG TAI CHAN MONASTERY
Page 209
An enormous Buddhist monastery, packed with artistic gems, elegant shrines and innovative architecture.

10 CROSS-ISLAND HIGHWAYS
Page 149, 212 & 308
The island's rough-hewn, cross-island highways guarantee white-knuckle, heart-stopping rides through the mountains.

11 SUN MOON LAKE
Page 200
A tranquil retreat of nature walks, cool breezes and calming views.

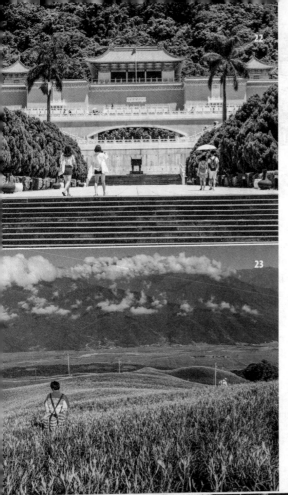

19 TAIPEI 101
Page 76

At 509m, Taiwan's tallest building dominates central Taipei, providing mind-blowing views of the surrounding area.

20 TAINAN
Page 232

The old capital of Taiwan, with its myriad temples, remains an important stronghold of Taiwanese culture.

21 MATSU ISLANDS
Page 372

Just off the coast of mainland China, these isolated islands are bastions of traditional Fujianese architecture, culture and cuisine.

22 NATIONAL PALACE MUSEUM
Page 71

View the former contents of Beijing's Forbidden City in this world-famous museum, an extraordinary collection of Chinese art and historic artefacts.

23 EAST RIFT VALLEY
Page 314

An idyllic landscape of rice paddies, fruit farms and small aboriginal hamlets, backed by two mountain ranges.

24 NIGHT MARKETS
Page 33

Taiwan's night markets are the best – and cheapest – places to try a selection of the island's famous "little eats".

Itineraries

The following itineraries span the entire length of this incredibly diverse island, from its modern cities to the jaw-dropping mountains of the central ranges. You may not be able to cover everything, but each itinerary guarantees rich insights into Taiwan's natural and historic wonders.

CLASSIC TAIWAN

This three-week tour takes in the east and west coasts, travelling from Taipei to Kenting.

❶ Taipei Home to the National Palace Museum, Taipei 101 and the Maokong teahouses – and *Din Tai Fung*'s addictive dumplings. **See p.52**

❷ Jiufen and Jinguashi Visit the historic Japanese mines and gold museum and sample a mind-bending array of "little eats". **See p.134**

❸ Taroko Gorge Taiwan's premier natural attraction offers a slice of Truku culture and the jaw-dropping sea cliffs at Qingshui. **See p.298**

❹ Taichung Cross the mountains to take in the best of Taiwan's tea culture. **See p.174**

❺ Sun Moon Lake Head back into the mountains to explore the temples and Thao culture of Taiwan's most scenic lake. **See p.200**

❻ Alishan National Scenic Area Explore tea plantations and Tsou villages and watch the sunrise over the "sea of clouds". **See p.219**

❼ Tainan Taiwan's historic capital is studded with ancient temples – and is also the best place to eat like an emperor. **See p.232**

❽ Kaohsiung Taiwan's second city boasts excellent seafood and a handful of historic sights, plus the possibility of day-trips to Foguangshan Monastery. **See p.252**

❾ Kenting National Park End your journey at the beach, with shimmering dunes and excellent surfing, diving and hiking. **See p.276**

EAST COAST ADVENTURE

The east coast is Taiwan's most enchanting and undeveloped region. Take up to three weeks for this itinerary, travelling from Hualien to Kenting.

❶ Hualien Start off in this laidback ocean city, home to Tzu Chi and *muaji* cakes. **See p.288**

❷ Hiking Taroko Gorge Get off the beaten path at Taroko with a hike along the challenging Lianhua Trail. **See p.303**

❸ Ruisui Hot Springs Head south to Ruisui in the East Rift Valley for some of Taiwan's most relaxing hot-spring pools. **See p.315**

❹ Amis Culture Return to the east coast, the ancestral home of the Amis tribe, and visit the Amis Folk Center in Duli. **See p.312**

❺ Donghe Make a stop at this sleepy Amis village to sample its celebrated Donghe *baozi* (steamed pork buns). **See p.310**

❻ Beinan Cultural Park Get a handle on Taiwan's Neolithic past at this fascinating archeological site. **See p.321**

❼ Ludao Take the ferry over to "Green Island" to snorkel, dive, or just lounge in its saltwater hot springs. **See p.325**

ABOVE FORMOSA BOULEVARD MRT STATION, KAOHSIUNG

❽ Lanyu This remote, beguiling island is home of the semi-subterranean houses and painted wooden canoes of the Tao people. **See p.331**

❾ Kenting National Park Rent a scooter and explore this park's wilder corners, from Baisha Bay to the Jiupengsha Dunes. **See p.276**

CULTURAL TAIWAN

Taiwan is a bastion of Chinese culture. This two-week tour takes in the best of its temples, museums, teahouses and old towns.

❶ Taipei Soak up ancient Chinese culture at the National Palace Museum, Longshan and Baoan temples and the *Wistaria Teahouse*. **See p.52**

❷ Pingxi Branch Rail Line Take the train to see historic mining towns, Japanese teahouses and a release of "heavenly lanterns". **See p.138**

❸ Sanxia Another easy day-trip from Taipei, Sanxia is home to revered Zushi Temple and a major Hakka museum. **See p.114**

❹ Beipu Head south to this small town near Hsinchu, the premier Hakka centre in the north, especially famed for its classical architecture, persimmon cakes and "cereal tea". **See p.159**

❺ Lugang Taiwan's most traditionally Chinese city boasts master woodcarvers, lantern makers and painters of Chinese fans. **See p.192**

❻ Tainan The former Dutch colony and base of Koxinga, the celebrated Ming dynasty general, is steeped in Chinese tradition. **See p.232**

❼ Meinong The centre of Hakka culture in the south specializes in Hakka food and blue clothing, but also traditional Chinese oil-paper parasols. **See p.264**

❽ Penghu Take a ferry to this island chain in the Taiwan Strait for the Qing dynasty forts, Twin Hearts Stone Weir and Erkan Traditional Village. **See p.340**

❾ Kinmen End your journey just off the coast of China at this island rich in traditional Fujianese culture dating back thousands of years. **See p.356**

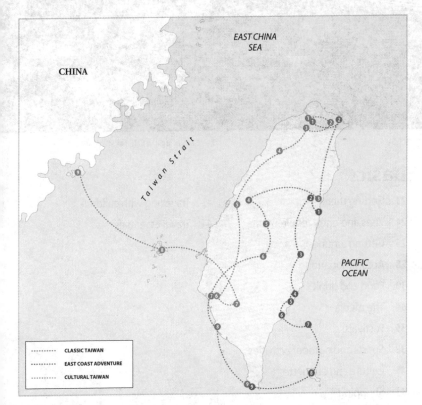

TRAIN IN ALISHAN NATIONAL SCENIC AREA

Basics

Getting there

Taiwan's main international gateway is Taiwan Taoyuan International Airport, located near the city of Taoyuan, about 50km southwest of the capital Taipei. The only other major international airport is at Kaohsiung, serving the country's second-largest city.

Although there are several nonstop flights to Taipei from North America and Europe, most trips will require a change of aircraft somewhere in Asia – **Hong Kong** is the closest and most convenient place, with dozens of regional carriers flying into Taipei and Kaohsiung daily. Numerous nonstop flights also operate between Taiwan and mainland Chinese cities such as Beijing, Shanghai and Guangzhou.

Flights from the UK and Ireland

There is a dearth of direct air connections between the **UK** and Taiwan, and the same is true from **Ireland** and continental Europe. Almost all travellers coming from Europe will need to make at least one stop, typically in Hong Kong or Bangkok.

China Airlines fly from London to Taipei via Amsterdam five days a week (16hr) for about £700–1000 return in peak season; they also fly to Taipei nonstop from Vienna and Frankfurt. EVA Air flies to Taipei from London via Bangkok for about the same price. From Ireland, you'll save money by taking a budget airline to London and connecting with one of the flights mentioned above.

Flights from the US and Canada

There are several daily flights to Taiwan from North American cities on both coasts. From the **US**, direct flights leave from Los Angeles, New York, Seattle and San Francisco, with the average return fare around US$1100–1300, depending on the time of year. Most nonstop flights from Canada operate out of Vancouver, but EVA Air also flies from Toronto once daily from Can$1600.

From Australia, New Zealand and South Africa

Almost all flights between **Australia** and Taiwan have a stopover somewhere else in Asia, with **Hong Kong** the best connected. Some of the cheapest fares to Hong Kong from Sydney are with Cathay Pacific. China Airlines has four weekly nonstop flights between **Sydney** and Taipei (9hr 45min) for

about Aus$1700 return and also fly nonstop from Brisbane four times weekly for about the same price. EVA Air flies to Taipei direct from Brisbane only, five times a week.

Flights from **New Zealand** are more limited, with carriers such as Air New Zealand, Cathay Pacific and Singapore Airlines flying from Auckland to Taipei via Hong Kong for around NZ$1500.

From China

With the "three links" now open to foreigners, direct air and sea travel between Taiwan and **China** offers some intriguing travel opportunities. **Flights** between Taipei and Beijing (3hr 15min) are served by several carriers, with tickets for around US$500 return or less, but you can also reach Shanghai (just 1hr 55min), Guangzhou (2hr) and numerous other Chinese cities nonstop. The primary **sea routes** are Fuzhou to Matsu (see p.374) and Xiamen to Kinmen (see p.358). If travelling to China from Taiwan, arrange a **Chinese visa** in Hong Kong or in your own country in advance – it's a lot of hassle to get one in Taiwan, as there are no Chinese consulates.

AIRLINES

Air Canada ⓦ aircanada.com.
Air France ⓦ airfrance.com.
Air New Zealand ⓦ airnewzealand.com.
All Nippon Airways (ANA) ⓦ anaskyweb.com.
American Airlines ⓦ aa.com.
British Airways ⓦ ba.com.
Cathay Pacific ⓦ cathaypacific.com.
Cebu Pacific Air ⓦ cebupacificair.com.
China Airlines ⓦ china-airlines.com.
Delta ⓦ delta.com.
EVA Air ⓦ evaair.com.
Emirates ⓦ emirates.com.
Finnair ⓦ finnair.com.
Hainan Airlines ⓦ hainanairlines.com.
Hong Kong Airlines ⓦ hongkongairlines.com.
JAL (Japan Air Lines) ⓦ jal.com.
Jetstar Airways ⓦ jetstar.com.
KLM (Royal Dutch Airlines) ⓦ klm.com.
Korean Air ⓦ koreanair.com.
Lufthansa ⓦ lufthansa.com.
Malaysia Airlines ⓦ malaysiaairlines.com.
Philippine Airlines ⓦ philippineairlines.com.
Qantas ⓦ qantas.com.
Royal Brunei ⓦ flyroyalbrunei.com.
Singapore Airlines ⓦ singaporeair.com.
South African Airways ⓦ flysaa.com.
Thai Airways ⓦ thaiair.com.
Tigerair ⓦ tigerair.com.

Turkish Airlines Ⓦ turkishairlines.com.
United Airlines Ⓦ united.com.
Xiamen Air Ⓦ www.xiamenair.com.

AGENTS AND OPERATORS

Absolute Asia Ⓣ 212 627 1950, Ⓦ absoluteasia.com. Features several country-wide luxury tours ranging from four to nine days.

Bamboo Trails Ⓣ 886 89 851 835, Ⓦ bambootrails.com. Based on Taiwan's East Coast, this foreign-run Taiwan specialist offers interesting and insightful professionally led tours to all corners of the island.

Goway Travel Experiences Ⓣ 1800 387 8850 or Ⓣ 416 322 1034, Ⓦ goway.com. Two- to eight-day tours of all the main sights: Taipei, Taroko Gorge, Sun Moon Lake and Kenting.

Greentours UK Ⓣ 01298 83563, Ⓦ greentours.co.uk. Offers excellent eighteen-day expeditions by bus and on foot through central Taiwan and Lanyu Island, with a focus on flora and fauna, for around £4795.

North South Travel UK Ⓣ 01245 608 291, Ⓦ northsouthtravel .co.uk. Friendly, competitively priced travel agency, offering discounted fares worldwide. Profits are used to support projects in the developing world, especially the promotion of sustainable tourism.

STA Travel Australia Ⓣ 134 782, New Zealand Ⓣ 0800 474 400, South Africa Ⓣ 0861 781 781, UK Ⓣ 0333 321 0099, US Ⓣ 800 781 4040; Ⓦ statravel.com. Worldwide specialists in independent travel; also student IDs, travel insurance, car rental, rail passes and more. Good discounts for students, under-31s and teachers.

Trailfinders Ireland Ⓣ 01 677 7888, UK Ⓣ 020 7368 1200; Ⓦ trailfinders.com. One of the best-informed and most efficient agents for independent travellers.

Wings Ⓣ 520 320 9868 or Ⓣ 866 547 9868, Ⓦ wingsbirds.com. Specialists in birdwatching tours that cover most of Taiwan.

Visas and entry requirements

Nationals of the UK, Ireland, US, Canada, Australia, New Zealand and South Africa do not require a visa for stays of up to ninety days. This **visa-free period** is for travel only – working is not permitted – and it cannot be extended under any circumstances. Citizens of these countries must have a passport valid for at least six months from the date of entry, a return or onward air ticket and no criminal record. For longer stays and other nationalities you can check information on various visa requirements at the Taiwanese legation in your home country, or at Ⓦ www.boca.gov.tw. The site also outlines the procedures for changes of visa status, such as from student to resident.

Embassies and consulates

Due to the pressures of the "**One China Policy**", only twenty countries (mostly small Pacific island and South American states) have full diplomatic relations with Taiwan under its official name – Republic of China. These states have proper embassies in Taipei, and likewise Taiwan has full missions in their capitals under the ROC name. Most other countries are represented in Taipei by an "economic and cultural" or "representative" office. Despite such names, however, these offices provide the same services as all other embassies and consulates.

Similarly, Taiwan is represented in most countries by **consular, information and trade offices**, but adding to the confusion is the fact that most don't have "Taiwan" or "Republic of China" in their names; caving in to pressure from the PRC, most countries insist that something such as "Taipei" is used instead.

TAIWANESE FOREIGN LEGATIONS

Australia Taipei Economic & Cultural Office Ⓦ teco.org.au; Unit 8, 40 Blackall St, Barton, ACT 2600, Canberra (Ⓣ 02 6120 2000); Level 46, 80 Collins St, Melbourne, VIC 3000 (Ⓣ 03 9650 8611); Suite 1902, Level 19, MLC Centre, King St, Sydney, NSW 2000 (Ⓣ 02 9223 3233).

Canada Taipei Economic and Cultural Office Ⓦ taiwanembassy. org/ca; 151 Yonge St, Suite 501, Toronto, ON M5C 2W7 (Ⓣ 416 369 9030); Suite 2200, PO Box 11522, 650 West Georgia St, Vancouver, BC V6B 4N7 (Ⓣ 604 689 4111).

Hong Kong Kwang Hwa Information and Culture Centre, Suite 4907, 49F Central Plaza, 18 Harbour Rd, Wan Chai (Ⓣ 852 2523 5555, Ⓦ taiwanculture-hk.org).

Ireland Taipei Representative Office, 8 Lower Hatch St, Dublin 2 (Ⓣ 01 678 5413, Ⓦ roc-taiwan.org/ie).

New Zealand Taipei Economic & Cultural Office. Level 21, 105 The Terrace, Wellington (Ⓣ 04 473 6474); Level 18, 120 Albert St, Auckland (Ⓣ 09 303 3903, Ⓦ roc-taiwan.org/nz).

Singapore Taipei Representative Office, 460 Alexandra Rd, 23-00 PSA Bldg 119963 (Ⓣ 65 6500 0100, Ⓦ roc-taiwan.org/sg).

South Africa Taipei Liaison Office Ⓦ roc-taiwan.org/za; 1147 Schoeman St, Hatfield, Pretoria (Ⓣ 012 430 6071); 1004, 10/F, Main Tower, Standard Bank Centre, Hertzog Blvd, Foreshore, Cape Town (Ⓣ 021 418 1188).

UK Taipei Representative Office Ⓦ roc-taiwan.org/uk; 50 Grosvenor Gardens, London SW1W 0EB, England (Ⓣ 020 7881 2650); 1 Melville St, Edinburgh EH3 7PE, Scotland (Ⓣ 0131 220 6886).

US Taipei Economic & Cultural Representative Office Ⓦ roc-taiwan.org/us; 4201 Wisconsin Ave, NW, Washington DC 20016 (Ⓣ 202 895 1800); 55 West Wacker Drive, Suite 1200, Chicago, IL 60601 (Ⓣ 312 616 0100); 3731 Wilshire Blvd, Suite 780, Los Angeles, CA 90010 (Ⓣ 213 389 1215); 1 East 42nd St, 4/F, New York, NY 10017 (Ⓣ 212 486 0088); other offices in Atlanta, Boston, Guam, Houston, Kansas, Miami, San Francisco and Seattle.

Getting around

Getting around in Taiwan can be ultra-convenient or infinitely frustrating, depending on where you are and the weather. Efficient trains, a vast network of buses and a plethora of domestic flights are available, while ferries connect the offshore islands.

While the mountains that bisect the island make for some convoluted travel logistics, for most travellers the biggest challenge comes down to **language**. Though signs in English – or at least in romanized script – are becoming more common, it still takes some planning to make your connections if you don't speak or read Chinese. One of the best ways around this is to ask someone to **write down** the name of your destination in Chinese so that you can show it to clerks in bus and train stations. Likewise, it can pay to have the name of your hotel and the sites you wish to visit written in Chinese in case you get lost.

By train

Almost all major cities and towns in Taiwan are connected by the efficient Taiwan Railway Administration (TRA) network of local and express trains, though travel in Taiwan was revolutionized with the opening of the separately managed **High-Speed Rail** (**HSR**) in 2007. While regular express trains can take over five hours between Taipei and Kaohsiung, it takes just one and a half hours via HSR. The latter only covers major cities on the west coast however,

---

while TRA trains run on both the **western** and **eastern** rail lines for about half the price of the high-speed trains. The TRA also maintains several slower, narrow-gauge **branch lines** that mostly transport tourists inland to Jiji (see p.197), Neiwan and Pingxi (see p.138).

Updated **timetable** and fare information is listed on the **Taiwan Railway Passenger Train Timetable**, which can be found at train station information centres, as well as some convenience stores and kiosks. To check schedules online or make bookings in advance, check the TRA's website at ⓦrailway.gov.tw.

Buying tickets

Train stations usually have separate **queues** for advance and same-day departures, as well as for cash and credit card purchases – this is usually labelled in English on the cashier's window. For shuttle journeys from main stations it's faster to use the **ticket machines** that are labelled in English. It's imperative that you **retain your ticket** when you get off the train, as you're still required to return it at the gate to exit the train station – if you lose it, you might have to pay a fine.

There are five classes of train, from express to local services. For the three fastest classes, it's often a good idea to buy your ticket **in advance** (either online or at the station), especially if you plan to travel on a weekend or public holiday, when all seats are commonly full. When no seats are available, you'll usually still be offered a ticket on all but the Taroko and Puyuma expresses. If you do have a standing-room-only ticket but manage to find a free seat, it's acceptable to sit there until the ticket holder turns up and politely asks you to vacate.

Train classes

Note that Taiwan's penchant for different forms of *pinyin* is perfectly illustrated by the rail system, with station names and even train classes written in a variety of styles. In this guide Hànyǔ Pīnyīn (see p.419) is the default, in line with government policy.
自強; Zìqiáng (usually written as Tze-Chiang). The fastest class of trains, which includes Taroko (太魯閣; tàilǔgé) and Puyuma Express trains (普悠瑪; pǔyōumǎ). All feature assigned seating, a/c and, in some cases, a dining car. No standing passengers allowed.
莒光; Jǔguāng (sometimes written as Chu-Kuang). The second fastest, also with assigned seating and a/c.
復興; Fùxīng (sometimes written as Fu-Hsing or Fusing). The third fastest, also with assigned seating. Has a/c but is not as comfortable as the higher classes.
普快車; "Local Express" (pǔ kuàichē). Short- to

DISTANCE CHART

The figures shown on this chart represent the total distances **in kilometres** between major cities in Taiwan. They are calculated on the shortest available route by **major road**, rather than as the crow flies.

	Changhua	Chiayi	Hsiunchu	Hualien	Kaohsiung	Keelung	Taichung	Tainan	Taipei	Taitung
Changhua	–	75	103	349	176	198	19	129	173	343
Chiayi	75	–	169	420	114	264	98	63	250	262
Hsinchu	103	169	–	249	272	95	84	232	70	443
Hualien	349	420	249	–	344	177	332	373	174	166
Kaohsiung	176	114	272	344	–	373	200	45	353	170
Keelung	198	264	95	177	373	–	179	327	25	343
Taichung	19	98	84	332	200	179	–	148	154	362
Tainan	129	63	232	373	45	327	148	–	302	217
Taipei	173	250	70	174	353	25	154	302	–	341
Taitung	343	262	443	166	170	343	362	217	341	–

medium-distance commuter train. Has a/c but no assigned seating.
區間車; "Local Train" (qūjiānchē). Short- to medium-distance commuter, which stops at all stations. A/c but no assigned seating.

Rail passes

Travellers with a valid International Student Identity Card (ISIC), or a Taiwan Youth Travel Card (YTC) can apply for a **Taiwan Rail Pass (TR Pass)** at all major train stations. Passes cost NT$599 for five days, NT$799 for seven days, and NT$1098 for ten days. If you intend to travel a lot this can be a good deal, though the catch is that the pass is only valid on non-reserved seats on jǔguāng or commuter trains, not zìqiáng or HSR.

Anyone can buy a **Taiwan Rail Card**, available in denominations of NT$1000 and NT$500, and which gives a ten percent discount on regular fares.

High-Speed Rail

Taiwan's superb **High-Speed Rail (HSR**; 台灣高鐵; táiwān gāotiě; @thsrc.com.tw) has cut the travelling times between Taipei and Kaohsiung by two-thirds. The train, one of the world's fastest, stops at twelve stations along a 349km track travelling at an average speed of about 300kmph. Note however, that apart from Taipei, most of the specially built stations are well outside city centres and mean an additional shuttle leg for travellers looking to stay in the heart of major cities. There are now stations at: Nangang, Taipei, Banqiao, Taoyuan, Hsinchu, Miaoli, Taichung, Changhua, Yunlin, Chiayi, Tainan and Zuoying (Kaohsiung). Various multi-day passes are available, which can present quite a saving if you plan to travel a lot on the HSR within a short space of time. The three-day pass costs NT$2200 and offers unlimited HSR travel during this period, but can only be bought by foreigners who will be in the country for less than six months, and it can only be purchased from selected agents (see @thsrc.com.tw for more details).

SAMPLE TRAIN FARES

Taipei–Hualien zìqiáng NT$440; jǔguāng NT$340.
Taipei–Kaohsiung (HSR to Zuoying) NT$1490; zìqiáng NT$843; jǔguāng NT$650.
Taipei–Taichung (HSR) NT$700; zìqiáng NT$375; jǔguāng NT$289.
Taipei–Tainan (HSR) NT$1350; zìqiáng NT$738; jǔguāng NT$569.
Taipei–Taitung zìqiáng NT$783; jǔguāng NT$604.
Kaohsiung–Taitung zìqiáng NT$362; jǔguāng NT$279.

By bus

Buses are generally cheaper than trains, and, with the exception of the HSR, can be much faster – provided you travel when traffic is light. In addition, the best bus companies have extremely comfortable air-conditioned coaches, with big cosy armchair-style seats, movies and an onboard toilet.

Bear in mind that the air conditioning is never turned off, so it can get chilly on board.

However, buses in **rural areas** are being dropped each year, as more Taiwanese tourists take to the roads in their own cars or on coach tours. For independent travellers, this makes already hard-to-reach mountain areas even more difficult to get to without your own transport.

In most cities, bus company **offices** are clustered around the train station, and their buses usually stop right outside the office. Be sure to save your ticket, as you are often required to return it to the driver before disembarking.

SAMPLE BUS FARES

City buses NT$10–20/sector.
Taipei–Alishan NT$620.
Taipei–Kaohsiung NT$435–817.
Taipei–Sun Moon Lake NT$470.
Taipei–Taichung NT$250–385.
Taipei–Tainan NT$350.
Chiayi–Alishan NT$230.
Kaohsiung–Meinong NT$136.
Kaohsiung–Kenting NT$334.

BUS COMPANIES

Aloha Bus ☏ 0800 043168, ⓦ aloha168.com.tw.
Free Go Bus ☏ 0800 051519, ⓦ setter.southeastbus.com.
Ho-Hsin Bus ☏ 0800 002377, ⓦ ebus.com.tw.
Kuo Kuang ☏ 0800 010138, ⓦ kingbus.com.tw.
Taoyuan Bus Corp ☏ 0800 053808, ⓦ www.tybus.com.tw.
Ubus ☏ 0800 241560, ⓦ ubus.com.tw.

By car

In more remote areas such as the cross-island highway routes and segments of the east coast,

TAIWAN TOURS

The **Taiwan Tour Bus** programme is an umbrella for a variety of guided bus tours, usually no longer than one day, and originating in several major cities. Organized by the Tourism Bureau through local tour operators, there's a huge variety of itineraries – these can be useful for those short of time, or for visiting places difficult to reach with public transport. **Prices** range from NT$1100 for half-day tours of Taipei to NT$1988 for day-trips to Taroko. You must reserve in advance; check ⓦ www. taiwantourbus.com.tw for more details.

hiring a car can be the most convenient way to get around. Driving in major cities can be stressful for inexperienced drivers, but anyone used to driving in big cities should find it manageable. Taiwanese drive on the right-hand side of the road, and the highway speed limit is 110kmph. On other roads, speed limits range from 50 to 70kmph – speed cameras and speed traps are common.

Foreign tourists renting a car in Taiwan will need an **international driver's licence** and **passport** for rentals of up to thirty days (you need a local licence for longer). **Prices** vary depending upon location, time of the week and the type of vehicle, but in general full-day rentals start from around NT$1800 with discounts of up to thirty percent usually given for multi-day rentals (except during public holidays). Rental prices commonly include insurance, but you may have to sign a blank credit-card voucher to cover speeding fines.

CAR RENTAL AGENCIES

Car-Plus ☏ 0800 222 568, ⓦ car-plus.com.tw.
Chailease Auto Rental ☏ 0800 588 508, ⓦ rentalcar.com.tw.
Hotai Leasing Corp ☏ 0800 024 550, ⓦ easyrent.com.tw.
Nice Rent A Car ☏ 0800 200 414, ⓦ www.nicecar.com.tw.
VIP Car Rental ☏ 02 2713 1111, ⓦ www.vipcar.com.tw.

TAXIS

Yellow **taxis** are widely available in towns and cities and are most easily secured by flagging one down on the street. Drivers should always use the meter for short journeys (flagfall typically NT$80), but can also be chartered for half- and full-day trips.

Uber was banned in Taiwan in 2017, but has since made a partial return in Taipei only, though just for licensed commercial drivers.

By scooter

The humble **scooter** remains the transport of choice in Taiwan, and is certainly the most convenient way to explore smaller cities and far-flung areas with little or no public transport. However, while renting a scooter is easy for Taiwanese or permanent residents, it's increasingly difficult for foreign visitors.

The main problem is that the shops that rent the scooters are responsible for any fines you may incur. Most scooter shops are family operations that are not able to chase foreigners overseas to get them to pay them back for these fines. Until the law is changed, many shops insist on seeing a valid **ARC** (**Alien Resident Certificate**), proof of permanent address in Taiwan and a local licence. Many shops seem unaware that foreigners can legally drive a

50cc scooter with an **international driver's licence**, though as private operators they are not obliged to do business with you in any case.

Having said that, there are several popular tourist spots where you can easily rent scooters – Little Liuqiu Island and Sanyi for example – by simply leaving your passport as security, and in others, you may be able to get locals to help you (this usually means your friendly homestay/hotel owner "guaranteeing" the rental). The average scooter rental is about NT$300–600 per day.

Another increasingly popular option at tourist hotspots is to rent an **electric scooter**, which is better for the environment, and does not require any kind of driving licence (although this may be set to change). Electric scooters generally cost a little more than regular scooters (usually NT$400–600/day), but there are no fuel costs, although in popular locations with limited charging stations, running out of charge is a real possibility.

Note that **traffic accidents** – especially those involving scooters – are the leading cause of death and injury to foreigners in Taiwan. The dangers of the country's roads are apparent from the moment you arrive: vehicles of all sizes, from giant buses to cars to scooters, all aggressively jockeying for position with reckless disregard for road rules. In fact, the only practice that seems to be universally accepted is that drivers are only responsible for **what lies ahead**, and monitoring what is happening behind or to one's side is almost completely unheard of. **Drive defensively**, and allow plenty of space between yourself and any vehicles in front of you.

By bike

The use of **bicycles** for short rides, day-trips and full-scale touring is becoming increasingly common across Taiwan, with designated cycle paths being built in tourist destinations and subsidized bike schemes in many cities (ⓦwww.youbike.com.tw in Taipei, ⓦ i.youbike.com.tw/en/f101.php in Taichung and ⓦwww.c-bike.com.tw in Kaohsiung). In places with such paths, bikes – ranging from basic three-speeds (usually NT$100/day) to multispeed mountain bikes (typically NT$200–400/day) – can easily be **rented**. While these rental bicycles are generally well maintained and fine for short rides on paved paths, they're not suited to touring, and those planning on covering longer distances should arrive with their own or buy or rent a higher-quality bike from a shop in a major city. Respected manufacturer **Giant** (ⓦgiant-bicycles.com) rents bicycles with panniers for longer trips, and allows for one-way drop-offs

(between certain destinations). Costs are usually NT$1500 for the first three days and then NT$200 per day thereafter for an entry level touring bike, or from NT$500 per day for a good-quality road bike.

Cycle touring is becoming increasingly popular, particularly along the dramatic East Coast and East Rift Valley (see box, p.308). Supported and self-guided rides are available through Grasshopper Adventures (ⓦgrasshopperadventures.com).

By boat

There are regular **passenger ferries** to Taiwan's **outlying islands**, although in winter many services are scaled back. Ludao (Green Island) and Lanyu (Orchid Island) are easily reached by ferry in good weather, while the Taiwan Strait islands of Little Liuqiu, the Matsu archipelago and the Penghu archipelago are accessible by ferry for much of the year. Ferry details are given in the relevant chapters.

By plane

With HSR offering real competition on the busy west-coast corridor, **flights** between the major cities in Taiwan have been dramatically cut back. Unless you're in a real hurry, flying isn't a great deal unless heading to Taiwan's **outlying islands** (particularly Kinmen, Matsu and Lanyu), when you'll save a lot of time by taking a plane.

Taipei's **Songshan Airport**, just to the north of central Taipei, operates services to many outlying islands, as well as daily flights to the eastern cities, including Hualien and Taitung. In addition, the **airports** in Chiayi, Kaohsiung, Taichung and Tainan operate several domestic routes. Prices are usually set wholesale by the airlines, so there's little point in going to an agent.

DOMESTIC AIRLINES

Daily Air Corp ☎ 02 2712 3995, ⓦ dailyair.com.tw.
Far Eastern Air Transport (FAT Air) ☎ 02 8770 7999, ⓦ www.fat.com.tw.
Mandarin Airlines ☎ 02 412 8008, ⓦ www.mandarin-airlines.com.
Uni Air ☎ 02 2508 6999, ⓦ uniair.com.tw.

Accommodation

Taiwan offers travellers a wide range of accommodation, from Spartan dormitories and weathered white-tile hotels to quaint, family-run homestays and plush five-star resorts.

Few Taiwanese travel alone, so there is a severe shortage of true **single rooms** with one single bed. In most cases, the Taiwanese equivalent is a room with a **queen-sized bed** suitable for most couples – and priced accordingly. A **double room** usually has a king-sized bed and is more expensive still. Some hotels have genuine twins (two single beds), but often the only choice with two separate beds will be a quad (ie. two double beds) and these rooms tend to be around 25–50 percent more expensive than a double.

Hotels

Basic **budget hotel** rooms cost as little as NT$700 per night at off-peak times. At this price, rooms are likely to be a bit tatty and damp, probably with cigarette burns on the furniture and a smell of stale smoke. Still, most of them will have an attached bathroom with shower, TV and phone.

Mid-range hotels usually cost NT$1500–3000, and standards generally vary in accordance with price. At the lower end, rooms are likely to resemble cleaner versions of budget hotels, often with the only difference being that they offer packets of tea and coffee in addition to cable TV. At the higher end, rooms should be clean and comfortable, with big bathtubs and/or shower cubicles, and **breakfast** is often included in the price. You're also more likely to encounter English-speaking staff.

All of the biggest cities, but especially Taipei, have international **five-star hotels** that feature giant beds with fine linen, business centres, fitness rooms, spa and massage services and luxury restaurants. Though discounts are sometimes offered, these hotels generally charge a minimum of NT$4000 for a standard room, and prices are often twice that.

Hot-spring hotels

Hot-spring hotels are all the rage in Taiwan, but standards vary wildly. Those in resorts close to big cities can be expensive, often charging NT$6000+ for rooms with **en-suite spring tubs**, while those further afield can offer the same amenities for half the price.

> **TOP 5 PLACES TO STAY**
> **Ambience Hotel, Taipei** See p.85
> **Butterfly Valley Resort, East Rift Valley**. See p.318
> **The Lalu, Sun Moon Lake** See p.205
> **Makung Traditional Homestay, Magong, Penghu** See p.348
> **Qinbi Holiday Village, Matsu** See p.381

Almost all offer **public pools**, which are free to paying guests and can be used by non-guests for what is usually a nominal fee. Many hot-spring hotels also rent spa rooms for shorter periods for those wishing to bathe in private without staying. Note that the quality of the spring water varies between resorts, and even between hotels at the same resort. In general, the older-looking hotels tend to be disappointing, often only having small bathtubs into which the spring water is piped through the tap. Meanwhile, newer – and considerably more expensive – hotels have been designed with a keener eye for aesthetics, with larger tubs made of marble or with Japanese-style wooden designs, plus a range of aquatherapy jets and sometimes even scented pools.

Homestays

So-called **"homestays"** (mínsù) have sprouted up all over Taiwan, particularly in scenic rural areas, where families have set up bed-and-breakfast-style businesses to take advantage of mounting tourist numbers. However, the nature of these homestays varies dramatically, and many are nothing more than tiny, family-run hotels – plus, **prices** tend to be on a par with mid-range to expensive hotels. Rooms are often in wings that adjoin the owners' houses, and breakfast, though provided, is typically not eaten with the family. However, places advertising themselves as homestays are nearly always clean and friendly, as well as exuding more character than most hotels. We list several homestays in this guide, but new ones are constantly opening, and are often listed on online booking sites. Although many aren't

---

ALTERNATIVE ACCOMMODATION

These days many people book their accommodation online, and while conventional hotels and homestays can be found at sites such as ⓦagoda.com and ⓦbooking.com, **sharing-economy options** can provide a very different perspective on a destination: AirBnB (ⓦairbnb.com), Vacation Rentals by Owner (ⓦvrbo.com) and Tripping (ⓦtripping.com) present everything from farmhouses to luxury villas, and Couchsurfing (ⓦcouchsurfing.com) offers free accommodation along with the chance to meet and spend time with locals (as they host guests).

ACCOMMODATION PRICES

Accommodation prices in Taiwan range from NT$300 for the cheapest dorm bed, through to over NT$10,000 for rooms at the best five-star hotels in big cities and tourist resorts. While rack rates can be alarmingly high, they are only charged during peak times, such as weekends, public holidays and the summer school break (and even then mostly just at beach resorts and the most famous attractions). By far the most expensive time to travel in Taiwan is during **Chinese New Year**, when rack rates can double. Hotels are often full at this time, so you should try to make bookings well in advance. Prices listed in this guide are for the cheapest double room on a weekday (Mon–Thurs & Sun). Unless otherwise mentioned, all accommodation listings have some form of **wi-fi** or internet connection – usually this is in-room, but sometimes only in public areas in cheaper hotels, homestays and hostels.

directly accessible by public transport, most offer **pick-up** services from the nearest train or bus station if you call in advance.

Hostels

Hostels are just about the only accommodation in Taiwan that could accurately be described as budget. **Dormitory** beds cost as little as NT$300 per night, with discounts often doled out for long-term stays. Many hostels also have a few **private rooms**; though invariably small, they can be good value, with some going for as low as NT$500 a night, even in big cities – these tend to be the preferred haunts of newly arrived English teachers, who often rent them on a weekly or monthly basis, so they can be hard to find.

Most hostels in Taiwan are now affiliated with Hostelling International (ⓦ hihostels.com), and will provide discounts to cardholders. The majority of hostels have laundry facilities, wi-fi and common TV rooms; some have communal kitchens.

Camping

Camping is increasingly popular in Taiwan, especially in national scenic and forest recreation areas. If you have your own gear, grass spots generally go for about NT$500–800, while those with raised platforms usually cost about NT$800–1000. Some campsites also offer **rentals**, with tents and sleeping bags and mats provided for around NT$800–1000 – which for groups is undoubtedly some of Taiwan's cheapest accommodation. Almost all of these types of camping areas have adjoining barbecue pits and public showers and toilets.

In **national parks** and other remote areas, camping is often your only option, though there are few designated sites, and low-impact methods are recommended – **campfires** should be forsaken in favour of cooking stoves, for example. As landslips

occur on mountain trails with frightening regularity, care should be taken when choosing where to pitch your tent, especially in rainy weather. The intensity of the island's rain can test the waterproofing of even the most high-end tents, so make sure you bring a tent with a high hydrostatic head (at least 2000mm), particularly if you'll be camping on bare earth (in which case a ground sheet is highly recommended). Taiwan Camping (ⓦ www.taiwancamping.net) is a great resource – the site has a map of the island showing hundreds of campsites, along with contact numbers, prices and reviews.

Food and drink

Taiwan offers a huge variety of cuisines, from Chinese and Taiwanese food to Japanese and indigenous dishes. Choices range from super-cheap night markets and street stalls, to wallet-draining restaurants featuring some of Asia's best chefs. In the major cities there's also plenty of Western food, from smart Italian cafés to all the familiar fast-food chains.

Taiwanese food

Taiwanese cuisine is difficult to define, and best thought of as an umbrella term for a huge variety of dishes and styles. Although Taiwanese cuisine is rooted in **Fujianese** cooking (from southern China), since 1949 many dishes have evolved from specialities originating in other parts of China. In addition, much of what's considered to be Taiwanese food, particularly cakes and desserts, was influenced by the **Japanese** during the occupation period. Being an island, Taiwan is particularly renowned for its **seafood** – **shellfish**, **squid** and **crab** are extremely popular, with **milkfish** a favourite in the south.

One of the classic dishes found all over Taiwan is

sānbēi, "**three cups**", a sumptuous blend of soy sauce, rice wine and sesame oil, seasoned with various spices, added to meat or tofu and usually served in a clay pot. Other national staples are **braised pork rice** (lǔròufàn) and **oyster omelette** (é a jiān). **Shaved ice** (tsuà bīng) **stalls** are another national institution: mounds of ice topped with fruits or traditional sweets such as red bean and sweet taro.

Local specialities

Every region, town and even village in Taiwan seems to have a **speciality**, eagerly dished out by local vendors. Tainan's signature dish is **dānzi mián**, a mixture of pork, noodles and egg or shrimp. **Fish balls** (yúwán) are most associated with Danshui, Kaohsiung (marlin), Tainan (milkfish) and Nanfangao (mahi-mahi). **Rice noodles** (mǐfěn) are noted in Hsinchu, while **Sichuan beef noodles** (niúròu mián) is a dish primarily associated with Taipei. Steamed or deep-fried **meatballs** (gòngwán) are best in Changhua and Hsinchu. **Turkey rice** (huǒ jīròufàn) is a Chiayi innovation while Shenkeng is Taiwan's **tofu** capital. The most infamous tofu dish is chòu dòufǔ, or **stinky tofu**, the smell of which sickens most foreigners but tastes delicious (it's actually fermented tofu cubes deep-fried in pig fat). In fact, Taiwan offers plenty of dishes most Westerners find revolting, including **pig intestines** and lǔ wèi, a mix of tofu and various internal organs of cows or pigs, simmered in a tasty broth and often eaten cold. Try them and you're bound to win the respect of the incredulous Taiwanese sitting next to you.

Hakka food

Hakka food, a type of Chinese cuisine associated with the Hakka people (see box, p.158), has become very popular in Taiwan – restaurants dish up classic favourites in all the major cities. Hakka cuisine is noted for its strong, rich flavours and salty, fatty ingredients, particularly **pork**, traditionally designed to fill hungry agricultural labourers. Favourites include **bǎntiáo** (fried noodles), bamboo shoots, braised stuffed tofu, **kèjiā máshǔ** (glutinous rice cakes rolled in peanuts) and fried pork intestines with ginger – this tastes a lot better than it sounds. One of the major culinary draws at Hakka tourist spots across the island is **léichá** (cereal tea), a tasty, thick blend of nuts and tea leaves.

Indigenous food

Indigenous food differs slightly between tribes, but the main ingredients tend to be the same.

> ## COOKING TOURS
> Taiwan's culinary diversity has attracted attention in recent years, and regularly features on international TV cooking shows. For travellers looking to explore the flavours of the island in depth, there are now a few companies offering **culinary tours** around the island. These tours typically include "master classes" with local chefs, visits to fresh produce markets and agricultural regions, and of course plenty of good food, both à la carte, and "à la street-stall". Bamboo Trails' Taiwan Taste Trail (ⓦ bambootrails.com) is recommended.

Ginger is often in soups and tea, while the most celebrated dish is undoubtedly "**mountain pig**" (shānzhū; wild boar), which is usually roasted. **Millet wine** (xiǎo mǐjiǔ) is mildly alcoholic and served at all times of the day, and **freshwater fish** is also a regular feature of aboriginal meals, served with mountain vegetables such as sweet potato, and bird's nest fern. **Bamboo rice** (zhútǒng fàn; rice cooked in bamboo tubes) is tasty but not really traditional food – rice arrived with Chinese immigrants in the seventeenth century.

Breakfast

Traditional **breakfasts** in Taiwan, particularly in the north and in the cities, follow a modified northern-Chinese style, with common items including dòujiāng (soybean milk), yóutiáo (foot-long dough fritters), dànbǐng (egg pancake), mántóu (steamed bread) and a variety of steamed buns (bāozi). You can usually find small hole-in-the-wall-type places or stalls serving these snacks in every neighbourhood, and while the formica tables and greasy-spoon atmosphere might be off-putting, the food is well worth a try. In south Taiwan, particularly in smaller towns, rice-based dishes are more common, and in Tainan it's not unusual to see people eating large meals of seafood and milkfish to start the day.

Regional Chinese cuisine

China's **regional cuisine** is well represented in restaurants all over Taiwan. The most respected northern school is **Beijing**, with its emphasis on bread, noodles, dumplings and **Beijing duck**, its most famous dish. It's rare to find places specializing in other northern styles: the handful of Shaanxi and

Xinjiang restaurants are not very authentic, though **Mongolian barbecues**, where you roast your own meat and vegetables on griddles placed in the middle of the table, are deservedly popular.

Eastern-style cuisine such as **Shanghainese** food is best known for xiǎolóngbāo or pork dumplings, and is big business in Taiwan; the craze for 1930s-style Shanghai restaurants and food has also made its way to the island, with favourites including eel, freshwater fish with corn and pine nuts (sōngrén yùmǐ), yellow croaker (huángyú) and drunken chicken (zuìjī). Cuisine based on Zhejiang and Jiangsu specialities, including **Hangzhou** food, which also features delicately flavoured freshwater fish, is fairly easy to find.

Southern cuisine is best epitomized by **Cantonese** food, a global favourite with colourful and varied ingredients, but fewer spices than other schools. Often associated with lavish banquet food such as shark's fin soup, **dim sum** (diǎnxīn) and the ubiquitous **roast meat** stalls provide a more affordable option. **Fujianese** food is closely related to Taiwanese; "Buddha Jumps over the Wall" is probably its most lauded (and expensive) dish, a rich stew of rare seafood and meats, but the most authentic seafood dishes are found on Matsu and Kinmen.

Sichuanese food is part of the Western school, the spiciest of all Chinese cuisines, with fiery chilli, black peppercorns and, if you're lucky, huā jiāo (Sichuan flower peppers) added to dishes such as mápó dòufù (a spicy meat and tofu stew), and chicken with peanuts (gōngbǎo jīdīng). Two Taiwanese obsessions are derivatives of Sichuan dishes: **beef noodles** (niúròu miàn) and **hotpot** (huǒguō). The latter has blossomed into a major obsession on the island, with Japanese, Cantonese, Mongolian and spicy hotpot variations; the main difference is the sauces and stock used to flavour

the water. Once you've chosen the sauce, you select your raw ingredients and boil them in a gas-fired cauldron. **Hunan** food, as spicy as Sichuan food but more oily and featuring dishes such as honey ham and minced pork, is not so common and is found primarily in the capital.

Japanese food

Japanese food is common in Taiwan, ranging from traditional, highly expensive restaurants in hotels, to cheap, local derivatives with a decidedly Taiwanese flavour – you'll also see plenty of Japanese snacks such as **onigiri** (sticky rice wrapped in seaweed) in local convenience stores. Japanese food traditionally revolved around **rice**, but today is associated with richer fare, usually involving **seafood**: the best-known is **sashimi** or raw fish, typically served on rice to create **sushi**, which in Taiwan can be very affordable and also sold in most supermarkets. Numerous restaurants specialize in **shabu shabu** (hotpot), curry rice, **ramen**, **soba** or **udon** noodles, **yakitori** (chicken kebabs), **tempura** (battered and deep-fried seafood and vegetables) and **teppanyaki** (stir-fried meat and vegetables).

Western food

The choice of **Western food**, especially in the big cities, continues to improve in Taiwan, but quality varies and many restaurants produce highly localized versions of the original cuisine. Bars and pubs often serve decent staples such as burgers, sandwiches and basic Tex-Mex favourites, while hotels offer more upmarket options. In cities such as Taipei, Taichung, Kaohsiung and Hualien, the choice of **French**, **Italian** and **American-style** food isn't bad, with plenty of expat chefs and talented locals opening restaurants

---

VEGETARIAN FOOD

Vegetarian food has a long history in Chinese culture and, as in China, is primarily associated with Buddhism. At the cheaper end of the scale, vegetarians will find plenty of food at **night markets**: roast corn-on-the-cob and sweet potatoes, tofu, and a huge range of fruits and nuts. Almost every city and town will have cheap **vegetarian buffets** where you can pile as many vegetables on your plate as you like – the price is calculated by weight but is rarely more than NT$200 for a large serving. The larger, more formal vegetarian **restaurants** tend to be Buddhist-inspired (identified by images of Buddha, Guanyin or lotus flowers on the walls). **Chinese vegetarian food** ranges from simple, fresh dishes of green vegetables to more elaborate combinations of herbs, roots and even flowers. One aspect of this might confuse foreign vegetarians, however: tofu and gluten are often cooked to reproduce the textures and flavours of meat (like roast pork). Taiwanese vegetarians, including many Buddhist monks, applaud these culinary skills. It can be hard to find decent non-meat options **in rural areas**, where rice and local vegetables will have to suffice: note that many sauces, even on vegetables, contain shrimp or fish.

– however, prices tend to be higher than local food. Breakfast remains a stumbling block though, and for many Taiwanese a "Western" breakfast comprises fried egg sandwiches, loaded with mayonnaise and spam, or pork hamburgers, sold at cheap roadside stalls and breakfast canteens (*Beautiful & Breakfast* is a nationwide chain). Five-star hotels in the big cities generally offer the best Western breakfasts.

Major **fast-food chains** including *Burger King*, *Domino's Pizza*, *KFC*, *McDonald's*, *Pizza Hut* and *Subway* can be found all over the country. *Starbucks* also has a major presence in Taiwan, and has spawned a large number of local **coffee-shop chains** such as *Dante*, *Donutes* and *85C*, which are invariably cheaper, and sometimes better than their international counterparts.

Other international food

Korean food is gaining popularity on the island, and tends to be a lot more authentic than Southeast Asian cuisine such as **Thai**, which is usually adapted to local tastes and blander than what you'd get in Bangkok. South Asian and **Indian** food, buoyed primarily by a small but growing Pakistani and Bangladeshi expat population, is becoming more available in Taiwan.

Where to eat

Taiwan's **night markets** (yèshì) are the best places to sample local food at budget prices, typically NT$30–50 per dish. They're usually located along streets lined with both permanent shops and temporary **stalls**, though in some cities, a few markets have specially built premises. Things only really get going after 5pm and start to wind down after 11pm, though many stay open till the early hours, especially at weekends. Language is not a problem – just point and get stuck in. The crowds can be suffocating at weekends, but that's all part of the experience and probably the reason why most night markets also feature foot massage centres. Cheap local **diners** and **buffets** (zìzhù cān) offer similar fare, the latter an especially good idea if you want to avoid having to order in Chinese. Hygiene standards are better than they seem at these places, and it's generally safe to drink water or tea served free on your arrival (which will have been boiled or purified).

If you fancy a stronger tipple with your food, give **beerhouses** (píjiǔ wū) a go. These atmospheric locations are good places to try Taiwanese snacks such as squid, steamed peanuts with small fish,

TOP 5 RESTAURANTS
Din Tai Fung, Taipei. See p.89
Epicurean Café, Orchid Island. See p.336
Cauliflower, Magong, Penghu. See p.349
Chikan Peddler's Noodles, Tainan. See p.246
Shengxing Inn, Sanyi. See p.166

fried oysters, fresh clams and fried prawns. **Teahouses** (see below) also usually serve food.

Restaurants

Restaurants in Taiwan, as in China, tend to be set up for **groups**: diners sit at large, round tables in order to share the sizeable plates of food on the menu. It's quite acceptable to dine alone, but with more people you'll be able to try more dishes. All the major hotels operate expensive but top-notch restaurants, their lavish buffets the best value if you want to splurge. Restaurants get going early in Taiwan, with breakfast places opening by 6am. Opening hours for restaurants are typically 11am–2pm and 5–8pm. In the countryside some places close by 7pm, though in the cities many will stay open till 9 or 10pm. **Prices** vary according to the quality of the establishment, but it's rare to pay less than NT$120 per dish, and more like minimum NT$300 at smarter places.

Ordering can be difficult if there's no English menu or English-speaking staff, but unless it's exceptionally busy someone will usually be able to help. Often there will be an English menu somewhere on the premises if you ask, and at street stalls pointing is usually sufficient. Chopsticks are de rigueur in all Chinese-style restaurants, but larger places will have knives, forks and definitely spoons if you ask. Most restaurants will serve filtered **water** or **tea** for no extra charge.

Drinking

Tea and teahouses

Taiwan produces some of the world's finest **tea**, and as a result is a good place to drink and buy various strains, particularly oolong (wūlóng chá, semi-fermented tea). **Lishan oolong**, grown at heights above 2200m near the town of Lishan, and **Dongding oolong**, produced around the town of Lugu in the heart of the country, are often considered the best teas in Taiwan. Relatively mild, Dongding oolong is dried for a brief period over a charcoal fire, giving it a subtle smoky flavour. Taiwan's other famous strain is **Oriental Beauty** (dōngfāng měirén chá or just "white oolong"), grown in Hsinchu and Miaoli counties and deriving its sweeter flavour from young leaves that have been bitten by tiny insects. This bite starts the oxidation of the leaves and adds the distinctive sweet and sour flavour. Other oolongs to look out for are Alishan "high mountain tea" (gāoshān chá), tiěguānyīn and bāozhǒng, the lightest and most floral of the strains. Taiwan also produces small amounts of green tea (lǜ chá) and black tea (hóng chá), especially around Sun Moon Lake.

Teahouses are an important part of contemporary Taiwanese culture, ranging from the traditional to the ultra chic, and Taiwan is regarded as a global leader in tea innovation: **bubble tea** (pàomò hóngchá) originated in Taichung, and the city remains home to some of the island's grandest teahouses, often huge establishments with carp ponds, miniature gardens and cosy pavilions.

Visiting a teahouse

At traditional-style teahouses, after choosing your tea type, you'll be given a teapot, a flask or kettle of hot water, several smaller pots and a bag of dried tea leaves, enough for several rounds. When it comes to **making tea** the traditional way, Taiwan is far less rigid than Japan, but although methods do vary around the country, the basic principles remain the same. The **first brew** washes the leaves and is poured away, while the **second** is drunk after a few seconds – the tea is poured out of the pot into a separate container before being served into small **drinking cups** (get your waiter to help if you get confused). These days you can usually order a range of meals and snacks with the tea.

Alcohol

Taiwan's tipple of choice is **beer** (píjiǔ), and the number one bestseller is state-owned **Taiwan Beer**. The Taiwanese are immensely proud of the brew (fairly average by international standards, although the Gold Label, jīnpái, is more quaffable), and you'll gain much kudos by drinking it, especially in rural areas. It's sold in cheap cans and large bottles in convenience stores and at food stalls, and in smaller bottles in bars in the cities. The island is also gradually expanding its range of **craft beers** (usually from NT$150), particularly in dedicated craft pubs and bars in the cities, but also in tourist hotspots such as Dulan's Highway 11. **Western brands** such as Budweiser, Heineken, and San Miguel are available in most bars and stores (along with all major Japanese brews) but a more diverse range of Irish, German, Belgian or British beers and ales is generally limited to pubs in the big cities.

Taiwan's national spirit is **gāoliáng jiǔ**, made from sorghum. **Kinmen Kaoliang Liquor** is its most celebrated incarnation, available at 38 or 58 percent proof. **Tunnel 88** is a slightly cheaper version (38 to 42 percent proof) made in Matsu. **Rice wines**, such as the **Shaoxing** variety made in Puli, tend to be too sour or sweet for Western tastes, and grape wines have become more popular, particularly in Taipei, where the annual release of Beaujolais Nouveau has become an important event for the fashion-conscious. It's expensive, thanks to heavy taxation, and you'll only get a good selection in the larger or Western-oriented supermarkets and speciality stores – red wines are far better represented than whites, and Antipodean and South American wines usually offer the best value in regular supermarkets.

Soft drinks and water

Canned **juices** are sold throughout the island, and there are plenty of fresh-fruit stalls. It's common to add milk, syrup and often sugar to juice drinks in Taiwan, so check before you order. Freshly pressed **sugar cane juice** is a delicious, sweet drink served by street vendors all over the country, while **papaya milk** is associated with Kaohsiung. Most supermarkets and convenience stores stock all the usual soft drinks, as well as fresh **milk** and a bewildering range of **soy** and **yoghurt drinks**; low-fat (or skimmed) and non-sugar versions of all of these are slowly becoming available. In the mountains, aiyu jelly (extracted from fig seeds) blended with lemon juice is a popular and refreshing drink.

Though considered potable in most places, **tap water** is a potential cause of minor stomach ailments, especially for first-time visitors – it's not a good idea to drink it unless it has first been boiled (many hotels provide an electric kettle for this purpose). If you're staying long-term you might want to take advantage of the **water dispensing machines** that are found in every town and city, which deliver reverse osmosis-filtered water for NT$1 per litre (bring your own container).

The media

As the only true democracy in the Chinese-speaking world, the Taiwanese media consistently exhibit a level of openness that is unheard of in Asia's other Chinese societies. Since the end of martial law in 1987, when the ban on independent newspapers was lifted,

there has been a rapid proliferation of print, news and entertainment media, with plenty of feisty political debate and steamy celebrity gossip. You'll need to read or speak Chinese to make the most of this, however; if not, you'll have to rely on a handful of English-language newspapers, magazines and websites.

Newspapers and magazines

There are three **daily English newspapers**, all of which have online editions: the **China Post** (Ⓦchinapost.com.tw), the **Taipei Times** (Ⓦtaipeitimes.com) and **Taiwan News** (Ⓦetaiwannews.com). The writing and editing standards of these papers are fairly high, and some of the domestic coverage can be quite incisive; however, international news is largely restricted to wire copy. All three have weekend **entertainment listings** and can be bought at bookshops, convenience stores, kiosks and business-class hotels. For deeper international news and business coverage, newspapers such as the **Wall Street Journal Asia**, the **Financial Times** and the **International Herald Tribune** can be found in five-star hotels and some news kiosks in Taipei. A limited selection of English-language magazines are available in big city bookstores (Caves, Eslite, Page One), HSR stations and airports.

Radio

There are more than 150 radio broadcasting companies in Taiwan, with regular domestic programming by medium-wave AM and VHF FM stations in Mandarin and other Chinese dialects, chiefly Taiwanese and Hakka. The only English-language **radio station**, International Community Radio Taipei (**ICRT**; Ⓦicrt.com.tw), broadcasts 24 hours a day at 100.7 MHz FM in northern and southern Taiwan, and 100.1 MHz FM in central Taiwan. Its broadcasts include a mix of Western pop music, news, talk shows and community service segments. It also carries some BBC World Service programmes, which are otherwise unavailable in Taiwan.

Television

Taiwanese **television** can offer travellers some interesting insights into nuances of the island's popular culture, with a host of variety and game shows, sitcoms, soap operas and films in Mandarin, Taiwanese and Hakka. Even if you don't speak Chinese, it's worth channel-surfing at least once, just to get a feel for what the locals watch. In terms of English-language programming, **cable TV** is available in most urban areas, offering an assortment of (generally American) channels.

Online Media

Social media including **Facebook** and the unstoppably popular domestic offering, **LINE** (Ⓦline.me/en), are increasingly used as a medium for information sharing, although these tend to be most relevant if you live in Taiwan and have connections and contacts on the island. **Focus Taiwan** (Ⓦfocustaiwan.tw) is a great resource packed with current news from around the island, and numerous **blogs** offer everything from travelogues to political commentary – one of the best is long-term expat Michael Turton's **The View from Taiwan** (Ⓦmichaelturton.blogspot.com).

Festivals

One of Taiwan's greatest attractions is the sheer range and depth of its festivals, all celebrated with passion and fervour. While the biggest ones are the traditional Chinese festivals – which double as public holidays – there is also an eclectic collection of religious festivals as well as an amazing array of time-honoured indigenous celebrations.

The majority of cultural and religious festivals follow the **Chinese lunar calendar**. As such, the actual Gregorian calendar dates on which they are celebrated tend to fluctuate significantly each year – in our **festivals calendar**, we have listed them under the Gregorian calendar month in which they are usually celebrated, with a note of their actual Chinese lunar calendar dates. We also specify which are **public holidays** (P), during which banks and government and private offices are closed, though many shops and restaurants remain open.

Indigenous festivals

Though Chinese traditional and religious festivals are routinely well publicized, many **indigenous celebrations** remain closely guarded **secrets**, and even local tourism officials are often confused about the actual dates on which they are observed. Villages typically stage their own celebrations, and **tribal elders** usually set the dates for these in accordance with a variety of factors. Further complicating this, established dates can be changed at the last minute in the face of inauspicious omens such as the sudden illness or death of a village elder. Finally, the truly authentic indigenous celebrations are taken very seriously, with ancient rituals performed with pinpoint precision. As such, most tribes don't want their traditions to become a spectacle for busloads of camera-toting tourists, so many – especially those along the east coast – make a concerted effort to hide their celebration dates from tourism officials. However, individual **travellers** or those in small groups are generally welcomed to events such as **harvest festivals** with open arms, often being invited to drink **local spirits** with the tribesmen. Those fortunate enough to experience these thriving cultures will see a side of Taiwan that most foreigners – and many Taiwanese – know precious little about, and it's well worth the effort to seek them out.

A festival calendar

JANUARY/FEBRUARY

Foundation Day/New Year's Day Jan 1 (P). Marks the founding of the Republic of China in 1911, but also gives a nod to the beginning of the Gregorian calendar year. Offices and schools are shut, with many remaining closed on Jan 2 & 3.

Chinese New Year (chūn jié) Lunar Jan 1–3 (P). Taiwan's most important festival, marking the start of the Chinese year. Celebrations centre mostly on family gatherings with lavish meals; "lucky" money in red envelopes is exchanged; fairs and public parades are held. Banks and government offices close for these three days, but many other offices close for longer (depending which days the festival falls on).

Qingshui Zushi's Birthday Lunar Jan 6. Commemorates the quasi-historical figure from Fujian, revered for his wisdom and munificence (see p.408). Main ceremonies at Zushi Temple in Sanxia, outside Taipei, including the ritual slaying of giant, over-fed "God Pigs".

Jade Emperor's Birthday Lunar Jan 9. Pays tribute to the chief Taoist deity, the head of celestial government thought to mirror that of imperial China (see p.408). Main ceremonies at temples in Taichung and Tainan.

Lantern Festival Lunar Jan 15. Marks the end of Chinese New Year festivities, but itself often lasts several days in big cities such as Taipei and Kaohsiung. Main activity is the public display of paper lanterns; in some cities, they're launched into the sky, most famously during the Heavenly Lantern Festival in Pingxi. Another popular event is the Beehive Rockets Festival in Yanshui near Tainan, where an almost 200-year tradition of setting off fireworks has transformed into an annual free-for-all. In Taitung county, all the fireworks and firecrackers are directed at one person (usually a young man), playing the role of Master Handan, as he is paraded along the streets on a palanquin.

FEBRUARY/MARCH

Peace Memorial Day Feb 28 (P). Instituted in 1997, and also known as "2-28 Memorial Day", it commemorates the 2-28 Incident (see p.394). **Wenchang Dijun's Birthday** Lunar Feb 3. Pays respect to the god of literature, revered by students and their parents ahead of exams.

Offerings of incense and wishes are written on colourful paper placed in glass jars.

Mayasvi Festival Usually early March. Tsou tribe celebration of warriors returning from battle, with rituals giving thanks to the god of war and the god of heaven. Hosted annually in rotation between Dabang and Tefuye villages.

Guanyin's Birthday Lunar Feb 19. The goddess of mercy's birthday is celebrated at Buddhist temples throughout the country, but the main place to mark the occasion is Taipei's Longshan Temple. The event is also celebrated at the Zizhu Temple in Neimen (near Kaohsiung), one of the most sacred sites for Taiwanese Buddhists. Its festival features a performance of the Song Jiang Battle Array, ritualized martial arts depicting symbolic battles with traditional weapons, including farm tools. **Youth Day** March 29. Pays tribute to the members of Sun Yat-sen's revolutionary uprising who were killed in the failed Canton Uprising against the imperial Qing government on March 29, 1911. Taiwan's president officiates at a public service at the Martyrs' Shrine in Taipei, and local governments hold similar ceremonies.

Queen Mother of the West's Birthday Lunar March 3. Honours the highest-ranking female deity, often portrayed as the Jade Emperor's wife (see p.409). Main festivities occur in Hualien (where it is celebrated on Lunar 18/7), the centre of her cult in Taiwan.

Supreme Emperor of the Dark Heaven's Birthday Lunar March 3. Pays respect to the controller of the elements, particularly fire, who is worshipped at some four hundred temples across Taiwan.

APRIL/MAY

Tomb Sweeping Day (qīngmíng jié) April 5 (P). Families visit cemeteries to clean graves of relatives and pay respects to their ancestors. In Taiwan, it's celebrated on the anniversary of Chiang Kai-shek's death. "Grave cakes" are offered and paper money is burned. **Baosheng Dadi's Birthday** Lunar March 15. Marks the birthday of Baosheng Dadi, the "Great Emperor who Preserves Life". Biggest celebration is held in Xuejia, north of Tainan.

Bunun Ear-shooting Festival Early May. Most important celebration of the Bunun tribe, traditionally a test of archery skills to mark the coming of age of the tribe's males.

Dajia Mazu Pilgrimage. This nine-day pilgrimage is one of the world's biggest religious festivals, with worshippers parading a caravan containing one of the island's most revered Mazu deities around a circuit before returning it to its mother temple in Dajia. Always preceding Mazu's birthday celebration, the pilgrimage is part of the month-long Dajia Mazu Culture Festival.

Mazu's Birthday Lunar March 23. One of Taiwan's most important folk festivals, celebrating the birthday of Mazu, goddess of the sea, the island's most popular folk deity. Mazu deities are returned to their "mother temples" on this day to be blessed and increase their spiritual powers. The liveliest celebrations are held at Dajia's Zhenlan Temple (see box, p.187), Beigang's Chaotian Temple (see p.216) and Lugang's Tianhou Temple (see p.193). **Labour Day** May 1 (P). Celebrates workers' rights and the eight-hour workday in line with international convention.

MAY/JUNE

Cleansing Buddha Festival Lunar April 8. Celebrates the birth of Buddha in accordance with the Mahayana school. Worshippers flock to

Buddhist temples island-wide, with monasteries such as Chung Tai Chan, Foguangshan and Dharma Drum hosting legions of devotees.

Kinmen City God Birthday Lunar April 12. Villagers carry statues of deities and parade the streets beating drums and gongs to scare off evil spirits.

Tainan City God Birthday Lunar April 20. Main festivities are held at the venerated Tainan City God Temple (see p.241).

Dragon Boat Festival (duānwǔ jié) Lunar May 5 (P). One of the three major Chinese holidays, featuring dragon boat races held in honour of the poet Qu Yuan who, according to legend, drowned himself in protest after being slandered by envious officials on this date in 280 BC. Races are held in most major cities, with international races in Taipei, Lugang, Keelung and Kaohsiung. The most distinctly Taiwanese are the indigenous-style races held in Erlong, near the east coast hot-springs resort of Jiaoxi.

Taipei City God Birthday Lunar May 13. Includes fireworks, elaborate dances by temple guardians and a lavish parade in which the deity is carried around the streets surrounding Taipei's City God Temple (see p.66).

JULY/AUGUST

Guan Di's Birthday Lunar June 24. Honours one of Taiwan's most admired deities, the red-faced patron of chivalrous warriors, misleadingly known as the God of War (see p.407). Ceremonies held island-wide, but Taipei's Xingtian Temple hosts the biggest.

Yimin Festival Lunar July. The most important annual observance of the Hakka people honours groups of Hakka militia from the late eighteenth century. The main celebration is held at the Yimin Temple in Fangliao, near Hsinchu, and is marked by offerings to ancestors, music and the ritual slaying of several dozen force-fed "God Pigs" – an increasingly controversial ceremony that is seldom witnessed by foreigners (see box, p.159).

AUGUST/SEPTEMBER

Amis Harvest Festival. One of the most colourful indigenous celebrations, centred on dancing, singing and coming-of-age rituals for young men. Although dates vary from year to year, the most important festival of the Amis tribe is generally held in late summer, often in August. Ask at villages north of Taitung.

Ghost Month Begins (guǐyuè) Lunar July 1. The time when the gates of hell are opened and spirits of "hungry ghosts" haunt the living (see p.404). Daily rituals include burning of incense and paper money, while major festivals are held in Keelung, Toucheng and Hengchun at the middle and end of the month. Traditionally this is seen as an inauspicious time for travel (especially by boat), but this belief is fading among the younger generation.

Ghost Festival (yúlán jié) Lunar July 15. Appeasement ceremonies held at temples across the island. Families offer flowers, fruit and three sacrificial offerings: chicken (or duck), pig and fish. Taiwan's most famous is the Keelung Ghost Festival, where an elaborate night parade is held before thousands of glowing "water lanterns" are released onto the Keelung River.

Ghost Month Ends Midnight Lunar July 30. On the last day of Ghost Month, the gates of hell close and hungry ghosts return to the underworld. In the month's last hour, contests in which men race to climb tall bamboo towers to collect meat and rice dumplings – are held; the most famous is in Toucheng near Yilan, while a similar event is also staged in Hengchun in the southwest.

Thao Pestle Music Festival. Held during the seventh lunar month in Itashao Village on Sun Moon Lake, members of the Thao tribe – Taiwan's smallest indigenous group (see p.403) – pound grain into a stone mortar with bamboo pestles, creating a traditional harmony.

Austronesian Culture Festival. Biennial international festival of indigenous cultures in Taitung, designed to instil pride and preserve traditions, using the example of indigenous peoples such as the Maori of New Zealand. The events span several months but dates are not consistent – the last two were Aug–Nov (2016) and May–Sept (2014).

SEPTEMBER

Armed Forces Day Sept 3. Honours all branches of Taiwan's military while also marking the end of China's eight-year War of Resistance against Japan. Big ceremonies at martyrs' shrines around Taiwan and military parades in the big cities.

Teachers' Day/Confucius's Birthday Sept 28. Pays tribute to teachers on the birthday of China's best-known educator and scholar, Confucius. Unique dawn ceremonies are held at Confucius temples nationwide, with the biggest at Taipei's Confucius Temple (see p.68).

SEPTEMBER/OCTOBER

Mid-Autumn Festival (zhōngqiūjié) Lunar Aug 15 (P). Also known as the "Moon Festival" – families gather in parks and scenic spots to admire what is regarded as the year's most luminous moon and to share moon cakes and pomelos, and (these days) to barbeque. Since the festival coincides with the autumn harvest, the Taiwanese also mark it by making offerings to the Earth God for a bountiful harvest.

Double Ninth Day Lunar Sept 9. Nine is a number associated with yang, or male energy, and on the ninth day of the ninth lunar month male strength is celebrated through activities including hill walking and drinking chrysanthemum wine; kite-flying is also popular. In 1966, the day was also designated as "Senior Citizens' Day", and has since come to be a time to pay respects to the elderly.

OCTOBER

Hualien Stone Sculpture Festival. Highlights the work of local and international stone sculptors (see p.288).

Sanyi Woodcarving Festival. Held in Taiwan's woodcarving capital to celebrate the craft. Includes ice-sculpting and carving contests (see p.165).

National Day Oct 10 (P). Also known as "Double Tenth Day", it commemorates the Wuchang Uprising that led to the overthrow of the Qing dynasty in 1911 by revolutionaries led by Sun Yat-sen. Military and public parades and fireworks displays are held in front of the Presidential Building in Taipei.

Retrocession Day Oct 25. Marks the official end of fifty years of Japanese colonial rule over Taiwan on October 25, 1945. The national flag is flown everywhere.

NOVEMBER

Rukai Black Rice Festival. The Rukai tribe's major festival, named in honour of what was once their staple diet. Offerings are made for abundant harvests, and it's a traditional time for marriage proposals and weddings. The biggest ceremony is held at Duona, usually in late November, in Maolin National Scenic Area (see p.267).

Ritual of the Short Black People. The most poignant expression of Saisiyat ("true people") identity, meant to appease spirits of a people the tribe are believed to have exterminated (see p.402). Major festival held every ten years, with a smaller one every two years.

Birth of Bodhidharma Lunar Oct 5. Honours the legendary Buddhist monk, also known as the Tripitaka Dharma Master, traditionally credited as the founder of the meditative Chan (or Zen as it's known in Japan and the West) school of Buddhism (see p.405). Rites performed at the Chung Tai Chan Monastery near Puli (see p.209).

Sun Yat-sen's Birthday Nov 12 (P). Marks the birthday of Sun Yat-sen, founder of the Republic of China and the Chinese Nationalist Party who is commonly considered to be the father of modern China.

Qingshan's Birthday Lunar Oct 22. Celebrates the birthday of the King of Qingshan (Green Mountain), who is believed to ward off pestilence and dispense justice in the underworld. Ceremonies held at Taipei's ornate Qingshan Temple (see p.65).

DECEMBER

Puyuma Ear-shooting Festival End of Dec. Celebration of the Puyuma tribe and traditionally a test of archery skills, marking the entry of boys into adulthood. Rituals held near Zhiben, to the south of Taitung.

Constitution Day Dec 25. Commemorates the passage of the Constitution of the Republic of China on December 25, 1946. The national flag is flown throughout the country, but these days Christmas is more often celebrated.

Sports and outdoor activities

One look at a relief map of Taiwan shows you its huge adventure sports potential; bisected by northeast Asia's highest mountains and with the rushing rivers and sheer cliffs of the east coast, this hidden paradise of outdoor pursuits is starting to attract more adventurous travellers from Asia and the rest of the world. As well as being a haven for trekkers and mountaineers, the island also offers excellent conditions for a range of activities, from cycling and kayaking to paragliding and surfing, with many grassroots operators springing up to meet the needs of travellers.

Hiking and trekking

Much of Taiwan is rugged wilderness that offers some of Asia's most amazing **hiking** and **trekking** possibilities. With an extensive network of national parks, Scenic Areas and forest reserves – all of which are laced with trails – the hardest part for most hikers is deciding where to start. There also are

eighteen **Forest Recreation Areas** in Taiwan, and while the trails in some of them have suffered extensive typhoon damage, others have well-marked paths with English signage. For more on these areas, visit the Forestry Bureau's website: Ⓦ recreation.forest.gov.tw.

A monumental effort is under way to link up many of Taiwan's major trails into an island-wide, north-to-south interlocking network known as the **National Trail System**. However, the series of typhoons that strikes the island each summer inevitably wipes out various sections of trail, often taking years to rebuild, so the project is perhaps overly optimistic. For more details on the trails that will make up the system, visit Ⓦ recreation.forest.gov.tw/RT_E/index.html.

Mountain climbing

With 258 mountains taller than 3000m and the **highest peaks** in northeast Asia (excluding some of the volcanoes on Russia's Kamchatka peninsula), you'd think Taiwan would be a mountaineering hotspot, but most of its stunning peaks are only tackled by a few climbers each year. Many of the trails are cut straight into the mountainsides and are thus extremely prone to dangerous **landslips** – especially during spring and summer rain – but apart from this most of the main routes up major peaks pose few technical challenges. Despite this, **mountain permits** are required for almost all of them (see box opposite).

By far the most famous peak is **Yushan** (Jade Mountain), which at 3952m is northeast Asia's highest. It's also one of the most accessible, thanks to a well-built, scrupulously maintained trail and one of Taiwan's most often-used mountain shelters. In good weather, reasonably fit climbers can ascend Yushan and its surrounding peaks without much difficulty (see p.227).

Taiwan's second-highest peak, the 3886m **Xueshan** (Snow Mountain), makes for a beautiful climb that often yields fantastic vistas of the mountains of Shei-Pa National Park and nearby Taroko National Park. During winter, Xueshan and the surrounding mountains that make up the majestic Holy Ridge often remain covered in awe-inspiring snow for months. The main trail to the summit is usually in excellent nick, and though the climb is steeper than Yushan, there are two mountain shelters that can help break up the journey (see p.171).

The favourite of almost every serious Taiwanese climber is **Nanhushan**, also known as "Nanhu Dashan". Tucked away in the far northwest corner of Taroko National Park, this gorgeous 3742m peak has been climbed by precious few foreigners (see p.304).

If you don't want to plan your own climb, try Tainan-based Barking Deer Adventures (☎0938 337 710, ⓦbarking-deer.com), or Kaohsiung-based Blue Skies Adventures (ⓦblueskiesadventures.com.tw) – the latter post upcoming group trip dates on their Facebook page (ⓦbit.ly/BlueSkyAdventures), but can also arrange private trips.

Mountain biking

With its hilly terrain and network of trails, Taiwan has excellent **mountain biking**, rivalling the best of North America and southern Europe. Heart-stopping downhill courses, technical rock gardens, jumps, berms and super-fast single track: the island has it all, and much is easily accessible from cities such as Taipei and Taichung. If you're an avid trail rider and plan to visit Taiwan for any length of time, it's worth bringing your bike with you (rental bikes tend not to be suitable for mountain biking). Check the archived website of the **Formosan Fat Tire Association** (ⓦformosanfattire.com) for details of bike shops such as **Alan's Mountain Bike** in Taipei (ⓦalansmountainbike.com.tw) – these are the best

---

MOUNTAIN PERMITS

One of the main reasons why relatively few foreigners climb Taiwan's tallest peaks – and as a result miss out on one of the island's most extraordinary features – is the astounding level of misinformation regarding **mountain permits**. Some Taiwanese and foreign expats talk about them as if they're next to impossible to obtain, and even some official sources insist the only way foreigners can climb major peaks is to join one of the regular weekend climbing excursions arranged by **outdoor shops** in major cities. While these shops will take care of the permit paperwork and can cut out most of the logistical planning – attractive options for non-Chinese-speakers with limited time – the downside is that you'll be shunted into a large **group** of complete strangers of varying experience and abilities. A better option is the expat-run companies such as Blue Skies and Barking Deer Adventures (see above), which organize smaller groups.

In fact, it's relatively straightforward to **arrange your own permits**, the process for which is continually being simplified for travellers. No longer is it necessary to hire a local **guide** for walks up the main mountains, although that is still advised for peaks that require technical climbing skills, as well as for multi-day treks across remote stretches of the parks. It's also now possible for individual climbers to obtain **solo permits**, although park officials are reluctant to issue these for more dangerous mountains, or during periods of heavy rain or snow.

In all cases, the easiest way to apply is **in person** at the headquarters of the relevant park, as this allows you to thoroughly explain your plan to conservation section officials. It also enables them to suss out your prior experience and climbing ability as well as inspect your kit. And while they're under no obligation to do so, park officials will sometimes prepare your permit more quickly if you apply in person.

APPLICATIONS

There are two kinds of permits: the standard **national park entry permit** (入園; rùyuán) and the **police permit** or **mountain entry permit** (入山; rùshān). Both are free. The latter is normally easy to obtain in person just before you start hiking, usually at the police station or checkpoint closest to the trail – you'll need an application form, three copies of your hiking itinerary and one copy of your passport and park entry permit.

Park permits, surprisingly, take more time. If you aren't able to apply in person, the best way for foreigners to apply is by completing the **application form online** and printing out the permit. The form must be received by the park seven to thirty days before the planned start of your climb, although there are special permit quotas for foreigners which can be made up to sixty days in advance. The Yushan National Park (ⓦysnp.gov.tw), Shei-Pa National Park (ⓦspnp .gov.tw) and Taroko National Park (ⓦtaroko.gov.tw) **websites** have the application process clearly mapped out in English – the Shei-Pa and Taroko sites have example forms to download, and a copy of the mountain permit application form.

In addition to providing your personal details, you'll need to briefly outline your proposed **itinerary**, including the expected date and time of your start and where you plan to spend each night: for **mountain cabins**, the park will reserve spaces for you, though usually you must bring your own sleeping bag and foam or air mattress. Once approved, officials will either fax or email the permit to you, and it can also be printed from the website.

places to hook up with local riders and join organized rides.

Cycle touring

Another two-wheeled activity for which Taiwan is well suited is **bicycle touring**. The dramatic "cross-island" roads that wind their way across the central mountain ranges offer remarkable alpine scenery and an honest cycling challenge to boot, although during heavy rains there can be dangerous rockslides and caution is essential on the road's many blind curves (note that the Southern Cross Island Highway remains closed). Although the highway that runs along the east coast from Taipei to Hualien is a tempting option, the road is choked with giant gravel trucks and runs through several long, dark tunnels, making for a very harrowing ride.

To see much of the island's best mountain and coastal scenery in one long ride, try a route that combines one of the central cross-island routes with the southern one: start at Sun Moon Lake or Puli and head north past Wushe until you reach Dayuling, then turn east and ride through the Taroko Gorge until you come out at Highway 9; go south to Hualien and then further south (either on Highway 193, Coastal Highway 11, or a mix of the two); the roads converge at Taitung, from where Highway 9 heads south and then across the mountains – branch off onto County Route 199 for the last section down to Kenting. Bicycle tour specialists Grasshopper Adventures (UK ☎020 8123 8144, US ☎818 921 7101, ⓦgrasshopperadventures.com) operate a variety of fully-supported bike tours accompanied by experienced guides.

Whitewater-rafting, kayaking and river tracing

Taiwan's steep mountains combined with heavy spring and summer rains often make for solid white-water-rafting and kayaking conditions, and its many narrow canyons offer exhilarating river tracing opportunities. Though many streams are too steep and technical for all but the most experienced kayakers, a few of the island's rivers are well known for **whitewater-rafting**. By far the most popular – and one of the safest – is the **Xiuguluan River**, which at 104km is eastern Taiwan's longest. The main 24km run begins in Ruisui, about midway between Hualien and Taitung on the East Rift Valley's Highway 9, and cuts through a gorge in the Coastal Mountain Range to finish just before the Pacific estuary at Dagangkou (see box, p.316). Bear in mind that if you

have rafted challenging rivers elsewhere in the world, you might find the Taiwanese approach is over-cautious, with operators using support rafts and speedboats, leading to a less exciting experience.

Hualien Outdoors (☎0989 512 380; ⓦhualien outdoors.org) organizes safe, professional adventure activities in the Hualien and Taroko region, including river tracing (NT$3000 per person, minimum of two).

If you prefer to negotiate your whitewater in a **kayak**, you can try several other less-commercialized rivers. Some kayakers put in at the headwaters of Taipei County's **Nanshi River** at Fushan, and paddle all the way down to Wulai, an elevation loss of about 200m. Another option is the **Beigang River** in Nantou County's Huisun Forest, which has a fast-but-short stretch of rapids. Contact **Paddle Around International** (ⓦwww.kayak.com.tw; Chinese-speaking only) or the **Aruba Outdoor School** (ⓦenaruba.blogspot.com) for lessons and tours.

Paragliding

The exhilarating sport of **paragliding** is popular in Taiwan, with a steady stream of fledgling pilots joining a dedicated community of die-hard expats and Taiwanese. Having said that, it's not a great place for **beginners** – clubs are unlicensed and unregulated, and flying sites can be tough for first-timers. Assuming you've done your initial training elsewhere, there are around six well-known flying sites scattered across the island, each with its own prime season, making it possible for local pilots to fly pretty much year-round. Two places vie for honours as Taiwan's top paragliding spot: Luye Gaotai, in the East Rift Valley near Taitung, and the Saijia Aviation Park in Pingdong County, not far from Kaohsiung. The **Saijia Aviation Park** was the first in Taiwan to open to paragliding and has the largest landing and best thermalling potential, but was officially closed in 2004 after a fatal accident involving a tandem passenger. At the time of writing, the private landowner was allowing flying to take place for a fee, but is awaiting a licence to make this legal – check with one of the visitor centres in Maolin National Scenic Area for the latest (see p.267).

Luye Gaotai, which generally has better conditions in summer, has two specialized take-off sites with rubber running-track surfaces and is the site of an international competition that attracts some of the world's most talented pilots. Along the northeast coast are some other popular paragliding sites, such as **Feicuiwan** (Green Bay) near Keelung, as well as **Yilan** and **Hualien**.

Diving and snorkelling

Taiwan's **scuba diving** and **snorkelling** spots are not nearly as famous as those of Southeast Asia, but a few of them are just as good. The top spots are **Kenting National Park**, Little Liuqiu Island, the Penghu Islands, and the superb Pacific islands of **Ludao** and **Lanyu**. However, while the Kenting area has numerous dive shops that offer scuba trips, some of the other spots have less reliable operators, and if you want to undertake serious dives in these areas it's best to arrange them in advance through one of the many scuba companies in major cities; Taiwan Dive based in Kaohsiung is a good place to start (Ⓦ taiwandive.com).

Some operators offer reasonably priced **scuba courses**, with basic open-water certification available for as little as NT$15,000 (in a group). If you know you'll be travelling to one or more of these islands, it's a good idea to bring your own **mask** and **snorkel**; fins are not essential, but in some places **neoprene boots** are necessary to keep from cutting your feet on the coral as you wade out. If you don't have your own kit, it's worth asking snorkelling shop owners if you can rent just the mask, snorkel and boots for a discounted rate and make your own way to the reef. In summer, there is little need for a wetsuit in Taiwan's warm tropical waters; though some shop owners may tell you that a wetsuit is needed to protect you from jellyfish, in most cases this is not necessary.

As for **marine wildlife**, the Pacific islands of Ludao and Lanyu are veritable treasure-troves of tropical fish and dolphins, and sightings of sea turtles and magnificent striped sea snakes are possible even while snorkelling (see box, p.332). Advanced scuba divers can see giant schools of **hammerhead sharks** off the southern tip of Ludao from January to March of each year. For more information, visit the Taiwan Dive website.

Kitesurfing and windsurfing

Taiwan is well known for its **windsurfing**, and **kitesurfing** is also rapidly gaining ground; the **Penghu Islands** (see p.340) are widely considered one of the world's top spots. Given the islands' unique flatness, the northeast monsoon winds that whip across the strait are especially powerful here, with wind speeds of up to 50 and sometimes even 60 knots possible in winter. The horseshoe-like shape of the Penghu archipelago generates a Venturi effect that squeezes every bit of the wind pressure, making it a spectacular place for slalom sailing, chop hopping and just pure speed.

While Penghu is packed with Taiwanese tourists in summer, due to the fierce winter winds it's practically deserted from October to March, save for the growing number of world-class windsurfers and kitesurfers who are making the islands part of their annual circuit. Visit Ⓦ liquidsportpenghu.com for organized tours.

Surfing

Although Taiwan's **surf** is not of the same calibre and consistency as the likes of Hawaii, Indonesia or Sri Lanka, anyone who has surfed the island on a good day will tell you that it can be nothing short of inspiring. Rideable waves can be found from tip to toe of Taiwan, but in general those that travel across the Pacific to crash against the eastern coastline are the ones to look out for – especially in the days preceding a **typhoon**. There are spots suited to all levels, from sandy beach breaks swarming with beginners to reef breaks that only the experienced should attempt. For advanced surfers, crowds aren't a major problem, as the only really big waves are at the vanguard of typhoons or during the winter when you'll need a wetsuit, especially in the north.

While there are some **surf shops** near the most popular beaches, these rent mostly longboards and only sell basics such as baggies, rash vests and wax, so bring your own board and back-up supplies if you're planning any serious surfing. The beaches best kitted out for travellers looking to surf (ie. where board rental, lessons, meals and accommodation are possible) are **Daxi** on the northeast coast (see box, p.145), **Dulan** and **Donghe** on the east coast (see p.310) and **Nanwan** and **Jialeshui** (see box, p.278) near the island's southern tip. There are several other possible surf spots along the east coast, but you'll need your own board, private transport, time to scout out the coastline and plenty of experience navigating reef. A few different companies now operate surf tours in Taiwan: Surf Taiwan (Ⓦ surftaiwan.com) is one of the most professional.

Culture and etiquette

Mainstream Taiwanese culture is a curious combination of traditional Chinese practices, modern commercialism and technological ingenuity, with a palpable Japanese influence left over from decades of colonial rule. Those

expecting stereotypical "Chinese" experiences akin to what can be had in mainland China are likely to be surprised and enchanted by the striking behavioural differences between the Taiwanese and their fellow Chinese neighbours.

Taiwanese people are unquestionably some of the friendliest in Asia, if not the entire world, and most foreign visitors are impressed by the often staggering level of **hospitality** from the moment they arrive.

If you're invited to someone's home, it's a good idea to bring a **gift**, usually something simple such as a tin of cookies, a basket of fruit, or a box of chocolates. Before entering someone's home, always remember first to remove your **shoes**, even if your host says it's not necessary.

Facing up to face

As in many parts of Asia, the concept of "**face**", the grey area between politeness and public pride, is an omnipresent reality in Taiwan, but foreigners who are thoughtful and sensitive to others are not likely to encounter serious problems. Many Taiwanese have travelled, studied or worked overseas and are somewhat accustomed to behaviour that could be categorized as "Western".

The best working rule is to avoid behaving in a way that causes someone to be embarrassed in front of others, or in front of you. Pointing out other people's mistakes or shortcomings, especially in public, is rarely appreciated and will usually precipitate the proverbial "loss of face". Losing one's **temper** in public and openly expressing anger is a sure-fire way to lose face, both for yourself, and the recipients of your outburst. Not only are such public displays of emotion likely to cause profound embarrassment, they often will convince others that you are uncivilized and undeserving of further attention or assistance. This doesn't mean that Taiwanese people don't get angry, but rather that there is a general belief in the virtue of self-control when dealing with others.

When Taiwanese are embarrassed or upset, they often will **smile** or giggle nervously, which can be confusing for the uninitiated foreigner. Understand that such smiles or laughter may well in fact be expressions of apology rather than amusement, and try to respond with a smile of your own.

Physical gestures and greetings

Visitors to Taiwan and many other Asian countries will notice that most people beckon to each other with their palms facing down, waving towards the ground, and travellers are well advised to emulate this – calling people towards you by rolling your fingers back with your palms up is widely considered to be crudely suggestive, particularly when a man is motioning towards a woman.

Although in Chinese tradition **shaking hands** was not the usual manner of greeting, Taiwanese men now commonly practise this custom, particularly in business circles. However, powerful or overly enthusiastic handshakes are considered aggressive and can cause bewilderment. Men and women generally don't shake hands upon meeting, opting instead for slight nods of deference, although this is changing and urban businesswomen are increasingly likely to offer their hands when meeting foreigners.

Business cards

Exchanging **business cards** (míngpiàn in Mandarin) is a Taiwanese obsession, even between people with no business intentions, and name cards with contact details can be very useful for any foreigner planning to spend time in Taiwan. Printing of business cards in Taiwan is cheap and quick; sophistication and detail are not essential – your telephone, email address and preferably your name in Chinese are sufficient.

When exchanging business cards or gifts, presenting them with **both hands** tells your counterpart that you are offering them unreservedly. To the contrary, passing business cards with one hand or flipping them across tables is viewed as uncultivated, flippant and even disrespectful. When receiving another's business card, it's considered respectful to read their name and title and, when appropriate, to praise them for their position on the career ladder. Avoid immediately putting cards in your wallet or pockets – even if you're only trying to secure them, such action is likely to be interpreted as a sign of uninterest. Also, **writing** on business cards – especially in red ink, which is typically reserved for letters of protest or angry remarks – is still a major faux pas in Taiwan. This should only be done when you need to jot down essential information, such as a mobile phone or hotel room number, and have nothing else to write on.

Superstition

One of the most fascinating features of Taiwan, and one that never ceases to amaze even the longest-term foreign expatriates, is how some of the most ancient of Chinese **superstition** has survived – and even thrives – in one of the world's most technologically advanced societies. This seeming paradox pervades everyday life in Taiwan – don't be surprised if you witness, say, a fashionable young computer salesman making elaborate offerings at a makeshift shrine in front of his trendy Taipei shop.

While most of the places of ancient lore are in mainland China, many of the traditional practices no longer exist there, stamped out during decades of Maoist revisionism and replaced primarily with conspicuous consumerism. And though traditional southern-Chinese beliefs such as those of the Cantonese have survived in places such as Hong Kong and Macau, nowhere are age-old Chinese superstitions – mostly Fujianese – more a part of everyday life than in Taiwan.

Bad omens

For the visitor, one of the most obvious aspects of this is the widespread belief in **bad omens**, and the lengths to which many Taiwanese will go to avoid them. Comments or jokes that imply **death** or disaster are almost certain to elicit visible cringes from those within earshot and can make some people decidedly edgy. For example, a seemingly innocuous statement such as "she's going to get herself killed walking in front of all that traffic," can imply in the minds of many Taiwanese that this will actually happen. This is not to say that warning people to be careful is taboo, but you should not follow up a warning with a statement of what could happen.

Actions that imply the notion that something untoward could happen are also widely avoided in Taiwan, which helps to explain why so many Taiwanese refuse to write **last wills** out of fear that such action could precipitate their own demise. Giving someone a **handkerchief** as a gift, for example, is not recommended as it implies that the recipient may soon have reason to cry. Likewise, things that are symbolic of death, such as **white flowers** – requisite at funerals – are to be avoided.

Even words or phrases that remind people of death can cause offence, with the most obvious of these being mispronunciations of the Chinese word for "**four**," (sì) which said in the wrong tone can mean "to die" (sǐ). Giving **clocks** as gifts also is unthinkable, as the Mandarin phrase "to give a clock" (sòngzhōng) sounds the same as that for "to attend a funeral".

Swimming

Another fairly common Taiwanese fear that in part can be chalked up to superstition is that of **deep water**. Many Taiwanese are unwilling to venture into water that is deeper than their heads, and most public swimming pools are no more than chest deep. Although this can be partially attributed to poor Taiwanese swimming standards – generally lower than those of most Western countries – for some it has more to do with the fear that discontented ghosts lurking beneath the surface could possess them. However, this belief is far less common among the young and is quickly dying out.

Shopping

Taiwan is one of Asia's best shopping destinations, offering everything from chic malls to traditional markets. Each of the major cities has a collection of malls and department stores where you can buy international brands (at international prices), although larger-sized women's clothing is still hard to come by. These malls also often have movie theatres and food courts, but typically don't open until 11am. At the other end of the spectrum, traditional markets sell everything from fruit and vegetables to jade and antiques; some of these markets only take place on certain days of the week or times of the day.

Everyday needs are easily sourced at the ubiquitous 24hr **convenience stores** (7-Eleven and Family Mart are the most prevalent) or, for more choice, at **hypermarkets** such as Carrefour and RT Mart. The widest choice of **toiletries** is at Watsons, which has branches in many towns and cities around the country. In tourist areas, there are invariably **regional specialities** (often food based) which locals buy in bulk. Taiwan is also regarded as a good place to pick up cutting-edge **electronics** at bargain prices – each of the major cities has an electronics market or street.

Haggling isn't common practice and is only really seen at tourist markets, where you might get a small discount.

Travelling with children

Taiwan is a first-rate family destination: safe, with good transport connections and lots of family-oriented attractions. Travelling to Taiwan with kids will also open up a world of local experiences;

family is the most important thing in Taiwan, and travelling with kids you'll find a warm and welcoming reception almost everywhere you go.

While never as overbearing as mainland China, the level of interest in your children (especially if they have blond hair and blue eyes) can sometimes be awkward, and can make even a simple trip to the supermarket into a major event; however, the other side of this is that you will often receive special treatment.

In practical terms, nappies and milk formula are widely available in convenience stores, supermarkets and baby shops, and cots can be provided in better hotels. Attractions and transport options often have discounted (or free) rates for children, depending on their age or height, and there are public playgrounds in most towns and cities.

Travel essentials

Costs

Taiwan is one of Asia's most developed countries, and, as such, is more expensive than, say, Thailand or Vietnam. Still, you'll find it considerably cheaper than Hong Kong, Japan or South Korea, and there are plenty of ways for inventive travellers to keep their costs to a manageable level. Although staying in Taipei can be challenging for backpackers on a tight budget, once you get outside the capital you'll find that prices typically run the gamut of budgets, from backpacker to mid-range to luxury traveller.

Accommodation ranges from as little as NT$300 (US$10/£7.50/€8.50) for a hostel dorm bed to NT$10,000 (US$338/£250/€280) for a room in a five-star resort, while **food** can cost as little as NT$30 (US$1/£0.75/€0.85) for basic street food such as noodles to easily more than NT$1000 (US$34/£25/€28) for a meal in a semi-posh sit-down restaurant. By staying in dorms or basic doubles and keeping to ordinary, working-class Chinese places to eat, most budget-conscious travellers should be able to keep their costs to around NT$1500 (US$49/£38/€43) per day, perhaps a bit more when undertaking long journeys.

Admission prices to museums and tourist sights are usually quite reasonable; government-run venues are typically cheap, while the cost of privately operated attractions varies wildly. Though discounts for museums and public performances are usually given to senior citizens and students, most travellers are unlikely to fit in the second category as foreign

student cards are generally not recognized. However, foreigners formally studying on a full-time basis in Taiwan qualify for **student cards** that will be honoured throughout the country.

Crime and personal safety

For the vast majority of foreign travellers and residents, Taiwan is an exceptionally safe place, and foreigners are seldom witnesses to – much less victims of – crime. By far the biggest threat to personal safety in Taiwan is **traffic accidents**, especially those involving scooters and motorcycles (see p.28), and foreigners should employ extreme caution while out on the roads.

All recreational **drugs** including marijuana are strictly illegal, and simple possession can lead to jail time and almost certain expulsion from the country. Police **raids** on clubs are common, especially in Taipei and Taichung, and in a few cases the police have taken all revellers to the station for urine tests.

Police departments in most big cities have **foreign affairs sections** that are normally staffed with English-speaking officers.

Customs

You're allowed to **import** into Taiwan up to 200 cigarettes or 25 cigars, and a one-litre bottle of liquor. Adults can bring in goods valued up to NT$20,000, and the duty-free allowance is up to NT$10,000. It's prohibited to import gambling articles, fruits, live animals, non-canned meat products and toy pistols, and **drug trafficking** can be punishable by death.

Electricity

Taiwan's electric current is **110V AC**, the same as the US, and the wall sockets are made for standard **American two-pin flat plugs**. Unless they're dual voltage (most mobile phones, cameras, MP3 players and laptops are), all Australian, British, European, Irish, New Zealand and South African appliances (as well as those from Hong Kong and mainland China) will need a voltage transformer as well as a plug adapter.

Health

As one of Asia's most developed destinations, Taiwan doesn't present many significant health risks for foreign travellers and residents – most visitors will find that using the same precautions they

EMERGENCY NUMBERS

The national number for **police** is ☎110, while the island-wide number for **general emergencies** such as fire or ambulance services is ☎119.

exercise in their home countries will be more than enough to keep them healthy during their stay and the worst you'll face is stomach upset, dehydration and heat stroke. Medical facilities in the big cities are of a high standard, although English-language abilities vary, so if you don't speak Chinese you may need the help of someone who does.

There are **pharmacies** in all Taiwanese towns, and most of them are of a high standard and offer a similar range of products to those in Western countries. Near the prescription windows there are sometimes counters offering treatment advice for a variety of ailments, but usually little if any English is spoken at these. In emergencies, you may wind up having to play a slightly embarrassing game of charades, acting out your ailment and pointing to the affected area – in such cases, the Taiwanese are invariably earnest and will try to help you without showing the faintest trace of amusement. Most pharmacies have a wide range of antibiotics.

There are **public health clinics** in most towns, and they are generally of a reasonable standard and can offer diagnoses and provide medication for most non-emergency conditions. Seeing a doctor at public clinics or hospitals is inexpensive (NT$500), but you'll be expected to **pay first** and then make the claim to your insurance company later. Private clinics in Taipei (see p.99), where most staff will speak English, can be much more expensive: expect to pay NT$1200 or more just to see a doctor.

For emergencies and serious illnesses, you should go to a **hospital** – all major towns have them, although if you have time, you should try to get to a major city as their hospitals are usually of a higher quality and there is a greater likelihood that English will be spoken. The best hospitals are in Taipei, Kaohsiung and Taichung, but Hsinchu, Tainan, Taitung, Chiayi and Hualien all have adequate facilities.

Dengue fever

There is no malaria in Taiwan, but **dengue fever**, a mosquito-borne viral disease with similar symptoms, has been a resurgent problem in recent years. There have been cases of dengue all over Taiwan, but over the past two decades it has been more common in the south, particularly in Kaohsiung and Pingdong counties. Outbreaks tend to occur after summer rains, when standing water stagnates, creating breeding grounds for the striped **aedes aegypti**. The peak period is June to October, but cases are increasingly occurring earlier in the year.

There is no dengue vaccine, nor are there any prophylactics against the disease, so the only way to prevent it is to avoid being bitten by mosquitoes. The mosquitoes that transmit dengue bite day and night, so you should use insect-avoidance measures at all times. Also known as "break bone fever", the onset of the disease is characterized by severe joint pain that gives way to high fever, sweating and pounding headaches. Some people may also develop a rash over their torso and limbs. There's no cure, but bed rest is recommended while the symptoms run their course, and paracetamol can help the headaches. The symptoms usually subside after several days of rest, but can return intermittently over the next several weeks. Although dengue is not life-threatening to adults, a more virulent strain called **dengue haemorrhagic fever** primarily affects young children and can be dangerous for infants.

SARS and "bird flu"

In 2003, Taiwan had the world's third-highest number of confirmed cases (346) of the potentially lethal **SARS** (Severe Acute Respiratory Syndrome) virus, resulting in 37 deaths, but there have been no confirmed cases since then.

Outbreaks of **avian influenza**, an infectious disease of birds caused by type A flu strains, have continued however. Although the so-called "bird flu" usually only infects birds and pigs, the number of humans being infected with a mutated form of the virus has been rising, especially in countries such as China and Vietnam, and there also have been cases in Taiwan. Most travellers aren't at much risk of bird flu, unless they visit poultry farms or markets selling live birds.

The **H1N1 Virus** (so-called "swine flu") pandemic in 2009 also affected Taiwan, with around forty people dying of the illness by mid-2010, but this was far fewer than in many Western countries.

Since the SARS outbreak, the practice of wearing **surgical masks** when suffering from colds and flu has become much more common in Taiwan.

MEDICAL RESOURCES

International Society for Travel Medicine ☎ 1404 373 8282, ⓦ istm.org. A full list of clinics worldwide specializing in travel health.

AUSTRALIA, NEW ZEALAND AND SOUTH AFRICA

Netcare Travel Clinics South Africa ☎ 082 911, ⓦ netcare.co.za. Travel clinics in South Africa.

Traveller's Medical and Vaccination Centre Australia ☎ 1300 658 844, ⓦ traveldoctor.com.au Lists travellers' medical and vaccination centres throughout Australia and New Zealand.

UK AND IRELAND

Hospital for Tropical Diseases Travel Clinic UK ☎ 020 3456 7891, ⓦ thehtd.org/travelclinic.aspx

MASTA (Medical Advisory Service for Travellers Abroad) UK ☎ 0330 100 4200, ⓦ masta-travel-health.com.

Tropical Medical Bureau Ireland ☎ 00 353 1 2715 200, ⓦ tmb.ie.

US AND CANADA

Canadian Society for International Health Canada ⓦ csih.org. Extensive list of travel health centres.

CDC US ☎ 1800 232 4636, ⓦ cdc.gov/travel. Official US government travel health site.

Insurance

It's essential to take out an insurance policy before travelling to Taiwan, as much to cover against theft and loss or damage to property as for illness and accidental injury. A typical **travel insurance policy** provides cover for the loss of baggage, tickets and – up to a certain limit – cash or cheques, as well as cancellation or curtailment of your journey. Most of them exclude injuries caused by so-called **dangerous sports** unless an extra premium is paid, and it's crucial to ensure that any borderline activities you're likely to engage in are covered. In Taiwan, this can mean cycling, mountain biking (trail riding), paragliding, river tracing, rock climbing, scuba diving, surfing, whitewater-rafting, windsurfing and even trekking. Given the likelihood that you'll find yourself driving or riding on the back of a motorcycle or **scooter** in Taiwan – especially if you plan to visit any offshore islands – you should make sure this activity is covered as well.

If you need to **make a claim**, you should keep receipts for medicines and medical treatment, including copies of signed medical reports clearly stating the diagnosis and prescribed treatment, in English if possible. In the event you have anything stolen, you'll need to visit the nearest police station and file a report for **stolen property**. Although this can be complicated in small towns where little English is spoken, police stations in the biggest cities usually have somebody on hand who can speak some English.

Finally, if your trip to Taiwan is part of a longer, multi-country journey, make sure that your policy covers Taiwan in the first place: some insurers will not provide coverage for Taiwan due to perceptions of military-political risk.

Internet

Taiwan is one of the world's biggest **internet** users, although most surfing is done via home computers, laptops and of course, smart phones, so internet cafés are not as common as might be expected. Most hotels, and many cafés, and public areas and buildings have free wi-fi which makes travelling with a smartphone or laptop worthwhile. Government buildings and visitor centres offer free wi-fi access to visitors signed up to i-Taiwan (ⓦ itaiwan .gov.tw/en). Visitor centres at airports, train stations and tourist destinations can help you to set up an account – you'll need to bring your passport.

In the more touristy bits of Taiwan, there are usually **internet cafés**. However, in most places – even in the big cities – you may be forced to enter the grisly world of the Taiwanese **computer game centre**. At these, you are likely to find a high-speed internet connection but you'll have to endure the background noises of automatic gunfire and enough secondhand cigarette smoke to make the Marlboro Man suffocate. **Prices** vary among computer game centres, but in general most charge about NT$20–30 per hour (sometimes double this in Taipei).

Laundry

Laundry services are easy to arrange but expensive at better hotels, but for travellers on a budget many hotels, hostels and homestays have coin-operated washing and drying machines. There are also plenty of self-service street laundrettes (洗衣; xǐyī), which generally open late, and where coin-operated machines cost NT$30–50 per load. Conventional "Chinese laundries" (where they do all the hard work) are less common and more expensive.

LGBT+ travellers

Despite the traditional underpinnings of Taiwanese society, **homosexuality** is no longer considered taboo and the perception of the LGBT+ community is far more progressive than that of most of its Asian neighbours. Though pockets of prejudice remain, public acceptance of homosexuality (and bisexuality) has grown markedly since the lifting of martial law in 1987, and there are now thriving gay

ROUGH GUIDES TRAVEL INSURANCE

Rough Guides has teamed up with WorldNomads.com to offer great travel insurance deals. Policies are available to residents of over 150 countries, with cover for a wide range of adventure sports, 24hr emergency assistance, high levels of medical and evacuation cover and a stream of travel safety information. Roughguides.com users can take advantage of their policies online 24/7, from anywhere in the world – even if you're already travelling. And since plans often change when you're on the road, you can extend your policy and even claim online. Roughguides.com users who buy travel insurance with WorldNomads. com can also leave a positive footprint and donate to a community development project. For more information, go to Ⓦroughguides.com/travel-insurance.

communities in big cities such as Taipei, Kaohsiung and Taichung. The country's **legal stance** towards homosexuals is widely considered the most advanced in Asia, with gays and lesbians enjoying most of the same freedoms as heterosexuals: there is no law against sodomy, and homosexual behaviour between consenting adults over the age of 16 in private is legal. On 24 May 2017, the Constitutional Court ruled that same-sex couples have a right to **marry**, and gave the Legislative Yuan two years to amend current marriage laws. According to the court ruling, if these amendments are not passed within two years, same-sex marriages will automatically become legal.

Much of this public enlightenment and legislative change has been the result of a concerted drive by Taiwan's homosexual community, which boasts more than thirty gay and lesbian organizations. The country's first **gay pride festival** was held in 1997 at the 2-28 Peace Park, a popular night-time cruising spot for gay men, and what was hailed as the first gay rights parade in the Chinese-speaking world was held in Taipei in 2003. The October 2015 parade attracted nearly eighty thousand people, making it the largest gay pride event in East Asia.

Indeed, **Taipei** has become a magnet for overseas LGBT+ tourists, elevating the city's status from the gay capital of Taiwan to a top gay destination in Asia. While the capital undoubtedly has the most sophisticated scene, with numerous bars, clubs and saunas specifically catering to gays and lesbians,

such venues are springing up in other major cities and same-sex couples are commonly seen in mainstream social establishments. Given this openness, gay and lesbian travellers should easily find places to hang out: some of the best-known venues in Taipei (see p.95) have information on gay clubs in other cities and often can provide you with their business cards. For current information on gay life in Taiwan check out Ⓦutopia-asia.com/tipstaiw .htm or Ⓦgaytaipei4u.com.

Unlike Thailand and the Philippines, Taiwan doesn't have a developed **transgender** community, and as such there is less understanding of transgender issues. However, in true Taiwanese spirit, all but the most ultra-conservative older generation tend to be open (or at least not overtly against) people's right to walk their chosen path – all the more so if they are foreigners, who are already considered to be something of an unfathomable entity. This said, transgender travellers are most likely to find acceptance and make friends in the gay bars and clubs of the big cities.

Living in Taiwan

Taiwan has long attracted foreigners to work or study. **Teaching English** is by far the most common form of employment, and while some simply use Taiwan to top up on cash before continuing their travels, others end up staying much longer, sometimes branching out into other businesses or making Taiwan their permanent home. However, teaching rates of pay have remained around the same level for over a decade, while regulations have tightened up and the cost of living has increased, making teaching in Taiwan a less popular option than it was in the early noughties. Though it's certainly harder to make a decent living teaching in Taiwan these days, there are still plenty of jobs for the determined. Unlike places such as Hong Kong and Singapore, where teachers with English accents are preferred, in Taiwan it is the **North American accent** that is almost universally desired, so Americans and Canadians comprise the majority of teachers. However, there are plenty of teachers from countries such as the UK, Ireland, Australia, New Zealand and South Africa, and if English is your first language and you have a degree it shouldn't be too hard to land a job.

Although it's possible to source jobs from your home country before you leave, it can be difficult to determine the legitimacy of the company from overseas and many prefer to simply pick the place where they most want to live and turn up to look for work – most towns and cities have English-language schools. In general, the best times to look are towards the end of summer and just after the Lunar New Year.

It's possible to teach a wide variety of **age groups** in Taiwan, from elementary school kids singing English songs, to businessmen looking to refine their formal English skills. However, probably the most plentiful job opportunities are with the ubiquitous **bushiban** (after-hours cram schools, mostly for teenagers). While these night-time language centres are a major employer of English teachers, some foreigners find teaching overworked and exhausted high-school kids to be depressing.

Qualifications, work visas and pay

To teach legally, you must have a **bachelor's degree** or the equivalent from an accredited university in an English-speaking country. It's not imperative to have **TESL** (Teaching English as a Second Language) or **TEFL** (Teaching English as a Foreign Language) certification, but it will bolster your credentials and make your job easier and more rewarding – in some cases it might also put you into a higher pay bracket.

Once you've found work and signed a contract, your school will apply for your **work visa**, which will qualify you for an **Alien Resident Certificate** (ARC) and basic health insurance. However, several nationalities, including Australians, New Zealanders, Canadians, French and British aged 18 to 30 are eligible to apply for a **working holiday visa** through the Youth Mobility Program which allows them to engage in part-time work while they travel for up to one year. Contact the Taiwan representative offices in your country or see the Bureau of Consular Affairs website (Ⓦboca.gov.tw) for more details.

Many schools pay on a monthly basis, so you may have to wait for your first payment and should come with enough money to live on for at least one month, and ideally enough to put down a deposit on a rental apartment and set yourself up (at least NT$40–50,000 total). Most jobs pay NT$600–700 per hour, with the amount of hours worked per week anywhere from fourteen to thirty; figure on earning NT$40,000 to NT$60,000 per month. Many teachers supplement their incomes – and try to dodge taxes – by taking side jobs that pay cash under the table, such as **private tutoring**. However, in the unlikely event that you are caught doing this, you are almost certain to be kicked out of the country.

The cost of a room in a pre-furnished shared **apartment** varies widely, but in general they range from NT$5000–12,000 per month in the big cities; one-bedroom apartments will be N$8000–15,000, and over NT$20,000 per month in Taipei.

Useful websites

The following **websites** have job listings, flats for rent and regularly updated information on issues affecting English teachers in Taiwan: Ⓦenglishintaiwan.com; Ⓦforumosa.com; Ⓦtealit.com. Another useful site with information for English teachers around the world, including Taiwan job postings, is Ⓦdaveseslcafe.com.

Maps

The best **English-language maps** of Taiwan are available from book and map stores internationally, although since the development of digital maps and GPS, many of the print ones are outdated – the most recent offering is Nelles (2015). Google Maps and Apple Maps are both reasonably accurate in Taiwan.

The **Taiwan Tourism Bureau** produces a series of maps covering the whole country which are available at visitor centres; while these aren't the most detailed, they're in English, regularly updated, and free. On the ground in Taiwan you can also source detailed local area and city maps, though the best of these tend to be in Chinese only.

Money

Taiwan's currency is the **New Taiwan Dollar** (NT$) or xīntáibì, although it's usually referred to by the generic Mandarin terms **yuán** or **kuài**. Notes come in denominations of NT$100, 200, 500, 1000 and (seldom seen) 2000, while coins come in units of NT$1, 5, 10, 20 and 50. The **exchange rate** has been fairly steady at around NT$30 to the US dollar for a number of years now; following the Brexit vote, it was NT$40 to the UK pound and NT$35 to the euro. You can check current exchange rates at Ⓦxe.com. Note that foreign currencies are hardly ever accepted in Taiwan.

Almost all cities and towns have **ATMs** from which travellers can withdraw funds using bank **debit** or **credit cards** – this is by far the most convenient and safe method of obtaining cash for daily expenses. Though some ATMs are only for domestic bank account holders, many support international systems such as Accel, Cirrus, Interlink, Plus and Star (always check for the correct logo). The most common ATMs – and the most useful to foreigners – are those of **Chinatrust Commercial Bank**, which allow cash advances from major credit cards and can be found in **7-Eleven** convenience stores throughout the country. Other banks with ATMs that recognize international cards are **Bank of Taiwan** and **International Commercial Bank of**

China (ICBC). Citibank and HSBC also have branches in Taiwan's biggest cities. Most **hotels** accept credit card payment, with Visa and MasterCard the most widely accepted. American Express and Diners Club also are fairly commonly recognized, though this is more the case in the big cities. Stores in most cities will accept credit card payment, although in many rural areas this is not possible.

Private **moneychangers** are rare in Taiwan, and if you need to exchange foreign currency you'll probably have to do so in a bank – in most towns, Bank of Taiwan will have a **foreign exchange counter**, and branches are usually centrally located. The most widely accepted currency for exchange is **US dollars**, followed by Chinese RMB, Hong Kong dollars, Japanese yen and British pounds.

Traveller's cheques are becoming increasingly outmoded in Taiwan and are probably more trouble than they're worth. Those cut in US dollars are the easiest to cash.

Phones

Domestic calls are easily made from private and public telephones; the latter come in two types: coin and card. Though there are still a few **coin booths** around, most of them only take NT$1, NT$5 and NT$10 coins; local calls cost NT$2 for up to two minutes (NT$6 for 2min calls to mobile phones), and you'll need a stack of coins for long calls. Far more common these days are **card phones** (prepaid **phone cards** can be bought in convenience stores and train stations in NT$100, NT$200 and NT$300 denominations) which can be used for both domestic and **international calls**. You can also make an overseas direct-dial call by first keying in ☎002, followed by the country code, area code and number. For operator-assisted international calls dial ☎100 or ☎0800 080 100 for international information (free). For domestic calls, there is no need to dial the area code when making calls within the same area code.

Mobile phones

Your **mobile phone** may already be compatible with the Taiwanese network, which is GSM 900MHz/1800MHz. Visitors from North America should ensure their phones are GSM/Triband and have the appropriate MHz capabilities.

Buying a SIM card

If your phone is not locked to a particular network, you'll save on roaming charges on your mobile phone by purchasing a local **SIM card**, which allows you to **pay-as-you-go**, though for longer stays it's even cheaper to sign a contract and pay monthly. SIM cards (with air-time) can be bought for as little as NT$600, and your new Taiwan number is usually activated within 24 hours. Taiwanese SIM cards allow you to receive incoming calls for free; you're only charged for the calls you make.

Chunghwa Telecom, FarEasTone and Taiwan Mobile are the biggest service providers, and all have desks at **Taiwan Taoyuan International Airport** (most close by 9pm). These stores can offer a variety of different short-term packages, and can also **rent you a handset**. If you miss the airport desks and can't find one of their stores elsewhere (usually located in most cities), try **7-Eleven** or hypermarket chain **Carrefour**, both of which also sell SIM cards. Look for a 7-Eleven where one of the clerks speaks English – as long as the shop is not busy, they'll usually be happy to walk you through the process.

Wherever you purchase your SIM card, you'll need your **passport** and another piece of **photo ID**. Longer term contracts require an ARC and proof of residence.

Photography

Taiwan is a photographer's paradise, with an endless line-up of subjects: spectacular landscapes, historic temples, festivals, atmospheric Chinese medicine shops and markets bursting with tropical fruit all vie for your attention. In modern Taiwan, everybody takes photos, all the time, and therefore you'll often find willing subjects, although stopping them from pulling a cutesy pose can be more difficult. In more traditional or remote areas (eg. Orchid Island) it is wise to use more discretion, and wherever you are, you should always ensure you have permission before taking people's photographs. Military installations are also a no-no for photos. If you're interested in a dedicated **photography tour**, east-coast based Bamboo Trails (🖥bambootrails.com) offers photography trips escorted by both a tour leader and professional photographer, with each day designed to focus on improving a particular skill.

Post

Taiwan's **postal service**, the state-owned **Chunghwa Post**, is speedy and reliable, offering a range of services that are user-friendly even if you don't speak Chinese. **Post offices** are located in all cities, towns and most villages, though **opening hours** vary in accordance with their size – expect most to be open from about 8am until 5pm

Monday to Friday and about 8.30am to noon on Saturday. In big cities the main branches may have longer hours (until 8pm on weekdays), while in small villages and rural locations hours are often shorter, with no weekend service. **Stamps** can be bought at post offices, convenience stores and even on line at ⓦ post.gov.tw, where you also can find a list of prices, branch addresses and opening hours.

Postboxes come in two colours: the red box is where you post overseas mail (in the left-hand slot) and Taiwan express mail (in the right-hand slot). Green boxes are for domestic surface mail (left) and local city mail (right).

Poste restante services are available at the main post offices of the large cities. Letters should be addressed to GPO Poste Restante, together with the city name – be sure to use the romanization for city names that is used in this book. They'll keep post for fifteen days before they start adding daily charges.

Smoking

Lung cancer has long been a leading cause of death in Taiwan, and in 2009 the government implemented some of the most stringent **anti-smoking laws** in Asia. Smoking is banned in all indoor public places, including transport systems, hotels, shopping malls, restaurants and bars, though the latter can get around this if they have open-air areas or smoking rooms with independent ventilation, completely separated from the non-smoking sections (bars that open after 9pm are also exempt). As of 2015, smoking while driving a car or scooter is also illegal; violators are subject to a fine of up to NT$600.

Studying Chinese

Foreigners have been coming to Taiwan to learn Chinese for decades, with many claiming that Taipei is the best place in the world to study **Mandarin**, as the version spoken here is far more intelligible than the heavily accented drawls of the Beijing dialect, for example. Be aware, however, that if you study in central or southern Taiwan – places where the Taiwanese dialect is commonly spoken – you are likely to hear highly corrupted forms of Mandarin in your daily activities, and this can complicate the learning process.

CHINESE LANGUAGE SCHOOLS

TAIPEI

Chinese Culture University Mandarin Learning Center Room 406, 4/F, 231 Jianguo S Rd Sec 2 ⓣ 02 2700 5858, ⓦ mlc.sce.pccu.edu.tw.

International Chinese Language Program National Taiwan University, 170 Xinhai Rd Sec 2, Daan ⓣ 02 2363 9123, ⓦ iclp.ntu.edu.tw.

Mandarin Training Center National Taiwan Normal University, 162 Heping E Rd Sec 1 ⓣ 02 7734 5130, ⓦ mtc.ntnu.edu.tw.

Taipei Language Institute 4/F, Taipei Roosevelt Center, 50 Roosevelt Rd Sec 3 ⓣ 02 2367 8228, ⓦ tli.com.tw.

TAICHUNG

Chinese Language Center at Donghai University Room 103, Language Building, 1727, Sec. 4, Taiwan Blvd, Xitun, 3 ⓣ 04 2359 0121, ⓦ clc.thu.edu.tw.

Fengchia University's Language Center 100 Wenhua Rd, Xitun ⓣ 04 2451 7250, ⓦ fcu.edu.tw.

National Chunghsing University 145 Xingda Rd S District ⓣ 04 2287 3181, ⓦ nchu.edu.tw.

Taipei Language Institute Taichung Center 4F-3, 489 Taiwan Blvd, Sec 2, West District ⓣ 04 2321 1998, ⓦ tli.com.tw.

KAOHSIUNG

Taipei Language Institute 2F, No. 507, Jhongshan 2nd Rd ⓣ 07 215 2965, ⓦ tli.com.tw.

Time

Taiwan is eight hours ahead of GMT (7hr ahead during BST), the same as Beijing, Hong Kong, Macau and Singapore. Daylight-saving time is not observed.

Tipping

On the whole, **tipping** at restaurants, bars and in taxis is not expected, although this is changing slowly in big cities. When you're travelling round the country you'll rarely be expected to tip, except perhaps in the occasional Western-oriented establishment, particularly those run by North American expats. Even then, many of these will levy a ten-percent **service charge** on your bill, obviating the need for any further gratuity. In some areas, such as Taipei's university district, you may receive a bill pointing out that a ten-percent service charge is not included, indicating that some sort of tip is expected. Bellboys at upmarket hotels always appreciate tips, as do tourist guides and tour leaders if you are on a group trip.

Tourist information

Taiwan's Tourism Bureau (ⓦ go2taiwan.net) operates a number of **overseas branches** (see opposite), with offices in Australia and the US offering basic leaflets on Taiwan's best-known attractions, while the main European office is in Frankfurt, Germany. There also are tourism offices scattered across Asia, with those in Hong Kong and Singapore offering the best range of English-language materials.

In Taiwan itself, reliable English information is a pretty mixed bag, especially considering the formidable number of **tourist information centres** around the island. Much of the material is simply translated directly from the original Chinese version, with literal interpretations that are more likely to leave tourists revelling in their literary merit than their usefulness. The most useful information sources are the **visitor centres** of the national parks and Scenic Areas, which often have educational overviews with English labelling and free pamphlets. Published under the auspices of the tourism bureau, the glossy bi-monthly **Travel in Taiwan** (W tit.com.tw) contains features on a variety of travel destinations and is worth seeking out. The free publication, which has **calendars of events** throughout the country, is available in many tourist information centres.

TAIWANESE TOURIST OFFICES ABROAD

Taiwan Visitors Association Friedrichstrasse 2-6, 60323 Frankfurt (T 49 69 610 743, W taiwantourismus.de).

Hong Kong Taiwan Visitors Association, Room 512, 5/F, Silvercord Tower 1, 30 Canton Rd, Tsim Sha Tsui, Kowloon (T 852 2581 0933).

US Taiwan Visitors Association, The Wilshire Colonnade Building, Suite 780, 3731 Wilshire Blvd, Los Angeles, CA 90010 (T 213 389 1158); 1 E 42nd St, 9/F, New York, NY 10017 (T 212 867 1632); 555 Montgomery St, Suite 505, San Francisco, CA 94111 (T 415 989 8677).

GOVERNMENT WEBSITES

Australian Department of Foreign Affairs W smartraveller.gov .au.

British Foreign & Commonwealth Office W gov.uk/ government/organisations/foreign-commonwealth-office.

Canadian Department of Foreign Affairs W voyage.gc.ca.

Irish Department of Foreign Affairs W foreignaffairs.gov.ie.

New Zealand Ministry of Foreign Affairs W mfat.govt.nz.

South Africa Department of Foreign Affairs W dfa.gov.za.

US Department of State W travel.state.gov.

Travellers with disabilities

Taiwan is making progress when it comes to accessible tourism, though overall the country remains woefully ill-equipped to accommodate travellers with **disabilities**. A good place to start is the **Eden Social Welfare Foundation** (T 02 2230 7715, W www.eden.org.tw), which specializes in helping people with disabilities in Taiwan. Eden operates a network of wheelchair-accessible buses – if you don't speak Chinese, someone at the foundation should be able to help you hook up with these. You should also get in touch with the **Taiwan Access for All Association** (T 02 2599 4649, W twacces-s4all.wordpress.com), a not-for-profit organization which has a special focus on accessible tourism; they can arrange hotels, transport, wheelchair rentals, assistants and organize excellent nature tours and day-trips all over the island, with English-speakers on hand as guides.

All stations and trains on the **Taipei MRT** (subway) are handicap-accessible, with special restrooms, ramps, elevators, extra-wide ticket gates and designated wheelchair areas on the trains. The **Kaohsiung MRT** has similar facilities. Most of the bigger hotels in Taipei can comfortably accommodate disabled travellers – *Sherwood*, *Fullerton*, *Grand Hyatt* and *Shangri-La's Far Eastern Plaza* among them. Major sights in Taipei shouldn't provide too many hassles: the National Palace Museum has handicapped-accessible restrooms and elevators, and getting around Taipei 101 and the Chiang Kai-shek Memorial is relatively straightforward.

However, most city streets and sidewalks pose formidable challenges, with consistently uneven pavements, steep inclines, steps and few access ramps to be found. Most of the older buildings remain frustratingly inaccessible for those with walking disabilities, and beyond Taipei, travelling can be tough going without the help of the above organizations.

Women travellers

Taiwan is an extremely safe country, and most **women travellers** here are unlikely to attract any special attention other than that usually paid to most foreign visitors. Still, it's always a good idea to be cautious when walking at night or through unlit areas such as underground tunnels, and, if possible, to take a friend with you. Late-night assaults on women by their **taxi drivers** are very rare but occasionally happen, and you should be attentive if you take a taxi at night by yourself. You'll minimize the possibility of being harassed if the driver knows he is accountable – calling for a cab and taking down the vehicle number is good practice, or if you hail one on the street you might visibly jot down the driver's name and vehicle number. Also, if you are carrying a mobile phone, make sure it's visible to the driver.

Taipei and around

1

Taipei and around

First-time visitors to Taipei (臺北; táiběi), Taiwan's political and financial heart and home to nearly three million people, can be forgiven for feeling a little discombobulated initially. Aside from the obvious Chinese influences, the city displays characteristics from Southeast Asia and Japan, too: Tokyo's order, energy and ramen joints; the motor scooters, street kitchens and hidden shrines of Ho Chi Minh City; Hong Kong's skywalks, pavement palm trees and decaying 1980s architecture. However, stay a little while, and you'll start to notice Taipei's own idiosyncrasies: locals slurping bubble tea and soybean milk (both Taipei creations), same-sex couples holding hands with a boldness that would be unacceptable in nearby nations, and gangs of businesspeople downing post-work beers at the ubiquitous "stir-fry" bar-restaurants. Throw in excellent museums and relaxing hot springs, all set against a backdrop of majestic mountains, and the sum total is one of the most pleasant cities in the Chinese-speaking world.

Though you could spend months here and still not absorb all the city has to offer, a week is usually enough to get a decent taster. Many tourists come solely to visit the mind-blowing **National Palace Museum**, but they risk missing out on a host of other attractions. Tour the **Presidential Building**, **National Taiwan Museum** and **Chiang Kai-shek Memorial Hall** to grapple with Taiwan's complex history, while **Longshan Temple** is the best introduction to its religious traditions. Further north, **Dihua Street** is packed with traditional stores, while **Baoan Temple** is one of the country's most elegant shrines, and the **Shunyi Museum of Formosan Aborigines** is an excellent introduction to Taiwan's indigenous peoples. East Taipei offers a change of pace and scenery, with **Xinyi** district a showcase of gleaming office towers and glitzy shopping malls, all of them overshadowed by cloud-scraping **Taipei 101**. Eating in Taipei is always memorable, with a huge choice of exceptional **restaurants**, **teahouses** and some of Taiwan's best **night markets**, while a vast range of department stores, specialist shops and antique stalls makes **shopping** in the city just as rewarding. To the north, **Yangmingshan National Park** and **Beitou** are where the best hikes and hot springs are located, while **Maokong** to the south provides a taster of Taiwan's wilder hinterland. There are also plenty of attractions in the wider city area, including the hot-spring baths of **Beitou**, the snack-shacks of **Tamsui**, and quaint **Sanxia**.

Highlights

❶ Baoan Temple Other religious sites get more tourists, but this temple is a work of art, packed with intricate carvings and exceptional craftsmanship. **See p.69**

❷ National Palace Museum One of the world's greatest museums, with an extraordinary collection of Chinese art and historical artefacts. **See p.71**

❸ Tapei 101 Take a super-fast lift to the top of Taiwan's tallest building for spectacular views of the city. **See p.76**

❹ Maokong Ride the cable car over the hills to the tea plantations of Maokong, home to alluring teahouses that stay open long into the night. **See p.78**

❺ Shilin Night Market Taipei's largest and most popular night market, with a vast array of cheap Taiwanese food, from garlic sausage to oyster omelettes. **See p.93**

❻ Wistaria Teahouse Sip oolong tea and absorb the historical ambience at Taipei's original teahouse. **See p.92**

❼ Beitou Soak up the hot-spring baths in one of Taiwan's oldest Japanese spas. **See p.99**

HIGHLIGHTS ARE MARKED ON THE MAP ON P.56

1

Brief history

People have lived in the Taipei Basin for thousands of years, but the modern city is an amalgamation of several villages brought together little over a century ago. The region's original inhabitants were the indigenous people known as the **Ketagalan**, but the Qing government in Beijing, having assumed control of Taiwan in 1683, granted farmer **Chen Lai-zhang** (from Quanzhou in Fujian, China), the first official licence to settle the Taipei area in 1709. More immigrants followed, leading to the creation of **Bangka**, Taipei's first Chinese settlement and today's Wanhua district. In 1853, new arrivals from Tong'an (Xiamen) clashed with more established settlers from Zhangzhou (both in Fujian) in what's known as the **Ding-Xia Feud**. The fight left 38 dead and led to the establishment of **Dadaocheng** (today's Datong) by the aggrieved Tong'an settlers.

Taipei (literally "North Taiwan", and actually pronounced *tai-bei*) Prefecture was created in 1875. The location of the city (initially referred to as "Chengnei" or city centre) was carefully chosen midway between Bangka and Dadaocheng so as not to provoke the rival clans. Construction of the city walls began in 1879, but, hampered by lack of funds, they weren't complete until 1884, marking the official **founding of the city**. When Taiwan was upgraded to a province of China in 1885, first governor **Liu Mingchuan** was already living in Taipei, but Dadun (modern Taichung), was chosen as the provincial capital. Liu started to develop Taipei regardless, building schools, establishing Taiwan's first railway and commissioning a British architect to construct the first bridge over the Tamsui River in 1888. Taipei was finally made **provincial capital** of Taiwan in 1894, on the eve of the **Japanese occupation** a few months later. The Japanese era (1895–1945) saw the emergence of modern Taipei – many of the capital's finest buildings were constructed in the first half of the twentieth century, and with the destruction of the city walls between 1900 and 1904, Bangka and Dadaocheng were gradually absorbed.

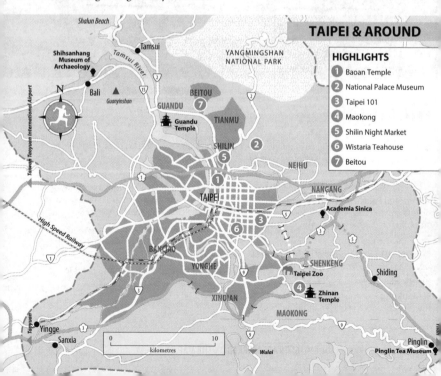

TAIPEI & AROUND

HIGHLIGHTS

1. Baoan Temple
2. National Palace Museum
3. Taipei 101
4. Maokong
5. Shilin Night Market
6. Wistaria Teahouse
7. Beitou

TAIPEI ORIENTATION AND ADDRESSES

Taipei's urban area sprawls for quite a distance; indeed, some would argue that the buildings don't finish until the far south of Taiwan. However, mercifully, the part that's of interest to tourists is rather small. The **old walled city**, which makes up much of what is now **Zhongzheng** district, is the de facto centre (even though it's geographically to the west) and contains a great number of notable sights and places to stay. Immediately to its west is **Wanhua** district, which features some important places of worship – both religious and commercial, since this is where the city's youth come to shop. Heading north you'll find the wide **Datong** and **Zhongshan** districts, while to the southeast is the **Da'an** area, which has plenty of places to eat and drink, thanks to the thousands of students at the nearby university. Then comes **East Taipei**, which includes the famous Taipei 101 building and its surrounding super-modern business and shopping area; some way to the southeast is **Maokong**, a mountain area famed for its tearooms and temples.

The **road layout** of the city is an elaborate grid, with the central point at the junction of Zhongxiao and Zhongshan roads just east of Taipei Station. Major roads leading east or west off **Zhongshan Road** have the suffix "East" or "West", while roads heading north or south from **Zhongxiao Road** and later **Bade Road** are similarly labelled "North" or "South". Roads are further divided into **sections** (Zhongxiao East has seven), and street numbers reset at the beginning of each section, so the section number is crucial when finding an address. Side streets off the main roads are known as "lanes": Lane 180, Zhongxiao East Road, Section 4, can be found by locating no. 180 on section four of Zhongxiao East Road – the lane should be right next to it. "Alleys" are the smallest units in the system, interconnecting with lanes and labelled similarly.

In February 1947, the **2-28 Incident** began here (see p.394), and in 1949 Taipei became the **capital of the Republic of China**, its population swollen by an influx of mainland Chinese – by 1967 it had topped 1.5 million, while today it's more like 2.7 million. These days being Taipei mayor is one of the nation's top jobs: Ma Ying-jeou, Lee Teng-hui and Chen Shui-bian all held the post before becoming president.

Zhongzheng

中正；zhōngzhèng

Renamed to commemorate Chiang Kai-shek in 1990, **Zhongzheng** district is where Taipei was born in the 1880s. Little remains of Liu Mingchuan's **old walled city** (城內; chéngnèi), as the walls and most of the early buildings were demolished by the Japanese (four gates survive). Indeed, it's the Japanese period that gives the area much of its historic character, most evident in its numerous government offices and the particularly distinctive **Presidential Building** southwest of **2-28 Peace Park**, another colonial legacy. Today's Zhongxiao, Zhongshan, Aiguo and Zhonghua roads follow the line of the old walls. Further south are the National Museum of History and **Chiang Kai-shek Memorial Hall**, one of Taipei's most famous landmarks.

The area is rather spread out, making it somewhat tedious to get around the many sights on foot, especially on a hot day – taxis can be tempting. Zhongzheng also punches a little below its weight in the restaurant department – most places focus on business customers, though there are a few good finds dotted around (see p.87).

Beimen

北門；běimén • Zhongxiao West Rd, Section 1 • Daily 24hr • Free • Beimen MRT

A good place to start a tour of the walled city is its old north gate, or **Beimen**. Completed in 1884 and also known as Chengenmen, its terracotta-coloured paint, sharp-pointed roof and traffic-heavy backdrop combine to provide a winning tradition-meets-modernity vista. Around sunset, if it's not raining, you'll find the gate surrounded by a phalanx of local photographers.

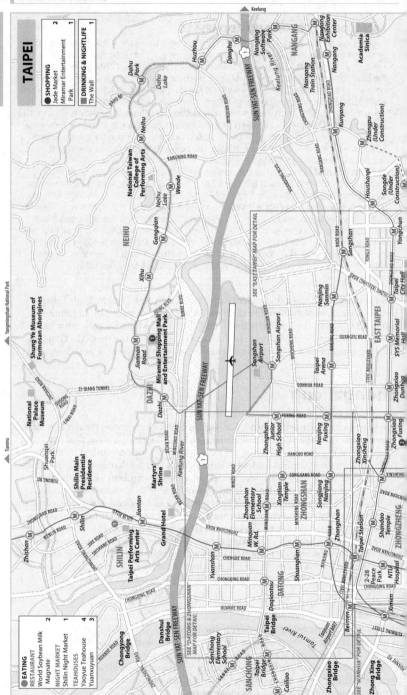

TAIPEI

● SHOPPING
Jade Market 2
Miramar Entertainment
Park 1

■ DRINKING & NIGHTLIFE
The Wall 1

● EATING
RESTAURANT
World Soybean Milk
Magnate 2
NIGHT MARKET
Shilin Night Market 1
TEAHOUSES
Yaoyue Teahouse 4
Yuanxuyuan 3

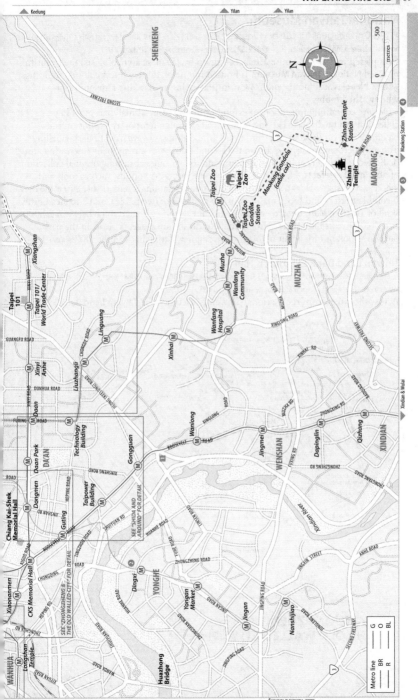

1

National Taiwan Museum

國立臺灣博物館; guólì táiwān bówùguǎn • 2 Xiangyang Rd • Tues–Sun 9.30am–5pm, last entry 4.30pm • NT$30 joint ticket with Taiwan Land Bank Exhibition Hall • ☏ 02 2382 2566, ⓦ www2.ntm.gov.tw • NTU Hospital MRT

Completed in 1915 to house artefacts dug up by Japanese archeologists, the beautifully restored **National Taiwan Museum** is housed in one of Taipei's finest colonial buildings, with a Neoclassical facade and 32 Corinthian columns flanking a magnificent whitewashed lobby.

Despite containing four floors of exhibition rooms, only a small part of its huge collection can be displayed at one time, mostly through temporary exhibits in the basement and on the first and third floors (these almost always have English labelling). The only permanent displays are on the second floor, with a marginally interesting area dedicated to Taiwan's animals and plants, and the far more absorbing original collection of **aboriginal artefacts**. Highlights include some rare píngpǔ finds, such as tools and wood carvings, as well as a small **prehistoric area** containing a remarkable ensemble of Neolithic pottery and tools, many from the Beinan site (see p.321), and a replica of the skull of **Tsochen Man**, unearthed in Tainan county and estimated to be between 20,000 and 30,000 years old. There's also permanent exhibition space, of sorts, in the park outside – look out for a pair of locomotive engines, dating back to the 1870s and 1880s.

Taiwan Land Bank Exhibition Hall

土銀展示館; tǔ yín zhǎnshì guan • 25 Xiangyang Rd • Tues–Sun 9.30am–5pm • NT$30 joint ticket with National Taiwan Museum • ☏ 02 2314 2699, ⓦ www2.ntm.gov.tw • NTU Hospital MRT

Across the street from the National Taiwan Museum is the **Taiwan Land Bank Exhibition**

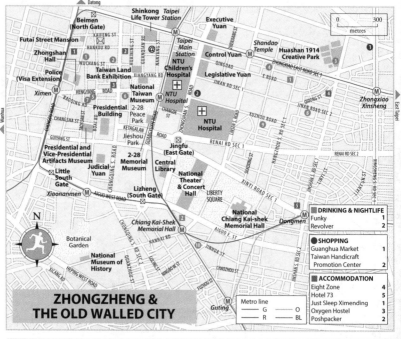

ZHONGZHENG & THE OLD WALLED CITY

● DRINKING & NIGHTLIFE	
Funky	1
Revolver	2

● SHOPPING	
Guanghua Market	1
Taiwan Handicraft Promotion Center	2

■ ACCOMMODATION	
Eight Zone	4
Hotel 73	5
Just Sleep Ximending	1
Oxygen Hostel	3
Poshpacker	2

Metro line	
— G	— O
— R	— BL

● EATING			CAFÉS		Old Park	6
RESTAURANTS		Fu Hang Soy Milk	4	Astoria	2	Snow King	1
		Old Wang's Beef		Mayor's Residence		TEAHOUSE	
Alleycat's Pizza	3	Noodles	7	Arts Salon	9	Cha for Tea	5
Daka	10	Shao Shao Ke	8				

Hall, another Neoclassical gem completed in 1933 for Nippon Kangyo Bank. It served as the Land Bank after World War II, and its huge two-storey vault has been converted into a cramped but illuminating exhibition on the building's history. The big crowd-pleaser here, though, is the **Evolution Hall**, with its array of giant dinosaur skeletons, T-Rex and two-storey sauropods among them. English is used throughout, and you can grab a coffee at the terrace upstairs.

2-28 Peace Park

二二八和平公園; èrèrbā hépíng gōngyuán • 3 Ketagalan Blvd (also Xiangyang Rd) • Daily 24hr • Free • NTU Hospital MRT

Behind the National Museum, **2-28 Peace Park** was created by the Japanese in 1899 and known as Taipei Park or New Park until 1997, when it was renamed to commemorate the tragic massacre that began on February 28, 1947 (see p.394). The park featured heavily in Pai Hsien-yung's groundbreaking novel *Crystal Boys*, which highlights the struggles of Taipei's gay community in the 1960s, but today it's a popular place for locals to stroll, have lunch and take photos. It contains several Qing dynasty and Japanese-era relics, though many of the latter have been torn down over the years, most notably Japanese Governor-General Kodama Gentaro's statue, destroyed to make way for the spire-like **2-28 Monument** in the centre of the park.

2-28 Memorial Museum

二二八紀念館; èrèrbā jìniànguǎn • 3 Ketagalan Blvd • Tues–Sun 10am–5pm • NT$20 (free on Wed) • ☎ 02 2389 7228 • NTU Hospital MRT

In the southeast corner of 2-28 Peace Park, the former home of Japan's colonial Taipei Broadcasting Bureau has been converted into the **2-28 Memorial Museum**, a fascinating if sobering place to learn about the 2-28 Incident and subsequent struggle for democracy in Taiwan. Apart from an informative video with English subtitles, the rest of the museum's extensive displays are labelled in Chinese only, so it's best to visit midweek, when there are fewer visitors, and ask for an English-speaking guide (free). The first-floor exhibits provide the historical context of the Incident, starting with the Japanese occupation, while the second floor recounts the major events of the massacre and subsequent "White Terror".

Presidential Building

總統府; zǒngtǒng fǔ • 122 Chongqing S Rd Sec 1; entrance at back of building at Boai and Baoqing roads • Mon–Fri 9am–noon; irregular "open house" events usually 8am–4pm • Free; reservations required three days in advance via website; ID required (passport preferred) • ☎ 02 2312 0760, ⓦ english.president.gov.tw • Ximen MRT

At the heart of what was once the old walled city lies the imposing redbrick facade of the **Presidential Building**, its 60m tower for years the highest point in Taipei. The president and vice president still work here and security is understandably tight – for visits on weekdays you must now make a reservation in advance. English-speaking guides are provided free of charge – it's not possible to tour the place without one, and many exhibits have Chinese-only captions.

Constructed between 1912 and 1919 by the Japanese to mimic British imperial architecture, the building served as the office of Japanese governor generals until 1945, assuming the function of Taiwan's presidential office from 1949. The first-floor rooms are arranged around two inner gardens that form the Chinese character for "sun" (日) when viewed from above (also the first character for "Japan"). Here you'll find an informative exhibition on all nineteen Japanese governor generals, including the fourth governor, **Kodama Gentaro** – the Taiwanese used to say "his spit is law", a fairly vivid indication that colonial rule wasn't all green tea and sushi at the time. The building also contains exhibits on Taiwan's five post-Japanese-era presidents, the history of the site itself, a basic history of the island and temporary art displays.

1

On a dozen or so Saturdays and Sundays throughout the year the building has an "**open house**" (no reservations required), which means you get to see some of the other areas (including the impressive Entrance Hall and Presidential Reception Room), wander around the first floor independently and take photographs (forbidden on weekdays).

Presidential and Vice-Presidential Artifacts Museum

總統副總統文物館; zŏngtŏng fùzŏngtŏng wénwùguǎn • 2 Changsha St Sec 1 • Mon–Sat 9.30am–5pm • Free • ☎ 02 2316 1000, ⓦ www.drnh.gov.tw • Ximen MRT

The second floor of the elegant building housing Taiwan's Academia Historica (國史館; guóshǐguǎn) serves as the **Presidential and Vice-Presidential Artifacts Museum**, a sort of political history museum combined with bizarre art gallery. The political bit can seem a little dry, with rooms dedicated to Taiwan's electoral process, the presidency, constitution and inauguration day; you can take the oath of office yourself next to a painting of Sun Yat-sen.

The more enticing section displays a range of **official gifts** to Taiwan's presidents, most pertinently a chunk of the Berlin Wall and a key to the city of Paris. You'll find a room housing presents from various Oceanian nations – including an outrigger canoe from the Marshall Islands – and another room of objects from Central America and the Caribbean. The limited sources of these gifts brings Taiwan's present-day predicament – it is recognised by nineteen mostly tiny UN member states, and dropping – sharply into focus.

National Museum of History

國立歷史博物館; guólì lìshǐ bówùguǎn • 49 Nanhai Rd • Tues–Sun 10am–6pm • NT$30 • ☎ 02 2361 0270, ⓦ www.nmh. gov.tw • Chiang Kai-shek Memorial Hall MRT

The **National Museum of History** was founded in 1955, the third in a series of ageing Ming and Qing dynasty replica buildings along this stretch of Nanhai Road. The bulk of its collection, largely comprising artefacts from central China, was transferred from the Henan Museum back on the mainland in 1949. If you've already been to the National Palace Museum, you might feel it's a waste of time coming here, but it's much smaller and easier to absorb – the extensive collection of **Shang and Zhou dynasty bronzes** is particularly impressive and the temporary exhibits usually have a Taiwanese focus, with a bias towards painting and calligraphy.

Chiang Kai-shek Memorial Hall

中正紀念堂; zhōngzhèng jìniàntáng • 21 Zhongshan S Rd • Daily 9am–6pm, changing of guard hourly 9am–5pm • Free • ☎ 02 2343 1100, ⓦ www.cksmh.gov.tw • Chiang Kai-shek Memorial Hall MRT

The collection of monumental architecture surrounding **Chiang Kai-shek Memorial Hall** is one of Taipei's grandest sights. It doesn't seem to matter that all this was completed in the 1980s – these buildings are some of the largest examples of classical Chinese architecture anywhere in the world.

Built as a shrine to commemorate the man who – admire him or loathe him – did more to create modern Taiwan than any other, the memorial hall sits at the centre of a grand plaza (known as "**Liberty Square**" since the DPP renamed it in 2007). The plaza's striking 70m octagonal roof is designed to resemble the Temple of Heaven in Beijing, and is covered with blue glazed tiles. Start by climbing the 89 granite stairs to the **main hall**, which contains a giant bronze statue of the Generalissimo under an elegant red-cypress-wood ceiling; though it seems a bit like a mausoleum, Chiang isn't buried inside. Inscribed onto the marble wall behind the statue are the three pillars of Chiang's political thought, loosely adapted from Sun Yat-sen's "Three Principles of the People": Science (科學; kēxué), Democracy (民主; mínzhǔ) and Ethics (倫理; lúnlǐ). The **changing of the guard** here is an elaborate ceremony that takes around ten minutes. Downstairs you'll find a series of renovated art galleries, while on the ground level exhibition rooms tell the story of Chiang's life through photographs, paintings and personal effects, though you might tire of the predictably flattering commentary. His two shiny Cadillacs are also on display. Don't miss the gift shop either, where Chiang's image – rather like Mao's in China – now adorns designer T-shirts, bags and trendy cards.

National Theater & Concert Hall

國家兩廳院; guójiā liǎngtīngyuàn • Liberty Square (21 Zhongshan S Rd) • Tours Mon–Fri 11am, 1pm & 3pm • Tours NT$100; book online at least a week in advance • ☎ 02 3393 9888, ⓦ npac-ntch.org • Chiang Kai-shek Memorial Hall MRT

The magnificent classical Chinese buildings flanking the CKS Memorial Hall either side of Liberty Square comprise the **National Theater**, closest to the MRT station exit, and the **National Concert Hall**. The two halls, with traditional hip-and-gable roofs, were completed in 1987. If you can't catch a show here, consider the illuminating one-hour tours, though these will be in Chinese only unless you make a special request by phone.

Huashan 1914 Creative Park

華山1914文化創意產業園區; Huáshān 1914 wénhuà chuàngyì chǎnyè yuánqū • 1 Bade Rd Sec 1 • Daily 10am–11pm, some galleries close at 6pm • Free • ☎ 02 2358 1914, ⓦ www.huashan1914.com • Zhongxiao Xinsheng MRT

The **Huashan 1914 Creative Park** occupies the grounds of the old Taipei Winery, built between 1914 and 1916 and abandoned in 1987. The site now makes for a pleasant afternoon of wandering, with the restored, high-ceilinged warehouses serving as performance spaces, artsy shops and temporary art exhibition halls. The annual **Simple Life Festival** is held here in December, and free concerts often take place over summer weekends.

Wanhua

萬華; wànhúa

Full of shopaholics, East Asian tourists and trendy locals, it may come as a surprise to learn that modern **Wanhua** district – bounded by Zhongzheng to the east and the Tamsui River to the west – is actually the oldest part of the city. Founded by immigrants from China in the early eighteenth century, the village was gradually absorbed by newly created Taipei in the 1890s. Originally known as **Bangka** or Manka in Taiwanese (from the Ketagalan word for "canoe"), its name was changed by the Japanese in 1920: the new characters read "Manka" in Japanese but "Wanhua" in Chinese.

Northern Wanhua is home to super-charged **Ximending**; this is where Taipei's teenagers come to have fun, and even on weekday evenings it can be packed with Mandopop fans checking out wannabe performers, and wearing the latest fads. There are several great places to eat (see p.87) within and around Ximending's pleasing pedestrianized zone.

Southern Wanhua has an altogether different atmosphere – home to several **temples** and **night markets**, this earthy area was once a major red-light district. While it's perfectly safe, you'll still see some seediness going on, though these days most commonly behind the veneers of teahouses and karaoke.

Covered sidewalks in Wanhua provide shelter from sun and rain, and the area's sights are best reached on foot.

Longshan Temple

龍山寺; lóngshān sì • 211 Guangzhou St • Daily 6am–10pm • ☎ 02 8252 0103, ⓦ lungshan.org.tw • Longshan Temple MRT

The most important of Wanhua's "big three" temples (the others being Qingshui and Qingshan), **Longshan Temple** is the ideal place to soak up Taiwan's vibrant religious traditions. Located a block north of the MRT station across Mangka Park, the temple

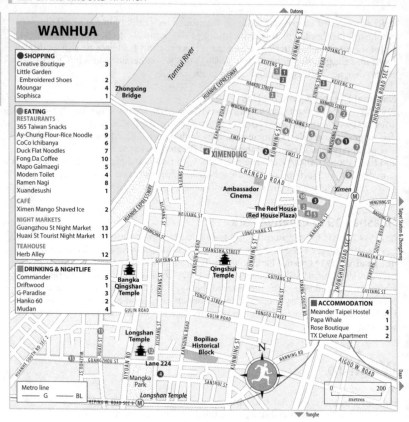

WANHUA

SHOPPING

Creative Boutique	3
Little Garden Embroidered Shoes	2
Moungar	4
Sophisca	1

EATING

RESTAURANTS

365 Taiwan Snacks	3
Ay-Chung Flour-Rice Noodle	9
CoCo Ichibanya	6
Duck Flat Noodles	7
Fong Da Coffee	10
Mapo Galmaegi	5
Modern Toilet	4
Ramen Nagi	8
Xuandesushi	1

CAFÉ

Ximen Mango Shaved Ice	2

NIGHT MARKETS

Guangzhou St Night Market	13
Huaxi St Tourist Night Market	11

TEAHOUSE

Herb Alley	12

DRINKING & NIGHTLIFE

Commander	5
Driftwood	1
G-Paradise	3
Hanko 60	2
Mudan	4

ACCOMMODATION

Meander Taipei Hostel	4
Papa Whale	1
Rose Boutique	3
TX Deluxe Apartment	2

was established in 1738 (making it Taipei's oldest), renovated 1919–1924 and partially rebuilt after US bombing destroyed much of the complex during World War II. It's principally a Buddhist temple dedicated to the Bodhisattva **Guanyin**, but there are more than a hundred deities worshipped here, mostly from the Taoist pantheon.

The main entrance on Guangzhou Street borders a pleasant courtyard, replete with artificial waterfall on the right-hand side. Before entering the temple proper, take a look at the two dragon pillars outside the **Front Hall**, the only bronze pair in Taiwan. Once inside you'll see prayer tables and worshippers facing the **Main Hall** in the centre where Guanyin is enshrined – the principal image of the goddess has proved virtually indestructible over the years, surviving local conflicts, earthquakes and even the US bombing. Note the two gold censers (incense burners) in front of the hall, with their vivid cast images of "silly barbarians lifting a corner of the temple", supposedly eighteenth-century depictions of the Dutch. This is the busiest part of the temple, but the deity-packed **Rear Hall** also receives a steady stream of visitors. The goddess Mazu is worshipped in the centre and fringed by guāngmíng lights, each representing a donation made in the hope of attracting good fortune. To the far right is a separate shrine dedicated to the gods of literature, primarily Wenchang Dijun in the middle, patronized by students and anxious parents at examination time. Guan Di occupies the shrine on the far left and in front of this in a side hall is a newer altar dedicated to the Matchmaker, a sort of Chinese cupid (see p.409).

Herb Alley

青草巷; qīngcǎo xiàng • Lane 224, Xichang St • Longshan Temple MRT

The narrow, L-shaped passage next to Longshan Temple has been dubbed **Herb Alley**, crammed with hundred-year-old stalls selling aloe vera, sweet basil, herbal teas (see p.92), lavender, Japanese knotweed (literally "tiger cane" in Chinese) and a variety of dried Chinese herbs and roots including "white-horse dung" – you'll probably smell it before you see it.

Bopiliao Old Street

剝皮寮老街; bōpíliáo lǎojiē • Lane 173, Kangding Rd (at Guangzhou St) • Tues–Sun 9am–9pm; Heritage & Culture Education Center Tues–Sun 9am–5pm • Free • ☎ 02 2336 1704, ✺ hcec.tp.edu.tw

One of Taipei's newest regeneration projects, **Bopiliao Old Street** comprises an artfully renovated Qing dynasty alley book-ended by two museums – extremely photogenic but unfortunately very empty, despite plans to rent the renovated shophouses to small shops and businesses. Just to the east, the **Heritage & Culture Education Center** at 101 Guangzhou St has a few family-friendly displays covering the history of the street.

Qingshan Temple

青山宮; qīngshāngōng • 218 Guiyang St Sec 2 • Daily 5.30am–9.30pm • ☎ 02 2382 2296 • Longshan Temple MRT

Established in 1854 by immigrants from Quanzhou, **Qingshan Temple** is dedicated to General Zhang, a quasi-historical figure from China's Three Kingdoms period, also known as "King of Qingshan" and a popular administrator. Admirers began to worship him after his death, and in time he was credited with special powers of protection – he was also the deity favoured by tea merchants in the area. Qingshan is enshrined amid an elaborate gold altar in the **Main Hall**; beyond here the **Rear Hall** houses various deities, but don't miss the temple's gold-painted **carvings**, particularly on the beams and third-floor ceiling, which are incredibly ornate.

Qingshui Temple

清水巖; qīngshuǐyán • 81 Kangding Rd • Daily 6am–9pm • ☎ 02 2371 1517 • Ximen MRT

At the end of a narrow lane bordered by a row of cheap food stalls, **Qingshui Temple** was founded in 1787 by immigrants from Anxi county in Fujian. The temple is dedicated to Chinese hero Chen Zhao-ying, another historical figure who was later deified. The temple was burned to the ground during the "Ding-Xia" Feud in 1853, but rebuilt by 1867 – the **Main Hall** has survived more or less intact since then and contains the seven original images of the deity brought from China. The most powerful is known as the "Penglai Divine Progenitor", whose nose is said to fall off in times of danger, only to miraculously reattach itself when the coast is clear. He's shared with the Qingshui Temple in Tamsui, spending six months in each place. Note the intricate artwork inside, particularly on the roof beams.

The Red House

西門紅樓; xīmén hónglóu • 10 Chengdu Rd • Tues–Thurs & Sun 11am–9.30pm, Fri & Sat 11am–10pm; art boutiques Tues–Thurs & Sun 2–9.30pm, Fri & Sat 2–10pm; art market Sat & Sun 2–10pm • Free • ☎ 02 2311 9380, ✺ www.redhouse.org.tw • Ximen MRT

The handsome **Red House**, a former redbrick market building and movie theatre completed in 1908 by the Japanese, now houses a series of **art boutiques**, a teahouse, a theatre, a live-music venue (*Riverside Live House*), and a small exhibition on the history of the site. The courtyard around the building is crammed with open-air bars (all gay-friendly; see p.95) and restaurants; an **art market** also runs here most weekends.

1

Datong

大同; dàtóng

Taipei's second oldest neighbourhood after Wanhua, **Datong** borders the Tamsui River north of Ximending. The district evolved from two villages; north of Minquan Road, **Dalongtong** was established in the early eighteenth century, while to the south **Dadaocheng** was created in 1853 by refugees from Wanhua. The latter flourished in the 1870s as tea exports boomed and foreign companies established bases on the wharf. Today it's an enticing place to wander, its narrow lanes littered with historic buildings, traditional shops and temples.

Historic **Dihua Street** (迪化街; díhuà jiē) runs parallel to the river, cutting through the southern half of Datong, and is crammed with photogenic shophouses built in Chinese Baroque style, many dating from the 1920s. At Chinese New Year, the street expands into an open-air emporium for traditional gifts and snacks. North of Nanjing Road the street is lined with silk and cloth stores, followed by the stalls of **Yunglo Market**, then shops dedicated to traditional Chinese medicine, herbs and dried foods.

Xiahai City God Temple

霞海城隍廟; xiáhǎi chénghuáng miào • 61 Dihua St • Daily 6am–8pm • ⓦ tpecitygod.org • Daqiaotou or Zhongshan MRT

The **Xiahai City God Temple** may be small, but it's one of Taipei's most venerated places of worship. Completed in 1859 by Tong'an (Xiamen) Chinese migrants to replace the one destroyed in Wanhua six years earlier, the main City God statue inside was brought to Taiwan from its hometown (Xiacheng) in China in 1821. The main shrine contains the revered City God image and his officials, but it's also the most popular place in Taipei to make offerings to the "**Matchmaker**", represented by a 43cm-high image of an old man with a long beard, in front and to the left of the main altar. Praying to this Chinese cupid is believed to result in finding your ideal partner in less than six months – should this tempt you, leaflets in English explain how you can make an offering. The side hall to the right of the main shrine contains Guanyin (nearest the entrance), the City God's wife next door (make-up is a common offering here) and at the end, an altar commemorating the 38 men (the yì yǒng gōng) killed saving the City God in the Ding-Xia Feud of 1853. The City God's birthday on Lunar May 13 (usually in June) is one of Taipei's biggest religious **festivals** involving fireworks, parades and traditional performances over several days.

Wang's Tea

有記名茶; yǒujì míngchá • 26 Lane 64, Chongqing N Rd Sec 2 • Mon–Sat 9am–8.30pm • Free • ☎ 02 2555 9164, ⓦ wangtea .com.tw • Zhongshan MRT

Housed in a beautifully restored building, **Wang's Tea** offers an enjoyable introduction to Taiwanese tea culture (though they don't always have English speakers). The tea merchant was first established in Fujian, China, in 1890 and opened here after the family fled the mainland in 1949 (they had already set up a branch in Dadaocheng in 1907). You can sample quality Taiwanese tea inside, and tour the factory at the back, where the aroma of

---

SHOPPING ON DIHUA STREET: HERBS, CRAFTS AND SHARK FIN

Dihua Street is justly famed for its magnificent ensemble of early nineteenth-century shop-houses, many of which have been run by the same family for generations – examples include the **Qianyuan Medicine Shop** (see p.98) and **Yong Xing**, a traditional ironmonger at number 288. Here and there you'll also find places selling shark fin – some in prodigious volumes; you should avoid buying anything from any such enterprises. There are also some newer, tastefully renovated stores, including **Artyard** pottery shop (see p.98) and **Sunrice**, a century-old rice shop which has reinvented itself in recent years (see p.99).

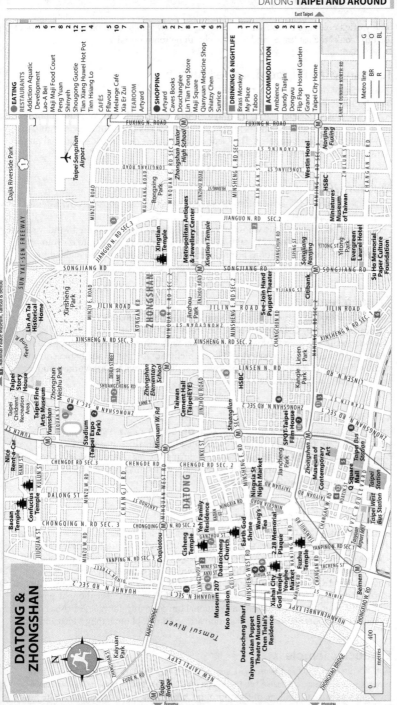

East Taipei

● EATING

RESTAURANTS

Addiction Aquatic Development	3
Lao-A Bei	6
Maji Maji Food Court	8
Peng Yuan	2
Shinyeh	12
Shougong Guotie	11
Tian Xiang Huwei Hot Pot	4
Tien Hsiang Lo	

CAFÉS

Fflavour	5
Melange Café	10
Xia Er Zui	7
TEAROOM	
Artyard	9

■ SHOPPING

Artyard	5
Caves Books	2
Douchanglee	7
Lin Tian Tong Store	8
Maji Square	1
Qianyuan Medicine Shop	6
Shiatzy Chen	3
Sunrice	4

■ DRINKING & NIGHTLIFE

Brass Monkey	3
My Place	1
Taboo	2

■ ACCOMMODATION

Ambience	6
Dandy Tianjin	3
Dongwu	2
Flip Flop Hostel Garden	5
Grand	1
Taipei City Home	4

Metro line	
G	
O	
BL	
BR	
R	

DATONG & ZHONGSHAN

1

freshly dried oolong is overpowering. You can also view the charcoal pits and barrels once used to "cook" the tea leaves, and visit the charming room upstairs.

Taiyuan Asian Puppet Theatre Museum

台原亞洲偶戲博物館; tái yuán yà zhōu ǒuxì bówùguǎn • 79 Xining N Rd • Tues–Sun 10am–5pm • NT$80 • ☎ 02 2552 9079, ⓦ taipeipuppet.com • Daqiaotou or Zhongshan MRT

A short detour off Dihua Street, the **Taiyuan Asian Puppet Theatre Museum** is housed in an atmospheric shophouse and is made up of three floors of exhibits devoted to Taiwanese and Asian **puppetry**. The Nadou Theatre next door hosts traditional puppet shows – check the website to confirm dates.

Museum207

迪化207博物館; díhuà 207 bówùguǎn • 207 Dihua St • Daily except Tues 10am–5.30pm • Free • ☎ 02 2557 3680, ⓦ museum207.org • Daqiaotou MRT

Housed in a restored building whose salmon-pink tiles and parsley-painted windows make it look rather edible, the new **Museum207** is certainly worth popping into on your way around Dihua Street. Exhibitions revolve every few months, but the real highlight is heading up to the top floor for superlative views over the surrounding's rooftops.

Cisheng Temple

慈聖宮; císhènggōng • 17 Lane 49, Baoan St (off Yanping St) • Daily 6am–8pm • Daqiaotou MRT

Dedicated to Mazu, **Cisheng Temple** dates from the 1860s when immigrants fleeing Wanhua to the south established it on the riverbank – it was moved to this location in 1914. Today it's a quiet, unassuming place, chiefly notable for its shady forecourt lined with Indian laurel trees and excellent seafood stalls, filled with local workers and mahjong players at lunchtime.

Dadaocheng Church

大稻埕教堂; dàdàochéng jiāotáng • 40 Ganzhou St • ☎ 02 2553 9741 • Daqiaotou MRT

Built in 1915 to replace the original established by Canadian missionary George Mackay, **Dadaocheng Church** was destroyed during the Japanese invasion. Its red brickwork has since been immaculately restored (with a massive, modern extension on the back), but there's little to see inside.

Museum of Contemporary Art

台北當代藝術館; táiběi dāngdài yìshùguǎn • 39 Changan W Rd • Tues–Sun 10am–6pm, but sometimes closes for up to two weeks between exhibitions; check website • NT$50 • ☎ 02 2552 3721, ⓦ www.mocataipei.org.tw • Zhongshan MRT

Occupying one of the most attractive Japanese-era buildings in the city, the **Museum of Contemporary Art** (MOCA) is an innovative modern art gallery, a short walk from Zhongshan MRT station. Constructed in the 1920s and 1930s, it served as an elementary school and Taipei's City Hall before opening as MOCA in 2001. The thought-provoking temporary exhibitions here feature international but primarily Taiwanese artists, and include contemporary painting, installation art, sculpture, photography, video and film.

Confucius Temple

孔廟; kǒngmiào • 275 Dalong St, entrance near junction with Kulun St • Tues–Sat 8.30am–9pm, Sun 8.30am–5pm; dance performances Sat 9am; traditional ceremonies Tues–Fri 9am & 4pm • ☎ 02 2592 3934, ⓦ www.ct.taipei.gov.tw • Yuanshan MRT

In what was once the village of **Dalongtong** (大龍峒; dàlóngtóng), famed as the home of scholars, Taipei's **Confucius Temple** is best known for hosting the world's most authentic annual celebration of Confucius's **birthday** on September 28 (see p.37). Though the great teacher is still revered in Taiwan, he's not associated with any of the daily rituals that make other temples so colourful, and on other days the temple is relatively peaceful. Built in South Fujianese style but laid out according to the original Confucius temple in Qufu (in China's Shandong province), the oldest buildings here were constructed between 1927 and 1939.

A short, signposted walk from the MRT, the temple is entered from the southwest via the **Hong Gate**, which leads into a garden with Minglun Hall on your left and the **Li Gate** just ahead; walk through this to get to the front of the main temple complex. The first building on your left is the ceremonial **Lingxing Gate**, while beyond this the **Yi Gate** fronts the central stone courtyard and **Dacheng Hall**, the most important part of the temple. Note the decorated cylinders on the hall's roof, symbolizing the bamboo containers used to hide Confucian classics during the Qin Emperor's fanatical "Burning of the Books" in 213 BC. The hall is typically bare inside: it contains a single tablet commemorating Confucius in the centre, and sixteen others for the Four Sages (including Mencius) and the Twelve Wise Men, all Confucian disciples, as well as various musical instruments used in ceremonies. The black tablet hanging from the beam above the shrine was written by Chiang Kai-shek and says "education for all". The courtyard is ringed by the **East and West Rooms**, containing the memorial tablets of 154 other Confucian disciples and scholars, while the **Chongsheng Shrine** at the back of the complex houses tablets venerating the first five generations of Confucius's ancestors.

Baoan Temple

保安宫; bǎoān gong • 61 Hami St • Daily 6am–10pm • ☎ 02 2595 1676, ⓦ baoan.org.tw • Yuanshan MRT

A few metres north of the Confucius Temple is **Baoan Temple**, Taipei's most beautiful shrine. Though there are many deities enshrined here, the principal figure is Baosheng Dadi, regarded as a god of medicine or healing (see p.408). Tradition maintains that immigrants from Tong'an (Xiamen) began worshipping here in 1742 and a simple shrine was completed in 1760, but the first official temple was constructed between 1805 and 1830. The temple won a UNESCO conservation award in 2003 in recognition of the incredible restoration work completed in the 1990s.

Before you go in, check out the painted wall carving inside the easternmost of the compound's three southern gates – it features Chinese hero Yue Fei having the words "Serve Your Country" being carved onto his back by his patriotic mother. Once inside you'll see the **Main Hall** across the courtyard, packed with numerous images of Baosheng and surrounded by statues of the **36 celestial officials**, carved between 1829 and 1834 and exceptionally rare pieces of temple art. The seven eye-catching **murals** that adorn the outer walls of the hall depict various Chinese legends and were completed in 1973. The **Drum Tower** on the left (west) side of the courtyard houses a shrine to the Birth Goddess, while the **Bell Tower** on the opposite side is an altar to Mazu. Shennong Dadi, the god of agriculture, is worshipped in the **Rear Hall**. The **Baosheng Cultural Festival** is usually held April to May and comprises several weeks of traditional performances leading up to **Baosheng's birthday** (Lunar March 15), including an extensive programme of Chinese opera and music in the evenings, and a boisterous parade the day before the main ceremony.

Zhongshan

中山; zhōngshān

Bounded by Fuxing Road in the east and maple-lined Zhongshan Road in the west, **Zhongshan** is a lively modern district covering much of the northern part of central

1

Taipei. Zhongshan is primarily a collection of residential neighbourhoods, shopping streets and offices with no discernible centre, its sights spread out and often best combined with attractions in other areas; Taipei's excellent **Fine Arts Museum** is close to the temples in Dalongtong, while the **Su Ho Memorial Paper Culture Foundation** lies much further south.

Taipei Fine Arts Museum

台北美術館; táiběi měishùguǎn • 181 Zhongshan N Rd Sec 3 • Tues–Fri & Sun 9.30am–5.30pm, Sat 9.30am–8.30pm • NT$30 (free Sat 5–8.30pm) • ☎ 02 2595 7656, ⓦ tfam.museum • Yuanshan MRT

If you only have time for one modern art gallery in Taipei, make it the **Taipei Fine Arts Museum**, a short walk from Yuanshan MRT. Its four floors primarily showcase modern Taiwanese art – though exhibitions change every few months, they usually include pieces from the museum's extensive permanent collection. This includes Chen Cheng-po's nostalgic *Street Scene on a Summer Day* and Liao Chi-chun's colourful oil painting *Courtyard with Banana Trees*, as well as works by Li Chi-mao, Lee Chun-shan and Yu Cheng-yao. The popular shopping and eating destination **Maji Square** (see p.88 & p.97) is a short walk from the museum.

Taipei Story House

台北故事館; táiběi gùshìguǎn • 181-1 Zhongshan N Rd Sec 3 • Tues–Sun 10am–5.30pm; Story Tea House Tues–Fri 11am–7pm, Sat & Sun 11am–9pm • NT$50 • ☎ 02 2587 5565, ⓦ storyhouse.com.tw • Yuanshan MRT

Built in 1914 as an opulent, Tudor-style private mansion for tea merchant Chen Chao-chun, the **Taipei Story House** is now a venue for rotating art exhibitions (previous themes have included the history of bridal gowns), and performances of *nanguan* music.

Lin An Tai Historical Home

林安泰古厝; línāntài gǔcuò • 5 Binjiang St • Tues–Sat 9am–5pm • Free • ☎ 02 2599 6026, ⓦ english.linantai.taipei • Walkable from Fine Arts Museum, but crossing Xinsheng Rd can be dangerous; it's best to take a taxi, or bus #R50 from museum or Yuanshan MRT

Set on the northern edge of Xinsheng Park, the **Lin An Tai Historical Home** is Taipei's oldest residential building. It was built by wealthy merchant Lin Hui-gong in 1783–85 and moved here from its original location in Daan district in 1983, to avoid destruction during a road-building project. The house is a pristine example of southern Fujian-style architecture from the Qing dynasty, though apart from a few pieces of furniture there's not much to see inside – the historic ambience is reduced further by the roar of jets coming into land at Songshan Airport, and the highway overpass at the back.

Xingtian Temple

行天宮; xíngtiān gong • 109 Minquan E Rd Sec 2, at Songjiang Rd • Daily 4am–10.30pm • ☎ 02 2503 1831, ⓦ www.ht.org.tw • Xingtian Temple MRT

Completed in classical Chinese style in 1967, **Xingtian Temple** is a fascinating place to observe **traditional rituals**. Dedicated to Guan Di, represented by a large statue in the **Main Hall**, the main attraction for locals is the smorgasbord of spiritual services on offer; these include píng ān dài (a charm worn around the neck), shōuhún (spiritual healing) and shōujīng (fortune telling by drawing lots). Most temples offer the latter, but here believers have a choice of one hundred readings dating back over eight hundred years, compared to the usual 64. Volunteers, often English-speaking and wearing blue robes (dào yī), are on hand to answer questions.

Su Ho Memorial Paper Culture Foundation

樹火紀念紙文化基金會; shùhuǒ jìniànzhǐ wénhuà jījīnhuì • 68 Changan E Rd Sec 2 • Mon–Sat 9.30am–4.30pm; paper-making Mon–Sat 10am, 11am, 2pm & 3pm • NT$100 (NT$180 with paper-making) • ☎ 02 2507 5535, ⓦ suhopaper.org.tw • Songjiang Nanjing MRT

One of Taipei's few craft-based museums, the **Su Ho Memorial Paper Culture Foundation** offers a welcome break between temples and department stores, and the chance to make your own traditional Chinese paper.

Crammed into this four-storey shophouse are tastefully presented displays on **paper-making** and Taiwan's paper industry, a mini paper mill and a gift shop. Though most of the labels are in Chinese, there's an informative English audio-guide included in the entry price. The "DIY" paper-making sessions can be a lot of fun, though usually require a group – if your visit coincides with a private tour group, you're welcome to join in.

Miniatures Museum of Taiwan

袖珍博物館, xiùzhēn bówùguǎn • 96 Jianguo N Rd Sec 1 • Tues–Sun 10am–6pm • NT$180, children NT$100 • ☎ 02 2515 0583, ⓦ www.mmot.com.tw • Songjiang Nanjing MRT

Especially popular with families, the **Miniatures Museum of Taiwan** is a slightly kitsch but absorbing collection of tiny palaces, cars, houses, intricate furniture, a mine and even the world's smallest television (it's about 2cm wide, and really does work). The craftsmanship on display is certainly impressive, and most items have English labels.

Shilin

士林; shìlín

The district of **Shilin**, north of the Keelung River, is the home of Taipei's biggest **night market** (see box, p.93), the phenomenal **National Palace Museum**, one of the world's finest collections of Chinese art and historical artefacts, and the huge and slightly outlandish **Taipei Performing Arts Center** (台北藝術中心; táiběi yìshù zhōngxīn), across from Jiantan MRT station. Designed by renowned Dutch architect Rem Koolhaas, the arts centre was due to open in 2015, but was still under construction at the time of writing; it should be open by 2019.

National Palace Museum

國立故宮博物院; guólì gùgōng bówùyuàn • 221 Zhishan Rd Sec 2 • Mon–Thurs & Sun 8.30am–6.30pm, Fri & Sat 8.30am–9pm; English guided tours daily 10am & 3pm • NT$250; audio-guides NT$100 • English tours free; reserve online • ☎ 02 2881 2021, ⓦ www.npm.gov.tw • From Shilin MRT station take bus #304, #R30 or minibuses #18 and #19 (10min); #R30 goes straight to the main entrance

The **National Palace Museum** is the most famous attraction in Taiwan, pulling in over two million visitors a year with its unparalleled collection of **Chinese art**, a priceless treasure-trove going back five thousand years. The museum also owns hundreds of documents, pieces of furniture, rare books and official decrees issued by the Imperial Chinese government, as well as masses of everyday items that provide a fascinating insight into life at court. Very little of this has to do with Taiwan of course – the contents are a legacy of Chiang Kai-shek's retreat from China in 1949, when the former Imperial art collection was shipped, crate by crate, across the Taiwan Straits. While the Forbidden City in Beijing (also known as the Palace Museum) has more items, the finest pieces ended up in Taipei, becoming a contentious and often heated political issue between the two countries. Note that parts of the museum can be utterly swamped by tour groups throughout the day; your best chance of avoiding the crowds is late on **Saturday evenings**.

The museum's collection of over 655,000 pieces is still too large for everything to be displayed at the same time (thankfully there's a new southern branch, focusing on Asian art, near Chiayi; see p.216), but there's always plenty on show. The museum is

1

arranged thematically, but there's often a chronological order within each section. It's perhaps most rewarding to start on the third floor and work down (although the tea room on the fourth floor is the best place to take a break); alternatively, the daily **tours** in English offer a more digestible introduction to the main exhibits.

The third floor

The **third floor** is split into east and west wings, respectively home to permanent exhibitions of **bronze** and **jade**, which together make up much of the museum's remarkable ensemble of **Neolithic** artefacts. There are also some temporary exhibition halls here, their focus usually on similar materials or particular timeframes.

The bronze halls

The real highlights on this floor are the collection of stunning **bronzes** from the **Shang and Zhou dynasties** (1600–221 BC), principally ritual vessels owned by the wealthy. Typical pieces include the cauldron-like dǐng, and sets of cast bronze bells (zhōng), which had a ceremonial function. The most celebrated exhibit is the **San P'an Basin** dating from the late Western Zhou dynasty (700–900 BC), a ritual water vessel with an invaluable 350-character inscription inside. Another illustrious piece, the **Maogong Ding** (máogōng dǐng), named after the Duke of Mao and engraved with five hundred characters, from the Zhou dynasty, has its own special gallery to the side. The **Qin and Han dynasties** (221 BC–220 AD) were the last to use ritual jades and bronzes, represented by the highly ornate zūn, or wine vessel.

The jade halls

During Neolithic times, jade was believed to be a medium for spirits, and as such was given special reverence. A collection of dazzling **jade** and stone carvings are spread across two **halls** here, including the exceptional *Jadeite Cabbage with Insects*, a delicate Qing dynasty jade carving made to look like bok choy.

The second floor

The **second floor**'s east wing is home to some sumptuous **ceramics** and antiquities, while the west wing is entirely devoted to temporary exhibitions culled from the museum's rare collection of silk-screen **painting** and **calligraphy**.

LOOT OR LEGACY – THE HISTORY OF THE PALACE MUSEUM

While the National Palace Museum continues to expand (mostly from donations), at its core remains the priceless collection of art and artefacts once owned by the Chinese emperors. The **Imperial collection** was formally established in the reign of the first Song dynasty emperor, Taizu (960–975), who seized the artwork owned by rulers he had defeated in battle; his brother and successor, Taizong (976–997), expanded the hoard considerably, commissioning new pieces and collecting ceramics, artwork and statuary from all over China. This very private collection ended up in Beijing's Forbidden City, and it wasn't until the last emperor **Pu Yi** was forced to leave in 1924 that it was opened to the public: it became the **National Palace Museum** one year later. After the Japanese invaded Manchuria, its precious contents were carted around the country by the Nationalist government, on and off, for almost sixteen years, but by 1949 defeat at the hands of the Communists looked certain. During one, tense night in February of that year, most of the collection was packed into crates and shipped from Nanjing to Taiwan, just weeks before the city fell. It's worth noting, however, that although the most valuable pieces were spirited across the Taiwan Strait, much was left behind. The retreat was meant to be temporary, and it took another fifteen years before the authorities, resigned to the status quo, decided to unpack the boxes and build a museum in 1965.

China, where many see the removal of the collection as looting, would love to see it returned to the mainland. There's little chance of that happening any time soon: most Taiwanese point to the destruction of artwork during China's **Cultural Revolution** in the late 1960s and claim that they have worked hard to protect important treasures that might otherwise have been lost.

The ceramic halls

China's "golden age", the **Tang dynasty** (618–907), is one of the few in Chinese history when plump women were considered attractive: the earthenware figures of suitably curvaceous court ladies are indicative of the period. Porcelain and ceramics also flourished in the **Song dynasty** (960–1279). Don't miss the rare rǔ yáo ceramic *Narcissus Basin* in bluish-green glaze, a container dating from the Northern Song dynasty. The **Ming dynasty** (1368–1644) sections feature the best of China's porcelain and ceramics, much of it from the famous kilns at Jingdezhen, over on the mainland in Jiangxi province. The intricate *Doucai Cup with Chickens* and *Blue-and-white Flat Vase with Figures* are considered the most accomplished pieces from the early part of the era.

The painting and calligraphic exhibitions

The museum's rare collection of silk-screen **painting** and **calligraphy** is truly magnificent, though exhibits are rotated regularly, with a three-month display limit usually imposed to guard against light damage. Keep your eyes peeled (and fingers crossed) for masterpieces from the **Song dynasty** (960–1279), when landscape watercolour painting was reaching its zenith: highlights of the collection include Fan K'uan's *Travellers Among Mountains and Streams*, the lyrical *Storied Mountains and Dense Forests* by Chu-jan and *Early Spring* by Guo Xi. The museum also has an extensive collection of Ming and Qing dynasty artwork, but it's essentially pot luck what you'll get to see at any given time – check the website for details.

The first floor

The **first floor** has permanent galleries dedicated to **Qing-dynasty furniture**, a vast array of **religious sculptural art**, and treasures from the Qing Imperial collection (mostly intricate **curio boxes**). Other galleries show rotating exhibits from the **rare books** and documents departments – perhaps not of that much interest to the casual overseas visitor, but certainly worth a peek.

Shung Ye Museum of Formosan Aborigines

順益台灣原住民博物館;shūnyì táiwān yuánzhùmín bówùguǎn • 282 Zhishan Rd Sec 2 • Tues–Sun 9am–5pm • NT$150 (or NT$320 combined with National Palace Museum) • ☎ 02 2841 2611, ⓦ www.museum.org.tw • From Shilin MRT station take bus #304, #R30 or minibuses #18 and #19

The **Shung Ye Museum of Formosan Aborigines**, 100m up Zhishan Road from the Palace Museum, is one of Taipei's most appealing museums, providing a thorough introduction to Taiwan's indigenous population. The museum tries to give an airing to the sixteen formally recognized tribes, but focuses on the nine most prominent: the Amis, Atayal, Bunun, Paiwan, Puyuma, Rukai, Saisiyat, Tao and Tsou. The collection isn't particularly large, but it's well presented, and videos covering the origins and current social situation of the various tribes on the **first floor** are excellent – just make sure you avoid school parties and tour groups because you'll miss most of the commentary. The **basement** is the most intriguing part of the museum, highlighting festivals, myths and rituals, with a special area dedicated to head-hunting and a selection of ceremonial weapons.

Shilin Main Presidential Residence

士林官邸正館;shílín guāndǐ zhèngguǎn • 60 Fulin Rd • **Residence** Tues–Sun 9.30am–noon & 1.30–5pm • NT$100; audio-guides free • **Gardens** Mon–Fri 8am–5pm, Sat & Sun 8am–7pm • Free • ☎ 02 2881 2512 • Shilin MRT

The most important of **Chiang Kai-shek**'s former estates, the **Shilin Main Presidential Residence** was built in 1950 – after years of lying derelict the old mansion was restored in 2011 and is now open to the public. The official rooms downstairs are filled with classical Chinese furniture (and paintings by Madam Chiang, aka Soong May-ling) but are a little artificial – the private rooms upstairs are more personal and most of the

1

items here are originals, including the bed Chiang Kai-shek died in in 1975, the room US vice-president Nixon used in 1953 and Madam Chiang's typically pink bathroom. The display of Madam Chiang's dresses and handbags always attracts plenty of attention, and indeed the whole site is a major attraction for Chinese mainland tour groups, so visit early if you want a tranquil experience. It's worth getting a free audio-guide in English at the entrance, as not much is labelled.

The lush **gardens** that surround the mansion, famed for their roses and plum blossoms, are equally popular, as is the **Victory Chapel** (1949; 凱歌堂; kǎigē táng) where the Chiangs prayed, and the **Ciyun Pavilion** (慈雲亭; cíyún tíng), built in 1963 to commemorate Chiang's mother.

National Revolutionary Martyrs' Shrine

忠烈祠; zhōngliècí • 139 Beian Rd (1km east of Jiantan MRT station) • Daily 9am–5pm; colour guard ceremonies daily 8.50am & 5pm, changing of the guard hourly 9am–4pm • Free • ☎ 02 2885 4162 • Bus #208, #247, #267 or #287 from Yuanshan MRT station, or a 10min walk from the *Grand Hotel*

Just north of the Keelung River is the **National Revolutionary Martyrs' Shrine**, the largest of similar memorials all over Taiwan, dedicated to more than three hundred thousand civilians and soldiers killed in struggles with the Qing dynasty, the Japanese and the Communists. It's also another reminder of Taiwan's official status as Republic of China – most of the people honoured here died on the mainland. The main gate sits on Beian Road, but you have to trudge across a vast plaza from here to get to the grand collection of buildings known as the Sanctuary. Completed in 1969 to resemble the Taihedian in Beijing's Forbidden City, the **Main Shrine** contains a central tablet that commemorates all those who died – Taiwanese visitors usually bow here. Note the painting of Sun Yat-sen to the left. Individual tablets are enshrined in the **Civilian Martyrs' Shrine** on the right side of the complex, or the **Military Martyrs' Shrine** on the left, the whole thing encircled by a walkway lined with paintings and boards describing every military campaign fought by the Nationalists. The **colour guard ceremonies** and hourly **changing of the guard** are extremely elaborate affairs, lasting more than fifteen minutes, and both highly photogenic.

Shida and around

Taking up the western chunk of Da'an, Taiwan's main **university district** is home to thousands of students from National Taiwan Normal University (known to all and sundry as "**Shida**") and National Taiwan University (the most prestigious in the land, and likewise usually referred to as "**Taida**"). Other than charming **Da'an Park**, there are few sights as such here, but the neighbourhood is highly valued by both locals and visitors, due to its popular restaurants, bars, cafés and tearooms. Contrary to what you

---

YONGHE – HOME OF SOYBEAN MILK

The suburb of **Yonghe** (永和; yǒnghé) has become synonymous with delicious **soybean milk** (dòujiāng) and associated breakfast snacks not just in Taiwan but throughout the Chinese-speaking world. In fact so many soybean shops in Taiwan and Asia use the word "Yunghe" in their name that even many Chinese don't know it's actually a suburb of Taipei. Soybean milk originated in China in the nineteenth century, becoming popular as a drink in the 1930s and imported to Taiwan when the Nationalists fled the mainland in 1949; Donghai ("East Ocean") was the original store, established in Yonghe in 1955. It became so successful that today, even in China, thousands of stores call themselves "Taiwan Yunghe Soybean Milk" in deference and it's become one of the country's most successful examples of what the Taiwanese call "selling back" to China. Donghai was renamed "World Soybean Milk Magnate" in 1968, and the present incarnation is still a great place to breakfast, a short walk north of Dingxi MRT station (see p.90).

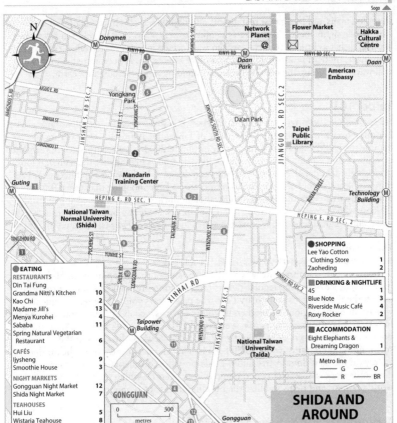

SHIDA AND AROUND

EATING

RESTAURANTS

Din Tai Fung	1
Grandma Nitti's Kitchen	10
Kao Chi	2
Madame Jill's	13
Menya Kurohei	4
Sababa	11
Spring Natural Vegetarian Restaurant	6

CAFÉS

Ijysheng	9
Smoothie House	3

NIGHT MARKETS

Gongguan Night Market	12
Shida Night Market	7

TEAHOUSES

Hui Liu	5
Wistaria Teahouse	8

SHOPPING

Lee Yao Cotton Clothing Store	1
Zaoheding	2

DRINKING & NIGHTLIFE

45	1
Blue Note	3
Riverside Music Café	4
Roxy Rocker	2

ACCOMMODATION

Eight Elephants & Dreaming Dragon	1

Metro line
— G   — O
— R   — BR

may expect of a student zone, the establishments here aren't all bargain-bucket places, and the area in general makes for surprisingly pleasant walking territory.

Da'an Park

大安公園; dàān gōngyuán • Entrances on Xinyi Rd, Jianguo South Rd Sec 2, Heping East Rd Sec 1 and Xinsheng South Rd Sec 1 • Daily 24hr • Free • ☎ 02 2885 4162 • Da'an Park MRT

The most pleasant expanse of greenery in central Taipei, **Da'an Park** is generally regarded by locals as something of a playground – walk around and you'll see rollerblading, skateboarding and jogging going on, as well as occasional games of mahjong, and morning *tai chi*. The park is usually a lot more peaceable than it may sound, especially given the fact that it's hemmed in by four major roads; the exceptions are New Year (both lunar and solar) and Christmas, when performances are usually held at the amphitheatre to the north end of the park.

East Taipei

East Taipei, comprising Songshan, Xinyi, part of Daan and the suburban district of Nangang, is the modern commercial heart of the city. Best known for Taipei's premier

1

shopping malls and its hippest restaurants and nightlife, it also has a handful of worthwhile sights tucked in between the office towers. **Xinyi** (信義; xìnyì) itself is a former wasteland that as little as twenty years ago was covered in sugar cane. Today it's plastered with malls, modern residential blocks and office towers – many connected with elevated walkways – including the famous **Taipei 101** building, once the tallest on earth.

Taipei 101

台北一零一; táiběi yīlíngyī · 7 Xinyi Rd Sec 5 · ☎ 02 8101 8899, ⓦ www.taipei-101.com.tw · Taipei 101/World Trade Center MRT

Looming over Xinyi, and indeed the whole of Taipei, the 508m-tall **Taipei 101** tower became the world's tallest building on completion in 2003 – it was surpassed six years later by Dubai's Burj Khalifa (828m). A whopping 101 storeys high (hence the name), it looks surprisingly delicate, given its size, having been designed by Taiwanese architect C.Y. Lee to resemble a stalk of bamboo. The tower sits atop a large shopping mall (see p.97), which remains up there with the best in the city, though the luxury shops, aimed at mainland Chinese who are no longer arriving in huge numbers, are now a bit empty. In the basement is a great food court, as well as a branch of *Din Tai Fung* (see box, p.90).

The observatory

Daily 9am–10pm, last entry 9.15pm · NT$600; Priority Pass NT$1200; audio-guide free

The entrance to the **observatory** is on the fifth floor of the shopping mall. Here, you have the choice of buying regular tickets (or collecting pre-booked ones), or splashing out on the more expensive Priority Pass. The pass allows you to sidestep the queues – which can be prodigious on weekends, going down as well as up – and zoom to the top in just 37 seconds in elevators that were, until 2016, the world's fastest. Up on the 89th floor, the indoor observatory provides unparalleled views of the city and the surrounding mountains, while you'll get a hair-raising perspective from the outdoor gallery on the 91st floor. A free audio-guide provides commentary on the views, but don't miss the massive steel-plated **damper** in the centre, which at 660 tonnes is the world's largest, and helps stabilize the building in case of typhoons.

National Dr Sun Yat-sen Memorial Hall

國立國父紀念館; guólì guófù jìniànguǎn · 505 Renai Rd Sec 4 · Daily 9am–7pm, art galleries close at 5pm; changing of the guard hourly 9am–6pm · Free · ☎ 02 2758 8008, ⓦ www.yatsen.gov.tw · SYS Memorial Hall MRT

Grandly located in a small park on the western edge of Xinyi, the **National Dr Sun Yat-sen Memorial Hall** is a striking postmodern re-creation of a classical Chinese palace, with concrete pillars and bright-yellow roof. It was completed in 1972 to preserve the memory of the founder of the Republic of China, and what's now referred to, in all seriousness, as "Sunology". A giant bronze statue of Sun Yat-sen guards the main entrance, where you can witness another solemn **changing of the guard** ceremony, often mobbed by mainland Chinese tourists – Sun is eulogized on both sides of the Taiwan Strait. On either side of the statue are rooms documenting Sun's life and his relationship with Taiwan (with English labelling), though you'll see scant mention of his influential wife, Soong Qing-ling, who sided with the Communists after his death and died in Shanghai in 1981. The rest of the building contains several **galleries** that showcase Taiwanese art.

Songshan Cultural & Creative Park

松山文創園區; sōngshān wénchuàng yuánqū · 133 Guangu S Rd (enter from Lane 553, off Zhongxiao E Rd Sec 4) · Park daily 8am–10pm; galleries daily 9am–6pm · Free · ☎ 02 2765 1388, ⓦ songshanculturalpark.org · Taipei City Hall MRT · **Red Dot Design Museum** · 臺北紅點設計博物; táiběi hóngdiǎn shèjì bówù · Tues–Fri 11.30am–5.30pm, Sat & Sun 9.30–5.30pm · NT$150 · ☎ 02 2748 0430, ⓦ en.red-dot.org · **Taiwan Design Museum** · 台灣設計館; táiwān shèjì guǎn · Tues–Sun 9.30am–5.30pm · NT$120, sometimes more for special exhibitions · ☎ 02 2745 8199, ⓦ www.tdm.org.tw

Taipei's old tobacco factory, built by the Japanese in 1937, has been transformed into the **Songshan Cultural & Creative Park**, a series of art shops, galleries and museums that aims to become the central design hub for the city. Much of the main building serves as showrooms for Taiwan's various design associations and societies, while temporary art and design shows take place in the adjacent warehouses. Permanent attractions include high-quality art and design stores, including a branch of Liuligongfang (see p.98).

The park also features a couple of museums: the **Red Dot Design Museum** puts on rotating exhibitions based on winners of the prestigious German-based Red Dot Design Awards, while the fascinating **Taiwan Design Museum** focuses on the history of Taiwanese product design since the 1930s, and occasionally puts on major exhibitions.

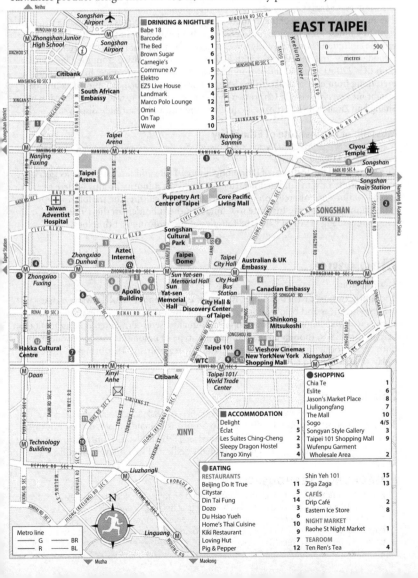

EAST TAIPEI

■ DRINKING & NIGHTLIFE	
Babe 18	8
Barcode	9
The Bed	1
Brown Sugar	6
Carnegie's	11
Commune A7	5
Elektro	7
EZ5 Live House	13
Landmark	4
Marco Polo Lounge	12
Omni	2
On Tap	3
Wave	10

● SHOPPING	
Chia Te	1
Eslite	6
Jason's Market Place	8
Liuligongfang	7
The Mall	10
Sogo	4/5
Songyan Style Gallery	3
Taipei 101 Shopping Mall	9
Wufenpu Garment Wholesale Area	2

■ ACCOMMODATION	
Delight	1
Éclat	5
Les Suites Ching-Cheng	2
Sleepy Dragon Hostel	3
Tango Xinyi	4

● EATING	
RESTAURANTS	
Beijing Do It True	11
Citystar	5
Din Tai Fung	14
Dozo	3
Du Hsiao Yueh	6
Home's Thai Cuisine	10
Kiki Restaurant	9
Loving Hut	7
Pig & Pepper	12
Shin Yeh 101	15
Ziga Zaga	13
CAFÉS	
Drip Café	2
Eastern Ice Store	8
NIGHT MARKET	
Raohe St Night Market	1
TEAROOM	
Ten Ren's Tea	4

Metro line
G — BR
R — BL

1

Academia Sinica

中央研究院; zhōngyāng yánjiùyuàn • 128 Academia Rd Sec 2 • ☎ 02 2782 2120, ⓦ sinica.edu.tw • From Nangang MRT station take bus #212, #270 or Blue #25 to the campus, or it's around 25min on foot from Nangang Exhibition Center MRT

The district of **Nangang** (南港; nángǎng), east of Xinyi, is home to **Academia Sinica**, one of Taipei's less-visited treasures. Founded in 1928 as China's foremost academic research institute, the Academia relocated to Taiwan with the Nationalists in 1949 and today the main campus contains a couple of fine museums clustered at the southern end.

Museum of the Institute of History and Philology

歷史文物陳列館; lìshǐ wénwù chénlièguǎn • Humanities Science Rd • Wed, Sat & Sun 9.30am–4.30pm • Free • ☎ 02 2652 3180, ⓦ museum.sinica.edu.tw

The Academia's **Museum of the Institute of History and Philology** is a remarkable treasure-trove of Chinese archeological finds, excavated by the institute in the 1930s. It's not huge, but the collection is magnificently presented. Among the most important artefacts are the "**wooden slips**" (tablets inscribed with Chinese characters), dating from the Han dynasty (206 BC–220 AD) and found at frontier fortresses in Gansu province. Inscribed with everything from official orders to the letters of ordinary soldiers, they provide a unique insight into everyday life in China two thousand years ago. The museum's collection of **Shang and Zhou dynasty bronzes** is equally impressive and beautifully displayed.

Museum of the Institute of Ethnology

民族學研究所博物館; mínzúxué yánjiùsuǒ bówùguǎn • Humanities Science Rd • Wed, Sat & Sun 9.30am–4.30pm • Free • ☎ 02 2652 3303, ⓦ ioe.sinica.edu.tw

The **Museum of the Institute of Ethnology** houses a rare and fascinating collection of artefacts from Taiwan's indigenous tribes and China's minority groups – there are special sections on folk religion in Taiwan, aboriginal culture, the trailblazing expeditions made by the Institute to China's southern borders in the 1930s and Dr Ling Shun-sheng (1901–1978), the founder of the Institute of Ethnology.

Maokong

貓空; māokōng

The southernmost district of Taipei is known as **Maokong**, one of Taiwan's oldest tea-growing areas and beloved for its hills, teahouses, temples and romantic night views of the city. Production of **tiěguānyīn** (a high-quality, semi-fermented oolong tea) began here in the 1880s, though **bāozhǒng** (another type of oolong) is just as prevalent. In both cases production is relatively small and it's "tea tourism" that brings in the cash today – the **Maokong cable car** is one of the biggest attractions in Taiwan.

Zhinan Temple

指南宮; zhǐnán gong • 115 Wanshou Rd • Daily 4am–8.30pm • Free • ☎ 02 2939 9922, ⓦ chih-nan-temple.org

The second gondola stop (after Taipei Zoo South) is **Zhinan Temple**, one of Taiwan's most important religious centres. Established in 1891, it blends Confucian, Taoist and Buddhist practices and features five main halls dedicated to a mixture of gods.

MAOKONG'S TEAHOUSES

Maokong's **teahouses** are predominantly scattered on this south side of the valley, all within walking distance of Maokong gondola station. Pots of tea usually start at NT$250 and can last most of the afternoon depending on how many people are in your group – expect to pay a cover charge of NT$70 or over per person at the better places, such as *Yaoyue Teahouse* (see p.92) and *Yuanxuyuan* (see p.92).

1

MAOKONG BY CABLE CAR

The 4km-long **Maokong Gondola** (貓空纜車; māokōng lǎnchē; ❶02 2181 2345, ⓦenglish. gondola.taipei) links Maokong and Zhinan Temple with Taipei Zoo, making the area a major tourist attraction. It's definitely the most appealing way to travel between the three sights, with gasp-inducing views of the jungle-smothered slopes and city beyond. The **base station** (Tues–Thurs 9am–9pm, Fri 9am–10pm, Sat 8.30am–10pm & Sun 8.30am–9pm) is a short walk from Taipei Zoo MRT station. You need to grab a "queue ticket" first, and enter when your time is called; you can use your EasyCard to pay (NT$20 discount on weekdays) or buy tickets at machines inside the station (one-way NT$120 to Maokong, NT$100 to Zhinan Temple and NT$70 between the temple and Maokong). The special cars with glass, transparent bottoms (貓纜之眼; māolǎn zhīyǎn), aka "**crystal cabins**", are a big hit and have their own queue and tickets (same price) – they go every 2–4min, but the wait can be much longer than for regular cars.

Make sure you get hold of a **map** first at the **visitor centre** at the Taipei Zoo base station (same hours as car service; ❶02 8661 7627). Be warned: the **wait** for a ride can be as much as three hours at peak periods, so get there early or check online (or the electronic screens at Zhongxiao Fuxing MRT station) before you go.

Follow the path from the gondola station, and the **Lingxiao Shrine** is the first temple you come to. It's also the most impressive architecturally, with several swirling levels and a multitude of gods inside (the Jade Emperor is on the top floor while the "Three Pure Ones" reside on the first floor).

Walk down the hill under the covered walkway and you'll come to the most important part of Zhinan, the **Chunyang Shrine** or **Original Hall**. This contains the chief deity, and the biggest draw for pilgrims, **Lu Dong-bin**, one of the "Eight Immortals" and a patron of barbers, though like many gods he's supposed to grant good health and general prosperity to all his believers. There's one exception: legend has it that Lu was rejected by the only female member of the Eight Immortals, Ho Hsien-ku, and driven by jealousy, he's been an incorrigible flirt ever since, making it bad luck for couples to visit the temple. The biggest shrine, and the stupa you can see all over the valley, is the much quieter **Daxiong Hall**, a short walk to the right (facing the Original Hall). This is a Buddhist temple, with gold statues of Sakyamuni Buddha, Amitabha and the Medicine Buddha in the main hall. You can walk back to the gondola station via the very steep road behind Daxiong Hall.

Before the cable car was built, the traditional way down from Zhinan was via the stone stairs in front of the Chungyang Shrine: the first section ends a short way down the mountain at a small Earth God shrine – turn right and follow the stone pathway, lined with Japanese stone lanterns, 900m to Lane 33, a short walk from Zhinan Road and the bus stop on the edge of Muzha. There are supposed to be 1185 or 1192 steps, depending on where you start counting.

Maokong Station

Daily 4am–8.30pm • Most tourist buses (NT$15) run daily 9am–8pm, every 10–30min

The final gondola station (at 299m) is **Maokong** itself, where you'll find a small group of snack stalls. From here, everything is well marked in English, with **teahouses** (see box opposite) divided into three colour-coded zones. Special tourist buses zip between destinations for those who don't fancy walking, though unless it's unusually hot, the lanes make for a pleasant stroll through small tea plantations. Turn left at the station and you'll eventually pass **Tian En Temple** (天恩宮; tiānēn gōng), a good example of an I-kuan Tao shrine, and the redbrick **Taipei Tea Promotion Center** (台北市茶推廣中心; táiběishì chá tuīguǎng zhōngxīn; 8–2, Lane 40, Zhinan Rd Section 3; Tues–Sun 9am–5pm; free; ❶02 2234 0568), 1.2km from the gondola station, which houses a small exhibition on the history of the area, and the tea-making process (plus free tea).

Taipei is Taiwan's biggest international gateway, and also has **transport connections** to just about everywhere on the island. It's best to buy **tickets** in advance if you're planning to travel at the weekend, when transport is jammed with locals pouring out of the city.

BY PLANE
TAIWAN TAOYUAN INTERNATIONAL AIRPORT

Most international flights to Taipei arrive at Taiwan Taoyuan Internatonal Airport (臺灣桃園國際航空站; táiwān táoyuán guójì hángkōngzhàn; ⓦtaoyuan-airport.com), near Taoyuan, 40km southwest of the capital. There are tourist service centres (daily 7.30am–11.30pm; ⓣ03 398 2194), ATMs and exchange counters in both terminals.

MRT to/from the city The new MRT line is now the fastest way into town, heading from both terminals directly to a large concourse connected to Taipei Station (every 15min, daily 6am–11pm; 36–38min; NT$160). If you're flying with China Airlines, you should be able to check in and drop off your hold luggage here before heading to the airport.

Buses to/from the city Several companies offer services into the city, with bus stations clearly signposted in each terminal. There are numerous routes to town (most daily 4.40am–11pm; NT$90–140), terminating at Taipei Station, Songshan Airport, Nangang Exhibition Center and more; allow around an hour for the journey. These buses pass other MRT stations on the way, so if you've a specific destination in mind, it's best to ask at a counter, where staff will identify the best route for you. Heading back to the airport, simply return to the closest bus stop – you can pay on the bus. There are also buses from the airport to non-Taipei destinations; for some points south you'll want to hop on the bus to Taoyuan HSR Station (every 5–10min, daily 6.20am–10.15pm; NT$30), just 6km away.

Taxis to/from the city Taxis are available at both terminals 24hr. All taxis use the meter – expect to pay NT$1100–1400 to the city centre (NT$320–350 to Taoyuan HSR Station). Heading back, you should be able to arrange a pick-up for a fixed rate of just NT$1000–1100, and therefore cheaper than flagging down a taxi – ask at your hotel.

SONGSHAN AIRPORT

Domestic flights and an increasing number of international flights (mostly from China, Japan and Korea) arrive at Songshan Airport (松山機場; sōngshān jīchǎng; ⓦwww.tsa.gov.tw), conveniently located at the top of Dunhua Rd on the northern edge of downtown Taipei. Facilities include a post office, banks, 24hr lockers (NT$120–360), ATMs and a visitor information centre (daily 8am–8pm; ⓣ02 2546 4741).

Getting to/from the city The metro station (see p.82) and local bus stops are just outside the terminal, but it's

less than NT$250 by taxi to and from most destinations in central Taipei. There are also express buses to Taiwan Taoyuan International Airport (NT$125).

BY TRAIN
TAIPEI STATION

Taipei Station (台北車站; táiběi chēzhàn) has trains to and from all major cities, including HSR services. The station is relatively easy to navigate for non-Chinese-speakers; there are ticket windows in the cavernous main hall, though it's usually faster to use the ticket machines (separate ones for local and express services). Taxis line up at the station entrance. There's a visitor information centre (daily 8am–8pm; ⓣ02 2312 3256) on the west side of the main ticket hall, while coin-operated left-luggage lockers are tucked away in the basement, with daily rates starting at NT$30 for a small backpack-sized locker and NT$70 for larger spaces. The maximum storage time is 72hr.

Destinations Changhua (22 express daily; 2hr 20min); Chiayi (HSR every 30min; 1hr 40min); Fulong (19 express daily; 1hr 5min); Hsinchu (HSR every 10–30min; 30min); Hualien (15 express daily; 2hr 50min); Kaohsiung (HSR every 30min; 2hr to the Zuoying terminal); Keelung (every 15–30min; 40min); Sanyi (6 daily; 2hr 20min); Taichung (HSR every 30min; 1hr); Tainan (HSR every 30min; 1hr 45min); Taitung (6 express daily; 5hr); Yilan (18 express daily; 1hr 30min); Yingge (every 6–20min; 25min).

BY BUS
TAIPEI BUS STATION

Most buses operate from the efficient Taipei Bus Station (臺北轉運站; táiběi zhuǎnyùnzhàn), part of the Q Square mall complex opposite the train station: some companies run frequent 24hr services to all the major cities on the west coast, while those heading to the east coast are less frequent. At the time of writing, buses that formerly used Taipei West Bus Station (demolished in 2016) were departing from temporary stops outside Taipei train station's #3 East gate; things may have changed by the time you read this – staff in the terminal or train station will be able to point you in the right direction. The main bus station has left-luggage facilities (NT$25–70 for 3hr).

Destinations from bus station Alishan (Fri & Sat 1 daily: March–Oct 8.45pm; Nov–Feb 9.45pm; 6hr 10min); Daxi (daily at 5.40pm); Hsinchu (every 30min; 1hr); Jiaoxi (hourly; 45min); Lugang (7 daily; 3hr 30min); Luodong (every 15–20min; 1hr); Puli (5 daily; 3hr 40min); Sun Moon

Lake (5–8 daily; 4hr); Taichung (every 30min–1hr; 2hr); Tainan (every 30min–1hr; 4hr 30min).

Destinations from train station Dharma Drum Mountain (every 15–30min; 1hr 40min); Jinshan (every 15–30min; 1hr); Kaohsiung (every 15–30min; 5hr 30min); Keelung (every 10–15min; 1hr); Yehliu (every 15–30min; 40min).

TAIPEI CITY HALL BUS STATION

Taipei City Hall Bus Station (市府轉運站; shìfǔ zhuǎnyùnzhàn) is located out east in Xinyi, right by Taipei City Hall MRT station. Left-luggage lockers are available at NT$20–50 for 3hr.

Destinations Dharma Drum Mountain (every 10–20min; 1hr 30min); Hsinchu (hourly; 1hr); Jinshan (every 10–20min; 1hr); Keelung (every 10–25min; 50min); Taichung (every 10–20min; 1hr); Tainan (hourly; 5hr); Taoyuan (every 10–20min; 40min); Yilan (every 10–15min; 40min).

BY FERRY

Weekend ferry tours connect Dadaocheng Wharf (大稻埕碼頭; dàdàochéng mǎtóu), at the end of Minsheng Rd in Datong (see map, p.67), with Tamsui to the north (Sat & Sun 10am & 1pm; NT$300); from there you can head on to Bali or Fisherman's Wharf (see p.109). You can buy tickets at a little booth by the wharf.

GETTING AROUND

The most convenient way to travel around Taipei is by **metro**, though **buses** are getting easier to use for non-Chinese-speakers. **Taxis** are not expensive for journeys within the centre, but it's best to avoid **driving** yourself unless you have nerves of steel. During the week, try to avoid the peak **rush hour** periods (8–9am and 5.30–7pm).

BY METRO

Travelling by Taipei Metro (see map opposite), also known as the MRT ("Mass Rapid Transit"; ⓦ english.trtc.com.tw), is by far the best way to get around. The system comprises several colour-coded lines and is continuing to expand. Services operate at short intervals from 6am to midnight every day, and are efficient, clean and fast; there are route maps in every carriage, though downloading a smartphone app to keep one in your pocket is always a good idea.

Fares Single-trip tokens cost NT$20–65 depending on distance travelled (usually NT$20–30 in the centre) and can be purchased from ticket offices or machines in the stations; if you're planning to stay longer than a week it's a good idea to buy an EasyCard or travel pass (see box below).

BY BUS

Taipei has an extensive bus network with destinations marked in English on the front of most buses, and electronic screens displaying the name of each stop once inside. English-language route maps can be obtained from MRT stations or visitor centres and fares are cheap at NT$15 per sector, which covers most journeys within the city; you can pay in cash, or use an EasyCard or travel pass (see box below). Note, however, that most bus stops have maps and timetables solely in Chinese, which means you'll have to plan ahead – Google Maps routes are usually accurate, and the Bus+ app has an English-language option.

BY TAXI

Taxis are plentiful within the city centre: the initial fare is NT$70 and is good for the first 1.5km, after which it's NT$5 for each additional 300m. After 11pm, an extra NT$20 is charged automatically and carrying luggage incurs another NT$10 fee. The meter is always used, the only exception being trips to the airport, which are often negotiated in advance. Taipei residents often complain about the city's number of unregistered taxis; for a guaranteed official one, call ☎0800 055850. Uber (ⓦuber.com), the smartphone ride share service, operates in Taipei, though it was banned for a time in 2017, and has since been curtailed.

BY BIKE

Taipei has invested heavily in its bike infrastructure of late, with lanes appearing across the city. However, getting around the city can be tough by bike, as you have to compete with pedestrians, parked motorbikes and more. The most appealing routes run along the river banks, though these can

---

EASYCARDS AND TRAVEL PASSES

If you're in Taipei for a while, it may be a good idea to invest in an **EasyCard** (ⓦeasycard.com.tw). Costing NT$100 (NT$80 of which is a refundable deposit), the card is available from machines or service counters in all MRT stations; value can be added in multiples of NT$100. It's valid for metro and bus services, and – if you register – the city YouBikes too (see opposite). Registering is easiest at a service desk, upon purchase, though you'll need a **Taiwanese phone number**.

There are plenty of other city **passes** on offer, from daily metro tickets (NT$150) to five-day passes covering the metro and bus systems (NT$700), but you'd have to do an awful lot of travelling around to make them worth the cost.

TAIPEI METRO

often be difficult to get to, or even downright dangerous – many of the relevant junctions from the main road are also motorbike gauntlets. Still, it's worth giving cycling a go; you can pick up a free map showing cycle paths from MRT stations. **YouBike** The YouBike public rental system (ⓦ taipei .youbike.com.tw) offers bikes at over 160 locations throughout the city. If you have a Taiwanese mobile number, you can sign up to become a member to use the system – you'll need to get an EasyCard first (see box opposite), and register for YouBike at the same time. Those without a local number will have to head to a bank of bikes and hope that their international bank card is accepted in the machines. The price is the same either way: NT$10 for each 30min, though this goes up for NT$20 after 4hr, and NT$40 after 8hr.

Other bike rental Non-YouBike rental kiosks (usually operated by Giant), along official riverside bikeways (Bali, Daodacheng Wharf, Dajia, Muzha, Jingfu Bridge) allow you to rent bikes from one place and return them at any other affiliated kiosk or shop (daily 8am–noon & 2–5.30pm; around NT$15–60/hr or NT$80–260 for 6hr). You need ID (passport – you may have to leave it with them), and may have to leave a deposit. The cycle maps available at MRT stations also show rental locations.

BY SCOOTER

Local firms are reluctant to rent scooters to foreigners in Taipei, though Bike Farm (ⓣ 0926 283 300, ⓦ bikefarm. net) is owned by an English expat and offers rentals for

1

CITY WI-FI

Much of Taipei is covered by the free **Taipei Free Public WiFi Access network** (**TPE-Free**); international visitors need to register online, then go to any of the city's visitor centres (see below), present a passport and get an account number with which to activate the service. An easier ad-based variant is in use in most MRT stations and on the trains themselves; put in a passport number, check the box, and click the first of the two Chinese-only options. Annoyingly, you do have to do this every time you log on. Many cafés and restaurants around town provide free wi-fi.

NT$500/day (minimum four days) and monthly rentals from NT$2200–2600, including all servicing. There's no shop; instead, staff will bring the bike to an MRT station on request. You'll need a passport and a NT$7000 deposit – and a bit of luck, since their bikes aren't great. We cover practicalities of riding scooters in Taiwan in Basics (see p.27).

INFORMATION

Tourist information Taipei City Government (ⓦenglish .tpedoit.taipei.gov.tw) runs thirteen visitor centres throughout town, including at the main train station, Songshan Airport, Taipei City Hall Bus Station (all usually daily 9am–9pm; ⓣ02 2723 6836) and several MRT stations (Beitou, Jiantan, Ximen and Yuashan; usually daily 9am–5pm). At any of them you can pick up free maps and

BY HOP-ON, HOP-OFF BUS

Hop-on, hop-off buses operated by Taipei Sightseeing (ⓣ02 8791 6557, ⓦwww.taipeisightseeing.com.tw) run along two routes: one north to Expo Park and the National Palace Museum, and the other east to Taipei 101 and surrounding sights; both then join up to travel around Zhongzheng and Wanhua. Tickets range from NT300 for 4hr to NT1200 for two days.

Discover Taipei (see below).

Magazines The free bi-monthly magazine *Discover Taipei* often has useful feature stories; you can find it at most tourist offices (see above), though sadly they still haven't got around to making online content. Most of the expat blogs to the city focus firmly on food – recommended ones include ⓦjaysuneatstaipei.com and ⓦhungryintaipei.blogspot.com.

ACCOMMODATION

Taipei has a plentiful supply of mid-range and luxury **hotels** scattered all over the city – however, beware of major trade shows such as Computex (May/June), which can lead to a shortage of rooms. Budget accommodation is also easy to find – Taipei offers a huge choice of **hostels**, many of which have capsule-style beds; beware when booking hostels online, since these are often marketed as cheap private rooms, when they're essentially dorms. Most of the cheap accommodation is concentrated in **Zhongzheng** and the area around the train station (convenient if arriving by bus or train), but in recent years a new crop of hostels has emerged in **Shida**, near the major universities and plenty of nightlife; and in **Datong**, one of the older and more enticing neighbourhoods. Note that all the places listed here (and throughout this guide) have free **wi-fi** in rooms, unless otherwise stated.

ZHONGZHENG

★**Eight Zone** 八方美學商旅 bāfāng měixué shānglǚ 8 Jinshan S Rd Sec 1 ⓣ02 2358 3500, ⓦwww .hotel8zone.com; Zhongxiao Xinsheng MRT; map p.60. Plush boutique hotel with stylish, individually decorated rooms, just a 5min walk from the MRT. There's a cool lounge bar, 24hr coffee and tea, huge plasma TVs, and jacuzzi tub and rainforest shower in the bathroom. You'll often be able to chop the rack rates in half, too. Breakfast included. NT$7700

Hotel 73 新尚旅店; xīnshàng lǚdiàn 73 Xinyi Rd Sec 2 ⓣ02 2395 9009, ⓦhotel73.com; Dongmen MRT; map p.60. Sleek boutique hotel with a modern but minimalist artsy theme: the walls above the beds feature quirky modern designs, while the room designs are monochrome in general but with bold flashes of colour. Light fittings are futuristic and the bathrooms feature lots of glass screens. Rates sometimes come down below

NT$2000 if booking online. NT$2800

★**Just Sleep Ximending** 捷絲旅西門町; jiésīlǚ xīméndīng 41 Zhonghua Rd Sec 1 ⓣ02 2370 9000, ⓦwww.justsleep.com.tw; Ximen MRT; map p.60. This budget boutique hotel lies on the boundary between bustling Ximending and the old city, with 150 simple but stylish rooms; spaces are small, but intelligently designed (like a capsule hotel, but without the capsules) so that it doesn't seem cramped. Each room comes with satellite TV, breakfast voucher and fridge; prices drop considerably midweek. Other branches around town. NT$4000

★**Oxygen Hostel** 奧斯金旅店; àosījīn lǚdiàn 100 Chongqing S Rd Sec 1 ⓣ02 2311 4567, ⓦfacebook .com/OxygenHostel; Ximen MRT; map p.60. About as cheap as central Taipei gets, with most beds in capsule-style berths which have USB ports and afford at least a modicum of privacy. It's surprisingly stylish for the price,

AIRBNB AND LONGER-TERM ACCOMMODATION

Many visitors to Taipei make use of **Airbnb** (wairbnb.com) as an accommodation resource. Most private rooms in the centre go for NT$500–1200/night, though you often get far more value for money when booking whole apartments (NT$750–1400). As in many cities around the world, Airbnb here is something of an unresolved issue – there were no real complaints from the hotel industry until tourist numbers from mainland China plummeted in 2016 (courtesy of changes in official policy from Beijing). Since then, industry lobbying has resulted in crackdowns on unlicensed hotels, and nobody is fully sure what the future holds. For now, Airbnb is still the best source of medium-term accommodation for foreigners in Taipei, though for longer stays you may wish to look at dedicated rental sites such as wrentaltw.com and wtaipei.craigslist.com.tw.

and the large common room and attached bar are great places to hang out. It's also in a winning location, right by the 2–28 Peace Park. Dorms NT$400

Poshpacker 鉑泊客旅店; bóbókè lǚdiàn 39 Chongqing S Rd Sec 1 ☎02 2375 5555, wwww .poshpackerhotel.com; Beimen or Taipei Main Station MRT; map p.60. If you want the atmosphere of a hostel but don't fancy sleeping in a dorm, this is the place for you – cheap private rooms (mostly rather small, and all with shared facilities), and a café-like common area downstairs. NT$1480

WANHUA

★**Meander Taipei Hostel** 台北漫步旅店; táiběi mànbù lǚdiàn 4–6/F, 163 Chengdu Rd ☎02 2383 1334, wmeander.com.tw; Ximen MRT; map p.64. Friendly, modern hostel with rustic aboriginal-themed decor, two spotless dorms and a stylish en-suite double. There's a coin laundry, shared kitchen and coffee machine, plus cable TV in the lounge, but no lift. Towels can be rented for NT$50. Dorms NT$600; double NT$1880

Papa Whale 46 Kunming St ☎02 2331 1177; Ximen or Beimen MRT; map p.64. Adventurously-designed hotel which has gone for boho-chic, drawing in moneyed tourists (mostly East Asian) with its stylish, spacious rooms, and fancy common areas including a courtyard pond and mini-library. Many guests end up mingling with locals at the attached *Driftwood* bar (see p.94). NT$5100

Rose Boutique 玫瑰精品旅館; méiguī jīngpǐn lǚguǎn 63-1 Xining S Rd ☎02 2381 9333, wwww .rosehotel.com.tw; Beimen MRT; map p.60. Cosy boutique hotel, a short walk from busy Ximending, with stylish, blond wood panelling and bathrooms, contemporary furniture and all the latest technology, from Japanese toilets to extended flat-screen TVs. Rate drops to NT$2200 or less on weekdays. NT$3600

★**TX Deluxe Apartments** 天時藝宿; tiānshí yìsù 46 Kunming St ☎02 2331 2986; Ximen or Beimen MRT; map p.60. Particularly popular with those who are staying more than a few days in Taipei, these spacious, modern apartments (but without kitchen facilities) are set above the *Papa Whale* hotel, though check-in is at the *Art Inn*, a mini-block west. Rates, which already compete with hostel

dorms if there are two of you, drop further to NT$1000 on weekdays. On the downside, rooms tend to be cleaned hurriedly. NT$1200

DATONG & ZHONGSHAN

★**Ambience** 喜瑞飯店; xǐruì fàndiàn 64 Changan E Rd Sec 1, ☎02 2541 0077, wambiencehotel.com.tw; Songjiang Nanjing MRT; map p.67. One of Taipei's plushest designer hotels, where rooms are decked out with sleek Philippe Starck and Ferruccio Laviani furniture, flat-screen TVs and a striking all-white colour scheme. You'll usually end up paying NT$3000 or less online. NT$4600

Dandy Tianjin 丹迪旅店天津店; dāndí lǚdiàn tiānjīn diàn 70 Tianjin St ☎02 2541 5788, wdandyhotel.com.tw; Zhongshan MRT; map p.67. Stylish business hotel, close to Zhongshan MRT station. The thirty rooms have a Scandinavian-style colour scheme – everything is white and blond wood – with flat-screen TVs. Free washers/dryers and breakfast included; book online for the best rates. NT$3800

Dongwu 東吳飯店; dōngwú fàndiàn 238 Yanping N Rd Sec 2 ☎02 2557 1261, wwww.dongwu-hotel .com; Daqiaotou MRT; map p.67. Business hotel situated in an interesting part of Datong, opposite the Tse Sheng Temple. Staff provide useful maps as well as information on local attractions and cheap eats. Rooms are modern and comfortable, with satellite TV. NT$2800

★**Flip Flop Hostel Garden** 夾腳拖的家長安; jiājiǎotuō de jiā chángān 122 Chang'an W Rd ☎02 2558 5050, wffh-garden.com; Taipei Main Station MRT; map p.67. Pretty much the best hotel in town: an admirably artsy affair where the "reception", common room and many walls throughout the building double as gallery space of sorts. Rooms are decent, there are events every week or so (often pulling in a fair few locals), and staff are super friendly; the cheaper original *Flip Flop Hostel* is also nearby, but this one is far snazzier and worth the extra cost. Dorms NT$550; doubles NT$1600

Grand 圓山大飯店; yuánshān dàfàndiàn 1 Zhongshan N Rd Sec 4 ☎02 2886 8888, wwww.grand-hotel.org; Yuanshan MRT; map p.67. The *Grand*'s soaring Imperial-style architecture and Chinese decor definitely

1

BEST OF TAIPEI'S ACCOMMODATION

Best for those on a tight budget
Oxygen Hostel (see p.84)
Coolest hostel Flip Flop Hostel Garden
(see p.85)
Best for fancy furnishings Ambience
(see p.85)
Best for longer-term stays TX Deluxe
Apartments (see p.85)
Best breakfast setting Les Suites

Ching-Cheng (see below)
Best-equipped beds Sleeping Dragon
Hostel (see below)
Artiest mid-range hotel Papa Whale
(see p.85)
Best for a retro vibe Solo Singer (see
p.101)
Best for hot-spring baths Full Moon
(see p.118)

have character, though the spacious rooms are a little worn for a five-star, and the spectacular views are only available for deluxe rooms and above. The historic *Yuan Yuan Teahouse*, still serving Madame Chiang's favourite red-bean cake, adds ambience. The inconvenient location is mitigated somewhat by the free shuttle bus to Yuanshan MRT station – and the fact that you're almost certain to pay far lower than the rack rates. Breakfast included. NT$8100

★**Taipei City Home** 台北CT屋; táiběi CT wū 7 Alley 5, Lane 172, Changan W Rd ⓦ taipeicityhome.weebly .com; Taipei Main Station MRT; map p.67. A traveller favourite, close to the train station, with two no-frills but cosy private rooms, two comfy dorms (with lockers and towels included), free breakfast and home-made brownies, a decent kitchen and the ever-friendly manager always on hand. Cash only, and they prefer you use hostel websites to make reservations. Dorms NT$550; doubles NT$1580

SHIDA & AROUND

Eight Elephants & Dreaming Dragon 八隻大象青年之家; bāzhī dàxiàng qīngnián zhījiā 1/F, 6 Alley 4, Lane 48, Jinjiang St ⓣ02 2368 0301, ⓦ eehostel.com; Guting MRT; map p.75. Cosy hostel with spotless dorms, single rooms and private en-suite with bathrooms in Taiwan's university district, handy for Guting MRT station. Kitchen, a/c and washing machine all included, and there's a cool basement chillout space. Dorms NT$440; doubles NT$1320

EAST TAIPEI

Delight 大來飯店; dàlái fàndiàn 432 Changchun Rd ⓣ02 2716 0011, ⓦ delighthotel.com.tw; Nanjing E Rd MRT; map p.77. Smart business hotel and one of the best bargains in the city, a short walk from the MRT station. Chinese art lines the corridors, and rooms have been decorated in a swish, contemporary style. Breakfast included. NT$4000

Éclat 台北怡亨酒店; táiběi yìhēng jiǔdiàn 370

Dunhua S Rd Sec 1 ⓣ02 2784 8888, ⓦ eclathotels.com; Daan MRT; map p.77. Small luxury hotel littered with expensive European art – perfect for a romantic getaway and serious splurge. The beds are extra soft, and rooms boast Starck chairs, Bang & Olufsen CD players, and an LCD TV in the bathroom so you can watch while enjoying the rainforest shower. NT$5000

★**Les Suites Ching-Cheng** 台北商旅 (慶城); táiběi shānglǚ, qìngchéng 12 Qingcheng St ⓣ02 8712 7688, ⓦ www.hotelsuitesching-cheng.com; Nanjing E Rd MRT; map p.77. Taipei's top boutique hotel, close to the MRT, with a sleek, contemporary Asian design and plenty of clever touches: a lounge offering free hot drinks and biscuits throughout the day, a 24hr computer room, and a bamboo-fringed garden for breakfast. Rooms feature modern Chinese art and canopy beds, with Japanese baths in superiors. Breakfast included, and you can get discounts of NT$2000 most days. NT$9200

★**Sleeping Dragon Hostel** 八隻大象青年之家; dùláigēn guójì qīngnián lǚshè 7/F, 399 Nanjing E Rd Sec 5 ⓣ02 8787 0739, ⓦ sleepydragonhostel.com; Nanjing Sanmin MRT; map p.77. Some rare good value in East Taipei, this hostel may look far from the action on a map, but is only a 7min walk from the MRT, and you can even walk all the way to Taipei 101 in half an hour. The colourful common room leads on to the dorms, and their super-sturdy, semi-enclosed bunk berths, which all somehow cram in a locker, shoe box, shelf, and even a fold-out desk. Breakfast included. Dorms NT$550

Tango Xinyi 台北柯旅天閣-信義館; táiběi kēlǚ tiāngé – xìnyì guǎn 297 Zhongxiao E Rd Sec 5 ⓣ02 2528 8000, ⓦ xy.tango-hotels.com; Yongchun MRT; map p.77. One of three slick chain boutique hotels in Taipei, with this one close to an MRT station and all the action in Xinyi. The stylish, contemporary rooms come with DVD and flat-screen TVs, whirlpool tubs and use of the heath club. Breakfast usually included. NT$9400

EATING

Taipei is one of the world's greatest showcases for **Chinese cuisine**. In addition to a vast array of **restaurants**, Taipei's vibrant **night markets** (yèshì) offer a bewildering range of dishes and excellent value for money (see box, p.93).

Another budget favourite are the "**Taiwan Buffets**" (自助餐; zìzhù cān) you'll see in every neighbourhood – these canteen-style places allow you to pile up as much food on your tray as you like, with each dish incurring a small charge (it's rarely more than NT$150 for a huge plateful). Slightly pricier at about NT$150 per dish, restaurant-bars known as **rechao** (熱炒; rèchǎo), or "stir fry", are a real Taipei institution – and many people go to these for the cheap beer even more than the food. Lastly, the city's **teahouses** (cháguǎn) are atmospheric places to eat light meals and sip Chinese-style tea. For expat foodie recommendations, try ⒲jaysuneatstaipei.com and ⒲hungryintaipei.blogspot.com.

RESTAURANTS

The capital's restaurants cover cuisine from every Chinese school of cooking, overlaid with Taiwanese specialities. Taipei also has more Japanese restaurants than any city outside Japan, while Western options, though still a bit hit-and-miss, have mushroomed in recent years – all the major fast-food chains are well represented if you get really desperate. Luxury hotels are the best places to splurge, and usually they cater to all tastes – buffets here are incredibly elaborate affairs, with gargantuan piles of food and correspondingly high prices.

ZHONGZHENG

Alleycat's Pizza 1 Bade Rd Sec 1 ☎02 2395 6006, ⒲alleycatspizza.com; Shandao Temple MRT; map p.60. This chain's pizzas impress even NYC aficionados – gooey mozzarella, crispy crusts and refined toppings such as goat's cheese, Italian chorizo and artichoke. Large (12 inch) ones cost NT$430–NT$530. This branch has the best location, nicely set in the Huashan 1914 Creative Park. Mon–Thurs & Sun 11am–11pm, Fri & Sat 11am–midnight.

★**Daka** 打咔; dǎ kǎ 43–47 Roosevelt Rd Sec 1 ☎02 3322 5589; Chiang Kai-Shek Memorial Hall MRT; map p.60. Perhaps the most famous *rechao* in town, heaving each evening with locals ordering a mixture of seafood and meat dishes (both from NT$150), rice (free; unlimited) and beer (as cheap as in the shops). A quintessential Taipei experience. Daily 4pm–2am.

Fu Hang Soy Milk 阜杭豆漿; fùháng dòujiāng 2/F, 108 Zhongxiao E Rd Sec 1 ☎02 2392 2175; Shandao Temple MRT; map p.60. Taipei's most famous breakfast place by far, with long queues, as people wait patiently on the staircase from early morning. Frankly, their fried dough-sticks (NT$25) and soybean milk (NT$30) aren't all that special, but the experience certainly is. Tues–Sun 5.30am–12.30pm.

★**Old Wang's Beef Noodles** 老王記牛肉麵; lǎowángjì niúròumiàn 15 Taoyuan St ☎0937 860 050; Ximen MRT; map p.60. This well-respected joint has been knocking out classic *hong shao*-style beef and broth

noodles since the 1950s (NT$110–220), and they're some of the best in the city. The second floor has more character than the ground level. Daily 8am–8pm.

Shao Shao Ke 勺勺客; sháoshàokè 27 Hangzhou S Rd Sec 1 ☎02 2351 7148; Shandao Temple MRT; map p.60. Laidback Shanxi-style restaurant with succulent lamb kebabs (NT$175) and soup with unleavened bread (pào mò; NT$175–200), a wonderful meal which is part DIY. You'll be given a disc of bread and an empty bowl, and after you fill the latter with peanut-sized chunks of the former, they whisk it away and return it full of broth, meat (lamb is the norm in Xi'an, the home of this dish), veggies and glass noodles. Tues–Sun 11.30am–2.30pm & 5.30–10pm.

WANHUA

365 Taiwan Snacks 365台湾小吃; 365 táiwān xiǎochī 34 Hanzhong St; Ximen MRT; map p.64. Two-floor snack venue busy with locals chowing down braised-pork rice (from NT$35), oyster omelette (NT$60) and other simple dishes – choose from the picture menu out front. Daily 11.30am–7pm.

Ay-Chung Flour-Rice Noodle 阿宗麵線; ā zōng miànxiàn 8 Ermei St ☎02 2388 8808, ⒲ay-chung .com; Ximen MRT; map p.64. A Taipei institution, this stall has been serving sumptuous rice noodles in paper cups (small NT$50; large NT$65) since 1975 – the added slices of pig intestine may not be to everyone's taste, but they're damn fine noodles. Take away or eat standing up on the street. Mon–Thurs 9am–10.30pm, Fri–Sun 9am–11pm.

CoCo Ichibanya Coco 壱番屋; Coco fānwū 49 Hanzhong St ☎02 2231 8820; Ximen MRT; map p.64. A great place for Japanese-style curry rice. Piece together your meal from the ingredients on the menu (including breaded chicken cutlet, cheese, okra, omelette and far more), choose your spice level (one to seven), and you're good to go; it'll cost NT$200–250. Daily 11am–9.30pm.

Duck Flat Noodles 鴨肉扁土鵝專賣店; yāròu biǎntuěr zhuānmàidiàn 98-2 Zhonghua Rd Sec 1 ☎02 2371 3918; Ximen MRT; map p.64. Cheap,

VEGETARIAN RESTAURANTS

Vegetarians are well catered for in Taipei, with numerous local diners serving Buddhist-inspired or cheap, buffet-style **vegetarian food**. As well as dedicated places including *Loving Hut* (see p.91), *Xuandesushi* (see p.88) and the *Spring Natural Vegetarian Restaurant* (see p.89), *Hui Liu* teahouse (see p.92) also has excellent organic vegetarian food, and some Western operations such as *Pig & Pepper* (see p.91) have veggie options.

1

no-nonsense local diner whose name is a relic of its past, as they actually use a different bird these days – delicious goose-meat noodles in soup (NT$60) and plates of sliced goose (from NT$300) are the only two things on the menu. Daily 9.30am–10.30pm.

Fong Da Coffee 蜂大珈琲; fēngdà kāfēi 42 Chengdu Rd ☎02 2371 9577; Ximen MRT; map p.64. Cosy coffee shop close to Ximen MRT, established in 1956 and always busy. Antiquated machinery grinds and roasts fresh espresso, cappuccino and frappes (NT$70–150) near the entrance. Daily 8am–10.30pm.

Mapo Galmaegi 麻蒲海鷗; mápú hǎiōu 4/F, 123 Xining S Rd ☎02 2312 9999; Ximen MRT; map p.64. Popular with Korean tourists who aren't keen on breaking away from home comforts, this large, upper-floor Korean restaurant allows you to barbecue meat at your own table (portions from NT$350), and also serves several types of *jjigae* (broth; NT$250) and *jeon* (savoury pancakes; NT$300). Daily 11.30am–2pm & 5–10pm.

Modern Toilet 便所主題餐厅; biànsuǒ zhǔtí cāntīng 2/F, 7 Lane 50, Xining S Rd ☎02 2311 8822, Ⓦ moderntoilet.com.tw; Ximen MRT; map p.64. The menu here is an unexceptional mix of Chinese and Western dishes, but you're either going to be amused or disgusted by the food at a restaurant whose slogan reads "Shit or food?". Offerings include a turd sub sandwich (NT$290), curry served in a fake toilet bowl (NT$270), and "poop" meatballs (NT$260). You have been warned. Mon–Fri 11.30am–10pm, Sat & Sun 11am–10pm.

★**Ramen Nagi** 豚骨拉麵凪; túngǔ lāmiàn zhǐ 6/F, 52 Hanzhong St ☎02 2370 2000, Ⓦ n-nagi.com.tw; Ximen MRT; map p.64. The Ximending area has more ramen places than you could count, but this one stands out from the crowd. Not only is it an offshoot of a venerable Shibuya noodle house, but it serves something called the "midorio" – like a normal ramen, but made with pesto,

powdered cheese, and chilli oil (NT$230). This may sound awful, but it found favour even in Tokyo, a city where ramen is perhaps the most important religion – once you go midori (green), you may never be satisfied by a normal ramen again. (Nagi do those too though, and they're also delicious.) Daily 11.30am–10pm.

Xuandesushi 玄德素食; xuándé sùshí 4 Lane 34, Hankou St Sec 2 ☎02 2314 4357; Ximen MRT; map p.64. Despite having "sushi" in the name and a steakhouse next door, this is the best (if the ugliest) pick of a small choice of veggie places on this narrow lane. Served buffet style and priced by weight (usually NT$70–120 for a paper tray-full), it avoids any menu confusion; the food's tasty, and the staff amiable. Mon–Fri 11.30am–3.30pm & 4.30–7pm, Sat 11.30am–2.30pm.

DATONG & ZHONGSHAN

★**Addiction Aquatic Development** 上引水產; shàngyǐn shuǐchǎn 18 Alley 2, Lane 410, Minzu E Rd ☎02 2508 1268; Xingtian Temple MRT; map p.67. Taipei's fish market now has a wonderful (and surprisingly swanky) stand-up dining area, at which you can enjoy the freshest sushi in town (sets NT$510–660); side-stalls sell urchins, oysters and other raw seafood. Daily 9.30am–midnight.

Lao-A Bei 老阿伯; lǎo ā bǎi 226 Dihua St Sec 1 ☎0955 341 050; Daqiaotou MRT; map p.67. There are precious few places to eat on Dihua St (see p.66), but this little eatery is thoroughly appropriate to the area's simple charm. Try their fish-ball soup (NT$55), or the rice or noodles with a fried garlic topping (NT$25–35). Mon–Sat 7.30am–3pm.

★**Maji Maji Food Court** MAJI MAJI集食行樂; MAJI MAJI jíshí xínglè 1 Yumen St; Yuanshan MRT; map p.67. Part of the Maji Square development in Expo Park, this strip of snack shacks has amazing variety – British-style oysters, Japanese takoyaki balls, Thai street

---

EAT YOUR WAY AROUND THE MAINLAND

Exploring Taipei's **restaurants** will allow your taste buds to travel across mainland China without having to pay a fortune and plough through red tape for a Chinese visa. The eating establishments in Taiwan's capital run the gamut of almost every regional cuisine, from Beijing duck and spicy Sichuan dishes to Cantonese *dim sum* (diǎnxīn in Mandarin). Yunnanese food is conspicuously absent; given how popular such restaurants have been in Beijing in recent years, this gap in the market may well soon be exploited.

BEST FOR...

Beijing hotpot *Beijing Do It True* (see p.90)

Xi'an paomo (soup with unleavened bread) *Shao Shao Ke* (see p.87)

Spicy Sichuan cuisine *Kiki Restaurant* (see p.90)

Super-spicy Hunan cuisine *Peng Yuan* (see opposite)

Refined Hangzhou cuisine *Tien Hsiang Lo* (see opposite)

Shanghai-style steamed dumplings *Din Tai Fung* (see opposite)

Hong Kong dim sum *Citystar* (see p.90)

Chinese dough-stick and soy-milk breakfast *World Soybean Milk Magnate* (see p.90)

food, Colombian arepas and empanadas, Canadian poutine, Mexican tacos and more. Mon–Thurs & Sun 11.30am–8.30pm, Fri & Sat 10.30am–9.30pm.

★ **Peng Yuan** 彭園; péngyuán 2/F, 380 Linsen N Rd ☎ 02 2551 9157; Shuanglian MRT; map p.67. Named after founder and celebrated chef Peng Chang Gui (who is said to have invented "General Tso's Chicken" or zuǒzōngtáng jī; NT$380), this banquet-style restaurant specializes in fiery Hunan cuisine. "Peng's Tofu" (péngjiā dòufǔ; NT$320), served with pork and chillies, is a must order, though everything else is also excellent. Daily 11.30–2pm & 5–9.30pm.

Shinyeh 欣葉台菜本店; xīnyè táicài běndiàn 34 Shuangcheng St ☎ 02 2596 3255, ⓦ www.shinyeh.com.tw; Zhongshan Elementary School MRT; map p.67. Celebrated Taiwanese restaurant chain with several branches in the city; this Shuangcheng branch is the original. The food is outstanding – expect to pay NT$100–200 for noodles or rice and NT$200–400 for a main dish. Specialities include fried oyster omelette, pumpkin congee and pork knuckle. Daily 11am–midnight.

Shougong Guotie 手工鍋貼; shǒugōng guōtiē 119 Huayin St; Zhongshan or Taipei Main Station MRT; map p.67. Taipei now has a huge central bus terminal, but in the dirty days of yore vehicles would pick up and drop off on Chengde Rd. This little shack was once used as a simple snack stop for boarding or alighting passengers, and though it's now more distant from the terminal, many still return to this day. Try a savoury, Beijing-style breakfast pancake (NT$25, or NT$35 with egg), and some soybean milk (NT$15). Daily 7.30am–5pm.

Tian Xiang Huwei Hot Pot 天香回味; tiānxiāng huíwèi 2/F, 16 Nanjing E Rd Sec 1 ☎ 02 2511 7275; Zhongshan MRT; map p.67. Popular málà (spicy hotpot) restaurant, Mongolian style. There's no English but the menu has pictures and it's basically a case of choosing which meat (NT$160–300) and vegetables (less than NT$100) to stick in the pot. Special "medicinal" pots (tastier than they sound) are NT$400. Daily 11.30am–2am.

★ **Tien Hsiang Lo** 天香樓; tiānxiānglóu B1, Landis Hotel, 41 Minquan E Rd Sec 2 ☎ 02 2597 1234; Zhongshan Elementary School MRT; map p.67. One of Taipei's most elegant restaurants, blending modern and classical design and offering an extensive menu of Hangzhou-style food including fried shrimps with Lóngjǐng tea leaves, drunken chicken and West Lake-style steamed fish. A la carte dishes start at around NT$320, with set menus from NT$1500. Daily noon–2.30pm & 6–10pm.

SHIDA & AROUND

Din Tai Fung 鼎泰豐; dīngtàifēng 194 Xinyi Rd Sec 2 ☎ 02 2321 8928, ⓦ www.dintaifung.com.tw; Dongmen MRT; map p.75. This Taiwan institution has been knocking out sumptuous dumplings for thirty years,

and its Shanghai-style food is still worth the hype. Try the legendary steamed pork dumplings (xiǎolóngbāo), which at NT$200 for ten are not bad value. Be prepared to wait (take a number). There's also a less crowded branch in the basement of Taipei 101 (see p.90). Mon–Fri 10am–9pm, Sat & Sun 9am–9pm.

Grandma Nitti's Kitchen 8 Lane 93, Shida Rd ☎ 02 2369 9751; Taipower Building MRT; map p.75. Great-value Western diner attracting local expats, students and young professionals since 1989. The all-day breakfast is first-rate, and the burritos, sandwiches and pasta dishes on offer make perfect brunch material (NT$200–300). Check out the rooftop terrace, and the dessert selection including cherry pies, cheesecake and choc-chip cookies (cakes NT$110–150). Mon–Sat 10am–11pm, Sun 10am–10pm.

Kao Chi 高記; gāojì 5 Yongkang St ☎ 02 2341 9984; Dongmen MRT; map p.75. A decent enough alternative to Din Tai Fung just around the corner (especially if you don't fancy queuing), with a wide selection of Shanghai-style food (drunken chicken, chicken soup and fried pork buns; NT$200–400) and steamed pork dumplings that are certainly not as tasty as those around the corner, but good nonetheless (NT$240 for ten). Daily 9.30am–10.30pm.

Madame Jill's 翠薪越南餐廳; cuìxīn yuènán cāntīng 11 Lane 24, Roosevelt Rd Sec 4 ☎ 02 2368 0254; Gongguan MRT; map p.75. Taipei's best Vietnamese restaurant, tucked away in the heart of Gongguan and offering cheap but mouthwatering favourites such as spring rolls, pho, curry chicken and spicy coconut beef with French bread (beef noodles from NT$150). Daily except Weds 11am–2.30pm & 5.30–9pm.

Menya Kurohei 麵食黑平; miànshí hēipíng 10-3 Yongkang St ☎ 02 2397 0787; Dongmen MRT; map p.75. Before eating at Menya Kurohei, you should understand two things about Japanese noodles. First, tsumeken (dry noodles served with dipping broth) is far easier to eat than boiling-hot ramen on a warm day; second, Japanese tantanmen (noodles with minced pork, in a spicy soup) is far better than the original Chinese version (dàn dàn miàn). Eat the evidence here from NT$170. Daily 11am–10pm.

★ **Sababa** 沙巴巴; shābābā 17 Lane 283, Luosifu Rd Sec 3 ☎ 02 2363 8009; Taipower Building MRT; map p.75. Established over a decade ago, which is somewhat miraculous for a place in the university area, this restaurant was founded by an Israeli, and is the best place in town for Middle Eastern delights including falafel, baba ganoush and hummus. Snacks rolled in freshly made, excellent pita bread will set you back NT$150 and up; full plates cost around NT$300. Daily 11.30am–10pm.

Spring Natural Vegetarian Restaurant 春天素食餐廳; chūntiān sùshí cāntīng 3/F, 177 Heping E Rd Sec 1 ☎ 02 2393 0288, ⓦ springfood.com.tw; Guting MRT; map p.75. Bright, contemporary buffet restaurant with a massive selection of veggie delights to choose from

1

(11.45am–2pm NT$500; 2.30–4.30pm NT$350; 5.45–9pm NT$600). Daily 11.45am–9pm.

★**World Soybean Milk Magnate** 世界豆浆大王; shìjiè dòujiāng dàwáng 284 Yonghe Rd Sec 2; Dingxi MRT; map p.75. Created in 1968, this was the place which kicked off Taipei's mania for soy milk – though a little out of the way, it's well worth coming to pay your respects. Late morning is best, once the breakfast rush is over; go Taiwanese and have a fried dough-stick with their utterly delicious soybean milk (NT$45 will get you both). Daily 24hr.

EAST TAIPEI

Beijing Do It True 北京都一处; běijīng dūyīchù 506 Renai Rd ☎02 2720 6417; SYS Memorial Hall MRT; map p.77. Cheerful Beijing-style restaurant, best known for its Chinese sesame buns served with sliced pork, fried "jumbo" dumplings and Beijing-style hotpot (NT$200–400). It's named after an old restaurant in Beijing, feted by Emperor Qianlong (this one was established in Kaohsiung in 1949 and moved here in the 1960s). Daily 11am–2pm & 5–9pm.

Citystar 京星港式飲茶; jīngxīng gǎngshì yǐnchá 2/F, 216 Dunhua S Rd Sec 1 ☎02 2741 2625; Zhongxiao Dunhua MRT; map p.77. Respectable *dim sum* restaurant that stays fairly busy all night, offering great views and in a convenient location on the corner of Dunhua and Zhongxiao roads. The Cantonese food is great value, too; many small plates go for around NT$100. Daily 24hr.

Din Tai Fung 鼎泰豐; dǐngtàifēng B1/F Taipei 101, 7 Xinyi Rd Sec 5 ☎02 8101 7799, ⓦdintaifung .com.tw; Taipei 101 / World Trade Center MRT; map p.77. The Taipei 101 branch of this Taiwan institution (see box below) is just as good as the original branch (see p.89), but you're unlikely to have to queue for anywhere near as long – sometimes not at all. Daily 11am–9.30pm.

Dozo 102 Guangfu S Rd ☎02 2778 1135, ⓦfacebook .com/Dozo.IzakayaBar; SYS Memorial Hall MRT; map p.77. Not exactly the most authentic Japanese *izakaya* (bar-restaurant) in town, but quite a trip nonetheless, with live drummers every night, a large, open-plan area, sunken tables and dark, minimalist decor. Offers a variety of Japanese sushi, rice, noodles and meat dishes for NT$120–380; for drinks, you can choose from some interesting house cocktails, Japanese "highballs" (whisky and soda), and giant towers of Asahi draft beer. Mon–Thurs & Sun 6pm–2am, Fri & Sat 6pm–3am.

★**Du Hsiao Yueh** 度小月擔仔麵; dùxiǎoyuè dànzǐmiàn 9-1 Yongkang St ☎02 3393 1325; Dongmen MRT; map p.77. Branch of a revered Tainan noodle establishment, established over a century ago. Deservedly popular, the dànzǐ noodles (NT$50 a bowl) are a must-order; also worth trying are the stewed duck eggs for NT$15, lǔ ròu fàn (stewed pork on rice) for NT$35 and fried shrimp rolls for NT$200. The decor is sleek, contemporary Chinese, and the chef cooks over charcoal-fired pots near the entrance. NT$100 minimum spend per person. Mon–Sat 11.30am–11pm, Sun 11.30am–9.30pm.

Home's Thai Cuisine 香米泰國料理; xiāngmǐ tàiguó liàolǐ 39 Lane 280, Guangfu S Rd ☎02 2778 6806, ⓦhomesthai.com.tw; Sun Yet-Sen Memorial Hall MRT; map p.77. A great choice for Thai food, with most of the chefs hailing from Thailand (plus a couple from Myanmar). The food tastes suitably authentic (most mains NT$350–500), and it's served in a highly attractive space. Daily 11.30am–2.30pm & 5.30pm–10pm.

Kiki Restaurant Kiki餐廳; kiki cāntīng 47 Lane 280, Guangfu S Rd ☎02 2781 4250; Sun Yet-Sen Memorial Hall MRT; map p.77. Trendy Sichuan restaurant with bright, contemporary decor and an extensive menu that provides a spiciness ratings for each dish; think spicy braised bean curd and stir-fried chicken with chilli

---

DIN TAI FUNG

Din Tai Fung is not only the most famous restaurant in Taipei; it's certainly the best-known in Taiwan, and quite possibly all of Asia. The place actually started life as a cooking-oil shop in 1958; when business started slowing down in 1970, founder Yang Bingyi hit on the idea of selling steamed, soup-filled xiǎolóngbāo dumplings as well as oil. These went down so well that the place expanded to become a full restaurant (see p.89) shortly afterwards, and things have been on the up ever since.

Much of *Din Tai Fung*'s fame outside the Chinese-speaking world came from a single newspaper article: in Jan 1993, the **New York Times** named it one of the world's top ten restaurants. The owners picked up this publicity and ran with it, opening up branches in the USA, mainland China, Korea, Australia and elsewhere; the Hong Kong branch ended up landing a **Michelin star** in 2010, which only added to the legend.

Far from having its reputation ruined locally by global popularity, Taiwanese people remain enormously proud of *Din Tai Fung*. Standards remain extremely high, perhaps best evident in their Taipei 101 branch (see p.90), where the dumplings are made in a glassed-off space by a team of almost two dozen chefs, clad in brain-surgeon-style masks and white gowns. Don't leave Taipei without trying the famed xiǎolóngbāo.

(NT$110–310). Daily 11.30am–3pm & 5.30–10.30pm (till 10pm Sun).

Loving Hut 愛家國際餐飲; àijiā guójì cānyǐn 30 Lane 280, Guangfu S Rd ☎02 2777 2711, ⓦlovinghut .com; map p.77. This popular vegan restaurant is part of a chain with several branches in Taipei. Expect a wide range of dishes, from wild-rice stew and soy steaks to pumpkin noodles and blueberry bagels. NT$220 will buy you a Singa-style *laksa*, or some Vietnamese spring rolls. Tues, Weds & Fri–Sun 11.30am–2.30pm & 5–9pm.

Pig & Pepper 15 Lane 295, Fuxing S Rd Sec 1 ☎02 2708 7899, ⓦpigandpepper.com.tw; Daan MRT; map p.77. Relaxed all-day brunch spot tucked away into a small lane; offerings include braised-pork egg benedict (NT$420) and Southwestern fried chicken and gravy (NT$350); all dishes come with a coffee or tea. Tues–Sun 11am–3pm & 6pm–10pm.

Shin Yeh 101 101 食藝軒; 101 shíyìxuān 85/F Taipei 101, 7 Xinyi Rd Sec 5 ☎02 8101 0185, ⓦshinyeh.com .tw; Taipei 101/World Trade Center MRT; map p.77. This celebrated Taiwanese restaurant chain now has a posh branch right at the top of Taipei 101 – it's worth a visit just for the experience of eating at such a lofty perch. The menu features staple *Shin Yeh* home-style Taiwanese food: their signature fried rice noodles, braised pork belly with bamboo shoots and the like (sets from NT$1500). Daily 11.30am–3pm & 5.30–10pm.

Ziga Zaga 2/F Grand Hyatt Taipei, 2 Songshou Rd ☎02 2720 1200; Taipei 101/World Trade Center MRT; map p.77. Set in the *Grand Hyatt*, this is Taipei's swankiest Italian restaurant, serving authentic pasta and pizza (NT$500–600), and main dishes from NT$800. The place turns into a jazz bar after 7.30pm, with live bands till 9.30pm (11.40pm Fri & Sat), but that's not necessarily the end of the entertainment – according to many locals, the hotel is haunted. Mon–Thurs & Sun11.30am–3pm & 6pm–10pm, Fri & Sat 11.30am–3pm & 6pm–1am.

CAFÉS
ZHONGZHENG

Astoria 明星咖啡廳; míngxīng kāfēitīng 2/F, 5 Wuchang St Sec 1 ☎02 2381 5589; Ximen MRT; map p.60. Established by emigre Russians in 1949, this expensive but charming old-school café serves decent coffee (from NT$200), cakes and light meals (afternoon tea from NT$330, daily 2.30–5pm). It was the closest thing Taipei had to a literary salon in the 1950s – some of the famous regulars who once dined here include writers Huang Chun-ming and Pai Hsien-yung – but these days it can come across as a little forlorn. Daily 10am–9.30pm.

Mayor's Residence Arts Salon 官邸藝文沙龍; guāndǐ yìwén shālong 46 Xuzhou Rd (no English signs) ☎02 2396 9510, ⓦwww.mayorsalon.tw; Shandao Temple MRT; map p.60. This gallery and café

has one of the most atmospheric settings in the city: a beautifully restored Japanese-style wooden house, once the home of Taipei's mayors. Serves up coffee and tea (NT$150 and up), light pasta dishes and lunch specials (from NT$480). Daily 9am–10pm.

Old Park 老牌公園號; lǎopái gōngyuánhào 2 Hengyang Rd ☎02 2311 3099; NTU Hospital MRT; map p.60. Venerable shop famed for its pastries (try the taro flavour) and especially its home-made sweet-and-sour plum juice (酸梅湯; suānméitāng; NT$30), served from a metal vat. Daily 10am–8pm.

★**Snow King** 雪王冰淇淋; xuěwáng bīngqílín 65 Wuchang St Sec 1 ☎02 2331 8415; Ximen MRT; map p.60. Forget the traditional Taiwanese desserts – this is the best sweetie place in town. Its creator became famed as the man who could make ice cream from anything, so why not avoid the regular flavours and go for jasmine, bitter melon, curry, sesame oil chicken, pork, or beer? Amazingly, even the weird ones work – try for yourself (NT$70–110 per ball). Daily noon–8pm.

WANHUA

Ximen Mango Shaved Ice 西門町芒菓冰; xīméntíng mángmāobīng 17 Hanzhong St ☎02 2388 8511; Ximen MRT; map p.64. Cheery dessert café specialising in things made with mango – the snow ice (NT$190) should feed two (they also have a green-tea-and-red-bean variety). They also have mango shake and mango juice (both NT$75). Daily 10am–11pm.

DATONG & ZHONGSHAN

★**Fflavour** 豐味果品; fēngwèi guǒpǐn 103 Dihua St Sec 1 ☎02 2557 6763; Daqiaotou MRT; map p.67. The aroma will hit as soon as you enter this fruit store, which has gone all fancy of late and now caters to young, hipster sorts, doling out smoothies and fruit juices (NT$150–250) made with fruit sourced from local farms. The choice of mango, avocado, red dragon fruit and the like can be tricky – go for whatever's in season (ie, most pungent). Daily 10am–7pm.

Melange Café 米朗琪咖啡館; mǐlǎngqí kāfēiguǎn 23 Lane 16, Zhongshan N Rd Sec 2 ☎02 2567 3787; Zhongshan MRT; map p.67. Of the many cafés on this newly trendy lane, this is the most popular – so much so that they've had to open another branch. This one's both prettier and marginally less busy; try the coffee made from beans sourced across the globe (NT$130–230), or go for teas, waffles, scones or mille-feuille. Mon–Fri 7.30am–10pm, Sat & Sun 8.30am–10pm.

Xia Er Zui 呷二嘴; xiá èr zuǐ 34 Ganzhou St ☎02 2557 0780; Daqiaotou MRT; map p.67. This place has been serving up old-fashioned shaved-ice bowls (think jelly, beans and cold noodles) and a variety of dumplings since 1954 (NT$45–60). Tues–Sun 9am–5.30pm.

SHIDA & AROUND

Ijysheng 一之軒; yīzhīxuān 53 Shida Rd ☎02 2362 0425; Taipower Building MRT; map p.75. This popular bakery sells Asian-style breads and twelve scrumptious flavours of máshǔ (glutinous rice cakes); they also do frozen versions (try the maple walnut), and a huge range of elaborate cakes, pastries and savoury snacks. Daily 7am–11pm.

Smoothie House 永康街思慕昔; yǒngkāngjiē sīmùxī 15 Yongkang St ☎02 2341 8555, ⓦsmoothie house.com; Dongmen MRT; map p.75. Hugely popular ice-dessert store; locals line up to dig into the "super fruits mix", made of strawberry, mango and kiwi fruit topped with fluffy ice and mango sorbet; or the version topped with panna cotta. Both are NT$210 and big enough to share. Daily 10am –11pm.

EAST TAIPEI

Drip Café 好滴咖啡; hǎodī kāfēi 26 Lane 553, Zhongxiao E Rd Sec 4 ☎02 2764 8181; Sun Yet-Sen Memorial Hall MRT; map p.77. East of Songshan Cultural Park (see p.77), this is a good pit-stop for pasta and sandwiches (often featuring some quirky ingredients; from NT$220), coffee, and desserts such as bubble-tea croissant ice-cream (NT$180). Daily 11.30am–10pm.

★**Eastern Ice Store** 東區粉圓; dōngqū fěnyuán 38 Lane 216, Zhongxiao E Rd Sec 4 ☎02 2777 2057; Zhongxiao Dunhua MRT; map p.77. The best place in East Taipei for traditional shaved ice (tsuàbīng), with a small seating area and a choice of four toppings for NT$60 (taro, peanuts, red bean, etc). Toppings also served as a hot dessert. Daily 11am–11pm.

TEAHOUSES
ZHONGZHENG

Cha for Tea 喫茶趣; chīcháqù 62 Hengyang Rd ☎02 2312 2828, ⓦwww.chafortea.com.tw; Nanjing E Rd MRT; map p.60. One of Taiwan's most popular teahouse chains, this branch is an easy introduction to the island's fine teas. A pot here will cost NT$165–350, and snacks are available too. Daily 11am–10pm.

WANHUA

Herb Alley 青草巷; qīngcǎo xiàng Off Xichang St; Longshan Temple MRT; map p.64. The streets to the east of Longshan Temple (see p.63) are home to well over a dozen small stands selling various kinds of tea and juice. You'll have to read Chinese to know what you're ordering (and some of the ingredients are mysterious even to locals), but there's no harm in asking to sample before you buy. From NT$20. Most stalls daily 8am–8pm.

DATONG & ZHONGSHAN

Artyard 民藝埕; mínyì chéng 67 Dihua St ☎02 2552 1367; map p.67. This pottery shop (see p.98) has a gorgeous, secluded tearoom on its upper level; around NT$250 per head. Mon–Wed & Sun 10am–7pm, Thurs–Sat 10am–11pm.

SHIDA & AROUND

Hui Liu 回留; huíliú 9 Lane 31, Yongkang St ☎02 2392 6707, ⓦhuiliu.info; Dongmen MRT; map p.75. Tranquil and elegant teahouse located on the corner of Yongkang Park, with wooden tables and beautiful handicrafts. Organic specialities include tiěguānyīn, bāozhǒng and wild Pu-Er tea, and there's an excellent vegetarian menu – avoid meal times if you just want to drink (around NT$380/pot). Daily 11.30am–10pm.

★**Wistaria Teahouse** 紫藤廬; zǐténglú 1 Lane 16, Xinsheng S Rd Sec 3 ☎02 2363 7375; Taipower Building MRT; map p.75. Taipei's most historic Japanese-era teahouse, Wistaria is best known for being the meeting place of artists and political dissidents post-1949, and where much of the movie Eat Drink Man Woman was shot. Sip tea (NT$250–350) – or a cooling plum juice – in the main room with simple wooden tables and chairs, or try the Japanese rooms with tatami mats further back. Daily 10am–11pm.

EAST TAIPEI

Ten Ren's Tea 天仁集團; tiānrén jítuán 174 Zhongxiao E Rd Sec 3 ☎02 2771 7370, ⓦtenren.com .tw; Zhongxiao Dunhua MRT; map p.77. Founded in 1953, this is one of the largest and most respected tea manufacturers in Asia, with stores all over the island. This branch, just off Dunhua Rd, also doubles as a simple café with a takeaway counter and a few chairs and tables inside, where you can sample the formidable range of teas (from NT$60 a cup). Daily 9am–10.30pm.

MAOKONG

★**Yaoyue Teahouse** 邀月茶坊; yāoyuè cháfǎng 6 Lane 40, Zhinan Rd Sec 3 ☎02 2939 2025. Beyond the Taipei Tea Promotion Center lies one of the best teahouses in Maokong, with rustic wooden pavilions and a series of outdoor terraces overlooking tea and bamboo plantations. The entrance is marked by a Chinese gate flanked by lanterns on the left side of the road. Service charges vary according to the time of day (NT$70–180/person), with teas extra (NT$220–NT$360); English menu available. Daily 24hr.

Yuanxuyuan 緣續緣; yuánxùyuán 16-2 Lane 38, Zhinan Rd Sec 3 ☎02 2936 7089. The closest place to the station, with a cosy, classical Chinese interior – its wooden booths overlook the valley and are set around an indoor fishpond bridged by stepping stones. Take the right-hand fork at the station – the teahouse is 50m on the right, marked by a "moongate" or round entrance.

TAIPEI'S NIGHT MARKETS

It would be a pity to visit Taipei without exploring at least one or two of its **night markets**, a quintessential component of the city's culinary life. Their stalls offer a vast range of cheap xiǎochī, or "little eats", and most things come in at NT$25–60 per order. Each stall has its own opening and closing times, but you're best off coming from 5pm–midnight.

★**Gongguan Night Market** 公館夜市; gōngguǎn yèshì Gongguan MRT; map p.75. Food stalls cram the lanes between Roosevelt and Tingzhou roads south and north of the MRT station. One must-try is *Lan's Steamed Sandwiches* (藍家割包; lánjiā gēbāo; pork buns; NT$50) at 3 Alley 8, Lane 316, Roosevelt Rd Sec 3 (look for the "Traditional Taiwan Snack" sign), but the most celebrated stall is *Chen San Ding Pearl Milk* (陳三鼎黑糖粉圓鮮奶; chénsāndǐng hēitáng fěnyuán xiānnǎi) at 10 Lane 316, selling the city's best bubble tea for NT$40.

Guangzhou St Night Market 廣州街夜市; guǎngzhōujiē yèshì Guangzhou St between Xiyuan Rd and Wuzhou St; Longshan Temple MRT; map p.64. Traditional outdoor market, with the best stalls on the junction with Wuzhou St: *Memory Aiyu Ice* (懷念愛玉冰; huáiniàn àiyù bīng; NT$35) has been serving cooling "aiyu" jelly drinks (àiyù bīng; NT$35) since 1951, made from the seeds of a fig-like fruit, while *Ding Ji Tempura* (頂級甜不辣; dǐngjí tiánbùlà; daily 11am–late) on the other side offers boiled Taiwanese-style squid tiánbùlà "tempura" (NT$45–60).

Huaxi St Tourist Night Market 華西街夜市; huáxījiē yèshì Between Guangzhou St and Guiyang St; Longshan Temple MRT; map p.64. This covered pedestrian-only street is half food and half CDs, bags, foot massages and jewellery. Try the juicy pork gēbo (NT$40) at *Yuanfang Steamed Sandwiches* (源芳割包; yuánfāng gēbāo; closed Wed) at no. 161. The street is traditionally famous for snake dishes

(it's also known as "Snake Alley"), though the gruesome "shows" no longer take place.

Raohe St Night Market 饒河街夜市; ráohéjiē yèshì; Raohe St between Tayou Rd and Bade Rd; Songshan MRT; map p.77. Try the delicious charcoal-baked Fuzhou beef pepper pies (húiāobǐng; NT$50) from *Fuzhou Shizu Pepper Buns* (福州世祖胡椒餅; fúzhōu shìzǔ hújiāobǐng; daily 3pm–midnight), near no. 249; *Dongfa Oyster Noodles* (東發號蚵仔麵線; dōngfāhào kēzǐ miànxiàn) at no. 94 (oyster noodles NT$60); and *Chen Dong Medicinal Spareribs* (陳董藥燉排骨; chéndǒng yàodùn páigǔ; mutton and ribs simmered in medicinal herbs for NT$70) at no. 160.

Shida Night Market 師大夜市; shīdà yèshì Longquan St, parallel to Shida Rd, from Lane 50 to Heping Rd; Taipower Building MRT; map p.75. An eclectic mix of fried chicken, crêpes, burritos, Chinese, Indian and Thai influences in a trendy area popular with students.

Shilin Night Market 士林夜市; shìlín yèshì 101 Jihe Rd ☎02 2881 5557; Jiantan MRT; map p.58. The city's biggest and oldest night market, dating from 1910, is now located in the basement of the Shilin public market (the latter is busiest in the mornings), and therefore weatherproof (and has a/c). Try the dàpíngbāo xiǎopíng (NT$40) at *Shilin Old Little Roll in Big Roll Shop* (士林老字號大餅包小餅; shìlín lǎozìhào dàbǐng bāo xiǎobǐng). The action continues in the lanes between here and Dadong Rd.

The cover charge is NT$120/person till 6pm, then NT$150 thereafter; teas range from NT$$300 to 350, with snacks from NT$100 (English menu available). Tues–Sun 11am–midnight.

DRINKING AND NIGHTLIFE

The **nightlife** in Taipei may underwhelm if you're used to larger Asian cities, but there's still a lot going on, including **lounge bars**, **speakeasies** and **craft breweries**, a wide selection of **live music** venues, and **nightclubs** attracting top international DJs. Bars and clubs are scattered throughout the city, but there are enough clusters to allow some stumbling around on foot. The university districts of **Shida** and **Gongguan** are prime hunting grounds for cheaper venues, there are some quirky choices around **Wanhua**, while upscale **East Taipei** is where you'll find many of Taipei's top lounge bars and clubs. For a good online guide, try ⓦ thirstyintaipei.com.

BARS
ZHONGZHENG
Revolver 1-1 Roosevelt Rd Sec 1 ☎02 3393 1678, ⓦ revolver.tw; Chiang Kai-Shek Memorial MRT; map p.60. One of the most popular expat hangouts in town, with

a selection of beers ranging from reasonably priced types (NT$130) to local craft options (up to NT$300). The outdoor area is a great mingling space. Also a live music spot of some repute (see p.94). Mon–Thurs 6.30pm–3am, Fri & Sat 6.30pm–5am, Sun 6pm–midnight.

1

WANHUA

Driftwood Papa Whale Hotel, Kaifeng St Sec 2 ☎ 02 2388 3699; Ximen MRT; map p.64. Hotel bar where the clientele is usually a mix of guests staying upstairs and sophisticated locals. A very good meeting spot (particularly the bar, half of the seating around which is open to the street), and drinks (including local craft beers) are fairly priced at NT$200 or so. Mon–Thurs & Sun 5–11.30pm, Fri & Sat 3pm–12.30am.

★**Hanko 60** 60 Hankou St Sec 2 ☎ 02 2381 0808, ⓦ facebook.com/Hanko60; Ximen MRT; map p.64. You won't see a sign for this self-proclaimed speakeasy – press the button by the door next to some old cinema posters, push your way through the curtains, and you'll be greeted by the sight of rich *cognoscenti* yapping over cocktails (NT$300–400). Pricey though the drinks are, they're also expertly made, many of them takes on (and sometimes even made with) Chinese tea. The only negative is that, for a speakeasy, it's frustratingly hard to mingle. Mon–Thurs & Sun 8pm–2am, Fri & Sat 8pm–3am.

DATONG & ZHONGSHAN

Brass Monkey 銅猴子; tónghóuzi 166 Fuxing N Rd ☎ 02 2547 5050, ⓦ brassmonkeytaipei.com; Nanjing E Rd MRT; map p.67. Popular pub with quality beers on tap and large servings of Western food on the menu. Big-screen TV means it's a popular expat venue for major sports events. Tues is salsa night, Wed is steak night and Thurs is ladies' night. Mon–Wed & Sun 5pm–1am, Thurs 5pm–4am, Fri & Sat 5pm–2am.

My Place 石洞運動酒吧; shídòng yùndòng jiǔbā 3-1 Lane 32, Shuangcheng St ☎ 02 2592 8122; Zhongshan Elementary School MRT; map p.67. Closest thing the Combat Zone has to an institution, this British-style pub is one of the oldest in the area, opening in 1975. Draft beer is NT$150 a pint and NT$600 a pitcher. Daily 7pm–3am.

SHIDA & AROUND

45 45酒吧; 45 jiǔbā 45 Heping E Rd Sec 1 ☎ 02 2321 2140; Guting MRT; map p.75. Student-favourite pub also popular with expats and locals, *45* is close to Guting MRT station and has two floors accessed via a narrow stairway from street level. Snack food and beers from NT$130. Daily 5.30pm–4am.

Roxy Rocker 搖滾客; yáogǔn kè 177 Heping E Rd Sec 1 ☎ 02 2351 8177, ⓦ facebook.com/TaipeiRocker; Daan MRT; map p.75. Cool bar with a rock 'n' roll theme (though reggae is also played), giant Led Zeppelin murals, great cocktails (from NT$200) and a special vinyl listening room with over ten thousand records of all genres to sample. Daily 8pm–4am.

EAST TAIPEI

Barcode 5/F, 22 Songshou Rd ☎ 0920 168 269; Taipei 101/World Trade Center MRT; map p.77. Something of a

hangout for beautiful people, with funky interiors and sublime cocktails (from NT$400) – the best reason to visit. Daily 9pm–2.30am.

The Bed 水煙館; shuǐyānguǎn 29 Alley 35, Lane 181, Zhongxiao E Rd Sec 4 ☎ 02 2711 3733; Zhongxiao Dunhua MRT; map p.77. Lounge bar with dark corners, comfy sofas, divans and a couple of beds to relax on amid the vaguely Indochinese decor: if the Vietnamese snacks and cocktails aren't enough, for NT$600 you can puff on a *shisha* (water pipe filled with fruit-flavoured tobacco). Daily 6pm–2am.

Carnegie's 卡奈基餐廳; kǎnàijī cāntīng 100 Anhe Rd Sec 2 ☎ 02 2325 4433, ⓦ carnegies.net; Xinyi Anhe MRT; map p.77. Big expat favourite (the original is in Hong Kong) and the place to come for dancing on tables and general drunken mayhem. It's also one of the best places for English pub food (mains NT$390–490), including all-day breakfasts. Mon, Tues & Thurs 11am–2am, Wed & Fri 11.30am–4am, Sat 10.30am–4am, Sun 10.30am–2am.

★**Commune A7** 3 Songshou Rd ⓦ www.communea7 .com; Taipei 101/World Trade Center MRT; map p.77. What a fantastic addition to the city this open-plan stall area has been. Most people come here for the snacks, but it makes a fantastic place to drink too, with outposts of several Taiwanese breweries, most pertinently Sunmai. You can sit where you like; try for a seat with a night view of Taipei 101. Mon–Thurs 3pm–midnight, Fri 3pm–1am, Sat & Sun noon–midnight.

Landmark 68 Zhongxiao E Rd Sec 5 ☎ 02 2722 0592, ⓦ taihubrewing.com; Taipei City Hall MRT; map p.77. A small bar with standing room only, this often feels like the nexus around which Taipei's craft-beer scene revolves. In reality, they usually only have a few of their house Taihu brews, with the remainder hauled from the UA. A jar will set you back NT$200–250. Mon–Thurs 5pm–11.30pm, Fri–Sun 3pm–1.30am.

Marco Polo Lounge 馬可波羅酒廊; mǎkěbōluó jiǔláng 38/F Shangri La's Far Eastern Plaza Hotel, 201 Dunhua S Rd ☎ 02 2378 8888 ext. 5952; Xinyi Anhe Rd MRT; map p.77. It's hard to beat the stunning views from this hotel cocktail bar, right across the city to Taipei 101. The drinks are pretty good, too. Mon–Thurs 2.30pm–1am, Fri & Sat 11.30am–1am.

On Tap 21 Alley 11, Lane 216, Zhongxiao E Rd Sec 4 ☎ 02 2741 5365, ⓦ ontaptaipei.com; Zhongxiao Dunhua MRT; map p.77. TV screens of all sizes packed into this amiable pub makes it a prime spot for viewing international sports events, but the pub grub (NT$300 or so) and imported beers (NT$170–260) are also pretty good. Daily 5pm–late.

LIVE MUSIC
ZHONGZHENG

Revolver 1-1 Roosevelt Rd Sec 1 ☎ 02 3393 1678,

ⓦrevolver.tw; Chiang Kai-Shek Memorial MRT; map p.60. While the downstairs bar is a foreigner hangout (see p.93), the upper level is much more Taiwanese in feel, with local hipsters taking in good live music most nights. Entry NT$200–1200. Mon–Thurs 6.30pm–3am, Fri & Sat 6.30pm–5am, Sun 6pm–midnight.

SHIDA & AROUND

Blue Note 藍調台北; lántiáo táiběi 4/F, 171 Roosevelt Rd Sec 3 ⓣ02 2362 2333; Taipower Building MRT; map p.75. This pioneer jazz club, established in 1974, is a little hard to find but well worth the effort for the cosy venue and quality live jazz (entry NT$300–350). The entrance is on Shida Rd: take the first doorway on the left after Roosevelt Rd and get the lift up. Daily 8pm–12.30am.

Riverside Music Café 河岸留言; héàn liúyán 2 Lane 244, Roosevelt Rd Sec 3 ⓣ02 2368 7310, ⓦriverside.com.tw; Gongguan MRT; map p.75. Live rock and jazz venue just off Roosevelt Rd. Shows start from 9.30pm most days (cover charge usually NT$300–400). Sister to the similar *Riverside Live House* at the Red House (see p.65). Wed–Sat 7pm–2am.

The Wall 這牆; zhèqiáng B1, 200 Roosevelt Rd Sec 4 ⓣ02 2930 0162, ⓦthewall.tw; Gongguan MRT; map p.58. Taipei's best live rock venue with acts playing most nights from 8pm (opens as a record store during the day), though it can close early once the music stops – check the website for times. Located just off the busy Roosevelt and Keelung Rd junction, next to a cinema entrance. Admission NT$300–500. Tues–Sun: shop 3–11pm, bar 8pm–2am; bands 8–11pm.

EAST TAIPEI

Brown Sugar 黑糖餐廳; hēitáng cāntīng 101 Songren Rd ⓣ02 8780 1110, ⓦbrownsugartaipei.com; Xiangshan MRT; map p.77. This jazz club and restaurant has a regular programme of acts from 9pm, reverting to a trendy nightclub after 1am. Packed at weekends, with a big cocktails and drinks list, it's tucked away behind the Capital Center: walk down the alley at the end of Songshou Rd. Daily noon–2am (2.30am weekends).

EZ5 Live House EZ5音樂餐廳; EZ5 yīnyuè cāntīng 211 Anhe Rd Sec 2 ⓣ02 2738 3995, ⓦwww.ez5.com .tw; Liuzhangli MRT; map p.77. Hosts up-and-coming Mando-pop singers backed by a live band every night,

anything from syrupy love ballads and rock to funky R&B. Daily 7pm–2am.

CLUBS

EAST TAIPEI

Babe 18 18 Songshou Rd ⓣ0930 785 018, ⓦfacebook .com/Babe18.Taipei; Taipei 101/World Trade Center MRT; map p.77. Not a classy venue by any means (is the name a giveaway?), but if all you want to do is drink and dance, then this might be the place for you: all-you-can-drink deals, a youthful crowd, and generic hip-hop and R&B. Wed–Sun 10pm–4am.

Elektro ATT4FUN, 12 Songshou Rd ⓣ02 7737 9887, ⓦfacebook.com/ElektroTaipei; Taipei 101/World Trade Center MRT; map p.77. Formerly *Spark*, this is the new big-hitter near Taipei 101 – dress flash, bring cash. Most people end up booking tables here, partly because the dancefloor is relatively small; as you may have inferred from the name, EDM is usually what's pulsing out of the quality sound system. Entry usually NT$700 on weekends (includes two free drinks); ladies' night Wed. Wed–Sun 10pm–4am.

★**Omni** 5/F, 197 Zhongxiao E Rd Sec 4 ⓣ0983 803 388, ⓦomni-taipei.com; Zhongxiao Dunhua MRT; map p.77. Many in Taipei's clubbing fraternity were distraught when the *Luxy* closed its doors in 2015, though its replacement doesn't disappoint – merging the previous venues three dance rooms into one huge hall, and sparing no expense on a design which has received international awards, this is up there with the most important clubs in the land. Mostly EDM, trance and house; entry usually NT$800. Wed, Fri & Sat 10.30pm–4.30am.

Wave 12 Songshou Rd ⓣ0911 439 897, ⓦfacebook .com/waveclubtaipei; Taipei 101/World Trade Center MRT; map p.77. Cheap, not too crowded, and more for locals than foreigners, this club plays hip-hop and house. Tickets (NT$400–800, depending on day and time) include several drinks vouchers. Wed–Sun 10pm–4am.

LGBT+ NIGHTLIFE

ZHONGZHENG

Funky B1, 10 Hangzhou S Rd Sec 1 ⓣ02 2394 2162, ⓦfunkyclub.looker.tw; Shandao Temple MRT; map p.60. Opened in 1991, this is the oldest gay club in town, with a mix of music and fashionable clientele, particularly popular with the lesbian crowd. Cover NT$300–450. Mon

---

LGBT+ TAIPEI

Taipei has come a long way since the dark old days depicted in Pai Hsien-yung's *Crystal Boys* (see p.417), and the city has a thriving **LGBT+ community**, with the most defined gay area being the courtyard of the Red House (see p.65) in Wanhua, aka "Rainbow Plaza" (彩虹廣場; cǎihóng guǎngchǎng); arrivals have certainly gone up since the legalization of same-sex marriage in 2017. Some of the most established and popular gay venues are listed here (see above), and you'll find plenty more at ⓦgaytaipei4u.com.

1

& Tues 9pm–3.30am, Wed & Thurs 9.30pm–4.30am, Fri–Sun 9.30am–5.30am.

WANHUA

Commander 2/F Red House Square, 47 Lane 10, Chengdu Rd ☎ 02 2388 0440; Ximen MRT; map p.64. On the upper level of Rainbow Plaza, this is a fetish/uniform bar – not (always) as intimidating as one might expect. Mon–Thurs 7pm–1am; Fri–Sun 7pm–2am.

G-Paradise Red House Square, 47 Lane 10, Chengdu Rd ☎ 02 2370 4978; Ximen MRT; map p.64. Japanese-style sake bar that attracts a slightly older clientele than sister bar *G-2 Paradise* nearby. Cash only. Daily 5pm–2am.

Mudan Red House Square, 47 Lane 10, Chengdu Rd

☎ 02 2370 0940; Ximen MRT; map p.64. Perhaps the most reliably boisterous of the line of near-identical street-level bars, with cheap happy-hour specials and some powerful cocktails. Mon–Thurs & Sun 5pm–1am; Fri–Sat 5pm–2am.

DATONG & ZHONGSHAN

Taboo 90 Jianguo N Rd Sec 2 ☎ 02 2518 1119, ⓦ www .taboo.com.tw; Xingtian Temple MRT; map p.67. Lesbian bars don't tend to last long in Taipei, but this one has stood the test of time; the cheap drinks help, and it gets pretty crowded on weekends, when sometimes there are themed nights. Wed, Fri & Sat 10pm–4am.

ENTERTAINMENT AND THE ARTS

Taipei has an incredibly vibrant **cultural life**, with a daily feast of exhibitions, shows, gigs, plays and traditional performances. Performance groups such as **U-Theatre**, **Cloud Gate** and **Han-Tang Yuefu** (see p.413), all based in the city, are world class. The best way to buy **tickets** is to approach the venue directly or visit one of the ERA ticket offices located in Eslite or Kingstone bookstores. You can also download an English order form from ERA's Chinese website (ⓦ ticket.com.tw).

CHINESE OPERA

National Taiwan College of Performing Arts 國立臺灣戲曲學校; guólì táiwān xìqǔ xuéxiào 177 Neihu Rd Sec 2 ☎ 02 2796 2666, ⓦ tcpa.edu.tw; Wende MRT; map p.58. While not aimed at foreigners, the students here put on various performances, including acrobatics and Beijing opera (the latter usually with English subtitles). NT$400–600 for the cheap seats.

TaipeiEYE 臺北戲棚; táiběi xìpéng Taiwan Cement Hall, 113 Zhongshan N Rd Sec 2 ☎ 02 2568 2677, ⓦ www.taipeieye.com; Minquan W Rd MRT; map p.67. An easily digested taster of Chinese performing arts, featuring various acts from aboriginal song and dance to Chinese puppetry and opera. It's firmly targeted at tourists but the standard is high – many of Taiwan's premier troupes perform here. Mon–Fri NT$550, Sat NT$880. Mon, Wed & Fri 8–9pm, Sat 8–9.30pm.

PUPPETRY

See-Join Hand Puppet Theater 敘舊布袋戲園; xùjiù bùdài xìyuán 8 Lane 144, Jilin Rd ☎ 02 2523 1118, ⓦ see-join.com.tw; Songjiang Nanjing MRT; map p.67. Performances are combined with traditional Taiwanese snacks and beer, served as you watch. Shows (NT$400, not including food) usually run Sat and Mon 7–8pm, and Tues noon–1pm; it's best to reserve in advance (online or by phone). Mon–Fri 11am–9pm, Sat & Sun 5–9pm.

CINEMAS

Taipei is loaded with cinemas, most of them packed at weekends. All the major Hollywood movies arrive in Taiwan soon after their US release dates and are rarely dubbed into Chinese; most tickets cost around NT$270–300. Ximending

is where you'll find the older and larger screens – check times in local English newspapers.

Ambassador Theatre 國賓電影院; guóbīn diànyǐngyuàn 88 Chengdu Rd (at Kunming St) ☎ 02 2361 1223, ⓦ www.ambassador.com.tw; Ximen MRT; map p.64. This cinema's huge screen is the biggest in the city.

SPOT-Taipei Film House 光點台北電影主題館; guāngdiǎn táiběi diànyǐng zhǔtíguǎn 18 Zhongshan N Rd Sec 2 ☎ 02 2511 7786, ⓦ www.spot .org.tw; Zhongshan MRT; map p.67. Arthouse cinema showing several movies daily (local and international), located in the former US consulate. It also houses a bookshop, café and bar with terrace.

Vieshow Cinemas 威秀影城; wēixiù yǐngchéng 20 Songshou Rd ☎ 02 8780 5566, ⓦ vscinemas.com.tw; Taipei 101/World Trade Center MRT; map p.77. A huge multiplex cinema in Xinyi, and one of the most popular places in town. They also have screens in Ximending and the bus terminal complex.

CONCERT VENUES

Western classical and Chinese music, especially *nanguan* (see p.413) is usually performed somewhere in Taipei year-round, and the standards are generally high – prices vary from show to show. Note that the Taipei Performing Arts Center (台北藝術中心; táiběi yìshù zhōngxīn) should be open across from Jiantan MRT station by 2019.

National Theater and Concert Hall 國家兩廳院; guójiā liǎng tīngyuàn Chiang Kai-shek Memorial Plaza, 21-1 Zhongshan S Rd ☎ 02 3393 9888, ⓦ npac-ntch.org; CKS Memorial Hall MRT; map p.60. This is where Taiwan's premier orchestra, the National Symphony

Orchestra, performs classical music – occasionally Chinese-style. Tickets start at NT$400.

Taipei Arena 台北小巨蛋; táiběi xiǎojùdàn 2 Nanjing E Rd Sec 4 ☎02 2577 3500, ⓦenglish.arena .taipei; Taipei Arena MRT; map p.77. This futuristic venue hosts major pop concerts, shows such as Disney on Ice and Cirque du Soleil, as well as sporting events.

Zhongshan Hall 中山堂; zhōngshān táng 98 Yanping S Rd ☎02 2381 3137, ⓦenglish.zsh.gov .taipei; Ximen MRT; map p.60. Taipei's oldest concert hall, completed in 1936 (the Japanese in Taiwan surrendered here in 1945), and a venue for traditional Chinese or classical music. Performances most evenings, though usually closed in July.

SHOPPING

Taipei is littered with huge **shopping malls**, most of them upmarket affairs located in East Taipei, while **traditional shops** tend to be in the older, western parts of the city. In addition to night markets and the shops listed below, **Ximending** is the place to check out Taipei street fashion. Elsewhere, the weekend **Jade Market** is a definite highlight, while **Guanghua Market** is computer-geek heaven.

DEPARTMENT STORES AND SHOPPING MALLS

Eslite 誠品書店; chéngpǐn shūdiàn 245 Dunhua S Rd Sec 1 ☎02 2775 5977; Zhongxiao Dunhua MRT; map p.77. Stylish department store packed with boutiques and housing Eslite Bookstore (2/F; 24hr), which has a decent English-language selection. They have a few similar establishments around town, including one by Songshan Cultural Park. Daily 11am–10.30pm.

Maji Square Maji集食行樂; Maji jíshí xínglè 1 Yumen St (at Taipei Expo Park) ☎02 2597 7112; Yuanshan MRT; map p.67. Designed by artists Harlem Yu and Eugene Yeh, and sometimes referred to as *Maji Maji*, this inventive shopping area features recycled materials and old containers housing snack stalls (see p.88). Daily noon–10pm.

The Mall 遠企購物中心; yuǎnqǐ gòuwù zhōngxīn 203 Dunhua S Rd Sec 2 ☎02 2378 6666, ⓦwww.themall.com.tw; Xinyi Anhe MRT; map p.77. This posh shopping centre contains a Shiatzy Chen store (see below) on the fourth floor, while on the fifth floor there's a Bamboola (bamboo gift boxes and cups), Tittot (glassware) and the Franz Collection's award-winning porcelain designs. In the basement is a City supermarket. Mon–Thurs & Sun 11am–9.30pm, Fri & Sat 11am–10pm.

Miramar Entertainment Park 美麗華百樂園; měilìhuá bǎilèyuán 20 Jingye 3rd Rd ☎02 2175 3456, ⓦwww.miramar.com.tw; Jiannan Road MRT; map p.58. This shopping centre in Dazhi, just north of the Keelung River, is crammed with all sorts of shops, as well as Asia's largest IMAX cinema screen and its second-largest Ferris wheel (daily 11am–midnight; NT$200/ride at weekends, NT$150 weekdays). Daily 11am–10pm.

Sogo 太平洋百貨; tàipíngyáng bǎihuò 45 Zhongxiao E Rd Sec 4 ☎02 2776 5555, ⓦsogo.com.tw; Zhongxiao Fuxing MRT; map p.77. Major Japanese department store selling just about everything, from designer clothes to steel woks. Daily 11am–9.30pm.

Taipei 101 Shopping Mall 台北101購物中心; táiběi 101 gòuwùzhōngxīn 7 Xinyi Rd Sec 5 ☎02 8101 8800, ⓦwww.taipei-101.com.tw; Taipei 101/World Trade Center MRT; map p.77. Taipei's smartest mall, jammed with boutiques, designer stores, restaurants and tearooms. The basement contains Taipei's largest food court, and Jason's Market Place (see p.98) for imported food. Mon–Fri 11am–10pm, Sat & Sun 10am–11pm.

CLOTHES

★**Creative Boutique** 10 Chengdu Rd; Ximen MRT; map p.64. Set in the Red House (see p.65) in the site of Taipei's first-ever enclosed marketplace, this is effectively a mini-mall of local craft and clothing – perhaps the most interesting stalls are those selling t-shirts with deliberately idiosyncratic Taiwanese designs. Tues–Sun 11am–10pm.

Douchanglee 1 Lane 16, Zhongshan N Rd Sec 2 ☎02 2581 9866, ⓦstephanedou.com; Zhongshan MRT; map p.67. Two floors full of chic, women's fashion in Stephane Dou and Changlee Yugin's boutique. Daily 10am–7pm.

Lee Yao Cotton Clothing Store 李堯棉衣店; lǐyáo miányī diàn 2 Lishui St ☎02 2396 7843, ⓦwww .leeyau.com.tw; Dongmen MRT; map p.75. Designer boutique popular with expats, specializing in traditional Chinese clothes with vivid floral designs. Prices range from NT$1000 to NT$10,000 (no English signs). Daily 11am–8.30pm.

Little Garden Embroidered Shoes 小花園; xiǎohuāyuán 70 Ermei St ☎02 2311 0045; Ximen MRT; map p.64. Venerable old store with roots in 1930s Shanghai, specializing in handmade embroidered shoes in classical Ming- and Qing-dynasty styles. Daily noon–6pm.

Shiatzy Chen 夏姿服飾; xiàzī fúshì 49 Zhongshan N Rd Sec 2 ☎02 2542 5506, ⓦshiatzychen.com; Zhongshan MRT; map p.67. Shiatzy Chen is Taiwan's top designer, famous for making chinoiserie and the *cheongsam* hip. You'll find branches in malls and upmarket areas all over the city, but this is the flagship store. Daily 10am–7pm.

Wufenpu Garment Wholesale Area 五分埔商圈; wǔfēnpù shāngquān Between Zhongxiao E Rd Sec 5 and Songren E Rd/Zhongpo N Rd; Houshanpi and

Songshan MRT; map p.77. Discount clothes market, choked with everything from brand-name designers (or at least good copies of them) to absolute kitsch, as well as a variety of accessories. Cash only. Most shops daily 1–10pm.

ANTIQUES, ARTS AND CRAFTS

If you're a serious buyer, the antique shops around Jianguo Rd between Renai and Xinyi make fascinating browsing; Lane 291 is lined with posh stores full of jewellery, paintings, carvings and statues (many are closed Mon). Heping East Rd Sec 1, east of Guting MRT station, is home to traditional Chinese calligraphy equipment stores.

Artyard 民藝埕; mínyì chéng 67 Dihua St ☎02 2552 1367; map p.67. Long shophouse dating from 1923 and now home to a craft store and a showcase for Hakka Blue pottery. There's a café out back, and a tearoom (see p.92) upstairs. Mon–Wed & Sun 10am–7pm, Thurs–Sat 10am–11pm.

★**Jade Market** 建國假日玉市; jiànguó jiàrì yùshì Under the Jianguo Elevated Freeway, between Renai and Jinan roads ☎02 2708 5931; Daan Park MRT; map p.58. Massive selection of jade jewellery, carvings and other antique stalls. Sat & Sun 9am–6pm.

Lin Tian Tong Store 林田桶電; líntiántōng diàn 108 Zhongshan N Rd Sec 1 ☎02 2541 1354; Zhongshan/ Taipei Main Station MRT; map p.67. Established in 1928 by Lin Xinju (it's still in the family) and specializing in Japanese-style tubs, basins and flowerpots made from *hinoki* cypress wood. The scarcity of such wood in Taiwan today accounts for the high prices, but even if you're not buying it's worth a quick look. Daily 10.30am–8.30pm.

Liuligongfang 琉璃工坊; liúligōngfǎng 346 Dunhua S Rd Sec 1 ☎02 2701 3165, ⊛liuli.com; Xinyi Anhe MRT; map p.77. Designer glass sculpture studio (also known as Liuli), founded by movie star Loretta Yang in 1987. There are also showrooms in most shopping malls. Daily 9.30am–8pm.

Qianyuan Medicine Shop 乾元行; qiányuán hang 71 Dihua St ☎02 2558 4291; Beimen MRT; map p.67. Set on charming Dihua St, this traditional Chinese pharmacy was established in 1875 and is still renowned for its powerful remedies. Mon–Sat 9am–6pm.

Songyan Style Gallery 133 Guangfu S Rd ☎02 2765 1388; Sun Yat-Sen Memorial Hall MRT; map p.77. Set on the eastern side of the main Songshan Cultural Park building, this store has an intriguing collection of crafts (and also clothing), all from the hands and minds of young Taiwanese designers. Daily 10.30am–6pm.

Taiwan Handicraft Promotion Center 台灣手工業推 廣中心; táiwān shǒugōngyè tuīguǎng zhōngxīn 1 Xuzhou St ☎02 2393 3655, ⊛handicraft .org.tw; NTU Hospital MRT; map p.60. The best place for standard Chinese arts and crafts, including jewellery, porcelain, tea, fans, *cloisonné* enamelware and even traditional clothing. Daily 9am–6pm.

Zaoheding 昭和町; zhāohédīng 60 Yongkang St; Guting MRT; map p.75. Compact warehouse packed with cheap antique stalls selling everything from old books and statues to pieces of furniture. Things starting winding down after 8pm. Daily 2–10pm.

CAMERAS, COMPUTERS AND ELECTRICAL EQUIPMENT

Taipei's "camera street" covers Hankou St Sec 1 and the section of Boai Rd south of Kaifeng St – here you'll find all the latest in high-tech photographic equipment.

Guanghua Market 光華商場; guānghuá shāngchǎng 8 Civic Blvd Sec 3 ☎02 2341 2202; Zhongxiao Xinsheng MRT; map p.60. Huge mall specializing in small retailers and wholesalers of computer parts, games and accessories. Taipei is a great place to pick up computer hardware at reasonable prices, though English is rarely spoken by sales assistants (or used in manuals) and systems may not always be compatible with your home country. Daily except Tues 10am–9pm.

BOOKS

★**Caves Books** 敦煌書局; dūnhuáng shūjú 58 Zhongshan N Rd Sec 3 ☎02 2599 1169; Yuanshan MRT; map p.67. Great local store with a good selection of China and Taiwan-related books, as well as reference/teaching materials, and a fair few Rough Guides too. Daily 11am–8pm.

Moungar 莽葛拾遺; mǎnggě shíyí 4 Lane 152, Guangzhou St (on Mangka Park) ☎02 2336 2717; Longshan Temple MRT; map p.64. Sells old CDs and has a small selection of secondhand English books, in a gorgeous converted Chinese shophouse close to Longshan Temple. Daily 11am–8pm.

FOOD & DRINK

★**Chia Te** 佳德鳳梨酥; jiādé fènglí sū 88 Nanjing E Rd Sec 5 ☎02 8787 8186; Taipei Arena MRT; map p.77. This place usually takes the biscuit, if you'll pardon the pun, for Taipei's best pineapple cakes. Most customers buy in bulk by the box (the cakes are also available in any 7-Eleven, though far less fresh), but you can buy them individually for NT$30. Daily 8am–9.30pm.

Jason's Market Place B1/F, 7 Xinyi Rd Sec 5 ☎02 8101 8701, ⊛www.taipei-101.com.tw; Taipei 101/World Trade Center MRT; map p.77. In the basement of the Taipei 101 mall, this is the city's best supermarket for imported food, and also has a wide range of Taiwanese craft beer. Daily 10am–10pm.

★**Sophisca** 22 Lane 50, Wuchang St Sec 2 ☎02 2772 1557; Ximen MRT; map p.64. From the outside this may look like any other shop in Ximending, but take a closer peek and you'll discover sweets in zany packaging, including chocolate in lipstick tubes, fruit candies in mini fruit crates, and even entire edible first-aid kits. Daily 9am–10pm.

★**Sunrice** 米日一里; mǐrì yīlǐ 296 Dihua St Sec 1 ☎ 02 2550 5567, ⓦ sunrice1923.com; Daqiaotou MRT; map p.67. The Yehjinfa rice-processing company has called this space home since 1923, though the fifth generation has decided to modernize – they have changed the original name and, in addition to rice, now sell other agricultural products. A sleek, modern space, where clever shelving minimizes the impact on the old building. Wed–Sun 11am–8pm.

DIRECTORY

Banks and exchange ATMs are on almost all major thoroughfares, as well as in most 7-Elevens, MRT stations and some *McDonalds*. Most banks exchange foreign currency.

Consulates Australia, 27–28/F, President Int'l Building, 9 Songgao Rd (☎ 02 8725 4100, ⓦ australia.org.tw); Canada, 6/F, Hua-Hsin Building, 1 Songzhi Rd, Xinyi (☎ 02 2544 3000, ⓦ canada.org.tw); South Africa, Suite 1301, 13/F, 205 Dunhua N Rd (☎ 02 2715 3251, ⓦ southafrica. org.tw); UK, 26/F President Int'l Building, 9-11 Songgao Rd (☎ 02 8758 2088, ⓦ gov.uk/world/taiwan); US, 7 Lane 134, Xinyi Rd Sec 3 (☎ 02 2162 2000, ⓦ ait.org.tw).

Hospitals and clinics Most hotels will be able to help contact doctors if you feel sick, and most downtown hospitals have staff who can speak English. The Taiwan Adventist Hospital at 424 Bade Rd Sec 2 (☎ 02 2771 8151, ⓦ tahsda.org.tw) has a special clinic for foreigners with English-speaking staff towards the back of the main building, known as the Priority Care Center (☎ 02 2776 2651) – it's NT$1700 for a walk-in registration and doctors are on duty Mon–Thurs 9–11.30am and 2–4.30pm, and 9–11.30am on Fri and Sun.

Pharmacies Taipei is littered with Traditional Chinese Medicine shops, but conventional Western non-prescription remedies (and toiletries) can be purchased in Watsons stores all over the city.

Post office The main Post Office is at 114 Zhongxiao W Rd Sec 1 (Fri–Mon 8.30am–9pm, Sat 9am–noon), but there are smaller branches all over the place.

Around Taipei

The mountains and river valleys that surround the capital are loaded with attractions, making for enticing day-trips or short breaks. The **hot-spring spas** of **Beitou** are some of Taiwan's best, while hikers should find plenty to keep them busy in **Yangmingshan National Park**. The old port towns of **Tamsui** and **Bali** contain a handful of historical sights, while **Wulai** and the towns to the southeast offer a taster of the island's mountainous interior. **Yingge** is a must-see for anyone with an interest in ceramics, and the temple at **Sanxia** is one of Taiwan's most beautiful.

Beitou

北投; běitóu

It can be tempting to think that the northern Taipei district of **BEITOU** sits atop some gigantic dragon's den – warm jets of steam billow out from umpteen drains and pipes, and an odd, copper-like smell hangs in the air. This is all on account of the area's bubbling sulphur-carbonate **hot springs**. Osaka merchant Hirada Gengo opened Beitou's first hot-spring inn in 1896, and during the Japanese occupation it became one of the island's most prominent resorts. The Japanese were particularly attracted to **hokutolite**, a mineral-laden stone formed by the springs, and bathers still come here to enjoy its therapeutic qualities.

Since Beitou is so close to central Taipei (just 20min by MRT), most visitors come for the day, taking a dip in one of the many **spas** in the area. However, the area's charming ambience is amplified after sunset, and it's certainly worth spending a night here – all the better to explore a smattering of sights recalling Taiwan's Japanese past, centred on **Beitou Park** (北投公園; běitóu gōngyuán), a swath of green following sulphuric Beitou Creek up the valley from Xinbeitou MRT station.

Ketagalan Culture Center

凱達格蘭文化館; kǎidágélán wénhuàguǎn • 3-1 Zhongshan Rd • Tues–Sun 9am–5pm • Free • ☎ 02 2898 6500

With around thirteen thousand aboriginal residents registered in the city, the **Ketagalan Culture Center** was established as a focus for the indigenous community in Taipei. Its

1

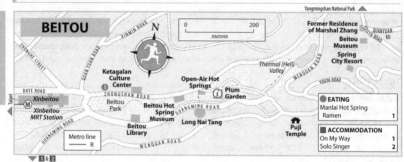

two floors of exhibits provide a decent introduction to Taiwan's sixteen aboriginal tribes with sculptures, everyday artefacts like smoking pipes, costumes and videos, and a particularly good section on the píngpǔ tribes (see p.399).

Beitou Library

台北市立圖書館北投分館; táiběi shìlì túshūguǎn běitóu fēnguǎn • 251 Guangming Rd • Mon & Sun 9am–5pm, Tues–Sat 8.30am–9pm • ☏ 02 2897 7682

With a sloping turf roof and sleek wooden design, the ecofriendly **Beitou Library** is reputed to be Taiwan's most energy-efficient structure – the building creates its own solar power and conserves rainwater. Opened in 2006 and designed by Taipei-based firm Bio Architecture Formosana, the library contains over sixty thousand books, including an English-language section.

Beitou Hot Spring Museum

北投溫泉博物館; běitóu wēnquán bówùguǎn • 2 Zhongshan Rd • Tues–Sun 9am–5pm • Free • ☏ 02 2893 9981

At the top of Beitou Park sits the **Beitou Hot Spring Museum**, housed in the attractively restored public bathhouse built in 1913, complete with stained-glass windows and original bathing pool in the basement. It's the best place to learn about the history of the area.

Plum Garden

梅庭; méitíng • 6 Zhongshan Rd • Tues–Sun 9am–5pm • Free • ☏ 02 2897 2647

Just beyond the Open-Air Hot Springs spa lies the **Plum Garden**, the latest of Beitou's Japanese-style mansions to be restored. Built as a private residence in the late 1930s, these days it houses the official visitor information centre, and serves as a memorial to revered scholar and calligrapher **Yu Youren** (1879–1964), who spent summers here between 1949 and his death (principally through rare photos and examples of his enchanting calligraphy).

Thermal Valley

地熱谷; dìrègǔ • Off Zhongshan Rd, near Guangming Rd • Daily 9am–5pm • Free

A lane off Zhongshan Road at the top end of Beitou leads to the **Thermal Valley**, also sometimes referred to as "Hell Valley". It's essentially a huge pool of bubbling, emerald-green spring water, and is especially impressive when shrouded in billowing clouds of steam – wintertime is particularly good for this. With an average temperature of 70°C, you'll understand why the lake is fenced off.

Beitou Museum

北投文物館; běitóu wénwùguǎn • 32 Youya Rd • Tues–Sun 10am–6pm • NT$120; English audio tours free • ☏ 02 2891 2318, ⊛ www.beitoumuseum.org.tw • A 20min uphill walk from central Beitou, or take bus #230 (which continues on to Yangmingshan)

It's a pleasant (if occasionally steep) walk up the Beitou valley to the **Beitou Museum**, another gorgeous Japanese-style structure now a **folk art** gallery and posh teahouse. The building started life in 1921 as the Kazan Hotel, but its tranquil wooden corridors and rooms feel more akin to a temple. The tatami room on the second floor is allegedly where Japanese kamikaze pilots had their final meals in 1945 – you'll be surprised how many locals (and Japanese tourists) still find this fascinating. Today the museum's permanent exhibition explains the building's history, while revolving folk art displays include everything from Taiwanese aboriginal artefacts to textiles, clothing and handicrafts from minority groups in mainland China. The exhibits are always visually stimulating, but you'll get more out of this (and the roster of cultural events held here) if you speak and read Chinese.

Former Residence of Marshal Zhang

少帥禪園; shàoshuài chányuán • 34 Youya Rd • Daily 10am–9pm, teahouse daily 1–6pm • NT$150 (can be used as credit in the restaurant and spa); private hot springs from NT$1200/hr • ☎ 02 2893 5336, ⊛ sgarden.com.tw • A 20min walk from central Beitou, or take bus #230 (which continues on to Yangmingshan)

Next door to the Beitou Museum, the **Former Residence of Marshal Zhang** was originally a Japanese hotel built in the 1920s – from the 1960s this was where **Zhang Xueliang** (instigator of China's Xian Incident) and his wife were held under house arrest. The old warlord was essentially held captive by the KMT from 1937 to 1990, emigrating to Hawaii in 1995 where he died in 2001. Today the house has the dubious honour of having the only Taiwanese tribute to Zhang (who is regarded as patriotic hero in China), a small exhibition in the old living room, together with an odd-looking bust and several examples of his calligraphy. The other main attraction is the **Little Six Teahouse** (小六茶鋪; xiǎoliù chápù) on top of the building, where sipping tea with grand views of Beitou below is the perfect way to end an afternoon (you can also sample the **hot springs** here in private rooms).

ARRIVAL AND INFORMATION
BEITOU

By metro Beitou is on the red Tamsui MRT line, easily accessible from central Taipei. The branch line to Xinbeitou (新北投; xīnběitóu or "New Beitou"), just a few minutes away, brings you closer to the main hotels and spas.

By bus The #S9 (every 40min) connects Beitou MRT station and Beitou Park with Yangmingshan National Park (see p.102); the more regular #230 will also get you near.

Tourist information The visitor information centre is housed in the Plum Garden (see opposite), 6 Zhongshan Rd (Tues–Sun 9am–5pm; ☎ 02 2897 2647).

GETTING AROUND

By bike There are plenty of YouBike stations for those who fancy pedalling around town.

On foot Beitou is pretty walkable, with some lovely interconnected park areas to stroll through

ACCOMMODATION

On My Way 途中青年旅舍滿來溫泉拉麵; túzhōng qīngnián lǚshè 82 Guangming Rd ☎ 02 2891 0230, ⊛ onmywayhostel.com. Good cheap option, with all the necessary hostel mod cons, including decent, attractively decorated dorms and an occasionally lively common room. Dorms NT$600, doubles NT$1600

★**Solo Singer** 7 Lane 21, Wenquan Rd ☎ 02 2891 8312, ⊛ thesolosinger.com. An absolutely wonderful choice, set in an old inn and former bordello from the 1950s. The place has been brought bang up to date, and delightful breakfasts (included) are served in a nearby café, but the place still exudes the best elements of its previous incarnations. Special rates often available; see website for details. NT$3000

EATING

★**Manlai Hot Spring Ramen** 滿來溫泉拉麵; mǎnlái wēnquán lāmiàn 1-8 Zhongshan Rd ☎ 02 2894 9588. Given Beitou's history and hot-spring focus, it somehow makes sense to eat Japanese food here, and the amount of such establishments indicates that there's plenty of demand. This place is a great choice, serving "Taiwanese-style" ramen from NT$130, and other cheap goodies including fried tofu (a bargain at NT$40) and hot sake (NT$100). Daily 11.30am–9.30pm.

1

BEITOU'S HOT-SPRING SPAS

Beitou's hot-spring water is piped into **spas** all over the valley, many doubling as attractive hotels – it can be expensive to stay the night, but most places offer affordable day-rates for their spa facilities. The places listed here are especially recommended, but you'll see plenty of perfectly decent modern hotels as you walk along Beitou Park. You'll normally be allowed to stay in the "public" pools (typically including sauna, steam room and a variety of hot and cold spring pools) as long as you like; private rooms with baths (and usually beds to relax in) are NT$700–3000/hour, depending upon where you go. We cover the practicalities of hot-spring hotels in Taiwan in Basics (see p.29).

Long Nai Tang 龍乃湯; lóngnǎitāng 244 Guangming Rd ☎ 02 2891 2236. Founded in 1907 and the oldest of Beitou's traditional Japanese bathhouses, this is a no-nonsense affair where you just strip off and get into the fairly basic separate male and female indoor stone baths (NT$150). Look for the white shack-like hut below the Open-Air Hot Springs. Daily 6.30am–9pm.

Open-Air Hot Springs 公共露天溫泉; gōnggòng lùtiān wēnquán 6 Zhongshan Rd ☎ 02 2893 7014. Also known as the Millennium Hot Springs, this is the cheapest outdoor spa in Beitou (NT$40), featuring several mixed-sex pools that close for cleaning at regular intervals through the day. There's no nudity here, and gents should note that unless they're

wearing Superman-style briefs or tight lycra shorts, they're probably not going to be let in. Nice location on the banks of the creek, but it can get crowded, especially at weekends. Coin-operated lockers available. Daily 5.30–7.30am, 8–10am, 10.30am–1pm, 1.30–4pm, 4.30–7pm & 7.30–10pm.

Spring City Resort 春天酒店; chūntiān jiǔdiàn 18 Youya Rd ☎ 02 2897 5555, ⓦ www.springresort.com.tw. Located high on the hills above Beitou and regarded as one of its top resorts, this modern five-star hotel offers stylish private bathhouses open 24hr (NT$600/hr/person), while you can access the shared outdoor spa (nine different pools) for NT$800 for the day. Daily 9am–10pm.

Yangmingshan National Park and around

陽明山國家公園; yángmíngshān guójiā gōngyuán

A comfortable day-trip from Taipei, **Yangmingshan National Park** sits on a geological fault line sprinkled with dormant **volcanoes**, **hot-spring spas** and well-marked **hiking trails**. The highlight is the climb up **Mount Qixing**, the park's highest peak, but it also contains important historical sights – Chiang Kai-shek built his first and last homes in Taiwan here. A park shuttle bus ferries visitors around the main attractions making it unusually accessible to non-hikers, so try to avoid visiting at weekends and during holidays, especially in the spring and summer flower-viewing seasons, when the park is at its busiest.

Yangmingshuwu

陽明書屋; yángmíng shūwū • 12 Zhongxing Rd • Daily: visitor centre 9am–4.30pm, tours 9am–1.30pm (1hr) • NT$80 • ☎ 02 2861 1444

The third stop on the park shuttle bus is **Yangmingshuwu**, the best-preserved of Chiang Kai-shek's fifteen former homes in Taiwan. From the bus stop it's a ten-minute walk down the hill to the **visitor centre** where you pick up a tour guide: tours (mandatory) take around an hour, though these are given in Chinese only. From here it's another short walk to the **house** itself, which was once surrounded by five hundred armed guards and several tanks.

Originally known as the Zhongxing Guesthouse, it was built in 1970 as a luxury hotel where the Generalissimo could host foreign dignitaries. Instead, it became the last home of the ailing president after Taiwan's withdrawal from the UN saw official visits dwindle. Inside it's an odd mix of classical Chinese decor, 1970s Western design (check out Madam Chiang's pink-tiled bathroom) and extreme security: the basement was bolstered by reinforced concrete to resist air attacks, with a series of escape tunnels leading to the gardens and beyond. The contents of the house – furniture and personal items – are authentic reproductions, including a small collection of Madam Chiang's own paintings.

Yangming Park

陽明公園; yángmíng gōngyúan • Hushan Rd

Twenty minutes' walk downhill from Yangmingshuwu (follow signs to the "Flower Clock") is **Yangming Park**, a popular subsection of the national park often packed out with tourists. The main attraction is **flowers**: in spring the gardens here are crammed with cherry blossoms and azaleas and the park is the main focus of February's popular **Yangmingshan Flower Festival**.

Grass Mountain Chateau

草山行館; cǎoshān xíngguǎn • 89 Hudi Rd (off Hushan Rd) • Tues–Sun 9.30am–5pm, restaurant 11.30am–1.30pm & 2.30–7pm • ☎ 02 2862 2404, ⓦ www.grassmountainchateau.com.tw

The handsome Japanese-style house dubbed the **Grass Mountain Chateau** was Chiang Kai-shek's first home in Taiwan in 1949 until his Shilin Residence was completed a year later, thereafter becoming one of his summer retreats. The building was originally a guesthouse belonging to Taiwan Sugar Corporation, and was renovated in the 1920s for Crown Prince Hirohito, who ended up staying here for just two hours in 1923. In 2003, it was turned into a series of **art galleries** and a **restaurant**, but tragically the whole place was burnt to the ground (in suspicious circumstances) in 2007. After a meticulous reconstruction it reopened in 2010 – the Japanese floors, screens and inner courtyard have been artfully re-created, while the former living room has become a small display area dedicated to Chiang.

Zhuzihu

竹子湖; zhúzi hú

Park shuttle bus stop number four is **Zhuzihu**, a dried-up lake now ringed with vegetable and flower farms, and best visited in December when the **calla lilies** are in bloom. Follow the signs along the road from the bus stop and you'll reach a junction after around 300m: this is the 4km loop road that circles the area, dotted with rustic **teahouses** and **restaurants**.

Xiaoyoukeng

小油坑; xiǎoyóu kēng

The seventh shuttle bus stop is **Xiaoyoukeng**, just off the highway in the centre of the park, which features a huge and highly photogenic sulphuric steam vent eating into the side of Mount Qixing. The spot feels remote, and it's pretty enough, though you're unlikely to want to stay too long.

Lengshuikeng

冷水坑; lěngshuǐ kēng • Hot springs: daily 6–9am, 10.30am–1pm, 2.30–5pm & 6.30–9pm • Free

Stop number nine is **Lengshuikeng**, where you'll find hot-spring baths – simply walk in and strip off (you're expected to be naked, and men and women are separated), leaving

---

CLIMBING MOUNT QIXING

At 1120m high, **Mount Qixing** (七星山; qīxīngshān; also transliterated as Mt Cising) is the loftiest in the park. The hike up takes about two hours from the visitor centre (2.4km) – the path is well marked and paved most of the way, though it gets pretty steep and exposed in places, and can be cool and cloudy on top. On a clear day, the views across the Taipei Basin and the sea to the north are spectacular. Once at the top, you'll grasp why the park area used to be known as "Grass Mountain" (cǎoshān) – the windswept peaks are covered in thick silvergrass. The park was later renamed in honour of the Ming dynasty philosopher Wang Yang-ming. Other routes up include the western path from Xiaoyoukeng (1.65km; see above), which is more dramatic, lined with yellow sulphurous rocks and steaming vents; while the eastern trail leads from Lengshuikeng (1.9km; see above).

1

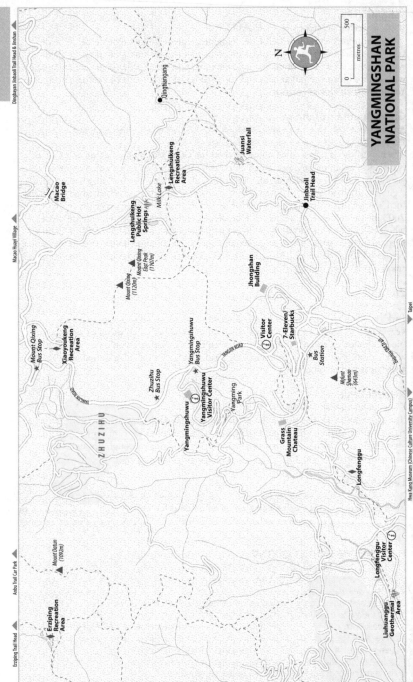

Dingbuyan Jinbaoli Trail Head & Jinshan

Macao Huayi Village

Anbu Trail Car Park

Erziping Trail Head

Hwa Kang Museum (Chinese Culture University Campus)

Taipei

YANGMINGSHAN NATIONAL PARK

N

0   500
metres

Qingtiangang

Juansi Waterfall

Milk Lake

Macao Bridge

Lengshuikeng Recreation Area

Jinbaoli Trail Head

Lengshuikeng Public Hot Springs

Mount Qixing East Peak (1107m)

Mount Qixing (1120m)

Jhongshan Building

Mount Qixing Bus Stop

Xiaoyoukeng Recreation Area

Visitor Center

7-Eleven/ Starbucks

Yangmingshuwu Bus Stop

YANGJIN ROAD

Zhuzihu Bus Stop

Bus Station

Mount Shamao (643m)

ZHUZIHU

Yangmingshuwu Visitor Center

Yangming Park

Yangmingshuwu

YANGJIN ROAD

Grass Mountain Chateau

Mount Datun (1092m)

Longfenggu

Erziping Recreation Area

Longfenggu Visitor Center

Liuhuanggu Geothermal Area

clothes on the shelves by the pool. The bus stops in front of the hot springs first, makes a small loop to Qingtiangang and returns to Lengshuikeng. Alternatively, you can walk the easy 1.8km trail to Qingtiangang (40min); the route passes by "**Milk Lake**" (niúnǎihú), so named on account of its unusual greenish-white sulphur surface.

Qingtiangang

擎天崗; qíngtiān gāng

The tenth bus stop is **Qingtiangang**, a wide, open plateau (actually an ancient lava terrace) noted for its silvergrass and herd of cattle: there's a short but pleasant loop trail here, as well as access to the more challenging **Jinbaoli Trail** (金包里步道; jīnbāolǐ bùdào; also known as Fisherman's Old Trail). The latter actually starts at the **Juansi Waterfall** (涓絲瀑布; juānsī pùbù) bus stop a few kilometres south of Lengshuikeng, and meanders its way 7km north to the small village of **Bayan** (八煙; bāyān) on Highway 2 – it's an enjoyable hike that can take half a day, but you'll have to catch the Taipei–Jinshan bus back from here or walk for another hour or so to Jinshan. From the waterfall stop, the shuttle bus completes the loop and ends up back at the bus station.

Longfenggu

龍鳳谷; lóngfènggǔ • 200 Quanyan Rd • Visitor centre daily 9am–4.30pm • Free • ☎ 02 2893 5580 • Take bus #230 heading to Beitou from Yangmingshan bus station and get off at the junction of Xingyi and Quanyuan roads near the visitor centre

South of the main park area on the road to Beitou, the **Longfonggu Visitor Center** is at the heart of the park's most dramatic volcanic scenery – a desolate landscape of sulphur plumes and bleached rocks. To the left of the centre is the **Longfonggu** area itself with paths leading down from the road and up to a series of hot springs, while ahead on your right is the **Liuhuanggu Geothermal Scenic Area** (硫磺谷地熱景觀區; Liúhuánggǔ dìrè jǐngguānqū), a valley laced with volcanic fumaroles and hot springs, but a longer walk along Xingyi Road.

Hwa Kang Museum

華岡博物館; huágāng bówùguǎn • Hsiao Fong Memorial Building, Chinese Culture University, 55 Huagang Rd • Mon–Fri 9am–4pm • Free • ☎ 02 2861 0511 • Bus Red #5 goes all the way into the campus (or it's a 10min walk along Aifu 2nd St then Huagang Rd from bus #260 University stop); it's the first building on the left as you enter the university

Easily tagged on to a day-trip to the park, the **Hwa Kang Museum** is located within the Chinese Culture University, just over 2km south of the park bus station. The museum's collection comprises almost fifty thousand historical artefacts from China and Taiwan, though only a fraction is displayed at one time. Highlights include work by painters **Zhang Da-qian** and **Pu Xin-yu**, prehistoric pottery and jade from the Beinan site (see p.321) and an original Tao canoe from Lanyu.

You can walk back into Taipei from here (allow an hour, at a leisurely pace) via **Tianmu Water Pipe Trail** (天母水管步道; tiānmǔ shuǐguǎn bùdào), which is clearly signposted on Aifu 3rd Street, not far from the main road. The trail snakes downhill for around 2km to the start of Zhongshan Road Section 7 in the suburb of Tianmu, where you can take bus #220 into the city centre.

Lin Yutang House

林語堂故居; línyǔtáng gùjū • 141 Yangde Blvd Sec 2 • Tues–Sun 9am–5pm • NT$30 • ☎ 02 2861 3003, ⓦ linyutang.org.tw • Bus #260 and Red #5 stop outside

Tucked away along the main road to Yangmingshan National Park is the **Lin Yutang House**, a small but atmospheric monument to one of China's greatest writers. Lin had a peripatetic career that saw him live in the West for many years, and in 1937 he topped the *New York Times* bestseller list for a year with *The Importance of Living*. He spent the last ten years of his life in this house, and died in 1976; he's buried in the garden. Lin's fame has faded somewhat, but the house is certainly special and commands a magnificent viewpoint over Taipei.

ARRIVAL AND DEPARTURE

By metro and bus The fastest way to Yangmingshan is to take the MRT to Jiantan and then catch Red #5 bus or #260 from Wenlin Rd just outside the station (every 7–13min; 20–30min). Buses from Jiantan terminate at the park bus station (just beyond 7-Eleven and *Starbucks*), close to several hotels with hot-spring spas. From Beitou, #230 also

YANGMINGSHAN NATIONAL PARK AND AROUND

heads to the park bus station, while Tourist Shuttle Bus #S9 goes all the way to Zhuzihu (all buses NT$15). Royal Bus #1717 (❶ 02 8295 7022) also runs a handy service from Taipei Bus Station to Jinshan (roughly hourly) that cuts straight across the park, via the park bus station and Zhuzihu; you can also catch these at Jiantan MRT station.

GETTING AROUND AND INFORMATION

By shuttle bus From the park bus station, the park shuttle bus #108 (Mon–Fri every 30–40min, Sat & Sun every 10–20min) provides a loop service to all the main points of interest in the park for NT$15/trip, or NT$60 for unlimited rides; buy tickets on board, or from the bus station office. Note that some buses stop at Erziping and return to the bus depot.
Visitor centres The main visitor centre (daily 8.30am–4.30pm; ❶ 02 2861 5741, ❻ www.ymsnp.gov.tw) is 700m from the park bus station – the first stop on the shuttle bus or a steep 15min hike (the sidewalk path goes all the way so there's no need to follow the road). The centre contains

several exhibition rooms and provides free information, but it's best to buy one of the more detailed maps from the shop if you intend to do a lot of hiking. Note that Xiaoyoukeng, Lengshuikeng and Qingtiangang have small visitor centres (daily 9am–4.30pm) and basic shops on site. All visitor centres are closed on the last Mon of each month.
Provisions Beyond the hotels and a couple of local diners near the bus station, eating options are limited in the park area (Zhuzihu and the Grass Mountain Chateau are your best bets), so stock up at 7-Eleven (just up from the bus station) if you want snacks.

Tamsui

Set on the northern bank of the Tamsui River, 20km north of Taipei, the old port town of **TAMSUI** (淡水; dànshuǐ) is hugely popular with local day-trippers and mainland tourists. The chief draw is the **food** – at the weekends you'll see thousands of Taiwanese trawling up and down its wharves and old streets eagerly stuffing themselves with local specialities (see box, p.112) and enjoying carnival games. However, Tamsui has plenty more to offer: it's packed with historical attractions that include **Fort San Domingo** and a small but fascinating collection of sights associated with Canadian missionary **George Leslie Mackay**.

Most of the action in Tamsui takes place along the **waterfront**, lined with cheap food stalls and packed at weekends. From the MRT station it's possible to walk or cycle quite a distance along the riverbank, beyond the **Tamsui Customs Wharf** (淡水海關碼頭; dànshuǐ hǎiguān mǎtóu), just below Fort San Domingo. Alternatively (or as part of a loop), take the inland route past some of the town's historical sights beginning with **Gongming Street**, just across from the MRT station.

Brief history

Tamsui means "fresh water", and it is thought to have been the name given to the area by early Chinese seafarers. The settlement was established around **Fort Santo Domingo** (the name is slightly different today), built by the Spanish in 1628 and later occupied by the Dutch. By 1662 the Dutch had been driven off the island, the village growing slowly as more Chinese immigrants started to arrive in the eighteenth century. Tamsui boomed after the Treaty of Beijing opened up the port to foreign trade in 1860 – **Robert Swinhoe**, the first British vice-consul, arrived a year later and a customs office was in operation by 1862. *Hongs* such as Jardine Matheson were soon busy exporting oolong and bāozhōng **tea**, but Tamsui's downfall was its lack of a deepwater harbour – from 1906 it began to lose precedence to Keelung and by the 1920s had become a relative backwater. Today, in addition to a healthy tourist trade, Tamsui is the home to three universities and growing numbers of Taipei commuters.

Tamsui Art & Cultural Park (Shell Story House)

淡水文化園區; dànshuǐ wénhuà yuánqū · 22 Bitou St · Tues–Sun 9am–6pm · Free · ❶ 02 2622 1928
One of the town's newest restoration projects, the **Tamsui Art & Cultural Park** lies just

behind Tamsui MRT station. Several old redbrick warehouses once used by the oil multinational Shell are being gradually transformed into a tranquil arts and crafts centre, with studios, shops, cafés and classical Chinese sculptures. The **Shell Story House** (殼牌故事 館; képái gùshìguăn) is a small permanent display with English labels about Shell's long role in Tamsui, beginning in 1897 (antique pumps, barrels, lanterns and the like).

Longshan Temple

龍山寺; lóngshān sì • 22 Lane 95, Zhongshan Rd (off Qingshui St) • Daily 5.30am–8.30pm • ☎ 02 2960 3456
Where Gongming Street meets Zhongzheng Road, a narrow lane leads into **Qingshui Street Market** (清水街市場; qīngshuǐjiē shìchăng), which has more character than the waterfront and features some tasty snack food, but closes in the afternoon. Turning left along Qingshui Street and then first right should take you to **Longshan Temple**, a peaceful shrine to Guanyin dating from 1858 (and not related to the one in Taipei), with unusually high wooden ceilings, Qing dynasty dragon columns and an elegant gold statue of the "Goddess of Mercy" herself in the main hall, protected on either side by the warriors Wei Tuo and Guan Yu.

Fuyou Temple

福佑宮; fúyòu gōng • 200 Zhongzheng Rd • Daily 5.30am–8.45pm • ☎ 02 2621 1731
The current incarnation of modest **Fuyou Temple** dates back to 1796, making it Tamsui's oldest and most important, primarily because of the historic inscriptions on its columns and steles (the one near the entrance on the left dates back to around 1722). The temple is dedicated to Mazu, which is not surprising given its proximity to the wharf – the park opposite affords magnificent views of Guanyinshan.

Teng Feng Fish Ball Museum

登峰魚丸博物館; dēngfēng yúwán bówùguăn • 117 Zhongzheng Rd • Daily 10.30am–7.30pm • Free • ☎ 02 2629 3312
The **Teng Feng Fish Ball Museum** is housed in one of the town's most popular fish-ball makers, in business since 1950 (though these premises are modern). Behind the usual stacks of fish crisps and "iron eggs" (see box, p.112) is a small display on the battles

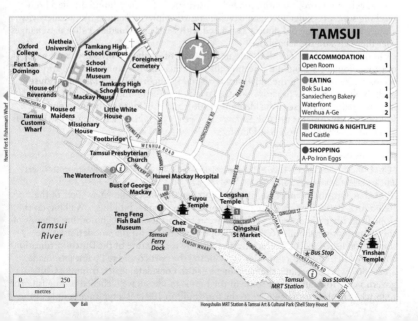

1

fought in Tamsui during the **Sino-French War** in 1884 (with English labels), and a less interesting exhibition on fishing and fish-ball making upstairs (Chinese only).

Mackay Street

馬偕街; mǎxié jiē

In the centre of the triangle where Zhongzheng Road meets Sanmin Street stands a bust of **George Mackay**, complete with gigantic beard, while just opposite is the narrow, unmarked lane known as **Mackay Street**. Along here on the right (no. 6) sits the white stone **Huwei Mackay Hospital** (滬尾偕醫館; hùwěi jiēīguǎn; Mon–Thurs 10am–5pm, Fri & Sat 10am–6pm, Sun 11am–6pm; free; ☎02 2629 2515), which Mackay opened in 1897. Today it houses a small exhibition on the great man (limited English commentary), as well as the *Mackay Café*. Next door at no. 8, the current **Tamsui Presbyterian Church** (淡水長老教會; dànshuǐ zhǎnglǎo jiāohuì) was built in 1933 on the site of the chapel Mackay established in 1890. It still attracts a sizeable congregation on Sundays.

The Little White House

小白宮; xiǎo báigōng · 15 Zhenli St · Mon–Fri 9.30am–5pm, Sat & Sun 9.30am–6pm · NT$80, joint ticket with Fort San Domingo and Hobe Fort · ☎02 2628 2865 · From Huwei Mackay Hospital, keep walking along Mackay St, turn right at the junction ahead, then follow the road uphill, over the footbridge and take the second lane on the left

Built between 1869 and 1876, the **Little White House** served as Tamsui's British-run customs officer's residence before becoming a Japanese clubhouse in 1900. The chalk-white colonial bungalow has been immaculately refurbished, though the rooms are a little bare – the exhibits inside do provide plenty of history and background on the site, but you may find more pleasure simply roaming around the gardens outside.

Oxford College

牛津學堂; niújīn xuétáng · 32 Zhenli St (Aletheia University) · Daily 9am–4pm · Free · ☎02 2621 2121 ext 1061

Mackay's original boys' school (the precursor of Tamkang School) was known as **Oxford College**, and you can still visit the humble college building (used 1882–1901) just inside the modern campus of Aletheia University. Concerned residents of Mackay's hometown in Oxford, Ontario, funded construction after they found out he'd been teaching students under a banyan tree. The restored interior is more like a gallery than a museum, displaying old photos associated with Mackay, Canadian cultural exchanges over the years and the school itself.

On the other side of Zhenli Road (and also part of Aletheia University) are a series of elegant colonial-style buildings technically off limits, though you are free to stroll along the path around them if the university is open. Highlights include: **Mackay's House** itself, built in 1875, its innards now displaying photos and implements pertaining to him; the redbrick **House of the Maidens** (1906); and the **House of the Reverends** (1909), which contains the *Bok Su Lao* café (see p.110). From here the road swings left, and leads downhill to Fort San Domingo.

Fort San Domingo

紅毛城; hóngmáo chéng · 1 Lane 28, Zhongzheng Rd · Mon–Fri 9.30am–5pm, Sat & Sun 9.30am–6pm · NT$80 for joint ticket with Little White House and Hobe Fort · ☎02 2623 1001 · Bus #R26

Touted as Tamsui's premier historic site, **Fort San Domingo**, known as "Fort of the Red-haired Barbarians" in Chinese, comprises two separate buildings. Walking up the slope from the main entrance, you'll arrive at the **fort** itself, though nothing remains of the **Spanish** original built 1636–38, a stone replacement for the wooden stockade they'd established in 1628. The current structure is a mixture of the **Dutch** fortifications completed in 1644 and renovations (including the portico and red paint job) made after 1867 when it became the permanent **British Consulate**, leased from the Chinese government. You can explore some of the rooms inside, all well labelled in English. The redbrick **consular residence** next to the fort (built in 1891) is a typical example of the colonial-style architecture of the time, with a couple of rooms furnished in reasonably authentic Victorian decor, and more exhibits related to the site. The Brits maintained a presence here until 1971.

Hobe Fort

滬尾砲臺; hùwěi pàotái • 34 Lane 6, Zhongzheng Rd Sec 1 • Mon–Fri 9.30am–5pm, Sat & Sun 9.30am–6pm • NT$80 for joint ticket with Little White House and Fort San Domingo • ☏ 02 2629 5390 • Bus #R26

Designed by a German architect and built for the Qing government between 1886 and 1889, **Hobe Fort** (aka Huwei Fort) never saw action – today it's a pristine example of a sizeable nineteenth-century gun fortification, though there's not much to do other than wander the main courtyard and clamber on the walls. The vaults inside contain a small exhibition on the French invasion of Tamsui during the **Sino-French War** in 1884.

Fisherman's Wharf

漁人碼頭; yúrén mǎtóu • Take bus #R26 from the MRT station (or along Zhongzheng Rd), or ferry from Tamsui pier (every 30min; 20min; NT$60)

Given a fancy makeover in 2003, the large marina and fishing harbour at the mouth of the Tamsui River, some 4km from Tamsui MRT station, is known as **Fisherman's Wharf**, though it remains of limited interest to most foreign tourists. The giant *Fullon Hotel* and various restaurants and shops surround the marina. It's a prime sunset-viewing location, but once you've strolled along the elevated boardwalk, admired the views and crossed **Lover's Bridge**, there's not much to do, although taking the ferry back to central Tamsui is a good way to get onto the river.

ARRIVAL AND DEPARTURE   TAMSUI

By MRT Tamsui is the last station on the Tamsui MRT line, just 35min from Taipei Station (NT$50), making it an easy day-trip from the capital.

By bus Tamsui is the main departure point for journeys into the North Coast Scenic Area, with the bus station conveniently located to the right of the MRT station and destinations and route numbers clearly labelled. The special North Coast Shuttle Bus (☏ 02 2432 3185) calls at all the main tourist attractions in the Scenic Area (Mon–Fri every hour, Sat & Sun every 30min; NT$15 per leg or NT$160 for all-day ticket), supplemented by Keelung bus #862, which essentially follows the same route all the way to Keelung, but misses out some of the tourist spots.

Destinations Baishawan (every 10–15min; 30–35min); Jinshan (every 10–50min; 1hr); Juming Museum (every 30min–1hr; 1hr 20min); Keelung (every 20–50min; 2hr); Sanzhi Visitor Center (every 10–15min; 30min); Shimen (every 10–15min; 40min); Teresa Teng Memorial Park (every 30min–1hr; 1hr); Yehliu (every 30min–1hr; 1hr 35min).

By ferry Ferries run from the pier – a short walk west from the MRT station – to Bali every 10–15min (10min; NT$23) and Fisherman's Wharf every 30min (20min; NT$60); buy tickets from the booths on the wharf before boarding (you can also use an EasyCard). Ferry tours to and from Taipei are far rarer, running only at weekends (see p.82).

GEORGE MACKAY (1844–1901)

Canadian missionary **George Leslie Mackay** is still fondly remembered in Taiwan for his pioneering work in the fields of education and medicine (he's famous for the somewhat gruesome achievement of having extracted over 21,000 teeth), as well as his primary task of establishing the **Presbyterian Church** in northern Taiwan. Born in Oxford, Ontario, in 1844, he came to Taiwan in 1871, and after a brief stint in Kaohsiung arrived in Tamsui in 1872. In 1878, Mackay married a local woman and settled in Tamsui, which remained his home until he died in 1901. Although there was considerable resistance to his early proselytizing efforts (vividly described in his 1895 memoir *From Far Formosa*), he gathered a sufficient number of disciples to build north Taiwan's first church here in 1882, as well as a **boys' school** (Oxford College). His educational legacy also continues at Tamkang High School (淡江中學; dànjiāng zhōngxué), where his grave now lies, together with those of his immediate family; it's at the far end of the campus, though you can only enter on Saturdays (10am–4pm).

GETTING AROUND AND INFORMATION

By taxi Taxis line up in front of the MRT station and have an initial fare of NT$70 for the first 1.25km (NT$5 per 250m thereafter). There are additional fixed charges of NT$30 between 6am and 11pm, and NT$50 between 11pm and 6am.

By bike There are plenty of YouBike stations here – cycle paths lead from Tamsui all the way up and down the coast, so you could even cycle here from Taipei if you so desired.

Tourist information Tamsui's helpful main visitor information centre (daily 9am–6pm; ☎ 02 2626 7613) is located in the MRT station (1 Zhonzheng Rd); there's a smaller post at the entrance to Fort San Domingo.

ACCOMMODATION

Open Room 欧朋侖旅店; ōupénglún lǚdiàn 9/F, 93 Zhongshan Rd ☎ 02 2621 8333, ⓦ www.openroom .com.tw. Not a bad choice at all if you feel like staying the night in Tamsui, *Open Room* may not look like much from the outside, but the rooms are very swanky for the price – coffee-coloured affairs featuring refrigerators, hair-dryers and everything else you'd expect of a four-star hotel. NT$2600

EATING

Tamsui's **snack food** is renowned throughout Taiwan (see box, p.112), but there are plenty of more "regular" places for a meal, juice or coffee. The waterfront makes a happy hunting ground.

Bok Su Lao 牧師樓; mùshī lóu 32 Zhenli St ☎ 02 2628 1212, ⓦ boksulao.com. In a fabulous location in the old redbrick "Reverend's House", built in 1909 and now part of Aletheia University, *Bok Su Lao* is the Taiwanese (Fujianese) pronunciation of the Chinese name of the building. Sit beneath elegant arches or in the tranquil garden and enjoy an iced coffee or sandwich (both NT$160). Tues–Thurs & Sun 10am–7pm, Fri & Sat 10am–9pm.

Sanxiecheng Bakery 三協成餅舖; sānxiéchéng bǐngpù 81 Zhongzheng Rd ☎ 02 2621 2177. Better known as "Chez Jean", this place has been producing pastries since 1935. Their hefty sesame cakes and famed dōngguā ròubǐng ("wax gourd meat pies") are delicious. You can usually sample everything before you buy. Daily 9am–7.45pm.

Waterfront 榕堤水灣餐廳; róngtí shuǐwān cāntīng 229-9 Zhongzheng Rd (on the waterfront) ☎ 02 2629 0052, ⓦ waterfront.com.tw. Stylish place overlooking the river, and a pleasant spot for a meal or just a drink, *Waterfront* is reminiscent of an upmarket Bali beach resort, with thatched *palapas*, designer sofas and wicker chairs. Serves mainly Western-style dishes (mains NT$500–850). Mon–Fri 11.30am–11pm, Sat & Sun 11.30am–1am.

Wenhua A-Ge 文化阿給; wénhuà āgěi 6-4 Zhenli St ☎ 02 2621 3004. Barebones snack stall near the Little White House, which has been cooking up sumptuous ā-gěi (tofu packets stuffed with vermicelli noodles, fried and smothered in rich, spicy seafood sauce; NT$40) for over a hundred years. The seating area is a little down the hill from the counter. Daily 9.30am–6.30pm.

DRINKING

Red Castle 達觀樓; dáguānlóu 6 Lane 2, Sanmin St (accessible via the 106 steps at the end of Lane 14, off Zhongzheng Rd) ☎ 02 8631 1168. Built by a wealthy tea merchant in 1899 in a colonial style reminiscent of the consular residence, today this historic spot houses a so-so Chinese restaurant and a café. Way up on the top floor, the café, which serves alcohol and is open till late, boasts one of the best views in Tamsui, and is especially enjoyable at sunset accompanied by a beer (from NT$140). Restaurant daily 11am–10pm; café Mon–Thurs & Sun 11am–midnight, Fri & Sat 11am–1am.

SHOPPING

A-Po Iron Eggs 阿婆鐵蛋; āpó tiědàn 135 Zhongzheng Rd ☎ 02 2625 1625. This simple but venerable store is a good place to buy Tamsui's famous "iron eggs" (tiě dàn; NT$100 for eight large ones) – this was supposedly the first place to sell the eggs, back in the 1970s. You can also buy fish crisps here (NT$50 a packet). Daily 9am–10pm.

Bali

八里; bālǐ

It's a short ferry ride from Tamsui to **BALI**, a fast-developing suburb of Taipei on the left bank of the Tamsui River. Bali was a thriving port in the eighteenth century, but after its wharves began to silt up in the 1840s, business moved to the other side of the river.

1

Today the riverbank has been developed into a series of parks dubbed **Shore-Community-Museum** (水岸．社區．博物館; shuǐàn-shèqū-bówùguǎn) by local authorities, but the real highlight is the **Shihsanhang Museum of Archaeology**, 4km further along the coast. The town itself is an unattractive mix of light industry and residential development, but the magical views of Yangmingshan across the river more than compensate.

Arriving by boat, you'll disembark at **Bali Old Wharf Street** (八里渡船頭老街; bālǐ dùchuántóu lǎojiē), a smaller version of Tamsui's promenade of snack stalls and carnival games.

Shihsanhang Museum of Archaeology

十三行博物館; shísānháng bówùguǎn • 200 Museum Rd (4km west of central Bali) • April–Oct Mon–Fri 9.30am–6pm, Sat & Sun 9.30am–7pm; Nov–March daily 9.30am–5pm • NT$80 • ☎ 02 2619 1313, ⓦ www.sshm.ntpc.gov.tw • Served by #R13 and #R22 buses from Longmi Rd (reached via the narrow lane opposite the ferry quay); alternatively it's a well-signed bike ride

Tucked away behind the pot-shaped domes of the local water treatment plant, the **Shihsanhang Museum of Archaeology** displays a remarkable collection of dig finds from 200 to 1500 AD. The building itself has won several awards, while the actual archeological site now lies within the treatment plant, and a small area of this is open to the public. The finds are particularly significant because it's the only prehistoric site in Taiwan to show evidence of **iron smelting**; in addition, **Tang dynasty coins** suggest the community traded with merchants from China. Perhaps the most intriguing object on display is the mysterious **anthropomorphic jar**, one of the few prehistoric artefacts ever found in Taiwan depicting a human face. The collection isn't huge but it's still impressive – it even includes **jade earrings** that experts believe were already 1000-year-old antiques when acquired by the people at Shihsanhang.

The museum also highlights the archeological process that lies behind the discoveries, including excavation techniques and how, crucially, the experts made their assumptions. The Shihsanhang site was abandoned five hundred years ago and its inhabitants remain a mystery – the logical conclusion that they were the ancestors of the Ketagalan, the aboriginal tribe that occupied the area when Dutch and Chinese settlers arrived in the seventeenth century, is still debated.

ARRIVAL AND GETTING AROUND   BALI

By bus To reach Bali from Taipei, take the MRT to Guandu and switch to the #R13 or #R22 bus (every 20–40min), just outside exit 1, which swings past the wharf area and then the museum in around 20min.

By ferry Ferries make the 10min journey from Tamsui Wharf to Bali every 10–15min (NT$23).

By bike Bikes can be rented from the outlet close to where the ferry docks (NT$200/day; photo ID required).

EATING

If you arrive in Bali by ferry, you'll come straight out at the bottom of a small road lined with **snack-food shacks**. Look out for fried squid and crab, as well as fried donuts and deep-fried crackers (some stuffed with creamy taro paste).

She Family Peacock Clam King 佘家孔雀蛤大王總店; shéjiā kǒngquègé dàwáng zǒngdiàn 22 Duchuantou St ☎ 02 2610 3103. Just across from the ferry pier, the main event here is in fact not clams, but large stir-fried green mussels (kǒngquègé; from NT$200) garnished with basil, making them look (apparently) like peacocks. Daily 11am–9pm.

Guanyinshan

觀音山; guānyīn shān

Dominating the skyline above Bali, **Guanyinshan** (612m) is the only part of the North Coast and Guanyinshan National Scenic Area (see p.122) south of the Tamsui River. It's the closest thing the Taipei region has to a holy mountain, supposedly resembling Bodhisattva Guanyin in repose, and littered with numerous temples dedicated to the Buddhist deity. Hundreds of temples in Taiwan have been constructed with andesite rock (known as Guanyin Stone) from the mountain over the years, but quarrying is now restricted – these days it's better known for **birdwatching** (particularly for hawks and eagles between March and May), and the panoramic views of the Taipei Basin from the top. **Hiking trails** crisscross the mountain, but the easiest way to climb the main peak is to start from **Lingyun Temple** (凌雲寺; língyún sì) on the south side and end up in Bali, where there are plenty of places to eat and you can catch the ferry back to Tamsui.

Tough Man Peak

硬漢嶺; yìnghàn lǐng • Peak is 4.6km from Bali Wharf

The summit of Guanyinshan is known as **"Tough Man Peak"**, said to encourage the scores of young army recruits who once trained here. It's actually 609m high, but the Yinghan Monument on top adds another 3m. From Lingyun Temple, it's 2km to the top via a well-signposted stone path that passes the larger **Lingyun Chan Temple** (凌雲禪寺; língyúnchán sì), built in 1909 but now looking a bit like a multistorey car park – its 11m statue of Guanyin in the main hall is one of Taiwan's largest.

From the peak it's 4.6km straight down to Bali Wharf along similarly well-marked paths and lanes – you should emerge on the main Bali highway (Longmi Rd) where you turn left and walk a further 600m to the narrow lane (Duchuantou St) leading to the wharf on the right.

ARRIVAL AND INFORMATION   GUANYINSHAN

By bus To reach the southern slopes of Guanyinshan, you're best off heading to Luzhou station, at the western end of the eponymous metro line (see map, p.83). From here, buses are more reliable than they are from central Taipei, since they have to cut through less traffic; take the #20 or #785 to the final stop at Lingyun Temple (every 40–50min; 20min).

Tourist information The Guanyinshan Visitor Center (daily 9am–5pm; ☏ 02 2292 8888, ⓦ www.northguan-nsa.gov.tw) has English-speaking guides, an exhibition room and video presentations on the mountain's volcanic origins, temples and history. It's another 1km along the road from Lingyun Temple, or an energetic 1.1km detour from the main trail down a steep path – you'll have to walk back the same way to reach the peak.

Yingge

鶯歌; yīnggē

Just 20km south of the capital, the historic town of **YINGGE** is best known today as Taiwan's premier **ceramics** manufacturing centre, overflowing with over eight hundred ceramic shops and factories. The industry was founded by a Fujian immigrant called **Wu An** – legend has it that he recognized the quality of the local soil in 1805 and invited his relatives to join him in a pottery-making venture. The Wu family dominated production thereafter, until the Jianshan Ceramic Cooperative broke their monopoly in 1921 and the Japanese introduced modern kilns in the 1930s. Yingge boomed in the postwar period, but like many traditional industries in Taiwan it declined in the 1980s, with tourism and the art trade keeping the dollars flowing today.

Yingge Old Street

鶯歌老街; yīnggē lǎojiē • From the Yingge Ceramics Museum, head back to the crossroads and continue under the railway bridge, taking the first left up a gentle slope (Jianshanpu Rd)

Jianshanpu Road, otherwise known as **Yingge Old Street**, was the birthplace of Yingge ceramics, though you won't see any old buildings here. Despite the palm trees and paved road, it's just a modern strip of pottery shops and snack stalls. Nevertheless, it is one of the best places in Taiwan to stock up on high-quality ceramics.

Yingge Ceramics Museum

鶯歌陶瓷博物館; yīnggē táocí bówùguǎn • 200 Wenhua Rd • Mon–Fri 9.30am–5pm, Sat & Sun 9.30am–6pm (closed first Mon of every month) • NT$80; free audio-guides available in English (photo ID required) • ☎ 02 8677 2727, ⓦ www.ceramics.ntpc. gov.tw • A 15min walk from the train station, or bus #702 (every 12–30min) stops close to the museum

The modern, stylish halls inside stylish **Yingge Ceramics Museum** tell you everything you'd ever want to know about Yingge's history and ceramics in general, with an additional exhibition on future prospects and the use of ceramics in advanced technology – everything has bilingual labels.

ARRIVAL AND GETTING AROUND

YINGGE

By train Getting to Yingge is easy: take any train heading south from Taipei Station (every 6–20min; 25min). The only trains that don't stop are the express services and high-speed trains.

By bus Moving on to Sanxia, take Taipei Bus #702 (every 12–30min) from near the ceramics museum on Wenhua Rd.

By taxi Taxis from Yingge train station to Sanxia cost around NT$200.

On foot From Old Street, an elevated pedestrian path heads towards the museum; the route becomes a regular pavement, then a boardwalk, along the way. Note that you can't walk across the bridge to Sanxia.

EATING

Fu Guei Tau Yuan 富貴陶園; fùguì táoyuán 96 Chongqing St ☎ 02 2670 5250; map opposite. Perhaps the only notable restaurant in town, an immaculately fancy affair serving a mix of Taiwanese and Western food (mains

from NT$400). Their teas and coffees (from NT$170) are served in delightful Yingge earthenware. Daily 11am–9pm.

SHOPPING

Tai-Hwa Pottery 臺華窯; táihuá yáo 53 Chongqing St ☎ 02 2678 0000; map opposite. Tai-Hwa is a major player in the Yingge pottery scene – they have no fewer than six branches here. This is the most interesting, with a

"Back to Golden Era" dynastic-style theme; around the corner at 16-1 Jianshanbu Rd, their "concept" store sells goods of a diametrically different ilk. Daily 11am–8pm.

Sanxia

三峽; sānxiá

Three kilometres south of Yingge across the Dahan River, **SANXIA** is the home of one of Taiwan's most lavish temples, and an atmospheric old street. In the nineteenth century, the town emerged as an important distribution centre for camphor and tea along the banks of the Sanxia River, later developing its own cloth-dyeing industry. By the 1970s these trades were in decline, and though agriculture is still an important part of the local economy, tourism has provided a much-needed boost. Sanxia is close enough to Yingge to walk, but don't try it – there's no footpath on Sanying Bridge.

Zushi Temple

祖師廟; zǔshī miào • 1 Zhangfu St (off Minquan St) • Daily 4am–11pm • ☎ 02 2671 1031

Tucked away in the heart of Sanxia, and facing the river in front of Zhangfu Bridge, **Zushi Temple** is dedicated to popular deity Qingshui (see p.408) and is one of Taiwan's most spectacular shrines. Though it lacks the grandeur and scale of larger temples, its ostentatious decor and intricate craftsmanship make this a unique showcase for temple art – for many connoisseurs it's the finest on the island. Though the temple dates from 1769 it has been rebuilt three times – the most recent renovation began in 1947, and is still ongoing. The **Main Hall** housing Qingshui's image is flanked by shrines to the Moon Goddess (tàiyīn niángniáng) on the left (symbolizing west) and

Sun God (tàiyáng xīngjūn) on the right (east). The key here is attention to detail: the temple beams are plastered in delicate carvings covered in real gold foil and it's one of the few shrines in Taiwan to use **bronze sculptures** throughout. The **dragon pillars** here are particularly ornate: there are supposed to be an incredible 156 inside, though not all have been completed – the six pillars in the central courtyard are regarded as the finest examples.

Sanxia Old Street
三峽老街; sānxiá lǎojiē

Minquan Street (民權街; mínquán jiē) lies 50m behind the Zushi temple, and south of here this becomes Sanxia's pedestrianized **Old Street**, where most of the redbrick shop fronts – over a hundred in total – date from the late nineteenth century. The Chinese Baroque architecture on display is extremely photogenic, but the shops sell mostly kitsch gifts and snacks.

ARRIVAL AND DEPARTURE   **SANXIA**

By bus Getting to Sanxia from Taipei can be a pain. There are direct buses, but since these can take forever, you're best off taking the #706 or #981 from Yongning MRT station (35min, if you're lucky; NT$15) to Fuxing or Wenhua roads, from where it's a short walk to the temple and Old Street. You might even be best off heading by train to Yingge (see opposite), and catching bus #702 (every 12–30min; NT$15) from there.

EATING

Hsi-Lai-Chen 喜徠珍古井餐廳; xǐláizhēn gǔjǐng cāntīng 40 Zhongshan Rd ☏ 02 8671 1798. The most atmospheric restaurant in central Sanxia occupies an 80-year-old shophouse with cypress wood beams and serves excellent green tea and light meals (NT$100–280). Scenes from the lauded 1978 Taiwanese movie *The Story of a Small Town* were filmed here. Daily 11am–9pm.

Kang Hsi Shuan Croissants 康喜軒金牛角; kāngxǐxuān jīnniújiǎo 44 Minquan St ☏ 02 8671 6396. The main purveyor of Sanxia "croissants" (complete with servers wearing cow-horn hats), available stuffed with a variety of fillings including red bean, plum and peanut (NT$25–35). Daily 8am–8pm.

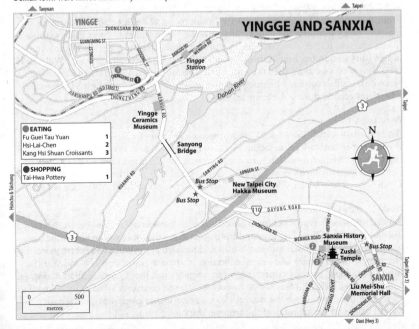

1

Wulai

烏來;wūlái

Lying in a valley 25km south of Taipei, **WULAI** is a popular day-trip from the capital, offering magnificent mountain scenery and northern Taiwan's highest **waterfall**. It's also a traditional home of the **Atayal** tribe, though the mixture of kitsch stores and dance shows on offer are aimed squarely at tourists. That said, the **museum** is definitely worth a visit, the **cherry blossoms** are magnificent in the spring, and a short walk beyond the tourist carnival lie quiet valleys and rivers offering some beautiful **hikes** and genuine Atayal villages. Wulai is also one of three popular **hot-spring** areas near Taipei (along with Beitou and Yangmingshan), though the main difference here is that it doesn't have that rotten egg smell. "Wulai" loosely translates as "hot spring", and comes from the Atayal word *urai*, meaning poisonous.

The bus from Taipei terminates right in front of **Wulai Village** – cross the bridge over the Tonghou River ahead to run the gauntlet of tourist shops, snack stalls and gift stores on **Wulai Old Street** (烏來老街; wūlái lǎojiē). This is where most of Wulai's cheaper accommodation and spas are located. At the end of Wulai Old Street you'll come to the Lansheng Bridge over the wider Nanshi River, which leads to the Log Cart (see below) and the road to the waterfall.

Wulai Atayal Museum

烏來泰雅博物館;wūlái tàiyǎ bówùguǎn • 12 Wulai Old St • Tues–Fri 9.30am–5pm, Sat–Sun 9.30am–6pm • Free • ☎ 02 2661 8162

The **Wulai Atayal Museum** is an absorbing introduction to the valley and the people who once dominated the area. Its three floors focus on the history, architecture and culture of the Atayal tribe, with explanations in English. Highlights include a collection of enormous curved Atayal hunting knives – some with highly decorative scabbards – and a description of "*tuxan*", the Atayal system of spiritual belief.

Wulai Special Scenic Area

烏來風景特定區 烏來瀑布;wūlái fēngjǐng tèdìngqū wūlái pùbù

From the Lansheng Bridge you can walk 1.6km to the **Wulai Special Scenic Area** in around twenty minutes; the road is rarely crowded on weekdays – after passing a row of hotels and spas it rises along the side of a deep and precipitous gorge smothered in jungle (this section has been dubbed "**Lovers' Walk**"). Just after you first spot **Wulai Falls** (烏來瀑布; wūlái pùbù) on the far bank, you'll come to the second tourist village. The view of the falls is certainly picturesque, and at 80m it's northern Taiwan's highest – best appreciated during the rainy season.

Wulai Log Cart

烏來台車;wūlái táichē • Daily: Jan–June & Sept–Dec 8am–5pm; July & Aug 9am–6pm • NT$50 one-way

If you'd rather not walk to the Scenic Area, you can get there in five minutes on the **Wulai Log Cart**, a miniature train that runs every few minutes along old tram tracks, built by Japanese forestry companies in 1928 and transformed into a tourist attraction in the 1960s – catch it in Wulai Village up the flight of steps next to *Helen Coffee* (see p.118).

Wulai Forestry Life Museum

烏來林業生活館;wūlái línyè shēnghuó guǎn • 1–2 Pubu Rd • Daily except Tues 9am–5pm • Free • ☎ 02 2661 6780

The history of the Wulai Log Cart and the communities that once worked here (the train was powered manually well into the 1960s) is chronicled at the **Wulai Log Forestry Life Museum**, with old photos and a small collection of artefacts (mostly post-World War II). Initially developed by the Japanese for its forestry potential, the "Qing Liu Yuan Aboriginal Culture Village" (酋長文化村; qiúzhǎng wénhuà cūn) was created in 1952 by local Atayal to try and promote tourism in the area: in 1966, a performance group was created and tourism has been the mainstay of the area ever since.

Yun Hsien Resort

雲仙樂園; yúnxiān yuèyuán • Resort daily 8.30am–5pm, cable car daily 8.30am–10pm; dance performances Sat & Sun 10.30–11.30am & 2.30–3.30pm • NT$220 (includes return cable car from station on Huanshan Rd) • ☎ 02 2661 6383

An odd and rather faded mixture of theme-park rides and gardens firmly targeted at families, tour groups and dating couples, **Yun Hsien Resort** lies beyond the top of Wulai Falls, reached via a genuinely spectacular **cable car** ride – the station is a short walk up the steps from riverside Pubu Street. The acclaimed **Lokah Cultural Troupe** of Atayal dancers perform here on weekends, and there's an expensive on-site hotel, Yun Hsien Hotel.

Doll Valley

娃娃谷; wáwágǔ • Xinxian Village • Daily 8am–5pm • NT$85 • ☎ 02 2661 7358

Scenic **Doll Valley** (also known as the Neidong National Forest Recreation Area) is a pleasant hour-long hike from Wulai Falls, along the edge of an increasingly wild and lush gorge; typhoon damage made the path a little too wild in 2016, and it remained closed at the time of writing, though things should be up and running again by 2019.

The valley's name has nothing to do with dolls; one theory is that it's a corruption of the original Chinese name "Frog Valley" – the Chinese characters for Doll Valley are very similar. Follow the main road along the Nanshi River for about twenty minutes from Wulai Falls until you reach the pedestrian suspension bridge and cross to the other side. From here the path follows the left bank of the river through **Xinxian** village, to another road and eventually the car park in front of **Neidong National Forest Recreation Area** (內洞國家森林遊樂區; nèidòng guójiā sēnlín yóulè qū). Once you've paid the entrance fee, the path passes the **Xinxian Falls** (信賢瀑布; xìnxián pùbù) on the right bank, before continuing past a dam and on to the mouth of Doll Valley itself, containing the middle and upper **Neidong Falls** (內洞瀑布; nèidòng pùbù) in a gorge off the main river. It's become a popular spot for swimming in recent years, but during the week it shouldn't be too busy. From here it's possible to follow paths further up the valley to the top of the falls, though you have to return to Wulai via the same route.

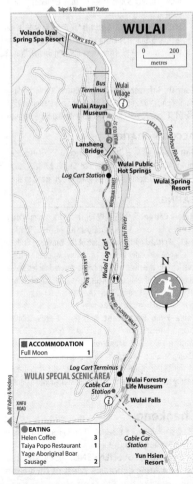

ARRIVAL AND INFORMATION
WULAI

By bus To get to Wulai from Taipei, take the metro to Xindian MRT station and turn right at the main exit to the bus stop just outside, from where you can catch the #849 to Wulai Village (every 20min; 30–45min; NT$15). At the weekend, it's better to catch the bus at Taipower MRT station to ensure a seat.

By taxi Taxis are expensive but they'll save a lot of time at the weekends, when there can be long lines for buses: fixed rates (clearly marked at taxi ranks) are NT$680 from Xindian to Wulai Old St; NT$270 between Old St and the cable car station; and NT$410 between Old St and Neidong/Doll Valley.

1

WULAI'S HOT SPRINGS

Hot springs are big business in Wulai, and most spas double as hotels – the cheapest places line Wulai Old Street, but these often have only indoor baths. You'll find another more contemporary, stylish cluster on the other side of the Nanshi River, along Wenquan Road. Wherever you go, **rates** are around NT$300–800 per session; prices tend to drop in the off-season (April–Sept), when Taipei is a bit like a huge steam room anyway.

Volando Urai Spring Spa Resort 馥蘭朵烏來渡假酒店; fùlánduǒ wūlái dùjià jiǔdiàn 3 Yandi Village ☎ 02 2661 6555, ⓦ volandospringpark.com; map p.117. For unabashed luxury, this is hard to beat, with Japanese-inspired rooms and private spas overlooking the river. Day-guests can pay NT$1260 (NT$1400 Fri & Sat) for 1hr in a private bathhouse with a view (for two people), and NT$850/day (NT$1000 Fri & Sat) for use of the lavish pools. The bus passes the hotel about 500m before the terminus. Pools 8am–11pm.

Wulai Public Hot Springs 烏來露天公共浴池; wūlái lùtiān gōnggòng yùchí By the Nanshi River; map p.117. From the Lansheng Bridge, Wulai's public hot-spring pools (free) are clearly visible on the riverbank – this is best when the river level is low, since you can make use of niches built into the riverbank. Tends to be busy with locals, even in poor weather; you'll need a swim suit. Daily 24hr.

★**Wulai Spring Resort** 烏來名湯溫泉會館; wūlái míngtāng wēnquán huìguǎn 36 Laka Rd ☎ 02 2661 6161; map p.117. Forget the utilitarian-sounding name – these pools are delightful. Set into a quieter, more natural part of the valley, the resort offers vistas of trees set to a soundtrack of cicadas buzzing in the distance. It's NT$500 for the public pools, or the same per person for a private one (1hr). Mon–Thurs & Sun 8am–10pm, Fri & Sat 8am–11pm.

Tourist information Wulai Visitor Center (daily 8am–6pm; ☎ 02 2661 6355) is near the bus station at 45-1 Wulai St (before you cross the bridge to Old St) – you can bathe your feet in a special hot-spring pool here. They stock the usual information, but English speakers are rare.

ACCOMMODATION

Full Moon 明月溫泉會館; míngyuè wēnquán huìguǎn 1 Lane 85, Wulai Old St ☎ 02 2661 7678; map p.117. Decent value, with spa baths attached to all of the pleasingly spacious rooms, and communal facilities elsewhere in the complex. Half-board NT$3600

EATING

Helen Coffee 海倫行動咖啡; hǎilún xíngdòng kāfēi 1 Lane 86, Wenquan Rd ☎ 02 2661 6392; map p.117. Perched on the other side of the Lansheng Bridge, this open-air café features a lovely wooden terrace overlooking the river, with umbrella-covered tables and a large menu of various coffees, teas and frappes from NT$80. Mon–Fri noon–5pm (or last customer), Sat & Sun 8am–9pm (or last customer).

Taiya Popo Restaurant 泰雅婆婆美食店; tàiyǎ pópó měishídiàn 14 Wulai Old St ☎ 02 2661 6371; map p.117. This Atayal-run joint (marked "Tayan Aboriginal Shop" in English), with its bamboo decor, is one of the better places to eat, though all the restaurants nearby serve up the same dishes: rice stuffed into bamboo tubes (zhútǒnggfàn; NT$50), fried or barbecued "mountain pig" (shānzhū; NT$200), fried fish and shrimp (NT$150), millet cakes (mua-ji; NT$100/box), iced hot-spring boiled egg (bīng wēnquán dàn) and lots of green vegetables. All the dishes here are nominally aboriginal, and very tasty. Daily 10am–10pm.

Yage Aboriginal Boar Sausage 雅各道地原住民山猪肉香肠; yǎgè dàodì yuánzhùmín shānzhūròu xiāngcháng) 84 Wulai Old St ☎ 0955 167796; map p.117. Lines form at the bottom of Wulai Old St at this celebrated stall selling authentic aboriginal-style boar (mountain pig) sausages (NT$35 each) with spicy sauce and raw garlic. Daily 11am–8pm.

Shenkeng

深坑; shēnkēng • Buses #660 and #251 stop on the opposite side of Muzha Rd Sec 4 from Muzha MRT station and take 15–25min to reach Shenkeng (every 15–30min)

The old town of **SHENKENG**, just above the Jingmei River, is an excellent place to gorge on Taiwanese delicacies. Most of the action takes place along **Old Street** (深坑老街;

shēnkēng lǎojiē), aka Shenkeng St, beginning near the bus stop on the main road (Beishen Rd Sec 2), marked by a 100-year-old banyan tree at its entrance, and continuing past **Jishun Temple** (集順廟; jíshùn miào) in the centre. The street has been beautifully restored, lined with ornate (and very photogenic) Chinese Baroque-style shophouses filled with local gifts, crafts and especially snacks. The chief speciality here is **tofu** (豆腐; dòufu), served up in a bewildering number of ways, from stewed tofu (hóngshāo dòufu) served from massive vats to tofu ice cream (dòufu bīngqílín).

EATING

A-Ju Taro Balls 阿珠芋圓; Azhū yùyuán 134 Shenkeng St ✆ 02 2662 6986. Best place for that traditional Taiwanese dessert on Old St: big bowls of taro balls in sweet sauce for NT$80–150. Daily 8am–9.30pm.

Gu Zao Cuo Shenkeng Tofu 古早厝豆腐美食料理; gǔzǎocuò dòufu měishí liàolǐ 140 Shenkeng St ✆ 02 2662 2534. Spacious, popular tofu restaurant that knocks out some potent chòu dòufu (stinky tofu) plus

tasty sliced cold chicken (báizhǎnjī) for NT$150–400. Daily 10am–8.30pm.

★**Jindading Teriyaki Tofu** 金大鼎串燒香豆腐; jīndàdǐng chuànshāo xiāngdòufu 162-1 Shenkeng St ✆ 919 294075. Tiny stall near the banyan tree at the start of Old St, selling "teriyaki" tofu on skewers for NT$35, topped with a creamy sauce and dipped in crushed peanuts and coriander. Daily 9am–10pm.

Pinglin
坪林; pínglín • Catch bus #923 to Pinglin outside Xindian MRT station (Mon–Fri hourly, Sat & Sun every 30min; 30–40min); bus #G12 also makes the same trip every hour, but takes a much slower route (1hr)

The small town of **PINGLIN** feels a million miles from Taipei, even with a steady trickle of tour buses rattling along its main street. In fact, it's only 20km from the edge of the city via the Taipei–Yilan Highway. Located at the bottom of the Beishi River valley it makes a good day-trip but is also the centre of an attractive region of hiking trails and smaller sights that really require your own transport (or bike) to explore fully. Pinglin is famous principally for its **tea**, much of which is bāozhōng oolong – you can see acres of tea bushes lining the hills that surround the town.

Pinglin Tea Museum
坪林茶葉博物館; pínglín cháyè bówùguǎn • 19-1 Shuisongqikeng, Shuide Village • Mon–Fri 9am–5pm, Sat & Sun 9am–5.30pm (closed on the first Mon of every month) • NT$80 • ✆ 02 2665 6035, ⟨ www.tea.ntpc.gov.tw

Across the river from the bus station, the **Pinglin Tea Museum** is the town's main attraction and a good introduction to everything connected with tea in Taiwan, beginning with its hazy, ancient Chinese origins. Tea rituals are explained, and the various strains detailed – invaluable for anyone interested in Taiwanese tea culture.

EATING

For cheap tea and food (fried **freshwater shrimps** and **fish** are the specialities here) head to Beiyi Rd leading out of town (the main road back to Xindian), where there's a huge choice of restaurants lining the roadside.

Cha Ding Tea House 甲鼎茶莊; jiǎdǐng cházhuāng 205 Beiyi Rd Sec 8 ✆ 02 2665 7390. Part

shop, part teahouse and part restaurant, this is the pick of the bunch in Pinglin. In addition to locally grown tea, they have a pretty wide range of Taiwanese food, including shellfish, meat dishes and noodle soup (most mains NT$90–200). You may have to resort to pointing if you can't read the Chinese menu. Daily except Weds 11am–6pm.

YEHLIU GEOPARK

North Taiwan

North Taiwan

Wild terrain, indigenous tribes and even wilder weather terrified early settlers, making north Taiwan one of the last parts of the island to be colonized. In 1949, the region was swamped by a huge influx of refugees from China, and today its jam-packed cities contain more Mandarin-speakers and their descendants than anywhere else in Taiwan, providing a high proportion of Kuomintang (KMT) support.

North Taiwan encompasses New Taipei City (the former Taipei county) plus Hsinchu, Miaoli, Taoyuan and Yilan counties, part of a densely populated **urban corridor** stretching from Keelung on the northeast coast to the fast-expanding cities of Taoyuan and Zhongli further west. Proximity to the capital means many attractions can be visited as a series of extended day-trips. Beyond this urban core lies a **dramatic coastline**, one of the north's most appealing features: the **North Coast and Guanyinshan National Scenic Area** and, further south, the **Northeast and Yilan Coast National Scenic Area** offer spectacular scenery and some decent beaches. Between the two areas, the port city of **Keelung** is set in a strategic harbour surrounded by ruined fortresses and is home to Taiwan's best night market, as well as its biggest annual Ghost Festival. Inland, the **Pingxi Branch Rail Line** winds its way through a lush mountain valley, past cascading **Shifen Falls** and **Pingxi** itself, home of Taiwan's most magical event, the release of hundreds of "heavenly lanterns" during the **Lantern Festival**. Nearby, the once booming mining towns of **Jiufen** and **Jinguashi** have been reinvented as tourist attractions, sporting atmospheric teahouses, snack stalls and museums.

Heading south, Hsinchu and Miaoli counties form the **Hakka heartland** of Taiwan, with **Beipu** providing ample opportunity to experience Hakka food, and **Sanyi** renowned as the country's foremost woodcarving centre. With more time and preferably your own transport, you can traverse the winding **Northern Cross-Island Highway**, connecting the historic streets of Daxi with Yilan on the east coast. **Yilan county** contains a handful of worthwhile stops, especially the plunging **Wufongqi Waterfalls**.

North Coast and Guanyinshan National Scenic Area

北海岸及觀音山國家風景區; běihǎiàn jí guānyīnshān guójiā fēngjǐngqū

Taiwan's rugged coastline between Tamsui and Keelung falls within the **North Coast and Guanyinshan National Scenic Area**, easily accessible from Taipei and a popular destination for day-trips (Guanyinshan itself is covered in Chapter 1). The northeast corner has the best scenery, with highlights including the **Dharma Drum Mountain**

KEELUNG NIGHT MARKET

Highlights

❶ Yehliu Geopark View the geological oddities peppering this jagged outcrop on the north coast. **See p.128**

❷ Keelung Night Market One of the island's best night markets, rich in seafood, tasty rice noodles and mouthwatering fruit ice stalls. **See p.133**

❸ Jiufen This stunning mountainside town is said to have inspired the bathhouse in Miyazaki's classic animated film, *Spirited Away*. **See p.134**

❹ Yilan County Surf along the dramatic coast, hike to waterfalls or sip Taiwan's own whisky and

beer, both made with mountain-fresh water. **See p.148**

❺ Hsinchu City Tucked away in this modern city, with a budding art scene and trendy café culture, is the heritage of one of north Taiwan's earliest settlements. **See p.153**

❻ Hakka culture Beipu and Shengxing are enchanting places to absorb Hakka culture, feast on excellent food and enjoy some *léichá* or "cereal tea". **See p.159**

❼ Lion's Head Mountain Scenic Area Be transported into wild nature, eulogised in the scripture of Buddhist shrines. **See p.160**

HIGHLIGHTS ARE MARKED ON THE MAP ON P.124

monastery, **Yehliu Geopark**'s fascinating rock formations and the entrancing modern sculptures at the **Juming Museum**.

GETTING AROUND   NORTH COAST AND GUANYINSHAN NATIONAL SCENIC AREA

BY BUS
North Coast Shuttle Bus The North Coast Shuttle Bus (Mon–Fri hourly, Sat & Sun every 30min; ☎ 02 2432 3185) offers a convenient service to all the main tourist attractions on the north coast, departing from the port town of Tamsui, reachable by MRT from Taipei. The shuttle bus is supplemented by Keelung bus #862, also from Tamsui, covering more or less the same route (with Sanzhi Visitor Center the notable exception). Note that journey times given below are from Tamsui.

Destinations Baishawan (every 10–15min; 30–35min); Jinshan (every 10–50min; 1hr); Juming Museum (every 30min–1hr; 1hr 20min); Keelung (every 20–50min; 2hr); Sanzhi Visitor Center (North Coast Shuttle Bus only; every 10–15min; 30min); Shimen (every 10–15min; 40min); Teresa Teng Memorial Park (every 30min–1hr; 1hr); Yehliu (every 30min–1hr; 1hr 35min).

Buses from Taipei West The #1815 Kuo Kuang bus from Taipei West Bus Station to Jinshan Youth Activity Center (every 15–30min; 1hr 30min) stops at Yehliu (1hr) and Jinshan (1hr 25min); some of these buses terminate at Dharma Drum Mountain, so check before you get on.

BY BIKE
Cycling the North Coast is a popular way to get around the area. On the northwest coast is the first of three cycle paths (金色水岸; jīnsè shuǐàn), which runs from Guanshan Park alongside the Tamsui River. The next path (fēngzhīmén; 風芝門) runs from Qianshuiwan Coast Park for 4.5km to Baishawan. On northwest coast is the Wanli (萬里; wànlǐ) to Jinshan (金山; jīnshān) route, which takes you 7.5km inland through verdant hills.

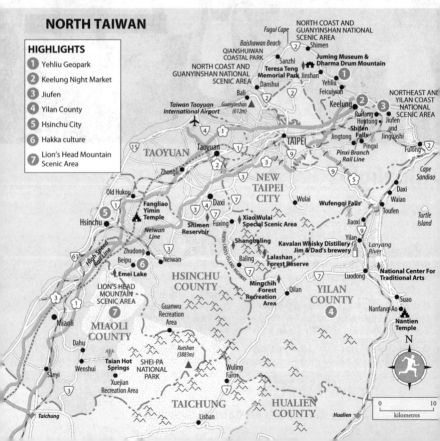

NORTH TAIWAN

HIGHLIGHTS
1. Yehliu Geopark
2. Keelung Night Market
3. Jiufen
4. Yilan County
5. Hsinchu City
6. Hakka culture
7. Lion's Head Mountain Scenic Area

Sanzhi

三芝; sānzhī

The small agricultural town of **SANZHI** is a tea- and rice-growing centre, best known in Taiwan as the birthplace of former president Lee Teng-hui. Attractions here are spread out and difficult to reach without your own transport, though the North Coast Shuttle Bus goes direct to the Sanzhi Visitor Center, the best place to start.

Sanzhi Visitor Center

三芝遊客中心; sānzhī yóukè zhōngxīn • 164-2 Butoukeng, Buping Village • Daily 9am–5pm • ☎ 02 8635 3640, ⓦ northguan-nsa.gov.tw • On North Coast Shuttle Bus route (see opposite)

2

The **Sanzhi Visitor Center** is 2km east of the town centre and home to a couple of enlightening museums, both with English labelling. The first recounts the history of the area and includes a section on the north coast's earliest inhabitants, the Ketagalan, while the **Gallery of Famous Sons** commemorates the town's most respected former residents, in particular **Lee Teng-hui**, Taiwan's first democratically elected president, who in 1923 was born in the **Yuanxing Residence**, a traditional Fujian-style three-sided home just outside the visitor centre.

Qianshuiwan Coastal Park

淺水灣; qiǎnshuǐwān • 11km north of Tamsui

Qianshuiwan Coastal Park, just west of Sanzhi, is the first beach destination on the North Coast Shuttle Bus route. Get off at either Daku or Siban to enjoy the bay, with its beach of rock and sand. The beach is popular with families who come for sunset, after which the numerous local restaurants and bars that line the shore soon fill up.

Baishawan

白沙灣; báishāwān • Visitor Centre daily 9am–5pm • ☎ 02 26364503, ⓦ northguan-nsa.gov.tw

The **beach** at **Baishawan**, five minutes up the coast by bus from Qianshuiwan, is free, has the finest white(ish) sand on the north coast, and is home to the main **visitor centre** for the whole Scenic Area. Next door, the family-friendly **North Coast Exploratorium** (Tues–Sun 9am–5pm; NT$30; ☎ 02 8635 5174) contains interactive displays about the ecology of the region. You can also wander along the boardwalk up to **Linshan Cape** (麟山鼻; línshānbí), a craggy finger of volcanic lava at the eastern end of the bay. There's not much point visiting during the cooler winter months, however.

Fugui Cape

富貴角; fùguì jiǎo

The next major stop after Baishawan, **Fugui Cape** is Taiwan's most northerly point, a rugged headland topped by a stumpy 14m lighthouse. The nearest bus stop is on the main road, a few minutes' walk from **Fuji Fishing Harbour** (富基漁港; fùjī yúgǎng), a compact and ramshackle dock crammed with fishing boats. A lively fish market (daily 10am–8pm) hugs the quayside, and there's a row of popular **seafood restaurants** nearby. The cape itself is a short walk from the back of the harbour, along the rocky coastline. **Fugui Lighthouse** (富貴角燈塔; fùguì jiǎo dēngtǎ) was built in 1949 and is generally off limits (as is the military radar station nearby), but the walk there offers wide ocean views and a chance to gaze at the cape itself, a battered jumble of rocks below the headland, often littered with driftwood.

Shimen

石門; shímén

Another 4km beyond Fugui Cape, **SHIMEN** is Taiwan's most northerly village and a convenient lunch stop. On the eastern side of Shimen lies the topographic feature that gave the village its name ("Stone Gate"), the **Shimen Cave** (石門洞; shímén dòng), a naturally eroded stone arch, just off the beach.

Temple of Eighteen Lords

十八王公廟; shíbā wánggōngmiào • 1-1 Neialibang (Hwy-2) • Daily 24hr • ☏ 02 2638 1818 • The shrine is a short walk from the bus stop on the main road, behind the highway bridge

Just under 4km east of central Shimen, the **Temple of Eighteen Lords** is a tiny shrine swathed in gold leaf. Despite its size, this is one of the most popular temples on the north coast – not least because worshipping here is meant to bring good luck in gambling or the lottery. Several legends are associated with the site, the official one being that the shrine was established in the late Qing dynasty to commemorate the faithful **dog** (the eighteenth "lord") of one of seventeen fishermen drowned at sea. When the bodies of the men washed ashore near Shimen, the dog was miraculously still alive, but, overcome with grief, it threw itself into its master's tomb as a sign of loyalty.

The **tomb** representing the eighteen is to the left side of the main hall, lined with cigarettes placed here for the fishermen's spirits to smoke, but to get a piece of the money-making action you'll need to get your hands on one of two bronze dog statues guarding them; touch the dog's mouth for general good luck, its feet for great wealth and the head to ensure your children grow up extra intelligent. Note that this tomb is a recently built reproduction – the real one is behind the shrine in the basement.

EATING   SHIMEN

Liu's Zongzi 劉家肉粽; liújiā ròuzòng 30 Zhongyang Rd ☏ 02 2638 1088. The main drag in Shimen (Zhongyang Rd) is lined with stalls selling the regional version of the classic zòngzi (rice dumplings wrapped in bamboo leaves; NT$25–30); locally dubbed ròuzòng, the Shimen interpretation can include chicken as well as minced radish – a delicious treat since the 1960s. Daily 9am–7pm.

Jinshan

金山; jīnshān

Some 12km south of Shimen, **JINSHAN** is the largest town on the north coast and a good place to grab lunch or take a dip in one of its numerous hot-spring resorts. The town sits behind a small promontory that divides its two popular but unexceptional beaches.

Jinbaoli Street

金包裡老街; jīnbāolǐ lǎojiē

Running parallel to the east of the main thoroughfare, Zhongshan Road, is Jinshan's Old Street, also known as **Jinbaoli Street** to commemorate the Ketagalan name for the area, and once the site of a busy riverside dock. Few old buildings remain, but it's a pleasant place to browse (the town is noted for its traditional cakes, wooden shoes and baked sweet potatoes and yams). The Traditional Medicine store at no. 26, and rice shop at no. 28 are its best examples of early twentieth-century architecture.

Cihu Temple

慈護宮; cíhùgōng • 16 Jinbaoli St • Daily 5am–9pm • ☏ 02 2498 2510

At the southern end of Jinbaoli Street is **Cihu Temple**, established in 1809 and dedicated to Mazu – it's the biggest temple on the north coast, containing a plethora of statues and one central gold-faced image of the main deity. The temple faces Minsheng Road, and turning left here takes you towards the **beach** – hail a cab or catch any bus that's heading this way if you don't fancy the 1.2-km walk over the hill.

Governor-General Hot Spring

舊金山總督溫泉; jiùjīnshān zǒngdū wēnquán • 196 Minsheng Rd • Daily 9am–midnight • Spa and hot-spring pool NT$300 • ☎ 02 2408 2628, ⓦ warmspring.com.tw

From central Jinshan, Minsheng Road leads to Shuiwei Fishing Port (水尾漁港; shuǐwěi yúgǎng) on the south side of the promontory, and Old Jinshan Beach or Jiatou Xialiao Beach (加投下寮海灘; jiātóu xiàliáo hǎitān), which is free, but often littered with flotsam. The best thing here is the **Governor-General Hot Spring**, housed in a grey Japanese-era building completed in 1939. The second-floor restaurant is a decent place to have lunch, while the outdoor pools are attractive (there's no accommodation).

2

ARRIVAL AND INFORMATION JINSHAN

By bus Buses from Tamsui and Keelung stop on Zhongshan Rd in the centre of town, while bus #1815 from Taipei terminates just outside the large grey reception building of Jinshan Youth Activity Center near the beach. The North Coast Shuttle Bus (see p.124) stops right outside the visitor centre.

Destinations Baishawan (40min); Dharma Drum Mountain

(10min); Keelung (30min); Shimen (20min); Taipei (1hr); Tamsui (1hr); Yehliu (10min).

Tourist information Jinshan Visitor Center (金山遊客中心; jīnshān yóukè zhōngxīn; daily 9am–5pm; ☎02 2492 2016, ⓦ northguan-nsa.gov.tw) at 171–2 Huanggang Rd, just outside the centre on the way to the beach, can provide local maps and information.

ACCOMMODATION AND EATING

The most celebrated local speciality is **duck noodles**; for something lighter, the stalls on Jinbaoli St serve up plenty of delicious **snacks**: bags of sweet-potato cubes in caramelized sugar (NT$50), potato crisps (from NT$80) and bags of sesame balls (málǎo; NT$100).

★**Jinshan Duck (Guangan Temple)** 金山鴨肉 (廣安宮); jīnshān yàròu/guǎngāngōng 104 Jinbaoli St. The best place to sample the local duck noodles is the bustling forecourt of this temple. Plates of duck, with special plum sauce and fresh ginger, as well as fried prawns, noodles and bamboo shoots cost NT$60 to NT$120. Grab your food, then head to the three numbered eating areas further down the street. Daily 9am–7.30pm.

Jinshan Youth Activity Center 金山青年活動中心; jīnshān qīngnián huódòng zhōngxīn 1 Qingnian Rd ☎02 2498 1190, ⓦ chinshan.cyh.org.tw. This centre offers a range of chalet accommodation, all clean and fairly spacious, as well as camping, with or without your own tent. Hot meals are available in the reception building. Camping (tent provided) NT$800, camping pitch NT$500, chalet NT$3000

Dharma Drum Mountain

法鼓山; fǎgǔshān • 555 Fagu Rd, 7th Neighborhood, Sanjie Village • Daily 8am–4pm • Free • ☎ 02 2498 7171, ⓦ dharmadrum.org
• The North Coast Shuttle Bus goes past the monastery entrance, and some #1815 Kuo Kuang buses from Taipei West Bus Station terminate here – a taxi from Jinshan should cost NT$200

Beautifully located in the hills above Jinshan, around 3km from the centre of town, **Dharma Drum Mountain** is an absorbing Buddhist educational complex and monastery with extensive gardens. Established in 1989 by respected monk and scholar Master Sheng Yen, it is Taiwan's newest Chan (Zen) Buddhist foundation. Visitors are welcome, but it's best to email in advance if you require a free **guided tour** in English.

From the main entrance, make your way up the hill to the Reception Hall where you'll find an information desk. From here, you can walk across to the adjacent Main Building: the third floor contains the **Founding History Memorial Hall**, which uses a suitably futuristic blend of Buddhist relics and modern technology to recount the history of Buddhism and the life of Master Sheng Yen, while the Glories of Dharma Drum Mountain on the next floor up is a vast but rather hagiographical portrait of the founder and scenes from his life. Another highlight is the **Great Buddha Hall** in the main temple of the complex, with its imposing bronze images of Sakyamuni Buddha (centre), the Medicine Buddha (right) and Amitabha Buddha (left), backed by ornate canopies carved by Japanese craftsmen.

Juming Museum

朱铭美術館; zhūmíng měishùguǎn • 2 Xishihu (Hwy 22-1), Jinshan • Tues–Sun: May–Oct 10am–6pm, Nov–April 10am–5pm; Main Building closes 15min before the rest of the site • NT$250, children under 6 free • ☎ 02 2498 9940, ⓦ www.juming .org.tw • The North Coast Shuttle Bus goes right to the museum; free shuttle buses leave Jinshan District Office (at the junction of Zhongshan Rd and Zhongzheng Rd) daily at 10.30am & 2pm (plus 12.30pm on Sat & Sun), returning 1.40pm & 5pm (plus 3.40pm on Sat & Sun); taxis from Jinshan should cost around NT$250

Opened in 1999 by Ju Ming, Taiwan's most celebrated sculptor, the **Juming Museum** lies over the ridge behind Dharma Drum Mountain. It's more a sculpture park than a museum, with most exhibits displayed around a series of landscaped gardens and ponds – it's obviously best to visit when the weather is good.

From the museum **service centre**, walk down through a gallery of sculptures by some of Taiwan's acclaimed artists, to the outdoor area. The first installations on display are usually taken from Ju Ming's **Living World Series**: anything from life-size parachutists cast in bronze to stainless steel swimmers (exhibits rotate). The real highlight, however, is the sculptor's most famous work: thirty giant pieces of his extraordinary **Taichi Series**, a collection of huge, chunky figures created in the late 1970s and early 1980s. The abstract, faceless bronze forms manage to convey intense movement and the controlled energy of the Chinese martial art without resorting to minute detail. The museum's pyramid-shaped **Main Building** is where much of Ju Ming's early Nativist woodcarvings are displayed, along with work from Yu Yu Yang, his teacher. English-language documentaries about the sculptor are screened here throughout the day.

Teresa Teng Memorial Park

邓丽君纪念公园; dènglìjūn jìniàn gōngyuán • Jinbaoshan Cemetery, 18 Xishihu (Hwy 23-1), Xihu Village • Daily 24hr • ☎ 02 2498 5900 • On North Coast Shuttle Bus route (see p.124)

Hugging the slopes above the Juming Museum, **Teresa Teng Memorial Park** in the Jinbaoshan Cemetery (金寶山陵園; jīnbǎoshān língyuán) has become a pilgrimage site for music fans from all over the world, as the last resting place of **Teresa Teng** (Dèng Lìjūn in Chinese), one of the most famous Chinese pop singers of all time – she died tragically in 1995, after an asthma attack at the age of 43. Her tomb is often littered with flowers, while her memorial garden features a life-size statue and a giant electronic keyboard that can be "played" by stepping on the keys. Her ten most famous hits (including *Will You Come Back Again?*) echo around the site on permanent loop.

Yehliu Geopark

野柳地質公園; yěliǔ dìzhì gōngyuán • 167-1 Gangdong Rd, Yehliu • Daily 8am–5pm • NT$80, children NT$40 • ☎ 02 2492 2016, ⓦ www.ylgeopark.org.tw • On North Coast Shuttle Bus route (see p.124)

Just to the north of the fishing village of **YEHLIU** (野柳; yěliǔ) lies **Yehliu Geopark**, home to a Martian-esque landscape of geological formations. Set on Yehliu Cape, the park commands stunning views across the bay to Jinshan and Yangmingshan beyond – hike to the end of the headland and you'll usually have the place to yourself. Unique rock formations litter the cape, due to years of weathering and seismic activity – the small **visitor centre** at the entrance shows English videos on the geology of the area. From here, well-marked **trails** lead along the 1.7km headland past all of the most famous formations: rocks that resemble tofu and ginger, the unique and mystifying candle rocks and the ubiquitous mushroom rocks, the most famous of which is the **Queen's Head** (女王頭; nǚwángtóu) – the original has become so weathered that there's a fibre-glass replica.

EATING

Shark Bites Toast 鯊魚咬士司; shāyú yǎo shìsī 167-3 Yeligangdong Rd ☎ 02 2492 2197. Just outside the geopark, this fast-food restaurant is clean, has a/c and offers a variety of Taiwanese and Western-style light bites. Try the shaved ice with mango ice cream (NT$180). Mon–Fri 10am–6pm, Sat & Sun 10am–8pm.

Keelung

基隆; jīlóng

The evocatively weathered port city of **KEELUNG**, sandwiched between verdant mountains and northern Taiwan's best natural harbour, is a strategic location that has been fought over by foreign powers since the seventeenth century. Home to around four hundred thousand people, its setting is picturesque and there's plenty to see: numerous **fortresses**, a legacy of the city's violent past, the **Fairy Cave**, one of Taiwan's most atmospheric shrines, an easy-to-navigate **night market** and the country's largest and most illuminating **Ghost Festival**, held every August.

The **harbour** remains the heart of the city, with all the main streets and buildings crammed between here and the mountains. The West Passenger Terminal is where cruise ships and Matsu ferries dock, while at the Maritime Plaza you can watch black kites swooping into the sea to catch fish. The vibrant area south of the waterfront is where you'll find Keelung's shops, temples and restaurants, while the city's other main attractions lie either east or west of the port.

Brief history

The **Spanish** first established an outpost on **Heping Island** near Keelung in 1626, when the area was inhabited by the **Ketagalan**, who called it "Kelang". In 1642 the Dutch kicked out the Spaniards after a bloody siege, but they abandoned their last stronghold in Taiwan in 1668. Chinese immigrants began to arrive in large numbers in 1723 and the town became an important **port** in the nineteenth century, making it a regular target for foreign powers; during the 1841 Opium War, a British squadron shelled the

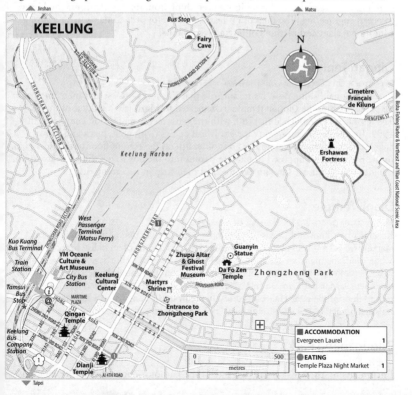

2

harbour, while in the Sino-French War the city was occupied by the French for eight months. The harbour was almost completely destroyed by Allied bombing at the end of World War II, but the post-war years saw a gradual rebuilding of its facilities – it's now Taiwan's second-biggest container port after Kaohsiung.

YM Oceanic Culture & Art Museum

陽明海洋文化藝術館; yángmíng hǎiyáng wénhuà yìshùguǎn • 4 Gangxi St • Tues–Sun 9am–5pm • NT$100, children NT$50 • ☎ 02 2421 5681, ⓦ ocam.org.tw

Located in the old headquarters of Yangming Marine Transport Corp, just opposite the train station, the **YM Oceanic Culture & Art Museum** is an artfully presented tribute to Keelung's long relationship with the sea. The second floor contains displays about navigation and the history of ancient vessels, while the other exhibitions change every six months and focus on a range of subjects connected with ships and the ocean, particularly with a Chinese or Taiwanese slant.

National Museum of Marine Science and Technology

國立海洋科技博物館; guólì hǎiyáng kējì bówùguǎn • 367 Beining Lu, Zhongzheng • Mon–Fri 9am–5pm, Sat & Sun 9am–6pm • NT$200, children NT$140 • ☎ 02 2421 5681, ⓦ www.nmmst.gov.tw • Bus #103, #791 or #1051 from the train station to Haikeguan stop

Located in in the eastern part of the city, in what had once been a thermal power plant, the impressive **National Museum of Marine Science and Technology** goes one step further in curating Taiwan's intimate relationship with the sea. Housed inside the main building are several detailed exhibits on everything from marine environmental issues to ocean engineering. The museum is heavily geared towards students, with a strong educational slant and plethora of interactive exhibits.

Qingan Temple

慶安宮; qìngān gōng • 1 Zhong 2nd Rd • Daily 6am–10pm • ☎ 02 2425 4626

As a traditional fishing port, it's no surprise that Keelung's busiest and most important place of worship, the **Qingan Temple**, is dedicated to Mazu (the Goddess of the Sea). The temple was established in 1780, with the most recent renovation completed in 1999. In addition to numerous ancient Mazu deities (with gold, black and brown faces), check out the shrine to five gods of wealth on the second floor of the Rear Hall, to the right. You're supposed to put a few coins into the box to get the gods' attention, the idea being you need to "invest" to enlist their help in becoming rich.

Dianji Temple

奠濟宮; diànji gōng • 27-2 Ren 3rd Rd • Daily 7am–10pm • ☎ 02 2425 2605

Keelung's best-known shrine is **Dianji Temple**, primarily because of the **Temple Night Market** (see p.133) held here. Established in 1875 on the site of an older shrine to the Water God, the main hall dates from 1923 and is dedicated to the Sage King Kaizhang (開漳聖王; kāizhāng shèngwáng) – his main image sits in the central shrine. The other main deity here is Marshal Tian Du (田都元帥; tiándōu yuánshuài), symbolized by a statue on the second floor of the Rear Hall, a historical figure from the Tang dynasty and a patron of xīpí music, a branch of běiguǎn (traditional "northern" music).

Zhongzheng Park

中正公園; zhōngzhèng gōngyuán • Xin 2nd Rd • Daily 24hr

Encompassing the hills on the east side of the harbour, **Zhongzheng Park** contains several religious and historic landmarks. The main trail passes several shrines and temples on the way up, skirting around the Martyrs' Shrine on the lower slopes and emerging at the **Zhupu Altar** (主普壇; zhǔpǔtán), the grand pǔdù (spirit offering) shrine which is the focus of Keelung's **Ghost Festival**. The shrine was completed in 1976 and is only opened during Ghost Month (usually Aug), when offerings and rituals made here are supposed to appease the "hungry ghosts" thought to wander the earth at this time.

If you can't experience the Ghost Festival, it's worth visiting the **Keelung Midsummer Ghost Festival Museum** (中元祭典文物館; zhōngyuán jìdiǎn wénwùguǎn; Tues–Sun 9am–5pm; free; ⊕02 2428 4242) on the first floor of the Zhupu Altar, a small but informative exhibition about the festival, with labels in English. From here it's a short walk up the final slope to Keelung's iconic 22m-tall **Guanyin Statue** – built on a panoramic spot facing the sea, it's now part of the unremarkable **Da Fo Zen Temple** (大佛禪院; dàfó chán yuàn) complex, built in 1969.

Ershawan Fortress

二砂灣砲台; èrshāwān pàotái · Shoushan Rd · Daily 24hr · Free · A 20min walk east of Da Fo Zen Temple; follow Shoushan Rd from the snack stalls behind the temple, taking a left turn at the first junction

Dating from 1840 but rebuilt several times, **Ershawan Fortress** is Keelung's largest fortress, though it's little more than a series of hefty gun emplacements – the path loops around the main battlements and barrack areas behind, passing a few old tombs and a line of steep steps leading to the original gate further down the slope. This has the words 海門天險 (hǎimén tiānxiǎn) inscribed on the front, which roughly translates as "Dangerous Sea-Gate". From here you can walk down the hill to Zhongzheng Road along the harbour and catch a bus back to the train station.

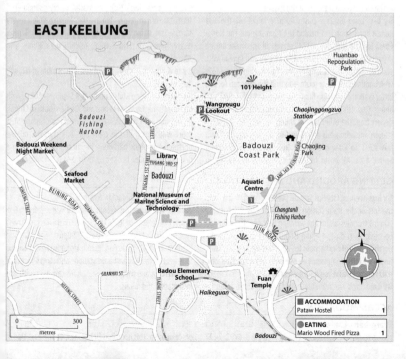

2

Cimetière Français de Kilung

法國公墓; fǎguó gōngmù • Zhongsheng Rd, just before the junction with Zhengfeng St • Daily 24hr • Free • Bus #101

One of Keelung's more unusual sites, the French Cemetery, or **Cimetière Français de Kilung**, is all that remains of the graves of over six hundred French soldiers killed during their occupation of the town in 1884–85. Estimates suggest that only 270 died as a result of fighting – the majority succumbed to diseases such as malaria, cholera and dysentery. Only a few of the original tombstones remain on the far right; the main stone monument was erected in 1954 when the French government transferred the graves of two senior officers who had died in Penghu to the cemetery. The two pillar monuments on site were erected by the Japanese. Ceremonies to commemorate the dead are still held here on November 11, led by official French government representatives from Taipei.

Fairy Cave

仙洞巖; xiāndòngyán • Zhongshan 4th Rd • Daily 6am–6pm • Free • Bus #301 (every 12–20min; 10min from the train station)

On the northern side of Keelung harbour, the **Fairy Cave** is actually a series of Buddhist shrines carved into the limestone caves facing the container port – the wall carvings provide the illusion of great antiquity, unusual in Taiwan, though the temple dates from the relatively recent Qing dynasty. The cave contains four shrines; the first is dedicated to Milefo, while the second cavern features an altar to Guanyin. Behind this, the main hall contains the three principal images of Buddha. To the left of the second cavern, a narrow passage through the rock takes you to another incense-filled shrine with a small stone effigy of Guanyin.

ARRIVAL AND DEPARTURE

KEELUNG

By train Regular local trains from Taipei (40min) arrive at the train station (基隆車站; jīlóng chēzhàn), located at the southwestern corner of the harbour.

By bus Long-distance buses from/to Taipei use the Kuo Kuang bus station just behind the train station. The North Coast Shuttle Bus (see p.124) serves all the main tourist attractions between Keelung train station and Tamsui MRT station; this service is supplemented by Keelung bus #862, which follows a similar route – to find the bus stop for the latter walk through Kuo Kuang bus station to the right and along Xiao 4th Rd. Other Keelung Bus Company services depart from the other side of Zhong 1st Rd from the train station, including bus #1013 to Jiufen and Jinguashi; and bus #791 to Fulong and the Northeast Coast National Scenic Area. All buses have their destinations marked in

English on the front.

Destinations Bitou (every 30min–1hr; 30–40min); Fulong (every 30min–1hr; 1hr); Jinguashi (every 30min–1hr; 40min); Jinshan (every 30min–1hr; 30min); Jiufen (every 30min–1hr; 30min); Taipei (every 30min–1hr; 1hr); Tamsui (every 30min–1hr; 1hr 30min); Yehliu (every 30min–1hr; 20min).

By taxi Taxis to Jinshan should cost a maximum of NT$400 (less to Yehliu).

By ferry Ferries to Matsu (daily at 9.50pm; 8–10hr), with onward connections to Fuzhou and Xiamen (both in China), depart from the West Passenger Terminal on Gangxi St, a short walk north of the train and bus stations, on the northern side of the harbour – buy tickets from the second floor. Tickets can be booked up to three days in advance.

GETTING AROUND AND INFORMATION

By bus Keelung City Bus Station (總站; zǒngzhàn) is to the left of the train station as you exit. Bus #101 (every 20min) trundles along Zhongzheng Rd beneath Ershawan Fortress, then on to Heping Island; #301 goes along the northern side of the harbour to Fairy Cave every 12–20min. Buses cost NT$15/journey – use your EasyCard (see box, p.82) or make sure you have exact change.

By taxi Taxis are available from the train station, but be

sure to negotiate the fare in advance.

Tourist information Keelung's useful Visitor Information Center (基隆市旅遊服務中心; jīlóngshì lǚyóu fúwù zhōngxīn; Mon–Fri 8.30am–5.30pm, Sat & Sun 9am–4pm; ⍉ 02 2428 7664, ⍈ tour.klcg.gov.tw) at 1 Gangxi St is next to the bus and train stations and stocks plenty of English-language material – staff here can help with bus information and hotels.

ACCOMMODATION

Evergreen Laurel 長榮桂冠酒店; chánglóng guìguàn jiǔdiàn 62-1 Zhongzheng Rd ⍉ 02 2427

9988, ⍈ evergreen-hotels.com; map p.129. The top place in town, this luxurious behemoth, on the east side of the harbour, has a green tower clearly visible from most points in the city. Rooms are comfy but a bit old-fashioned, with all the usual five-star amenities and stellar views from the higher floors. NT$3999

Pataw Hostel女巫国际背包客栈; nǚwū guójì bēibāo kèzhàn. Lane 369, Beining Rd, Zhongzheng District ☎886 974006188, ✉ourbest100@yahoo.com.

tw; map p.131. The best deal in the city, this hostel is located in a fishing village right on the coast, a 15min drive east from downtown. It's popular with the student crowd and those visiting to sail or snorkel. Dorms contain bunks with tent canvases on the top. Check-in after 6pm. Dorms NT$500

EATING

Mario Wood Fired Pizza 瑪利歐柴窯披薩; mǎlìōu cháyáo pīsà 45-6, 369 Xiang, Beining Rd ☎02 2469 0603; map p.131. This Italian place, run by locals, serves up not-half-bad pizzas and Italian staples for around NT$400. However, its principal selling point is its location in the coastal park, with staggering views of craggy hills surrounding the sea. Daily 11am–10pm.

★**Temple Plaza Night Market** 廟口夜市; miàokǒu yèshì Ren 3rd Rd, between Ai 3rd Rd and Ai 4th Rd ⓦmiaokow.org; map p.129. Keelung's night market is one of Taiwan's culinary highlights and by far the best place to

eat in the city. The market dates from the late Japanese occupation era and fronts Dianji Temple; each stall advertises its main dishes in English, and it's open around the clock. The ice and fruit stalls are refreshing in summer, and the thick soups, meatballs, oyster omelettes, curry rice and rice-flour noodles (mǐfěn) are especially recommended – try the "pot side scrapings" (thick rice noodles in a mixed seafood broth; NT$20–50) at *Ding Bian Cuo* (鼎邊趖; dǐngbiānsuō), one of the oldest stalls in the market, located at nos. 25-1 and 27-3. Daily 24hr.

Jiufen and Jinguashi

The historic gold-mining towns of **Jiufen** and **Jinguashi** occupy stunning hillside locations with sensational views of the northeast coast. Jiufen is justifiably renowned for its tasty **snack food** and atmospheric **teahouses**, though despite the hype, the town itself is architecturally fairly typical, more "shabby chic" than classical Chinese. From Jiufen, the main road runs 2km over the Mount Keelung ridge to Jinguashi, a major tourist destination in its own right. There, most of the town's mining-related attractions have been absorbed into the **Gold Ecological Park**, an ambitious project that combines restored Japanese buildings with old mines and temples.

Brief history

Gold was discovered in the Keelung River in 1889, and by 1896 the Japanese had begun mining in the area, dividing the land split by Mount Keelung between two government-run companies named after the officers in command: the concession operated by **Tanaka Group** became **Jinguashi**, while **Fujita Group** developed **Jiufen**. The gold ore on the Jiufen side was less pure and in 1899 the Japanese began to lease the concession to local entrepreneur **Yen Yun-nien** who founded the Taiyang Mining Corp in 1920 and began sub-leasing smaller chunks of land to Chinese prospectors. As a consequence, Jiufen developed haphazardly as a series of independent claims, gaining a reputation as a get-rich-quick town, or **Little Hong Kong**, in the 1930s.

Taiyang ceased all operations in Jiufen in 1971, and though artists started to settle here in the early 1980s, the good times seemed to be over – until **Hou Hsiao-hsien**'s 1989 movie *City of Sadness* (悲情城市; bēiqíng chéngshì), in large part shot in a then-atmospheric Jiufen, changed all that. The film was the first to make reference (indirectly) to the 2-28 Incident (see p.394) and won the Golden Lion at the Venice Film Festival. Overnight the town became a must-see attraction, creating the tourist carnival that still exists today. One of its admirers is Hayao Miyazaki, who used Jiufen as inspiration for the village in his Japanese anime hit *Spirited Away* (2001).

In contrast, the Japanese maintained direct control over Jinguashi until 1945, and the town developed in an orderly, pragmatic fashion. Its silver and especially **copper** deposits, discovered in 1905, became far more important than gold – by the 1930s the town was home to around eighty thousand people, with the hills honeycombed by a staggering 600km of tunnels. Mining finally ceased in 1987 when debts bankrupted the state-owned Taiwan Metal Mining Company – there's still gold in the hills but it's become too expensive to extract commercially.

Jiufen

九份; jiǔfèn

The narrow backstreets of **JIUFEN** are generally vehicle-free and, away from the busier areas, local life proceeds remarkably undisturbed. Most visitors get off the bus adjacent to the Gerding Parking Area at the top end of town, proceeding downhill straight into **Jishan Street** (基山街; jīshān jiē) to gorge on its vast array of **snacks** (see p.138). Keep walking along Jishan Street and you'll eventually reach Jiufen's most picturesque thoroughfare, **Shuqi Road** (豎崎路; shùqí lù), actually a series of stone steps slicing through the middle of town and lined with teahouses and old, photogenic Chinese-style buildings. Walk downhill to the junction with Qingbian Road (輕便路; qīngbiàn lù), turn left and in around 250m you'll come to a small square in front of the entrance to **Taiyang No. 5 Tunnel** (五番坑; wǔfān kēng), an evocative relic of Jiufen's mining days blasted out of the rock in 1935 and closed in 1971 – it's locked up but you can still peer through the bars. Retrace your steps to Shuqi Road and a short walk in the other direction along Qingbian (at Qiche Rd) you'll see gaudy **Chenghuang Temple** (城隍廟; chénghuáng miào), housing Jiufen's City God and remodelled many times since the first shrine was established here in the 1920s.

Shengping Theater

昇平劇院; shēngpíng jùyuàn • 137 Qingpian Rd • Mon–Fri 9.30am–5pm, Sat & Sun 9.30am–6pm • Free • ☎ 02 2496 9926

Tucked away at the junction of Shuqi and Qingbian roads, the **Shengping Theater** is another relic of Jiufen's golden years, built in 1934 and remodelled in 1961. Inside, the old redwood chairs have been restored, along with the stone walls and stage/screen, while small exhibits – old tickets, movie posters and the like – line the walkways.

Mount Keelung

基隆山; jīlóngshān

Rising high above both Jiufen and Jinguashi, **Mount Keelung** is an inactive volcano named by Chinese sailors who thought it resembled a chicken coop (pronounced "jilongshan" in Mandarin Chinese). On a fine day, the short but steep hike to the summit (588m) offers a spectacular panorama of towns (allow 30–40min for a leisurely hike up from the trailhead on Qiche Rd).

Jinguashi

金瓜石; jīnguāshí

Nestling in a small valley, just over the hill from Jiufen, **JINGUASHI** has only a handful of inhabitants and plenty of atmospheric alleys and streets to explore. Much of the old village is preserved within the absorbing **Gold Ecological Park**, an industrial heritage area that covers the western half of the valley.

Quanji Temple

勸濟堂; quànjì táng • 53 Qitang Rd • Daily 7am–7pm • ☎ 02 2496 1273

Sitting on the eastern side of the valley, **Quanji Temple** – rebuilt in 1933, based on an 1896 original – is noted principally for its bronze statue of Guan Di (the main god worshipped inside), which at 10.5m is one of the tallest in Asia, though the statue is also a modern creation, completed in 1991. The lane to the left of Quanji Temple leads 200m up to an abandoned smoke tunnel and **Baoshi Mountain** (報時山; bàoshí shān), which is just a

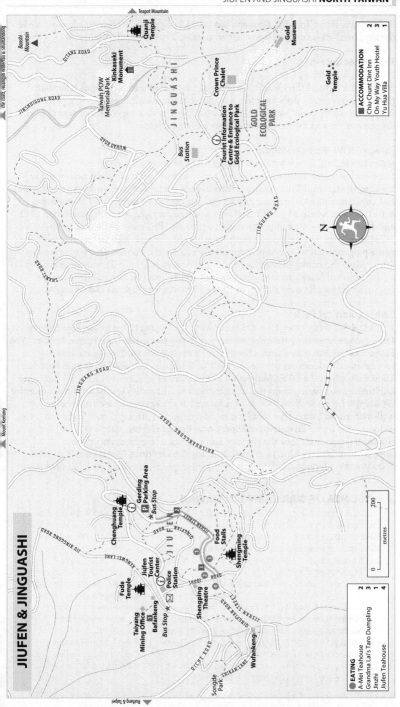

JIUFEN & JINGUASHI

Teapot Mountain
Baoshi Mountain
The coast, Huangjin Waterfall & Shuinandong
Mount Keelung
Ruifang & Taipei

Quanji Temple
QITANG ROAD
Kinkaseki Monument
Taiwan POW Memorial Park
JINSHUIGONG ROAD
WUHAO ROAD
J I N G U A S H I
Gold Museum
Crown Prince Chalet
Bus Station
Tourist Information Centre & Entrance to Gold Ecological Park
GOLD ECOLOGICAL PARK
Gold Temple
JINGUANG ROAD
SHANLU ROAD
JINGUANG ROAD
RUISHUANGGONG ROAD
MAIN ROAD

N

Chenghuang Temple
Gerding Parking Area
Bus Stop
JIU BINGGONG ROAD
FENGWEI LANE
Fude Temple
JIUFEN
Jiufen Tourist Center
Police Station
QINGBIAN ROAD
JISHAN STREET
Food Stalls
Shengping Temple
Taiyang Mining Office
Bafankeng
Bus Stop
Shengping Theatre
TUNR ROAD
Wufankeng
QINGBIAN ROAD
JISHAN STREET
SHIKAN LANE
Songde Park

ACCOMMODATION
Chiu Chunt Dint Inn 2
On My Way Youth Hostel 3
Yu Hua Villa 1

EATING
A-Mei Teahouse 2
Grandma Lai's Taro Dumpling .. 3
Jinzhi 1
Jiufen Teahouse 4

0   200
metres

lookout over the valley and "**Yingyang Sea**" (陰陽海; yīnyáng hǎi) below – the iron ore in the river here has stained the water yellow, creating a two-tone effect in the bay.

Teapot Mountain

茶壺山; cháhú shān

Steps to the right of the Quanji Temple lead to the trailhead for **Teapot Mountain** (580m), which really does look like a teapot if you're standing in the right place. It's a steep 2km climb to the summit along a stone path, with a rope-assisted scramble across the scree at the top, from where the views are magnificent.

Taiwan POW Memorial Park

金瓜石戰俘營; jīnguāshí zhànfúyíng • 40 Qitang Rd • Daily 24hr • Free • ⓦ powtaiwan.org

Steps lead downhill from Quanji Temple to a narrow lane: turn right here and you'll come to the tranquil **Taiwan POW Memorial Park** containing the Kinkaseki Monument and the remnant of a Japanese prisoner of war camp (see box below). A **memorial** marks the area where 1135 Allied POWs were incarcerated between November 1942 and March 1945 – the camp was known simply as "Prisoner of War Camp No. 1" or "Kinkaseki", the Japanese name for Jinguashi. The site now includes an eternal flame and a poignant statue of two prisoners by Wu Zong-Fu, dubbed *Partnership*, erected in 2011, while the names of over four thousand prisoners held in Taiwan are inscribed on a 17m polished black granite memorial wall. From here you can wander through Jinguashi, across the river and up to the Gold Ecological Park via **Old Qitang Alley**.

Gold Ecological Park

新北市立黃金博物館; xīnběi shìlì huángjīn bówùguǎn • 8 Jinguang Rd • Park (including Gold Museum) Mon–Fri 9.30am–5pm, Sat & Sun 9.30am–6pm (closed first Mon of every month) • Free • Benshan Fifth Tunnel Tours: Tues–Fri 9.30am, 1.30pm & 3.30pm, Sat & Sun 9.30am, 10.30am, 1.30pm, 3.30pm & 4.30pm • NT$80 • ☎ 02 2496 2800, ⓦ www.gep.ntpc.gov.tw

Occupying the slopes on the western side of Jinguashi, the **Gold Ecological Park** (also known simply as the "**Gold Museum**") is a mixture of museums and restored mining buildings, most dating from the Japanese period. The park's **tourist information centre** (遊客服務中心; yóukè fúwù zhōngxīn) is located at the entrance, and from here well-marked walkways lead to all the main sights. The principal trail leads past a row of food stalls to the **Environment Educational Center** (環境館; huánjìng guǎn) containing exhibits about the geology and ecology of the area, and a short introductory film. Behind here you'll find the **Crown Prince Chalet** (金瓜石太子賓館; jīnguāshí tàizǐ bīnguǎn), a distinctively Japanese guesthouse built in 1922 for Prince

---

PRISONER OF WAR CAMPS IN TAIWAN

Thailand's "death railway" is notorious in the English-speaking world (in part thanks to the film *Bridge on the River Kwai*), but few people are aware that the Japanese operated at least fifteen **POW camps** in Taiwan during World War II. More than 4300 men were incarcerated on the island, most of them British or Commonwealth troops captured in Hong Kong or Singapore, Dutch from Indonesia and Americans from the Philippines. Life was as brutal for the POWs here as anywhere else in Asia, with each camp revolving around a system of forced labour: in Camp No. 1, also known as **Kinkaseki** (金瓜石戰俘營; jīnguāshí zhànfúyíng) and the biggest, prisoners were forced to work in the Japanese copper mine in appalling conditions, while those at **Taichu Camp** (Camp No. 2), near Taichung, worked on a massive flood channel – many died from starvation, disease and ill-treatment. The camps were largely forgotten after the war, but thanks to a long campaign by former prisoners and expats living in Taiwan, a **memorial** was erected at the Kinkaseki site in 1997, and in 1999 the Taiwan POW Camps Memorial Society was formed to research all POW camps on the island (ⓦ powtaiwan.org). Several plaques have since been erected all over Taiwan, and a short memorial service takes place at Kinkaseki every year around November 11.

Hirohito's state visit the following year, though in the end he never made it up the mountain. Just before the Gold Museum, the **Benshan Fifth Tunnel** (本山五坑; běnshān wǔkēng) is a 180m section of renovated mine complete with wax exhibits – you have to join a tour to go inside. From here it's a short but steep walk up to the ruined **Gold Temple** (黃金神社; huángjīn shénshè), a Japanese Shinto shrine built in 1933 and later destroyed by fire.

Gold Museum

黃金館; huángjīn guǎn • Gold panning: daily 10.30am, 11.30am, 1.30pm, 2.30pm & 3.30pm • NT$100

2

Housed in the former Taiwan Metal Mining Company building at the end of the old rail track beyond the Benshan Tunnel, the **Gold Museum** focuses on the area's mining history. The highlight for many tourists is the chance to touch the **world's largest gold bar**, located on the second floor; at 220kg, it was worth just under US$10 million in early 2015. Suitably motivated, you can sign up for **gold panning** on the third floor. You're guaranteed to find gold dust – the museum adds some to each batch. There is also a small exhibition in the museum dedicated to the Kinkaseki POW camp.

Shuinandong

水湳洞; shuǐnǎn dòng • Jinshui Rd • Sat & Sun bus #826 passes the falls, otherwise it's a steep 30min walk down from the Gold Museum

Further down the Jinguashi River valley from the Gold Ecological Park, in the area known as **Shuinandong**, the remains of the old **copper refinery** (十三遺層; shísān yícéng or "Thirteen Levels" in Chinese), completed in 1933 and shuttered in 1981, make for a dramatic postindustrial landscape: the three serpent-like pipelines running up the mountainside are the world's longest smoke vents. The **Huangjin Waterfall** (黃金瀑布; huángjīn pùbù or "Golden Falls") nearby also gets its name from the iron and copper deposits in the river. Get oriented at the **Shuinandong Visitor Center**.

ARRIVAL AND DEPARTURE | JIUFEN AND JINGUASHI

BY BUS

Buses drop off at stops all along Qiche Rd in Jiufen, but it's best to wait until the stop at the top of the hill (Gerding Parking Area, near Jishan St) and walk downhill. Moving on, pick up buses at the junction of Qiche Rd and Shuqi Rd near the visitor centre. Buses to Jinguashi terminate on the eastern side of the valley at Quanji Temple.

From/to Taipei From Taipei, the fastest option to both towns is to take a train to Ruifang (every 30min–1hr; 45min), then switch to bus 788 to Jinguashi (20min), which first stop at Jiufen (15min). Buses depart from the opposite side of Mingdeng Rd from Ruifang station's main (west) exit; you'll need to walk a few blocks to the junction with Minquan St to find the bus stop (on the way back buses drop off in front of the station).

From/to Keelung Bus #1013 leaves Keelung (outside the train station) every 15min and takes around 30–40min to reach Ruifang, Jiufen and Jinguashi.

From/to Houtong Ultra-convenient bus #826 runs Sat & Sun only every 30min between Houtong, Jiufen, Jinguashi and Shuinandong.

Taiwan Tourist Shuttle Bus The Taiwan Tourist Shuttle Bus-Golden Fulong Route connects Jiufen, Jinguashi and Shuinandong with Fulong and other destinations along the coast: one-day tickets are NT$50 (or NT$15/trip), and buses run every hour Mon–Fri and every 30min on weekends.

BY TAXI

Taxis from Ruifang station operate under a fixed-rate system: NT$180 to Jiufen and NT$240 to Jinguashi.

GETTING AROUND AND INFORMATION

By bus Buses run frequently (every 15–30min; 5–10min) between Jiufen (along Qiche Rd) and Jinguashi (Quanji Temple and Gold Museum).

Tourist information The Jiufen Tourist Center (九份遊客中心; jiǔfèn yóukè zhōngxīn; daily 8am–6pm; ☎02 2406 3270) at 89 Qiche Rd (the main road towards the lower end of the town), has a small but informative exhibition and

English-language brochures; near Chenghuang Temple further up the hill, the Qingbian Road Visitor Center at 194 Qingbian Rd (daily 9am–9pm; ☎02 2497 3949) offers a similar spread of information. The Shuinandong Visitor Center (水湳洞遊客中心; shuǐnǎndòng yóukè zhōngxīn) is at 155-3 Dongding Rd (Tues–Sun 9.30am–5.30pm; ☎02 2486 1588).

ACCOMMODATION

JIUFEN

Chiu Chunt Dint Inn 九重町客棧; jiǔchóngdīng kèzhàn 29 Jishan St ☎02 2496 7680, ⊕9cd.com .tw; map p.135. Stylish, centrally located place above a Western-style café, with a traditional theme and comfy, elegant twins – the cheapest twins are small but a good deal on weekdays. NT$2300

On My Way Youth Hostel 途中國際青年旅舍, túzhōng guójì qīngnián lǚshè 23 Wushi ☎955 353228, ⊕onmywayhostel.com; map p.135. This lovely hostel tucked away off Jishan St is one of the few budget choices around. The welcoming manager leads free evening hikes. Coffee, tea and a simple breakfast are included. Check-in after 4pm. Dorms NT$600

Yu Hua Villa 御華山莊; yù huá shānzhuāng 23 Lane 8, Shuqi Rd; map p.135. ☎02 2406 3731, ⊕yes-go.com.tw. Friendly B&B in a delightful house perched on the slopes below the main drag, with helpful owners (the Lin family) who speak good English and a playful house cat, qiúqiú. There are comfy rooms, home-cooked breakfasts and gorgeous views. It's a steep walk up, but you can take the bus. NT$2700

EATING

Sampling the famous **snacks** on **Jishan St** (基山街) is an essential part of any visit to Jiufen; try the fish-ball soup, taro balls and roasted mushrooms. There are plenty of snack shops, local delicacy specialists and tourist novelty stores, hawking everything from ginger tea to charcoal chocolates. At the snack stalls expect to pay an average of NT$30–60 per dish. Business hours vary, but as a rule of thumb in Jiufen, places open and close early, from around 7am to 7pm.

JIUFEN

A-Mei Teahouse 阿妹茶酒館; āmèi chájiǔguǎn 20 Shixia Lane (above 121 Shuqi Rd) ☎02 2496 0833; map p.135. On the right as you descend the steps below Jishan St lies this multistorey Chinese palace with black wood and red lanterns. This spot featured heavily in *City of Sadness* – a faded board showing the Chinese characters for the film marks the steps up to the entrance and is a favourite photo spot for Taiwanese tourists. The teahouse across the street at no. 35 also claims a connection with the movie, though this seems to be more tenuous. Daily 8.30am–1am.

Grandma Lai's Taro Dumpling 賴阿婆芋圓; lài āpó yùyuán 143 Jishan St ☎02 2497 5245; map. p.135. A particular favourite for dessert lovers, *Grandma Lai's* serves sweet potato and tarot balls in soup (NT$40) – a Jiufen must-try. Daily around 7am–7pm.

Jinzhi 九份金枝紅糟肉圓; jiǔfèn jīnzhī hóngzāo ròuyuán 112 Jishan St ☎02 2496 0240; map. p.135. A big hit since it opened back in 1994, this snack joint sells sumptuous translucent-rice meatballs, stuffed with herb-infused pork and bamboo shoots flavoured with rice wine (around NT$50). Vegetarian equivilants, stuffed with tofu, can be found just across the street. Daily around 7am–7pm.

Jiufen Teahouse 九份茶坊; jiǔfèn cháfāng ☎02 2496 9056, ⊕jioufen-teahouse.com.tw; map p.135. *Jiufen Teahouse* is one of the highlights of Jiufen. It occupies the gorgeous old mining bureau's headquarters, which dates back over a century (though the teashop opened in 1991) – make sure you get a wooden booth with a view, or have your tea outside on the terrace. There's a NT$100 charge per person, in addition to the price of a tea set (NT$400–900), but the ambience, views and service make up for the cost. The tea (in 37.5g bags), warmed on charcoal, lasts for hours – you can take the leftovers home. Daily 10.30am – 9.30pm.

Pingxi Branch Rail Line

平溪支線; píngxī zhīxiàn

The scenic **PINGXI BRANCH RAIL LINE** makes a rewarding day-trip from Taipei, winding its way almost 13km up the Keelung River valley to the atmospheric village of Jingtong and passing through the old mining communities of Pingxi and Shifen. For much of the twentieth century this was the heart of Taiwan's **coal industry** (the line was completed in 1921 by the Japanese) and, though the mines have all now closed, you'll find several reminders of its industrial past scattered around the valley. These days, however, it's the mountain scenery, **hiking trails** and **waterfalls** that attract most of the tourists. The valley is also the location for one of Taiwan's most captivating **lantern festivals**.

Houtong
猴硐; hóudòng

The first stop on the Pingxi Branch Rail Line is **HOUTONG**, a virtually abandoned mining village 4.5km and five minutes down the track from Ruifang. This is the latest Taiwanese post-industrial site to get the tourism treatment, its eerie old buildings and pits being transformed into the **Houtong Coal Mine Ecological Park**, though rather bizarrely, it has also developed a reputation as a "**cat village**" (猴硐貓村; hóudòng māocūn), thanks to the hordes of feral moggies that thrive here. Across the specially decorated bridge, **Guangfuli** (光復里; guāngfùlǐ), south of the train station features a dedicated "cat village" visitor centre, cutesy "cat houses" and loads of cartoonish cat sculptures, with over a hundred real cats lounging on the steps and pathways. No one really knows the reason for the cat connection; the popular theory is that once the mine closed in the late 1990s, the now-abandoned pet cats were taken care of by one or two kind individuals, and the cats rapidly reproduced.

Houtong Coal Mine Ecological Park
猴硐煤礦博物園區; hóutóng méikuàng bówùyuánqū • Free • Tourist information centre daily 9am–6pm • ☎ 02 2497 4143

The Houtong area developed as a mining centre in the 1890s, with the major Rui-san Mining opening in 1934 – the last pit closed in 1990, devastating the local community. What remains of the mining infrastructure has been converted into the **Houtong Coal Mine Ecological Park**, a series of museums and ruins spread along the valley either side of the village. Get oriented at the **tourist information centre** near the station, set in the old coal plant office built by the Japanese in 1935. Here you can get information on all the local temples, Japanese Shinto shrines and mountain trails to explore.

Next door to the visitor centre, at 44 Chailiao Rd, the **Vision Hall** (愿景馆; yuànjǐng guǎn; daily 9am–6pm; free; ☎02 2497 4143) contains background on the history of the area. Nearby, looming over the village and train station, is the half-ruined hulk of the **Coal Preparation Plant**, built in 1920. Just under 1km southwest along the riverbank stands the reconstructed **Sand Drying Building** (烘沙室及干部浴室; hōngshāshì jí gànbù yùshì; Mon–Fri 9am–11.30am & 1.30–5pm, Sat & Sun 9am–5pm; free), featuring exhibits in English on the fascinating ecology and geology of the area. The

---

RIDING THE PINGXI BRANCH RAIL LINE

The **Pingxi Branch Rail Line** starts at the coastal town of **Baodouzi** (八斗子; bādòuzǐ), though most people begin the journey at Ruifang (瑞芳; ruìfāng) – connected by express trains to Taipei (45min) or frequent buses from Jiufen and Keelung. The Pingxi Line runs along the main line for 8km to Sandiaoling before breaking off and following the upper Keelung River valley to Jingtong (45–55min). You can buy an all-day **Pingxi Line pass** at Ruifang Station for NT$80, or pay per journey – the maximum is NT$29 (one-way) for the Ruifang to Jingtong trip (trips between Jingtong, Shifen and Pingxi are just NT$15). Trains **depart** Ruifang at roughly hourly intervals from 5.20am to 9.12pm; the last train leaves Jingtong at 10.12pm.

You'll find a handy **visitor information centre** inside Ruifang Station (daily 9am–6pm; ☎02 2497 3813).

PINGXI BY BUS

An alternative from Taipei is to take the #795 **bus**, which connects Muzha with Jingtong, Pingxi, Shifen and Shifen Visitor Center (40min to Pingxi; 50min to Shifen; NT$45, EasyCard accepted), and join the train from there. The bus departs from the opposite side of Muzha Road from Muzha MRT station (clearly marked in English) at 7.15am, 8.20am, 9.45am, 10.20am, 11am, 11.20am and thereafter roughly every hour until 10.40pm (more frequently Sat & Sun). The last bus leaves Shifen for Muzha at 8.35pm. Buses pass through Shenkeng, another worthwhile stop (see p.118).

Bus #826 runs Sat & Sun only (9am–6.30pm) every 30min between Houtong, Jiufen, Jinguashi and Shuinandong (NT$15).

building connects to the **Miners Memorial Hall** (礦工紀念館; kuànggōng jìniànguǎn; Mon–Fri 9am–11.30am & 1.30–5pm, Sat & Sun 9am–5pm); this 1960s bathhouse has a display showing just how grim life in the mines could be – women worked alongside the men till 1964, and black lung disease was rampant.

There's another park **visitor centre** (daily 8am–noon & 1–5pm; ☎02 2497 4143), 700m northeast of Houtong station along Chailiao Road, which has a little more background on the area, but isn't worth the walk if you've already visited the above attractions.

Shifen

十分; shí fēn

Three stops from Houtong, the village of **SHIFEN** gets swamped at weekends by tourists who come primarily to gawp at its celebrated **waterfall**, located back towards Ruifang, on the eastern side of Shifen. The village is also a good place to see and launch "heavenly lanterns" which are sold at several shops along the railway line.

Coal Mine Museum

新平溪煤礦博物園區; xīnpíngxī méikuàng bówùyuánqū • 5 Dingliaozi, Xinliao Village (off Shifen St) • Tues–Sun 9.30am–5pm • NT$200 • ☎02 2495 8680

Shifen's **Coal Mine Museum** (aka "New Pingxi Mine Ecological Park") is a worthy detour en route to Shifen Waterfall; follow the train tracks through the centre of the village, then Shifen Street as it bears left, and you'll pass the entrance a short walk ahead. The museum is actually the abandoned New Pingxi Coal Mine and processing plant, the whole thing eerily frozen in time from the day the miners stopped working in 1997. The site has two parts. The main entrance stands beside the old processing plant, and from here a trail follows a conveyor belt, still littered with coal, up a slope and to the beginning of a narrow-gauge rail line. Here you board a train for the bone-shaking, painfully slow 1km ride to the second area at the mine head, where you'll find a collection of exhibition rooms (Chinese labels only) and the **mineshaft** itself, the most interesting part of the site – you can walk 100m into the mountain.

Shifen Waterfall

十分瀑布; shí fēn pùbù • 11 Gankeng • Daily 9am–7pm • Free

The town's pride and joy, **Shifen Waterfall** is a fifteen-minute walk from the visitor centre, along a trail that starts at the back of the building and crosses the river twice before rejoining the rail tracks. En route you'll pass **Eyeglass Hole Waterfall** (眼鏡洞瀑布; yǎnjìngdòng pùbù), named after the two hollows that have been eroded into the rock behind it. The main falls are 15m high and 30m wide, not quite Niagara, but impressive nonetheless, and wonderfully photogenic, especially in full flood (usually Oct–March).

INFORMATION   **SHIFEN**

Tourist information Shifen Visitor Center (十分遊客中心; shífēn yóukè zhōngxīn; daily 8am–5.30pm; ☎02 2495 8409) has maps, information and a small café.

The centre lies 1.5km back along the tracks from Shifen station via Ruiping Rd, and across a bridge over the Keelung River (all well signposted).

ACCOMODATION AND EATING

Aztecas Mexican Grill 阿斯塔可墨西哥餐; āsītǎkě mòxīgē cān 176 Shifen St ☎02 2495 8638. A Tex-Mex joint in the least likely of all places, this small restaurant is the retirement project of Johnson Lee, who returned from the US to his native village. The food (NT$120 for a burrito, chips and soft drink) is pretty average, but the owner is hospitable, speaks some English and offers travel advice. Daily 10am – 9pm.

Lou-A-Chu 樓仔厝; lóuzǎicuò 3 Gang, 74 Shifen St ☎02 2495 8602, ⓦlouachu.okgo.tw. Near the Jingan suspension bridge, occupying a historical building dating back to 1922, this guesthouse and café oozes charm and is full of coal industry memorabilia. Out on the terrace you can enjoy a Taiwan oolong tea (NT$180), and overnight accommodation is available in one of the mine-themed boutique rooms. NT$2300

Pingxi

平溪; píngxī • If you're arriving by bus rather than on the Pingxi Branch Rail Line, note that you'll be dropped on Jinguan Rd, just across the river from Old St

The penultimate stop on the Pingxi Branch Rail Line, **PINGXI** is one of the valley's most atmospheric villages, though there's not much to see beyond the Guanyin Temple unless you visit during the **Lantern Festival**, when the village (along with Shifen) is home to one of Taiwan's most mesmerizing spectacles (see box below). From the station, Zhonghua Street leads down to narrow **Pingxi Old Street** (平溪老街; píngxī lǎojiē), lined with gift shops and decent places to eat, though the options can be limited Monday to Thursday.

2

EATING

PINGXI

Corner 28 街角28; jiējiǎo 28 28 Zhonghua St ☏ 0919 946 425. This extremely cute wooden chalet overlooks the train tracks. Try the tasty cakes, which you can wash down with coffee or tea. Cash only. Sat 11am–9.30pm (sometimes opens other days).

Pingxi Taro Ball Shop 平溪芋圓店; píngxī yùyuándiàn 23 Pingxi St, near the junction with Zhonghua St ☏ 02 2495 2108. Humble old food stall

selling simple but tasty bowls of taro ball desserts for NT$40–60. Daily 8am–10pm.

Red Turtle Noodles 紅龜麵店; hóngguī miàndiàn 10 Gongyuan St, the lane on the other side of Old St from Zhonghua St ☏ 02 2495 1286. Simple canteen selling bowls of tasty noodles and braised tofu from NT$40. Daily 8am–6pm.

Jingtong

菁桐; jīngtóng

The old mining village of **JINGTONG** is another reminder of the valley's industrial past – mining ceased here in 1987. It's the final stop on the line or a 1.8km walk from Pingxi station, along the road that follows the tracks. The small wooden **train station**, built in 1931 by the Japanese, stands on narrow **Old Street** (Jingtong St), lined with small shops and snack stalls. You'll also notice hundreds of small bamboo wind chimes (zhútǒng fēnglíng) hanging all over the place (check out the tree back along the tracks), inscribed with messages; the practice is supposedly in memory of two local lovers and is popular with young couples who hang them up for luck – you can write your own for NT$40.

Jingtong Mine Museum

菁桐礦業生活館; jīngtóng kuàngyè shēnghuóguǎn • 117 Jingtong St • Tues–Sun 9.30am–5pm • Free • ☏ 02 2495 2749

Just to the left of the train station is the **Jingtong Mine Museum**, which displays information about the area and the old mine, with a few mining artefacts (mostly old photos and maps), though there are no English labels. The building itself once served as railway staff dormitories.

THE SKY LANTERNS OF PINGXI

The **Pingxi Sky Lantern Festival** (ⓦpingxiskylantern.tw) celebrates the end of Chinese Lunar New Year, usually in February or early March. During that time, hundreds of **"heavenly lanterns"**, or tiāndēng are released into the night sky above Pingxi and Shifen – it's an enchanting sight, but you'll need to arrive early (the first mass launch is usually at 6.30pm) and brave serious crowds to enjoy it. The lanterns are lit by flames, and they rise up like balloons, each one representing a wish: white symbolizes peace, pink means happiness and orange is wealth. Outside of the festival, you can buy and launch individual lanterns (NT$150–200) from stalls near Pingxi train station on Zhonghua Street – at weekends you'll probably see them being launched right on the tracks, though the sight of them littering the countryside might put you off joining in.

2

SCALING THE PEAKS OF PINGXI

Pingxi is surrounded by some tantalizing **hiking trails**. Walk through the village and across the river to the main road – turn left here and in a few metres you should pass a signposted trail on the right leading to **Putuo Mountain** (普陀山; pǔtuóshān; 450m) and **Xiaozi Mountain** (孝子山; xiàozǐshān; 360m), both just 1km away (allow 2hr round-trip for each trail). The summit of the latter is one of the most dramatic on the island; a steep tower of rock scaled by steel ladders – the views are impressive, but don't try the climb on a wet day.

Coal Mine Memorial Park

煤礦紀念公園; méikuàng jìniàn gōngyuán • 50 Jingtong St • Daily 24hr • Free

The area above and behind Jingtong station is dominated by the **Coal Mine Memorial Park**, the remains of the Shidi Mine that closed in 1979. A path on the other side of the tracks leads first to the derelict coal preparation plant (1921), topped by a small café, and, further up the hill, the ruins of the mine-head buildings and the main tunnel, sealed by an iron-bar gate.

Pingxi Guesthouse of Taiyang Mining Company

臺陽礦業公司平溪招待所; táiyáng kuàngyè gōngsī píngxī zhāodàisuǒ • 167 Jingtong St • Mon 10am–5pm (and nominally Tues–Sun 10am–5pm) • Mon free; Tues–Sun (if open) NT$150 • ☎ 02 2495 2782 • Over-13s only

Old Street officially ends at the main road (Shuangjing Rd) overlooking the bridge, where buses stop – turn right here, and take the lane down to the Keelung River and the **Pingxi Guesthouse of Taiyang Mining Company**, a beautifully restored Japanese house built in 1939. Formerly, but erroneously, known as the **Crown Prince Hotel**, the building actually served as a club and guesthouse for the Taiyang Mining Company. In 1986, the building was sold to current owner Wang Zhen to become a Buddhist learning centre (真樸齋; zhēnpǔ zhāi), but after accepting public funds for a massive restoration, in 2012 Wang agreed to open the showcase Japanese property to limited public visits.

EATING AND DRINKING   JINGTONG

★**Palace Tea House** 皇宮茶坊; huánggōng cháfāng 5 Baishi Village ☎ 02 2495 2021. One of several beautifully preserved old Japanese dormitories built around 1938 on the other side of the Keelung River, this enticing restaurant and teahouse offers a choice of tables with tatami mats or chairs – you can order tea (NT$350–500 per pot) or light meals such as stewed chicken with basil (NT$280). English menu available. To get here, walk around the Pingxi Guesthouse and cross the river: turn immediately right then left up an alley and you'll see it on the right. Wed–Sun 10.30am–9pm.

Northeast and Yilan Coast National Scenic Area

東北角暨宜蘭海岸國家風景區; dōngběijiǎo jìyílán hǎiàn guójiā fēngjǐngqū

The **Northeast and Yilan Coast National Scenic Area** incorporates some of Taiwan's most spectacular coastal scenery, stretching 102.5km from Nanya, just east of Jiufen, to Suao. Accessible by bus or train, the area can be covered as a series of lengthy day-trips from Taipei or Keelung, though **Fulong**, with its attractive **beach**, is a gateway to the region (and home to the Scenic Area **visitor centre**) and a more convenient base for longer stays. Highlights include the network of **hiking trails** between Bitou Cape and Longdong and the surfing hotspot of **Daxi**. To the south, the towns of **Jiaoxi** and **Luodong** (just outside the Scenic Area proper) are worthy detours before heading on to Hualien.

GETTING AROUND   NORTHEAST AND YILAN COAST NATIONAL SCENIC AREA

BY BUS

The northern section The Taiwan Tourist Shuttle Bus-Golden Fulong Route (ⓦ www.gold-fulong.com.tw) runs between the Fulong Visitor Center and Ruifang station via Aodi, Longdong, Bitou and the Jiufen area. One-day tickets are NT$50 (or NT$15/trip); buses run every hour on weekdays (9am–4pm) and every 30min on weekends (8am–4pm). There's also bus #791 from Keelung to Fulong (daily every 30min–1hr 30min; 1hr), which stops at Bitou (30–40min), Longdong (35–45min) and Aodi (45–50min). Catch it at the Keelung bus stop, opposite the train station (see p.132) – the bus should be marked in English. **The southern section** For destinations south of Fulong you can pick up daily Kuo Kuang buses (#1811/1812) from Taipei West Bus Station: these stop outside the 7-Eleven in Fulong (near the train station) at 10am, 11am, noon, 4pm, 7.30pm and 10pm, before passing all the major attractions as far south as Luodong.

BY TRAIN
Fulong is accessible from Taipei by frequent express trains. Trains continue south from here to Daxi, Jiaoxi, Luodong and Hualien.

Bitou Cape
鼻頭角; bítuó jiǎo

BITOU (鼻頭; bítóu) is a small fishing community that lies at the trailhead to **Bitou Cape**, a rugged outcrop of layered sandstone and one of Taiwan's most scenic pieces of coastline. Arriving from Keelung, get off the bus before the tunnel on the edge of the village. From here there's a choice of two **hiking trails**. The **Lighthouse Trail** (燈塔線; dēngtǎ xiàn; 1.2km) starts across the bridge over the road, but for the best **views** head back into the village for the **Ridge Valley Trail** (稜谷線; lénggǔ xiàn; 1.1km), which starts on the right side of the harbour near the temple. All the trails are well marked in English – the latter rises steeply over the top of the cape to join the main trail on the southern side. There's the 12m-tall **Bitou Cape Lighthouse** (鼻頭角燈塔; bítóujiǎo dēngtǎ) at the end, but it's the magnificent views that make the hike worthwhile.

Longdong
龍洞; lóngdòng

From the Bitou Cape Lighthouse, follow the **Coastal Trail** (0.8km) along the seashore, passing a cluster of bizarre geological formations to **Longdong Bay Park** (龍洞灣公園; lóngdòngwān gōngyuán; June–Oct Mon–Fri 8am–5.30pm, Sat & Sun 7am–6pm; NT$100; ☎02 2490 9258), a series of sea-fed swimming pools next to the main road. From here it's another 2km around the bay to **LONGDONG** village – the stone pools here are abalone farms. Longdong's popular **rock climbing** area (龍洞岩場; lóngdòng yánchǎng) is a further 1.5km around the next cape, the 30m sandstone cliffs packed with climbers at weekends. The start of the trail to **Longdong Coastal Park** is clearly marked back in the village, climbing 100m above the cliffs and providing several stunning viewpoints. The trail ends at the main road and a bus stop 4km from **Aodi** (澳底; àodǐ), a largely unattractive fishing port famous for its wholesale fish market (daily 5–9am) and the **seafood restaurants** that line its main street.

Fulong
福隆; fúlóng

Just under 6km south of Aodi, **FULONG** has one of north Taiwan's best **beaches**, with heaps of fine sand surrounded by a ring of lush mountains and several enticing **cycle trails**. It's also the most convenient place to stay on the northeast coast, and famous in Taiwan for its **lunchboxes** or biàndāng, typically grilled pork or fish with a boiled egg, several types of vegetables and rice. Since 1999 Fulong has also been home to the **Ho-Hai-Yan Rock Festival** (held over three days in mid-July; free), whose mainly Taiwanese and Japanese bands attract up to half a million visitors.

Fulong Beach
福隆海水浴場; fúlóng hǎishuǐ yùchǎng • 40 Fulong St • June–Oct daily 9am–5pm • NT$100 • ☎02 2499 2381

The main entrance to **Fulong Beach** – a long spit of sand at the mouth of the Shuangxi River – is just beyond the visitor centre, next to the *Fullon Hotel*. Though it's officially

2

THE CAOLING HISTORIC TRAIL

The **Caoling Historic Trail** (草嶺古道; cǎolǐng gǔdào) is a 9.7km path that cuts across the hills between Fulong and Dali – it's a beautiful walk with mesmerizing views of the ocean at its southern end, and is easily covered in half a day. The trail incorporates the only remaining section of a stone trail, built in 1807 by Taiwan's first settlers, to link Tamsui with Yilan; the most historic sight en route is the **Tiger Tablet**, a stone flamboyantly engraved with the Chinese character for "Tiger". The story goes that military official Liu Ming-deng made the carving in 1867 in allusion to the mythical powers tigers have to control powerful winds: you'll probably see why this is appropriate when you reach the head of the pass nearby.

The trail can be tackled in either direction, though the steepest climb is the 2.8km between Dali and the pass – the route climbs more smoothly from Fulong, which also has more convenient rail connections. A new 3.5km route links Fulong to the head of the main trail; from **Fulong station** walk to the main road and turn left – you'll see the first sign about 150m further along directing you back under the tracks. In **Dali** (大里; dàlǐ), the trail ends at the back of the surprisingly large **Tiangong Temple** (天公廟; tiāngōng miào), 33 Binhai Rd Sec 7, dedicated to the Jade Emperor and a popular pilgrimage site. Just next door, at 11 Binhai Rd Sec 7, the **Dali Visitor Center** (大里遊客中心; dàlǐ yóukè zhōngxīn; daily 9am–5pm; June–Aug 8.30am–5.30pm; ☏ 03 978 0727) houses decent exhibitions on the area and particularly its Ketagalan inhabitants, but only in Chinese. Dali train station is a short walk along the main road.

open June to October, during which time there's a fee; if you approach the beach via the southern end of the village, you'll find a free section which is open all year round. The sand is fine, but tends to get covered in flotsam in winter, when it's not cleaned. While **swimming** is the main draw here, the beach sometimes gets waves suitable for **surfing**.

Caoling Tunnel Bikeway

舊草嶺自行車隧道; jiùcǎolǐng zìxíngchē suìdào • Daily: June–Sept 8.30am–5.30pm; Oct–May 8.30am–5pm • Free

The **Caoling Tunnel Bikeway** is the most popular cycle path in the area, a 5km ride beginning at the train station, taking in the 1924 Japanese railway tunnel (2.1km) and ending with stupendous views of Turtle Island at the **Shicheng Scenic Area** (石城觀景區; shíchéng guānjǐngqū) and coffee shop. Note that a 19km bike lane along Provincial Highway 2 (the coast road) links Shicheng with Fulong, creating a 27km loop via **Sandiaojiao** (三貂角; sāndiāo jiǎo), Taiwan's most easterly point.

Yanliao Beach Park

鹽寮海濱公園; yánliáo hǎibīn gōngyuán • 45 Yanhai St • Daily 9am–6pm • May–Oct NT$90; Nov–April NT$60 • ☏ 02 2490 3991 • Information boards in English and Chinese

As well as the Caoling Tunnel Bikeway, the other worthwhile ride in Fulong is the Longmen–Yanliao Bikeway (龍門鹽寮自行車道; lóngmén yánliáo zìxíngchē dào), a 4km trail across the Longmen Suspension Bridge over the Shuangxi River and through the dunes, north to **Yanliao Beach Park** (where bikes must be left at the entrance). This beautiful beach is part of Taiwan's longest continuous stretch of sand (3km) and is the spot where the **Japanese invasion** force landed in May 1895 – a stone monument (鹽寮抗日紀念碑; yánliáo kàngrì jìniànbēi) commemorates those who died resisting the occupation, while information boards describe the main events of the initial invasion.

ARRIVAL AND INFORMATION	FULONG

By bus Taiwan Tourist Shuttle Bus-Golden Fulong Route buses (see p.137) and Keelung buses terminate in the car park at the visitor centre.

By train The train station is in the centre of town at 2 Fulong St, a short walk from the main drag (Xinglong St).
Destinations Daxi (hourly; 13–20min); Jiaoxi (every 30min–1hr; 26–35min); Luodong (every 30min–1hr;

50–55min); Hualien (8 daily; 2hr–2hr 30min); Taipei (every 30min–1hr 4min–1hr 12min).

Tourist information The main Northeast Coast Scenic Area Visitor Center (福隆遊客中心; fúlóng yóukè zhōngxīn; daily: Jan–May & Oct–Dec 9am–5pm; June–Sept 8.30am–5.30pm; ☏ 02 2499 1210, ⓦ www.necoast-nsa.gov.tw) is on the edge of town at 36 Xinglong St. To get there from the train station, walk to the main road and turn left – you'll see the centre across the car park on your right.

There's plenty of information available and several exhibition rooms inside.

ACTIVITIES

Surfing You can usually rent surfboards (NT$600/day) and bodyboards (NT$300/day) at shops close to the train station, including Being Outdoors (地球人戶外休閒家; dìqiúrén hùwài xiū xián jīa; ☎ 02 2499 1372 or ☎ 0919 575372; ☻ being0125@gmail.com).

Cycling Rent bicycles (NT$100/day) from the shops outside the train station; the bike paths around Fulong are well marked in English.

ACCOMMODATION AND EATING

Beijing Outdoor 地球人戶外休閒家; dìqiú rénhù wàixiū jiānjiā 16 Fulong St. ☎ 24991392. This foreigner-friendly B&B, situated not far from the train station, offers simple, clean rooms, a pleasant coffee shop and surf lessons (price negotiable). NT$1200

Fullon Hotel Fulong 福容大飯店; fúróng dàfàndiàn 41 Fulong St ☎ 02 68907722, ⓦ fullon-hotels.com.tw. This rather imposing luxury hotel opened in 2016 and now dominates the coastline. There are indoor and outdoor swimming pools, three restaurants, hot spring suites and Japanese-style villas. NT$7000

Longmen Campsite 龍門露營區; lóngmén lùyíng qū 100 Xinglong St ☎ 02 2499 1791. The biggest campsite in Taiwan, offering tents for up to four, pitches for those bringing their own tents and chalet-type rooms. Plenty of water-based activities are on offer, including fishing and rafting. There are showers, a swimming pool (NT$60) and a small shop on site. Bike rental costs NT$80/hr; it's NT$70 to enter the site and access the facilities if you're not staying there. Tents for up to 4 NT$800, camping pitches NT$650, chalets NT$2300

Xiangye 鄉野便當; xiāngyě biàndāng 1 Fulong St ☎ 02 2499 1417. The most famous place to sample Fulong's celebrated biàndāng lunchboxes (NT$60) is at this venerable shop just outside the train station entrance. Daily 7am–7pm.

Daxi and Waiao

大溪; dàxī

Some 24km southwest of Fulong, **DAXI** is a once tranquil town that has become one of Taiwan's premier **surf centres** (not to be confused with the Daxi on the North Cross-Island Highway). It is widely considered to have the most consistent beach break

SURFING PRACTICALITIES IN DAXI AND WAIAO

Several surf shops in Daxi and Waiao offer **surfing packages** that include accommodation, meals, lessons and board rentals; if you just want to hire a board, expect to pay around NT$600 per day.

DAXI

Jeff's Surf Shop 衝浪俱樂部; "Jeff's" chōnglàng jùlèbù 100 Binhai Rd Sec 5; ☎ 936 529 090, ⓦ facebook.com/JeffSurf/TW. Run by Jeff Sun (aka Máo Gē), one of Taiwan's seminal surfers, this place offers excellent two-day/one-night surfing packages for NT$3500, including meals and board rental.

Spider Surf Club 台灣蜘蛛衝浪俱樂部; táiwān zhīzhū chōnglàng jùlèbù 96 Binhai Rd Sec 5; ☎ 936464686, ⓦ spidersurfing.com. Next door to Jeff's, Spider is popular with young surfers who spend weekends in the cheap but dingy basement a/c dorm (cheaper out of season). Their two-day/one-night surfing costs NT$3000, and the club's website has limited English information on daily conditions. Shop daily 8am–7pm (Sat & Sun only outside of summer). Dorms NT$300

WAIAO

Rising Sun Surf Inn 236 Binhai Rd Sec 2; ☎ 03 977 0933, ⓦ risingsunsurfinn.com. English-speaking staff at here can hook you up with boards, lessons and accommodation. One-day surf lesson packages start at NT$1500; boards are NT$500/day. Dorms NT$500, doubles NT$1500

Johnny Rose Surf School 強尼玫瑰衝浪學校; qiángní méiguī chōnglàng xuéxiào 213, Sec 2 Binhai Rd; ☎ 0937 823583, ⓦ jrsurf.com. Run by local surfer Johnny Hu, this is Waiao's one-stop surf shop. From board shorts to sun glasses, this is the place to get kitted out for your surf safari. They also run surf classes – check the website for details.

> ## GUISHAN ISLAND
>
> From **Toucheng**, one train stop south of Waiao, the Kuo Kuang bus #1877 from Yuan Shan or Nangang Exhibition stations connects with Wushi Harbour. From here, you can take a boat (daily 9am and 1pm; NT$1200) to the offshore island of **Guishan** (龜山島; guīshāndǎo) otherwise known as **Turtle Island**. The best time of year for dolphin-watching trips (NT$1200) is March to October. Some hotels, including *Rising Sun* (236, Section 2, Binhai Rd, ☎ 03 977 0933, ⓦ risingsunsurfinn.com) can help book your trip, or you can book a trip independently by calling (☎ 02 2499 115) or following advice on the tourist bureau website: ⓦ eng.taiwan.net.tw.

in northern Taiwan, and the waves on the edge of town in **Honeymoon Bay** (蜜月灣; mìyuè wān) hold great appeal for experienced and novice surfers alike. With typically hollow faces, the waves still have enough power and speed to lend themselves to shortboards and quick take-offs. Although Daxi can be surfed year-round, the biggest waves occur in **winter** – particularly in March – when faces of up to 3m can be had, though the water is cold at this time and you'll definitely need a wetsuit.

A ten-minute train ride away, along the black volcanic sands of **WAIAO** (外澳; wàiào) there is also developing a surf scene; the best breaks are off the beach 500m north from the train station. In winter, the waves here are fast, and not really recommended for beginners.

ARRIVAL AND DEPARTURE
DAXI AND WAIAO

By train Daxi is just 15min from Fulong by train (hourly). From the station, cross the street after you exit: the surf shops are about 100m to the left, while the beach is about 500m down the road to the right. Waiao is two stops south of Daxi (and 22–30min from Fulong).

EATING

★**Drifters Pizza Pub** 漂流者外澳披薩吧; piāoliúzhě wàiào pīsàbā 231, Sec 2, Binhai Rd, next to Waiao Station ☎ 0938 330735, ⓦ drifterspizza@ gmail.com. This bodacious Waiao surfer haunt is run by Californian surfer Garrett Bell. As well as craft beer (NT$170) and tasty pizzas (NT$270–350), *Drifters* hosts parties and bands on Sat and Sun, making it popular with Taipei weekenders. Daily except Weds 11am–11pm.

Jiaoxi

礁溪; jiāoxī

Some 20km south of Daxi, the inland resort town of **JIAOXI** is best known for its **hot springs** and the spectacular **waterfalls** just outside the city. Jiaoxi's bicarbonate hot-spring water is clear and odourless, and is piped into the dozens of **spa hotels** in town. Jiaoxi is celebrated for the relatively humble **spring onion pancake** (cōngyóubǐng) and its annual crop of zesty kumquats (jīnjú).

Wufengqi Falls

五峰旗瀑布; wǔfēngqí pùbù • Wufeng Rd, 3.5km west of Jiaoxi train station • Daily 24hr • Free • ☎ 03 988 0940 • Taxis should charge around NT$140 from central Jiaoxi (make sure you take your driver's number if you want a ride back)

Comprising three separate cascades, the **Wufengqi Falls** are among the most impressive in Taiwan. The upper two falls are thin threads of water plummeting dramatically over sheer, moss-smothered bluffs at least 30m high – the first falls are the highest and most spectacular. A paved pathway leads some 550m to the top, but it's a steep climb. Just before the trailhead is a line of **food stalls** selling an assortment of snacks and drinks, usually including the area's famed crop of **kumquats** (NT$50/bag).

Jiaoxi Hot Springs Park

礁溪溫泉公園; jiāoxī wēnquán gōngyuán • 16 Gongyuan Rd • Daily 24hr (usually closed 7–9am for cleaning) • Footbaths free; Forest Baths NT$150 • ☎ 03 987 2403

Jiaoxi is littered with hot-spring spas, but the most atmospheric place for a dip is the **Jiaoxi Hot Springs Park**, a newish area of pools and baths in the style of a plush Japanese spa just ten minutes' walk from the train station. The footbath area near the entrance is free, but to enjoy the beautiful **Forest Baths** (森林風呂; sēnlín fēnglǚ) you need to pay the admission charge. Note that most Taiwanese bathers opt to go nude.

ARRIVAL AND INFORMATION   JIAOXI

By train Jiaoxi station (礁溪車站; jiāoxī chēzhàn) is at 1 Wenquan Rd, near Zhongshan Rd in the centre of town. Numerous services run from/to Taipei (1hr 10min–2hr 20min) via Fulong and south to Hualien (1hr 5min–2hr).

By bus Kamalan buses run frequently from/to Taipei Bus Station (45min), and continue to Luodong (15–20min). Buses drop you at 150 Jiaoxi Rd Sec 5, a short walk from the train station. The useful Taiwan Tourist Shuttle Bus-Jiaoxi Route runs from the train station to the Jiaoxi Hot Springs

Visitor Center and the Wufengqi Falls (Mon–Fri 8am–5pm hourly, Sat & Sun 8am–5.30pm every 30min; NT$20 one-way).

Tourist information The well-stocked Tourist Information Center of Jiaoxi (礁溪溫泉會館/遊客服務中心; jiāoxī wēnquán huìguǎn/yóukè fúwù zhōngxīn; Mon–Fri & Sun 9am–5.30pm, Sat 9am–8pm; ☏ 03 987 2403) is located inside the Jiaoxi Hot Springs Park at 16 Gongyuan Rd.

ACCOMMODATION AND EATING

Chuan Tang Hotel 川湯溫泉養生館; chuāntāng wēnquán yǎngshēngguǎn 218 Zhongshan Rd Sec 2 ☏ 03 988 0606, ⓦ www.chuang-tang.com.tw. One of the most elaborate public bathing complexes in town is the first hotel on the right after you exit the train station (the sign just says "Hotel" in English). Rooms feature a sleek, contemporary design, and non-guests can use its several bathing pools with massage showers for NT$300 (open 24hr). NT$3600

Guan Xiang Century Resort Hotel 礁溪冠翔世紀溫泉會館; jiāoxī guānxiáng shìjì wēnquán

huìguǎn 6 Lane 66, Renai Rd ☏ 03 987 5599, ⓦ www.hotspring-hotel.com.tw. This plush hotel boasts huge Japanese-style rooms with hardwood floors and spa pools. Non-guests can use the lavish spa facilities for NT$500 (daily 8am–10pm). NT$7200

Jiaoxi Spring Onion Pancake 礁溪柯氏蔥油餅; jiāoxī kēshì cōngyóubǐng 128 Jiaoxi Rd Sec 4 ☏ 0972 158603. Try Jiaoxi's famous deep-fried snack at this much-loved stall (going since 1970), with a choice of three different sauces and an egg topping (NT$25–30). Mon–Fri 9am–6.30pm, Sat & Sun 9am–7pm.

Yilan

宜蘭市; yílánshì

The county capital of **YILAN** is a pleasant if unremarkable Taiwanese city. If you're staying here, it's worth visiting the **Dongmen Night Market** (東門夜市; dōngmén yèshì; daily from 5pm), a five-minute walk west of the historic train station, where a variety of snacks and knickknacks are on sale. Most visitors come to Yilan to visit the nearby **Kavalan Distillery** (Yuanshan Rd; Mon–Fri 9am – 6pm, Sat & Sun 9am–7pm; free; ☏ 02 2368 8750, ⓦ www.kavalanwhisky.com), where the country's most famous single malt, named after an indigenous Taiwanese group, is produced. Book ahead if you want a free guided tour in English; free tastings take place every half an hour. Further up the road, **Jim & Dad's Brewing Company** (Yuanshan Rd; daily 11am–6pm; ☏ 03 922 7199, ⓙ janddbrewing.com) produces Taiwan's premium craft beer. The brewery has an affiliated taproom where you can sample and then stock up on made-in-Taiwan lagers, ales and stouts.

ARRIVAL AND INFORMATION   YILAN

By train Yilan Station (宜蘭車站; yílán chēzhàn) is at 1 Yilanshi, Guangfu Rd. Frequent daily services run from/to Taipei (1hr 15min–2hr 25min). To get to the distillery or brewery, take bus #1751 from the railway station to shānshēngōu (山深溝) or bus #752 or #1786 from the transfer coach station to Yuanshan Branch, Taipei Veterans Hospital (內城園山榮民醫院, nèichéng yuánshān róngmín yīyuàn); taxi from Yilan Station

(20min; NT$250–300).

By bus Kemalan buses (瑪蘭客運; mǎ lán kèyùn) run regular coaches to Taipei Bus Station from Yilan Transfer Station, by the train station (around 1hr; NT$137).

Information Yilan's tourist office (☏ 03 931 2152) is conveniently housed just outside the train station (daily 9am–8pm).

ACCOMMODATION

Hang Khau 行口文旅; hángkǒu wénlǚ 239 Kangle Rd ⊕ 03 936 3610, ⊛hangkhauhotel.com. This is a real find in Yilan and one of the best places to stay in the city – it's a café, travel bookstore and hotel in one. A stone's throw from the station, and with numerous places to eat and drink just beyond the hotel's doors. Dorms NT$660, doubles NT$2400

Luodong

罗东; luódōng

2

Around 10km and a short bus or train ride south of Jiaoxi is the humdrum town of **LUODONG**, the smallest in Yilan county. There's not a great deal to see or do beyond the sizable **night market** (罗东夜市; luódōng yèshì; daily from 6pm), at ten-minute walk west of the train station, but you'll need to stop off at Luodong to get to the National Centre for Traditional Arts.

National Center for Traditional Arts

国立传统艺术中心; guólì chuántǒng yìshù zhōngxīn • 201 Wubin Rd Section 2, just off Provincial Highway 2 • Daily 9am–6pm; exhibition hall Mon noon–6pm, Tues–Sun 9am–9pm • NT$150 • ⊕ 03 9508 341, ⊛ en.ncfta.gov.tw

The **National Center for Traditional Arts**, located 7km east of the train station, is a privately run centre with daily **performances** of Chinese opera, folk dance and acrobatics. There's a **Folk Art Boulevard**, which is lined with shops selling expensive handmade crafts such as wooden slippers, tea sets, glassware, candles, finger puppets, fans and jewellery. The interesting **exhibition hall** has in-depth explanations of many traditional arts, including those of various aboriginal tribes. The complex also includes a coffee shop and convenience store, as well as a couple of snack bars.

ARRIVAL AND DEPARTURE   LUODONG

By train Luodong station (罗东车站; luódōng chēzhàn) is right in the centre of town at 2 Gongzheng Rd (at Zhanqian Rd). Numerous services run from/to Jiaoxi (17–20min) and Taipei (1hr 15min–3hr) via Fulong and Hualien (50min–1hr 30min).

By bus Kamalan buses run frequent services between Luodong and Taipei Bus Station – the bus station in Luodong is at the back of the train station at 229 Chuanyi Rd Sec 3. The useful Taiwan Tourist Shuttle Bus-Dongshan River Route connects Luodong train station with the National Center for Traditional Arts every 30min.

By taxi Taxis from Luodong station to the National Center for Traditional Arts should cost around NT$250 one-way.

ACCOMMODATION AND EATING

Luodong Night Market 罗东夜市; luódōng yèshì Minsheng East Rd between Zhongzheng and Xingdong roads. If you end up spending the night here, check out the local night market, which crams the streets and lanes along this part of Minsheng East Rd and is known for its cooked lamb stalls and iced desserts. Times differ, but various stalls open daily 2pm–3am.

Sun Sweet Hotel 山水商务饭店; shānshuǐ shāngwù fàndiàn 75 Heping Rd ⊕ 03 956 8755. Spotlessly clean and excellent value, with simple but stylish rooms, comfortable beds, free wi-fi and cable TV. it's also close to the train station and night market. Simple Taiwanese breakfast included. NT$1680

Northern Cross-Island Highway

北部横贯公路; běibù héngguàn gōnglù

The **Northern Cross-Island Highway** (Provincial Highway 7) is one of three spectacular routes that cross the mountainous interior of Taiwan, connecting the western plains with the east coast. The northern route starts in **Daxi**, around 35km south of Taipei, and follows the Dahan River before crossing the lofty Xueshan range and joining the main Yilan-to-Lishan road at **Qilan**, 120km away in Yilan county.

GETTING AROUND   **NORTHERN CROSS-ISLAND HIGHWAY**

BY CAR
You'll need your own transport to complete the whole route, as buses only travel as far as Shangbaling.

BY BUS
Taiwan Tourist Shuttle Bus The Taiwan Tourist Shuttle Bus-Cihu Route (Mon–Fri 9am–4pm hourly, Sat & Sun 8am–5.30pm every 30min) connects Zhongli train station with Daxi (1hr 4min), the Daxi Mausoleum (1hr 10min) and Cihu (1hr 13min); the last bus departs from Cihu at 5.30pm Mon–Fri and 7pm Sat & Sun. The Xiao Wulai Route (daily 8.30am, 9am, 9.30am, 10am, noon & 1.30pm) connects

Zhongli Station with the same destinations (30min faster) but ends up at the Xiao Wulai waterfall (1hr 20min). Day-passes are NT$150 (or NT$18/trip).

Public buses From Daxi bus station you can catch regular onward services to Cihu (20min) and hourly buses to Fuxing (45min). Buses to Shangbaling (1hr 30min) depart at 7.40am & 11.30am, returning at 9.50am and 1.30pm.

BY TAXI
Taxis are supposed to use the meter – reckon on NT$160 to Cihu from Daxi bus station, and at least NT$500 to Baling.

Daxi
大溪; dàxī

The official starting point for the Northern Cross-Island Highway is the historic town of **DAXI**, worth a pit stop for its two old streets lined with ornate Chinese Baroque architecture (this Daxi is not to be confused with the east-coast surfing centre). From the bus station, **Zhongyang Road** (中央路; zhōngyāng lù) is to the left of the main entrance, crammed with small stores and a daily wet market in the mornings. Walk north (right) up here to the end and you should hit **Heping Road** (和平路; hépíng lù), Daxi's gorgeous **Old Street**, crammed with craft stores, teashops and restaurants. The elaborate facades on display are some of the best preserved in Taiwan, most dating from the grand redevelopment of the town that began in 1912, the finely carved arches and beams etched with the names of the trading companies that once operated here. Many of the stores sell Daxi's most celebrated snack, **preserved tofu** (豆干; dòugān), which is usually flavoured and much tastier than it sounds.

The "Culture Resort of the Jiang's"
兩蔣文化園區; liǎngjiǎng wénhuà yuánqū

From Daxi, Provincial Highway 7 runs southeast to the village of **CIHU** (慈湖; cíhú), centre of what Taoyuan county has dubbed the "**Culture Resort of the Jiang's**", a collection of several sites associated with the Chiang family. Since his death in 1975, the influence of **Chiang Kai-shek** has faded – here at least his reputation has been rehabilitated and jazzed up with fancy marketing which has transformed the old dictator's image into a fashion concept, much like that of his old foe Mao Zedong.

Daxi Mausoleum
大溪陵寢; dàxī língqǐn • 1268 Fuxing Rd Sec 1 (Hwy 7), 2km north of Cihu • Daily 8am–5pm • Free • ☎ 03 388 3552 • Buses stop nearby

In 1988, Chiang's son and former president **Chiang Ching-kuo** was buried at the **Daxi Mausoleum**, actually completed in 1962 as an office of the president and the first site you'll hit coming from Daxi itself. Its sombre style and simple Chinese decor, with central courtyard, should prepare you for his father's tomb – they were designed to look very similar.

Daxi Visitor Center
大溪遊客中心; dàxī yóukè zhōngxīn • 1268 Fuxing Rd Sec 1 (Hwy 7), 2km north of Cihu • Daily 8am–5pm • ☎ 03 388 4437 • Buses stop nearby

Opposite Daxi Mausoleum is the **Daxi Visitor Center**, which has a small exhibition about Chiang Ching-kuo and his Russian-born wife **Chiang Fang-liang** (born Faina

Ipat'evna Vakhreva), who died in 2004 and whose remains also rest at the Daxi Mausoleum.

Cihu Sculpture Memorial Park

慈湖紀念雕塑公園; cíhú jìniàn diāosù gōngyuán • 1097 Fuxing Rd Sec 1 (Hwy 7) • Daily 8am–5pm • Free • ☎ 03 388 2201

From the Daxi Visitor Center you can walk along the pleasant 2km Touliao Eco-walking Trail to Cihu along Caoling Creek, past Niujiaonanpi Lake and through the remarkable **Cihu Sculpture Memorial Park**, studded with a vast collection of around two hundred Chiang Kai-shek statues "donated" (ie torn down) from other parts of Taiwan.

Cihu Visitor Center

慈湖遊客中心; cíhú yóukè zhōngxīn • 1097 Fuxing Rd Sec 1 (Hwy 7) • Daily 8am–5pm • Free • ☎ 03 388 4437

The enlightening **Cihu Visitor Center** contains a small exhibition highlighting Chiang Kai-shek's illustrious career in China and Taiwan – it's definitely worth a look before trudging up to the mausoleum site itself.

Cihu Mausoleum

慈湖陵寢; cíhú língqǐn • 1097 Fuxing Rd Sec 1 (Hwy 7) • Daily 8am–5pm • Free • ☎ 03 388 3552

At the end of a short trail from the Cihu Visitor Center (past Cihu or "Lake Kindness" itself) lies the simple but elegant **Cihu Mausoleum**, where Chiang Kai-shek was entombed in a black marble sarcophagus in 1975 – this was actually one of his many summerhouses, built in 1959 because the lake reminded him of his childhood home in China. Plans to move the great man (and his son) closer to Taipei seem to have been shelved; in any case, the idea was always to rebury them in China after reunification.

Fuxing

復興; fù xīng

Around 10km south of Daxi, the small town of **FUXING** is the first stop on Northern Cross-Island Highway proper, with an obvious **Atayal** influence, and is the best place to stay the night. Fuxing was also the home of yet another of Chiang Kai-shek's ubiquitous summerhouses, **Jiaobanshan Villa**, an elegant mansion which sadly burnt down in 1992.

Jiaobanshan Park

角板山公園; jiǎobǎnshān gōngyuán 133-1 Zhongzheng Rd • Daily 9am–5pm • Free • ☎ 03 3821678

Jiaobanshan Park is a pleasant, leafy space studded with modern sculptures commemorating the old villa, with views across the Dahan River valley and an exhibition hall with old photos and documents on aspects of Chiang Kai-shek's life here, his military career and his lesser-known family life. There's also a section on the paintings of Madam Chiang. Elsewhere in the park you can visit an informative display on Taiwan's camphor industry in an old wooden camphor storage house (樟腦收納所; zhāngnǎo shōunà suǒ), the 100m-long "war-readiness tunnel" (戰備隧道; zhànbèi suìdào) and the **Family Member Remembrance Pavilion** (思親亭; sīqīn tíng), which is supposed to have reminded Chiang of his hometown (Xikou in China).

ACCOMMODATION | **FUXING**

Fuxing Youth Activity Center 復興青年活動中心; fù xīng qīngnián huódòng zhōngxīn 1 Zhongshan Rd • ☎ 03 382 2276, ⌨ fuhsing.cyh.org.tw. Operated by China Youth Corp, this budget hotel occupies a superb location overlooking an arm of Shimen Reservoir. The rooms are simple but comfortable (with space for four people), all en suite with TVs, breakfast and magnificent views from the more expensive rooms on the top floor. Japanese-style tatami rooms (with mats on raised platforms rather than beds) are cheaper. Tatami rooms **NT$1050**; doubles **NT$3200**

Xiao Wulai Special Scenic Area

小烏來風景區; xiǎowūlái fēngjǐngqū · 42 Yisheng Village · **Scenic Area** Daily 8.30am–4.30pm · Free (NT$100 parking) · **Skywalk** Tues–Sun 8am–5pm · NT$50; apply in advance online at ⑳ skywalk.tycg.gov.tw/Skywalk

From Fuxing, the North Cross-Island Highway follows a series of gorges created by the Dahan River deep into the Xueshan range, with the scenery becoming increasingly wild and rugged. Around 4km from Fuxing, the **Xiao Wulai Special Scenic Area** contains the 50m **Little Wulai Falls** (小烏來瀑布; xiǎowūlái pùbù), Taiwan's most picturesque waterfall, 2km off the main highway.

You can walk down to the river in front of the falls from the main road near the tollbooth via a steep path, or check out the views from the transparent **skywalk** (小烏來天空步道; xiǎowūlái tiānkōng bùdào) of reinforced glass (a hanging bridge suspended 70m over the falls). Try to avoid visiting at the weekends, when the site gets mobbed by tour groups.

Shangbaling

上巴陵; shàngbālíng

South of Xiao Wulai, the North Cross-Island Highway becomes narrower, ending up as a winding, single-track road. Buses go as far as the village of **Baling** (巴陵; bālíng), at the bottom of the valley and lined with several basic places to eat, and sometimes on to the Atayal settlement of **SHANGBALING**, a further 200m up the mountain on a side road. The village is perched on a narrow ridge, often shrouded in mist, and has a single street lined with cheap restaurants and places to stay if you get stuck (be sure to try the fresh honey peaches or shuǐmìtáo here).

Lalashan Forest Reserve

拉拉山國有林自然保護區; lālāshān guóyǒulín zìrán bǎohùqū · Daily 7am–6pm; visitor centre daily 9am–6pm · NT$100 · ☎ 03 394 6061 · Zhongli bus #5301 departs Taoyuan (Fuxing Rd, near the train station) at 6.30am and noon, dropping off at Linbankou (3hr 30min), at the start of the reserve (but still around 3km from the old tree trail) – buses return at 9.30am and 3.30pm; bus #5090 and #5091 only go as far as Baling; buses also run from Daxi to Shangbaling

Also known as Daguanshan, **Lalashan Forest Reserve** lies 6.5km beyond the village of Shangbaling, an incredibly atmospheric reserve of giant red cypress trees or "God Trees" (shénmù), 1550m up in the mountains and 12.5km from the main highway. The small **visitor centre** here marks the start of a 3.7km **trail** taking in 22 of the biggest trees and viewpoints. The trees survived undiscovered during the period of intense logging initiated by the Japanese – most are between 500 and an astonishing 2800 years old, with the tallest topping out at 55m.

Mingchi Forest Recreation Area

明池國家森林遊樂區; míngchí guójiā sēnlín yóulèqū · Daily 6.30am–5pm · NT$120 · ☎ 03 9894106

The North Cross-Island Highway climbs to its highest point (1250m) near the **Mingchi Forest Recreation Area**, a tranquil alpine-like mountain retreat (free of tour buses), set around a small lake. The area was once a lumber station and is surrounded by more giant hardwoods and "God Trees". Beyond Mingchi, the road drops steeply for 17km through thickly wooded slopes to another forest reserve at **Qilan** (棲蘭; qílán) and the end of the highway: turn left for Yilan, Luodong and the east coast, and right for Lishan and the Wuling Recreation Area.

ACCOMMODATION AND EATING   MINGCHI FOREST RECREATION AREA

Mingchi Mountain Hostel 明池山莊; míngchí shānzhuāng 8 Yingshi Village ☎ 03 989 4104. This resort hotel is relatively expensive but the rooms and rustic cottages are very cosy; it's extremely tranquil and also contains an attractive restaurant and café. NT$3900

Hsinchu

新竹; xīnzhú

Just 86km from Taipei, **HSINCHU** is one of the wealthiest cities in Taiwan, largely as a result of the huge revenues generated by the **Science Park**, the country's answer to Silicon Valley, where Taiwanese tech firms including D-Link, Nuvoton and Realtk are based. Yet in the centre of town you can explore the remnants of one of north Taiwan's oldest cities, with plenty to offer visitors: **temples**, **ancient architecture** and **traditional food stalls** reflect the city's historic roots, while reimagined industrial spaces, such as the **Railway Art Warehouse**, highlight Hsinchu's cultural clout. It's also the gateway to the heart of Taiwan's **Hakka country**, centred on the town of Beipu.

2

Hsinchu has a compact centre, easily explored on foot. The **East Gate** (東門; dōngmén), a short walk north from the train station along Zhongzheng Road, the city's main commercial street, is its most distinctive landmark. The gate was completed in 1829 and is the only section of the old city walls to survive. A couple of blocks north of here, the **old city moat** has been transformed into a flower-filled park between Linsen Road and Zhongyang Road, where it merges into Qinshui Park; it's an attractive place to wander, especially at night, lined with coffee shops, stores and restaurants. The **old town** lies west of the moat, and still contains a smattering of historic sights and temples.

Hsinchu Image Museum

文化局影像博物館; wénhuàjú yīngxiàng bówùguǎn • 65 Zhongzheng Rd • Tues–Sun 9.30am–noon, 1.30–5pm & 6.30–9pm; film screenings usually from 7pm Wed–Sun • NT$20 • ☎ 03 528 5840

Just north of the East Gate, **Hsinchu Image Museum** occupies an old cinema built in 1933. The actual museum is very small, comprising a couple of exhibition rooms behind the Movie Hall. You can take a peek inside the latter, but it's more interesting to watch one of the old Taiwanese films screened here. The museum ticket includes entry to the film playing that day.

Chenghuang Temple

城隍廟; chénghuáng miào • 75 Zhongshan Rd, at Beimen St • Daily 4.30am–10.30pm • ☎ 03 5223666

Hsinchu's most important place of worship is **Chenghuang Temple**, surrounded by food stalls and attended by a constant stream of visitors. The stalls form the city's best **night market** (see p.156) and add to the boisterous atmosphere – during festivals locals like to eat here while traditional opera is performed in the courtyard. Built in 1748, much of the temple's current beauty stems from the restoration of 1924: look out for the iron abacus and lurid depictions of hell on the walls, a warning to would-be criminals. The large black-faced City God image in the **Main Hall** is said to be the most senior in Taiwan, while the City God's wife and two sons are worshipped in the Rear Hall.

Beimen Street

北門街; běimén jiē

Running north from Chenghuang Temple, **Beimen Street** is the city's most atmospheric thoroughfare and its earliest commercial street, lined with old shops, restaurants and teahouses. Just off the street there's a small alleyway known as the **Dark Street** (暗街仔; ànjiēzǎi) with a wooden plaque proclaiming this to be "the birthplace of Hsinchu City, founded in 1711". Don't miss the old puppet store, **Guoda** (國達民俗藝品; guódá mínsú yìpǐn) at no. 109, and just beyond Beida Road, on the right, **Xing Chun** (杏春; xìngchūn), a Traditional Chinese Medicine shop at no. 156. Beyond Changhe Temple is a row of dilapidated but charming Qing dynasty buildings; the two best maintained are the **Jinshi Mansion** (進士第; jìnshìdì) at no. 163, which was built in 1838 for Zheng

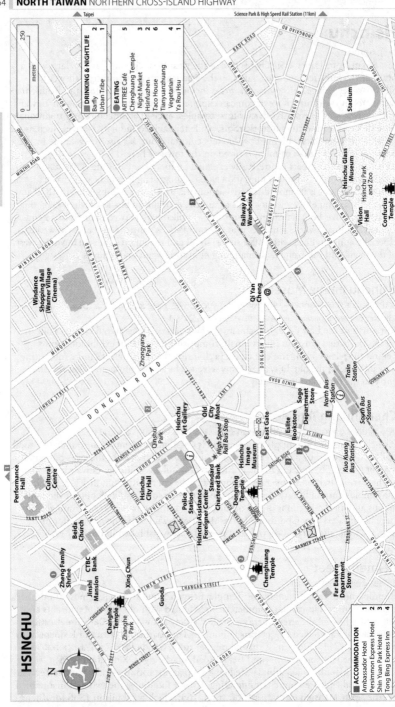

HSINCHU

Taipei

Science Park & High Speed Rail Station (11km)

0 metres 250

DRINKING & NIGHTLIFE	
Barfly	2
Urban Tribe	1

EATING	
ARTTREE Café	5
Chenghuang Temple	3
Night Market	2
Hsinfuzhen	6
Taco House	4
Tianyuanzhuang	
Vegetarian	
Ya Rou Hsu	1

ACCOMMODATION	
Ambassador Hotel	1
Persimmon Express Hotel	2
Shin Yuan Park Hotel	3
Tong Bing Express Inn	4

Stadium

Hsinchu Glass Museum

Hsinchu Park and Zoo

Vision Hall

Confucius Temple

Railway Art Warehouse

Qi Yan Cheng

Windance Shopping Mall (Warner Village Cinema)

Zhongyang Park

Train Station

Sogo Department Store

North Bus Station

South Bus Station

DONGDA ROAD

Hsinchu Art Gallery

Old City Moat

High Speed Rail Bus Stop

East Gate

Eslite Bookstore

Kuo Kuang Bus Station

Performance Hall

Cultural Centre

Qinshui Park

Hsinchu City Hall

Police Station

Hsinchu Assistance Foreigner Center

Standard Chartered Bank

Hsinchu Image Museum

Dongning Temple

Beida Church

Zheng Family Shrine

Jinshi Mansion Hotel

CTBC Bank

Xing Chun

Guoda

Changhe Temple

Zhanghe Park

Chenghuang Temple

Far Eastern Department Store

Yong-Xi (who became the first Taiwanese jìnshì, or official, in 1810), and the **Zheng Family Shrine** (鄭氏家廟; zhèngshì jīamiào) at no. 175 (completed in 1853), both closed to the public.

Changhe Temple

長和宮; chánghé gōng • 135 Beimen St • Daily 4am–10pm

Hsinchu's "outer" Mazu temple, **Changhe Temple** was built in 1742 next to a long-silted-over wharf (the nickname refers to its position just outside the old city walls). Mazu is enshrined in the **Main Hall**, flanked by Wenchang Dijun on the left and Guan Di on the right. The Rear Hall is dedicated to Guanyin, while the attached shrine to the right of the Main Hall is known as **Shuixian Temple** (水仙宮; shuǐxiān gōng) and dedicated to the Water God or the Great Yu, mythical founder of the Xia dynasty (2205–1766 BC), China's first.

Railway Art Warehouse

新竹市鐵道藝術村; xīnzhú shìtiě dàoyì shùcūn • 64 Huayuan St • Tues–Sun 9am–6pm • Free • ☎ 03 5628933

Adjacent to the train tracks, the **Railway Art Warehouse**, built in 1941, was once a vegetable market and now stands as an example of the city's burgeoning cultural scene. In 2004, the space was converted into a series of art galleries which play host to a large number of rotating exhibitions and events, as well artists in residence.

Hsinchu Park

新竹公園; xīnzhú gōngyuán • 295 Gongyuan Rd (main entrance on Dongda Rd) • Daily 24hr • To walk there, take the underpass to the right of the train station (opposite Sogo), then turn right and immediately left upon exiting the tunnel; walk across the car park to Nanda Rd and turn left to Dongda Rd

The cluster of attractions centred on **Hsinchu Park**, southeast of the station (which includes a small zoo, a dusty Confucian temple and a weekend flower market), tends to attract more tourists than the old town, though only the Glass Museum has much appeal.

Hsinchu Glass Museum

玻璃工藝館; bōlí gōngyì guǎn • 2 Dongda Rd Sec 1 • Tues–Sun 9–5pm • NT$50 • ☎ 03 562 6091, ⊛ glassmuseum.moc.gov.tw

Built by the Japanese in 1936 to serve as a clubhouse, the **Hsinchu Glass Museum** is now an innovative mixture of glass art exhibitions and permanent displays on the history and use of glass. The most interesting installations are the reinforced glass bridge on the second floor, and the **Jail of Glass** on the first floor with its glass walls, bars and even a glass toilet.

ARRIVAL AND DEPARTURE   **HSINCHU**

BY TRAIN

Hsinchu train station, built in 1913 and Taiwan's oldest, is at the southern end of the city centre at 445 Zhonghua Rd Sec 2, a short walk from East Gate.

Destinations Kaohsiung (express every 10–30min; 3hr 30min–5hr 30min); Sanyi (18 daily; 55min); Taichung (express every 10–30min; 55min–1hr 30min); Taipei (express every 15–30min; 1hr 5min–1hr 40min).

BY HSR

Hsinchu's HSR station (☎ 03 612 1000) is 11km east of the city at 6 Gaotie 7th Rd in Zhubei, linked to the centre of Hsinchu by bus or train: note that there is a free shuttle bus

(every 20–30min), but this only links the HSR station to Zhubei train station (25min), not Hsinchu itself.

Connections to/from central Hsinchu To get to central Hsinchu from the HSR station, take Kuo-Kuang bus #1782 (hourly at 18min past the hour 7.18am–8.18pm; 25min); buses terminate at "Dongmen Market", which means Zhongzheng Rd near the Hsinchu Municipal Image Museum, and return from the other side of Zhongzheng Rd at 10min past the hour. Alternatively, local trains to central Hsinchu run from Liujia Station adjacent to the HSR station (twice every hour, times vary; 20min); return trains depart Hsinchu train station at 17min and 47min past the hour.

Connections with the Taiwan Shuttle Bus Note that

2

the Taiwan Shuttle Bus-Lion's Head Mountain Route stops at the HSR station on the way to Beipu (NT$68) and the Lion's Head Mountain Visitor Center ($99): buses depart hourly 8.22am–3.22pm on weekdays and every 30min on weekends (one-day pass NT$100).

Destinations Kaohsiung (every 30min; 1hr 25min); Taichung (every 30min; 25min); Tainan (every 30min; 1hr 10min); Taipei (every 30min; 35min).

BY BUS

All the major bus stations line Zhonghua Rd near the train station in central Hsinchu. Kuo Kuang and How Tai are among the companies offering services to (and from) Taipei, Taichung and points further south. There are no direct buses to Taiwan Taoyuan International Airport; take a bus to Zhubei and change there, or go via the HSR to Taoyuan station, which has shuttle bus connections to the airport.

North Bus Station Hsinchu Bus Company's North Bus Station is on Zhonghua Rd, opposite Sogo, with infrequent services (#5621) to Xinpu or "Shinpu" (新埔; xīnpǔ; for Yimin Temple) at 7.45am, 9.40am and 10.30am (30min).

South Bus Station For Zhudong (竹東; zhúdōng; 40min), where you can catch onward services to Beipu, head to the South Bus Station, just to the left of the train station. Buses also depart for Toufen (#5614), Taipei (NT$130; 1hr) and Taichung (NT$150; 1hr) from here.

GETTING AROUND

By bus City buses (marked in English and Chinese) depart from several different stops around the train station, though you're unlikely to need them for sightseeing within the city.

By taxi Taxis are plentiful in the centre of town (the meter starts at NT$100). Like Taipei, most streets in Hsinchu are clearly marked in hànyǔ pīnyīn.

INFORMATION

Tourist information The best place for information and help in English is the Hsinchu Tourist Information Centre in the train station (daily 9am–8pm; ☎03 525 8977) – there's a smaller desk at the HSR station (daily 6am–11pm). The Hsinchu Foreigner Assistance Center (新竹地區外國人協助中心; xīnzhú dìqū wàiguórén xiézhù zhōngxīn; Mon–Fri 8am–5pm; ☎03 521 6121, ⓦ www.hccg.gov.tw/en/) at 120 Zhongyang Rd is also helpful.

ACCOMMODATION

Ambassador Hotel 新竹國賓大飯店; xīnzhú guóbīn dàfàndiàn 188 Zhonghua Rd Sec 2 ☎03 515 1666, ⓦ ambassadorhotel.com.tw. Hsinchu's top five-star hotel plays host to a steady stream of business visitors and occupies the 9th–24th floors of the city's tallest building, above the Shinkong Mitsukoshi department store. Rooms are modern, stylish and very comfortable, with extras including an indoor swimming pool and some excellent restaurants. NT$4450

Persimmon Express Hotel 柿子紅快捷旅店; shìzihóng kuàijié lǚdiàn 3 Lane 3, Datong Rd ☎03 522 3232. Stylish, contemporary budget option in the centre, near the old moat and a row of cool restaurants and bars – rooms come in a variety of themes, from kitsch Tudor to modern art and graffiti. All are simple and clean with breakfast included. NT$900

Shin Yuan Park Hotel 新苑庭園大飯店; xīnyùan tíngyuán dàfàndiàn 11 Datong Rd ☎03 522 6868, ⓦ shinyuan-hotel.com.tw. Comfortable mid-range option, not far from the East Gate and the train station. Rooms are relatively spacious, with bright but outdated blond wood decor in the cheaper ones. NT$2780

Tong Bing Express Inn 東賓快捷旅店; dōngbīn kuàijié lǚdiàn 4 Sunlin St ☎03 522 3161, ⓦ tongbing3161@yahoo.com.tw. A stone's throw from the train station, this budget option has gaudy, some might say colourful rooms, some without windows but most en suite. These are irrefutably humble lodgings, but you won't find a cheaper or better located hotel in town. Book ahead for best rates. NT$680

EATING

Eating in Hsinchu can be a lot of fun, as the city is renowned for its culinary **specialities**: pork meatballs in soup (gòngwántāng), rice noodles (mǐfēn) and stuffed meatballs (ròyuán) – especially at the **food stalls** in and around Chenghuang Temple and along Beimen St.

★**ArtTree Café & Bar** 藝術咖啡吧; yìshù kāfēi bā 37 Dongda St ☎03 562 0905, ⓦ facebook.com/ArtTree CafeBar. Near the Railway Art Warehouse, this hip café is popular with the artsy crowd. A bar atmosphere emerges in the evenings, when Strongbow cider is available (NT$160). Tea and coffee from NT$100. Daily 10.30am–10.30pm.

★**Chenghuang Temple Night Market** 75 Zhongshan Rd (inside the temple courtyard). Stalls to try include *Wang's Oyster Omelet* (王記蚵仔煎; wángjì ézǐjiān) which faces the main hall and specializes in oyster omelets for NT$50; just opposite, *Ah-Cheng Rice Noodles* (阿城號米粉; āchéng hào mǐfěn) knocks out rice noodles and pork meatballs from NT$45. Outside on Dongmen St, *Kuo's Spring Roll* (郭潤餅; guōrùnbǐng) has been selling delicious rùnbǐng (spring rolls stuffed with pork, dried shrimp and mushroom; NT$35) since 1906. Daily 10am–10pm.

Hsinfuzhen 新復珍; xīnfùzhēn 6 Beimen St ❶03 522 2205. Opposite Chenghuang Temple, this venerable cake-maker was established in 1898 and is famous for its deep-fried zhúqiàn bǐng (or "*chu chan*") meat cakes (NT$35), a pastry filled with a tasty blend of onion and pork, and sprinkled with sesame seeds – the sweet/sour combination is perfectly balanced. Food is labelled in English. Daily 8am–8.30pm.

Taco House 32 Sheng Li Rd ❶03 522 2261. Popular with expat teachers and foreigners employed in the science park, this lively Tex-Mex fast-food restaurant does reasonable burritos (NT$70), tacos (NT$40) and quesadillas (NT$95), as well as American-style sides such as mashed potatoes (NT$40). Daily 11am–10pm.

Tianyuanzhuang Vegetarian 田園莊素食; tiányuánzhuāng sùshí 2 Wenchang Rd ❶03 5233839. A short walk from the East Gate, this lovely hole-in-the-wall Buddhist diner oozes ambience. The walls are adorned with tourist photos of the area. To order, remove a wooden tag from the wall and give it to the owner, who is also the chef. If you can't read Chinese, just point at what you want. A vegan fried rice is NT$80, and no dish exceeds NT$95. Take-away or eat-in. Daily 11.30am–8pm.

★**Ya Rou Hsu** 鴨肉許; yāròu xǔ 212 Zhongzheng Rd ❶03 525 3290. One of Hsinchu's most famous local diners, this place has been serving duck noodles (thin or thick style) and plates of roast duck for over forty years; the secret is the mouthwatering special sauce. Lots of imitators in Hsinchu, but this is the best. Noodles NT$60. Daily 11am–4am.

DRINKING AND NIGHTLIFE

You'll find numerous **bars** downtown that cater primarily to local tastes: karaoke, TVs, plenty of Taiwanese snacks and a limited selection of bottled beers and cocktails. Most open after 7pm and don't close until well into the early hours. A good place to start is Minzu Rd, Lane 33, aka "**bar alley**".

Barfly 44 Renai St ❶03 533 5939. The place to go for a good night out in Hsinchu, with darts, table football and a good mix of locals and foreigners. Mon–Sat 8pm–2am.

Urban Tribe 22 Wuling St ❶03 532 0029, ⓦfacebook.com/UrbanTribeTW. A bit of walk from the centre of town, but well worth it if you're in the mood for a relaxing evening. This is Hsinchu's premier craft beer joint, offering a choice of brewed-in-Taoyuan lagers, pilsners and ales. The Water Buffalo IPA (NT$100/180) is a must try. Coffee and snacks also available. Daily 10am–11pm.

Neiwan Line

內灣線; nèiwānxiàn • Stalls open at 10am • NT$42 one-way from Hsinchu to Neiwan

Rolling inland from North Hsinchu Station into the verdant northern interior, the **NEIWAN LINE** makes a worthwhile day-trip from Hsinchu. One of three branch lines built during the Japanese colonial era, it was closed for five years during construction of the nearby Liujia line. Into 2011, it reopened with much fanfare as a tourist attraction. The route passes through Hsinchu suburbs and abandoned factories before ascending into a canvas of bamboo groves and palm trees.

Hexing Station

合興站; héxīngzhàn

Three stops before the end of the line, **Hexing Station** is nicknamed the "Station of Love", and was twinned with Japan's Kofuku "Happiness" Station in 2016. The old station house is home to a romance-themed gift shop selling heart-shaped trinkets, while next to the tracks an old train carriage has been converted into *Felicite Café* (小甜日心; xiǎotiánrìxīn), selling the best lemon tart (NT$59) anywhere in Taiwan.

Neiwan

內灣站; nèiwānzhàn

The last stop on the line and a highlight of the route, **Neiwan** is a picturesque Hakka hamlet surrounded by steep forested mountains. The streets are dotted with snack stores – while you're here, try the wild-ginger-flower rice dumplings (NT$35) sold at Auntie Jane's and Mama Luo's, both located on the old street opposite the station. A short walk out of town takes you to the Neiwan Bridge, which crosses a large ravine. On the opposite side, the **Venice-Neiwan Hotspring Resort** (daily 8am–11pm) offers a soothing hot tub for two for just NT$700.

Hakka country

Stretching southeast from Hsinchu, **Hsinchu country** is home to large numbers of **Hakka** people: though the ethnic group accounts for roughly fifteen percent of Taiwan's population, eighty percent of Hsinchu claims Hakka ancestry. **Beipu** is the most famous Hakka town in north Taiwan, while the **Yimin Temple** near Xinpu is the centre of Hakka religious life on the island.

Fangliao Yimin Temple

枋寮義民廟; fāngliáo yìmín miào • 360 Yimen Rd Sec 3 (County Road 17), Xinpu • Daily 6am–9pm • Xinpu buses pass the temple; the last bus back to Hsinchu leaves around 6pm

The **Fangliao Yimin Temple**, around 10km northeast of Hsinchu (just outside Zhubei), is the original and most important yìmín temple in Taiwan, serving as the spiritual centre for the Hakka community on the island. The temple commemorates the Hakka militia killed during the Lin Shuangwen Rebellion of 1786–88: legend has it that the oxen pulling the cart laden with dead soldiers stopped at this site and refused to move any further. The bodies of almost two hundred militiamen were buried here as a result, and you can still see the vast **burial mound** at the rear of the temple. A shrine was built on the site soon afterwards. The **auxiliary burial mound** to the right of the original contains the bodies of over a hundred Hakka volunteers killed fighting during the Dai

---

THE HAKKA

Known as kèjiārén in Chinese ("guest families", or hak-kâ ngin in the Hakka language), the **Hakka** (客家人) are an ethnic subgroup of the Han Chinese family, with their own language, customs and traditions. Originally from the northern Chinese provinces of Henan and Shanxi, Hakka people began coming to Taiwan in the seventeenth century and have since developed a particularly strong identity. At first, Hakka migrants settled in Taipei county and along the western plains, but by the nineteenth century they had moved to the areas in which they predominate today: the mountainous parts of Taoyuan, Hsinchu and Miaoli counties, and in the Kaohsiung-Pingdong area. Though few Hakka are farmers today, they're still regarded as hard workers and have a reputation for producing some of the island's top **scholars** and **writers**: famous Hakka people include ex-president Lee Teng-hui, Soong Mei-ling (Chiang Kai-shek's wife) and film director Hou Hsiao-hsien.

Hakka people subscribe to the same **religious beliefs** as other Chinese groups in Taiwan, but they also have their own special gods and festivals. The worship of the **Yimin** (義民; yìmín; mostly in north Taiwan) is unique to Taiwan, while the island also has around 145 temples dedicated to the **Three Mountain Kings** (三山國王; sānshān guówáng), protective spirits of the Hakka and a tradition that came from Guangdong.

The **Council for Hakka Affairs** was created by the government in 2001 to help preserve Hakka culture on the island, and to ensure its language survives: there are several dialects spoken in Taiwan, with sìxiàn being the most important, and the one you'll hear on train announcements. **Hakka TV** (客家電視台; kèjiā diànshìtái), a 24hr station, has been on air since 2003.

> ## GOD PIGS
>
> One of the most controversial of Taiwan's traditional religious practices is the rearing of "**God Pigs**" (神豬; shénzhū) – unfortunate hogs that are fed to grotesque size over a few years, often so large they can no longer walk. The pigs are used as offerings to the gods – it's a particularly Hakka custom, used mostly at the Yimin Festival when literally hundreds are sacrificed. Pigs are killed the day before, by knife, and the carcass stretched over a metal cage so that it looks disturbingly similar in size to a small bus. It doesn't take much imagination to work out why animal rights activists get upset about this: cases of force-feeding, alleged ill-treatment and the relatively simplistic method of slaughter have led to increased calls for a ban over the years. Hakka groups say that it's a traditional part of their culture and that the pigs are well cared for. While it's true that the tradition of offering pigs goes back to the 1830s, the official "contest" to see who has the biggest, as well as the intensive, modern factory methods, are relatively new.

2

Chao-chun Rebellion (1862–65). All the dead warriors are venerated as gods (yìmín means "righteous people"), symbolized by the wooden tablets at the main altar.

There are three major **temple festivals** each year: the **Spring Festival** before Tomb Sweeping Day on April 5, the **Autumn Festival** at the end of October or beginning of November, and the most important, the **Yimin Festival** on Lunar July 20 – this is one of the few religious festivals to have originated wholly in Taiwan and features the infamous "God Pigs" (see box above).

Beipu

北埔; běipǔ

Lying around 20km southeast of Hsinchu, just north of the Lion's Head Mountain Scenic Area, the small town of **BEIPU** is the centre of Hakka culture in north Taiwan, the counterpart of Meinong in the south. Though it's a bit touristy these days, the compact area of old buildings and teahouses around Citian Temple and **Old Street** (Beipu St; 北埔街; běipǔ jiē) drips with rustic charm, has loads of places to try léichá (see box, p.160), and makes an easy excursion from Hsinchu or even Taipei.

Citian Temple

慈天宮; cítiān gōng • 1 Beipu St • Daily 5.30am–7pm

Established at the end of Old Street in 1835 (but remodelled in 1846 and 1876), **Citian Temple** is the town's main centre of worship. The facade is especially rich, adorned with ornate figurines and the roof a series of dramatically curved flying eaves/buttresses and snaking/bright/fiery dragons. The Main Hall is dedicated to Guanyin, flanked by tablets on the right representing the sānguān dàdì (Three Great Emperor-Officials) and on the left, the sānshān guówáng (Three Mountain Kings), all Hakka favourites.

Old Beipu

Beipu's oldest and most appealing buildings are crammed into a relatively small area around the Citian Temple, a mixture of traditional red- and mud-brick Chinese houses, well worth exploring. To the south, the **Zhongshu Tang** (忠恕堂; zhōngshù táng), built in 1922, is a charming Qing dynasty house with an unusual Baroque facade. Many houses are linked to the wealthy **Jiang family** – patriarch Jiang Xiou-nuan built the grand **A-Hsin Jiang Residence** (姜阿新宅; jiāngā xīnzhái) in the 1940s just to the north of the temple on Miaocian Street (廟前街; miàoqián jiē) in a blend of Western and Japanese styles. Like most of the buildings here, it's still privately owned and closed to the public. Beyond here, at 6 Jhongjheng Rd 9 (at Miaocian) is the simple traditional building known as **Jinguangfu** (金廣福; jīnguǎngfú), the old community hall built in the 1830s, and opposite, the more elaborate compound of **Tianshui Tang** (天水堂; tiānshuǐ táng), a huge Hakka-style mansion dating from 1832 and still occupied by the

2

LÉICHÁ – "CEREAL TEA"

Beipu is the best place in Taiwan to sample léichá (擂茶), or **"ground tea"**, a popular Hakka drink with origins in ancient China. Its modern incarnation is one hundred percent contemporary Taiwan, however: a green tea mixed with a paste of peanuts, sesame, pumpkin and sunflower seeds. It's delicious and very filling (it's sometimes called "**cereal tea**"), but the twist is that you get to prepare it yourself. DIY sessions are offered at most of the teashops in town, and in general you are expected to at least have a go – the staff are sometimes reluctant to pitch in. After a few minutes you'll understand why; the raw ingredients are placed into a ceramic bowl and must be pounded into an oily paste with a giant wooden pestle, a process which takes a strong arm, or preferably, several. The tea is usually served with Hakka-style *muaji* (*máshǔ* in Mandarin), sticky rice rolled in ground peanuts.

Jiang family. Jhongjheng Road becomes a narrow alley east of here, containing some of the town's most atmospheric **teahouses**.

ARRIVAL AND DEPARTURE   BEIPU

BY BUS

Buses stop in Beipu at the junction of Nansing St (南星街; nánxīng jiē) and Jhongjheng Rd (中正路; zhōngzhèng lù) next to the OK Mart (the town uses Tongyong Pinyin signage), a short walk from the old part of town. Turn right on Nansing and you'll hit Beipu St at the next junction.

Taiwan Shuttle Bus The easiest way to get to Beipu is to catch the Taiwan Shuttle Bus-Lion's Head Mountain Route from Hsinchu HSR station or from Zhubei train station (8am–3pm: Mon–Fri hourly, Sat & Sun every 30min; one-day pass NT$100). The last bus leaves Beipu St for the return journey at 5.25pm Mon–Fri and 6.25pm Sat & Sun.

From/to central Hsinchu To get to Beipu from central Hsinchu you must first catch a bus to Zhudong (竹東; zhúdōng), then take bus #5610 to Beipu from the Zhudong bus station (every 20–30min; 15min).

ACCOMMODATION AND EATING

Almost every teahouse and restaurant in Beipu serves classic **Hakka food**, such as salty pork (xián zhūròu) and cereal tea (léichá), with another speciality, "persimmon cakes" (dried persimmon; shí shìbǐng).

★**Beipugo Guesthouse** 北埔口民宿; běibùkǒu mín sù 168 Buxiangnanxing St ☎03 580 4121. Right at the entrance to the town, this smart and airy guesthouse offers traditional fan-cooled rooms. The main selling point is the fine view of the surrounding countryside, which can be enjoyed from the communal terrace. Downstairs, an affiliated antiques shop sells Hakka handicrafts and heirlooms. NT$1200

Lord Jiang's Persimmon Cakes 姜太公柿餅; jiāngtàigōng shìbǐng 24 Miaocian St ☎03 580 5270. Celebrated purveyor of "persimmon cakes", with dried fruit available for around NT$30–50 for a small box. Daily 9am–6pm.

★**Puyu Hakka Tea** 璞鈺擂茶; púyù léichá 8 Xiangmiaoqian Rd ☎31 580 2250, ✉letea123@gmail .com. If you only visit one restaurant in Bepu, make it this one. Cereal tea and local handicrafts are beautifully packaged in the shop, while the restaurant dishes up Buddhist vegetarian food with a Hakka twist. Daily 9am–7pm.

The Well 水井; shuǐjǐng 1 Jhongheng Rd ☎03 580 5122. Beipu's most atmospheric teahouse is at the eastern end of Jhongjheng Rd, where it becomes very narrow; it's a tranquil Qing dynasty building, with stone walls, wooden ceilings, ticking antique clocks and rustic tables and chairs. Tea, coffee and Hakka meals are available from NT$150 (English menu). Daily 10am–6pm.

Lion's Head Mountain Scenic Area

獅頭山國家風景區;shītóushān guójiā fēngjǐngqū

The Buddhist temples of the **Lion's Head Mountain Scenic Area** have been attracting pilgrims since the Qing dynasty. The area is shaped like a rectangle, with an area of 242 square kilometres divided between Miaoli and Hsinchu counties. Its most accessible **hiking trails** and **temples** are clustered around **Lion's Head Mountain** (shītóushān) itself, in the northern half of the area, and along the Zhonggang River valley just to the south. The region is also the home of the **Saisiyat** people (see p.402). It's possible to see everything in a fairly long day (combining two Taiwan Shuttle Bus routes), but there are a few places to break the journey. The other main section worth checking out is **Emei Lake**, dominated by the immense **statue of Maitreya Buddha**, one of Taiwan's highlights.

Lion's Head Mountain Recreational Area

獅山遊憩區; shīshān yóuqì qū

2

The main attractions in the northern section of the region are loosely grouped within the **Lion's Head Mountain Recreational Area**, anchored by the informative **Lion's Head Mountain Visitor Center** (see p.162), where the buses terminate. There are a couple of easy **hikes** from here: the 1.7km **Tengping Historic Trail** (藤坪古道; téngpíng gǔdào) is a lush, forested path rich in birdlife, while a few metres further along the main road takes you to the signposted 1.3km path to **Shuilian Cave** (水濂洞; shuǐliándòng) – the cave is noted for the sheet of water dripping across its mouth (the "water curtain"), and tiny **Fanyin Temple** (梵音寺; fànyīn sì) inside.

Lion's Head Mountain Historic Trail

獅山古道; shīshān gǔdào

The most popular hike from the visitor centre is the **Lion's Head Mountain Historic Trail** (3.5km); the **trail can be closed** after heavy rain, so check before starting out. It's a scenic, 4km path over the hills to Quanhua Temple, lined with stone slabs and weaving past eleven temples, as well as smaller shrines, statues and calligraphy inscribed onto the rocks. Many of the temples are carved into the limestone cliffs, but most of the original buildings were destroyed during the Hsinchu earthquake of 1935, and what you see today are faithful reproductions. The path and main sites are well marked in English. At Wangyue Pavilion (望月亭; wàngyùe tíng) not far from **Yuanguang Temple** (元光寺; yuánguāng sì), about 2.5km from the visitor centre, a trail spur leads 700m to the summit of **Lion's Head Mountain** (492m) itself, with sweeping views of the valley from the top (the peak does vaguely resemble a lion's head). Back on the main trail, the path drops steeply into the Zhonggang River valley for the final 1km to Quanhua Temple.

Quanhua Temple

勸化堂; quànhuà táng • 242 Shishan Village • Daily 6am–8pm • ℡ 03 782 2020 • Shuttle buses (see p.162) running between the visitor centre and Nanzhuang stop by Quanhua Temple (15min from each)

Established in 1900, **Quanhua Temple** is a spectacular cluster of classical-style halls perched on the hillside, its tiered structure providing a wonderful close-up perspective of the elaborate, dragon-covered roofs and beams. The temple is the only nominally Taoist place of worship on the mountain, primarily dedicated to the Jade Emperor and Guan Di, but, in true Taiwanese style, there are also shrines to Confucius and Sakyamuni Buddha. It's a beautiful location, and a good place for lunch.

Nanzhuang

南庄; nánzhuāng

Midway up the Zhonggang River valley and 10.5km from the main visitor centre, **NANZHUANG** is a small, atmospheric Hakka village that once was a major coal-mining and logging centre. Today it mostly caters to tourists, with well-preserved Japanese-era wooden houses and an official Old Street. It also has an excellent hot-springs spa blessed with odourless sodium bicarbonate spring water, and some great places to eat.

2

Maitreya Monastery (Nature Loving Wonderland)

大自然文化世界; dàzìrán wénhuà shìjiè • 1 Joyful Rd, Huguang Village, Emei • Sat & Sun 9–11.30am & 1.30–4.30pm (Tues–Fri only open for groups of more than 15 people) • Free • ☎ 03 621 4596, ⓦ naturelovingwonderland.org • To get to Emei Lake by public transport, you'll have to first take a bus to Zhudong (see Beipu, p.160) and take Hsinchu Bus #5609 (8 daily 6.55am–6.40pm; NT$52) towards Shanzhu Hu (珊珠湖; shānzhū hú); ask to get off at Fuxing Elementary School (40min), near the Xiao Mao Pu Drawbridge – you'll see the statue from here

A reservoir created from the Emei River, **Emei Lake** (峨眉湖; éméi hú) occupies the far northwestern corner of the Scenic Area and contains a couple of islands in its centre. Despite the tourist hype, it's not big or especially beautiful, and the main reason to come here is to wonder at the 72m-high bronze **Maitreya Buddha Statue** (彌勒大佛; mílè dàfó) on one of the islands. In 2001, the World Maitreya Great Tao Organization began construction of the statue – said to be the tallest of its kind in the world – and the gigantic **Maitreya Monastery** (聖地建築; shèngdì jiànzhù), aka "Nature Loving Wonderland". Visitors can take a look at the phenomenal Main Shrine, with its ceiling of interwoven glass tiles and copper plates, and peruse the related exhibits at the Universal Family Cultural Exhibition Center, inside the giant statue itself. Known as mílèfó, Maitreya Buddha is the chubby, smiling incarnation of Buddha popular throughout Taiwan.

ARRIVAL AND INFORMATION

BY BUS

TAIWAN SHUTTLE BUS

Lion's Head Mountain Route Buses (Mon–Fri 8am–3pm hourly, Sat & Sun every 30min; one-day pass NT$100) run from Zhubei train station and Hsinchu HSR Station to the Lion's Head Mountain Visitor Center; the last bus back leaves the visitor centre at 5pm on weekdays and 6pm weekends.

Nanzhuang Route Buses (Mon–Fri 9.30am–3.30pm hourly, Sat & Sun 8am–5pm every 30min–1hr) run from Lion's Head Mountain Visitor Center to Quanhua Temple, at the end of the main hiking trail (15min), then on to Nanzhuang (30min). A one-day pass is NT$50.

LION'S HEAD MOUNTAIN SCENIC AREA

TOURIST INFORMATION

Lion's Head Mountain Visitor Center The main visitor centre (獅山遊客中心; shīshān yóukè zhōngxīn; daily 8.30am–5.30pm; ☎ 03 580 9296, ⓦ www.trimt-nsa. gov.tw) is in the northern part of the Scenic Area, around 6km south of the village of Emei. English-language materials and an informative video are available, but the exhibits here are labelled in Chinese only.

Nanzhuang Visitor Center There's a small but helpful visitor centre (南庄遊客中心; nánzhuāng yóukè zhōngxīn; daily 8.30am–5.30pm; ☎ 03 782 4570) at 43 Datong Rd on the main road into Nanzhuang.

ACCOMMODATION AND EATING

Lao Jin Long 老金龍; lǎojīn lóng 1 Minzu St (at Zhongzheng Rd), Nanzhuang ☎ 03 782 2168. This long-established spot at the southern end of the village serves excellent Hakka food, with set meals from NT$500 – these typically include local trout, as well as classic pork and bamboo dishes. Mon & Wed–Fri 11am–2pm, Sat & Sun 11am–7pm.

Quanhua Temple 勸化堂; quànhuà táng 242 Shishan Village ☎ 03 782 2563. The temple canteen serves decent vegetarian meals with a view; breakfast costs NT$60, lunch and dinner are both NT$80. Expect lots of greens, bamboo shoots, excellent miso soup, plenty of tofu

and bottomless bowls of rice. Meals are free for guests staying at *Shishan Dalou*. Daily 6.30–8am, noon–1pm (2pm Sat & Sun) & 5.30–7pm.

Shishan Dalou 獅山大樓; shīshān dàlóu Quanhua Temple, 242 Shishan Village ☎ 03 782 2563. Quanhua Temple runs a small budget hotel on site, which offers slightly faded but clean private rooms, all en suite with flatscreen cable TV (hot water from 4pm only). The real highlight, however, is the balconies, which all have excellent views of the valley below, especially beautiful in Feb when the cherry blossoms flower. NT$1000

Taian Hot Springs

泰安溫泉區; tàiān wēnquánqū

Straddling the Wenshui River just to the south of Lion's Head Mountain Scenic Area, **TAIAN HOT SPRINGS** is one of Taiwan's most attractive resorts, offering visitors an enticing combination of **hill walks** and rejuvenating **hot springs**. It's no longer a tranquil haven, however – plenty of tour buses and large groups come here to enjoy the outdoor activities. As a result, hotels tend to be pricey, but don't be put off: all are open for public bathing, so you don't have to stay overnight to enjoy the waters, and the area rarely feels crowded, especially on weekdays. Miaoli Route 62 winds for 12km alongside the Wenshui River before reaching the main hot-springs village of **Jinshui** (錦水; jǐnshuǐ).

ARRIVAL AND DEPARTURE
TAIAN HOT SPRINGS

Getting here without your own transport is tough. One relatively easy option is to **rent a scooter** in Sanyi, about a 1hr ride away. By **public transport**, you'll need to first take a **train to Miaoli** (苗栗; miáolì), and then catch a **bus to Dahu** (大湖; dàhú; hourly; 50min); from Miaoli train station walk straight ahead about 50m and you'll find the bus station on your right.

BY BUS, TAXI OR HITCHING
From Dahu or Wenshui There are two local buses a day from Dahu on to Taian Hot Springs (Mon–Fri only), but the schedule is erratic, so you're better off trying to get a taxi from Dahu (NT$500) or at the village of Wenshui (汶水; wènshuǐ), around 50min from Miaoli. If you plan to stay at one of the Taian hotels, they can help you arrange taxis from Dahu or Wenshui.

From Provincial Hwy 3 You can get off the Miaoli bus 1km south of Wenshui on Provincial Highway 3, at the junction with Miaoli Route 62 (the stop is known as "fǎyúnsì" (法雲寺), but the busy 7-Eleven here is the main landmark. From here you can walk up Route 62 for 200m or so to the Shei-Pa National Park Headquarters (see box, p.166), then either hitch a ride to Taian or get staff to call a taxi for you.

TAIAN HIKING TRAILS

There are several **hiking trails** around Taian, but bear in mind that most of the paths are very steep, leaving them vulnerable to landslips during heavy rains; be sure to ask locals about the latest trail conditions before setting out.

SHUIYUN WATERFALL

The area's easiest hike – though one not to be attempted in rainy weather – is to the **Shuiyun Waterfall** (水雲瀑布; shuǐyún pùbù), a shimmering cascade hidden behind a bend along the Wenshui River. The route begins at the car park at the end of Miaoli Route 62 (2km beyond the village). A gravel trail continues for another kilometre or so before it reaches the **Shuiyun Suspension Bridge** (水雲吊橋; shuǐyún diàoqiáo), which you must cross in order to reach the trail proper. After crossing the bridge, climb the wooden steps for a couple of hundred metres until the trail enters the forest and splits into two directions (with signs in Chinese): the left-hand fork leads to the top of Hushan, while the right-hand path drops down to the river trail to the falls. Take the right-hand trail for about 50m until you reach another sign pointing to the left; follow this path for a few minutes until you reach a rocky outcrop along the riverbank. If you look closely at the rock's edge you'll find a rope you can use to lower yourself to the riverbed. From here, keep to the left side of the river to reach the Shuiyun Waterfall, about 1.5km upstream: the easiest line to follow is marked by **bamboo poles** stuck deep into the ground and crested with red flags. Allow at least one and a half hours to make the return trip from the car park.

HUSHAN

The steep path to the top of **Hushan** (1492m; 虎山; hǔshān) is the area's most challenging and rewarding hike. The ascent is strenuous and suitable only for fairly fit and experienced hillwalkers. From the left-hand fork beyond the Shuiyun Suspension Bridge, the trail winds through a cool, shaded forest before cutting sharply up to the top of Hushan (flagged with **ribbons**). Close to the top, the trail crosses the rocky riverbed that can fill up rapidly in the rainy season, and you must walk up the riverbed itself for about 100m before reconnecting with the trail; here it's essential to look for the trail ribbons tied to overhanging tree branches in order to keep to the path. On clear days, the **views** from the top of Hushan can be stupendous. From the car park at the end of Route 62, allow yourself three to four hours for the return hike, depending on fitness level.

INFORMATION

Hiking information The *Tenglong Hot Spring Villa* is the best place to get information about trail conditions (you'll usually find someone who speaks English); the safety of the trails varies widely depending on the weather, so it's a good idea to ask here before setting out.

Services There are no ATMs in Jinshui, so be sure to take enough cash – if you're stuck, there's a Chinatrust Commercial Bank ATM in the 7-Eleven back at the junction of highways 3 and 62. If you're planning to do some hiking in Taian, you could also stock up on some trail snacks at the 7-Eleven, as there is only one shop in Jinshui (at the *Tenglong Hot Spring Villa*) and it's a bit pricey.

ACCOMMODATION AND HOT SPRINGS

Though plush hot-spring **hotels** and **homestays** line much of Miaoli Route 62, **Jinshui** has the best range, all within easy walking distance of the main trails. Most are expensive, but you should be able to snag discounts on weekdays. Hotels tend to have a **public bathing area**, usually gender-segregated nude pools open late into the evening.

Sunrise Hot Spring Hotel 日出溫泉渡假飯店; rìchū wēnquán dùjià fàndiàn 34 Henglong Shan ☎ 03 794 1988, ⓦ hothotel.com.tw. Stylish rooms with a slight aboriginal theme and attached stone-slab bathing tubs. The lavish communal outdoor bathing pools are open to the public (daily 8am–10pm; NT$450); those seeking greater luxury can rent private two-person spa rooms (NT$1400/1hr). About 1km further up the road from

Tenglong Hot Spring Villa. NT$5500

Tang Wei 湯唯溫泉民宿; tāngwéi wēnquán mínsù 72-2 Henglong Shan ☎ 03 794 1885, ⓦ tangwei .com.tw. Modern Euro-style chalet right on the river, offering a wide range of rooms, from the fairly cheap and simple (but still with flat-screen TVs) to lavish cabins. Hot-spring pools are open to non-guests Mon–Fri 4–10pm (NT$250), Sat & Sun 2–10.30pm (NT$300). NT$1100

Sanyi and around

三義; sānyì

Tucked away in the south of Miaoli county, **SANYI** is Taiwan's **woodcarving** centre. Apart from the **Sanyi Wood Sculpture Museum**, the town's main attractions are its numerous woodcarving (mùdiāo) shops, selling a vast range of work from religious icons to kitsch souvenirs squarely aimed at the tourist trade. The built-up area south of the station is the original and fairly unattractive town centre, while most of the woodcarving shops lie a further 2km to the south, where Zhongzheng Road is known as **Shuimei Street**. Tucked away in the hills to the southeast, **Shengxing** offers some beautiful hiking, historic Hakka teahouses and the photogenic ruin of **Longteng Bridge**. The village is halfway along a 16km loop of old rail line between Sanyi and Houli (后里; hòulǐ), abandoned in the 1990s.

Sanyi Duck Factory

三義鴨箱寶; sānyì yā xiāngbǎo • 176 Chonghe Rd • Mon–Fri 9am–5pm, Sat & Sun 9am–6pm • Free; duck painting NT$250–1100 ☎ 03 787 2076

Heading south along Zhongzheng Road from the train station, there's not much to see in the main part of Sanyi; turn left on County Route 130, then first right beyond the rail tracks on Miaoli Route 49 towards Shengxing. Just ahead you'll see signs (in Chinese) to the **Sanyi Duck Factory**, just off the main road. Local carvers sell a wide range of multicoloured wooden ducks, birds and animals here, and you can paint your own model in a warehouse next door – the whole process takes about two hours.

Shuimei Street

水美雕刻街; shuǐměi diāokè jiē

At the southern end of Sanyi, Zhongzheng Road becomes **Shuimei Street**, the town's main commercial woodcarving area. It's crammed with over two hundred shops stretching for almost 1km, and is a good place to browse for gifts – though the most visually striking pieces are often big and expensive, there are plenty of smaller, more affordable artwork on display.

Sanyi Wood Sculpture Museum

三義木雕博物館; sānyì mùdiāo bówùguǎn • 88 Guangsheng Village • Tues–Sun 9am–5pm • NT$80 • ☎ 03 787 6009, ⓦ wood.mlc.gov.tw • The museum is clearly signposted in English off Zhongzheng Rd, 2.7km from the station

Showcasing the best of local carving, the **Sanyi Wood Sculpture Museum** is a modern building at the end of a small strip of woodcarving shops, many doubling as teahouses and cafés. This is **Guangsheng Village** (廣聲新城; guǎngshēng xīnchéng), purpose-built to accommodate Taiwan's finest wood sculptors, in order to pool their artistic (and tourist-attracting) synergies – it's also the focus of the month-long **Sanyi Woodcarving Festival**, usually held between August and October. The museum houses a small exhibition on the history of woodcarving and a collection of absorbing sculptures on the higher floors.

Shengxing

勝興; shèngxīng • A 15min taxi ride from Sanyi Station or 45min cycle

Around 3km beyond Sanyi and fun to cycle to is the attractive Hakka village of **SHENGXING**, particularly appealing in the spring when the area's distinctive white **tung flowers** (tónghuā) are in bloom. Shengxing was once an important transport hub for the **camphor oil** industry, but a new tunnel meant mainline trains bypassed the village in the late 1990s. Today the area has been rebranded as the Jiushanxian Agricultural Area and the tourist industry is booming, which means weekends and holidays the place turns into a bit of carnival; visit on a weekday if possible.

The **old station**, completed in 1911 and once Taiwan's highest mainline stop at 402m, is a picturesque wooden building at the bottom of the narrow main street. The road back up the hill is lined with teahouses and stores serving Hakka food, snacks and souvenirs. There are some good **hikes** in the nearby national forest park, though most visitors seem content to amble up and down the old train tracks, taking selfies.

Longteng Broken Bridge

龍騰斷橋; lóngténg duànqiáo

From Shengxing village centre, it's a pleasant ride or walk to **Longteng Broken Bridge**, just under 6km to the southeast. The hike along the old rail tracks is mostly level – head south through the 726m tunnel near Shengxing station. The bridge is a redbrick viaduct that collapsed during the Hsinchu earthquake of 1935, now a romantic ruin, overgrown with weeds and bushes and surrounded by lush, wooded hills. Assuming you have a scooter, you can loop back to Sanyi from here via Miaoli Route 51, which rejoins Provincial Highway 13 at the southern and more interesting end of town.

ARRIVAL AND DEPARTURE
SANYI AND AROUND

By train Sanyi train station (三義車站; sānyì chēzhàn) is inconveniently located at the far northern end of town, just off the main street, Zhongzheng Rd (Provincial Hwy 13).

Destinations Hsinchu (18 daily; 50min); Taichung (18 daily; 35min); Taipei (3 express daily; 2hr 30min).

GETTING AROUND

By scooter or bicycle As the area is too spread out to see everything on foot, you may want to rent a bicycle or scooter. Jian Guang (建光; jiànguāng; ☎ 03 787 1879; no English signs and little English spoken) at 162-2 Zhongzheng Rd, opposite the station, is pretty relaxed about renting to foreigners; all you need is a driving licence, though with no ARC (see p.27) you'll need to leave your passport with them. Rates are NT$350–400/day, and you won't need more than NT$70 for petrol. They also rent high-quality bicycles for NT$200/day.

By taxi Taxis charge NT$200 from Sanyi to Shengxing (one-way).

ACCOMODATION AND EATING

Sanyi Sakura Resort 三義櫻花; èryì yīnghuā 1–18 Lane 8, Bagu St, Sanyi ☎03 500 6896, ⓦfacebook.com/SanyiClub. More boutique hotel than resort, this is still one of the few solid accommodation options in Sanyi. Conveniently located just down the hill from the Wood Sculpture Museum, rooms have all mod cons, en-suite bathrooms and great views of the surrounding countryside. Breakfast included. NT$4000

★**Shengxing Inn** 勝興客棧; shèngxīng kèzhàn 72 Lane 14, Shengxing Village ☎03 787 3883.

Shengxing's oldest and most attractive restaurant, on the right just up the slope from the station, was adorned with red bricks taken from the Longteng Bridge after the 1935 earthquake. Sumptuously prepared Hakka dishes include the bamboo and pork dish, special tofu and the succulent duck or zhīsù yāròu (mains NT$200–400). Léichá (see box, p.160) costs NT$100/person (DIY), or NT$250 for a bowl made for you. Menus are in Chinese only, but the owner's wife speaks English. Daily 9am–8pm; meals from 10.30am.

Shei-Pa National Park

雪霸國家公園; xuěbà guójiā gōngyuán

An unapologetically rugged reserve of mountain peaks and raging rivers, **SHEI-PA NATIONAL PARK** is one of Asia's most pristine expanses of wilderness. Stretching across almost 770 square kilometres of the magnificent **Xueshan range**, Taiwan's third-largest national park is studded with stunning peaks, 51 of them higher than 3000m – putting them on a par with most of the European Alps. The park's highest peak is the range's namesake: **Xueshan** (Snow Mountain), which at 3886m is the second-tallest mountain in northeast Asia. Despite its lofty height, it's one of the island's most accessible and rewarding climbs, with an extremely well-maintained **trail** that is typically open for most of the year. This path is also a grandiose gateway to the park's other mountain highlights, such as the precipitous **Holy Ridge** that extends north from Xueshan to the 3492m **Dabajianshan**, whose distinctive pyramid shape has made it one of the country's most celebrated peaks.

Seasonal conditions vary, but in general the **best time** for hiking or climbing in Shei-Pa is October to December and late February to April. The May rains and the frequent typhoons that hit the island from June to September can cause severe damage to the trails, making landslips a concern. Though winters are cold and the main peaks are usually covered with **snow** from late December to mid-February, for experienced climbers with proper gear this can be the most rewarding time to visit.

Wuling Recreation Area

武陵遊樂區; wǔlíng yóulèqū · Mon–Fri NT$130, Sat & Sun NT$160, cash only (valid 2 days)

The only section of Shei-Pa accessible by public transport, the **WULING RECREATION AREA** is the base for Xueshan climbs and is a worthwhile destination in its own right. Commonly known as **Wuling Farm** (武陵農場; wǔlíng nóngchǎng), the area was

---

SHEI-PA VISITOR CENTER

Shei-Pa National Park Headquarters (雪霸國家公園管理處; xuěbà guójiā gōngyuán guǎnlǐchù) and its **visitor centre** (Tues–Sun 9am–4.30pm; ☎03 799 6100, ⓦwww.spnp .gov.tw) are inconveniently located along Miaoli Route 62 just off Provincial Highway 3, about 2km from the town of Wenshui on the way to the Taian Hot Springs. The visitor centre has two exhibition halls that give an excellent bilingual overview of the park's most notable attractions and show films (Tues–Sun). On most days, English-speaking staff are on hand and can provide you with park **maps** as well as more detailed topographical maps (Chinese only) of trails in the Xueshan area. Those wishing to climb mountains within the park can apply here for national park **entry permits**, although you must submit your application seven working days before the proposed start date of your climb (see box, p.170).

established as an **orchard** in 1963 by retired KMT soldiers, and still draws domestic tourists looking to buy freshly plucked peaches, pears and apples.

Many tourists drive up the main road, stopping at various orchards along the way to pick fruit, until they reach the **Wuling Suspension Bridge** (武陵吊橋; wǔlíng diàoqiáo). It's possible to walk the entire distance, but it's about 10km each way, so make sure you have enough time for the return journey.

Beyond the suspension bridge the road leads to the trailhead for one of the area's best-known hikes, to **Taoshan Waterfall** (桃山瀑布; táoshān pùbù). The 4.5km walk climbs about 450m before reaching the 50m-high cascade; allow two to three hours for the return journey.

2

ARRIVAL AND DEPARTURE   WULING RECREATION AREA

BY BUS

It's essential to check all current departure times (with the local tourist office if you don't speak Chinese) before making plans, as mountain bus routes are especially liable to change.

From/to Taipei E-go Bus runs direct to Wuling Farm daily at 7.20am, arriving at 11.20am; the bus returns at 2pm.

From/to Yilan The simplest way to reach Wuling by public transport is to take one of the two daily Kuo-Kuang buses (7.30am & 12.40pm; 2hr 45min) that run from the east-coast city of Yilan (宜蘭; yílán). These buses stop in Wuling before heading on to Lishan (梨山; líshān). Yilan can be reached by express train from Taipei (every 30min–1hr; 1hr 5min–1hr 20min); the town's bus station is 150m

from the train station (left as you exit). Heading back, buses depart from Lishan for Wuling and Yilan at 8.30am and 1.30pm, departing from Wuling at around 9.10am and 2.10pm, but get to the bus stop well in advance just in case. At Lishan (which is 29km and 20–30min south of Wuling), you can catch a bus to Taroko Gorge and Hualien.

From/to Taichung From Taichung's Fengyuan bus station, a bus departs daily for Lishan at 8am, arriving around 2pm; connecting services for Wuling leave Lishan at 4.50pm (20–30min). Heading back to Taichung, buses leave Wuling at 6.30am, and Lishan at 8am. The bus stops at Puli on the way at around 11.20am, where you change for Sun Moon Lake.

INFORMATION

Tourist information The Wuling Visitor Center (武陵遊客中心; wǔlíng yóukè zhōngxīn; Tues–Sun 9am–4.30pm; ☎04 2590 1350, ⓦwww2.wuling-farm

.com.tw), 4 Wuling Rd, provides a basic map of the Wuling Farm area.

ACCOMMODATION

Hoya Resort Hotel 武陵富野渡假村; wǔlíng fùyě dùjiàcūn 3–16 Wuling Rd ☎04 2590 1399, ⓦwww. hoyaresort.com.tw/wuling. Set on a hill to the left of the road after you enter the recreation area, this upmarket package-style resort includes breakfast and dinner buffets in its room rates. The restaurant is for guests only. NT$6600

★**Wuling Farm Campground** 武陵農場露營天地; wǔlíng nóngchǎng lùyíng tiāndì ☎04 2590 1470, ⓦwww2.wuling-farm.com.tw. Well-maintained

campsite near the Xueshan trailhead, with hot showers and the on-site *Forest Coffee Bar* serving set breakfast, lunch, dinner and snacks. As well as pitches for those with their own tent, they offer raised-platform tents with mattresses for four people, and cabins. For those in need of some creature comforts, the campsite's affiliated hotel has rooms and villas on offer. Pitches NT$1000/person; tents NT$1300/person; cabins NT$2500/person; doubles NT$3500

Xueshan

雪山; xuěshān

The 3886m-high **Xueshan** is one of Asia's most scintillating climbs, and though it takes a modicum of planning, it's well worth the effort. An exceptionally fit walker could make the nearly 22km journey from the trailhead to the peak and back in one long day, but most climbers choose to take their time and spend a night in the free **369 Cabin**. For those with more time and their own camping equipment, this trail can be the gateway to a two- to three-day circuit over the hair-raising **Holy Ridge** and on to **Dabajianshan** – without question one of Taiwan's top treks.

It's best to arrive the day before you're scheduled to set out to allow plenty of time to

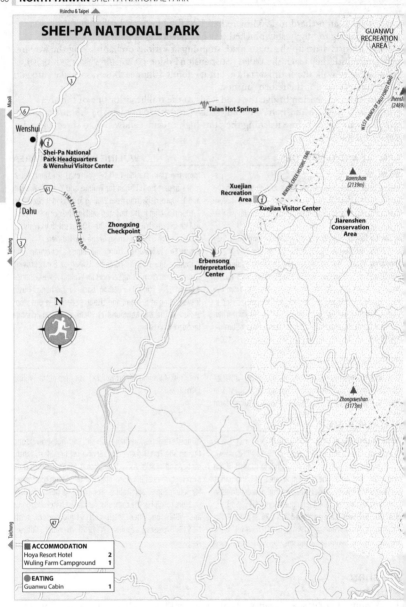

SHEI-PA NATIONAL PARK

Hsinchu & Taipei

Miaoli

GUANWU
RECREATION
AREA

Taian Hot Springs

Wenshui

Shei-Pa National
Park Headquarters
& Wenshui Visitor Center

WEST BRANCH OF DAJIA FOREST ROAD

Jhensi
(2489)

Jiarenshan
(2139m)

Xuejian
Recreation
Area

Xuejian Visitor Center

Jiarenshen
Conservation
Area

Dahu

Taichung

ZHONGXING FOREST ROAD

Zhongxing
Checkpoint

Erbensong
Interpretation
Center

N

Zhongxueshan
(3173m)

Taichung

47

ACCOMMODATION
Hoya Resort Hotel   2
Wuling Farm Campground   1

EATING
Guanwu Cabin   1

check in and to arrange **transport** to the **trailhead**. It's a 7km walk along the main road from the visitor centre to the trailhead, and, though the scenery is pleasant, the walk adds considerable time and distance to the climb and could make it a challenge for some hikers to make it to the *369 Cabin* by nightfall. If the park rangers are free, they might offer to drop you off at the trailhead the following morning; otherwise, you'll have to arrange a shuttle and pick-up with your hotel.

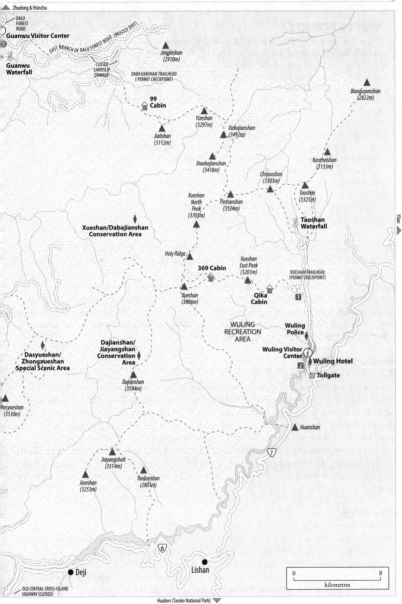

The climb

From the Xueshan trailhead (雪山登山口; xuěshān dēngshānkǒu), it's 2km to the **Qika Cabin** at 2463m (七卡山莊; qīkǎ shānzhuāng; free), which has pit toilets and a nearby tap with a fresh water supply. From here it's a steep 5km climb, mostly up stone steps, to the *369 Cabin* – allow between two to five hours depending on your fitness. Once you reach Xueshan's **East Peak** (雪山東峰; xuěshān dōngfēng; 3201m), the trail becomes

2

SHEI-PA PERMITS

To climb anywhere in Shei-pa National Park you'll need to arrange a **national park entry permit** (入園; rùyuán; apply in advance) and **police permit** or **mountain entry permit** (入山; rùshān; handed out by local police stations on the spot) to make any of these climbs – you'll find more details on the permit system in Basics (see box, p.39). The Shei-Pa **website** also has the application process clearly mapped out in English. Though applications for the park entry permit are technically supposed to be received **seven to thirty working days** before the proposed start date of your climb, in practice they are often approved within a few days, and if you turn up to the park headquarters to apply in person (foreigners are allowed to do this), the staff are likely to prepare your permit much more quickly.

Before you begin your climb, you must pick up your **mountain entry permit** at the **Wuling Police Squadron** (武陵警察小隊; wǔlíng jǐngchá xiǎoduì; ☎ 04 2590 1117), a few hundred metres north along the main road from the visitor centre, on the left-hand side. You'll need an application form (from the Shei-Pa website), three copies of your hiking itinerary, and one copy of your passport and park entry permit. The rangers are also likely to inspect your kit to ensure that you have the necessary **equipment**.

more gradual and gives good views directly west across the valley to the Holy Ridge. About 1km further is the **369 Cabin** (三六九山莊; sānliùjiǔ shānzhuāng), which overlooks a giant valley and a vast plain to the north, making for an ideal place to relax and soak up the scenery – in late afternoon clouds often roll into the valley, creating the spectacular "**sea of clouds**" phenomenon. There are no designated sleeping spaces, so you're free to grab whatever bunk you fancy. Near the cabin are pit toilets and a tap with fresh water – a convenient place to replenish your **drinking water**, as there are no other reliable sources between here and the summit.

Xueshan Main Peak
雪山主峰; xuěshān zhǔfēng

Many climbers set their alarms for as early as 3am to ensure they can cover the remaining 3.9km to **Xueshan Main Peak** before dawn, and indeed watching the sun rise here, over a pinkish-blue sea of clouds below, is an ethereal experience. However, the summit can be phenomenal at any time of day, and if there's a large crowd getting up early for the sunrise it's worth sleeping in and heading to the top a bit later, when you can have it all to yourself. Average walkers should be able to complete this stage in two to three hours. It's important to try to reach the top by midday to allow yourself plenty of time for the descent to the trailhead, which can take anywhere from four to five hours.

Holy Ridge
聖稜線; shèngléng xiàn

From Xueshan Main Peak it's also possible to set out across the **Holy Ridge** from where you can carry on north to **Dabajianshan** or head east to **Taoshan** and back down to the Wuling Recreation Area. However, the Holy Ridge is precarious in places and there are some steep fixed-rope sections, so it's really only suited to more experienced climbers. It's essential to ask the park rangers in Wuling about the latest trail conditions and the weather forecast – the ridge is highly exposed and lightning is a real danger here.

Guanwu Recreation Area
觀霧遊樂區; guānwùyóulèqū

At around 2000m in elevation, **Guanwu Recreation Area** is cool and densely vegetated, with one of Taiwan's most humbling old-growth forests and the island's only **Sassafras Conservation Area**. If wilderness walks are what you're after, it's well worth the effort to get here; in addition to having the safest trail to **Dabajianshan** (permits required), it offers several shorter **hikes** that on clear days can yield splendid vistas of the park's highest mountains – especially those along the Holy Ridge. The best is the 1.5km trail to the **Guanwu Waterfall** (觀霧瀑布; guānwù pùbù), which drops delicately down a near-vertical 30m rock face.

Dabajianshan

大霸尖山; dàbàjiānshān

For most hikers, the journey to spectacular **Dabajianshan** takes a minimum of three days, with two overnight stays in the **99 Cabin**. To reach the original **trailhead** (at 1750m) from the visitor centre, you'll need to hike around 20km of the generally flat east branch of the earthen Dalu Forest Road (vehicles may be able to traverse this section in future – check in advance). The climb to the cabin, which sits at about 2700m, is fairly steep, and most walkers stop here for the night, rising well before dawn for the slog to the summit. However, as Dabajianshan has sheer faces on all sides, it's not possible to go to the very top: though the park installed **metal railings** on one side to make the ascent possible, a couple of climbers fell off and they had to be closed. Most walkers return to the *99 Cabin* and spend a second night there before hiking down to the road the next morning.

ARRIVAL AND INFORMATION

By car To get to Guanwu you'll need to have your own transport. The area is around 60km southeast of Hsinchu via County Route 122 and the winding Dalu Forest Road (allow 2hr by car). At the 15km point you'll pass the Yuanshan Checkpoint (雲山檢查哨; yúnshān jiǎncháshào), where you need to get your mountain

GUANWU RECREATION AREA

entry permit (free).

Tourist information Guanwu Visitor Center (觀霧遊客 中心; guānwù yóukè zhōngxīn; Tues–Sun 9am–4.30pm; ☎ 03 727 6300), just inside the park entrance at the 26km mark, is where you should enquire about trail conditions.

ACCOMMODATION AND EATING

99 Cabin 九九山莊; jiǔjiǔ shānzhuāng This large overnighting facility is 2800m up on the Dabajianshan trail. You'll need a permit to stay here; book ahead at Guanwu Visitor Center. NT$200

Guanwu Cabin 觀霧山莊; guānwù shānzhuāng Dalu Forest Rd, km 28 ☎ 03 224 163. Originally built for loggers, this rustic cabin has been transformed into a restaurant serving basic meals (no accommodation).

Central Taiwan

SUN MOON LAKE

Central Taiwan

Bounded by the densely populated cities of the north and the lush tropical plains of the south, central Taiwan is a region defined by mountains: its mighty ranges contain a vast array of mesmerizing landscapes, from the beauty of Sun Moon Lake and Alishan National Park to the awe-inspiring peak of Yushan, northeast Asia's tallest mountain. The rugged appeal of this wilderness is matched by the friendliness of the communities who have made a way of life here for centuries. To the west, the mountains recede to the coastal plains, and modern Taiwan in the shape of the prosperous cities of Taichung, Changhua and Chiayi, but glimpses of the past are everywhere.

Taichung, gateway to the region, is one of the most dynamic cities in the country. To the south, the flat river plains are rich in traditional Chinese culture; worship of Taoist deity Mazu, Goddess of the Sea, is more intense here than in any other part of Taiwan. The towns of **Beigang** and **Dajia** are home to the most important Mazu temples on the island, and the annual Dajia Mazu Pilgrimage is Taiwan's largest religious festival. **Lugang** is one of Taiwan's oldest towns, a living museum of temples, narrow streets, master craftsmen and delicious street food, while the Great Buddha Statue in Changhua is one of Asia's biggest. **Sun Moon Lake**'s splendid natural beauty is sometimes marred by the sheer number of visitors who make their way here, but there's so much in this area that you can always escape the crowds. South of the lake, the **Jiji train line** rolls past bucolic scenery, while **Xitou Forest Recreation Area** presents impossibly picturesque bamboo landscapes. North of Sun Moon Lake, at the centre of the island is the township of **Puli**, home to the mind-boggling **Chung Tai Chan Monastery**, a staggering monument to contemporary architecture and Zen Buddhist philosophy.

Further south lies the town of Chiayi and, to its east, the narrow valleys and traditional Tsou villages of **Alishan National Scenic Area**, which has an array of attractive and highly individual homestays. Alishan borders the **Yushan National Park**, offering a more challenging hiking experience, though the stunning path up its main peak is tackled by thousands of visitors every year.

This chapter covers Changhua, Chiayi, Nantou, Taichung and Yunlin counties; visitors should note that although **getting around** the coastal plains is straightforward given the north–south transport links, accessing remote parts of the interior can be tricky without your own transport.

Taichung

台中; táizhōng

Spread over the flat coastal plains west of the mountains, **TAICHUNG** is Taiwan's third-largest city, the unofficial capital of central Taiwan and an important transport hub for the region. It is also one of the country's most attractive cities to live in: the climate is drier, the streets greener and less crowded than Taipei or Kaohsiung.

The 921 Earthquake p.180	Lalu Island p.200
Taichung street snacks p.185	Talking some Tsou p.219
Mazu Holy Pilgrimage p.187	Alishan's red cypress trees p.222
Lugang's living heritage p.194	Yushan wildlife p.227

DAJIA MAZU PILMIGRAGE

Highlights

❶ **921 Earthquake Museum** Informative and poignant memorial to the devastating quake that hit Taiwan in 1999, with high-tech exhibits built around the hauntingly stark ruins of a junior high school. **See p.177**

❷ **Dajia Mazu Pilgrimage** The annual Mazu Pilgrimage to celebrate Taiwan's "patron saint" is an exuberant celebration involving hundreds of thousands of people. **See box, p.187**

❸ **Lugang** Historic town with bags of charm, old streets, craft shops, temples and tasty "little eats". **See p.192**

❹ **Sun Moon Lake** The ancestral home of Taiwan's smallest aboriginal tribe, the Thao, the area around this glistening turquoise lake is some of the most gorgeous scenery in the country. **See p.200**

❺ **Chung Tai Chan Monastery** Taiwan's largest Buddhist temple complex is an incredible blend of modern engineering and dazzling traditional craftsmanship. **See p.209**

❻ **Alishan National Scenic Area** Explore a lush, mountainous region sprinkled with alluring homestays, Tsou villages and pristine hiking trails. **See p.219**

❼ **Yushan National Park** The ascent of Yushan, northeast Asia's highest mountain, is one of the country's highlights: a spectacular hike through the clouds with mind-blowing views. **See p.227**

HIGHLIGHTS ARE MARKED ON THE MAP ON P.176

Taiwanese **tea culture** is very much in evidence; the city has an appealing mix of elegant classical teahouses and stylish contemporary cafés.

Taichung covers a vast area and is divided into eight districts, but it's simplest to think of the city as having two parts: the centre and the west. The older parts of Taichung lie mainly in Central District, around the train station (though spreading east- and northwards), and holds attractive remnants of the Japanese colonial past alongside a smattering of unusual **temples**, as well as traditional food stalls, shops and cheap hotels. In contrast, the **modern city** is concentrated in the west, home to most of Taichung's international hotels, restaurants and nightlife, as well as the **National Taiwan Museum of Fine Arts**, a world-class contemporary art gallery, the otherworldly edifice of

CENTRAL TAIWAN

HIGHLIGHTS

1. 921 Earthquake Museum
2. Dajia Mazu Pilgrimage
3. Lugang
4. Sun Moon Lake
5. Chung Tai Chan Monastery
6. Alishan National Scenic Area
7. Yushan National Park

the new Taichung National Theatre, and further out, I.M. Pei's iconic **Luce Memorial Chapel**, another striking piece of modern architecture.

Taiwan Boulevard (台灣大道; táiwān dàdào), which starts at the main train station, is the main east–west thoroughfare connecting the two main parts of the city and providing a route to the freeway, Donghai University and the harbour (24km out). Beyond Taichung's suburbs, the chief attractions are **Dajia** and its famous **Mazu Pilgrimage**, and the **921 Earthquake Museum**.

Brief history

Taichung traces its origins to a military post and village known as **Datun**, established in 1733 on the site of today's Taichung Park, but the modern city is an amalgam of several places. Datun was briefly the **capital of Taiwan** after the island became a province of China in 1885, but local infrastructure was poor and Taipei, which was the provisional capital, assumed the official role in 1894. After the Japanese occupied Taiwan in 1895 the city's name was changed to Taichung, or "Central Taiwan" and development began in earnest, with Englishman William Barton hired to design the new road layout for the city. The economy boomed in the 1970s and 1980s, with manufacturing and shoemaking in particular leading the way, and by the 1990s the commercial centre of the city had drifted west towards Taichung Port (Taiwan's second largest).

Central and eastern Taichung

The formerly shabby **old centre** (中區; zhōngqū) around the main train station is gradually being gentrified, and is where you'll find Taichung's traditional shopping streets and food stalls, as well as its finest **Japanese colonial buildings**, some of which have been beautifully restored. It is easily explored on foot. The main street, Zhongshan Road, runs northwest from the station. To its north is **Jiguang Street** (激光街; jīguāngjiē), lined with clothes shops and snack stalls. To its south, **Electronic Street** (電子街; diànzǐjiē) is crammed with numerous electronic and computer stores which get going after noon. Ziyou Road (aka **cake street**; see box, p.185) leads up to Taichung Park where Old Taichung spills over into **North District** (北區; běiqū), home of several significant temples.

Stock 20

台中二十號倉庫; táizhōng èrshí hào cāngkù • Lane 37, Sec 4, Fuxing Rd • Take the underpass under the station • Tues–Sun 10am–5pm • Free • ☎ 04 2220 9972, ⓦ stock20.boch.gov.tw

On the south side of the train station, itself an attractive building completed in 1917, **Stock 20** is an innovative arts centre converted from old train warehouses. The galleries have eight to ten shows per year by the resident artists – check the website or call for details (Chinese only).

Taichung Municipal Office Building

台中市役所; táizhōng shìyìsuǒ • 97 Minquan Rd • Tues–Sun 10am–9pm • Free

The city's most stately colonial architecture sits proudly on the western side of Minquan Road. Built in 1911 with a handsome Neoclassical portico and domed roof, **Taichung Municipal Office Building** is an elegant white building that was the original City Hall. It now operates as an attractive gallery for temporary art and history exhibitions.

921 Earthquake Museum of Taiwan

九二一地震教育園區; jiǔèryī dìzhèn jiàoyùyuánqū • Tues–Sun 9am–5pm • NT$50 • ⓦ 921emt.nmns.edu.tw • Bus #50 to Kengkou, or a Nantou-bound bus from Fengyuan bus station via Zhongxing (中興新村; zhōngxīng xīncūn; every 30min); tell the driver you want to get off at Guangfu Xingcun (光復新村站; guāngfù xīncūn zhàn), from where it's a short walk to the museum

In the village of Kengkou (坑口; kēngkǒu), roughly 14km south of Taichung train station, the **921 Earthquake Museum of Taiwan** is an evocative, sobering introduction to the damage and destruction wrought by the massive earthquake of 1999, particularly in this part of the country. Though it has attracted criticism from people who say it ignores the controversial aspects of the 921 Earthquake (such as substandard building construction), it's informative and very moving. The museum is centred on the former site of **Guangfu Junior High School** – most of the (thankfully, empty) school collapsed during the quake. Ruined school buildings

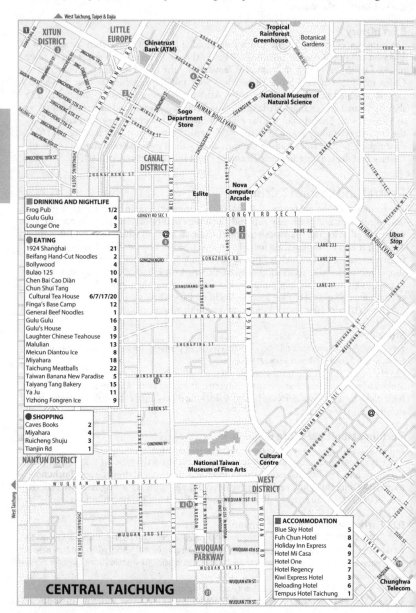

DRINKING AND NIGHTLIFE

Frog Pub	1/2
Gulu Gulu	4
Lounge One	3

EATING

1924 Shanghai	21
Beifang Hand-Cut Noodles	2
Bollywood	4
Bulao 125	10
Chen Bai Cao Diàn	14
Chun Shui Tang Cultural Tea House	6/7/17/20
Finga's Base Camp	12
General Beef Noodles	1
Gulu Gulu	16
Gulu's House	3
Laughter Chinese Teahouse	19
Malulian	13
Meicun Diantou Ice	8
Miyahara	18
Taichung Meatballs	22
Taiwan Banana New Paradise	5
Taiyang Tang Bakery	15
Ya Ju	11
Yizhong Fongren Ice	9

SHOPPING

Caves Books	2
Miyahara	4
Ruicheng Shuju	3
Tianjin Rd	1

ACCOMMODATION

Blue Sky Hotel	5
Fuh Chun Hotel	8
Holiday Inn Express	4
Hotel Mi Casa	9
Hotel One	2
Hotel Regency	7
Kiwi Express Hotel	3
Reloading Hotel	6
Tempus Hotel Taichung	1

CENTRAL TAICHUNG

form the outdoor area of the museum; on both sides of them are two futuristic exhibition halls packed with interactive displays labelled in English and Chinese. The **Chelungpu Fault Gallery** crosses the actual fault line – a clearly visible ridge created by the quake that cuts across the running track; while the **Earthquake Image Gallery** features audio-visual images of the quake and its aftermath, climaxing in hourly shows in a huge theatre.

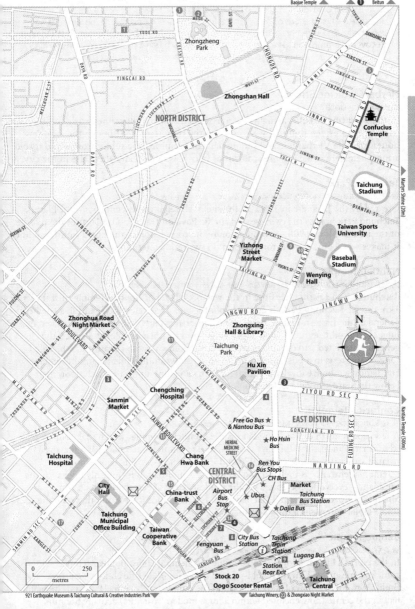

> **THE 921 EARTHQUAKE**
>
> All over Taiwan, but particularly in the central part of the country, you'll hear about the **921 Earthquake** (九二一大地震; jiǔèryī dàdìzhèn): the 7.3-magnitude quake ripped across the island at 1.47am on September 21, 1999, killing 2455 people, injuring more than 8000 and destroying 50,652 buildings. It's also known as the **Chi-Chi Earthquake** – the epicentre was beneath the town of Jiji, 12.5km west of Sun Moon Lake. In fact, many of the casualties in Nantou county were victims of an aftershock five days later that measured 6.7 on the Richter scale, flattening buildings weakened on September 21.
>
> Despite the heroic efforts of rescue services in the days after the disaster, the government was criticized for its slow response. In the aftermath, it established the **921 Earthquake Post-Disaster Recovery Commission** to help affected areas, but many building contractors responsible for illegal construction – blamed for many of the deaths – have never been prosecuted.

Herbal Medicine Street

草藥街; cǎoyàojiē

Herbal Medicine Street is actually a whole series of narrow alleys lined with Traditional Medicine stores, ten minutes' walk north of the train station. Although the area now houses sizeable Vietnamese and Indonesian communities, the subtle aromas and torpid atmosphere here make it more redolent of Old Taiwan than anywhere else in the city.

Taichung Park

台中公園; táizhōng gōngyuán • Gongyuan Rd • Daily 10am–9pm • Free

Created by the Japanese in 1903 on the site of the eighteenth-century fort of Datun, **Taichung Park** houses the twin-peaked **Hu Xin Pavilion** (湖心亭; húxīntíng) in the middle of the lake. Built in 1908 to commemorate the completion of the north–south rail line, it makes a welcome retreat from the sun on sweltering afternoons.

Nantian Temple

南天宮; nántiān gōng • Ziyou Rd • Daily 6am–10pm • Bus #61 from the city bus station

Taichung's East District has little in the way of sights, but **Nantian Temple**, just under 1km east of Taichung Park, is certainly photogenic. Dedicated to Guan Di, a (deified) general of the Eastern Han dynasty, the Main Hall is fairly typical, but it's backed by a huge, garish 48m statue. Seated above a tiger and swathed in colourful robes, the general is depicted stroking his beard – he's also known as the "Beautiful Whiskered One" – and rests in a posture said to convey great wisdom, while his bright red face and hands symbolize loyalty and bravery. You can climb up to the sixth floor, just below the statue, to take a closer look.

Confucius Temple

孔廟; kǒngmiào • 30 Shuangshi Rd Sec 2 • Tues–Sun 9am–5pm • Bus #50, #65

A few blocks north of Taichung Park is the **Confucius Temple**, which makes up in scale what it lacks in history. Taiwan's second-largest Confucian temple, it is a massive, palatial structure completed in 1976 and is still in near-pristine condition. Its ceremonial entrance is the **Lingxing Gate** on Lixing Road, but this only opens for the president – everyone else enters via the modest "**Gate of Perceiving Virtue**" on Shuangshi Road. The central **Dacheng Hall** is a magnificent structure that contains a single tablet commemorating Confucius.

Baojue Temple

寶覺寺; bǎojuésì • 140 Jianxing Rd • Tues–Sun 9am–5pm • Bus #82

In the North District, **Baojue Temple** is one of Taichung's most popular temples – tourists come to gape at the 27m-high gold-painted statue of mílèfó (the chubby Maitreya Buddha) to the far right of the compound. The temple was built in 1928 and the main hall in the centre (now enclosed within a huge modern structure) actually honours

Sakyamuni Buddha. Japanese tourists tend to congregate around the small pavilion and stele to the left, next to the remembrance hall; some Taiwanese fought for Japan in World War II, and this is where many of them were interred after being killed overseas. The calligraphy on the stele is an epitaph written by former president Lee Teng-hui, whose brother was killed fighting for the Japanese.

West Taichung

This area is comprised of sprawling Nantun, Xitun and West districts beyond Wuquan Road (五權路; wǔquán lù) and Beitun District to the north. It is where you'll find more of the modern Taichung, where the most cosmopolitan restaurants and attractions are located.

National Museum of Natural Science

國立自然科學博物館; guólì zìrán kēxué bówùguǎn • 1 Guanqian Road • Tues–Sun 9am–5pm, no entry after 4.30pm • Exhibition Halls NT$100, Science Center NT$20, Botanical Gardens NT$20 • ☏ 04 2322 6940, ⊕ nmns.edu.tw • Buses #301–308

For Taiwanese tourists, the gargantuan **National Museum of Natural Science** is Taichung's top attraction. It's a very family-friendly experience, despite the lack of much labelling in English. Behind the main complex, the striking **Tropical Rainforest Greenhouse** (熱帶雨林溫室; rèdài yǔlín wēnshì) has become a city landmark, thanks to its 31m-high steel and glass exterior and lush rainforest inside, complete with simulated rainfall, while the **National Botanical Gardens** (國立植物園; guólì zhíwùyúan) surrounding the greenhouse are a very pleasant place to relax.

National Taiwan Museum of Fine Arts

國立台灣美術館; guólì táiwān měishùguǎn • 2 Wuquan W Rd Sec 1 • Tues–Fri 9am–5pm, Sat & Sun 9am–6pm • Free • ☏ 04 2372 3552, ⊕ ntmofa.gov.tw • Buses #30, #40, #56, #71 or #75 from the city bus station or Renyou bus #89 from Luchuan East St

An essential visit for anyone with even

WEST TAICHUNG

● SHOPPING
International Art Street ... 1
Tianmu Jade Market ... 2

■ DRINKING & NIGHTLIFE
18TC ... 2
Gordon Biersch
  Brewery Restaurant ... 1
X-Cube ... 3

■ ACCOMMODATION
Hung's Mansion
  Hotel ... 1
Tango Taichung ... 2

● EATING
Geng Du Yuan ... 1
Wu Wei Tsao Tang ... 2

a vague interest in Taiwanese and Chinese art, the **National Taiwan Museum of Fine Arts**, in West District, contains a series of galleries displaying a wide range of both Taiwanese and international work. Most of the exhibits change every few months and tend to have English explanations, though the permanent gallery introducing the history of Taiwanese art on the first floor is presented solely in Chinese.

Wanhe Temple

萬和宮; wànhégōng • Wanhe Road Sec 1 • Daily 6am–10pm • Bus #75

Modern **Nantun District** (南屯; nántún) covers a vast swath of southwest Taichung, but its roots go back to the late seventeenth century. It's here you'll find the city's oldest place of worship, **Wanhe Temple**. The current structure, which comprises three main halls and is dedicated to Mazu (see box, p.187), was begun in 1726 on the site of a shrine built in 1683, but has been renovated many times – the intricate *koji* (jiāozhītáo) figurines set into the walls are especially vivid here.

Wenchang Temple

文昌公廟; wénchānggōng miào • 116 Wenwu Rd • Daily 5.30am–8.30pm • Bus #75

Nantun's **Wenchang Temple** is the modern sister temple of an older shrine in Beitun. The two-storey temple is dedicated not only to Wenchang Dijun (the "Emperor of Passing Exams"), but also Guan Di and Sakyamuni Buddha, and is popular with students: the box in front of the main altar is stuffed with photocopies of test applications and ID cards.

National Taichung Theatre

台中國家歌劇院; táizhōng guójiā gējù yuàn • Huilai Rd Sec 2 • Mon–Thurs & Sun 11am–9pm, Fri & Sat 11.30am–10pm • Free; guided tours NT$100 (daily in Chinese, or in English with 2 weeks' notice) • ☏ 04 2251 1777, ⊕ en.npac-ntt.org • Buses BRT#302, #303, #304, #306 or #307

Completed in 2016, the **National Taichung Theatre** is the jewel in the city's architectural crown. From the outside, its imposing blend of smooth concrete and tinted glass draws you in, where the cavernous entrance hall looks fresh from a Star Wars set. Designed by award-winning Japanese architect Toyo Ito, the theatre took eleven years to build – and it's easy to see why. The entire building is supported by its uniquely curved walls; the level of detail is astounding, and, as you'd expect, the acoustic quality is excellent. There are surprises at every turn, from the bold volcano in the sixth-floor **Sky Garden** to more subtle touches, such as painted butterflies whose edges draw the facial profiles of the workers that built the theatre. Possibly the biggest drawcard is the rose-hued **Grand Theatre**, which can seat over two thousand people, but this can only be visited if you attend one of the three daily performances – see the website for show schedules and tickets. There are also several smaller art spaces and theatres, plus on the fifth floor is a trendy café and a shop selling artsy curios and designer goods.

Luce Memorial Chapel

路思義教堂; lùsīyì jiàotáng • 181 Taiwan Blvd Sec 3 • ☏ 04 2359 0121 • Buses #301–308 run from the city bus station via Tunghai University, and there's a free shuttle from the HSR Station

Xitun District (西屯區; xītún qū) covers a massive chunk of northwest Taichung, its main attraction being the elegant **Luce Memorial Chapel** within the grounds of **Tunghai University** (東海大學; dōnghǎi dàxué), around 9km from the train station. Designed by lauded architect I.M. Pei, it's a breathtaking piece of engineering: completed in 1963 and named after the American Presbyterian missionary Henry Winters Luce, its graceful tent-like structure resembles an inverted ship's hull or, more appropriately, praying hands; it still functions as the university's Christian chapel. The **university grounds** are also worth exploring if you have time, as this is one of the most attractive campuses in Taiwan, with Tang dynasty-themed buildings, and the main avenues lined with Phoenix trees and blossoms.

ARRIVAL AND DEPARTURE   **TAICHUNG**

BY PLANE

Taichung Airport (台中航空站; táizhōng hángkōngzhàn; ☎04 2615 5000; ⓦwww.tca.gov.tw) is a tedious 20km northwest of the city centre, near the village of Xishi (西勢, xīshì). To get into the city, take a taxi (NT$750) or Taichung Bus #9 or #302. As well as domestic services, Taichung airport has flights to an increasing number of destinations in China and Asia with budget carrier Hong Kong Express.

Domestic destinations Hualien (3 weekly; 50min); Kinmen (9–10 daily; 50min); Magong (6–9 daily; 40min); Nangan (2 daily; 1hr 5min).

BY TRAIN

Taichung is almost midway on the western train line between Taipei and Kaohsiung, and the train station (台中火車站; táizhōng huǒchēzhàn) sits in the old centre of the city, close to all local and long-distance bus stations and served by frequent taxis. The train station was being extended and fitted with a sleek new roof at the time of writing, and this is due to be completed by 2019.

Destinations Changhua (22 express daily; 12–15min); Chiayi (19 express daily 50min–1hr 10min); Ershui (1 express daily; 40min); Kaohsiung (19 express daily; 1hr 50min–2hr 50min); Tainan (19 express daily; 1hr 20min–2hr 5min); Taipei (22 express daily; 1hr 40min–2hr 30min).

BY HIGH-SPEED RAIL

The HSR Station (高鐵台中站; gāotiě táizhōngzhàn; ☎04 4066 0000, ⓦthsrc.com.tw) is located at 8 Zhanqu 2nd Rd, in Wuri (烏日; wūrì), 7km southwest of the city centre. You can take the free shuttle bus from here into the city (daily 6.35am–12.10am, every 15–20min; 50min), which terminates at Taichung Park via Sogo, or pay around NT$15 for a local train; these depart regularly from the connecting Xinwuri station (新烏日車站; xīnwūrì chēzhàn) and take 10min to get to the main train station. There are also buses to Changhua (30min), Lugang (1hr) and Sun Moon Lake (1hr), and plenty of taxis (NT$250 into the city and around NT$1000 to Sun Moon Lake).

Destinations Chiayi (every 20–30min; 25–40min); Kaohsiung (frequent; 45min–1hr); Tainan (every 20–30min; 45min); Taipei (frequent; 50min–1hr).

BY BUS

There are two main places where long-distance buses arrive and depart in Taichung: the Chao Ma area (朝馬; cháomǎ) near the freeway and, more conveniently for most travellers, the streets around the main train station. If you are staying in western Taichung you can alight at Chao Ma or along Taiwan Blvd.

BUS STATIONS

The new Taichung Bus Station (台中客運站; táizhōng kèyùn zhàn) is just a few minutes' walk to northeast of the train station, and operates Taichung Bus and Kuo Kuang (☎04 2222 2830) services. From here there are regular services to Taipei, Taiwan Taoyuan International Airport, Chiayi, Tainan and Kaohsiung, plus some more local destinations including Puli and Beigang. Other buses leave from a range of small depots nearby on Jianguo Rd; Ubus (☎04 2226 3034) offers similar destinations. Also on Jianguo Rd, a little west of the railway station, is Fengyuan station (☎04 2287 7732), with buses for Dajia and the 921 Earthquake Museum. CH Bus (☎04 2225 9631) is to the north on Shuangshi Rd, with frequent services to Puli, while Nantou Bus (☎04 2225 6418) a little further north offers the most reliable service to Sun Moon Lake (via Puli) and has daily services to Qingjing Farm. Ho Hsin (309 Fuke Rd, Xitun District; ☎04 2463 5163) operates frequent minibuses to Lugang (via Taiwan Blvd, stopping at Sogo and Chao Ma) as well as Taipei, Tainan and Kaohsiung.

Destinations Changhua (frequent; 30min); Chiayi (hourly; 1hr 30min); Dajia (frequent; 1hr); Kaohsiung (hourly; 2hr 30min); Lugang (frequent; 1hr); Puli (every 20min; 1hr); Qingjing Farm (3 daily; 3–4hr); Sun Moon Lake (hourly; 1hr 30min); Tainan (hourly; 2hr); Taipei (hourly; 2hr); Taiwan Taoyuan International Airport (hourly; 2hr).

3

GETTING AROUND

Taichung's long-awaited **metro** is due to open with two lines by the end of 2020, but until then a combination of bus, taxi and walking is the best way to explore the city.

By bus Taichung City Bus (ⓦcitybus.taichung.gov.tw) operate services across the city. Most buses display destinations and announce stops in English, but timetables and maps at bus stops are provided solely in Chinese. Most journeys should cost the standard single-sector fare of NT$20. The main city bus station (台中汽車站; táizhōng qìchēzhàn) is just opposite the entrance to the train station (don't mistake it for any of the inter-city stations above). Numerous buses (including #301–#308) ply Taiwan Blvd from here.

By taxi Taxis are a good way to get around: the meter starts at NT$85 but you'll usually pay less than NT$250 for trips across the city centre.

By car Driving around Taichung isn't advisable, but renting a car to explore the surrounding area offers much more flexibility than relying on public transport. Discounted daily rates start from around NT$1700; there are rental outlets at the airport, HSR and train stations, including:

Avis (☎03 656 5990, ⓦavis-taiwan.com) and Car Plus (☎04 3601 5775, ⓦcar-plus.com.tw), both at the HSR Arrivals Hall; and Hotai Motor Company, 152 Jianguo Rd (☎04 2227 5500, ⓦeasyrent.com.tw).

By bike In 2014, Taichung introduced YouBike (ⓦi.youbike.com.tw), a public cycle rental programme. Bikes cost from NT$10/30min for the first 4hr and are available at the train station, City Hall, Taichung Park, and dozens of other locations around Taichung (see website for a map).

By scooter Driving a scooter around central Taichung can be a hair-raising and potentially dangerous experience for the uninitiated, but it can be useful if you plan to explore the hinterlands, or further afield to Sun Moon Lake. There are several scooter rental shops along near the train station which will rent to foreigners equipped with an international driving licence. Oogo (126 Fuxing Rd; ☎04 2220 8972, ⓦoogo.com.tw), behind the station, charges NT$300/half day, or NT$500/24hr for a 125cc scooter.

INFORMATION AND TOURS

Tourist information Taichung's helpful visitor information centre (台中火車站旅遊服務中心; táizhōng huǒchēzhàn lǚyóu fúwù zhōngxīn; daily 9am–6pm; ☎04 2221 2126, ⓦtravel.taichung.gov .tw) is near the main exit of the train station. Free wi-fi is available if you show your passport.

Travel agent Whose Travel (3F, 106 Huamei W St Sec 1, ☎04 2292 2320, ⓦwhosetravel.com) are English-speaking travel agents who offer all sorts of domestic and international itineraries.

ACCOMMODATION

OLD CENTRE

★**Blue Sky Hotel** 藍天飯店; lántiān fàndiàn 38 Shifu Rd ☎04 2223 0577, ⓦ1969blueskyhotel.com; map p.178. Previously a dilapidated old hotel, new ownership has breathed life back into this wonderful property which now offers elegantly styled rooms at very reasonable prices. The owner is clearly a fan of Art Deco, and has gone out of his way to make this place unique, with original touches at every turn – from the front desk, which is made from an old boiler, to the jukebox in the upstairs lounge. **NT$2700**

Fuh Chun Hotel 富春大飯店; fúchūn dàfàndiàn 1 Zhongshan Rd ☎04 2228 3181; map p.178. This budget hotel, opposite the train station, has rooms that are clean and come with TVs and wi-fi, but are otherwise basic and a bit worn. The prices and friendliness of the staff make it just about worthwhile for short stays. **NT$750**

Holiday Inn Express 智選假日飯店; zhì xuǎn jiàrì fàndiàn 94 Ziyou Rd Sec 2 ☎04 3505 9898, ⓦhiexpress.com; map p.178. In a good location just across from Taichung Park, this chain hotel has modern, comfortable, good-value rooms – though no fridges or bathtubs in the standard rooms. **NT$2500**

Hotel Mi Casa 米卡沙旅店; mǐ kǎ shā lǚdiàn 8 Alley 5, Lane 149, Fuxing Rd Sec 1 ☎04 2229 5353, ⓦmi-casa .com.tw; map p.178. Tucked away behind the train station in a surprisingly leafy location, this hotel has clean, compact, tasteful rooms, the best of which have balconies (NT$1800). The trendy, popular *Mi Café* is also on site. **NT$1500**

Hotel Regency 集賢大飯店; jíxián dàfàndiàn 17 Zhongshan Rd ☎04 2229 1171; map p.178. A good, cheap option close to the train station, this place has dated but cleanish rooms with cable TV, a/c and hot water. **NT$780**

Kiwi Express Hotel 台中奇異果快捷旅店; táizhōng qíyìguǒ kuàijié lǚdiàn 441 Taiwan Blvd Sec 1 ☎04 2229 4466, ⓦrs-kiwihotel.com; map p.178. An excellent-value hotel on the edge of downtown, with contemporary Asian murals on the walls of its compact, modern rooms. The ample breakfast buffet of Chinese and Western food is served in a stylish dining area. **NT$1380**

★**Reloading Hotel** 綠柳町文旅; lǜliǔtīng wénlǚ 55 Zhongshan Rd ☎04 2221 7668, ⓦreloading-hotel .com; map p.178. Opened in 2013, this cool, sophisticated hotel in the old centre has compact but comfortable standard doubles, while twin doubles ($2200) and deluxe rooms ($2500) offer more space. All rooms are decorated in bright white, with abstract art on the walls. **NT$1900**

WEST DISTRICT

★**Hotel One** 台中亞緻大飯店; táizhōng yàzhì dàfàndiàn 532 Yingcai Rd ☎04 2303 1234, ⓦwww .hotelone.com.tw; map p.178. Taichung's most stylish accommodation resides in the city's tallest skyscraper (designed by Kohn Pedersen Fox). Rooms are equipped with DVD players, iPod docks, printers and huge workstations, while superior rooms feature bathtubs with grand city views. Service is also top-notch, and there's a lounge bar on the 29th floor – although there's no swimming pool, surprisingly. Look for discounts online. **NT$6348**

XITUN

Hung's Mansion Hotel 台中商旅; táizhōng shānglǚ 593 Taiwan Blvd Rd Sec 3 ☎04 2255 6688, ⓦhungsmansion.com; map p.181. One of Taichung's flashiest boutique hotels, right out on the edge of the city. The spacious rooms come with giant 42in flat-screen TVs, DVD players and bathrooms equipped with quirky Japanese technology – think automatic toilets and massage showers. **NT$3800**

Tempus Hotel Taichung 永豐棧酒店; yǒngfēngzhàn jiǔdiàn 9 Taizhonggang Rd Sec 2 ☎04 2326 8008, ⊛www.tempus.com.tw; map p.178. Taichung's most elegant luxury hotel is spread over three buildings, with the cheapest rooms situated in the oldest block. The best rooms are decked out with natural wood and designer furnishings, the bathrooms swathed in marble. Facilities include access to the Mandara Life Club, a lavish spa and pool, as well as several swanky restaurants. NT$4300

NANTUN

★**Tango Taichung** 柯旅天閣台中; kēlǔ tiāngé táizhōng 525 Dadun Rd ☎04 2320 0000, ⊛www .tango-hotels.com; map p.181. Ultra-hip boutique chain (the suites have jacuzzis with huge TVs), a bit far from the old centre but worth the taxi fare; even the standard rooms are very stylish. There's a health club and spa, and the staff all speak English. A big Western breakfast buffet is provided, and there are plenty of shops and restaurants in the area. NT$3300

EATING

Taichung is an excellent place to gorge on both Taiwanese and international food. Traditional restaurants are concentrated in the old centre, with most of the more cosmopolitan options in the west: trawl the **Wuquan Parkway** (美術綠園道; měishù lǜyuándào) for a good selection, or the **Canal District** (河堤區; hétíqū) south of Taiwan Blvd. Taichung is also home to Taiwan's most successful **teahouse** chains and its most innovative drinks: bubble tea (pàomò hóngchá, a frothy black tea) was created around 1983, and pearl milk tea (zhēnzhū nǎichá, a milky tea with large chewy tapioca balls in the bottom) in 1987. Both are extremely sweet and served either hot or cold.

RESTAURANTS AND CAFÉS

OLD CENTRE

Chen Bai Cao Diàn 陳百草店; chén bǎicǎodiàn 12 Caoyaojie; map p.178. Located on the central junction of atmospheric Herbal Medicine St, this is a good spot to take a breather and a refreshing iced herbal tea (baicaochá; NT$15). Daily 8am–6.30pm.

★**Malulian** 瑪露連; mǎlùlián 235 Formosa Blvd Sec 1 ☎04 2228 8359, ⊛malulian.com.tw; map p.178. In business since 1971, this remains the best shaved-ice establishment in the old centre, with a good selection of fresh, tasty toppings (three with each order), such as creamy taro, almond pudding, red bean and various fruits (NT$50). Tues–Sat 10.30am–9pm, Sun 10.30am–7pm.

Miyahara 宮原眼科; gōngyuán yǎnkē Zhongshan Rd ☎04 2227 1926; map p.178. Housed in a grandly remodelled Japanese-era eye hospital, the elegant second-floor restaurant here specializes in Taiwanese cuisine, with traditional dishes such as three-cup chicken (NT$450) and stewed pork knuckle (NT$300), but also serves a full afternoon tea (NT$1280 for two) and quality teas and coffees. On the ground floor, an ice-cream parlour offers a huge selection of flavours including Lugu green tea, native guava, raisin mascarpone and 100 percent West African chocolate, to name but a few (NT$90 for a single scoop); at peak times queues go around the block. Even if you don't eat here, it's still worth browsing the department-style store, beautifully decked out with tall wooden cabinets, and with interesting local speciality foods for sale. Restaurant daily 11am–2pm, 2–5pm (afternoon tea only) & 5–9pm; store and ice-cream parlour daily 10am–10pm.

Taichung Meatballs 台中肉丸; táizhōng ròuwán 529 Fuxing Rd Sec 3 ☎04 2220 7138; map p.178. This big, busy, no-nonsense local diner has been serving deep-fried meatballs since the 1930s. They come in small bowls (NT$40) and have a gooey, sticky texture – their translucent skin is made of a taro and rice mixture. Filled with pork and bamboo shoots, they're topped with a delicious sweet-and-sour sauce. Daily 10.30am–8pm.

TAICHUNG STREET SNACKS

Taichung's night markets offer a good introduction to the local specialities: one of the best and most convenient is local favourite **Zhongxiao Night Market** (忠孝夜市; zhōngxiào yèshì; map p.178) on Zhongxiao Road. Further north, **Zhonghua Road Night Market** (中華夜市; zhōnghuá yèshì; map p.178) consists mostly of seafood stalls – you pick your dinner then sit down while they cook it (NT$40–60). For a more eclectic range of traditional and Western snack food, try the stalls crammed along **Yizhong Street** (一逢甲文華夜市中街; yīzhōngjiē; map p.178), open from lunchtime and popular with students. Also popular with students (and tourists) is **Fengjia Wenhua Night Market** (逢甲文華夜市; féngjiǎ wénhuá yèshì; map p.181), but it's a long way from the old centre. Travellers with a penchant for something sweeter won't be disappointed, with Ziyou Road (自由路; zìyóu lù), and Minquan Road (民權路; mínquán lù) crammed with **cake shops** selling suncakes (tàiyáng bǐng) – flat, crumbly pastries filled with sweet wheatgerm, honey or taro paste (NT$20–30).

3

Taiyang Tang Bakery 太陽堂老店; tàiyángtáng lǎodiàn 25 Ziyou Rd Sec 2 ☎04 2220 0012, ⓦsunbooth.com.tw; map p.178. One of the oldest cake shops on Cake St, this place sells individual suncakes from NT$28 and boxes of ten from NT$200. Daily 8am–10pm.

Ya Ju 雅居健康素館; yǎjū jiànkāng sùguǎn 39 Gongyuan Rd ☎04 2226 5505; map p.178. A modern and spotlessly clean Buddhist-inspired vegetarian restaurant, with round wooden tables and calligraphy on the walls. The menu offers a decent selection of Chinese food, but there's no English menu – point to the photos instead (NT$150–300 per dish). Daily 11am–2pm & 5.30–9pm.

NORTH DISTRICT

Beifang Hand-Cut Noodles 北方館; běifāngguǎn 154 Meide St ☎04 2235 8632; map p.178. Popular local lunch stop for traditional "knife-cut" noodles, thicker than usual, deliciously flavoured with big chunks of beef (NT$110). It's located on the north side of Zhongzheng Park – turn right off Xueshi Rd before the junction with Jianxing Rd. No English spoken. Daily 11am–2pm & 5–8pm.

Bulao 125 不老125 bùlǎo 125 125 Shuangshi Rd Sec 1 ☎04 2227 0125; map p.178. This two-storey colonial house was once the mayor's residence and is now home to Bulao 125, a senior welfare foundation which uses the building to showcase the incredible adventures of its elderly members – which include riding motorbikes around the island, kayaking and playing baseball. It's a lovely airy space, and there's a café operated by members and staff, where the menu features vegetables grown in the garden and lots of pickles. Set meals (NT$189) consist of noodles, soup, dessert and tea, and they also serve afternoon tea. Mon–Fri 10am–5.30pm, Sat & Sun 9.30am–5.30pm.

General Beef Noodles 將軍牛肉大王; jiāng jūn niúròu dàwáng 158 Xueshi Rd ☎04 2230 5918; map p.178. The chef at this cheap and cheerful canteen has won culinary awards for his version of the Taichung classic, beef noodles (NT$80–100), and it's definitely one of the best. No English spoken. Daily 11am–2pm & 4–10pm.

Taiwan Banana New Paradise 香蕉新樂園; xiāng jiāo xīn lèyuán 111 Shuangshi Rd Sec 2 ☎04 2231 7890; map p.178. An old train carriage marks the entrance to this kitsch, fun Taiwanese restaurant. Inside, tables are scattered along a reproduction of a 1930s street evoking old Taichung, the walls decorated in memorabilia (main dishes NT$120–300, dim sum NT$60–80, drinks NT$50–100). Daily 11.30am–9.30pm.

Yizhong Fongren Ice 一中豐仁冰; yīzhōng fēngrén bīng 1 Yucai St, at Shuangshi Rd; map p.178. Popular with students, this small shaved-ice stall offers surprisingly delicious combinations of plum ice shavings, kidney beans and ice cream (NT$25–35). Daily 10am–10pm.

WEST DISTRICT

1924 Shanghai 新月梧桐; xīnyuè wútóng 123 Wuquan W 3rd St ☎04 2378 3181; map p.178. One of Wuquan Parkway's many stylish, themed restaurants, with a focus on Shanghai and Jiangsu food – try the Wuxi spareribs (NT$380), or the king oyster mushrooms in basil and ginger (NT$280). The atmospheric interior recalls the fashionable Shanghai of the 1920s and 30s, with old posters, wooden tables and antiques, and has been used as a period film set. Daily 10am–10pm (main courses 11am–2pm & 5.30–9pm).

Bollywood 魔力屋印度料理; móliwū yìndù liàolǐ 1026 Jianxing Rd ☎04 2319 2828; map p.178. Appealing Indian restaurant, turning out classics including samosas (NT$60), bhel puri (NT$180), aloo jheera (NT$320), and chicken jalfrezi (NT$390), plus a few twists on the traditional – Bollywood fish and chips (NT$350) have a lightly spiced batter and come with a coriander dipping sauce. Daily 11am–2.30pm & 4.30–10pm.

Finga's Base Camp 風格; fēnggé 173 Xiangsheng South Rd Sec 1 ☎04 2472 0965, ⓦfingastaiwan.com; map p.178. This popular café-deli has moved location but continues to turn out tasty international food including burgers, sandwiches, salads (all NT$200–300) and Italian and Mexican dishes (NT$300–600). The new location has indoor and outdoor seating, and also serves freshly baked bread, and good coffee as well as soft drinks, beers and wine. Breakfast is served till noon. Mon–Fri 10am–10pm, Sat & Sun 8am–10pm.

Gulu Gulu 咕嚕咕嚕音樂餐廳; gūlūgūlū yīnyuè cāntīng 2 Lane 13, Wuquan W 4th St ☎04 2378 3128; map p.178. This fun restaurant is set inside a renovated colonial-era house owned by a Paiwan singer and serves authentic indigenous food which will bring you as close to the mountains of southern Taiwan as is possible. Try the grilled mountain boar (barbecued on Dawu slate), or set meals (NT$280–380) and millet wine. Live music from 6.30pm. Daily 11.30am–2pm & 5pm–10pm.

Gulu's House 咕嚕好吃; gūlū hǎochī 48 Jingming Rd ☎04 2327 1393; map p.178. Popular French restaurant with a sophisticated selection of dishes prepared by hospitable French owner Arthur. Standouts include the New Zealand beef fillet (NT$680), free-range rack of lamb (NT$580) and Toulouse sausages with mashed potatoes, onion sauce and Dijon mustard. Wine list NT$650–1500. Daily 6–9.30pm, Sat & Sun also noon–2.30pm.

Meicun Diantou Ice 美村點頭冰; měicūn diàntóu bīng 176 Meicun Rd Sec 1 ☎04 2301 2526; map p.178. Best shaved-ice shop in this part of town, with lavish piles of fruit and ice topped with condensed milk and coconut syrup – try the fresh mango, taro or "diantou ice", with three types of seasonal fruit (NT$80). Daily noon–11pm.

TEAHOUSES

Chun Shui Tang Cultural Tea House 春水堂人文茶館; chūnshuǐtáng rénwén cháguǎn 30 Siwei Rd ☎04 2229 7991; 17 Lane 155, Gongyi Rd ☎04 2302 8530; 9 Dadun 19th St (at Jingming 1st St) ☎04 2327 3647; 186 Fuxing Rd Sec 4 (inside Taichung Central) ☎04 2227 2712, ⓦchunshuitang.com.tw; map p.178. The Siwei Rd branch of this pleasant teahouse is where bubble tea was invented and where pearl milk tea was introduced, after the owner's mother mixed gelatine balls from her market stall with leftover tea. It later became the first Chun Shui Tang chain store and retains much of its original character. The English menus offer a huge number of drinks (NT$60–220) and their perfect accompaniment, brown-sugar cake (NT$55). Daily: Siwei Rd 8am–10pm; Gongyi Rd 8.30am–10.30pm; Dadun 19th St 8.30am–11pm; Fuxing Rd 9am–10pm.

Geng Du Yuan 耕讀園書香茶坊; gēngdúyuán shūxiāng cháfāng 109 Shizheng Rd ☎04 2251 8388; 520 Chongde 9th Rd, Beitun District ☎04 2422 4099; map p.181. Another Taichung chain, Geng Du Yuan's design is based on classical Suzhou gardens, with tatami mats, fishponds, waterfalls, bridges and cosy tearooms; pots of oolong tea start at NT$200, snacks from NT$60. Daily 9am–midnight.

★**Laughtear Chinese Teahouse** 悲歡歲月人文茶館; bēihuān suìyuè rénwén cháguǎn 29 Daquan St ☎04 2371 1984, ⓦlaughtea.com.tw; map p.178. An exquisite, tiny, wooden teahouse, with tatami mats, screen doors and Japanese decor. Features a range of special infusions including white hair oolong, sweet osmanthus honey, and green and mountain teas (NT$280 per pot). Light Chinese meals from NT$300. Daily 11am–9pm.

★**Wu Wei Tsao Tang** 無為草堂; wúwéi cǎotáng 106 Gongyi Rd ☎04 2329 6707; map p.181. Taichung's most atmospheric classical teahouse, surrounded by trees and beautifully arranged around a traditional fishpond, with wooden corridors lined with Chinese art. Teapots for one start at NT$240. Daily 10.30am–9.30pm.

DRINKING AND NIGHTLIFE

Fri and Sat nights in Taichung are raucous affairs, with a whole host of **pubs**, sophisticated **lounge bars** and hip **nightclubs** to choose from. Most of the action takes place on the west side of town in the Canal District or further afield, making taxis the easiest way to get between bars.

MAZU HOLY PILGRIMAGE

The annual eight-day **Mazu Holy Pilgrimage** from **Zhenlan Temple** (鎮瀾宮; zhènlángōng) in Dajia (大甲; dàjiǎ) to **Fengtian Temple** (奉天宮; fèngtiāngōng) in Xingang (新港; xīngǎng) is one of the greatest of all Taiwan's religious festivals. The event has also become a veritable media circus, attracting ambitious politicians and even street gangs who in the past have ended up fighting over who "protects" the goddess during the procession. The pilgrimage has its origins in the early nineteenth century, when Taiwanese pilgrims would cross the Taiwan Strait to the Mazu "mother temple" in Meizhou in Fujian every twelve years.

THE PROCESSION

The core **procession** comprises a series of palanquins in which Mazu and other senior Taoist deities are ferried 300km through rice fields and small villages, the roads lined with believers who kneel to allow Mazu's palanquin to pass over them for luck. Stops are made at smaller "branch" temples to enhance the power of local deities, and a constant stream of free drinks and food is handed out to the pilgrims trudging along behind. If you want to experience the mayhem you'll need to plan ahead: the best locations to watch the procession are in **Dajia** itself, when it leaves town and returns eight days later; or in **Xingang** at the end of the third day, when the town becomes a massive carnival of parades and traditional performers. The statue remains in Xingang for a day of celebrations (confusingly termed "Mazu's birthday", though the official birthday is Lunar March 23) before embarking on its four-day journey back to Dajia.

PRACTICALITIES

Unfortunately, it's hard to know when the parade will start until a few weeks before: the day of departure is determined by "throwing blocks", on the eve of the Lantern Festival (usually in January or February) – the way the wooden blocks land provides the answer. The parade itself usually takes place in April in the period leading up to Mazu's official birthday (see ⓦwww.dajiamazu.org.tw). Dajia Bus Company runs **minibuses** from Taichung train station (on the corner of Jianguo and Chenggong roads) to Dajia throughout the day, but you can also pick them up on Taiwan Boulevard.

BARS

Frog Pub 青蛙的店; qīngwādediàn 105 Huamei W St Sec 1 ☎04 2321 1197; 30 Yuding Rd ☎04 2203 0182 ⓦbit.ly/FrogPub; map p.178. Popular bar doubling as a Mexican restaurant, with one branch in a prime location in the heart of the Canal District, and another few kilomtres east. Relaxed café-style interior, with Taiwan Beer (NT$180) and Heineken (NT$210) on tap and tacos for NT$250 (mains NT$200–300). Free wi-fi. Mon–Thurs 11am–midnight, Fri & Sat 11am–2am.

Gordon Biersch Brewery Restaurant 鮮釀餐廳; GB xiānniàng cāntīng 13F Shinkong Mitsukoshi Department Store, 301 Taiwan Blvd Sec 3 ☎04 2259 5488, ⓦgordonbiersch.com.tw; map p.181. Congenial microbrewery and restaurant, serving handcrafted German and Czech-style lagers (NT$280 buys you a 100ml sampler of six different beers) and gourmet versions of hearty pub food such as burgers, sandwiches and pasta (from NT$400). Mon–Fri 11am–midnight, Sat & Sun 10.30am–midnight.

CLUBS AND LIVE MUSIC

18TC 38 Daguan Rd ☎0932 674 483, ⓦwww.18tc.com.tw; map p.181. One of Taichung's hottest venues and packed most nights, *18TC* features local and international DJs spinning a good mix of house and serious hip-hop for a young, lively crowd. Cover charge NT$300–500, including a drink or two; sometimes free entry for women. Daily 10.30pm–4am.

Gulu Gulu 咕嚕咕嚕音樂餐廳; gūlūgūlū yīnyuè cāntīng 2 Lane 13, Wuquan W 4th St ☎04 2378 3128; map p.178. Owned by the Paiwan singer Jang Kn Jang (Chinese name Qiu Jinming), this fun café-bar has live indigenous music from 6.30pm, often with performances by Jang himself. Daily 10am–2pm & 5pm–12.30am.

Lounge One 忘廊; wànglángng 29F, 532 Yingcai Rd ☎04 2303 1234, ⓦhotelone.com.tw; map p.178. Sophisticated sky bar in upscale *Hotel One*, with live music on Fri and Sat nights. Cocktails include the refreshing but potent Tea Mule (NT$350). Mon–Thurs & Sun 6pm–1am, Fri & Sat 6pm–2am.

X-Cube 41 Daguan Rd ☎0920 080 993 ⓦfacebook.com/XCube.club; map p.181. Around the corner from *18TC*, this is another popular club catering to a mainstream crowd. Cover charge (NT$200–500), which usually includes a free drink. To book a table you'll need to guarantee a minimum spend of NT$1000 per person. Tues–Sat 10.30pm–4am.

SHOPPING

Caves Books 12 Guanqian Rd, ☎04 2326 5559, ⓦcavesbooks.com.tw; map p.178. Part of an island-wide chain, this bookstore has a decent English-language section on the third and fourth floors, and heaps of ESL material. Daily 10am–9pm.

International Art Street 國際藝術街坊; guójì yìshù jiēfāng 2.5km west of the university; map p.181. An appealing place to spend an afternoon, this zone houses a cluster of small boutiques, craft shops, cheap clothes stores, teashops, furniture emporiums and art studios. Daily 10am–7pm.

Miyahara 宮原眼科; gōngyuán yǎnkē 20 Zhongshan Rd ☎04 2227 1927, ⓦmiyahara.com.tw; map p.178. A selection of teas and traditional snacks are on sale at this shop in a renovated Japanese-era hospital; a great place to browse, regardless of whether you buy anything. Daily 10am–10pm.

Ruicheng Shuju 瑞成書局; ruìchéng shūjú 4–33 Shuangshi Rd Sec 1 opposite Taichung Park; map p.178. Though the current shop is modern, established in 1912, this is supposedly Taiwan's oldest bookshop, specializing in Buddhist texts. It's a good place to buy gifts and stationery. Daily 10am–9pm.

Tianmu Jade Market 文心玉市-天目城; wénxīn yùshì tiānmù chéng 957 Wuquan West Rd; map p.181. The relocated Jade Market remains a great place to buy all kinds of jade items (as you'd expect), from inexpensive trinkets to beautifully sculpted pieces of art. A little bargaining is de rigueur. Mon & Thurs–Sun 9.30am–8pm.

Tianjin Rd 天津成衣街; tiānjīn chéngyī jiē North District, east of Daya Rd as far as the canal; map p.178. The city's fashion hub, Tianjin Rd has clothes from Taiwan, Hong Kong and Japan, and is also a major wholesale centre. Daily 9.30am–8pm.

GALLERIES

The Cultural Centre 文化中心; wénhuà zhōngxīn 600 Yingcai Rd; map p.178. Several exhibition halls featuring primarily local, contemporary painters, though there are also rooms dedicated to traditional porcelain, pottery and jade. Also has a periodicals reading room with English-language magazines. Free entry. Tues–Sun 9am–9pm.

Taichung Cultural & Creative Industries Park 台中文化創意產業園區; táizhōng wénhuà chuàngyì chǎnyè yuánqū 362 Fuxing Rd Sec 3; map p.178. The abandoned warehouses and factory buildings of the former winery, south of the station, have been developed into an atmospheric contemporary art centre. Free entry. Daily 10am–6pm.

DIRECTORY

Banks There are plenty of banks and ATMs throughout the city, and most 7-Elevens have Chinatrust ATMs: Citibank, 242 Zhongming S Rd ☎ 04 2372 6601 & 570 Taiwan Blvd Sec 2 ☎ 04 2313 1861; HSBC, 162-166 Wuquan West Rd Sec 1 ☎ 04 3603 6399.

Hospital The biggest hospital in town is China Medical University Hospital (中國醫藥大學; zhōngguó yīyào dàxué; ☎ 04 2205 2121 at 2 Yude Rd, off Xueshi Rd in North District).

Internet Most hotels have internet access, and there are numerous 24hr internet cafés (usually charging NT$20/hr) in the area around Fengjia University.

Pharmacies Watson's chain branches at 88–90 Jiguang St in the old centre (daily 10am–11pm; ☎ 04 2223 9369) and 154 Jingcheng Rd (daily 10am–10.30pm; ☎ 04 2310 2438).

Post The main post office is at 86 Minquan Rd (Mon–Fri 8.30am–9pm, Sat 9am–noon).

Changhua

彰化; zhānghuà

Just to the southwest of Taichung, **CHANGHUA** is best known for the **Great Buddha Statue** that overlooks the city centre from its lofty perch atop the **Baguashan** hill. But while this is certainly Changhua's most remarkable attraction, the city has many other charms, from imaginative culinary specialities to its engrossing temples. Most of the noteworthy sights are concentrated in the middle of town, between the train station and Baguashan to the east, and a walk down narrow **Chenleng Road** will take you near most of them.

Yuanqing Temple

元清觀; yuánqīngguān • 207 Minsheng Rd • Daily 8am–6pm

A few minutes south of the train station lies the ornately carved **Yuanqing Temple**. It was originally built in 1763 by settlers from southern China, and is primarily dedicated to worship of the chief Taoist deity, the **Jade Emperor**. In previous centuries, it was the site of an intense annual ten-day festival in the deity's honour. An extensive renovation began in 1866, taking some twenty years to complete, leaving the temple in the colourful form it is in today.

Confucius Temple

孔廟; kǒngmiào • Kongmen Rd • Daily 8am–5.30pm

The stately **Confucius Temple** is one of the oldest in Taiwan. First built in 1726, this ageing complex is a quiet haven in the heart of the city, its symmetrical layout of halls and courtyards emblematic of a classical Confucian temple. Flanking the entrance to the main **Dacheng Hall** is a pair of stone columns, beautifully carved with dragon motifs. There is English signage inside.

Great Buddha Statue

大佛像南天宮; dàfóxiàng nántiāngōng • 24hr • Walk along Kongmen Rd, beyond the Zhongshan Rd crossing, and follow the signs

Rising majestically on the city's eastern fringe is the 92m **Baguashan** (八卦山; bāguàshān), from the top of which its crowning glory – the **Great Buddha Statue** – keeps a constant vigil over the town. The Buddha sits at the edge of the **Baguashan Scenic Area** (八卦山風景區; bāguàshān fēngjǐngqū), a tranquil park interspersed with short walkways leading to pavilions and city vantage points. Towering 22m above its brightly coloured lotus-flower base, the statue has become one of Taiwan's most recognizable landmarks since its construction in 1961. It is made entirely of reinforced concrete and has a hollow, six-storey interior; you can go inside to check out the **dioramas** depicting the stages of Buddha's life. Behind the statue to the east is the three-storey **Great Buddha Temple**, the top floor of which is a superb place to watch the sun set over the Great Buddha's shoulders.

Nantian Temple

南天宫; nántiān gōng • 12, Lane 187, Gongyuan Rd Sec 1 • Daily 8am–5.30pm • NT$50

Not your average temple, Changhua's **Nantian Temple** offers three floors of gory delights, with a good helping of kitsch for good measure. No doubt the cutting edge of technology back in the 1970s, these days the animated life-size figures depicting scenes from Buddhist hell look more than a little dated, but the subject matter, which includes everything from men being dunked in pots of boiling oil to others being impaled, easily holds your attention. It's a little tricky to find – look for the green signs (with Nantian Temple in Chinese) directly opposite the main entrance to Baguashan, then follow the road down the hill for five minutes.

ARRIVAL AND INFORMATION CHANGHUA

By train Regular express trains from Taipei and Kaohsiung stop at Changhua train station, at the western edge of downtown. Changhua HSR Station opened in late 2015; however, its location 30km south of the city means it is of little use to those wanting to visit Changhua – Taichung HSR Station is closer (13km).
Destinations Chiayi (29 express daily; 1hr–1hr 30min); Kaohsiung (28 express daily; 2hr 10min–3hr 25min); Taichung (23 express daily; 10–20min); Tainan (28 express daily; 1hr 35min–2hr 35min); Taipei (31 express daily; 2hr–3hr 40min).
By bus Ho Hsin, Kuo Kuang and Ubus all have regular

express bus services from Taipei to Changhua's bus station (across Zhongzheng Rd from the train station). Changhua Bus runs frequent buses from here to Taichung and to neighbouring Lugang (30min), but you'll need to look out for the Chinese characters on the front (鹿港).
Destinations Lugang (frequent; 30min); Taichung (frequent; 30min); Taipei (hourly; 2hr 30min).
Tourist information There's a handy visitor centre (Mon–Fri 9am–noon & 1–5pm, Sat & Sun 8am–noon & 1–6pm; ☎04 728 5750) inside the train station, with friendly, English-speaking staff and maps covering Changhua's attractions, most of which are easily visited on foot.

ACCOMMODATION

Formosa Hotel 全台大飯店; quántái dàfàndiàn 668 Zhongzheng Rd Sec 2 ☎04 725 3017, ⓦformosahotel.com.tw. About 2km south of the train station, the *Formosa* has plush doubles and a range of amenities. Room rates include use of the hotel's fitness room, internet access and free bicycle rental (up to 3hr). NT$2200
Rich Royal Hotel 富皇大飯店; fùhuáng dàfàndiàn 97 Changan St ☎04 723 7117, ⓦfuhong .com.tw. This garish place has ageing, themed rooms but

appealing prices and helpful, friendly staff; it remains a good budget option. NT$1000
Soul Map Hostel 心旅地圖青年旅館; xīnlǚ dìtú qīngnián lǚguǎn 2F, 230 Sanmin Rd ☎0985 680 812, ⓦsoulmaphostel.com. This new hostel, just a short walk from station, is owned by a friendly local who speaks good English, and offers dorms and doubles with en-suite bathrooms; there's also a communal kitchenette. Dorms NT$500, doubles NT$990
Taiwan Hotel 台灣大飯店; táiwān dàfàndiàn 48

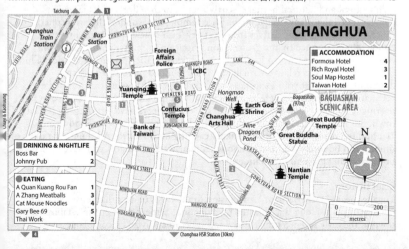

CHANGHUA

ACCOMMODATION	
Formosa Hotel	4
Rich Royal Hotel	3
Soul Map Hostel	1
Taiwan Hotel	2

DRINKING & NIGHTLIFE	
Boss Bar	1
Johnny Pub	2

EATING	
A Quan Kuang Rou Fan	1
A Zhang Meatballs	3
Cat Mouse Noodles	4
Gary Bee 69	5
Thai Work	2

Map labels: Taichung; Changhua Train Station; Bus Station; SANMIN ROAD; ZHONGZHENG ROAD SECTION 1; CHENGGONG ROAD; Foreign Affairs Police; GUANGFU ROAD; LANE 644; GUANGFU ROAD; YONGLE ROAD; ICBC; Yuanqing Temple; CHENLENG ROAD; Hongmao Well; Earth God Shrine; Baguashan (97m); BAGUASHAN SCENIC AREA; HEPING ROAD; Confucius Temple; Changhua Arts Hall; Great Buddha Temple; Bank of Taiwan; KONGMEN RD; Nine Dragons Pond; Great Buddha Statue; THONGHUA ROAD; TAIPING STREET; ZHONGZHENG ROAD SECTION 2; TONGQING STREET; Chiayi & Kaohsiung; GUASHAN ROAD; YONGLE STREET; DONGMIN STREET; Nantian Temple; MINQUAN ROAD; GONGYUAN ROAD SECTION 1; NANGUO ROAD; HUASHAN ROAD; N; 0 200 metres

Zhongzheng Rd Sec 2 ☏04 7224 681, ⊛www .hoteltaiwan.com.tw. Recently refurbished in trendy, modern style, this hotel has clean, spacious doubles, twins and singles, and is conveniently located. **NT$1750**

EATING

Changhua provides several culinary adventures, known for its "**cat-mouse noodles**" (niau-qī mi in Taiwanese), kuàngròufàn (stewed pork rice, known elsewhere in Taiwan as lǔròufàn) and legendary meatballs (bàh-wán in Taiwanese).

A Quan Kuang Rou Fan 阿泉爌肉飯; āquán kuàngròufàn 216 Chenggong Rd ☏04 728 1979. This is the city's most renowned stewed pork rice joint; the pork comes in one big piece, with a thick rind (NT$40). Daily 7am–1.30pm.

A Zhang Meatballs 阿璋肉圓; āzhāng ròuyuán 144 Changan St ☏04 722 9517. At the intersection with Chenleng Rd, this is a great place to sample bàh-wán (NT$40). The meatballs are served in a translucent coating of glutinous rice, and are filled with ingredients such as pork, shredded bamboo, mushrooms, egg yolk and, for the brave, pig's liver. Daily 9am–11pm.

Cat Mouse Noodles 貓鼠麵; māoshǔmiàn 223 Chenleng Rd ☏04 726 8376. Named because the restaurant's founder was said by his friends to have mouse-like mannerisms (and the Taiwanese word for "mouse" sounds like the Mandarin word for "cat"). A bowl of noodles costs NT$40; as well as their novel name, they are notable for the refreshingly non-oily soup in which they are served. Daily 9am–9pm.

Gary Bee 69 人美式餐廳 彰化店; rénměishì cāntīng zhānghuà diàn 51 Yongfu St ☏04 7276 969. For a break from Changhua's Taiwanese delicacies, try this friendly diner. It serves up tasty Western dishes including burgers (NT$150–300), wraps, salads and shakes. Free wi-fi. Mon–Fri 11am–2.30pm & 5–9pm, Sat & Sun 11am–9pm.

Thai Work 私房泰; sīfáng tài 53 Yongfu St ☏04 727 7588. A lovely old Japanese-era house converted into an attractive Thai restaurant, serving red and green curries (NT$228), seafood, soups and salad. Daily 11am–2.30pm & 5–9.30pm.

DRINKING AND NIGHTLIFE

Changhua doesn't have much by way of nightlife, though there are a few pubs on Chenleng Rd.

Boss Bar 135 Chenleng Rd ☏93 590 6667. A small bar that gets lively on weekends; Jinpai costs NT$180 and your sixth bottle is free. Daily 8.30pm–3am.

Johnny Pub 56 Gongyuan Rd ☏92 701 0767. A cosy, quiet bar on the edge of town, with Jinpai for NT$150 and occasional live music. Daily 8.30pm–5am.

Lugang

鹿港; lùgǎng One of Taiwan's oldest port towns, **LUGANG** has preserved much of its architectural and cultural heritage, partly thanks to the efforts of its famously conservative inhabitants. Lugang's historic **temples** are wonderfully atmospheric, but much of the town's fame derives from its tasty local **snacks** and its traditional **handicrafts**, fashioned by the greatest concentration of master craftsmen in the country. But while the town is eulogized in Taiwan as the epitome of classical China, the historic centre is relatively small and is surrounded by modern urban development. Adjust your expectations accordingly and Lugang can still make a fascinating trip from Changhua or Taichung – all the more so if you choose to stay overnight and see the old town when all the day-trippers have left. Lugang is a large town, but the historic centre is a thin wedge bordering **Zhongshan Road** from **Tianhou Temple** in the north to **Wenkai Academy** in the south. All the main points of interest can be reached as part of a long circular walk, though if you have time it can be a rewarding place to just wander.

Brief history

Lugang means "**Deer Harbour**," an allusion to the herds of deer that once roamed the Changhua plains, long since hunted to extinction. Settlers from Fujian established the town in the early seventeenth century, and it became Taiwan's second largest (after

Tainan) for most of the 1700s. Lugang's decline began in the late nineteenth century as the harbour began to silt up (the Lugang River is now a long walk from the old part of town, and the sea is several kilometres away). By 1895 Lugang was closed to major shipping: the town rapidly became a conservative backwater in the years that followed, avoiding the modernization engulfing the rest of the west coast until the late 1970s, when tourism gave the economy a much-needed boost.

Tianhou Temple

天后宮; tiānhòu gōng • 430 Zhongshan Rd • Daily 6am–10pm

Established in 1591, **Tianhou Temple**, at the northern end of Zhongshan Road, is one of the oldest temples in Taiwan, though the first stone temple here was completed in 1647 and the current buildings are a result of renovations completed in 1936.

Much of the temple has a palpably archaic feel, and its intricate **stone carvings**, original woodwork and religious artefacts make it one of the country's most authentic. Before you go in, take a look at the gold-painted carvings of foreigners on the beams on either side of the main gate: those in clogs are supposed to be wicked Dutch

3

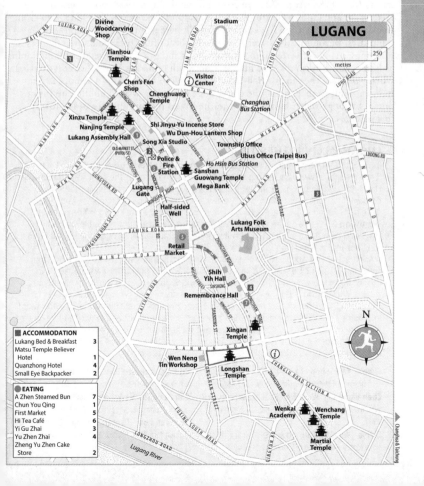

LUGANG

ACCOMMODATION
Lukang Bed & Breakfast	3
Matsu Temple Believer Hotel	1
Quanzhong Hotel	4
Small Eye Backpacker	2

EATING
A Zhen Steamed Bun	7
Chun You Qing	1
First Market	5
Hi Tea Café	6
Yi Gu Zhai	3
Yu Zhen Zhai	4
Zheng Yu Zhen Cake Store	2

colonizers. The **Main Hall** inside houses the chief Mazu deity (known as the "black-faced goddess" after being exposed to incense smoke for centuries), which is said to be one of six original statues from the Mazu mother temple in Meizhou, brought to Taiwan by Admiral **Shi Lang** in 1683. It's the smallest statue in the main shrine, honoured by several imperial tablets from various emperors hanging from the beams above. The altar through the doorway on the right honours Jing Zhu Gong, a local Land God, while the Birth Goddess is worshipped on the left side – this arrangement is repeated in all Lugang's major temples.

Old Market Street

古市街; gǔshì jiē

Lugang's official Mazu shrine on Wenkai Road, known today as **Xinzu Temple** (新組宮; xīnzǔgōng; daily 6am–9pm), marks the start of a series of narrow roads collectively known as **Old Market Street**, which form Lugang's most atmospheric neighbourhood. The initial stretch is Putou Street (pútóu jiē); on your left down here is **Nanjing Temple** at no. 74 (南京宮; nánjīnggōng), dedicated to Guan Di and dating from 1784. At no.72 is an assembly hall built in 1928, now home to the **Lukang Art and Culture Centre** (鹿港藝文館; lùgǎng yìwénguǎn; Tues–Sun 9am–5pm; free), which houses a modest collection of Chinese paintings, calligraphy and sculptures. Beyond it, the street is lined with beautifully preserved Qing dynasty buildings, many converted into touristy shops and cafés, but several still functioning as homes and workshops. The final section south of here is Yaolin Street (yáolín jiē), where you'll see the modest **Half-Sided Well** (半邊井; bànbiān jǐng) at no. 12. The well was built so that the public could share the spring water bubbling up inside one of Lugang's richer homes and is testimony to the munificence of the town's former elites.

LUGANG'S LIVING HERITAGE

In 1985, the Ministry of Education established the **Folk Art Heritage Awards**, also known as "Living Heritage Awards", to recognize the country's top craftsmen: the first winner, **Li Songlin** (1907–98), was from Lugang and is regarded as the greatest master craftsman of them all, primarily in woodcarving. Many of his works can be seen in Lugang's temples – Lugang has since had five more "folk arts masters" winners, more than any other town in Taiwan. **Chen Wanneng** (1942–) won the award in 1988 for his ornate tin sculptures, visible at Chen Wanneng'Workshop, although he now lives in Taipei. Traditional pieces can be seen at Chen's Fan Shop and at Wan Neng Tin Workshop.

Another talented woodcarver of the Quanzhou school is **Zhenyang** (1946–), who won the award in 1992. **Shi Zihe** (1935–) is also a woodcarver and a winner of the award in 1994 – you can see the master at work in his Divine Woodcarving Shop. Famous principally for his religious statues, **Wu Qingbo** (1931–) is a fifth-generation woodcarver and was an award winner in 1987. Finally, **Wu Dun-hou** (1925–) was a celebrated creator of traditional lanterns who won the award in 1988; he passed on the tradition to his son, whose works can be viewed at Wu Dun-hou Lantern Shop. Chen Chao-zong has received many awards for his exquisite, hand-painted fans, but he's not yet an official designated "Living Treasure". Though many of the workshops are open during regular working hours in the daytime, it's best to call ahead to arrange a visit.

Chen's Fan Shop 陳朝宗手工; cháozōng shǒugōng 400-1 Zhongshan Rd ☎04 777 5629.

Chen Wanneng' Workshop 陳萬能錫舖; chén wànnéng xípù 635 Zhanglu Rd Sec 7 ☎04 777 7847.

Divine Woodcarving Shop 施 扇自和佛店; shīshànzìhé fódiàn 655 Fuxing Rd ☎04 777 4502.

Shi Jinyu Incense Store 施金玉香舖; chén shī jīnyù xiāngpù 327-1 Zhongshan Rd.

Wan Neng Tin Workshop 萬能錫舖; wànnéng xípù 81 Longshan St ☎04 778 2877.

Wu Dun-hou Lantern Shop 吳敦厚燈舖; wúdūnhòu dēngpù 310 Zhongshan Rd ☎04 777 6680.

Nine-Turns Lane

九曲巷; jiŭqūxiàng • Look for the lane heading south from around 183 Minzu Rd

Legend has it that **Nine-Turns Lane** is named after the ninth month, September, when its thin, crooked alleyways offered protection from the chill winds, but most scholars believe it simply ran unevenly behind houses that stood along Lugang's harbour front. There's not a lot to see but it's one of the town's more appealing areas – especially the intriguing passageway that crosses the lane further south, known as **Shih Yih Hall** (十宜樓; shíyílóu) where Lugang's literati would, as the English sign explains, "recite poetry and partake in alcoholic revelry". The lane ends on Xinsheng Road but it's possible to follow redbrick alleys south from here, past the elaborate round window of the **Remembrance Hall** (意樓; yìlóu), and **Xingan Temple** (興安宮; xīngāngōng), Lugang's first Mazu shrine, before eventually reaching Sanmin Road near Longshan Temple.

Lukang Folk Arts Museum

鹿港民俗文物館; lùgăng mínsú wénwùguăn • 152 Zhongshan Rd • Daily 9am–5pm • NT$130 • ☏ 04 777 2019, ⓦ lukangarts.org.tw • The museum is a down a narrow lane by the side of the police station at no. 108

Housed in a 1920s Baroque mansion, once home to the mighty **Koo family**, one of Taiwan's richest and most influential, **Lukang Folk Arts Museum** contains a fascinating collection of artwork and everyday artefacts from the Qing and early Japanese period. Most of the objects reflect the lives of the very wealthy and, presumably, the Koos themselves. Patriarch **Koo Xian-Rong** established Lugang's salt industry in the 1890s and the family still wields considerable economic clout, controlling giants such as Taiwan Cement and Chinatrust Commercial Bank.

Longshan Temple

龍山寺; lóngshān sì • Daily 5am–10.30pm

Longshan Temple is one of the most famous Buddhist temples in Taiwan. What it lacks in size it makes up for in artistic beauty, especially its exquisite dragon pillars and **woodcarvings** – check out the amazing eight trigram windows in the **main entrance hall** and the roof beams above. The temple is principally dedicated to Guanyin, a deity and Bodhisattva associated with mercy and compassion, and traces its origins to a shrine founded in 1653. It was moved to the current site in 1786, when the area was outside the town and much quieter.

The temple was flattened by the 921 Earthquake (see box, p.180), triggering a massive restoration project that ended in 2009; everything was meticulously replaced exactly the way it was before the quake, from the exceptional artwork right down to the faded paintwork. The **Main Hall** holds the most revered images of Guanyin in the centre, whilst the **Rear Hall** is dedicated to several Buddhist bodhisattvas.

Wengkai Academy

文開書院; wénkāi shūyuàn • Daily 6am–6pm • Free

Part of a tranquil cluster of Qing dynasty buildings a block south of Longshan Temple, surrounded by pleasant parkland, **Wenkai Academy** was once a school and is now preserved as a monument. Built in 1827, it served as the focus not only for young scholars but also for Lugang's literati for much of the subsequent 150 years.

ARRIVAL AND DEPARTURE   LUGANG

By bus Frequent buses from Changhua and Taichung (some directly from the HSR station) terminate at the small bus station on Fuxing Rd (just north of Minquan Rd), but it's better to get off on Zhongshan Rd. Minibuses from Taichung (every 30min) also travel along Zhongshan Rd before terminating at the Ho Hsin bus station at 208

Minquan Rd. Coming from Taipei, you'll need to change buses in Taichung

Destinations Changhua (every 15min; 30min); Taichung (every 30min; 1hr); Taichung HSR (every 2hr; 1hr).

INFORMATION

Tourist information Lugang currently has two visitor centres (daily 9am–6pm; ⓦlukang.gov.tw), with maps and local information: the north area is covered at 488 Fuxing Rd (☏04 784 1263) and the south area at 2 Qingyun Rd (☏04 775 0830).

Banks ATM and banking facilities for non-Taiwanese bank account holders are limited in town, so make sure you bring cash with you. There's a Mega Bank with an ATM which accepts foreign cards at 254 Zhongshan Road.

ACCOMMODATION

Lukang Bed & Breakfast 天二鹿行館; tiānèrlù xíngguǎn 46 Chunhui St ☏04 777 4446, ⓦlkbnb. com.tw. Just off Fuxing Rd, this five-storey B&B isn't exactly idyllic, but it does offer some of the most comfortable rooms within walking distance of the old town. Most have gaudy, European-style furnishings, but all have cable TV and balconies, and there are a couple of "traditional" Chinese rooms. NT$2450

Matsu Temple Believer Hotel 后宫香客大楼; tiānhòugōng xiāngkè dàlóu 475 Zhongshan Rd ☏04 775 2508. This pilgrims' lodge just north of Tianhou Temple is housed in a pristine modern building and has basic, comfortable rooms in a variety of configurations. No

wi-fi or breakfast available. NT$1300

Quanzhong Hotel 全忠旅社; quánzhōng lǚshè 104 Zhongshan Rd ☏04 777 2640. The cheapest private rooms in town, the *Quanzhong* has small, faded doubles, or newer, bigger rooms for NT$1600. NT$900

Small Eye Backpacker小艾人文工坊背包客栈; xiǎo ài rénwén gōngfāng bèibāo kèzhàn 46 Houchi Lane ☏0972 359 566. A decent budget option in an attractive old building, *Small Eye* has mixed and female-only dorms with privacy curtains, as well as communal areas, and a small courtyard patio. The owners sometimes arrange talks and tours of the local area – ask at reception. Dorms NT$570

EATING

Lugang specializes in xiǎochī or "little eats": favourites include **oyster omelettes** (é a jiān) and "**shrimp monkeys**" (xiāhóuzi; mud shrimp fried with basil). Lugang's **cakeshops** and bakeries are renowned for their sweet specialities: **ox-tongue biscuits** (niúshébǐng) are a sweet flat pastry that vaguely resembles a tongue. All of these can be tried at the stalls and restaurants in front of Tianhou Temple.

A Zhen Steamed Bun 阿振肉包; ā zhèn ròubāo 71–73 Zhongshan Rd ☏04 777 2754. Always popular for its delicious pork buns with mushrooms (ròubāo; NT$15), this place shuts when they run out. Daily 9am–6.30pm.

Chun You Qing 春有晴; chūn yǒu qíng South of the Assembly Hall on Old St ☏04 777 6861. An attractive café with outdoor seating in an original Qing dynasty courtyard, complete with plenty of reminders of yesteryear including an old bike, a sewing machine and a well. There's an English menu offering passable representations of burgers and pasta dishes (NT$219–259). Daily 10am–6pm.

First Market 第一市场; dìyī shìchǎng Minzu Rd. An atmospheric place to experience some of the town's culinary treats with a host of speciality stalls. The most popular include *Sheng Chao Wu Wei* (生炒五味; shēngchǎo wǔwèi) at no. 171, named after its main dish, a broth of shrimp, cuttlefish, pork, mushrooms and bamboo shoots (NT$30); and, around the corner at no. 193, *Longshan Noodles* (龍山麵線糊; lóngshān miàn xiànhú), cooking up delicious vermicelli noodles with pork and dried shrimp (NT$25). Daily 6am–9pm.

Hi Tea Café 孩提咖啡; háití kāfēi 134 Zhongshan Rd ☏04 777 9657. This lovely little café makes a great spot to

take a break from sightseeing. The owner's father has a coffee plantation up in the Nantou hills and the café offers first-rate Taiwanese tea and coffee (NT$40–250). They also have bagels (NT$40–60) and waffles (NT$100–200).

Yi Gu Zhai 怡古斋; yígǔzhāi 6 Putou St (Old Market St) ☏04 775 6413. In a narrow shophouse with wooden benches and Qing dynasty decor, this atmospheric café serves hot beverages and teas of all kinds, notably the delicious rice-powder tea (miànchá; NT$40). Used as baby food in days of old, it's a thick, sweet drink best sampled cold. Daily 10am–6.30pm.

Yu Zhen Zhai 玉珍斋; yùzhēnzhāi 168 Minzu Rd ☏04 777 3672. This venerable cake shop was founded in 1877 by Fujianese immigrant Zheng Cui, and is home of the phoenix-eye cake (fènghuáng yǎngāo), phoenix-egg cake (fènghuáng sū) and the comparatively prosaic green-bean cake (ludòugāo; NT$35). Daily 8am–11pm.

Zheng Yu Zhen Cake Store 郑玉珍饼铺; zhèngyùzhēn bǐngpù 23 Old St ☏04 778 8656. Managed by the fourth generation of the Zheng family, this is a great place to sample Lugang's famous cakes (boxes from NT$90) – the first Zheng was head chef at *Yu Zhen Zhai*. Daily 10am–7pm.

The Jiji Branch Rail Line

集集線鐵道; jíjíxiàn tiědào

One of the country's four **narrow-gauge railways** that have been preserved for tourists, the **JIJI BRANCH RAIL LINE** begins southeast of Changhua and stretches 29.5km to an old depot near Sun Moon Lake. It chugs its way through tranquil countryside, stopping at a handful of **historic towns** that offer glimpses of a Taiwan that is fast disappearing. Much of the area is linked by easily navigable **bike paths** and dotted with a growing number of family-run **homestays**, many in restored traditional homes.

First opened in 1922 by the occupying Japanese to transport construction materials to Sun Moon Lake, the railway begins in the quaint town of **Ershui** – about thirty minutes by train from Changhua – and runs east through **Jiji** and **Shuili** before terminating in the rustic old village of **Checheng**, just south of Sun Moon Lake.

Ershui

二水; èrshuǐ · Frequent trains from Taichung (daily 45–50min) and from all stops along the Jiji Branch Rail Line (12 daily; 50min from Checheng)

The official starting point of the Jiji Branch Rail Line, **ERSHUI** is a town with considerable allure, thanks to its bucolic surroundings and a **cycle path** that winds through several kilometres of farmland, much of it **betel nut plantations**. The paved route – meant to be for cyclists only, but also used by cautious local motorists – passes a number of folk shrines and some wonderfully well-preserved traditional houses. To get to the beginning of the bike path, turn right after you exit the train station and walk about 200m until you reach the railway crossing to your right; cross the tracks and the path begins immediately to your right.

Fongbo Trail

A short taxi ride (N$100–150) or 20min walk from the Ershui visitor centre, where you can buy maps

The **Fongbo Trail** (豐柏山步道; fēngbǎishān bùdào) starts at **Fongbo Square** (豐柏廣場; fēngbǎi guǎngchǎng), essentially a car park a couple of kilometres north of Ershui train station. From here, a path leads through the **Taiwan Macaque Protection Area** (台灣獼猴保護區; táiwān míhóu bǎohù qū), home to an estimated three hundred of the energetic, bluish-grey-haired **monkeys**. Feeding them is strictly prohibited, though plenty of visitors ignore this rule, and as a result the monkeys can be a touch aggressive; keep your distance and keep food well hidden; the best time to see them is 10am–noon or 2–3pm. The path climbs gently for about 2km up the **Songbo Ridge** (松柏嶺; sōngbǎi lǐng), at the top of which are fine views and the **Shoutian Temple** (受天宮; shòutiān gōng), dedicated to Taoist deity Xuanwu, Supreme Emperor of the Dark Heaven (xuántiān shàngdì).

Jiji

集集; jíjí · Fourth stop on the Jiji Branch Rail Line, 20km from Ershui

The rustic charms of tourist-friendly **JIJI** draw in droves of visitors searching for remnants of the Japanese colonial era. The best preserved of these is **Jiji Station** itself (集集火車站; jíjí huǒchēzhàn). Built in 1933, it was badly damaged in the 921 Earthquake (see box, p.180) and was completely rebuilt; the same red-cypress beams and planks were used (although the main pillars were reinforced with steel), and its black-glazed roof tiles were replaced with those retrieved from other Japanese-era buildings in the area. There are plenty of snack stalls around it, serving Jiji's signature culinary speciality, stinky tofu (chòu dòufǔ). Most of Jiji's attractions are accessible via a series of **bike paths** (1.5–2.9km, forming a loop around the town), which are clearly marked with metal signs in the shape of a bicycle; maps are available at the visitor centre (see p.199).

Junshi Park

軍史公園;jūnshǐ gōngyuán • 1km east of Jiji train station • 24hr • Free

Tiny **Junshi Park** was created as part of a tourism drive following the 921 Earthquake. The park serves as an outdoor museum of military history and is filled with an impressive array of decommissioned equipment, including tanks, anti-aircraft artillery launchers, a cargo plane and a fighter jet.

Wuchang Temple

武昌宮;wǔchāng gōng

One of the most fascinating sights along Jiji's main cycle-path loop is the **Wuchang Temple**, which rose to prominence, ironically, after collapsing in the 921 Earthquake. The symmetrical fashion of its collapse is intriguing – its lower walls gave way, yet its ornate, multitiered roof remains almost completely intact, including its guardian statues, which now watch over the ruins.

Shuili

水里;shuǐlǐ • Penultimate stop on the Jiji Branch Rail Line; buses from and to Sun Moon Lake (hourly 6am–6pm; 30min) and Puli (1hr) from the Green Transit bus station; share taxis go to and from Taichung station

The biggest stop on the Jiji branch line, 7.3km from Jiji, is the former logging town of **SHUILI**. Known as the gateway to Sun Moon Lake, it is also home to the **Yushan National Park Headquarters** and its main visitor centre.

Shuili Snake Kiln

水里蛇窯;shuǐlǐ shéyáo • 41 Dingkan Lane • Daily 8am–5.30pm • NT$150 • ☎ 049 277 0967 • From Shuili train station, take a Puli-bound bus; buses between Checheng, Shuili and Sun Moon Lake stop on the main road, from where it's a 10min walk up to the ticket office

Once a major pottery producer, the **Shuili Snake Kiln** was established on the outskirts of town in 1927. Since the advent of plastics, it has rebranded itself as a tourist attraction. The kiln does, however, continue to produce exquisite pottery (including commissioned items for the exclusive shop Lalu in Sun Moon Lake), which is for sale. Visitors will see the giant linear kiln (hence the name), and the world's largest vase (almost seven metres tall) – plus there's a chance to try your hand at your own pottery.

Checheng

車埕;chēchéng • Last stop on the Jiji branch line; buses to and from Sun Moon Lake (35min) via Shuili (hourly 8.50am–6pm; 5min)

The Jiji Branch Rail Line terminates at the handsome wooden station at **CHECHENG**, rebuilt with precious cypress wood after the 921 Earthquake destroyed the old building and most of the village. Originally developed by the Japanese as a **logging centre**, the first timber factory was built in 1933, but by the 1970s the business had virtually collapsed. Since 2000 the village has been sensitively redeveloped as an ecofriendly tourist centre within the Sun Moon Lake Scenic Area, backed by a stunning ridge of mountains.

The dual focus of the village today is the **Lumber Pond**, ringed by attractively restored timber buildings, and **The Grove** (林班道; línbāndào; Mon–Fri 10am–6pm, Sat & Sun 9am–7pm). The latter is a shopping mall containing places to eat; the **Lohas Warehouse** (樂活倉庫; lèhuó cāngkù), selling sustainable products; and the **Experience Factory** (體驗工廠; tǐyàn gōngchǎng), where NT$250 gets you a DIY kit (a bit like an IKEA flat-pack) to build a Finnish spruce wood stool.

Checheng Wood Museum

車埕木業展示館; chēchéng mùyè zhǎnshìguǎn • 110–112 Minquan Lane • Mon–Fri 9.30am–5pm, Sat & Sun 9.30am–5.30pm; NT$40 • ☎ 049 287 1791

The **Checheng Wood Museum** is housed in a huge cypress-wood shed above the old timber workings, with carvings, exhibits on the history of the village and a slowly developing Railway Park, featuring old steam engines from the early twentieth century.

Checcheng Winery

車埕酒莊; chēchéng jiǔzhuāng • 118 Minquan Lane • Daily 9am–5.30am • Free • ☎ 049 287 0399

Visit the **Checcheng Winery**, a small local producer of plum wines, and take a wander past the distillery vats to the tasting room upstairs. There, free samples of plum wine are handed out in the hope that you'll buy one of the surprisingly delicious bottles.

ARRIVAL AND DEPARTURE   THE JIJI BRANCH RAIL LINE

By train The Jiji Branch Rail Line begins at the town of Ershui, a stop on the Western Rail Line, roughly halfway between Changhua and Chiayi. Trains arrive at the old station in the heart of town, where you'll also find the visitor centre and plenty of eating and bike rental options.

Destinations (from Ershui) Checcheng (12 daily; 50min); Chiayi (frequent; 40–55min); Kaohsiung (12 express daily; 2hr 35min–2hr 50min); Taichung (frequent; 45min–1hr); Tainan (15 express daily; 1hr 45min–2hr 10min).

GETTING AROUND

By train There are twelve daily services between Ershui and Checcheng (50min) in either direction, which stop at all five stations between the two (Yuanquan, Zhuoshui, Longquan, Jiji and Shuili). Tickets cost NT$90 for a full Ershui–Checcheng ticket, and are priced accordingly for stations in between (eg NT$29 from Ershui–Jiji); they can be bought at stations or on the train itself. Shuili and the railway's eastern terminus at Checcheng are both connected

to nearby Sun Moon Lake by shuttle bus; Shuili also has buses for the hot springs at Dongpu.

By bike Bicycles can be rented from just outside Ershui station (NT$50/hr) and from several shops opposite Jiji train station (NT$100/day), where scooters and electric scooters are also available (from NT$250/hr). Cycle paths run along the railway – especially appealing from Jiji onwards.

INFORMATION AND SERVICES

Tourist information Ershui's tiny but helpful visitor centre (Mon–Fri 9am–5pm, Sat & Sun 8am–4pm; ☎ 04 879 8129), just outside the station on the right, is usually manned by English speakers and has hand-drawn maps of the town in English. Jiji's large and friendly visitor centre (集集旅客服務中心; jíjí lǚkèfúwù zhōngxīn; 162 Minsheng Rd; daily 9am–6pm; ☎ 049 276 4625) is a short walk from Jiji station and has free wi-fi. The useful Checcheng Visitor Center is in the middle of the village at 36

Minquan St (daily 9am–5pm; ☎ 049 277 4981); it can help with visits to Sun Moon Lake from here.

Banks International credit and debit cards are accepted by the Chinatrust Commercial Bank ATMs in the 7-Eleven stores at Ershui (10 Guangwen Rd, 200m from the train station on the left) and Shuili (just outside the train station); and by the Taiwan Cooperative Bank ATM at Jiji (174 Minsheng Rd).

ACCOMMODATION AND EATING

ERSHUI

★**Fire-Burning Noodles** 火燒麵; huǒshāo miàn 724 Yuanji Rd Sec 3 ☎ 04 879 2608. A simple and friendly diner whose name is derived from the fiery wok used to fry the main dish – a sumptuous plate of fried pork noodles costs just NT$35. Wed–Sun 10.30am–7pm.

JIJI

Grandma's Stinky Tofu 阿婆臭豆腐; āpó chòu dòufǔ 7 Zhibin St. The best place to try stinky tofu in Jiji, *Grandma's* is a no-frills canteen on a small alley just across Minsheng Rd from the *JiJi Hotel*. For over forty years, this place has served only two items: chòu dòufǔ (stinky tofu; NT$45) topped with lightly stir-fried cabbage, and steaming bowls of dried duck's blood soup (NT$25). Daily from 3pm.

JiJi Hotel 集集大飯店; jíjí dàfàndiàn 113 Minsheng Rd ☎ 049 276 0778. The closest accommodation option to the train station, with basic, bright, clean doubles and a rather institutional ambience. **NT$1800**

Laowu Pig's Foot King 老五豬腳大王; lǎowǔ zhūjiǎo dàwáng 285 Minquan Rd ☎ 049 276 0034. Basic canteen popular with locals for its pig's trotters which are fried and stewed in soy sauce, apples and plums. Daily 9am–6pm.

Mountain, Fish, Water 山魚水渡假飯店; shānyúshuǐ dùjiǎ fàndiàn 205 Chenggong Rd ☎ 049 276 1000. North of the old centre opposite the Junior High School, this provides Jiji's best accommodation. Rooms have big, comfortable beds, flat-screen TVs and a slick modern Chinese design. **NT$2280**

Xitou Forest Recreation Area

溪頭森林遊樂區; xītóu sēnlín yóulèqū

A series of well-marked trails run through the magical landscapes of **XITOU FOREST RECREATION AREA**, taking in rivers, pine and gingko trees, bamboo thickets and an impressive 180m canopy walkway set 22m above the ground (known as the "Sky Walk"). There are also some pleasant cafés and places to stay here, spanning the range of budgets from camping up to five-star. Its proximity to Taichung, Sun Moon Lake and Jiji makes Xitou very popular as an escape from the summer heat, especially at weekends, but at other times it can be wonderfully tranquil.

ARRIVAL AND INFORMATION   XITOU FOREST RECREATION AREA

By bus Buses between Shuishe and Xitou Forest Recreation Area run in both directions (every 2hr, 7am–5.30pm), calling at Shuili and Jiji along the way: Xitou is a feasible day-trip from Sun Moon Lake or stops on the Jiji Branch Rail Line.

Tourist information At the Recreation Area's entrance is a visitor centre (daily 7am–5pm; ☎ 049 261 2210) where you can buy maps and entry tickets (Mon–Fri NT$160, Sat, Sun & hols NT$200).

ACCOMMODATION

Le Midi 米堤大飯店; mǐdī dàfàndiàn 1 Midi St ☎ 049 261 2222, ⌨ www.lemidi-hotel.com.tw. White-capped bellboys greet guests at this high-end property surrounded by bamboo groves, just below the entrance to the Recreation Area. Inside it's all mock-European splendour and plenty of facilities: pool, gym, spa, cinema, kids play room and ATM. Popular with Taiwanese honeymooners, rooms are well appointed with large windows, which make

the most of the verdant views. NT$4699
Xitou Campsite 溪頭露營休閒區; xītóu lùyíng xiūxiánqū Above Parking Lot 1 ☎ 049 2612 580. An extensive campsite stretching up a steep hillside, just inside the entrance to the forest park. There are several communal cold-water shower and toilet blocks, plus a central reception area with hot water showers (NT$60), a basic shop, and electronics charging points (free). NT$500

EATING

The village at the bottom of the Recreation Area has a host of snack stalls, shops and restaurants.

Forest Nine 森林巷九號; sēnlín xiàng jiǔ hào ☎ 049 2612 709. A surprisingly sophisticated café-restaurant within the park area, great for taking a break

from the trails. The menu includes set meals (NT$220), eggs Benedict (NT$110) and Shanlinxi tea (NT$150 per pot). Daily 9am–5pm.

Sun Moon Lake

日月潭; rìyuè tán

Hemmed in by lush tiers of mountains in the heart of Taiwan, **SUN MOON LAKE** is the island's largest freshwater body, its calm, emerald-green waters creating some of the country's most mesmerizing landscapes. The lake's name was inspired by its distinctive shape, with a rounded main section likened to the sun and a narrow western fringe compared to a crescent moon. Encircling it all is a 33km road (and a series of cycling

LALU ISLAND

Tiny **Lalu Island** (拉魯島; lālǔdǎo), just off Sun Moon Lake's southern shore is the most sacred site of the indigenous **Thao** people, who believe the spirits of their ancestors dwell there. For decades, the island served the purposes of tourism, hosting a shrine containing Taiwan's largest **Matchmaker** statue (see p.409). After the 921 Earthquake, there was considerable political pressure for the island to be returned to the Thao, and in 2000 it was renamed Lalu in accordance with tribal tradition. Its shores are now protected, and only the few remaining Thao are allowed to set foot on it – tourist boats generally circle the island.

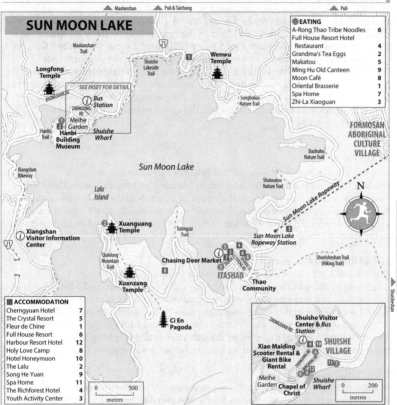

SUN MOON LAKE

EATING

A-Rong Thao Tribe Noodles	6
Full House Resort Hotel Restaurant	4
Grandma's Tea Eggs	2
Makatou	5
Ming Hu Old Canteen	9
Moon Café	8
Oriental Brasserie	1
Spa Home	7
Zhi-La Xiaoguan	3

ACCOMMODATION

Cherngyuan Hotel	7
The Crystal Resort	5
Fleur de Chine	1
Full House Resort	6
Holy Love Camp	8
Harbour Resort Hotel	12
Hotel Honeymoon	10
The Lalu	2
Song He Yuan	9
Spa Home	11
The Richforest Hotel	4
Youth Activity Center	3

and hiking trails), dotted with fascinating **temples** and picturesque **pavilions**, each offering a unique perspective on the waters below, while the **cable car** provides a stupendous panorama of the whole lake. The lake is also the ancestral home of the **Thao** (pronounced "Shao", meaning "people"), Taiwan's smallest officially recognized aboriginal tribe (see p.403).

Given its abundant beauty and range of attractions, Sun Moon Lake attracts large crowds throughout the year. It's a prime draw for mainland tourists, especially at weekends, and hotel rates skyrocket accordingly. Weekdays, particularly in winter, are the best time to visit. **Shuishe**, on the northern shore, is the hub for all transport, and is the traditional base from which to explore. On the opposite side of the lake, **Itashao** is home to the displaced Thao population from Lalu Island (see box opposite), and has developed into a tourist centre in its own right. It offers plenty of hotels and restaurants but manages to remain quieter than bustling Shuishe.

Swimming in the lake is allowed on only one day each year, when at least ten thousand yellow-capped Taiwanese (and a fair few foreigners) take to the waters for the annual **Sun Moon Lake Swimming Carnival**, a 3km cross-lake race that takes place around the Mid-Autumn Festival, usually in September.

Brief history

Until the early twentieth century, the lake was a shallow marsh called **Shuishalian**. In 1919, the Japanese started work on a **dam** for hydroelectric power, finally flooding the area in 1934 – and destroying the last traditional Thao community that had clung to the slopes of pyramid-shaped **Lalu Island** in the marsh's centre. Those inhabitants were forced to move to the lake's south side. After 1950, the Chinese ruler **Chiang Kai-shek** made the lake his favoured summer retreat, spurring further development that continued into the 1970s. In 1999, the 921 Earthquake severely damaged much of the lakeside infrastructure, levelling hotels and restaurants and rendering some hiking trails temporarily impassable. However, the tourist villages on the lake's northern and southern shores were gradually rebuilt and the area now bustles with visitors year-round.

Shuishe

水社; shuǐshè • Buses from Alishan, Checheng, Puli, Shuili, Taichung and Taipei stop here (see p.204)

On Sun Moon Lake's northern shore lies its booming commercial centre, **SHUISHE**, a handy base from which to explore the area with buses to all the lake's main attractions. It has plenty of accommodation options and some serene lake views – the covered viewpoint provided by **Meihe Garden** (梅荷園; méihé yuán), accessed by stone steps just to the west of Shuishe's wharf, is a particularly good vantage point.

Hanbi Building Museum

涵碧樓博物館; hánbìlóu bówùguǎn • 142 Zhongxing Rd, Shuishe • Daily 8am–6pm • Free

The **Hanbi Building Museum** has a fascinating collection of black-and-white photos of Chiang Kai-shek and a host of foreign luminaries who visited him at his lake retreat. The Chinese leader and his wife once occupied a private residence on the hilltop where *The Lalu* hotel now stands. The museum also provides an insight into Sun Moon Lake's history, with old photos that predate the dam's construction, giving a glimpse of what the triangular-shaped Lalu Island looked like before it was mostly submerged.

Longfong Temple

龍鳳廟; lóngfèng miào • 1km west of Shuishe, along Provincial Highway 21 • Daily 7am–7pm • ☎ 049 285 6818

The **Longfong Temple** is best known for the **Matchmaker** statue that sits in a separate shrine just outside the entrance. The statue – Taiwan's largest Matchmaker image – was originally placed on Lalu Island in a small shrine built in the 1960s, and was a fashionable place for group weddings on National Day. After the 921 Earthquake, however, it was removed from the island and taken to its present location. It's still extremely popular with Taiwanese couples.

Maolanshan Trail

貓蘭山步道; māolánshān bùdào • Trail begins at the northwest edge of Shuishe

The **Maolanshan Trail** is a paved, steep 3km road that winds from the edge of Shuishe up the mountainside. It traverses lovely terraces of Assam black tea bushes on its way upwards to a **weather observatory** (氣象站; qìxiàngzhàn) built on the mountaintop by the Japanese in 1940.

Wenwu Temple

文武廟; wénwǔ miào • 24hr • ☎ 049 285 5122 • Frequent shuttle buses daily from Shuishe

The imposing **Wenwu Temple** is perched on a hill overlooking the Sun Moon Lake's northeastern shore. The temple is dedicated primarily to learning and is thus popular with students, who come here to pray before important examinations. In the Rear Hall is a statue commemorating **Confucius**, in front of which is a table covered by candle jars filled with red-paper wishes written by students. The temple's other highly venerated deity is **Guan Di** (the red-faced one depicted in the Main Hall). Heading up to the rooftop viewing platforms at the top of the Confucius Hall will reward you with a magical vista of the ornate, bright orange roofs giving way to the sparkling lake, backed by pagodas and mountains.

Sun Moon Lake Ropeway

日月潭纜車; rìyuètán lǎnchē · Daily 10.30am–4pm (last entry 3.30pm) · NT$300 return · Frequent shuttle buses daily from Shuishe and Wenwu Temple

The **Sun Moon Lake Ropeway** is the lake's newest (and most popular) attraction. The Swiss Doppelmayr cable car glides across the Bujishan peak to the Formosan Aboriginal Culture Village, a 1.8km journey that takes around ten minutes. Most visitors come back the same way. Even if the Culture Village doesn't interest you, it's worth taking the ride for the gasp-inducing views over the lake (it rises to 1044m on Bujishan), trumped only by the seven-hour Shuisheshan hike (see below). Arrive early or late in the day (but before 3.30pm) to avoid a lengthy wait.

Formosan Aboriginal Culture Village

3

九族文化村; jiǔzú wénhuàcūn · NT$780 · ☎ 049 289 8835, Ⓦ nine.com.tw · Frequent shuttle buses daily from Shuishe and Wenwu Temple and via Sun Moon Lake Ropeway

The **Formosan Aboriginal Culture Village** is a rather touristy showcase for the culture of Taiwan's primary indigenous tribes; it also houses a theme park and European-style garden. Despite the rather artificial feel, the grounds are wooded and pleasant, it can be a lot of fun for children, and the park is certainly an earnest attempt to preserve indigenous culture – one third of employees are from indigenous communities. Note that the park sometimes closes the ticket office when it reaches its maximum capacity (a mere twenty thousand people).

Itashao

伊達邵; yīdáshào · Frequent shuttle buses from Shuishe, Wenwu Temple and Sun Moon Lake Ropeway

On the lake's southern fringe is **Itashao**, a major tourist centre that thrives mostly on the dying remnants of Thao culture. Numerous shops sell traditional Thao handicrafts and items associated with the tribe's folklore – there's a lively but Sinicized forty-minute Thao **song and dance show** at the Chasing Deer Market (逐鹿商集; zhúlù shāngjí; 11.20am, 2.20pm & 5.20pm; free) at the end of Itashao Street. The main village is now eighty percent ethnic Chinese, and the dwindling Thao population of about six hundred remains largely segregated, tucked away behind the tourist shops in a collection of corrugated iron huts. This **makeshift settlement** was set up to house the Thao who had lost their homes in the 921 Earthquake, and there still has been no agreement on where a permanent Thao village should be located. Today the only way to be sure of meeting true Thao people is to wander around this deprived area, but this can be a somewhat voyeuristic activity, and we don't recommend it. Just behind the settlement is the beginning of the Shuisheshan Trail.

Although it has developed considerably in recent years, Itashao still manages to feel quiet compared to Shuishe, especially at night, and its proximity to many of the lake's attractions makes it a decent alternate base to its busier rival.

Shuisheshan Trail

水社山步道; shuǐshèshān bùdào · The trail has two entrances, one by the Youth Activity Centre, and the main trailhead at the edge of the Thao settlement behind Itashao, marked by a large stone monument inscribed with the word "Thao" in English

For hikers, the highlight of any visit to Sun Moon Lake is the challenging 5.6km climb to the top of **Shuisheshan** (水社山; shuǐshèshān) – a seven-to-eight-hour return journey. By far the area's tallest mountain (2059m), the summit provides dizzying **panoramas** of the lake and its environs. The **Shuisheshan Trail** is suited to experienced, fit hikers and should only be attempted in clear weather, as the mostly dirt path is very steep in places, with few trail signs in English. That said, in several sections where the route is unclear, **ropes** tied to tree branches show you the way, and you can stop for rests at conveniently placed benches and wooden decks. Ask about trail conditions in the Shuishe visitor centre and aim to set out early for the best views from the summit.

The trail begins with wide stone steps that lead several hundred metres to a fork, where a Chinese sign marks the junction with the other trailhead. Turn right (left would take you back down to the Youth Activity Center), and after a gruelling hike through bamboo groves, hardwood forest and thick rhododendron bushes, you must shimmy over a series of big **quartz boulders** to reach the top of **Bujishan** (卜吉山; bǔjíshān), from where you can see the entire lake and a wide flood plain beyond, as well as the nearby city of Puli.

Xuanguang Temple and Xuanzang Temple

Xuanguang Temple 玄光寺; xuánguāng sì • Daily 7.30am–5.30pm • ☎ 049 285 0325 • **Xuanzang Temple** 玄奘寺; xuánzàng sì • Daily 7.30am–5pm • ☎ 049 285 0220 • Frequent boats daily from Shuishe (last return ferry to Shuishe departs at 5pm) and shuttle buses from Shuishe, Wenwu Temple, Sun Moon Lake Ropeway and Itashao

On a narrow peninsula jutting into Sun Moon Lake's southern shoreline, two places of worship, Xuanguang and Xuanzang temples, sit 800m apart along the Qinglong Trail. Both pay homage to Xuan Zang, a Chinese monk famed for his epic seventeen-year journey to India during which he secured over six hundred Buddhist sutras before returning to China to start work on translating them. This journey was immortalized as the storyline of the classic tale *Journey to the West*. Be sure to visit *Grandma's Tea Eggs* (see p.207) for a snack when exploring Xuanguang Temple.

The smaller of the two, **Xuanguang Temple** is closer to the lakeshore and was built to house what is claimed to be a sliver from Xuan Zang's skull. It is said to have been looted from Nanjing by the Japanese and taken to a temple in Saitama prefecture in Japan before being returned to Chiang Kai-shek's government in 1955, prompting the construction of the temple. This temple was soon deemed too small for such an important relic and in 1965 it was transferred to its present location, the grander **Xuanzang Temple** further up the hill. The temple now houses several precious relics that many Buddhists believe are among Asia's most sacred. These relics are enshrined in two miniature gold pagodas in the temple's main hall, with the jewel-encrusted middle pagoda holding several tiny, hardened kernels that some believe came from the ashes of **Buddha** himself, while the small pagoda on the right contains the revered shard of Xuan Zang's skull.

Ci En Pagoda

慈恩塔; cíēntǎ • 24hr • Easiest to reach with your own transport, but also accessible via the Qinglong Trail (2.5km) from Xuanguang and Xuanzang temples

Crowning the hill behind the Xuanzang Temple is the nine-tiered **Ci En Pagoda**, which the Chinese leader Chiang Kai-shek had built in memory of his mother in 1971. One of the lake's major landmarks, the pagoda is accessed via a 700m paved pathway and commands outstanding views. The 46m-high pagoda's base is at an elevation of 954m, making the top exactly 1000m above sea level. From this point, one can look down on the Xuanzang Temple, Lalu Island and across the lake to *The Lalu* hotel, all three of which are on the same axis – which is most auspicious for *feng shui* believers. Ringing the **giant bell** that hangs inside the top of the pagoda is considered mandatory for Taiwanese tourists.

ARRIVAL AND DEPARTURE SUN MOON LAKE

By bus Buses to Sun Moon Lake terminate at the station next to the visitor centre in Shuishe, on the lake's northwest side.

To/from Taipei Kuo Kuang runs direct buses from Taipei at

7am, 8am, 8.30am, 10am, 3pm and 5pm; returning buses depart 7.40am, 9.20am, 11.20am, 1.20pm, 2.20pm and 4.20pm (3hr 30min).

To/from Taichung and Puli Nantou Bus runs bus #6670

from Taichung Station (7.20am, 8.40am, 11am, 1.35pm & 3.35pm; 2hr 15min) to Sun Moon Lake via Taichung HSR Station and Puli, and there are also frequent services from Puli with Nantou and CH Bus. Among the Jiji Branch Rail Line towns, there are buses to Shuishe from Shuili (25min) and Checheng (30min).

To/from Alishan Two direct bus services cover the stunning route from Alishan to Shuishe (1pm & 2pm; 8am & 9am in the other direction; 3hr). If you miss the bus, a more circuitous route involves taking a bus from Alishan to Chiayi, a train to Ershui, then switching to the Jiji rail line to Shuili (from where there are buses to Shuishe).

Destinations Alishan (2 daily; 3hr); Checheng (8 daily; 30min); Puli (frequent; 30min); Shuili (14 daily; 25min); Taichung (frequent; 1hr 30min–2hr); Taipei (6 daily; 3hr 30min–4hr).

GETTING AROUND

By shuttle bus Regular shuttle buses (☎ 049 298 4031) leave from Shuishe bus station (daily 6.40am–5.20pm; Sat & Sun 3 extra services including 5.40pm), and make a clockwise circuit of the lake, stopping at Wenwu Temple, Sun Moon Lake Ropeway, Itashao and Xuanguang Temple (30min) before making the return trip; you can buy a day-pass (NT$80) or single tickets (NT$32 per section).

By scooter Xiao Maiding at 163 Zhongshan Rd in Shuishe (daily 8am–6pm; ☎ 049 220 1163) rents out scooters for NT$200/hr or NT$800/day, and also have electric scooters and a range of bicycles.

By bike Following the loop around the lake (around 30km) is the most enjoyable way to experience it, especially since a series of bike trails were constructed, meaning that around a third of the ride is off the road. Avoid weekends, as both roads and trails are busier. Giant (daily except Thurs: May–Oct 6am–7pm; Nov–April 7am–6pm; ☎ 049 285 6713), below the visitor centre, has the best-quality bikes, but also the most expensive. Prices start at NT$200/hr or NT$800/day. Shuishe's Zhongxing car park (where the Xiangshan cycling trail starts) has cheaper bike rental outlets; you'll also find them on the main road in Itashao. All of the bike rental places (and the visitor centre) have maps showing the main routes.

By ferry Ferries (☎ 049 285 5120) usually shuttle around the lake in a clockwise direction, from Shuishe Wharf (水社碼頭; shuǐshè mǎtóu), to Itashao Pier, Xuanguang Pier and back again (Mon–Fri 9am–4.30pm, every 45min; Sat & Sun 9am–5pm, every 30min). Each segment costs NT$100, or it's NT$300 for a complete loop (discounts are often available). You can take your bike on board for an additional NT$100 per trip, but not all boats have enough room, so check at the visitor centre first. Note that the ferries only skirt Lalu Island (between Xuanguang and Shuishe); only Thao people may visit.

By rowing boat For closer views of the lake, rowboats for two people can be rented at the end of the Zhongxing car park, near the visitor centre (NT$200/hour).

INFORMATION

Tourist information The Shuishe Visitor Center (水社遊客中心; shuǐshè yóukè zhōngxīn; daily 9am–6pm; ☎ 049 285 5353) at 163 Zhongshan Rd has been downgraded since the opening of the grand Xiangshan Visitors Center (向山遊客中心; xiàngshān yóukè zhōngxīn; daily 9am–5pm; ☎ 049 285 5668), 3km to the south. The former is more convenient for visitors without their own transport. There's another visitor centre at the ferry pier in Itashao (伊達邵 遊客中心; yīdáshào yóukè zhōngxīn; daily 8am–6pm; ☎ 049 285 0289). All three (⊕ sunmoonlake.gov.tw) are staffed by English speakers, and have English-language maps and leaflets.

Services The 7-Elevens in Shuishe and Itashao have Chinatrust ATMs, and there's free wi-fi in and around the visitor centres.

ACCOMMODATION

Sun Moon Lake's **accommodation** is heading upmarket – some of Taiwan's most expensive hotels are here. The most appealing hotels in both Shuishe and Itashao face the lake, and many have lake-view rooms with balconies. **Room rates** rise dramatically during summer, as well as at weekends and public holidays, but camping is also an option.

SHUISHE
Harbour Resort Hotel 碼頭休閒大飯店; mǎtóu xiūxián dàfàndiàn 11 Minsheng Rd ☎ 049 285 5143, ⊕ sunmoonhotel.com.tw; map p.201. Next to the wharf entrance, *Harbour Resort* has bright, jazzed-up balcony rooms with great lake views. NT$2500
Hotel Honeymoon 蜜月樓渡假飯店; mìyuè lóu dùjiǎ fàndiàn 116 Zhongshan Rd ☎ 049 285 5349, ⊕ honeymoon.okgo.tw; map p.201. On the main road through town, this cheap and cheerful place offers comfortable, kitsch rooms with fridges and cable TV. NT$1400

★**The Lalu** 涵碧樓; hánbì lóu 142 Zhongxing Rd ☎ 049 285 5311, ⊕ www.thelalu.com.tw; map p.201. Pure indulgence – all suites have large living and bathroom areas, with big balconies commanding superb lake views. The presidential suite costs a whopping NT$78,700. There's an infinity pool (heated in winter) whose water seems to

3

spill straight into the lake, a spa where you can soak in petal-filled perfumed baths or have a massage, plus a fitness room, teahouse and three restaurants. NT$16,800

★**Song He Yuan** 松鶴園大飯店; sōnghèyuán dàfàndiàn 137 Zhongshan Rd ☎049 285 6547; map p.201. Just off the main drag, this hotel's clean, comfortable and spacious doubles come with kettle and TV; breakfast (included) is Chinese, though it comes with toast. A favourite with foreigners on a budget – you'll usually get a discount (singles for as low as NT$800), though rates are NT$600 higher at the weekends. NT$1000

Spa Home 精緻旅店; jīngzhì lǚdiàn 95 Zhongshan Rd ☎049 285 5166, ⍵spahome.com.tw; map p.201. Near the junction of Zhongshan and Minsheng roads, this boutique hotel has sleek, stylish doubles dressed up with black beechwood furnishings; rooms facing the lake have balconies. There's also a restaurant and, as the hotel name suggests, a spa. NT$5100

ITASHAO

Cherngyuan Hotel 澄園旅店; chéngyuán lǚdiàn Itathao St ☎049 285 0062, ⍵www.cherngyuan.com. tw; map p.201. Quality small hotel with spacious, comfortable rooms, many of which look out over the lake (from NT$3720). Breakfast (included) is served in the rooftop restaurant, which enjoys tremendous views. NT$2400

The Crystal Resort 晶澤會館; jīngzé huìguǎn 3 Shuishalian St ☎049 700 8188, ⍵www.thecrystal. com.tw; map p.201. Plush boutique hotel right on the waterfront near Itashao Pier, with twenty luxurious rooms. Lakeside rooms have balconies, huge bathtubs and a coffee machine, while those at the back are a little smaller. All rooms have DVD players. The hotel also runs *Crystal Inn* next door, which has more affordable rooms (from NT$2200). NT$8600

Full House Resort 富豪群渡假民宿; fùháoqún dùjiā mínsù 8 Shuixiu St ☎049 285 0307, ⍵fhsml.idv. tw; map p.201. A three-storey timber building fronted by a peaceful garden restaurant, *Full House* has a quirky, offbeat charm, its halls and cosy cabin interiors decorated with portraits painted by the owner's wife. Lake-view rooms with balcony are extra (NT$3200). NT$2200

★**The Richforest Hotel** 力麗儷山林會館; lìlì lì shānlín huìguǎn 31 Shuixiu St ☎049 285 0000, ⍵sunmoonlake.lealeahotel.com/en; map p.201. Owned by the LeaLea chain, which also has a newer property right next door, his huge chalet-like complex has Canadian maple-wood interiors that have been tastefully refurbished. The best rooms have gorgeous lake views (from NT$9000), and hotel amenities include a swimming pool, sauna, fitness room, pool table and even a mahjong room. NT$7800

OTHER LAKESIDE OPTIONS

★**Fleur de Chine** 雲品酒店; yúnpǐn jiǔdiàn 23 Zhongzheng Rd ☎049 285 6788, ⍵fleurdechinehotel. com; map p.201. Incredibly plush lakeside retreat, with a choice of lakeside (NT$19000) or mountain views, all with French windows, private balcony and a natural hot spring bathtub. Rooms come with fluffy bathrobes and LCD TVs, and rates include breakfast and dinner. Half board NT$16,500

Holy Love Camp 聖愛營地; shèngài yíngdì 261–10 Zhongzheng Rd (Hwy-21A km 9.5) ☎049 285 0202, ⍵facebook.com/HolyLove.SunMoonLake; map p.201. This rustic lakeside retreat in a secluded cove northwest of Itashao Village is a haven for watersports devotees in summer, with canoeing, pedal-boating and windsurfing the main activities. There is no parking, so you need to arrange to be picked up by boat in Shuishe or Itashao. Bookings must be made in advance by phone. Dog lovers only (they keep a colony). Entry fee of NT$150 per person. Dorms NT$650, camping pitches NT$600

Youth Activity Center 青年活動中心; qīngnián huódòng zhōngxīn 101 Zhongzheng Rd ☎049 285 0070, ⍵www.cyh.org.tw; map p.201. A few kilometres northeast of Itashao, just off the main road around the lake, this hotel is popular with school groups and can be very noisy at times. However, its large, clean rooms – some Japanese style – are great value, especially for groups. Book online for the best rates. NT$1800

EATING

There are plenty of **restaurants** in Shuishe and Itashao, most of them serving standard Chinese fare. Individual travellers are best off heading straight to Shuishe's Minsheng Rd, where there are a few small establishments serving basics such as fried rice and noodles, or Itashao's Yiyong St (義勇街; yìyǒngjiē), packed with snack stalls selling sausage, roast quail and other aboriginal favourites. There's also a *Starbucks* on the edge of Shuishe with great lake views.

SHUISHE

★**A-Rong Thao Tribe Noodles** 阿榮邵族麵店; āróng shàozú miàndiàn 18 Minsheng St ☎049 285 6876; map p.201. Small aboriginal restaurant serving up delicious bowls of "Thao-Tribe Noodles" and fried bird's-nest fern. Daily 11am–2pm & 5–7.30pm.

Ming Hu Old Canteen 明湖老餐廳; mínghú lǎocāntīng 15 Minsheng St ☎049 285 5182; map p.201. This unassuming place serves up tasty Chinese staples such as fried rice and noodles (NT$90–150), and the friendly staff speak some English. Daily 11am–2pm & 5.30–8pm.

Moon Café 明月湖畔庭院咖啡館; míngyuè húpàn tíngyuàn kāfēiguǎn 23 Minsheng St ☎ 049 285 6726; map p.201. Pleasant and deservedly popular outdoor café overlooking the lake. Simple menu offering pizzas and waffle combo meals (NT$160–250), plus decent coffee (from NT$90). Daily 11.30am–7.30pm.

Oriental Brasserie 東方餐廳; dōngfāng cāntīng The Lalu, 142 Zhongxing Rd ☎ 049 285 5311; map p.201. One of The Lalu's major restaurants, the Oriental is open to non-guests and features pricey contemporary Western cuisine throughout the week (mains from NT$800). Its set lunches (from NT$900; noon–2pm) are popular. Daily 7am–11pm.

Spa Home 餐廳; Spa Home cāntīng 95 Zhongshan Rd ☎ 049 285 5166; map p.201. More upmarket than the places on Minsheng Rd, this restaurant has a big balcony with good lake views and specializes in Japanese hotpot and Italian dishes, with delicious home-made pastries and cocktails (NT$200 minimum). Daily 11am–8pm.

ITASHAO AND AROUND

★**Full House Resort Hotel Restaurant** 富豪群渡假民宿餐廳; fùháoqún dùjiā mínsù cāntīng 8 Shuixiu St ☎ 049 285 0307; map p.201. This arty establishment prides itself on Chinese-Western fusion dishes made completely from local and seasonal ingredients (pork stew, lamb or beef sets from NT$240). For groups, there are banquet menus (3–10 dishes, NT$1980–6380), which feature president fish fresh from the lake (delicious but bony) and make use of fresh fruit (pork with sweet basil and pineapple, for example). They also have a wine list, and good coffee. Guests can eat in the ground-floor restaurant or the garden café, both of which are packed full of quirky objets d'art. Daily noon–3pm & 5–8pm.

★**Grandma's Tea Eggs** 阿婆茶葉蛋; āpó cháyèdàn Xuanguang Temple; map p.201. These "Sun Moon Lake Eggs" (NT$10), hugely famous in Taiwan, are stewed in tea and mushrooms for 24hr and are the most popular snack at Sun Moon Lake – queues regularly form beneath Xuanguang Temple (on the waterfront). On busy days, they can sell up to an astonishing thirty thousand eggs. Daily 9.30am–5.30pm or till sold out.

Makatou 瑪蓋旦; mǎgàidàn 39 Itathao St ☎ 049 285 0523; map p.201. Grab a table by the water and order from a menu of local "Thao" fare, which is tasty even if it's not necessarily authentic: delicious wild boar, chilli fish, bamboo shoots and millet wine (NT$150 for big dish). English menus available, with photos. Daily 9am–7.30pm.

Zhi-La Xiaoguan 支蠟小館; zhīlà xiǎoguǎn 87 Yiyong Rd ☎ 049 285 0095; map p.201. No-frills place that serves delicious fried shrimp and fish from upwards of NT$70. No English menu. Daily 8am–7pm.

Puli

埔里; pǔlǐ

In the heart of Taiwan and surrounded by mountains, sprawling **PULI** is an easy day-trip from Sun Moon Lake, and lies at the start of the spectacular road to Wushe and **Hehuanshan**. The best reason to visit is the mind-blowing **Chung Tai Chan Monastery** on the outskirts of town, one of Taiwan's most remarkable sights. Puli's other attractions are mostly located in the north or northwestern corners of town, a long way from the bus station and traditional centre along **Zhongzheng Road**, so the best way to explore them is with your own transport. Most of these attractions are associated with traditional manufacturing and crafts that have flourished here for decades, and are linked to the surrounding natural resources: the town once produced eighty percent of Taiwan's **lacquer** and was the centre of a flourishing **paper** trade; it is still home to Taiwan's most famous **Chinese wines**.

Longnan Museum of Natural Lacquer Ware

龍南天然漆博物館; lóngnán tiānránqī bówùguǎn • 211 Beiping St • Tues–Sun 9am–noon & 1.30–6pm • Free; DIY workshops NT$350 (1hr 30min) – call in advance for sessions in English • ☎ 49 298 2076, ⓦ longnan.us

Tucked away on the western edge of downtown Puli, the **Longnan Museum of Natural Lacquer Ware** is the only remaining enterprise in Taiwan making traditional lacquers; these are so durable that the owners claim they'll last for a thousand years. The museum contains a small display area with a variety of lacquered artefacts (including a 2500-year-old cup), and a shop that sells excellent gifts. However, the place is most popular with groups for its **DIY workshops**.

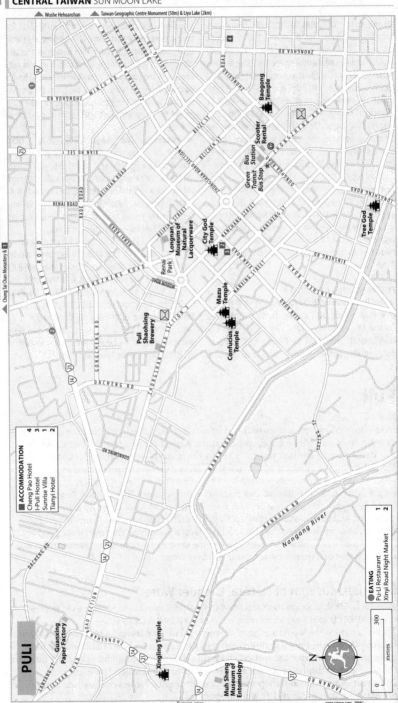

PULI

ACCOMMODATION
Cheng Pao Hotel 4
I-Puli Hostel 3
Sunrise Villa 1
Tianyi Hotel 2

EATING
Pu-Li Restaurant 1
Xinyi Road Night Market 2

Wushe Hehuanshan

Taiwan Geographic Centre Monument (50m) & Liyu Lake (2km)

Chung Tai Chan Monastery & T

Baogong Temple

Scooter Rental
Bus Station
Green Transit Bus Stop

Tree God Temple

Longnan Museum of Natural Lacquerware
City God Temple
Renai Park

Mazu Temple

Puli Shaohsing Brewery

Confucius Temple

Nangang River

Guanxing Paper Factory

Xingling Temple

Muh Sheng Museum of Entomology

Taichung

Sun Moon Lake

N

0 metres 300

Puli Shaohsing Brewery

埔里紹興酒廠; pǔlǐ shàoxīng jiǔchǎng • 219 Zhongshan Rd Sec 3 • Daily 8.30am–5pm (Sat & Sun till 5.30pm) • Free • ☎ 049 290 1649

The **Puli Shaohsing Brewery** is the home of the **Puli Winery Corp**, producer of the famous **Shaohsing wine**, originally from the town of the same name in Zhejiang, China. It's one of Puli's most popular attractions and often crawling with tourists stocking up on all manner of wine-related products, from Shaohsing ice cream and cake to Shaohsing sausage, sold on the first floor of the main building. Mildly intoxicating foods apart, there's not a lot to see here: the second floor contains exhibits on the winery and the devastation wrought by the 921 Earthquake, but English descriptions are limited.

Guangxing Paper Factory

廣興紙寮; guǎngxīng zhǐliáo • 310 Tieshan Rd • Daily 9am–5pm • NT$50; workshops NT$220 • ☎ 049 291 3037

Located on the western fringes of Puli, off the end of Zhongshan Road, **Guangxing Paper Factory** is an attractive series of open-air workshops where you can observe the laborious process of making paper by hand. Paper goods, including flavoured edible paper, are sold in the small gift shop, and there's an exhibition room at the back, but otherwise it's primarily set up for frequent workshops held by school groups; individuals can have a go too though, and you'll get to keep the paper you make.

Muh Sheng Museum of Entomology

木生昆蟲博物館; mùshēng kūnchóng bówùguǎn • 6–2 Nancun Rd • Daily 8am–5.30pm • NT$120 • ☎ 049 291 3311

West of town, just off the main highway to Taichung, the **Muh Sheng Museum of Entomology** is a curious relic of Puli's once highly lucrative butterfly trade. The museum was established by **Yu Mu Sen** (1903–74), who started working for the Japanese as a butterfly catcher in 1919, and contains two floors packed with an assortment of live and dead butterflies, huge moths, insects and scorpions. Before you reach the main building, you can walk through a greenhouse thick with **bird-winged butterflies**, Taiwan's largest species.

Taiwan Geographic Center Monument

台灣地理中心碑; táiwān dìlǐ zhōngxīnbēi • Around 2.5km northeast of the town centre, at the junction of Zhongshan and Xinyi roads on the outskirts of Puli

The **Taiwan Geographic Center Monument** lies in a park at the foot of **Hutoushan** (虎頭山; hǔtóushān; 555m). The monument is inscribed with the lines "clear water, clear mountain", written by ex-president Chiang Ching-kuo in 1979, but the actual centre point of Taiwan is on the top of the hill, a short but steep walk along the path behind this – a plaque up here marks the spot first identified by the Japanese in 1906. From here you can continue walking to tranquil **Liyu Lake** (鯉魚潭; lǐyútán; allow 1hr).

Chung Tai Chan Monastery

中台禪寺; zhōngtái chán sì • Daily: March–Oct 8am–5.30pm, Nov–Feb 8.30am–5pm • Free • ☎ 049 293 0215, ⓦ ctworld .org.tw • Book a tour (1hr 30min) 3–7 days in advance by downloading the reservation form on the website and then faxing it to ☎ 049 293 0836; taxis charge NT$200 from the centre of Puli

Just a few kilometres north of Puli, the **Chung Tai Chan Monastery** is one of the world's most lavish modern monuments to Chan Buddhism, fusing ancient tradition with contemporary building techniques. Designed by C.Y. Lee (the architect of Taipei 101), at an estimated cost of US$110 million, the monastery is worth a good half-day of exploring.

Chan is better known as "Zen" in the West, though you'll see few signs of the more austere Japanese version of the practice here. Chung Tai founder **Grand Master Wei Chueh** began a life of simple meditation in the 1970s in the mountains of Taipei county, and established Chung Tai Chan Monastery in 1987. Today he is head of **Chung Tai World**, a Buddhist order that includes several monasteries and over eighty meditation centres located throughout Taiwan and the world.

The monastery

The **monastery** complex is dominated by the massive, 37-floor central building, surrounded by a series of ancillary halls and statues. The 150m central tower is its most distinctive feature, flanked by two sloping dormitory wings and topped by an ornate gold pearl, set on gilded lotus leaves.

From the entrance, it's a short walk to the main building and the **Hall of Heavenly Kings**, with its impressive 12m-high guardians and colourful Milefo (the chubby, smiling incarnation of Buddha) statues. They protect the **Great Majesty Hall** where Sakyamuni Buddha is enshrined – this incarnation represents the historical Buddha and is carved from Indian red granite. To the right is **Sangharana Hall**, where in typically eclectic Taiwan style, Taoist deity Guan Di is enshrined as temple protector; to the left you'll find a statue of Indian monk Bodhidharma (or Damo, the 28th Buddhist patriarch and founder of the Chan school, also credited with bringing kung fu to Shaolin) in the **Patriarch Hall**, along with the inscribed religious lineage of the temple's founder, Wei Chueh. To go further than here, you'll need to have arranged a tour in advance.

Great Magnificence Hall and Great Enlightenment Hall

The fifth floor contains the **Great Magnificence Hall**, housing a graceful statue of the Rocana Buddha, crafted from white jade and sitting on a gold-covered thousand-petal lotus platform, representing the virtue of wisdom. From here it's customary to walk up to the ninth floor via a series of inclined corridors, eventually leading to the **Great Enlightenment Hall**. Everything here is brilliant white: the ceramic glass walls and floor, the doors, ceiling and even the statue of the Vairocana Buddha, which represents the spiritual or "dharma" body.

Hall of 10,000 Buddhas and beyond

The sixteenth floor is usually as far as most tours go: the **Hall of 10,000 Buddhas** contains a seven-storey teak wood pagoda, facing Puli through two giant windows. The walls of the hall are decorated with twenty thousand tiny copper Buddha statues. From here you can descend down the pilgrims' staircase, or if you're lucky, continue up into the sacred higher levels of the monastery – this will depend on the mood of your guide. The 31st floor is the **Sutra Treasury Pavilion**, containing the monastery's most valuable texts and decorated with soft jade carvings, while the very top, the 37th floor, is known as the **Mani Pearl**. The shell is made of titanium, but the interior of the ball is a simple shrine finished in wood containing a small Buddha statue and is rarely open to visitors.

Chung Tai Museum

Tues–Sun 9am–5pm • NT$200

Even if you haven't booked a tour, you can visit the impressive **Chung Tai Museum** next to the monastery's main building. The museum houses an extensive collection of modern and ancient **artwork** on the first floor – particularly noteworthy are the ancient stone carvings, many "liberated" from China over the years, and there are also temporary displays which change every few months.

ARRIVAL AND DEPARTURE

By bus Puli is only accessible by buses, all of which stop at the station on Zhongzheng Rd in the centre of town. Kuo Kuang (☎049 298 2131) runs buses from Taipei (West Station). CH Bus and Nantou Bus (☎049 299 6147) have frequent services from Taichung and on to Sun Moon Lake. Moving eastwards from Puli, there are frequent buses for Wushe and Qingjing Farm.

Destinations Qingjing Farm (12 daily; 1hr 10min); Shuili (14 daily; 1hr); Shuishe (frequent; 30min); Taichung (frequent; 1hr 10min); Taipei (hourly; 3hr 10min); Wushe (frequent; 50min).

GETTING AROUND

By taxi Since the discontinuation of Puli's tourist buses, the only way to get around is by taxi or your own transport. Taxis charge NT$150–200 for most journeys in town. It's best to negotiate a rate for at least half a day if you're planning to see all the sights (around NT$4000 for a full day).

By scooter Directly opposite the bus station is a handy scooter rental shop (daily 8am–8pm; ☎049 242 2929; NT$600/day, discounts for longer rentals); you'll need an international driving licence.

ACCOMMODATION

Cheng Pao Hotel 鎮寶大飯店; zhēnbǎo dàfàndiàn 299 Zhongxiao Rd ☎049 290 3333, ⓦchengpao.com.tw; map p.208. Now over 20 years old, this remains the best hotel in town, with three hundred comfortable rooms and a decent pool and gym. A 20min walk from the bus station. NT$2400

I-Puli Hostel 永樂園青年旅館; yǒng lèyuán qīngnián lǚguǎn 83 Xi'an Rd, Sec 1 ☎049 290 0102; map p.208. This 1940s hotel was converted into a hostel in 2015 and has bright, airy, male and female dorms with lockers and also some (windowless) twin rooms. The hostel is in a good location in the centre of town, and has friendly,

English-speaking staff. Dorms NT$550, doubles NT$1100

Sunrise Villa 眉溪曉莊; méixī xiǎozhuāng 2–5 Shoucheng Rd ☎049 299 3038; map p.208. An upscale homestay just outside Puli, surrounded by paddy fields and a small stream, and with tastefully decorated rooms that have views across the plain. The only drawback is its relative isolation – you'll need your own transport to get here. Discounts of 25 percent during the week. NT$2400

Tianyi Hotel 天一大飯店;tiānyī dàfàndiàn 89 Xian Rd Sec 1 ☎049 299 8100; map p.208. Recently renovated central hotel with English-speaking staff. Rooms are modern and comfortable and feature bold prints. NT$2080

EATING

In addition to the places listed below, **Donghua Rd** is lined with cheap "Taiwan buffet" diners. **Wudun Rd** and the streets around **Renai Park** also have plenty of restaurant choices, while **Renai Rd** itself has a few bars which can be lively on weekends.

Pu-Li Restaurant 金都餐廳; jīndū cāntīng 236 Xinyi Rd ☎049 299 5096; map p.208. It's worth the trip up to the north of town to experience Puli's "flower cuisine". Recipes focuses on healthy local ingredients including mountain mushrooms, white water bamboo and red sugarcane. Justly renowned for its lavish banquets, simple sets for two start at NT$800, but it's best experienced

Chinese-style, in a big group (from NT$3000 for ten). Daily 11am–2pm & 5–8pm.

Xinyi Rd Night Market 信义路夜市; xìnyì lù yèshì Xinyi Rd; map p.208. North of the centre, this is the best place to sample Puli's street-food offerings, such as stinky tofu, oyster omelettes, sausages and fishballs. Fri–Sun 6–11pm.

Provincial Highway 14

台14線;tái14xiàn

A spectacular, winding road through the clouds, **Provincial Highway 14** is one of Asia's highest, passing the 3000m mark at its uppermost point. With the original **Central Cross-Island Highway** closing indefinitely following the 921 Earthquake, Highway 14 from Puli is the only link between central Taiwan and the east coast. Only a few **buses** connect Puli and Lishan (see p.214), so having your own transport makes a huge difference here. When driving, be aware that the road is very narrow at points and has precipitous drops, especially after Qingjing Farm. In winter, your vehicle might require snow chains – check the forecast before setting out.

Wushe and around

霧社;wùshè

The highway follows the Mei River valley from Puli to **Wushe**, an Atayal village and location of the infamous "incident" of 1930 (see p.392), though only a small monument in the centre marks the tragedy. Wushe is the best place to eat on this side of the mountains (or fill up on petrol). It is the nearest town to the **Aowanda National Forest Recreation Area** (奧萬大國家森林遊樂區; àowàndà guójiā sēnlín yóulè qū; daily 8am–5pm; Mon–Fri NT$150, Sat, Sun & hols NT$200; ☎049 297 4511). Although it is not an easy drive, it is worth a visit between December and January, when the leaves of its magnificent maple trees change colour quite spectacularly. Wushe is also convenient for the nearby **Lushan Hot Springs** (廬山溫泉; lúshān wēnquán), a pleasant resort area nestled in the upper valley with plenty of hotels, odourless, acidic sodium carbonate waters (40–90ºC) and outdoor public pools at the spring source.

Qingjing Skywalk

清境天空步道清境農場; qīngjìng tiānkōng bùdào • 20km drive northeast of Wushe • Daily 7.30am–5pm • NT$50 • Buy tickets online at ⓦ nantou.welcometw.com

The region's newest attraction, **Qingjing Skywalk** is an elevated walkway spanning 1.2km and offering mesmerizing mountain vistas from start to finish. The skywalk was opened in 2017 and immediately became a must-see on tour-bus itineraries, meaning that the four thousand visitor capacity is often reached during the peak summer season. Although a limited number of tickets are available for purchase on the day, it's best to book in advance online.

Qingjing Farm

清境農場; qīngjìng nóngchǎng • 1km further north from Qingjing Skywalk • Daily 8am–5pm • Mon–Fri NT$160; Sat, Sun & hols NT$200 • ☎ 049 280 2748, ⓦ cingjing.gov.tw

Qingjing Farm, at 1750m, is one of the most popular of Taiwan's veterans' farms, and covered with fruit orchards, cattle fields and flower gardens. The road here is lined with pricey "European-style" **homestays**, which resemble alpine chalets, and various restaurants taking advantage of the stunning views across the valley.

Hehuanshan National Forest Recreation Area

合歡山森林遊樂區; héhuānshān sēnlín yóulè qū

The final stretch of Highway 14 to **Hehuanshan National Forest Recreation Area**, on the western edge of **Taroko National Park**, is the most scenic. The road snakes between the western (3416m) and eastern peaks (3421m) of Hehuanshan, the mountain that is the focal point of the Recreation Area; its western peak is easily reached in a couple of hours, via a gentle walk from the road. The car park opposite the eastern peak is one of the best places in Taiwan to see snow during the winter, and consequently often very busy. The aptly named *3158 Café* here serves coffee and snacks.

Lishan

梨山; líshān

Perched on the southeastern fringe of Shei-Pa National Park, the tiny village of **LISHAN** is a superb place for an overnight stop. Home to an idyllic community of apple and pear growers, its name means Pear Mountain. The village is at a height of 1945m and is surrounded by picturesque **tea plantations**, nationally famous for the sweet, fragrant oolong tea they yield.

ARRIVAL AND INFORMATION

PROVINCIAL HIGHWAY 14

By car Hiring your own transport is recommended – non-Taiwanese residents will find this easiest in Taichung (see p.183) or Hualien (see p.295).

By bus Public transport is limited, so be sure to check times and services in advance. Two bus companies run a daily bus terminating at Lishan, calling at several useful stops: Fengyuan Bus (☎ 04 2523 4175, ⚑ www.fybus.com.tw) from Taichung (9.10am; 6hr), via Dongshih, Puli,

Wushe, and Dayuling; and Hualien Bus (⚑ hualienbus.com.tw), from outside Hualien train station (8.40am; 5hr), via Tianxiang, Luoshao and Dayuling.

Tourist information Lishan has a small visitor centre (daily 8.30am–5.30pm; ☎ 04 2598 1331), just up the hill behind the fruit market in the middle of the village, which has Chinese maps of the area and the latest information on bus times.

ACCOMMODATION AND EATING

HEHUANSHAN NFRA

Songxue Lodge 松雪樓; sōngxuě lóu ☎ 049 2522 9696. At 3158m, this is Taiwan's highest hotel, and offers a range of rooms including mountain-view doubles (NT$3200) and quads. All rooms have balconies, and dinner and breakfast are included in the price. The restaurant is also open to non-guests. *Songxue* also runs nearby *Huaxue Lodge* (滑雪山莊; huáxuě shānzhuāng) which has dorm beds for NT$1200 including breakfast and dinner. Half board <u>NT$2900</u>

LISHAN

Swallow Castle 飛燕城堡渡假飯店; fēiyàn chéngbǎo dùjià fàndiàn 46 Minzu St ☎ 04 2598 9577. Although the rooms are a little ostentatious, this is the best place to stay in Lishan, and the splendid mountain views from the windows are more than enough to divert your attention from the tacky decor. Dinner (extra) is available if reserved in advance. There also are some Chinese food stalls across the street where you can get basic rice and noodle dishes. <u>NT$2800</u>

Chiayi and around

嘉義; jiāyì

Backed by the tantalizing peaks of Taiwan's mighty central mountain ranges, **CHIAYI** is the gateway to the Alishan National Scenic Area and Yushan National Park, as well as being home to one of the country's most famous Mazu temples at Beigang. Just north of the Tropic of Cancer, it marks the beginning of Taiwan's tropical south and, as one of the island's earliest cities, has plenty of historic temples and lively markets. Chiayi's commercial heart lies along Zhongshan Road, east of the train station, while its older parts lie further to the southeast.

Immigrant farmers from Fujian established the first settlement in the area in 1621, though the city formally dates from 1704, when the county government was moved here and the first wooden city walls were built. The area was originally called **Chu-lô-san** in Taiwanese, a transliteration of *Tirosen*, a **Hoanya** word (one of the pingpŭ tribes; see p.399). Following the Lin Shuangwen Rebellion of 1787–89, Emperor Qianlong renamed the town Chiayi, an honorific title meaning "praising them for their loyalty" to reward the inhabitants for resisting the rebels. During the Japanese occupation, it gained the epithet "**city of painting**", when masters such as Wu Meiling and Chen Cheng-po spearheaded the first **Nativist** art movement. Chiayi is now the largest city and commercial centre of Chiayi county.

Chenghuang Temple

城隍廟; chénghuáng miào • 168 Wufong North Rd, 1.5km from the railway station • Daily 6am–10pm

The city's most popular shrine is **Chenghuang Temple**. Established in 1715 in honour of Chiayi's City God, the current buildings date from 1940. The most valuable object inside the **Main Hall** is the plaque above the central altar, which translates as "Protector of Taiwan and the Ocean", awarded to the temple by Emperor Guangxu in 1887. The ceiling is particularly impressive – the woodcarvings here and the dragon pillars are exquisite, and the *koji* pottery figures set into the walls (behind glass) are deservedly well-renowned.

Chiayi Park

嘉義公園; jiāyì gōngyúan • Eastern end of Zhongshan Rd • **Historical Relics Museum** 嘉義史蹟資料館 • Tues–Sun 9am–5pm • Free • ☎ 886 5271 1647, ⓦ www.cabcy.gov.tw • **Sun-Shooting Tower** 射日塔; shèrìtǎ • Wed–Sun 9am–9pm • NT$50

The sprawling **Chiayi Park** is the city's largest green space. The eastern part of the park was once a Japanese Shinto shrine built in 1943 – two of its elegant cypress-wood temple buildings have been preserved and now function as the **Chiayi City Historical Relics Museum**. Its main hall was once the shrine's purification hall – the chamber in which a devotee would fast and prepare before making their offering. Just beyond the museum is the 62m-high **Sun-Shooting Tower**, which offers panoramic views of the city from its eleventh-floor observation deck, which also houses a café. The tower's design was inspired by the giant Sacred Tree in Alishan (see p.223): its aluminium shell mimics the wood grain of the tree and its centre has a tall empty space that references the crack in the tree's middle.

Jiuhuashan Temple

九華山地藏庵; jiǔhuáshān dìzàngān • 455 Minquan Rd, north of Zhongshan Rd • Daily 6am–10pm • Free

Jiuhuashan Temple is dedicated to **Dizang Wang**, a Bodhisattva usually depicted as a Buddhist monk who is revered as a guardian of children but confusingly known as the King of Hell (see p.409). Established in 1697, the structure was undergoing restoration at the time of writing. When it re-opens you should be able take the elevator up to the top of its **seven-storey pagoda** for a great panoramic view of the old city.

Museum of Chiayi City

嘉義市立博物館; jiāyì shìlì bówùguǎn • 215 Zhongxiao Rd • Tues–Sun 9am–5pm • Free • ☎ 05 278 0303 • A 20min walk to the northeast of the train station, along Linsen West Rd and across the railway lines

A lavish, modern facility containing well-presented exhibitions on geology, fossils and art, the **Museum of Chiayi City** is labelled in Chinese only, but is nonetheless the best place to view Chiayi's striking **stone monkeys** (shíhóu; second floor). Local sculptor Zhan Long started the fad in 1973, when he began to carve monkeys from fossilized

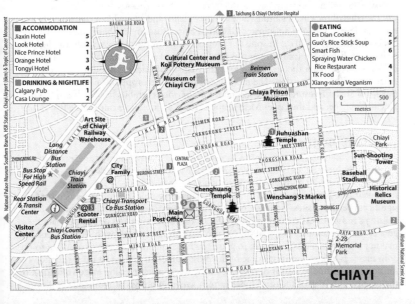

rocks found in the Pachong River, and the sculptures have since become the city's most celebrated motif.

Cultural Center and Koji Pottery Museum

文化中心; wénhuà zhōngxīn / 交趾陶館; jiāozhǐtáoguǎn • 275 Zhongxiao Rd • Tues–Sun 8.30am–5.30pm • Free

A statue of the artist and political martyr Chen Cheng-po sits outside the **Cultural Center**. It is home to a library and several galleries exhibiting the work of contemporary local and international artists. The most interesting part of the centre, however, lies in the basement: the **Koji Pottery Museum** is an excellent introduction to the ancient craft used extensively in temples to create detailed tableaux from famous Chinese stories or operas, and is crammed with stunning examples. The history of *koji* is described, as well as some of its most lauded practitioners such as Yeh Wang (1826–1887), a master craftsman born in Chiayi county. The exquisite **dragon plate** is a must-see, created by Kao Chi-ming, Chiayi's most famous contemporary *koji* artist.

Chiayi Prison Museum

獄政博物館; yùzhèng bówùguǎn • 140 Weixin Rd • Tues–Sun 9am–5pm; guided tours at 9.30am, 10.30am, 1.30pm & 2.30pm (Mandarin only) • Free • ☎ 05 362 1873

Built in 1919 and in operation until 1998, Chiayi's former prison is one of only five remaining Japanese prison buildings in Taiwan. A white archway marks the entrance to the **Chiayi Prison Museum**, behind which lies the guard's central control office. Cells are set out along three corridors which fan out from the control office, with raised patrol walkways above each corridor. The only way to visit is by joining one of the free guided tours – Chinese-speakers will gain a real insight into what life was like for those incarcerated here; English-language tours may be available if requested in advance.

National Palace Museum Southern Branch

故宮南部院; gùgōng nánbù yuàn • Taibao City, 13km west of Chiayi • Tues–Sun 9am–5pm; English guided tours at 10.30am & 2.30pm • NT$250; audio tours in English NT$100 • ☎ 05 362 0777, ⊕ www.npm.edu.tw

On the edge of the city, set amidst lakes and parkland, and housed in a curved swathe of metal and glass, the long-anticipated **National Palace Museum Southern Branch** finally opened at the end of 2015. In spite of facing criticism for the perceived political decision to focus on Pan-Asian (rather than specifically Chinese) arts, the museum is as impressive as it is popular. Major themes spread over the three floors include Buddhist art, ceramics, Asian tea culture and textiles. The most highly revered pieces appear on rotation in the **Gallery of Stellar Treasures** on the second floor – previous exhibits have included the prized Jadeite Cabbage, and the jasper Meat-shaped Stone. There's also a café on the first floor.

Chaotian Temple

朝天宮; cháotiāngōng • 178 Zhongshan Rd, Beigang • Frequent buses depart from Chiayi bus station to Beigang bus station (45min); turn right after you exit, take the first left and carry on for about 200m until you reach the rear of the temple

The otherwise unexceptional town of **Beigang** (北港; běigǎng), a short bus ride northwest of Chiayi, is worth a visit for the **Chaotian Temple**, one of Taiwan's most significant religious sites. Built in 1694 to enshrine what many consider to be the country's most powerful image of the goddess Mazu, the temple is one of the island's greatest **mother temples** (see p.406). As such, it's constantly filled with worshippers, making it the best place in Taiwan to grasp the fundamental importance of Mazu to the Taiwanese, as well as featuring some of the most exuberant temple art on the island. The most dramatic time to visit is during one of the weekends preceding **Mazu's birthday**, on the twenty-third day of the third lunar month, when hundreds of thousands of devotees besiege Beigang for the goddess's annual **inspection tour**; the image is paraded around town to a chaotic backdrop of fireworks, lion dances and stilt performers.

ARRIVAL AND DEPARTURE

BY PLANE

Chiayi airport (嘉義航空站; jiāyì hángkōng zhàn; ☏ 05 286 7886, ⓦ www.cya.gov.tw) is just over 6km south of the city near the village of Shuishang – it's best to take a taxi to the centre (around NT$200).

Destinations Kinmen (1–2 daily; 50min); Magong (1 daily; 30min).

BY TRAIN

Chiayi train station (嘉義火車站; jiāyì huǒchēzhàn) is on the western side of the city centre at 528 Zhongshan Rd – all the major bus stations are nearby. Regular express trains connect it to Taipei, Taichung, Tainan and Kaohsiung. Chiayi is also the start of the scenic Alishan Forest Railway, although it is currently only running between Chiayi and Fenqihu (Mon–Fri 9am, Sat 9am & 10am, Sun 9am, 9.30am & 10am; 2hr 20min; NT$384; ☏ 05 225 6918), from where you can board a bus to Alishan (daily 11.30am & 12.50pm; 1hr; NT$96). It is hoped that the Fenqihu–Alishan section will reopen at some point in the future – ask at the visitor centre for the latest information.

Destinations Changhua (29 express daily; 1hr–1hr 30min); Ershui (frequent; 45min–1hr); Fenqihu (2–3 daily; 2hr 20min); Kaohsiung (29 express daily; 1hr 15min–2hr); Taichung (19 express daily 50min–1hr 10min); Tainan (29 express daily; 30min–1hr 5min); Taipei (25 express daily; 2hr 35min–5hr 15min).

BY HIGH-SPEED RAIL

Chiayi HSR Station (高鐵嘉義站; gāotiě jiāyì zhàn) is inconveniently located in Taibao at 168 Gaotie W Rd; free BRT shuttle buses head into the city centre (every 20min; 25min), stopping at the back of the train station, before running along Chuiyang and Wenhua roads and terminating at Chiayi Park. Note that you can take normal pay-buses from the HSR Station direct to Alishan, Beigang and Budai (for the Penghu ferry; see p.343).

Destinations Kaohsiung (frequent; 30min); Taichung (every 30min; 20–35min); Tainan (every 20–40min;

20min); Taipei (every 30min; 1hr 30min).

CHIAYI AND AROUND

BY BUS

Main bus station (嘉義市先期交通轉運中心; jiāyìshì xiānqí jiāotōng zhuǎnyùn zhōngxīn) The long-distance bus station is at the back of the train station, facing Boai Rd Sec 2 at the end of Zhongming Rd. Kuo Kuang offers the cheapest rides to Taipei, Taichung and Tainan, while more luxurious buses are run by Aloha and Ubus to Taipei and by Ho-Hsin to Taipei, Taichung and Kaohsiung. Buses depart daily every 15–30min.

Chiayi County Bus Station (嘉義縣公共汽車站; jiāyìxiàn gōnggòng qìchēzhàn) This station is to the right as you exit the front of the train station, and has daily buses to Alishan Forest Recreation Area (hourly 6am–2pm; 2hr 30min) via Xiding and Shizhuo. Other locations in the Alishan Scenic Area are served less frequently: Fenqihu (6.55am, 9.25am & 2.55pm); Ruili and Ruifeng (9.15am & 4.15pm); and Dabang (5.45am, 10.55am, 4.55pm) daily. There are also three services daily from Chiayi HSR station to Alishan (10.10am, 11.40am, 1.10pm).

Chiayi Transport Co Bus Station (嘉義客運總站; jiāyì kèyùn zǒngzhàn). At 503 Zhongshan Rd (between Xingrong Rd and Xirong Rd), this station has regular services to Guanziling Hot Springs (關仔嶺; guānzǐlǐng; hourly), Beigang (北港; běigǎng; daily; every 10–15min), Yanshui (daily; hourly) and Budai Port (布袋港; bùdàigǎng; daily). The Budai Port bus leaves to coincide with Penghu boat departures (see p.343): currently buses leave at 8am (1hr–1hr 10min), stopping at the HSR Station around 20–30min after leaving the centre.

Destinations Alishan Forest Recreation Area (hourly 6am–2pm; 2hr 30min); Beigang (every 10–15min; 45min); Budai (daily at 8am; 1hr 30min); Dabang (3 daily; 2hr); Guanziling (hourly; 1hr); Kaohsiung (frequent; 1hr); Tainan (frequent; 30min); Taipei (frequent; 3hr 30min).

GETTING AROUND

By taxi Taxis are abundant in the city centre; the meter starts at NT$100, with trips to Chiayi Park around NT$150 from the station (locals negotiate rates at around NT$100 per trip).

By scooter You can rent scooters from shops on the corner of Renai, Zhongzheng and Zhongshan roads, although most won't hire to foreigners unless they have a Taiwanese licence: just right out of the train station, try Love Scooter Rental (愛騎機車出租; ài qí jīchē chūzū; 534

Zhongshan Rd; daily 7am–11pm; ☏ 05 222 2189), which offers 125cc scooters for NT$400/24hr. It's relatively hassle-free for foreigners – you'll need an international licence and a passport.

By car Avis (daily 8am–9.30pm; ☏ 03 656 5990, ⓦ avis-taiwan.com), Car Plus (daily 8.30am–9.30pm; ☏ 05 310 5225, ⓦ car-plus.com.tw), and Hotai Motor Company (daily 7am–11pm; ☏ 05 310 3555; ⓦ easyrent.com.tw) are all at the HSR Station.

INFORMATION

Tourist information There is a visitor information centre (daily 8am–5pm; ☎05 225 6649, ⓦwww.cyhg.gov.tw) with brochures and maps at the train station. Chiayi is slowly introducing hànyǔ pīnyīn street signs, though you are likely to see tōngyòng and other systems still in use.

ACCOMMODATION

Jiaxin Hotel 嘉新大飯店; jiāxīn dàfàndiàn 685 Zhongzheng Rd ☎05 222 2280; map p.215. Opposite the *Tongyi Hotel*, cleaner and a bit smarter than some of the other budget hotels in the area, with newly renovated rooms and decent showers, but still rather basic. NT$600

Look Hotel 兆楽客商旅; lèkè shānglǚ155 Linsen West Rd ☎05 228 5999; map p.215. Opened in 2012, this is one of central Chiayi's best hotels. Rooms are sleek, modern and comfortable, if a bit kitsch. Note that some of the cheapest "elite" rooms are windowless, so it's worth spending the extra few hundred NT$ on a standard room (NT$2280). NT$1980

Nice Prince Hotel 耐斯王子大飯店; nàisī wángzi dàfàndiàn 600 Zhongxiao Rd ☎05 277 1999, ⓦwww.niceprince.com.tw; map p.215. This is Chiayi's most extravagant hotel, where rooms are decorated in an aboriginal theme and have flat-screen TVs; the hotel has several decent restaurants, including Japanese, though it's not particularly convenient for downtown. NT$5100

Orange Hotel 桔子商旅; jiézǐ shānglǚ 168 Wenhua Rd ☎05 216 2323, ⓦorangehotels.com.tw; map p.215. Part of a growing chain, the *Orange* in Chiayi opened in 2016. Housed in a former bank, it's in a great location directly across from Central Plaza and close to the night market. Although it is principally a mid-range hotel, with simple but attractive doubles and twins, they also have two-, four- and six-bed dorms that link to a smart communal living room and kitchen. The only downside is that some dorms are windowless. Dorms NT$700, doubles NT$2300

Tongyi Hotel 統一大飯店; tǒngyī dàfàndiàn 720 Zhongzheng Rd ☎05 225 2685; map p.215. Simple but adequate budget hotel not far from the station, with ageing but reasonably clean rooms – all with TVs and showers, though the cheapest rooms are very small. NT$700

EATING

The centre of Chiayi is packed with places to eat, with street stalls lining Renai Rd just across from the train station. The city's main **night market** is on Wenhua Rd, with the busiest concentration of stalls south of Zhongshan Rd and north of Xueyang Rd.

En Dian Cookies 恩典酥本舖; ēndiǎnsū běnpù 221 Zhongshan Rd ☎05 238 7898; map p.215. "Square cookies" are a Chiayi speciality, and this tiny shop is the city's best place to buy them. The butter cookies are considered the most authentic, but chocolate is also good (small packets NT$55). Daily 9am–10pm.

Guo's Rice Stick Soup 郭家粿仔湯; guōjiā guǒzǐtāng 148 Wenhua Rd ☎05 225 6214; map p.215. Fantastically delicious rice soup that's one of the tastiest treats in the city; don't be put off by the ingredients, which include slow-boiled pig intestines (NT$30). Daily 9am–5.30pm.

Smart Fish 林聰明沙鍋魚頭; lín cōngmíng shāguō yútóu 361 Zhongzheng Rd, between Wenhua and Guanghua roads ☎05 227 0661; map p.215. The place to try rich and especially fragrant fish-head stew (NT$70–90), a local delicacy that's crammed with chunks of giant silver carp, cabbage, mushrooms and bean curd; the dish's power lies in the broth, which is utterly addictive. Daily 2.30–10pm.

Spraying Water Chicken Rice Restaurant 噴水火雞飯; pēnshuǐ huǒjīfàn 325 Zhongshan Rd ☎05 222 2433; map p.215. In spite of their chosen English name, this is the oldest restaurant serving Chiayi's signature speciality – small bowls of turkey rice (雞絲飯; jīsīfàn) – for NT$45. The dish can be found all over the city, but this no-nonsense place is an old favourite with locals and tourists alike, well located near the Central Fountain (pēnshuǐ) roundabout. Daily 9am–9.30pm.

TK Food 老楊方塊酥; lǎoyáng fāngkuàisū 506 Zhongshan Rd ☎05 222 4619; map p.215. Lauded for its sweet cookies since the 1970s (small bags for NT$40), *TK Food* is just across from the train station, so a lot more convenient if you can't make it to *En Dian Cookies* – though not quite as good. Daily 9.30am–9.30pm.

Xiang-xiang Veganism 香香素食; xiāngxiāng sùshí 126 Minquan Rd ☎05 271 5756; map p.215. Near Jiuhuashan temple, this great-value vegetarian restaurant is operated by young, energetic staff. As well as Taiwanese dishes (sesame noodles NT$40) there are also Korean (*kimchi* fried rice NT$70), Japanese, and Thai dishes on the menu, and eggs can be added on request. Photos of the old streets of Chiayi in the 1930s and 1940s add a nostalgic touch to the otherwise modern interior. Daily 11am–2pm & 4–9pm.

DRINKING

Chiayi doesn't have too much in the way of nightlife but there are a few **pubs and bars**, some of which serve Western meals and snack food.

Calgary Pub 卡加利美式餐飲; kǎjiālì měishì cānyǐn 19, Lane 351 Guohua St ☎ 05 227 0389; map p.215. The town's main watering hole, attracting a mix of locals and expats, this place occupies a century-old Japanese-era sawmill and warehouse featuring furniture cut from the original lumber. The cheap beers are complemented by burgers, pizzas and Mexican food. There's live music on Fri and Sat, something of a rarity in Chiayi. It's on a narrow lane off 224 Linsen West Rd, just before Guohua St. Tues–Sun 7.30pm–2am.

Casa Lounge 512 Daya Rd Sec 2 ☎ 0922 822 673; map p.215. Two blocks south of Chiayi Park, this cosy cocktail bar is a local artist hangout and plays a mix of Taiwanese hip-hop, rock and pop, along with a few foreign tunes thrown in for good measure. The owner is a master cocktail-maker; his creations include "around the world", which features eleven different liquors and a splash of fruit juice (NT$350). Daily 8pm–2am.

DIRECTORY

Banks Several banks with ATMs are clustered at the main roundabout on Zhongshan Rd. Citibank has a branch at 320 Chuiyang Rd (☎ 05 227 5100).

Hospital The Chiayi Christian Hospital (☎ 05 276 4994, ⊕ www.cych.org.tw) at 539 Zhongxiao Rd (Provincial Highway 1) has English-speaking doctors with walk-in clinics (Mon–Sat).

Internet access Near the train station, Xingji Internet (星際網際館站前店; xīngjì wǎngjì guǎnzhàn qiándiàn) at 578 Renai Rd is open 24hr and provides internet access for NT$20/hr.

Pharmacies Watson's has branches at 379 Zhongshan Rd (daily 10am–11pm; ☎ 05 223 6952) and 300 Renai Rd (daily 10am–10pm; ☎ 05 225 4776).

Post The main post office is at 107 Zhongshan Rd in the eastern part of the city, but there's a branch near the station at 647 Zhongzheng Rd.

Alishan National Scenic Area

阿里山國家風景區; ālǐshān guójiā fēngjǐngqū

Stretching from the foothills of western Taiwan all the way to the Yushan National Park, the extraordinarily diverse **ALISHAN NATIONAL SCENIC AREA** covers some 420 square kilometres of picturesque tea plantations, tranquil homestays and inviting Tsou aboriginal villages. Confusingly, there is no single mountain called Alishan; the actual peak that attracts the most viewers at sunrise is named **Zhushan**. It's the centrepiece of the **Alishan Forest Recreation Area**, the region's main tourist hub, which most Taiwanese refer to – similarly confusingly – as just "Alishan".

The spectacular **Alishan Forest Railway** is one of the scenic highlights of Taiwan, but sadly only half of it was running at the time of writing, due to successive typhoon damage. First destroyed by Typhoon Morakot in 2009, the line was ready to re-open in 2015, but then Typhoon Dujuan hit, and set plans back to the drawing board. In the meantime, visitors can enjoy a ride from Chiayi as far as Fenqihu and then bus the last leg to Alishan, or take a short ride on the Zhushan and Sacred Tree branch lines from the Forest Recreation Area itself.

Ruili

瑞里; ruìlǐ • Chiayi–Ruifeng buses stop at Ruili twice daily in either direction (9.15am & 4.15pm / 6am & 1pm), although it's worth hiring your own transport to make the most of this area; most of the homestays (see p.225) are located along Route 166

Perched precipitously above a sheer cliff-face and surrounded by tea plantations, the

---

TALKING SOME TSOU

Although most **Tsou** today speak Chinese as their first language, if you learn a few Tsou words before you visit Alishan, you'll definitely elicit a few smiles. The most commonly used word is *aveoveoyu* ("aview-view-you"), which literally means "my heart is happy" and is used both as a general greeting and also for "thank you". Similarly, *yokioasu* ("yoki-a-soo") means "good health" or "good luck" and is often used when saying goodbye. Other words you might be able to use are *mafe* ("ma-fey"; delicious) and *emi* ("emee"; millet wine).

picturesque village of **RUILI** is a relaxing place to gaze out upon the highland scenery while sipping cups of fragrant tea, or to roam along hiking trails. Nature walks near the village link all of Ruili's main scenic attractions, ranging from short paths leading to pristine waterfalls, or longer historic trails to nearby towns.

From March to June each year, the slopes around Ruili come alight at night, when thousands of **fireflies** (yínghuǒchóng) put on a nightly performance, considered by many to be the most magnificent of its kind in Taiwan.

Yuantan Natural Ecological Park

圓潭自然生態園區; yuántán zìrán shēngtàiyuán qū

It takes around an hour to walk the complete circuit of the **Yuantan Natural Ecological Park**, which encompasses the botanical gardens and three picturesque waterfalls. Near the visitor centre, which is a good place to break up your journey, a steep downhill trail leads to the most impressive of the three, the **Yuantan Falls** (雲潭瀑布; yúntán pùbù).

Fenqihu

奮起湖; fènqǐhú • A daily train runs from Chiayi (Mon–Fri 9am, Sat 9am & 10am, Sun 9am, 9.30am & 10am; 2hr 20min; NT$384; 05 225 6918) and from Alishan (1pm), and frequent local buses run from Shizhuo; alternatively, you can walk 6.5km south from Ruili via a hiking trail.

A former train repair station, **FENQIHU** makes a popular pit-stop on the way to Alishan. The compact village spills down the hillside immediately south of the train station and bus stop, its narrow **Old Street** (奮起湖老街; fènqǐhú lǎojiē) lined with curious snack shops and restaurants (see p.226). The **Fenqihu Garage** (奮起湖車庫; fènqǐhú chēkù), down the tracks from the station, houses a couple of American-made steam engines from the early twentieth century, while the **Exhibition Room of Culture and History of Fenqihu** (奮起湖文史陳列室啟用; fènqǐhú wénshǐ chénlièshì qǐyòng; daily 9am–5pm; free), further down the slope, houses some odd bits and pieces commemorating the village's past, housed in a nicely restored wooden house from the Japanese era.

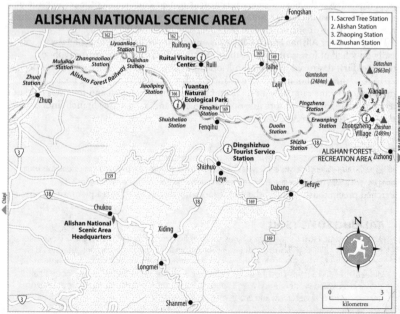

Fenqihu hiking trails

Fenqihu's shorter **hiking trails** feature wooden boardwalks, steps and English-language signage; the **Logging Trail** (木馬棧道; mùmǎzhàn dào; 700m) and the **Fenqihu Walking Trail** (1.2km) offer bracing hikes through forests of bamboo with stupendous views. But the area's main hike is the energetic climb up **Datongshan** (大涷山; dàtòngshān; 1976m), which in clear weather offers extraordinary sunrise views. The trailhead is about 4km east of Fenqihu along Chiayi Route 155. Just past the trailhead, the path splits into two, with the right-hand fork leading to the **18 Arhats Cave** (十八羅漢洞; shíbāluóhàn dòng) – a sizeable maze-like sandstone rock formation – just less than 2km further. The left-hand path winds to the top of Datongshan and is a moderate climb of 1.7km that takes about thirty minutes.

Dingshizhuo Tea Terraces

頂石棹; dǐngshízhuō • Around 40km from Chiayi and 25km from Alishan on Highway 18 • Buses between Chiayi and Alishan pass through Shizhuo; Shizhuo is served by regular buses (20min) from Fenqihu

Shizhuo (石棹; shízhuō) is an important junction, with Route 169 heading north to Fenqihu and south to Dabang. There's a 7-Eleven and plenty of cheap canteens, but little to see in the village itself. However, the nearby **Dingshizhuo** area, located above Highway 18 at around 1450–1700m, offers several marked trails for hiking, which afford enticing vistas of misty oolong **tea terraces** and a large patch of lush forest. Look for the turning at km 63.5 and then head to the tourist service centre for maps showing the nearby Dingshizhuo Trail and Tea Trail. There are over twenty **homestays** in the area, making it another great place to stay, and the tea is becoming a major attraction, with several accommodation options offering tours of the farms and tea tastings.

Dabang

達邦; dábāng • South of Shizhuo via County Route 169, along the Zengwun River valley • Three buses a day from Chiayi (5.45am, 10.55am and 4.55pm), departures in the other direction at 8am, 2.10pm & 7.10pm; schedules are unreliable, so check at the visitor centre (see p.224)

DABANG is the closest thing the indigenous Tsou people have to a capital, and one of the best places to get a feel for contemporary Tsou life – it's a sleepy place during the week, full of colourful wooden and corrugated-iron cottages. There are a few local cafés and a couple of major streets, but the highlight is the large **Kuba Ta Tapangu** (tapangu means village) in the centre. With its red-cypress frame raised on stilts and its thatched roof, the *kuba* or sacred hall is a visual reminder of indigenous Taiwan's cultural links with the South Pacific. You can't go inside – only male members of the Tsou tribe can enter.

Tefuye

特富野; tèfùyě • 2km west of Dabang; only accessible by private transport, or on foot

The village of **TEFUYE** feels a little isolated. It contains the second Tsou **kuba**, a couple of churches and some excellent trails. You can walk uphill from here to **Zizhong** (自忠; zìzhōng), 6.3km along the **Tefuye Old Trail** (特富野古道; tèfùyě gǔdào), lined with beautiful *hinoki* cypress trees and bamboo. You'll have to hike back or arrange a lift from Zizhong to Alishan; alternatively, it's much easier to walk down in the other direction.

Alishan Forest Recreation Area

阿里山森林遊樂區; ālǐshān sēnlín yóulèqū • NT$300 for foreigners, car pass NT$100, scooter NT$20 • Served by buses from Chiayi, Taipei, Shuishe and Fenqihu (see p.224); most buses stop just outside the 7-Eleven in Zhongzheng car park

The **ALISHAN FOREST RECREATION AREA** is the National Scenic Area's premier attraction. Its pristine alpine forests are dotted with (mostly) easy walking paths and several superb scenic views of the surrounding mountains and the surreal "sea of

ALISHAN'S RED CYPRESS TREES

While the area's cherry blossoms are indeed a moving sight, most of these trees ironically inhabit a still-visible cemetery of once-mighty **red cypresses**, logged by the occupying Japanese in the early twentieth century, in order to turn them into thousands of smoothly lacquered **tea tables**. In place of these ancient giants, many of which were well over 2000 years old when they were felled, the Japanese planted an assortment of their cherished sakura cherry trees. Sadly, apart from taking perfunctory photos before a handful of celebrated cypress stumps, most Taiwanese tourists pay scant attention to them, instead rushing to admire the cherry blossoms in an unwitting salute to the Japanese colonial legacy.

clouds" sunrise. However, what attracts most tourists to the Recreation Area is its **cherry trees**, which come into full bloom from mid-March to mid-April. During this period, the area is inundated with ten thousand visitors a day, choking the walking trails and making accommodation scarce. If you visit during this season, it's advisable to come during the week, though hotel and food prices skyrocket for the entire period. The area is especially cherished by busloads of mainland Chinese tourists – the Taiwanese folk song ālǐshān de gūniáng (*Alishan Girl*) dates back to 1949 and remains wildly popular among middle-aged Chinese (you'll probably hear them singing it).

The Forest Recreation Area begins just beyond the turning for Tatajia and Yushan, at a 24-hour **tollgate**. Around 300m further on, public buses terminate at the main tourist centre, clustered around a sprawling car park and known simply as "Alishan", though technically this is **Zhongzheng Village** (中正村; zhōngzhèngcūn). Up Zhushan Forest Road, to the east of Zhongzheng Village, is an area known as **Xianglin Village** (香林村; xiānglín cūn) where you'll find more upscale accommodation as well as the main hiking trails (see opposite); vehicles need special passes to drive beyond the gate on Zhushan Forest Road. Bear in mind that given the area's 2200m **altitude**, it can get cold here even in the height of summer, and afternoons tend to be quite chilly once the usual midday mists roll in.

Zhushan and the Sea of Clouds

祝山; zhùshān • Zhushan Sunrise Train: Alishan Forest Railway Station • Daily before dawn; check current departure times with your hotel staff, who can also arrange a wake-up call • NT$150 one-way (30min); tickets for the following day go on sale at 4.30pm

The most popular place to watch the sunrise and the famous "sea of clouds" (云海; yúnhǎi) is from the top of the 2489m **Zhushan**. The quickest way up is via the **Zhushan Sunrise Train** (祝山觀日火車; zhùshān guānrì huǒchē), which leaves well before dawn each morning from the main Alishan Forest Railway Station near the car park, stopping at **Zhaoping Station** (沼平車站; zhǎopíng chēzhàn) a few minutes later. During peak periods it's worth buying your ticket the day before. Despite the crowds, the carnival-like atmosphere on the train can be fun.

Once at the **summit**, expect to hear a barrage of Mandarin-language tourist information, blasted through a screechy loudspeaker, while the first appearance of the sun will be signalled by the simultaneous clicking of thousands of camera shutters. Dozens of **food vendors** with pushcarts sell breakfast items such as boiled eggs and heated tins of coffee. There's a pleasant teahouse a ten-minute walk beyond Zhushan Station, where you can enjoy a decent cup of tea before your walk (or train ride) back down.

Zhushan Sunrise Trail

祝山觀日步道; zhùshān guānrì bùdào

An alternative to the bustling sunrise train, the peaceful **Zhushan Sunrise Trail** gently climbs through a beautiful old-growth cedar forest en route to the summit. The turn-off for the trail is on the side of the road between Zhongzheng and Xianglin villages, a few hundred metres before you get to Zhaoping station; allow about an hour for the walk. There are no lights along the trail, so it's necessary to bring a torch.

Dui Gao Yue Forest Trail

對高岳森林浴步道; duìgāoyuè sēnlínyù bùdà • The path begins alongside the train tracks; 1.65km one-way

Closed for repairs at the time of writing, the **Dui Gao Yue Forest Trail** is set to reopen in 2018. Walking back down from Zhushan, look for a right at the first big bend in the road, from where begins a lovely detour through evergreen forest, before it dead-ends at a **pavilion** overlooking the nearby valley.

Alishan loop trails

Sacred Tree Line train • 12 daily; 15min • NT$100 one-way

The forest recreation area also has several **loop trails** well signposted in English, offering leisurely one- to three-hour hikes through the thick forests that cover the slopes around the resort area: depending on the season, the paths are littered with flowers and blossoms, while a cluster of monuments reflects the Japanese impact on the area. You can also combine a walk with the **Sacred Tree Line** (神木線; shénmù xiàn), another small-gauge train line that runs daily from the main station to the Sacred Tree Station.

3

Tree Spirit Monument

樹靈塔; shùlíngtǎ

The lower loop path begins on the road just beyond the *Alishan House* hotel: a short path on the left takes you to the main circuit. Walking clockwise you'll first pass the **Tree Spirit Monument** on your right, a Shinto shrine built by the Japanese in 1915 to appease the spirits of the decimated forests.

Alishan Museum

阿里山博物館; ālǐshān bówùguǎn • Daily 8.30am–4.30pm • Free

The **Alishan Museum** is an old wooden Japanese building that has been converted into a small display area for old woodworking machinery, tools and saws used in the cultivation of the area, alongside examples of mountain flora and fauna and a collection of Tsou artefacts.

Ciyun Temple

慈雲寺; cíyún sì • 24hr • Free

On the main lower loop trail, **Ciyun Temple** is another Japanese shrine, built in 1919 and housing a bronze Sakyamuni Buddha given to Emperor Taisho by the king of Thailand one year before; the statue is said to be filled with gold dust. The path drops from here to the Sacred Tree Station.

Giant Tree Trails

Giant Tree Trail 1 (600m) begins at Ciyun Temple and cuts across the lower loop, down to the **Sacred Tree** (阿里山神木; ālǐshān shénmù), an enormous red cypress that is over three thousand years old, and which was venerated by the Tsou. One of Taiwan's most beloved tourist attractions, its trunk is still visible but it is no longer living, having been laid to rest in 1997. Walking alongside the train tracks will bring you to the start of **Giant Tree Trail 2** (closed at the time of writing, but set to re-open soon), which involves a steep uphill climb through yet more giant cypresses, and emerges at the Shouzhen Temple.

Shouzhen Temple

受鎮宮; shòuzhèn gōng • 24hr • Free

Firecrackers from the atmospheric **Shouzhen Temple** regularly echo through the surrounding woods. The temple was rebuilt in 1969 and is the biggest in the area, primarily dedicated to the Supreme Emperor of the Dark Heaven. The temple and roadside here are lined with food stalls specializing in wasabi products – you can buy everything from the root itself through to nose-burningly hot white-wasabi peanuts.

Alishan Trail

阿里山遊覽步道; ālǐshān yóulǎn bùdào

From the Shouzhen Temple, the **Alishan Trail** starts with a climb up to the **Magnolia Garden** (木蘭園; mùlán yuán) and past **Two Sisters Pond** (姊妹潭; jiěmèitán), named after a legend of two broken-hearted Tsou girls who drowned themselves here. From here, there are several routes back to the main road and the village that cut through **Plum Tree Garden** (梅園; méi yuán). This area was the site of the original Alishan settlement: after the great fire of 1976, development moved to the current site in Zhongzheng Village and the devastated area was converted into a park. In the late afternoon, the terrace outside the *Alishan Gou Hotel* is one of the best places to view the sunset and sea of clouds over the valley.

Tatajia

塔塔加; tǎtǎjiā • Minibus tours: daily about an hour before sunrise (4.30am in the summer); 3hr return trip • NT$300/person • Pickup from your hotel

Those wanting to get further into the mountains to watch the often-spectacular sunrise at **Tatajia**, just inside Yushan National Park, can book a slot on one of the pre-dawn **minibus tours** that leave from Zhongzheng Village every morning. Tatajia is also the start point for the exhilarating climb up Yushan (see p.228).

ARRIVAL AND DEPARTURE   ALISHAN NATIONAL SCENIC AREA

Provincial Highway 18, a winding 70km road, connects Chiayi in the west to Alishan in the east: it cuts more or less through the middle of most of the National Scenic Area's sights. By public transport, a combination of buses from Chiayi and the picturesque Alishan Forest Railway is the best way to get across the area.

BY BUS

From Chiayi Chiayi County Bus Station (嘉義縣公共汽車站; jiāyìxiàn gōnggòng qìchēzhàn) has buses to Alishan Forest Recreation Area (10 daily, 6am–2pm; 2hr 30min) via Xiding and Shizhuo. Other locations in the Alishan Scenic Area are served less frequently: Fenqihu (daily 7.10am, 9.40am & 3.10pm); Ruili and Ruifeng (daily 9.15am & 4.10pm); and Dabang (daily 5.45am, 10.55am & 4.45pm). There are also three bus services from Chiayi HSR station to Alishan (daily 10.10am, 11.40am, 1.10pm).

From Taipei Kuo Kuang runs buses from Taipei West Bus Station to Alishan Forest Recreation Area on Fri & Sat (March–Oct 8.45pm; Nov–Feb 9.45pm; 6hr). Buses return at 11.30am on Sat and Sun.

From Sun Moon Lake There are now two direct bus services covering the stunning route from Shuishe to

Alishan (daily 8am & 9am, returning 1pm & 2pm) – tickets can be purchased at *Shin Shin Homestay* (see p.226). There is also a more circuitous route: take a bus to Shuili and switch to the Jiji rail line (hourly; see p.197); at Ershui you can catch trains to Chiayi (frequent; 40–55min) from where there are buses to Alishan.

BY TRAIN

The 86km narrow-gauge Alishan Forest Railway (阿里山森林鐵道; ālǐshān sēnlín tiědào; Mon–Fri 9am, Sat 9am & 10am, Sun 9am, 9.30am & 10am; 2hr 20min; NT$384; ☎ 05 225 6918) starts in Chiayi but at the time of writing was only operational up to its halfway point at Fenqihu, from where you can board a bus (daily 11.30am & 12.50pm; 1hr; NT$96) to Alishan. Check with the visitor centre in Chiayi, or ⊛ www.ali-nsa.net for the latest information.

GETTING AROUND

By minibus An electric minibus service now operates between Alishan Visitor Centre, Zhaoping and Xianglin

stations. It operates daily 8am–5pm and costs NT$50 for a single journey, or NT$80 round-trip.

INFORMATION

Ruili The Ruitai Visitor Center (瑞太遊客中心; ruìtài yóukè zhōngxīn; 1 Ruili Village; daily 8.30am–5pm; ☎ 05 250 1070) can provide Chinese-language hiking maps. Better information as well as English leaflets and maps can be found at the Yuantan Visitor Centre (圓潭遊客中心; yuántán yóukè zhōngxīn; daily 8.30am–5pm; ☎ 05 250 2026) at Km71.5 on Route 122,

which also has a café and exhibits on local flora and fauna. **Dingshizhuo Tea Terraces** The Dingshizhuo Tourist Service Station (頂石棹旅遊服務中心; dǐngshízhuō lǚyóu fúwù zhōngxīn; daily 9am–5pm; ☎ 05 256 2565) is signposted from Route 169 and has basic trail maps in English. **Dabang** The tiny visitor centre kiosk (達邦中心;

dábāng yóukè zhōngxīn; daily 9am–5pm; ☏ 05 2511982) can provide basic information on buses, accommodation and trails.

Alishan Forest Recreation Area On the opposite side of the car park is the visitor information centre (daily 8am–5pm; ☏ 05 267 9917), with English-language exhibits and a movie on the area's main attractions, as well as free English maps, brochures and transport information. Alishan's other tourist amenities are around or near the car

park, including a very ornate post office (Mon–Fri 8am–noon & 1–4.30pm; ☏ 05 267 9970) with currency exchange and an ATM, although this only accepts Taiwan-issued cards.

Tatajia The Tatajia Visitors Centre (塔塔加; tǎtǎjiā yóukè zhōngxīn; daily except Tues 9am–4.30pm) offers information, maps, a simple display on local wildlife, and a café on the second floor.

ACCOMMODATION

RUILI

The best places to stay are the village's superb homestays. In addition to offering pick-ups from the bus or train station, most can prepare home-cooked meals made from local ingredients.

A-Han Holiday Resort 阿漢的家民宿; a hàn dejiā mínsù 79 Ruili Village, Route 166 ☏ 05 250 1011 or ☏ 0932 981 526. A decent mid-range option set in an attractive wooden building. A fish pond and small tea field, a short walk from the hotel, belong to the hotel. The owner also operates a more expensive place across the road (*Xian Xian*), with grander wood-panelled rooms (NT$4800). **NT$2400**

Clear Moon Guesthouse 明月大船的家; míngyuè dàchuán de jiā 48 Ruili Village, Route 166 ☏ 05 250 1626 or ☏ 0937 699 338. Rooms here surround a courtyard backed by an enormous family shrine. The friendly owners make their own plum wine and are keen to share it with guests. They only open on weekends when they offer a package that includes one night's stay, three meals and an area tour – but you must call in advance to arrange this. Full board **NT$1500** per person

Over the Rainbows 遇見彩虹; yùjiàn cǎihóng 10 Ruili Village, Route 166 ☏ 05 250 2185 The best budget option in Ruili, this three-storey lodge has fan-cooled Western- and Japanese-style quads (NT$2880), some with balconies commanding sweeping views of the valley below. A handful of new shipping container doubles are also available – compact, but clean and comfortable and with a/c. The owners can arrange meals and night-viewing tours of the local fireflies, in season. **NT$2560**

Yejianghua Vacation Village 野薑花渡假村; yějiānghuā dùjiàcūn 1–3 Ruili Village, Route 166 ☏ 05 250 1095. Conveniently located right next to the Ruitai Visitor Centre, this friendly hotel has beautiful wooden cabins overlooking lush green tea fields dropping away to the valley below. They also have cheaper but perfectly comfortable rooms in a concrete building over the road. Doubles **NT$1600**, cabins **NT$2600**

FENQIHU

Arnold Janssen Activity Center 奮起湖楊生愛諾德 活動中心; fènqíhú yángshēng àinuòdé

huódòng zhōngxīn 26 Fenqihu ☏ 05 256 1134, ⊚ aj-centersvd.myweb.hinet.net. This Catholic hostel, down the hill from the train station, is Fenqihu's only real budget option. As well as dorms and basic doubles, singles (NT$500; shared bathrooms) and a smarter quad room with TV (NT$2000) are also on offer. Dorms **NT$300**, doubles **NT$800**

Fenqihu Hotel 奮起湖大飯店; fènqíhú dàfàndiàn 178 Fenqihu ☏ 05 256 1888. The town's best-known hotel, with a wide range of Japanese-style wooden-floored rooms, including some with traditional cedar tubs, although the cheapest are windowless. It's famous for its filling "railway lunchbox", and its gregarious owner knows the history of Fenqihu inside out. **NT$1680**

YaWho Hotel 雅湖山莊; yǎhú shānzhuāng 112 Fenqihu ☏ 05 256 1097. Located just off the far western end of the train platform, the cheap and cheerful *YaWho* has spartan but clean Japanese-style doubles and twins with large beds and TVs from NT$1200. There's also a ten-person room (NT$3000). The owner sells *aiyu* jelly on Old St during the day. **NT$1200**

Yeashow Hotel 雅琇山莊; yǎxiù shānzhuāng 150 Fenqihu ☏ 05 256 1336. Just down the steps to the left of Old St, the shiny *Yeashow* has very friendly management and small, carpeted rooms that are good value. **NT$1200**

DINGSHIZHUO TEA TERRACES

Lauya Restaurant & Guesthouse 神禾景觀餐廳民 宿; shénhé jǐngguān cāntīng mínsù Highway 18, Km65, just beyond Shizhuo ☏ 05 256 2341, ⊚ lauya .com. A fabulous wooden chalet with a stunning veranda high above the valley. The guesthouse features homely all-wood rooms with decks, and the tasty breakfast (included) can be served in the early hours of the morning if you're catching the sunrise train. Reservations essential. **NT$2600**

XIDING

The village of Xiding (隙頂; xìdǐng) at around Km54 on Highway 18, is a great place to stay, with a growing number of homestays perched in the tea fields above the main road.

★**Alishan Season Star** 四季星空; sìjì xīngkōng ☏ 0960 091 683, ⊚ seasonstar.com.tw. This

3

European-style, luxurious homestay has spacious rooms inspired by Neoclassical French interiors (one has a loft with a spiral staircase). It faces a tea plantation and a bamboo grove, with sensational views of the mountains across the valley. Owner Gordon Fang speaks English and piles on the French inspiration for breakfast and afternoon snacks (included); dinner is extra. NT$2890

DABANG
Keupana Homestay 給巴娜民宿; gěibānà mínsù 108 Dabang Village, on the Tefuye Rd ☎ 05 251 1688. On the edge of the village, this simple but appealing homestay has small, brightly painted doubles, triples, quads and six-person rooms in a modern building surrounded by flowers, a *hufu* (wooden pavilion) and views. NT$1200

ALISHAN FOREST RECREATION AREA
Most of the Forest Recreation Area's hotels are located in Zhongzheng Village, where you'll find a row of faceless mid-range establishments at the base of the hill, along with a few cheaper homestays. Reservations are essential during peak times. Higher-end accommodation can be found in Xianglin Village (香林村; xiānglín cūn), up Zhushan Forest Rd. Note that some mid-range and cheaper hotels only have hot water at certain times – enquire when checking-in.

ZHONGSHAN VILLAGE
Alishan Catholic Hostel 阿里山天主教福若瑟服務中心; ālǐshān tiānzhǔ jiāofú ruòsè fúwù zhōngxīn 57 Zhongshan Village ☎ 05 267 9602. The only budget accommodation in Alishan is down a narrow lane just after the tollgate on the left, in an area known as Zhongshan Village, which has cheap but basic doubles. NT$1200

ZHONGZHENG VILLAGE
Gau Shan Ching Hotel 高山青賓館; gāoshānqīng bīnguǎn 43 Zhongzheng Village ☎ 05 267 9988.

Hotel with very friendly management and clean, if slightly cramped, rooms; includes a Chinese breakfast in its rates. Some of the rooms have interior windows or no view, so ask for a room at the front. The staff speak limited English, but can help you book bus tickets to Tatajia and Chiayi. NT$1750
Shermuh Hotel 神木賓館; shénmù bīnguǎn 50 Zhongzheng Village ☎ 05 267 9511. Warm and friendly small hotel with compact, but clean and well-appointed rooms. Breakfast is in the form of a voucher for one of the restaurants in the main car park. NT$2560
★ **Shin Shin Homestay** 欣欣民宿; xīnxīn mínsù 24 Zhongzheng Village ☎ 05 267 9748. Friendly home-stay on the edge of the main car park, and a better deal than most of the older hotels. The cosy wooden cabin-like rooms all have en-suite bathrooms and TV; rates vary with room size and number of guests, and almost double at weekends and holidays. Breakfast not included. NT$1500

XIANGLIN VILLAGE
Alishan Gou Hotel 阿里山閣大飯店; ālǐshān gé dàfàndiàn 1 Xianglin Village ☎ 05 267 9611, ⊕ agh.com.tw. A stone's throw from Zhaoping Station, this modern hotel boasts a terrace that's become a favoured spot for viewing the sea of clouds. The hotel is divided into two sections: the older building B has well-priced doubles, while building A is a new addition and has comfortable quad rooms (NT$3600) with two double beds, fridge, TV and attractive bathrooms. The hotel's location makes for an easy early-morning stumble to catch the sunrise train, and a shuttle bus also connects it with Zhongzheng Village. NT$1690
Alishan House 阿里山賓館; ālǐshān bīnguǎn 16 Xianglin Village ☎ 05 267 9811, ⊕ alishanhouse.com.tw. This is the area's top hotel, split into two wings: the older Japanese-era historic wing; and a more luxurious modern block with chic rooms and balconies (NT$9800), plus a spa on the tenth floor. If you have a reservation, their shuttle will pick you up at the bus station. NT$7200

EATING

FENQIHU
Fenqihu's Old St is one of the best places to eat in all Alishan, though many places tend to close or operate short hours mid-week; most places are open on Sat. Local culinary delights such as *aiyu* jelly (àiyùbīng), made from a gel squeezed from fig seeds, the famous "railway lunchbox" (tiělù biàndāng), a compact arrangement of meat, boiled egg, rice and vegetables, and local wasabi (shānkuí) are all worth seeking out.
★ **Aishan Aiyu Jelly** 愛山屋野生愛玉店; àishānwū yěshēng àiyù diàn 107 Old St. This small stall at the end of Old St features thirst-quenching *aiyu* jelly drinks, made with freshly picked fruit from the

mountains nearby (from NT$25). Daily 9am–6pm.
Aiyu Uncle 愛玉伯ㄟ厝; àiyù bó de cuò. The most atmospheric place to sip tea and eat snacks in Fenqihu is this old teahouse tucked away in the narrow lanes below Old St. It's difficult to find – if you can't see the signs (Chinese only), ask someone. Daily 9am–6pm.
★ **Dengshan Shitang** 登山食堂; dēngshān shítáng 168 Old St ☎ 05 256 2666. The town's best-known maker of delicious biàndāng, with lunchboxes starting at NT$70 for a simple takeaway, and fancy pots (NT$120–150) that come with homemade soup. It's right by the station and features a unique ordering system, where you pay and receive change through slots, get an old

train ticket in return and grab your food when the bell rings, before sitting down to eat in the wooden dining room. Daily 9am–6pm.

Fenqihu Hotel 奮起湖大飯店; fènqíhú dàfàndiàn 178 Old St ☎05 256 1888. Famous producer of the ubiquitous lunchbox, which now has a national franchise to sell its biàndāng through 7-Eleven. NT$100 takeaway or NT$120 dine-in. Daily 7.30am–7.30pm.

Mary Store 瑪莉商店; mǎlì shāngdiàn 143 Old St ☎05 256 1566. This small store sells their own mixes of sweet-ginger and longan teas (NT$200) – drink samples are handed out for free. Daily 8am–6pm.

Tian Mei Zhen 天美珍火車餅專賣店; tiānměizhēn huǒchēbǐng zhuānmàidiàn 142 Old St ☎05 256 1008. Established in 1943, this lauded cake-maker knocks out boxes of "train cakes" (húhuǒchēbǐng; pastries with train images embossed on the crust and fillings such as green bean, red bean and green tea, sweetened with wild honey) for NT$120, and the crumblier gūzǎowèi hànbǐng cakes for NT$100. Daily 8am–9pm.

DABANG

Jiejiao Canting 街角餐廳; jiējiǎo cāntīng Village Centre ☎05 251 1545. In the heart of the village, this attractive open-sided bamboo café is popular with locals and serves biàndāng (NT$70–80) and coffee. Daily except Thurs 10am–7pm.

ALISHAN FOREST RECREATION AREA

You'll find plenty of restaurants dotted around Zhongzheng Village, and the better hotels, including *Alishan House*, also have their own. As well as standard Chinese fare, many of the places in town also serve mountain specialities including wild mushrooms, boar and deer. There's a 7-Eleven in the car park where you can buy drinks and snacks for your hikes.

★**The Great Beauty of Rihchu** 日出有大美; rìchū yǒudàměi 30 Zhongzheng Village ☎05 267 9958. Set to a cutesy theme, this place serves several fine teas (NT$180) and superb hotpots containing various meats and piled high with vegetables, pumpkin, bamboo shoots and dumplings (NT$280–500). English menu available. Daily 11.30am–2.30pm & 5.30–8.30pm.

Shanbin Canting 山賓餐廳; shānbīn cāntīng 19 Zhongzheng Village ☎05 267 9633. Cosy little booth-restaurant, serving hotpots (NT$350–500) and tasty mountain vegetables as well as Chinese classics such as beef and green peppers (NT$130) and sweet-and-sour ribs (NT$150). English menu available. Daily 11am–8.30pm.

Yushan National Park

玉山國家公園; yùshān guójiā gōngyuán

Taiwan's most untarnished breadth of backcountry, **YUSHAN NATIONAL PARK** is an archetypal mountain wilderness with a seemingly endless proliferation of 3000m peaks, separated by yawning river valleys. The park is Taiwan's largest by far, covering over three percent of the country and accessible by road from three sides. It is revered by Taiwanese conservationists, who have worked tirelessly to protect its natural treasures since its establishment in 1985. Sheltering six distinct vegetation zones, the park contains more than half of the island's endemic plant species, as well as some of Asia's rarest animal species (see box below).

But the park is primarily known for the majestic **Yushan** (Jade Mountain) – the tallest peak in northeast Asia at 3952m. Climbing to the summit is an exhilarating experience, and not as challenging as it might sound, although obtaining a permit requires significant advance planning. Spring and autumn are generally considered the best seasons for climbing, but you should always come prepared for fickle

YUSHAN WILDLIFE

Yushan National Park is home to many of Asia's rarest-seen animals. Chief among these is the elusive **Formosan Black Bear**, an omnivorous beast that mostly roams the foothills below 2000m. These bears are hardly ever encountered and seldom spotted by humans, although there have been more frequent sightings in recent years, particularly on the Walami Trail (see p.316). Much more visible is the profusion of **deer species**, some of which can be seen by watchful trekkers, especially on the northern fringes of Yushan, near the beautiful high-altitude meadows of **Badongguan**. The most commonly seen of these is the diminutive **Formosan Reeve's Muntjac**, recognizable by its tan coat and stubby, single-pronged antlers.

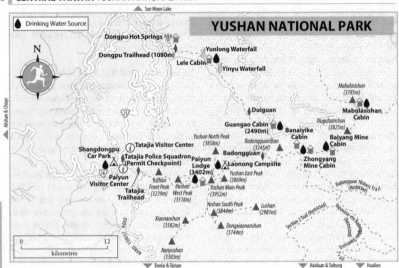

weather. The park is also, nominally at least, the homeland of the **Bunun** tribe, who remained semi-independent until they were brutally crushed by the Japanese in the 1920s.

The park's entry points and information centres are spread widely, making it seem like several different parks. If you're planning to climb Yushan, your gateway into the park will be either **Tatajia** (from Alishan/Chiayi) or **Dongpu** (from Sun Moon Lake). From Tatajia, the climb is easier and much more heavily trafficked, while the Dongpu approach is longer and more physically demanding but was closed after Typhoon Morakot and at the time of writing had yet to reopen. Tatajia is also famed for its spectacular sunrise views, and pre-dawn minibuses depart Alishan's hotels every day to ferry tourists to see it. The **Nanan** section of the park is covered in Chapter 5 (see p.316).

Climbing Yushan from Tatajia

塔塔加; tǎtǎjiā • Mountain entry permits must be filled out at the Paiyun Visitor Center (排雲遊客中心; páiyún yóukè zhōngxīn): you can drive straight to the Shangdongpu (上東埔; shàngdōngpǔ) car park near the visitor centre in your own vehicle; or take an Alishan–Tatajia sunrise minibus (see opposite), asking the driver to let you off early for the Paiyun Visitor Center

By far the easiest, most popular route up Yushan is from nearby **Tatajia**, along a well-maintained trail that is probably Taiwan's most famous hike. Although many Taiwanese will tell you it's an arduous two-day return climb, in reality a reasonably fit walker with an early start could make the 22km return journey from the **Tatajia Trailhead** (塔塔加登山口; tǎtǎjiā dēngshānkǒu) to the main peak in one long day. Most people start very early, hike up to *Paiyun Lodge*, then sleep for a few hours before making the summit ascent for sunrise and returning straight back down to the trailhead. Another option is to arrive late, stay at *Dongpu Lodge* (2600m) to acclimatize, and then set off early the next morning, giving plenty of time to appreciate the majesty of the scenery.

Whichever plan you favour, you will need to complete **permit** practicalities beforehand (see opposite) at the Paiyun Visitor Center. Once these are complete, you can take a park minivan (daily 6am–5pm) to the trailhe ad itself, another 2.8km along Nanxi Forest Road, saving you the walk, which otherwise adds about an hour to your journey each way.

The trail

From the Tatajia Trailhead (2610m) to the *Paiyun Lodge* (3402m) is an 8.5km walk of moderate intensity, with a fairly gradual ascent. If you reach the lodge quickly, you can stash your bag inside and make a speedy ascent of Yushan's **main peak** (玉山主峰; yùshān zhǔfēng), a steep 2.4km climb with an elevation gain of over 500m. Alternatively, you could first climb the lower 3518m **west peak** (玉山西峰; yùshān xīfēng) and return to the lodge for the night. Bear in mind that most Taiwanese hikers set their alarms for around 2am to allow ample time to reach the summit before **sunrise**. Sunrises from the top of Yushan can be truly inspiring. However, during busy periods you might consider sleeping in and waiting until the crowds start their descent; you'll have more chance of solitude at the top and will spend less time waiting at bottlenecks along the trail.

ARRIVAL AND DEPARTURE YUSHAN NATIONAL PARK

Arrival Tatajia is where your exploration of Yushan National Park is most likely to begin. It's around 20km east of the Alishan Forest Recreation Area (see p.219). There is no public bus service from Alishan to Tatajia, but there are hotel-run, pre-dawn minibuses from Alishan and Zhongzheng Village that take tourists to Tatajia Visitor Center each morning. For the Paiyun Visitor Center, ask the driver to let you off about 1km before the minibus's destination at Tatajia.

Departure Returning to Alishan is difficult: you'll need to pre-arrange a return pick-up, or you'll end up having to hitchhike, or walk to the police post to beg for a lift. For considerably more money than the minibuses, you can hire your own driver in Alishan to take you to the Paiyun Visitor Center and back (ask at your hotel). Renting a scooter or car at Chiayi (see p.217) is another alternative.

INFORMATION AND PERMITS

Park information For those climbing Yushan, visiting the Paiyun Visitor Center (排雲遊客中心; páiyún yóukè zhōngxīn; daily 6.30am–4pm; ☎049 270 2228), 1km from Alishan, is essential. If not, there is also the Tatajia Visitor Center (塔塔加遊客中心; tǎtǎjiā yóukè zhōngxīn; 9am–4pm, closed second and fourth Tues of the month; ☎049 270 2200), 19km from Alishan at the end of Highway 18, which has English maps, audiovisual presentations and an exhibition hall with information on the nearby mountains and local flora and fauna. The Yushan National Park Headquarters and its main visitor centre (300 Zhongshan Rd Sec 1; daily 9am–4.30pm; ☎049 277 3121, ⊕www.ysnp.gov.tw) is located in Shuili, near Sun Moon Lake.

Applying for permits You'll need a national park entry permit (入園; rùyuán) in advance to climb Yushan; you can apply online (⊕www.ysnp.gov.tw) in advance. To be sure of a permit, avoid weekends and Jan & Feb, when the trail is often closed. Applications are accepted 30–120 days in advance and only 92 permits are granted per day, of which 24 are reserved for foreigners wanting to climb Mon–Thurs & Sun; apply as early as possible. The permit costs NT$480, which includes a bed at *Paiyun Lodge*. It is also possible to apply for a one-day permit, but you'll need to provide proof that you've previously climbed a 3000m+ peak.

Mountain entry permit Once you have a park entry permit, you'll also need a separate mountain entry permit (入山; rùshān) from the Paiyun Visitor Center (see above). For this you'll need to submit your passport and three copies of your hiking plan and route map.

Organized climbing trips You can take some of the hassle out of the permit and transport situation by arranging the trek through Blue Skies Adventures (☎0982 858 316, ⊕blueskiesadventures.com.tw) who post upcoming group trip dates on their Facebook page, but can also arrange private trips.

ACCOMMODATION

Dongpu Lodge 東埔山莊; dōngpǔ shānzhuāng Below Shandongpu car park, Tatajia ☎0932 832 077. At 2600m, this simple government-run dorm lodge allows hikers to acclimatize before beginning the Yushan ascent, but is also popular with visitors hiking other trails. It can fill up fast, especially on weekends – book in advance. Hot water until 10pm. NT$300

Paiyun Lodge 排雲山莊; páiyún shānzhuāng Yushan. Dorm "beds" here are foam on wood, so you might want to bring your own roll mat. The lodge has drinking water, sleeping bags for hire (NT$300), and provides four meals per day, if reserved in advance (dinner NT$300, other meals NT$150). Included in permit fee.

South Taiwan

KAOHSIUNG

South Taiwan

Languid, tropical south Taiwan is a world away from Taipei, a land of betel nut plantations, pineapple groves and sandy beaches. The southern plains are home to Taiwan's oldest Chinese settlements, a bastion of Taiwanese culture with a correspondingly high proportion of independence supporters – the counties of Tainan, Kaohsiung and Pingdong are Democratic Progressive Party (DPP) strongholds and the Taiwanese language is spoken everywhere in preference to Mandarin. The lush southern mountains offer plenty of gorgeous scenery, and are predominantly inhabited by the Bunun, Paiwan and Rukai tribes. Much of the region's exuberant culture is encapsulated in its festivals: some temples hold elaborate boat-burning ceremonies every three years, while the horizontal firework display at Yanshui is a chaotic but exhilarating event held during the Lantern Festival.

Tainan is an essential stop on any tour of Taiwan. The former capital is crammed with ornate temples, engaging historical sights and some of the best snack food in the country. From here, the **Southern Cross-Island Highway** snakes east across the mountains to Taitung, a dramatic and perilous route which has remained closed since Typhoon Morakot struck in 2009, although the hot-spring village of Baolai, at its western gateway, is readily accessible. South of here, **Maolin National Scenic Area** was also badly damaged by Morakot, but has gradually been getting back on its feet, and offers magical scenery and traditional Rukai slate villages at Duona, Sandimen and Wutai.

   Kaohsiung, the biggest city in the south, is evolving from its grimy, industrial past to emerge as a modern, international city, while retaining its laidback, friendly character. Close by you'll find the impressive monastery at **Foguangshan** and, across the Gaoping River, the idyllic rural scenery of **Meinong**. Just south of Kaohsiung, the port of Donggang is famed for its tuna and boat-burning festival and is also the jumping-off point for the intriguing coral island of **Little Liuqiu**, 15km off the coast. The narrow stub of land at the foot of Taiwan is dominated by **Kenting National Park**, centred on the bustling main resort town, within easy reach of a host of white-sand and surf beaches.

Tainan

台南; táinán

Historic **TAINAN**, just a few kilometres inland from the southwest coast, is a city of ancient monuments, delicious food and, above all, **temples**: there are more gods worshipped, and more festivals and rituals observed in Tainan than in any other place in Taiwan. Much of this is a legacy of its two-hundred-year history as Taiwan's capital city – during the seventeenth century, the city was the last independent outpost of China's **Ming dynasty**.

MAZU DEITY, KAIJI TIANHOU TEMPLE, TAINAN

Highlights

❶ **Tainan** Taiwan's former capital is home to an abundance of historic but lively temples, along with appealing colonial remnants and some of the country's best street food. **See p.232**

❷ **Kaohsiung** Currently enjoying something of a renaissance, Taiwan's friendly second city is well worth a visit for its riverside walkways, lively cafés, harbour views and excellent seafood. **See p.252**

❸ **Foguangshan** Spend a day exploring the galleries, museums and elegant temples of this massive Buddhist monastery. **See p.264**

❹ **Meinong** The heart of Hakka culture in the south, Meinong is a perfect pastiche of rural Taiwan, best explored by bicycle. **See p.264**

❺ **Little Liuqiu Island** Kick back and enjoy the alluring rock formations on this tranquil coral island. **See p.271**

❻ **Kenting National Park** Hire a car or scooter and explore Taiwan's southernmost national park, with pristine surf beaches and stunning coastal scenery. **See p.276**

HIGHLIGHTS ARE MARKED ON THE MAP ON P.234

The oldest and most absorbing parts of Tainan are **Anping**, on the west side of town by the sea, and the cultural zones in the heart of the old city; the latter were created specifically to make things easier for visitors, with English information, signs and maps. The **Chihkan, Dong-an Fang, Five Canals** and **Confucius Temple cultural zones** contain the richest concentration of sights – reckon on spending at least two days to do them justice.

Brief history

The ancestral home of the Siraya píngpǔ tribe, Tainan began its modern history with the **Dutch**, who established **Fort Zeelandia** in 1624 on a sandbar off the coast. At that time, the site of the modern city's western half was under water, part of a huge lagoon ringed by a chain of sandy islets. The Dutch called the area "Tayouan" and made it the capital of their colony. In 1662, however, they surrendered to the superior forces of Ming general Zheng Chenggong, better known as **Koxinga** (see box, p.240). During the period of **Zheng family rule** that followed (1662–83), Tainan prospered, and many of its finest temples were constructed to befit its status as an independent Chinese kingdom. In 1664, one of the last descendants of the Ming royal family, the **Prince of Ningjing**, moved to the city. When the Zhengs surrendered to Chinese admiral Shi Lang in 1683, the city became known as **Taiwan-Fu** and was made prefectural capital of the island.

In 1823, a devastating storm led to the silting-up of the lagoon, and **Anping** (the site of Fort Zeelandia) became permanently joined to the mainland. The Treaty of Beijing (1860) paved the way for foreign merchants to trade camphor, tea and opium in Anping, but after the Japanese occupied Taiwan in 1895 the sale of opium and camphor became a government franchise and, with the port silting up further, by 1911 most merchants had left. When Taiwan became a province in 1885, the city became known as **Tainan-Fu**, or "South Taiwan" and lost its capital status to Taipei. Today it is Taiwan's fourth-largest city, with a population of around 770,000. In February 2016, the city was rocked by a 6.4 earthquake, causing the death of 117 people, almost all of who died in a single, poorly built high-rise in Yongkang district.

Chihkan Cultural Zone

赤崁文化園區; chìkǎn wénhuà yuánqū

The **Chihkan Cultural Zone** covers the northern part of the old city and is home to some of Tainan's finest temples and **Chihkan Tower**, a collection of Qing dynasty pavilions in the northern section of the old city, which is the best place to start.

Chihkan Tower

赤崁樓; chìkǎn lóu • 212 Minzu Rd Sec 2 • Daily 8.30am–9pm; music performances Wed–Sun 7.30–9pm, weather permitting – check at the visitor centre • NT$50 (includes performances) • ☎ 06 220 5647

West of the train station on Minzu Road, **Chihkan Tower** marks the site of **Fort Provintia**, built by the Dutch in 1653. The fort was captured by Koxinga in 1661 prior to his siege of Fort Zeelandia. After the Dutch defeat, the site was gradually abandoned until a Fujian-style temple pavilion was built on the ruins in 1875. Originally a **Sea God Temple**, the base of the pavilion is lined with **nine steles** sent to the city by Emperor Qianlong, praising the defeat of the Lin Shuangwen Rebellion of 1786–88 (see p.389); inside is a small exhibition (Chinese only) on Koxinga and the old Dutch fort. The pavilion beyond is the **Wenchang Pavilion** which houses an exhibition detailing the Qing civil service system, and a shrine to the fourth "Wenchang" or literature god, Kui Dou Xingjun (kuídǒu xīngjūn), said to aid those taking the old imperial civil service examinations. Supposedly based on a real person, he is said to have failed the examinations three times simply because the emperor was repulsed by his hideous looks – the poor scholar committed suicide and has been venerated ever since. Evening classical and traditional music performances are sometimes held in the grounds.

Kaiji Tianhou Temple

開基天后宮;kāijī tiānhòu gōng • 12 Zhiciang St • Daily 6am–9pm

Kaiji Tianhou Temple is a real gem: established in 1662, it is Tainan's oldest temple to Mazu, goddess of the sea (there are nearly a thousand in Taiwan). The shrine is decorated with fascinating artwork, such as the "barbarian" figures holding up the eaves of the corners, but the real highlight is the shrine to **Guanyin** at the back. This contains one of three celebrated images of the Bodhisattva in Tainan, the gold statue blackened with incense smoke over the years, her graceful pose capturing the ethos of Buddhist serenity.

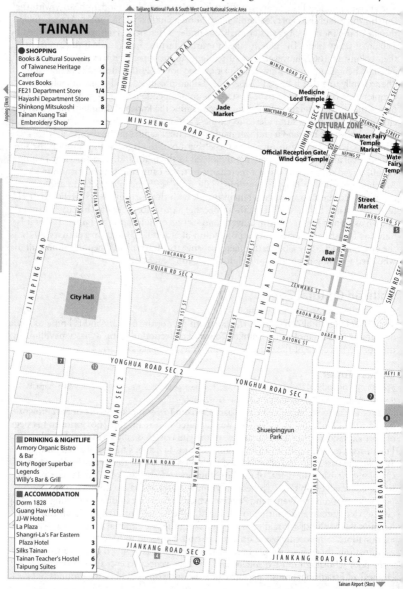

4

TAINAN

● **SHOPPING**
Books & Cultural Souvenirs of Taiwanese Heritage	6
Carrefour	7
Caves Books	3
FE21 Department Store	1/4
Hayashi Department Store	5
Shinkong Mitsukoshi	8
Tainan Kuang Tsai Embroidery Shop	2

■ **DRINKING & NIGHTLIFE**
Armory Organic Bistro & Bar	1
Dirty Roger Superbar	3
Legends	2
Willy's Bar & Grill	4

■ **ACCOMMODATION**
Dorm 1828	2
Guang Haw Hotel	4
JJ-W Hotel	5
La Plaza	1
Shangri-La's Far Eastern Plaza Hotel	3
Silks Tainan	8
Tainan Teacher's Hostel	6
Taipung Suites	7

Taijiang National Park & South West Coast National Scenic Area

Anping (3km)

Medicine Lord Temple
Jade Market
FIVE CANALS CULTURAL ZONE
Water Fairy Temple Market
Official Reception Gate/ Wind God Temple
Water Fairy Temp
Street Market
Bar Area
City Hall
Shueipingyun Park
YONGHUA ROAD SEC 2
YONGHUA ROAD SEC 1
JIANNAN ROAD
JIANKANG ROAD SEC 3
JIANKANG ROAD SEC 2

Tainan Airport (5km)

Official God of War Temple

祀典武廟; sìdiǎn wǔmiào • 229 Yongfu Rd Sec 2 • Daily 5am–9pm

The striking peach-coloured walls opposite Chihkan Tower belong to Tainan's **Official God of War Temple**. One of the city's most attractive temples, dedicated to god of war **Guan Di**, it originally served as the Prince of Ningjing's private gardens, built in 1665. He is said to have brought one of the images of the deity with him from China, but the temple was formally established in 1690, when it took on its current form. The **Main Hall** at the front of the complex contains the shrine to Guan Di, with an aged wooden

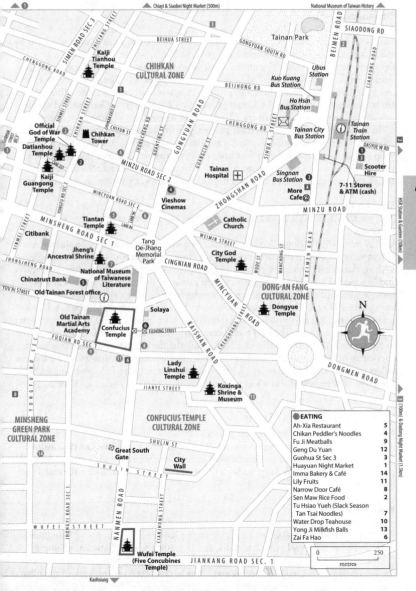

EATING

Ah-Xia Restaurant	5
Chikan Peddler's Noodles	4
Fu Ji Meatballs	9
Geng Du Yuan	12
Guohua St Sec 3	3
Huayuan Night Market	1
Imma Bakery & Café	14
Lily Fruits	11
Narrow Door Café	8
Sen Maw Rice Food	2
Tu Hsiao Yueh (Slack Season Tan Tsai Noodles)	7
Water Drop Teahouse	10
Yong Ji Milkfish Balls	13
Zai Fa Hao	6

tablet hanging from the beams above the entrance – carved in 1794, it reads 大丈夫 (dà zhàngfū) or "Great Man", an allusion to the fierce-looking god below. The **Rear Hall** contains tablets representing three generations of Guan Di's ancestors: on the left you'll see a small scroll inscribed with a bamboo engraving and poem said to have been penned by the general himself, although this is not the original – it's a rubbing from his tomb in China. To the left of here is a side hall containing another of Tainan's three captivating images of **Guanyin**, while around the back sits a plum tree allegedly planted by the Prince of Ningjing.

Datianhou Temple

大天后宮; dàtiānhòu gōng • Lane 227 • Daily 5am–9pm

Standing on the site of the Prince of Ningjing's palace, **Datianhou Temple** was built by the Qing victor Shi Lang to honour the goddess Mazu, whom he believed had delivered victory in 1683. The atmospheric **Main Hall** is packed with numerous Mazu deities, while the **stele** embedded in the wall to the right was commissioned in 1685 by Shi Lang to commemorate his triumph. The **dragon pillars** here are rare Ming originals from the time of Ningjing – this part of the temple is thought to have served as the private shrine where the last of the Mings would worship his illustrious ancestors.

The **Rear Hall** is dedicated to Mazu's parents, previously serving as Ningjing's actual residence but more famous for its grisly association with his concubines – they're supposed to have hanged themselves from the beams above, after hearing of Shi Lang's victory. The shrine to the left of the main hall contains another exceptional **Guanyin** figure, this one black-faced and robed in gold, set majestically within an attractive grotto.

Tiantan Temple

天壇; tiāntán • 16 Lane Alley 84, Zhongyi Rd Sec 2 • Daily 5am–10pm • Minimum donation of NT$100 expected for "Red Head Masters" rituals

Dating from 1854, **Tiantan Temple** is one of Tainan's most important. Despite the name ("Temple of Heaven"), the main building is a fairly typical south Fujian-style temple, with an elaborately carved facade and vivid dragons embellishing the double-eaved gable and hip roof of the Main Hall. The temple is primarily dedicated to the **Jade Emperor**, but operates more like a spiritual department store, with more deities and festivals than any other in Tainan. The **Main Hall** is where the Jade Emperor is worshipped and, as is traditional, the god is symbolized by a tablet with his name on it – he's too powerful to be represented by a statue. The **Rear Hall** is crammed with smoke-stained deities: the shrine in the centre is dedicated to the San Guan Dadi, the three imperial officials of Taoism, overseeing heaven, earth and sea, but the hall's most animated occupants are the **fortune tellers** or "Red Head Masters", spirit mediums who are employed to communicate with the gods. Wearing white shirts and red headgear, they perform rituals for visitors.

Five Canals Cultural Zone

五條港文化園區; wǔtiáogǎng wénhuà yuánqū

The old merchant quarter west of Simen Road is known as the **Five Canals Cultural Zone**. The neighbourhood was established beyond the old city walls in the eighteenth century as traders tried to keep up with the retreating lagoon, although the canals are long gone.

Water Fairy Temple

水仙宮; shuǐxiān gōng • Water Fairy Market, Guohua St • Daily 6am–9pm

The **Water Fairy Temple Market**, accessible from Guohua Street (opposite Gonghua St), is packed with meat and vegetable stalls, and contains the tiny **Water Fairy Temple**, dedicated to the five water lords of ancient Chinese tradition. Squeeze inside to view the intricately carved wooden beams and Chinese characters on the back of the pillars flanking the altar; uncovered in 2004, these etchings, which had been shielded behind plaster for hundreds of years, describe the origin of the temple.

Medicine Lord Temple

藥王廟; yàowáng miào • Shennong St • Daily 5am–6pm

West of the Water Fairy Temple Market, narrow **Shennong Street** (神農街; shénnóng jiē) is perhaps Tainan's most traditional and photogenic road, with ramshackle wooden houses and, at its western end, the **Medicine Lord Temple**. This small shrine, established in 1646, commemorates a doctor from the Tang dynasty: his statue sits in the Main Hall, flanked by two pages, one holding medical books, the other a bottle of medicine.

Confucius Temple Cultural Zone and around

孔廟文化園區; kǒngmiào wénhuà yuánqū

The southern half of the old city falls within the **Confucius Temple Cultural Zone**, littered with temples and historic sights, principal among which is the Confucius Temple itself. There are also plenty of interesting cafés and restaurants in the area – handy for taking a break from the sights.

The Confucius Temple

孔子廟; kǒngzǐ miào • Nanmen Rd • Daily 8.30am–5.30pm • Free; Dacheng Hall NT$25 • ⓦ confucius.culture.tw

Established in 1666 and rebuilt many times, the **Confucius Temple** is Taiwan's oldest and most revered Confucian shrine. With its russet-red walls, classical architecture and languid tree-lined forecourt, it's one of the most charming structures in the city, laid out in traditional style. As you enter from Nanmen Road, the tower in the far right-hand corner is the **Wenchang Pavilion** (文昌閣; wénchāng gé; maximum ten people at a time), a three-storey pagoda completed in 1715. You can clamber up the narrow stairs to see the simple shrines to Wenchang Dadi, the god of literature, on the second floor and Kui Dou Xingjun on the top floor. Nearby stands the **Hall of Edification** (明倫堂; mínglún táng), a school for those preparing to take provincial-level exams in the Qing period.

Dacheng Hall

大成殿; dàchéngdiàn • NT$25

The central **Dacheng Hall**, with its distinctive double-eaved swallowtail roof, is at the heart of the complex. It's simply decorated inside, with just one tablet dedicated to Confucius, inscribed "Great Teacher Spirit Tablet". As is customary, on each side are tablets to his disciples, but what makes this temple unique is the twelve boards hanging from the beams, each beautifully inscribed by various emperors and leaders of Taiwan. Qing dynasty Emperor Kangxi (ruled 1661–1722) wrote "Teacher of all Generations" on an olive-green tablet directly above the main shrine; former Kuomintang (KMT) president Chiang Kai-shek wrote the blue tablet to the right of the main altar; while at the front right is the newest offering from current president of Taiwan Tsai Ing-wen.

National Museum of Taiwanese Literature

國家台灣文學館; guójiā táiwān wénxuéguǎn • Nanmen Rd • Tues–Sun 9am–6pm • Free • ⓣ 06 221 7201, ⓦ www .nmtl.gov.tw

Just north of the Confucius Temple, the **National Museum of Taiwanese Literature** occupies the former City Hall, a striking Neoclassical building built by the Japanese in 1916. It's been beautifully restored and houses a small exhibition detailing the history of the building and a series of informative display rooms on the development of Taiwanese literature since the Japanese occupation. All the major authors are covered, with special sections on **Li Ang** (best-selling feminist writer) and pioneer **Lai He** (one of the first poets to use Taiwanese). Permanent exhibitions are labelled in English, but temporary shows tend to be Chinese only.

Great South Gate

大南門; dànánmén • Nanmen Rd • Daily 8.30am–5.30pm • Free

Fifteen minutes' walk south of the Confucius Temple on Nanmen Road, the **Great South Gate** is the best remaining example of Tainan's old defences. The double gate was completed in 1835 to replace the former wooden stockade and the compound is now home to a pleasant café. In the surrounding parkland, the **Forest of Steles** is the largest collection of historic memorial stones in Taiwan. There are 63 steles in all, some of which were used as headstones, while others laid down the law: carved edicts prohibit soldiers from beating peasants, and warn against using the moat as a public sewer.

Wufei Temple

五妃廟; wǔfēi miào • 201 Wufei St • Daily 8.30am–9pm

Set in a peaceful park a couple of blocks south of the Confucius Temple Cultural Zone, the Temple of the Five Concubines (aka **Wufei Temple**) is dedicated to the five concubines of the Prince of Ningjing, who committed suicide rather than submit to the Qing dynasty in 1683. They were buried here, in what was once a cemetery outside the city walls – the burial mound is behind the temple. The tiny shrine a few metres to the left of the temple is the **Yi Ling Jun Shrine** (義靈君祠; yìlíngjūn cí) which commemorates the two eunuchs who also committed suicide.

Koxinga Shrine

延平郡王祠; yánpíng jùnwáng cí • 125 Kaishan Rd • Daily 8am–5.30pm; museum daily 9am–5pm • Free • ☏ 06 213 5518

Dedicated to the Ming dynasty general still venerated on both sides of the Taiwan Strait, the **Koxinga Shrine** sits in a small park. The shrine is to the right of the park entrance under the memorial arch, and fronted by a massive statue of the general atop a stallion. Koxinga died in Tainan in 1662, but his body was eventually returned to China. Local people set up a small shrine on this spot to remember him, and an official shrine was built in 1874. The buildings you see today were rebuilt in northern-Chinese style in 1963.

The side corridors are lined with tablets commemorating Ming dynasty officials and generals, while the main shrine, complete with a gracious statue of Koxinga, sits in the centre. The **Rear Hall** contains shrines to Koxinga's Japanese mother (centre) and the Prince of Ningjing (right), while Koxinga's grandson Zheng Kezang is remembered on the left. Also on site, the **Koxinga Museum** contains two floors of temporary exhibits, usually with a historical theme.

THE LEGACY OF KOXINGA

The life of Zheng Chenggong, known as **Koxinga** in the West (a bastardization of guóxìngyé, a title given to him by one of the last Ming princes), is a complex mixture of fact, myth and politics. Born in 1624 in Japan to a pirate Chinese father and a Japanese mother, he was taken to Fujian in China when he was 7 and given a strict Confucian education. After the fall of the Ming dynasty in 1644, Fujian became the centre of **resistance** to the new Qing rulers, and Koxinga rose rapidly through the ranks of the military, eventually becoming the leader of the entire resistance movement. In 1658 he was defeated in Nanjing, which prompted a tactical **retreat to Taiwan**, and in 1661 he led a sizeable fleet across the straits to remove the Dutch. Contrary to popular belief, the siege of Fort Zeelandia was characterized by a series of blunders, Koxinga's overwhelmingly superior forces taking nine months to oust the defenders. The general died a few months later in 1662, most likely from malaria and, although he was initially buried in Taiwan, his body was taken back to China with his son in 1699. On the island he became known as kāishān wáng, "Open Mountain King", for his supposed role in developing infrastructure and opening up the country for Chinese immigrants; Koxinga is worshipped as a folk god – there are around 63 temples dedicated to him across the island.

Lady Linshui Temple

臨水夫人廟; línshuǐ fūrén miào • 16 Jianye St • Daily 6am–8.30pm

Just across from the Koxinga Shrine, on Jianye Street, **Lady Linshui Temple** is one of Tainan's most popular shrines, particularly with women. The temple was established in 1736 to worship the Birth Goddess, but in 1852, three female deities known as the "three ladies" (sānnǎifūrén) were added: Lady Linshui has since become the main deity, worshipped in the incredibly elaborate **Main Hall** and flanked by images of her 36 assistants, three for each month. Linshui is supposed to protect unborn children, babies and pregnant mothers – women often pray here for protection during childbirth.

Dong-an Fang Cultural Zone

東安坊文化園區; dōngānfāng wénhuà yuánqū

South of the train station, the **Dong-an Fang Cultural Zone** covers a swathe of eastern Tainan which includes the Grand East Gate, and a couple of absorbing temples both associated with the Chinese underworld.

Dongyue Temple

東嶽殿; dōngyuè diàn • 110 Mincyuan Rd • Daily 5.30am–9.30pm

Dongyue Temple was established in 1673, and is principally dedicated to the Great Emperor of East Mountain. He decides to which of the eighteen levels of hell to banish sinners, based on the City God's report, and holds court in the **Front Hall**. Dizang Wang occupies the **Middle Hall**, with lurid murals of hell on the walls, while the **Rear Hall**, permanently gloomy and always quiet, is the home of the "Great Emperor of Fengdu" (fēngdū dàdì), the deity who rules over hell itself.

City God Temple

城隍廟; chénghuáng miào • 133 Cingnian Rd • Daily 6am–5pm

North of the Dongyue Temple, the **City God Temple** was built in 1669 and is said to be the oldest City God temple in Taiwan. The sombre black tablet hanging from the beams in the **First Hall** reads "Here You Come", meaning everyone will be judged in time. The City God uses an abacus to calculate individual misdeeds – you can see it behind you, hanging above the entrance. Also note the shackles and torture instruments on the back of main pillars here – supposedly a deterrent to any mischief-makers.

Anping

安平; ānpíng • 4km west of the old centre • Anping can be reached by city bus #2 from the south bus station opposite the train station, or on Anping tour bus #88 or #99 from Tainan Park; alternatively, take a taxi (NT$200), or cycle here along the Yanshui River

Lying west of the old centre, where the city once met the sea, **Anping** is one of the oldest non-indigenous settlements in Taiwan: this is where the Dutch built their first fortress in 1624, and where Koxinga defeated them 38 years later. Anping is also famed for its street eats, and the narrow historic thoroughfare of **Yanping Street** (延平街; yánpíng jiē) is lined with tourist shops and snack-food stalls. The streets north of here are the best places to see Anping's "**sword lions**" (ānpíng jiànshī), elaborate hand-painted images, usually above the doors of traditional houses, of lions with swords in their mouths, thought to protect the occupants. The whole area is eminently walkable (see the tourist office's walking tour map).

Anping Fort

安平古堡; ānpíng gǔbǎo • Main entrance on Guosheng Rd, just off Gubao St • Daily 8.30am–5.30pm • NT$50 • ☎ 06 226 7348

At the heart of Anping is **Anping Fort**, the site of Fort Zeelandia, the first Dutch settlement in Taiwan. The only substantial Dutch remains are parts of the **outer wall**

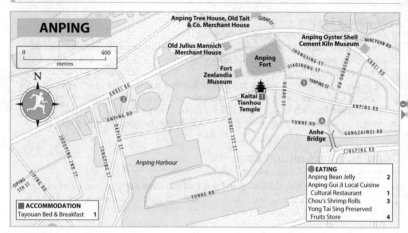

along the road in front of the fort – the imposing redbrick fortifications you see today were built by the Japanese. Check out the **Fort Zeelandia Museum** (熱蘭遮城博物館; rèlán zhēchéng bówùguǎn) across from the entrance, which traces the history of the fort and the Dutch presence here, as well as recounting recent archaeological digs. You can clamber up to the top of the fort, where there's an ugly modern observation tower, and a small exhibition room with models of the old fort and a copy of Koxinga's treaty with the Dutch (in Chinese).

Kaitai Tianhou Temple

開台天后宫; kāitái tiānhòugōng • 33 Guosheng Rd • Daily 5am–10pm

Just south of Anping Fort, **Kaitai Tianhou Temple** was established in 1668 but has been rebuilt many times, most recently in 1994. Its chief claim to fame is the senior **Mazu deity** inside (the large statue in the middle of the back row): this is said to be one of three images Koxinga brought with him from the holy Mazu shrine at Meizhou in China.

Anping Oyster Shell Cement Kiln Museum

安平蚵灰窯文化館; ānpíngé huīyáo wénhuàguǎn • 110 Anbei Rd • Tues–Sun 9am–5pm • Free

North of Anping Fort, the **Anping Oyster Shell Cement Kiln Museum** is the only remaining example of what was once a booming industry in Anping: the production of "oyster ash", the key ingredient (along with sugar and sticky rice water) in cement used for building houses. The kiln and main buildings have been expertly restored, with English explanations.

Old Tait & Co Merchant House and Anping Tree House

英商德記洋行; yīngshāng déjì yángháng / 安平樹屋; ānpíng shùwū • 106–8 Gubao St • Both daily 8.30am–5.30pm • NT$50 (includes both attractions) • ☎ 06 391 3901

A twenty-minute walk west of Anping Fort, the **Old Tait & Co Merchant House** dates from 1867, and houses an excellent museum focussing on the Dutch period in Tainan (1624–61), with hands-on exhibits and explanations in English. Next door, and accessed with the same ticket, **Anping Tree House** is an abandoned warehouse that once belonged to a British *hong* (trading company), and is now engulfed by a massive banyan tree, which makes for an otherworldly and photogenic environment, popular with visiting school parties. There's not much inside the ruined interior, but walkways take you across the top towards the Yanshui River, where white egrets often feed.

FROM TOP TIANHOU TEMPLE, CIJIN ISLAND, KAOHSIUNG (P.256); SALT PAN, TAINAN (P.232) >

Eternal Golden Castle

億載金城; yìzǎi jīnchéng • 3 Guangzhou Rd • Daily 8.30am–5.30pm • NT$50; swanboats NT$100/30min • ☎ 06 295 1504 • City bus #19 from the south bus station opposite the train station, or tour bus #88 from Tainan Park

Around 3km south of Anping Fort, the **Eternal Golden Castle** was commissioned by the Qing authorities in 1876. It was designed by French engineers, built with material from Fort Zeelandia and equipped with British cannons, although only one of the artillery pieces you see today is genuine, identified by the gunsight on the barrel in the northeast corner. The fortress saw action in the Sino-French and Japanese wars, but was abandoned during the Japanese occupation. Today, it has been well restored, with plenty of English labelling; clamber over the fortifications and take a trip in one of the pedal-powered "**swanboats**" (天鵝船; tiāné chuán) around the moat.

National Museum of Taiwan History

國立臺灣歷史博物館; guólì táiwān lìshǐ bówùguǎn • 250 Changhe Rd Sec 1, Annan District • Tues–Sun 9am–5pm (last entry 4.30pm); park daily 5am–10pm • NT$100, sometimes discounted to NT$80; audioguides (30min–1hr 30min) NT$100, plus ID or NT$1000 deposit • ☎ 06 356 8889, ⊕ en.nmth.gov.tw • Bus #18 from Tainan train station (40min)

Eight kilometres north of the city centre, the **National Museum of Taiwan History** offers an insightful introduction to the island's diverse and tumultuous history. Featuring state-of-the-art displays and techniques, the museum takes visitors on a chronological journey, aided by the use of scarily life-like mannequins. Three different audioguides allow you to choose how deeply you want to delve. There's also an impressive Children's Hall, and the museum itself is set in a huge and attractive **park** with nature trails, lakes and birdwatching sets. Allow at least a couple of hours for a visit.

ARRIVAL AND DEPARTURE

TAINAN

BY PLANE

Tainan Airport (臺南機場; táinán jīchǎng; ☎ 06 260 1016) is 5km south of the city at 775 Jichang Rd, a short taxi (NT$200–250) or bus ride (NT$18) from the centre; most hotels will arrange a pick-up. The airport has connections to the Taiwan Straits islands, Hong Kong and Ho Chi Minh City.

Taiwan destinations Kinmen (3 daily; 50min); Magong (4 daily; 30min).

BY TRAIN

REGULAR TRAINS

Tainan Train Station (台南火車站; táinán huǒchēzhàn) is located on the eastern edge of the city centre and is served by express trains running along the west-coast line to Chiayi, Kaohsiung, Taichung and Taipei.

Destinations Chiayi (29 daily; 30min–1hr); Kaohsiung (3 daily; 30min–1hr); Taichung (19 daily; 1hr 30min–2hr); Taipei (25 daily; 3hr–6hr).

HIGH-SPEED RAIL

Tainan HSR Station (高鐵台南站; gāotiě táinánzhàn) is located at 100 Gueiren Blvd in Gueiren (歸仁; guīrén), 10km southeast of the centre, and connected to the city by three buses (free); to get downtown take the Tainan Park (台南公園; táinán gōngyuán) bus to the train station (every 20min;

30–40min). Taxis (around NT$400–500) are provided by Taiwan Fast-Link (☎ 0809 005 006) and you can also rent cars here.

Destinations Chiayi (every 30min; 20min); Kaohsiung (every 30min; 15min); Taichung (every 30min; 40–55min); Taipei (every 30min; 1hr 30min–2hr).

BY BUS

Most long-distance buses arrive at and depart from offices on the left side of Beimen Rd Sec 2, north of the train station: Ho Hsin (☎ 06 227 0777) at no. 25 operates services to Taipei and Taoyuan at regular 30min intervals (24hr); buses to Taichung and Chiayi leave from a second Ho Hsin office a few shops up the road at no. 49. Kuo Kuang (☎ 06 222 5641) at no. 43 also has Taichung and Taipei buses, while Ubus (☎ 06 282 1551) at no. 71 offers 24hr services to Taipei and Taichung. Buses for the Southwest Coast National Scenic Area (including Nankunshen and Beimen) depart from the Jiali bus station at 198 Wenhua Rd (☎ 06 722 3613). For other destinations in Tainan county, you're best off with your own transport.

Destinations Chiayi (every 30min; 1hr); Kaohsiung (every 30min; 1hr); Nankunshen (hourly; 2hr); Taichung (every 30min; 2hr 30min); Taipei (every 30min; 4hr 30min); Taoyuan (every 30min; 4hr).

GETTING AROUND

By bus City buses, run by Kaohsiung Bus, are relatively easy to use in Tainan, with English timetables at some bus stops, and bus announcements and electronic signs in English, although you're unlikely to need them within the old centre. The main bus stations line the roundabout on Chenggong Rd across from the train station; from the south station you can pick up bus #2 to Anping and Fort Zeelandia, red bus #3 to Tainan Airport and #19 to the Eternal Golden Castle; the bus to the HSR Station normally departs from the north side. Tour buses #88 and #99 run between Tainan Park and Anping, and #99 continues on to Taijiang National Park and the Southwest Coast National Scenic Area (see p.249).

By car There are several car rental outfits at both train stations: Car Plus at the HSR Station (☎06 600 006, ⓦwww.car-plus.com.tw) and 115 Beimen Rd Sec 2 (daily 8.30am–8.30pm; ☎06 223 5566); Chailease Auto Rental at the HSR Station (☎06 602 5599, ⓦrentalcar.com.tw)

and 101 Beimen Rd Sec 2 (daily 8.30am–8.30pm; ☎06 225 1655).

By scooter A number of scooter rental shops are clustered near the train station, many of which will only hire to those with Taiwanese licences, but the store at 46 Fubei St (☎06 22223 919) will accept international licences (you'll need to show your passport). Prices are NT$400/day for a 125cc bike.

By bike Tainan is fast developing a cycle path network, especially around Anping, and has a citywide bike rental system, T-Bike (ⓦtbike.tainan.gov.tw). You can rent T-bikes for NT$10/30min using a credit card (or iPass) at various locations around the city including the train station, Koxinga Shrine, Chihkan Tower and Eternal Golden Castle, and drop them off at a different station. See the website for full details and rental locations.

By taxi For trips outside the centre it's more convenient to take a taxi – the initial fare is NT$85. If you can't flag one down, try at the train station.

INFORMATION

Tourist information The small visitor centre (daily 7.30am–7pm; ☎06 229 0082, ⓦwww.twtainan.net) next to the train station exit has a decent selection of English-language material. There's also a helpful information centre (Tues–Sun 8.30am–5.30pm) on the second floor of the Old

Tainan Forest Office (台南山林事務所; táinán shānlín shìwùsuǒ) on Youai St, across from the Confucius Temple.

Street signs The city uses tōngyòng pīnyīn, with streets marked in English and Chinese.

ACCOMMODATION

Tainan has plenty of **accommodation** conveniently located in the centre of the city, within walking distance or a short taxi ride from the station and most of the sights. There are good mid-range and high-end choices, but hostels are few and far between, and many of the budget hotels are fairly uninspiring.

AROUND THE TRAIN STATION

★**Dorm 1828** 台南青年守則; táinán qīngnián shǒuzé 28 Lane 18, Dasyue Rd Sec 1 ☎06 276 2740, ⓦdorm1828.com; map p.236. A saviour for backpackers, *Dorm 1828* offers the creature comforts of home in a cosy building nestled into the backstreets in the university quarter. As well as five- and eight-bed dorms, there are also doubles and twins (with shared bathrooms), plus a communal kitchen, and plentiful English-language advice. Dorms NT$550; doubles NT$1400

Guang Haw Hotel 光華大旅社; guānghuá dàlǚshè 155 Beimen Rd Sec 1 ☎06 226 3171; map p.236. A short walk south of the station, next to Caves Books, this is Tainan's best budget hotel and has English-speakers on the front desk. The compact, dated rooms have TVs, and bathrooms come with a tub and hand-held shower. Extras include breakfast and free internet access, while YHA cardholders get a small discount. NT$1060

La Plaza 天下大飯店; tiānxià dàfàndiàn 202 Chenggong Rd ☎06 229 0271, ⓦlaplaza.com.tw; map p.236. This old hotel has been redesigned in elegant modern-Chinese style, with sleek fittings, Chinese art and

grey-stone bathrooms; the deluxe rooms are more like mini-suites. Also offers free breakfast, a gym and coin laundry. NT$2280

★**Shangri-La's Far Eastern Plaza Hotel** 台南香格 里拉遠東國際大飯店; táinán xiānggélǐlā yuǎndōng guójì dàfàndiàn 89 Dasyue W Rd ☎06 702 8888, ⓦshangri-la.com; map p.236. Tainan's top luxury hotel, tucked away above the FE21 shopping mall opposite the train station. Service is first rate and rooms are huge and elegantly finished in soothing tones. As well as a gym, the upper-level pool deck is an enticing extra. Online specials can make this a great deal. NT$3600

DOWNTOWN TAINAN

★**JJ-W Hotel** 佳佳西市場旅店; jiājiā xīshìchǎng lǚdiàn 11 Jhengsing St ☎06 220 9866, ⓦjj-whotel .com.tw; map p.236. Fabulous boutique hotel fusing traditional Chinese style with postmodernist design, luxury and sheer surrealism. Each room has a different design, loosely based on traditional Chinese themes: think lofts, old closets, flat-screen TVs, floor-to-ceiling windows, crazy Thai furniture and lots of glass and marble. NT$2560

4

Silks Tainan 台南晶英酒店; táinán jīngyīng jiŭdiàn 1 Heyi Rd ⊕06 213 6290, ⓦwww.silksplace-tainan.com.tw; map p.236. Tainan's latest upscale offering, *Silks Tainan* enjoys a great location in the heart of the shopping district, and only a 15min walk from the Confucius Temple. The hotel's 255 rooms are modern and subtly styled in muted grey tones, with wooden floors and bathtubs, plus there are plenty of amenities including a small outdoor infinity pool, a fitness centre, a bar and several restaurants. NT$5060

Tainan Teacher's Hostel (Confucius Inn) 教師會館; jiāoshī huìguǎn 4 Nanmen Rd ⊕06 214 5588, ⓦtainan-teachers-hostel.com.tw; map p.236. Decent mid-range option in central Tainan, with pieces by teachers from the local art college on the walls, and a bakery in the lobby. The small but comfy en-suite doubles have desks, and rates include a basic breakfast and use of the washing machine. NT$1700

ANPING

Taipung Suites 臺邦商旅; táibāng shānglǚ 199 Younghua 2nd St ⊕06 293 1888, ⓦwww.taipungsuites.com.tw; map p.236. Located near City Hall, between Anping and downtown, this plush boutique hotel is well worth the short taxi or bike ride from the centre, with a fabulous roof deck and stylish rooms with flat-screen TVs and DVD players. There are discounts for singles, and plenty of restaurants nearby. NT$3300

★**Tayouan Bed & Breakfast** 台窩灣民居; táiwōwān mínjū 25 Guosheng Rd ⊕06 228 4177, ⊕0953 600 871, ⓦtayouan.com.tw; map p.242. Cute little B&B in a refurbished traditional-style home, built in 1947 by the current owner's grand-father. The four small but cosy rooms are Japanese style, with raised wooden platforms and simple futon mattresses. Bathrooms (three showers) and TV room are shared; single rooms available (NT$1000). Call the mobile phone number for a reservation (essential). Look for the sign opposite Kaitai Tianhou Temple. NT$2000

EATING

Tainan is famous for its excellent **street food** (see box below), available at numerous downtown restaurants and food stalls – or take a taxi out to **Huayuan Night Market** (see p.248). For **Western food** such as burgers or fish and chips, Tainan's pubs are your best bet.

CHIHKAN CULTURAL ZONE

Ah-Xia Restaurant 阿霞飯店; āxiá fàndiàn 7 Lane 84, Jhongyi Rd Sec 2 ⊕06 225 6789; map p.236. Popular with locals, this venerable restaurant serves Chinese banquet-style food with lots of fish and crab on the menu. One-person set meals are available (NT$800) but this place is best experienced in a group, in order to sample a good range of dishes. Try the glutinous rice with crab, and assorted cold dishes – a complete set (ten dishes) will be at least NT$6500. Tues–Sun 11am–2pm & 5–8pm.

★**Chikan Peddler's Noodles** 赤崁擔仔面; chìkǎn dānzǐmiàn 180 Minzu Rd Sec 2 ⊕06 220 5336; map p.236. Renowned for its peddler's noodles (NT$60), this inviting restaurant also turns out a smorgasbord of Tainan specialities, including garlic sausages (NT$70), coffin bread

(NT$90), shrimp rolls (NT$70), taro cake and milkfish. The open kitchen downstairs allows you to watch as individual portions of the noodles are prepared, and there's old-school seating on two floors and outdoors. Daily 11am–2pm & 5–9pm.

Guohua St Sec 3 國華街三段; guóhuájiē sānduàn Guohua St Sec 3; map p.236. South of the junction with Minzu Rd, this street is lined with famous stalls. On the corner at 19 Minzu Rd Sec 3 is *Jinde Spring Rolls* (金得春捲; jīndé chūnjuǎn; daily 7am–5pm) with plump spring rolls (lùmpiā) for NT$40, and *Brother Yang Starfruit Juice* (楊哥楊桃湯; yánggē yángtáo tāng) selling tangy starfruit juice next door (NT$20). On the other side, at 181 Guohua St, is *A-Song Meat Buns* (阿松割包; ā-sōng gēbāo) selling guàbāo (pork in

---

TAINAN'S STREET EATS

Tainan has a reputation for its traditional **Taiwanese** cuisine and many of its dishes are **street favourites** that are famous island-wide. Dānzǐmiàn (or "**peddler's noodles**" with pork, egg and shrimp) is probably the best-known dish, created in 1895 by hawker Hong Yu Tou – the name recalls the shoulder poles he used to carry the noodles to market, while the brand he created, "Slack Season", is a reference to the slow season for fishermen (typically spring and summer typhoon season), when his noodles were a way to make food last; several shops claim to be descended from his original stall.

Coffin Bread (guāncáibǎn, literally "coffin board" in Chinese; hollowed-out thick toast filled with a creamy mix of vegetables and seafood) is another Tainan speciality, a dish concocted in the 1950s when US troops were stationed nearby; but the city's **other snack foods** are equally renowned, including milkfish, eel noodles, oyster omelettes and shrimp rolls.

bun with sate sauce; NT$70–90 for two); ask for lean meat (shòuròu). 8am till they run out, usually around 5–6pm.

Sen Maw Rice Food 森茂碗粿; sēnmào wǎnguǒ 228 Minzu Rd Sec 2 ☎06 214 3389; map p.236. Appealing old Tainan diner, with wooden school desks for tables, and antiques on the walls including porcelain bowls signed by Taiwan celebrities. The main dish here is wah gwuǐ (NT$30), a tasty meat pudding with pork, egg and mushroom. English menu available. Daily 9am–9pm.

Zai Fa Hao 再發號; zàifā hào 71 Mincyuan Rd Sec 2 ☎06 222 3577; map p.236. Best place to sample zòngzi (sticky rice wrapped in bamboo leaves), with tasty mushroom and fresh pork fillings served in an old, no-nonsense store (NT$100). Daily 10am–8.30pm (closed every second Tues of the month).

CONFUCIUS TEMPLE CULTURAL ZONE

Fu Ji Meatballs 福記肉圓; fújí ròuyúan 215 Fucian Rd Sec 1 ☎06 215 7157; map p.236. Close to *Lily Fruits* and opposite the Confucius Temple, this old canteen sells delicious pork meatballs (bah-wán), in a glutinous rice wrapping – the slightly spicy sauce is delicious (NT$40 for two). No English menus. Daily 6.30am–6pm.

Imma Bakery & Café 322 Shulin St Sec 2 ☎06 214 2102; map p.236. This Israeli-Taiwanese bakery created quite a buzz when it opened in 2009, bringing real, freshly made bread, pies, baguettes, pastries and cookies to Tainan. The café also serves classic Middle Eastern dishes including *falafel*, *hummus* and *shakshouka* (NT$399), plus great coffee. There's also a branch in the Simen Shinkong Mitsukoshi department store. Tues–Sun 9am–10pm.

★**Lily Fruits** 莉莉水果店; lìlì shuǐguǒ diàn 199 Fucian Rd Sec 1 ☎06 213 7522; map p.236. Tainan's most famous tsuàbīng (shaved-ice) stall since 1947 (second generation); also sells an incredible range of fresh tropical fruits including guava, star fruit and mangoes served sliced, as juice, with soybean pudding or on ice (NT$25–100). Traditional red-bean toppings also served along with indulgent banana and chocolate. Daily 11am–10.30pm.

★**Narrow Door Café** 窄門咖啡; zhǎimén kāfēi 2/F, 67 Nanmen Rd ☎06 211 0508; map p.236. A tiny passageway (a real squeeze at 38cm wide) leads to this lovely old Japanese-era house with wooden floors and tables. It's one of the most atmospheric cafés in town, with great views of the Confucius Temple: coffees and teas go from NT$160, snacks and cakes from NT$120, and there's excellent Hakka spicy chicken for NT$350 and Hakka DIY *léichá* (cereal tea) for NT$150. Daily Mon–Fri 11am–11pm.

★**Tu Hsiao Yueh (Slack Season Tan Tsai Noodles)** 度小月擔仔麵; dùxiǎoyuè dānzǐmiàn 16 Jhongjheng Rd ☎06 223 1744; map p.236. This small

dānzǐmiàn restaurant was fully renovated in 2016, but the fifth generation of the founder's family continue to turn out some of the best noodles (NT$50) in the city, cooked up on a traditional stove near the entrance. They also serve classic grilled milkfish (NT$180), meatballs (NT$35) and braised duck eggs (NT$15). Daily 11am–9.30pm.

Yong Ji Milkfish Balls 永記虱目魚丸; yǒngjì shīmù yúwán 82 Kaishan Rd ☎06 222 3325; map p.236. This 85-year-old shop serves excellent lǔròufàn and fish-ball soup, and is justly lauded for its shīmùyú (milkfish) and sweet hóngchá (black tea). Note the early closing time. Daily 6.30am–1pm.

YONGHUA ROAD

Geng Du Yuan 耕讀園; gēngdú yúan 23 Yonghua Rd Sec 2 ☎06 295 0099; map p.236. A bit of a trek, but one of the most elegant classical teahouses of this Taichung chain, set in an atmospheric wooden building with cosy booths, goldfish pond and excellent pots of tea from NT$150. Daily 9.30am–midnight.

Water Drop Teahouse 滴水坊; dīshuǐ fāng 168 Yonghua Rd Sec 2 ☎06 293 2188; map p.236. Cheap, expertly prepared Buddhist vegetarian food, inside the Tainan branch of Foguangshan Monastery. Main dishes around NT$100, with plenty of fine teas. It's also worth ascending the steps next to the café entrance for a look at the Big Buddha Hall (take your shoes off). Tues–Sun 11am–2pm & 5–8pm.

ANPING

Anping Bean Jelly 安平豆花; ānpíng dòuhuā 433 Anbei Rd ☎06 391 5385; map p.242. Old-school wooden canteen knocking out delicious soybean pudding, or *dòuhuā* for over fifty years: try it with lemon juice or red beans (NT$35). They also serve coffee. The only downside is the location – it's a short taxi ride or a 20min walk from Anping Fort. Daily 8am–midnight.

Anping Gui Ji Local Cuisine Cultural Restaurant 安平貴記地方美食文化館; ānpíng guìjì dìfāng měishì wénhuàguǎn 93 Yanping St ☎06 222 9794; map p.242. Rustic tables and tiny stools with simple menu of Tainan favourites including coffin bread (NT$60), milkfish congee (NT$60), shrimp rolls (NT$60) and shrimp dumplings (NT$50); get a set (NT$159) for a taster of all the main dishes. English menu. Mon–Fri & Sun 11am–5.30pm, Sat 11am–7pm.

★**Chou's Shrimp Rolls** 周氏蝦捲; zhōushì xiājuǎn 408 Anping Rd ☎06 280 1304; map p.242. Tainan institution cooking up sublime shrimp rolls, lightly fried in batter, tempura-style (NT$60 for two), and bowls of delicious noodles (NT$50). It has a fast-food-style system with two floors of seating and a posh restaurant on the third floor. Halfway to Anping from downtown: taxis should be NT$150 from the station. Daily 10am–10pm.

4

Yong Tai Sing Preserved Fruits Store 永泰興蜜餞行; yǒngtàixīng mìjiànháng 84 Yanping St; map p.242. This historic store has been running, incredibly, since the Qing dynasty, and is still popular for its sticky, sweet snacks (boxes from NT$150). Daily 11.30am–9pm.

DRINKING AND NIGHTLIFE

Tainan has plenty of places for a drink, though things tend to be quiet during the week. **Haian Rd Sec 2** (海安路二段; hǎiānlù èrduàn), between Minsheng and Fucian, is the current **nightlife** district, lined with chilled-out **bars** and **cafés** with open-air seating.

Armory Organic Bistro & Bar 兵工廠; bīnggōng chǎng 82 Gongyuan S Rd ☎ 0979 502 470; map p.236. This longstanding two-floor bar has recently rebranded itself as a bistro but remains a popular watering hole come evening time, serving bottled beer (from NT$100) and cocktails (NT$200). The international food menu includes everything from quesadillas to steaks. Daily 8pm–late.

Dirty Roger Superbar 141 Dongmen Rd Sec 1 ☎ 06 274 7003; map p.236. The best thing about this pub, a Tainan institution, is the huge collection of records lining the walls (nearly 25,000 in all, plus 15,000 CDs) – if you see something you'd like to hear, ask the owner (a music history professor) and he's likely to put it on. Beers cost NT$150. Daily 7pm–2am.

SHOPPING

Books & Cultural Souvenirs of Taiwanese Heritage 台灣建築與文化資產出版社; táiwān jiànzhù yǔ wénhuà zīchǎn chūbǎnshè 57 Nanmen Rd; map p.236. Just across from the Confucius Temple, this store has a few English-language books on Taiwan. Mon–Fri 9am–6pm.

Carrefour 家樂福; Jiālèfú 16 Jhonghua W Rd Sec 2 ☎ carrefour.com.tw; map p.236. French hypermarket chain stocking all of the usual daily needs. Daily 10am–10pm.

Caves Books 敦煌書局; dūnhuáng shūjú 159 Beimen Rd Sec 1 ☎ cavesbooks.com.tw; map p.236. Caves has a good selection of English-language books on the fourth floor. Daily 10am–9pm.

FE21 Department Store 60 Gongyuan Rd; map p.236. Upscale department store (with another branch on Cianfong Rd). Daily 11am–10pm.

Hayashi Department Store 63 Jhongyi Rd Sec 2 ☎ 06 221 3000 ☎ www.hayashi.com.tw; map p.236. Tainan's first department store was established by a Japanese immigrant in 1932, and housed the city's first elevator.

DIRECTORY

Banks Most 7-Elevens have Chinatrust ATMs, and Citibank has a branch at 83 Yongfu Rd Sec 2 (☎ 06 223 1181).

Hospital English-speaking staff and doctors can be found at National Cheng Kung University Hospital (成大醫院; chéngdà yīyuàn; ☎ 06 235 3535) at 138 Shengli Rd.

NORTH OF THE CENTRE

Huayuan Night Market 花園夜市; huāyuán yèshì Junction of Hewei Rd Sec 3 and Hai'an Rd Sec 3; map p.236. North of downtown, this is Tainan's biggest and most popular night market, worth the taxi ride out for the vast array of local snacks on offer. Daily 7pm–midnight.

Legends 28 Beimen Rd Sec 2 ☎ 06 222 2420, ☎ legendstw.com; map p.236. Another Tainan stalwart, *Legends* is popular for its live music, performed from a stage set to a backdrop of brickwork and banyan. As well as beers and cocktails (NT$180), there's a food menu with Western staples such as chicken wings and pizzas. Tues–Sun 7pm–late.

Willy's Bar & Grill 葳芝二壘酒吧; wēilì èrlěi jiǔbā 321 Jiankang Rd Sec 2 ☎ 06 291 1050; map p.236. Cosy sports bar with free wi-fi, 1980s table-top video games, pool table upstairs, imported beers (NT$150) and excellent food: pizzas (NT$280–330), burgers and Tex-Mex classics. Shows all the major sports events on a huge TV screen. Tues–Sun 7pm–3am.

After the departure of the Japanese at the end of the World War II, the building became the office for the Taiwan Salt Company, but then spent decades derelict before being restored and re-opened in 2014. Though the style and fittings hark back to the Japanese era, the products within are high-end Taiwanese products, with a focus on design. There's also a café on the fourth floor. Daily 11am–10pm.

Shinkong Mitsukoshi 新光三越; xīnguāng sānyuè Tainan Place, 658 Simen Rd ☎ skm.com.tw; map p.236. A full-scale department store with all of the big international brands (even Harrods), a Cineplex and an extensive food court. Daily 11am–10pm.

Tainan Kuang Tsai Embroidery Shop 光彩繡莊; guāngcǎi xiùzhuāng 186-3 Yongfu Rd Sec 2 ☎ 06 227 1253; map p.236. Opposite the Official God of War Temple, this old store is full of brightly coloured fabrics used in temple festivals, clothing and puppets since 1941 – visitors are welcome to look around and take photos. Daily 8am–10pm.

Internet access *More Café* at 129 Beimen Rd Sec 1, a short stroll from the station, offers free wi-fi and two terminals (NT$25/hr). It's open 24hr and is a real café too (coffee NT$45).

Post office The main post office is at 6 Chenggong Rd, not far from the train station.

Southwest Coast National Scenic Area and around

南濱海國家風景區; nánbīnhǎi guójiā fēngjǐngqū

Taiwan's flat, marshy **southwest coast** stretches between Tainan and the Hukou Wetlands in Yunlin county. Encompassing both the **Southwest Coast National Scenic Area** and **Taijiang National Park**, the area contains some of Taiwan's oldest religious sites, remnants of a once thriving salt industry, several mangrove swamps and hundreds of oyster farms, which make for superb seafood and birdwatching.

GETTING AROUND AND INFORMATION

THE SOUTHWEST COAST

By car or scooter The easiest way to explore the region is with your own transport, which can be rented in Tainan (see p.245).

By bus Buses for the Southwest Coast National Scenic Area (including Nankunshen and Beimen) depart from the Jiali bus station at 198 Wenhua Rd (● 06 722 3613), while Tainan tour bus #99 serves Taijiang National Park.

By bike The whole region is accessible by bike, but the most cycle-friendly area is Taijiang National Park, which has around 30km of bike trails. You can rent bikes in Anping and Tainan (see p.245).

Tourist information The Southwest Coast National Scenic Area Visitor Center at 119 Jioucheng, Beimen Village (北門; běimén; daily 9am–5pm; ● 06 786 1000), can offer information and advice. For online information, see ● swcoast-nsa.travel.

Taijiang National Park

台江國家公園; táijiāng guójiā gōngyuán

Taijiang National Park covers the coastline immediately north of Anping, from the south bank of the Yanshui River to Qingshan Fishing Harbour, overlapping with the Southwest Coast National Scenic Area at its northern end. Once an inland sea, the wetland park is particularly noted for the endangered **black-faced spoonbill** (hēimiàn pílù), but also contains historical attractions.

Sihcao Wetlands

四草綠色隧道; sìcǎo lǜsè suìdào • Boats leave from behind Dajhong Temple: Mon–Fri 10am & 2pm, Sat & Sun 8am–3pm • NT$200 for the Green Mangrove Tunnel ride (30min) • ● 06 284 1610

Just over the Sihcao Bridge from Anping you can board pontoon boats for rides through the **Sihcao Wetlands**. Half-hour trips through the "**Green Mangrove Tunnel**" – a picturesque waterway cutting through a variety of mangrove species – offer the chance to see birds, fiddler crabs and mudskippers among other wildlife. In addition, longer trips out into the broader watercourses beyond are also possible. Boats leave when full, which means frequent departures on weekends and holidays, but can make for long waits on weekdays.

Orthodox Luermen Holy Mother Temple

正統鹿耳門聖母廟; zhèngtǒng lùěrmén shèngmǔ miào • 160 Chengan Rd • Daily 4am–9pm

Just west of Highway 17, a couple of kilometres south of the Zengwen River, the **Orthodox Luermen Holy Mother Temple** was originally just a thatched hut built by fishermen, rebuilt by Koxinga, and subsequently expanded to become one of the largest temples in the world and certainly the biggest dedicated to Mazu. It's worth a visit if you're passing by, particularly during festival times.

Taiwan Salt Museum

台灣鹽博物館; táiwānyán bówùguǎn • County Route 176 • Daily 9am–5.30pm (last entry 4.30pm; closed first Mon of the month) • NT$130 • ● 06 780 0990

The coastline north of Tainan is littered with saltpans, most abandoned after the industry collapsed in the 1990s. A few kilometres west of the town of **Qigu** (七股; qīgǔ), on

County Route 176, you'll see the two pyramid towers of the **Taiwan Salt Museum** and the salt mountains beyond. The museum has three floors of innovative displays covering the salt-making process and the history of the area, but English labelling is limited.

Qigu Salt Mountains

七股鹽山;qīgū yánshān • Qigu • Daily: March–Oct 9am–6pm; Nov–Feb 8.30am–5.30pm • NT$50, NT$100 with car • ☎ 06 780 0511, ⊕ cigu.tybio.com.tw

The two **Qigu Salt Mountains** comprise one 60,000-tonne, 20m-high pile, now dirty brown and scaled via a path cut into the rock-hard sodium crystals, and a slightly smaller mound of imported salt from Australia, pristine white and treated like snow by frolicking tourists. The area is a bit of a carnival at weekends, with stalls selling surprisingly tasty **salt popsicles** in smoked plum, egg yolk, almond and walnut flavours (NT$20), and even a pool where you can float, Dead Sea-like, in the brine. Nonetheless, it's one of the most bizarre sights in Taiwan, and worth the trek out.

Black-faced Spoonbill Reserve

黑面琵鷺保護區;hēimiàn pílù bǎohùqū • Exhibition Centre Tues–Sun 9am–4.30pm • Free • ☎ 06 788 1180

North of the Zengwen River estuary, the **Black-faced Spoonbill Reserve** is a 300-hectare wetland which attracts a large number and variety of migratory birds. Every year in September up to a thousand black-faced spoonbills begin to arrive here from Korea, returning north in March. The reserve has a bird-spotting pavilion and an exhibition centre, and can arrange guide services.

4

ARRIVAL AND INFORMATION	**TAIJIANG NATIONAL PARK**
By bus You can get to the park on Tainan tour bus #99, which has services stopping at Sihcao, the Orthodox Luermen Holy Mother Temple, the Salt Museum and the Qigu Salt Mountains (NT$18/ride); during the winter birdwatching months (Oct–April) the service	extends to Liukong Visitor Center and the Black-faced Spoonbill Reserve. **Park information** The new park headquarters is at 118 Sihcao Boulevard, north of the Sihcao Bridge (Mon–Fri 8.30am–5.30pm ☎ 06 284 2600, ⊕ www.tjnp.gov.tw).

Nankunshen Da Tian Temple

南鯤身大天府;nánkūnshēn dàtiānfǔ • Nankunshen Village • Daily 5am–10pm

Three kilometres north of Beimen, in the equally small village of **Nankunshen** (南鯤身; nánkūnshēn) lies the **Nankunshen Da Tian Temple**. It's the most important shrine in southern Taiwan and the centre of Wang Ye worship on the island, heading an

---

YANSHUI BEEHIVE FIREWORKS

An otherwise sleepy town, a short drive inland from Nankunshen, **Yanshui** (鹽水; yánshuǐ) attracts thousands to its annual **firework festival** (鹽水蜂炮; yánshuǐ fēngpào), one of Taiwan's most famous. The event takes place fifteen days into the Chinese lunar calendar – usually in February. What makes this pyrotechnic display unique is that the fireworks – lodged in over two hundred walls or "**beehives**" the size of a truck – are fired horizontally into the crowds creating a cacophony of noise, fire and smoke throughout the night. **Protective gear** (helmet, earplugs, jacket, gloves, towels and tape to fill in the gaps) is essential if you want to participate, but note that the crowds can be suffocating: around three hundred thousand people attend, and the numbers have grown so much that the event is now held over two nights, the first of which tends to be bigger and better. The tradition began in 1885, when locals paraded an image of Guan Di around the town to ward off a cholera epidemic; their prayers were answered only after shooting off a tonne of fireworks to "wake" the god. Each year during the Lantern Festival (Feb), Guan Di is once again paraded around the town before the fiery climax. The nearest train station is Xinying, from where there are frequent **buses** to Yanshui. On the nights of the event there are direct buses from Chiayi and Tainan.

organization of around seven thousand branch temples. Established in 1662 and rebuilt on this site in 1817, the temple is dedicated to five senior Wang Ye gods: Li, Tsi, Wu, Chu and Fan, each with their own birthday and special annual festival attracting thousands of pilgrims (the biggest is on Lunar April 26 and 27). The original wooden statues of the gods are said to have arrived by unmanned boat, miraculously driven by the wind from China in the early seventeenth century, and have since ensured abundant fish-hauls, good health and all-round prosperity for the fishermen in the village.

Guanziling

關仔嶺; guānzǐ lǐng

Tucked away in the northeast corner of Tainan county but easily accessible from Chiayi (and Tainan with your own transport), **GUANZILING** boasts beautiful scenery, unusual hot springs and a bizarre natural wonder. The Japanese started to develop the area in 1902 – the spring water is a rare type found in only two other places (Japan and Sicily). It contains alkali and iodine, has a light sulphuric smell and a greyish "muddy" colour.

Most of the spas and hotels are located within the **upper** and **lower village** on County Route 175, south of the junction with County Route 172, but apart from a few attractive **hiking trails** here, the real highlights of the area lie in the hills outside Guanziling within the **Siraya National Scenic Area** (西拉雅國家風景區; xīlāyǎ guójiā fēngjǐngqū; ⓦ www.siraya-nsa.gov.tw). The most appealing way to reach Guanziling is via County Road 174/175, also known as **Dongshan Coffee Road** (東山咖啡公路; dōngshān kāfēi gōnglù), which begins at Nanxi and makes its way north through a hilly boulder-strewn landscape of prime coffee- and orange-growing country – it's worth stopping at one of the attractively poised coffee shops along the way.

Water Fire Cave

水火洞; shuǐhuǒ dòng • 4.5km from the upper village – take the right-hand fork (Route 172) off Route 175

Though some distance from the upper village, it's worth the effort to get to the **Water Fire Cave** – a small cleft in the hillside with a pool of bubbling **spring water**. The flames smothering the rocks above the pool are a truly remarkable sight, particularly at night when you can see the full extent of the blaze, and may have the place to yourself. The flames are fuelled by spontaneously igniting natural gas which seeps out of the rock. The stone carving just above it is the "Water Fire God".

ARRIVAL AND DEPARTURE
GUANZILING

By car or scooter It's much easier to explore this part of Taiwan if you have a car or scooter – both of which can be rented in Chiayi, Tainan or Kaohsiung.

By bus The Chiayi Transport Co Bus Station (嘉義客運總

站; jiāyì kèyùn zǒngzhàn) has hourly services from Chiayi to Guanziling Hot Springs (daily 7am–5.40pm). Buses pass through the lower village first before terminating in a car park at the start of the upper village.

ACCOMMODATION

Guanziling's hot-spring spas all offer **accommodation** and places **to eat**, though it's usually possible to sample their spa facilities by paying day-rates.

Jing Leh Hotel 靜樂館; jìnglèguǎn 17 Lower Village ⓣ 06 682 2678. This is the most historic place in town, established in 1902 with Japanese-style rooms and white-tiled spa bathrooms, located across the river at the bottom end of the lower village. Private spa rooms cost NT$400/hr for non-guests. <u>NT$1500</u>

King's Garden Villa 景大渡假莊園; jǐngdà dùjiā

zhuāngyuán 56 Upper Village ⓣ 06 682 2500, ⓦ myspa.com.tw. Beyond *Toong Mao* at the very top of the village, this is Guanziling's best hotel, a sprawling collection of comfortable rooms, duplexes and villas. The resort has a good selection of hot springs, plus a fish spa and a decent-sized swimming pool. The on-site restaurant has a pleasant outdoor seating area which offers great

views and serves claypot chicken and a host of mountain dishes. Non-guests can use the springs for NT$350, or NT$450 on weekends (daily 9am–10pm). NT$4000
Toong Mao Spa Resort 統茂溫泉會館; tǒngmào wēnquán huìguǎn 28 Upper Guanziling Village

📞 06 682 3456, 🌐 toongmao.com.tw. A short walk uphill from the bus station, this modern behemoth has smart, comfortable rooms. The public pools are open 7.30am–10pm ($320). NT$2740

EATING

The region is famous for its **claypot chicken** restaurants which are easily identified by the large clay pots outside, and typically charge from NT$600 for a whole chicken.

Guimuwu 檜木屋; guìmùwū 43-2 Upper Village 📞 06 682 2205. Local restaurant with a cosy wooden interior featuring old family photos, and friendly staff serving the speciality claypot chicken (NT$600). Daily 11am–2pm & 5–9.30pm.
Rock Top Café 岩頂自然休閒防; yándǐng zìrán

xiūxián fáng 65 Upper Village 📞 06 682 3339. On the main road out of the upper village, this cool garden café has all the local specialities including great coffee and claypot chicken (NT$600), plus some interesting innovations – try the coffee sausages (NT$200). Daily except Weds 10am–10pm.

Kaohsiung

高雄; gāoxióng

Taiwan's second city, and one of the largest container ports in the world, **KAOHSIUNG** has undergone a dramatic metamorphosis in recent years, from polluted industrial centre of two million people to a green city of lush parks, waterside cafés, art galleries and museums all linked by a spanking new transport system. This said, Kaohsiung hasn't quite completed the transformation yet, and its pollution is still regularly the worst on the island. In the summer of 2014, the city's industrial legacy hit international headlines when a series of underground gas explosions ripped through central Lingya district, tearing apart roads, destroying buildings, killing 31 people and injuring hundreds more: a terrible tragedy that would have been far worse if the explosions had taken place during the day.

The older districts of **Yancheng**, **Cijin Island** and **Zuoying** contain plenty of historic sights and traditional snack stalls, and the latter is also home to pretty **Lotus Lake** and its band of gaudy temples and statues. Modern Kaohsiung is best taken in with an evening stroll along **Love River**, through the trendy Pier 2 arts district, or with a visit to the soaring **85 Sky Tower** close to its bustling **shopping districts**. To take a break from the city, hike up to the ridge of hills known as **Shoushan**, home to Kaohsiung's famously capricious troupe of monkeys.

Brief history

The oldest parts of Kaohsiung are Cihou Village on **Cijin Island**, established in the early seventeenth century, and the suburb of **Zuoying**, created by Koxinga in the 1660s as county capital, a position it maintained until the late eighteenth century. Cihou, and the harbour as a whole, was known as Takau, and remained a sleepy backwater until the port was opened up to foreign companies by the Treaty of Beijing in 1860, attracting merchants eager to exploit the south's growing **sugar trade**. Foreign trade had its dark side however: by the time the Japanese had assumed control of the city in 1895, a quarter of adult males in the south were addicted to opium. The Japanese imposed an Opium Monopoly in 1897, which effectively destroyed Western dominance of the sugar trade. They also began a major modernization programme, completing the harbour and docks in 1908 and opening the Takau Ironworks, Taiwan's first iron and steel mill, in 1919. Although the city was heavily bombed by US planes in 1945, the port was rebuilt and by the late 1970s Kaohsiung was Taiwan's premier industrial centre. In 1979, the **Kaohsiung Incident** was a defining moment in Taiwan's struggle for democracy (see box, p.255), and today the city remains a DPP stronghold.

National Science & Technology Museum

KAOHSIUNG

SHOUSHAN NATURE PARK

National Sun Yat-Sen University (Campus)

GUSHAN DISTRICT

Yuanheng Temple

Shoushan Zoo

Love River

Martyrs' Shrine

Train Station

Kaohsiung Vision Hall

Kaohsiung Main Station

City Family

eSoho

Formosa Boulevard

Sinsing Night Market

Central Park

Red Line

HSBC

Jianguo Bridge

Music Center

Kaohsiung Museum of History

San Shan Temple

Temple of God of War, Education

Xiahai City God Temple

City Council

ICBC

Bank of Taiwan

Zhongheng Bridge

Electric gondolas pier

Kaohsiung Film Archive

Holy Rosary Cathedral

Renai Park

Wufu Bridge

Love Pier

LRT Glory Pier

Bars

LRT Love Pier

LRT Line

Blue Path

Pier2 Art Centre

Yanchengpu

YANCHENG DISTRICT

Sanduo Shopping District

Vieshow Cinemas

SANDUO RD COMMERCIAL DISTRICT

Citi bank

85 Sky Tower

Kaohsiung Cultural Center

HAMASEN

Penghu Ferry Terminal

LRT Peng Lai Pier 2

LRT Hamasen

Orange Line

Sizihwan

Fisherman's Wharf

Kaohsiung Harbour

Chihou Lighthouse

Cijin Ferry Pier

Chou Ferry Pier

Gushan Ferry Pier

British Consulate at Takao

North Gate

Tianhou Temple

CIJIN VILLAGE

CIJIN ISLAND

Cijin Fishing Port

Magong

Pier 21 & Singang Ferry Wharf

Airport (Siam) & Kenting

EATING

Aroma Mutton Pot	3
ArtCo	9
City of Steamed Glutinous Rice	6
Gan's Frozen Taro	12
Hamasen Black Marlin Fish	8
Ball King	
J Café at Urban Spotlight	7
Kaohsiung Milk King	5
Kaohsiung Pearl Barley King	4
Liuhe Road Night Market	2
Old Capital City Dumplings	1
Tea and Art	10
Top Grade Vegetarian Noodle Shop	11

DRINKING & NIGHTLIFE

Beerbee	2
Black Dog Pub	4
Bottoms Up Saloon	5
Brickyard	3
Lamp	6
Lighthouse Bar & Grill	1

★ BUS STATIONS

Aloha Bus	5
City (local buses)	2
Ho Hsin Bus	6
ibus	7
Kaohsiung Bus	1
Kuo Kuang	3
Ubus	4

■ ACCOMMODATION

85 Sky Tower Hotel	9
Ambassador Hotel	4
City Suites	7
Cozy Planet Hostel	6
Grand Hi-Lai Hotel	8
Hotel Kindness	1
Hotel Kingdom	5
Hotel Skoal	3
TW Hostel	2

● SHOPPING

Caves Books	3
Dream Mall	4
Jade Market	1
Sanfenghong Traditional Covered Market	2
Taroko Park Mall	5

0   metres   500

4

85 Sky Tower

高雄85大樓; gāoxióng 85 dàlóu • 1 Zihciang Rd Sec 3 • Viewing deck daily 9am–10pm • NT$150 • ☎ 07 566 8000 • From the train station bus #100 passes the tower as it runs down Sanduo Rd, or it's a 5min walk from KMRT R8 Sanduo Shopping District (exit 2)

One of Taiwan's iconic buildings, the **85 Sky Tower** looms 347.5m over downtown Kaohsiung, its striking two-legged structure based on the Chinese character 高 (gāo, meaning tall, as in *gaoxiong* – tall hero – the city's modern name). It was the tallest building in Taiwan from 1997 until 2003 when Taipei 101, also designed by C.Y. Lee, was completed. Floors 46 to 70 are given over to the upmarket *Sky Tower Hotel*, while the 74th-floor **viewing deck** provides a mesmerizing panorama of the city and the harbour, especially at night.

Love River and Yancheng

愛河; àihé / 鹽埕; yánchéng

The once grim and gritty banks of **Love River** on the western edge of the city centre have become spruced-up promenades in recent years, with the area between Jhongjheng and Wufu roads lined with open-air cafés, parks and a riverside bike trail stretching all the way to Lotus Lake. The west bank of the river marks the beginning of **Yancheng**, one of Kaohsiung's oldest neighbourhoods and crammed with some of its most traditional shopping streets and food stalls, plus some worthwhile museums and a trendy arts district.

Kaohsiung Museum of History

高雄市歷史博物館; gāoxióngshì lìshǐ bówùguǎn • 272 Jhongjheng Rd Sec 4 • Tues–Sun 9am–5pm • Free • ☎ 07 531 2560 • KMRT O2 Yanchengpu or bus #248

The imposing former City Hall, built under Japanese rule in 1938, was converted into the **Kaohsiung Museum of History** in 1998. The bulk of the labelling is in Chinese, but there's enough English to make a short visit worthwhile. The first floor charts the history of the city and the old City Hall, while a special 2-28 Incident exhibition covers the bloody events of 1947 from a Kaohsiung perspective.

Kaohsiung Film Archive

高雄市電影圖書館; gāoxióngshì diànyǐng túshūguǎn • 10 Hexi Rd • Tues–Sun 1.30–9.30pm • Free; show your passport to view films • ☎ 07 551 1211, ⊕ kfa.kcg.gov.tw • A short walk north of Kaohsiung Bridge on the west bank of Love River

An interesting rainy-day option, particularly for film buffs, the **Kaohsiung Film Archive** contains a library of almost six thousand Chinese and international films along with personal TVs for viewing them, all for free. There's also a movie theatre with at least one daily screening, although you should check in advance if English audio or subtitles will be featured.

Pier 2 Art Centre

駁二藝術特區; bóèr yìshù tèqū • 1 Dayong Rd • ⊕ pier-2.khcc.gov.tw/eng • KMRT O2 Yanchengpu

Established in 2001, the **Pier 2 Arts Centre** has grown up to become a thriving hub of modern arts housed both within and outside of the huge graffiti-covered old

---

RIDING THE LOVE BOAT

Solar-powered "**Love Boats**" (愛之船; àizhī chuán; every 15min: Mon–Thurs 3–10pm, Fri 3–10.30pm, Sat & Sun 9am–10.30pm; NT$150) from **Love Pier** (愛碼頭; ài mǎtóu) silently ease their way up and down the river for twenty-five minutes between Wufu and Jhongjheng bridges (with stops at the *Ambassador Hotel* and Renai Park). This is a highly enjoyable way to see the city from a different perspective. The ride is particularly atmospheric at **night**, when you can also opt to take an **electric gondola** (daily 4–10pm; NT$200) that sets off from a jetty at the western end of Minsheng 2nd Road.

THE KAOHSIUNG INCIDENT

The **Kaohsiung Incident** (高雄事件; gāoxióng shìjiàn) of December 1979 was a political watershed, often regarded as the beginning of Taiwan's democratic revolution. Opposition to Taiwan's one-party state had been growing in the 1970s and, in an apparent concession, President Chiang Ching-kuo agreed to hold legislative **elections** in 1979 – but at the last minute he cancelled them. On Human Rights Day (Dec 10) a rally was organized in Kaohsiung in protest, the activists spurred on by the arrest the night before of two workers for *Meilidao* ("Beautiful Island" in English), a clandestine anti-establishment publication. Police were brought in to disperse the crowds and violent scuffles ensued. In the aftermath, almost every member of the unofficial opposition was arrested, culminating in the 1980 trial of the "**Kaohsiung Eight**". Most were jailed for lengthy periods, but the trial was widely publicized – as a result the defendants garnered a great deal of sympathy, ultimately creating a wider base for democratic reform.

Today, the list of those involved reads like a "Who's Who" of Taiwanese politics, many becoming leaders of the **Tangwai** (dǎngwài; Outside Party) movement and later the Democratic Progressive Party: Chen Shui-bian (president 2000–08) and Frank Hsieh (former Kaohsiung mayor and premier) were lawyers on the defence team, while Annette Lu (vice-president 2000–08) served five years in jail.

warehouses set just back from the harbour. Brightly coloured statues line the main paths, while exhibits within the various warehouse galleries are constantly changing, and there are plenty of cafés to take a break and watch the crowds wander by. Various large-scale events take place here during the course of the year, including Megaport (⑩megaportfest.com) a two-day outdoor music festival in March.

4

Shoushan Nature Park

壽山自然公園; shòushān zìrán gōngyuán • Take a taxi to the trail behind Longquan Temple (龍泉寺; lóngquán sì) on Lane 51 off Gushan 3rd Road – bus #245 also stops a short walk from the entrance

The line of hills due west of the city centre forms the **Shoushan Nature Park**, named after the peak of Shoushan (356m), a popular hiking spot. The southern end of the ridge is home to the Shoushan Zoo, Martyrs' Shrine and Yuanheng Temple, a huge Buddhist monastery; while the northern section, often referred to as "Monkey Mountain", is best known for its eight hundred or so **Taiwanese macaques** or rhesus monkeys, the densest such population in Taiwan. Although it's strictly forbidden to feed them, people still do so, with the result that the troupes can get aggressive; don't bring food, and keep a safe distance. During the week it's far less crowded.

Hamasen and the coast

哈瑪星; hāmǎ xīng • Buses #99 & #248

Built on reclaimed land north of the harbour during the Japanese period, the historic neighbourhood of **Hamasen** was once the business centre of Kaohsiung, claiming the city's first post office and police station, but is now packed with harbourside cafés. Hamasen's **Gushan Ferry Pier** (鼓山輪渡站; gūshān lúndùzhàn) offers the quickest boat route across to Cijin Island (see p.256). West of Hamasen, Kaohsiung's most accessible **swimming beach**, Siziwan (西子灣; xīzǐ wān), borders the beautifully located Sun Yat-sen University Campus.

British Consulate at Takao

打狗英國領事館; dǎgǒu yīngguó lǐngshìguǎn • 20 Lianhai • Daily 9am–9pm • NT$100 • ☎07 525 0100 • Bus #99

Facing the ocean on the western side of the city, the **British Consulate at Takao** occupies a strategic point high above Lianhai Road – it's a steep climb from the bus stop up to the main entrance. Contrary to what you'll read on site, evidence suggests that the redbrick colonial mansion was built between 1878 and 1879, and served as a base from which the British could administer customs until 1895, before being abandoned in 1910. Today there's a small **exhibition room** inside which contains paintings relating to the first British consul and zoologist, **Robert Swinhoe**, and several of the Taiwanese animals named after him.

Kaohsiung Harbour

高雄港; gāoxióng gǎng • Kaohsiung Shipping Company short cruises: every hour Sat & Sun 1–4.30pm (one-way 25min); dinner cruises daily 5.30pm • One-way NT$80; dinner cruises NT$700 • ☎ 07 332 0998

Kaohsiung Harbour has been extensively redeveloped over the past two decades, converting it from a grubby port zone into a leisure hub, complete with cafés and shops, plus a cycling trail along old rail tracks from Pier 1 to Pier 22, although this was off limits at the time of writing due to ongoing construction work for the new light-rail system. A great way to see the harbour is on one of Kaohsiung Shipping Company's **harbour cruises** from Singuang Ferry Wharf (新光碼頭; xīnguāng mǎtóu) or Cijin Ferry Station (旗津碼頭; qíjīndǎo) mǎtóu) which provide terrific views across the city's skyline.

Cijin Island

旗津島; qíjīndǎo • Frequent ferries (daily 6am–midnight) make the 5min journey from Gushan Ferry Pier in Hamasen to Cijin (NT$15; bikes NT$10); alternatively you can reach Cijin on a 25min harbour cruise from Singuang Ferry Wharf (see p.260), or by taxi via the under-harbour tunnel

The long sliver of **Cijin Island** lies between Kaohsiung Harbour and the sea, southwest of the city centre. It's the oldest part of the city, with plenty to keep you busy for half a day, but the best reason for a trip out here is to enjoy the **views**. Most attractions are easily accessible on foot, but Cijin also has 15km of **cycle paths**.

GETTING AROUND	**CIJIN ISLAND**

By bike Bike rental is available at the shops opposite the ferry wharf for NT$100/hr; most of these places will provide you with a map of the island.

Tianhou Temple

天后宮; tiānhòu miàoqián lù gong • Daily 5.30am–10pm

Just a short walk from the Cijin ferry wharf on Miaocian Road, **Tianhou Temple** is the oldest in Kaohsiung, established in 1673 and dedicated to Mazu. Note the wángchuán or "spirit ship", a model boat and shrine to the left of the main hall, dedicated to three Wang Ye gods thought to protect the village from disease.

Seafood Street

Miaocian Road (廟前路; miàoqián lù) crosses the island from the harbourside to the ocean, and is also known as **Seafood Street**, lined with restaurants offering a huge variety of fish and shellfish: pick out what you fancy and they'll cook it for you.

North Cijin

On the island's northwest corner, the redbrick and concrete gun emplacement of **Cihou Fort** (旗後砲台; qíhòu pàotái; daily 8am–5pm) was built on this strategic hill in the 1870s and taken by the Japanese after a short but fierce gun battle in 1895. A few hundred metres north of here a path ascends the hill on Cijin's northeastern tip, leading to the **Cihou Lighthouse** (旗後燈塔; qíhòu dēngtǎ; April–Oct Tues–Sun 9am–6pm; Nov–March Tues–Sun 9am–5pm), built in 1883 and still in use today – the views, which often encompass huge, passing container ships, are magnificent.

Zuoying

左營; zuǒyíng • Trains to Zuoying Station (左營車站; zuǒyíng chēzhàn; don't go to Xinzuoying) depart from Kaohsiung Station every 10–20min (6min); alternatively, take the KMRT to R15 Ecological District (紅線生態園區站; hóngxiàn shēngtài yuánqūzhàn) or bus #55; on weekends a special tour bus (NT$50) makes a circuit of Zuoying's main attractions, starting at the HSR station

Founded in the seventeenth century, **Zuoying** is today a lively suburban district full of trendy restaurants and bars, 5km north of downtown. The main attraction is **Lotus Lake**, but Zuoying is also home to the **Museum of Fine Arts**, and is the HSR terminus.

Lotus Lake

蓮池潭; liánchí tán • From Zuoying Station, cross the main road and walk straight up Shengli Rd (勝利路; shènglì liántán huáshuǐ zhǔtí lèyuán lù) to the lake, or take bus #35 from the KMRT station (R15 Ecological District); you can also cycle here from downtown Kaohsiung on the Love River bike trail

One of Kaohsiung's most popular attractions, **Lotus Lake** is surprisingly small at just 1.5km long and 500m wide, but is ringed by a handful of monuments, picturesque temples and pagodas, interspersed with plenty of snack stalls. Shady lakeside paths and a **bike trail** encircle the lake and there is decent English-language signage.

Little remains of old Zuoying, which once stood south of the lake, although the city wall is the best preserved in Taiwan. Known as the **Old Wall of Fengshan County** (鳳山舊城; fēngshān jiùchéng), it was completed in 1826 using bits of coral – you can see a section of the wall on Shengli Road, a few metres beyond the lake's southwestern corner.

Lotus Wakepark

蓮潭滑水主題樂園; liántán huáshuǐ zhǔtí lèyuán • Opposite 46 Xinzhuangzi Rd • Mon–Fri noon–sunset, Sat & Sun 10am–sunset • NT$500/30min on 100m course, NT$1100/full day on 531m course (NT$300 weekend surcharge); board rental NT$300–600 • ☏ 07 581 1566, ⓦ lotuswakepark.com

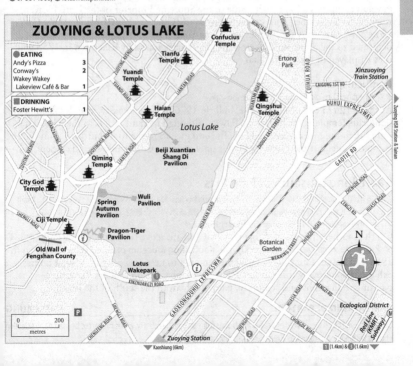

On the southern edge of the lake, the **Lotus Wakepark** offers cabled wakeboarding from beginners to experts, with a two-tower (100m) cable and a five-tower (531m) cable with obstacles. Also on site is the chilled *Wakey Wakey Lakeview Café and Bar* (see p.262), a great place for a meal or drink, regardless of whether you end up getting wet.

Dragon Tiger Pavilion

龍虎塔；lónghǔ tǎ · Liantan Rd · Daily 8am–6.30pm · Free

In the southwest corner of the lake, the **Dragon Tiger Pavilion** consists of an impressive pair of pagodas, accessed through gaudy dragon and tiger statues, which have become one of the city's most photographed landmarks. The pagodas were built in 1965 as an extension to **Ciji Temple** (慈濟宮；cíjì gōng) opposite. For good luck, enter through the dragon's mouth and exit via the tiger; inside are garish scenes of heaven and hell.

Spring and Autumn Pavilions

春秋閣；chūnqiū gé · Liantan Rd · Daily 8am–5pm · Free

A third of the way up Lotus Lake's western shore is the simply adorned **Spring and Autumn Pavilions**, two towers built in 1953 and fronted by a statue of Guanyin on top of a giant, garishly decorated dragon. **Wuli Pavilion** (五里亭；wǔlǐ tíng), further out in the lake, was added in 1978. All three pavilions are linked to the imposing **Qiming Temple** (啟明堂；qǐmíng táng; daily 4.30am–10pm) on shore, established in 1909, and rebuilt in the 1970s, dedicated principally to Guan Di, but hosting an array of gods including a bearded Confucius at the back of the main altar.

Beiji Xuantian Shang Di Pavilion and Yuandi Temple

Beiji Xuantian Shang Di Pavilion 北極玄天上帝廟；běijí xuántiān shàngdì miào · Daily 8am–5pm · Free · **Yuandi Temple** 元帝廟；yuándì miào · Daily 6am–10pm

Halfway along Lotus Lake's western edge, the impressive **Beiji Xuantian Shang Di Pavilion** comprises a 22m-high statue of the Supreme Emperor of the Dark Heaven, reached via a pier lined with characters from the Chinese classic *Creation of the Gods* (*Feng Shen Yan Yi*). A short walk west along Yuandi Road is **Yuandi Temple**, also dedicated to the Supreme Emperor, the chief image found by fishermen in 1758 and now displayed in the central altar.

Confucius Temple

孔子廟；kǒngzǐ miào · Liantan Rd · Tues–Sun 9am–5pm

At the northern end of Lotus Lake, built in 1976 in Song dynasty style, Kaohsiung's **Confucius Temple** is the biggest in Taiwan, although its status refers to the whole site rather than the main Dacheng Hall. The entrance to the central courtyard is on the left (western) side, but the Dacheng Hall is only open on Confucius's birthday (Sept 28).

Kaohsiung Museum of Fine Arts

高雄美術館；gāoxióng měishù guǎn · 80 Meishiguan Rd · Tues–Sun 9.30am–5.30pm · Free · ☎ 07 555 0331, ⓦ kmfa .gov.tw · Bus #205 stops at the Kaohsiung Municipal United Hospital (高雄市立聯合醫院；gāoxióng shìlì liánhé yīyuàn) nearby, and bus #73 runs from the HSR station to the museum

On the southern fringes of Zuoying, located in attractive **Neiweipi Cultural Park** (內惟埤 文化園區；nèiwéipí wénhuà yuánqū), the **Kaohsiung Museum of Fine Arts** was opened in 1994 and houses four floors of galleries, enough to keep you busy for several hours: exhibits change every three months, but the emphasis is on modern Taiwanese painting, calligraphy and sculpture, particularly from the south of the island.

ARRIVAL AND DEPARTURE   **KAOHSIUNG**

Taiwan's second city is well served by **trains** and **buses** from around the country, and is connected by **plane** to a selection of cities within Taiwan, as well as a number of international destinations.

BY PLANE

KAOHSIUNG INTERNATIONAL AIRPORT

Kaohsiung's airport (高雄國際航空站; gāoxióng guójì hángkōng zhàn) has numerous daily flights to Taipei, Magong (Penghu), Hong Kong, and mainland China. You can also fly to Hualien, Kinmen, the southern Penghu Islands of Qimei and Wangan, and an increasing array of international destinations (within Asia). The airport has international and domestic terminals, with several banks and ATM machines; both terminals have visitor information centres (domestic daily 9am–9pm; international daily 9am–12.30am; ☎ 07 805 7888) in the arrival halls.

Getting to/from downtown The airport is connected to the main train station via KMRT and by an hourly bus service. A taxi to/from the centre will cost around NT$250–350.

Getting elsewhere in Taiwan Buses for Kenting (2hr 30min) leave from the airport every hour. For other destinations you'll need to head to the bus, train or HSR terminals.

Domestic destinations Hualien (1 daily; 55min); Kinmen (8 daily; 1hr); Magong (15 daily; 35min); Qimei (2 daily; 35min); Wangan (2 weekly; 40min).

BY TRAIN

BY REGULAR TRAIN

Kaohsiung Train Station (高雄火車站; gāoxióng huǒchēzhàn) is at the northern end of the city centre: the KMRT station entrance is just outside, allowing speedy connections to the rest of the city. City buses leave from the terminal outside, where it's also easy to catch a taxi. Coin lockers are available at the train station and come in three sizes (up to 3hr). Most long-distance buses terminate along Jianguo Rd, close to the train station.

Destinations Chiayi (29 daily; 1hr–1hr 50min); Fangliao (for Kenting; 11 daily; 1hr–1hr 20min); Pingdong (37 daily; 15–25min); Taichung (19 daily; 1hr 50min–2hr 50min); Tainan (31 daily; 30min–55min); Taipei (24 daily; 3hr 35min–7hr); Taitung (12 daily; 2–3hr).

BY HIGH-SPEED RAIL

Zuoying HSR Station (高鐵左營站; gāotiě zuǒyíng zhàn) is at 105 Gaotie Rd, 5km north of downtown; from here, you can get into the city centre by KMRT, or take a train from the adjacent Xinzuoying train station. Taxis into the city cost around NT$200–250. Frequent services link all high-speed stations along the west coast including Taichung, en route to Taipei.

Destinations Chiayi (every 30min; 33min); Taichung (every 20min; 45min–1hr10min); Tainan (every 30min; 15min); Taipei (every 30min; 1hr 35min–2hr 15min).

BY BUS

Kaohsiung is well served by buses (see box below), including round-the-clock services to and from Taipei and Taichung.

Destinations Baolai (3 daily; 3hr); Chiayi (every 30min; 1hr 30min); Donggang (every 30min–1hr; 1hr); Fangliao (every 30min–1hr; 1hr); Foguangshan (every 30min; 40min); Kenting (every 15–30min; 2–3hr); Liugui (14 daily; 2hr 20min); Meinong (hourly; 1hr); Taichung (every 20–40min; 2hr 30min); Taipei (every 20min–1hr; 5hr); Taitung (4 daily; 4hr).

4

BUS COMPANIES AND SERVICES

Bus services from Kaohsiung do not operate from a single bus station – instead, **bus companies** have their own **depots**, many of them clustered together close to the train station: **Jianguo 2nd Road**, just east of the station, is your best bet for a variety of intercity and local services.

Aloha 261 Jianguo 2nd Rd ☎07 267 5640, ⓦwww.aloha168.com.tw. Runs the best buses in the country, with super-comfortable services to Taipei via Taichung.

Ho Hsin 255 Jianguo 2nd Rd ☎07 236 0209, ⓦebus.com.tw. Luxury buses to Chiayi, Taichung and Taipei.

ibus 289 Jianguo 2nd Rd ☎0800 889 116, ⓦibus. com.tw. Runs buses to Donggang and Kenting.

Kaohsiung Bus 高雄客運; gāoxióng kèyùn 245 Nanhua St, at the junction with Jianguo 2nd Rd ☎07 746 2141. Frequent services to Foguangshan, Meinong, Donggang and Kenting as well as hourly buses to Liugui in the Maolin National Scenic Area.

Kenting Express iBus, Kaohsiung Bus, Pingdong Bus (屏東客運; píngdōng kèyùn) and Kuo Kuang now run a combined "Kenting Express" 24hr service to Kenting, stopping at Fangliao, Checheng, Hengchun and Nanwan en route. Catch buses at the iBus stop or Kaohsiung Bus depot; they also leave Zuoying HSR Station from bus stop no. 1, before heading into the city, and some stop at the airport on the way to Kenting.

Kuo Kuang 306 Jianguo 2nd Rd ☎07 235 2616. Offers the cheapest services to Taipei (every 20min–1hr) and Taichung (every 20–40min), plus four daily buses to Taitung via Fangliao.

Ubus 265 Jianguo 2nd Rd ☎07 715 7458, ⓦubus. com.tw. Offers the same services as Kuo Kuang, at slightly higher rates.

BY FERRY

Taiwanline Taihua Ferry (台華輪; táihuá lún) operates four to five weekly services between Kaohsiung and Magong (4–5hr; NT$860; ☎ 07 561 5313). The terminal is in Hamasen District, off Binhai Road at Fisherman's Wharf, connected to the train station by bus #248.

GETTING AROUND

Kaohsiung's sights are scattered all over the city, so you'll need to use public transport (or taxis) to **get around**; most streets are clearly marked in tōngyòng pīnyīn at junctions.

By metro The city's metro KMRT (高雄捷運環狀輕軌; gāoxióng jiéyùn; ⓦ www.krtco.com.tw) and expanding LRT system (環狀輕軌; huán zhuàng qīngguǐ) are the best way to get around, although they don't go everywhere. Two MRT lines – Red (with stops R3 to R24) and Orange (stops 01 to 014) – crisscross the city (meeting at Formosa Blvd), from Gangshan in the north to the airport and Siaogang in the south, and from Sizihwan in the west to Daliao in the eastern suburbs. The LRT, which will eventually encircle the entire city, at the time of writing had one line open from Lizhinei (green line C1) in the east to Kaohsiung Exhibition Centre (green line C8) in the west, and intersects the Red Line at Kaisyuan (R6/C3). Buy single tokens (NT$20–65) from machines in the station, or use an EasyCard (see p.82). Sample fares from the train station are NT$25 to the HSR Station, NT$20 to Sizihwan and NT$35 to the airport. Services run 6am–midnight, with trains every 4–6min during peak hours.

By bus The Kaohsiung City Bus Station (高雄市公共汽車站; gāoxióngshì gōnggòng qìchēzhàn; ☎ 07 749 7100, ⓦ ibus.tbkc.gov.tw) is in front of the train station: timetables are in Chinese, but you can look for bus numbers and bilingual destinations on the front of the buses. Bus #248 (History Museum, Hamasen and Gushan Ferry Pier) and #100 (Liuhe Night Market, 85 Sky Tower and Sogo) depart from here. Fares are NT$12 with exact change required, so it's simpler to pick up an EasyCard.

By car Driving isn't recommended within the city, but can be worthwhile to explore the hinterlands. Car rental outlets include Car Plus (☎ 0800 222 568, ⓦ car-plus.com.tw) and Hotai Leasing (☎ 0800 024 550, ⓦ easyrent.com.tw), which both have offices at the airport and HSR Station (Car Plus also has a downtown office near the train station at 264 Jianguo 2nd Rd.

By scooter The following places will rent scooters to foreigners with an international licence: 555 Scooter Rental at 8, Lane 317, Linsen 1st Rd (☎ 0975 177 141, ⓦ 555scooters .com); Louis's Scooter Rental at 28-20 Zhouzi East St (☎ 0935 055 094). Both offer daily (NT$350–500), weekly (NT$1200–1500) and monthly (NT$2500–3000) rental.

By bike The Kaohsiung City Public Bike scheme (☎ 0800 255 995, ⓦ www.c-bike.com.tw) allows you to rent a bicycle with a credit card or EasyCard from one location and drop it at another; bikes are located along subway lines and Love River, with the major centre at Love Pier. The first 30min are free and then each subsequent 1hr 30min costs NT$10 if paying with an EasyCard, or NT$20 with a credit card. For more durable bikes, try Giant (☎ 07 553 1412) at 2218 Zhonghua 1st Rd, which has rentals from NT$200/day.

By taxi Taxis are plentiful and reasonably priced: the initial fare is NT$85, then NT$5 per 250m thereafter.

INFORMATION AND TOURS

Tourist information Kaohsiung has several visitor centres scattered around the city, with convenient branches in the train station (daily 10am–7pm; ☎ 07 236 2710), airport (daily 9am–12.30am; ☎ 07 805 7888), and at the HSR Station (daily 8.30am–8.30pm; ☎ 07 862 9110). There is also a branch at 110 Shengli Rd, Lotus Lake (daily 10am–7pm; ☎ 07 588 2497).

Organized tours British-owned Bamboo Trails (☎ 0970 782 393, ⓦ bambootrails.com) can arrange in-depth tours of the beautiful and diverse surrounding area including Foguangshan, Meinong, Baolai and Kenting, as well as a host of less well-known spots.

ACCOMMODATION

AROUND THE STATION

★**Hotel Kindness** 康橋商旅; kāngqiáo shānglǚ 44 Jianguo 3rd Rd ☎ 07 287 5566, ⓦ kindness-hotel .com.tw; KMRT R11 Kaohsiung Main Station; map p.253. Excellent mid-range option with branches all over the city; this one is near the train station. Rooms are small but modern, spotless and equipped with comfy doubles, flat-screen TVs and a small desk. The bathrooms feature massage showers. Buffet breakfast included; bikes are available to rent. NT$2000

Hotel Skoal 世國商旅; shìguó shānglǚ 64 Minjhuheng Rd ☎ 07 287 6151, ⓦ www.skoalhotel .com.tw; KMRT R11 Kaohsiung Main Station; map p.253. Decent budget hotel, with small and basic but clean and modern rooms. Within walking distance of the station; also has free laundry and free bike loans. NT$1380

TW Hostel 橙舍好舍青年旅舍; chéngshè hǎoshè qīngnián lǚshè 40 Jianguo 3rd Rd ☎ 07 288 8028, ⓦ twhostel.com; KMRT R11 Kaohsiung Main Station; map p.253. Well-located hostel, just a few minutes' walk from the train station, with four-, six- and eight-bed mixed and female-only dorms as well as en-suite single rooms and doubles. Communal facilities include a kitchen, laundry, lockers and shared computers (and printer). Dorms NT$500; singles NT$800; doubles NT$1200

DOWNTOWN
85 Sky Tower Hotel 君鴻國際酒店85; jūnhóng guójì jiǔdiàn 85 1 Zihciang 3rd Rd ☎07 566 8000, ⓦ85sky-tower.com; KMRT R8 Sanduo Shopping District; map p.253. Formerly the *Splendor Hotel*, *85 Sky Tower* remains a good upmarket choice for its incredible city and harbour views. The hotel occupies floors 46–70 of the eponymous tower – the higher you go the greater the price. There's also a gym and a range of classy restaurants and bars. The entrance is on Singuang Rd; check-in on the 39th floor. NT$4150

Cozy Planet Hostel 精緻背包客棧; jīngzhì bèibāo kèzhàn 8F, 331 Zhonghua 4th Road ☎0921 576 577, ⓦcozy-planet.com; KMRT R9 Central Park; map p.253. This recently renovated backpacker hostel has welcoming English-speaking staff and enjoys a good location near Central Park and Xinjuejiang shopping area. The dorms and private rooms are clean, plus there's some outdoor space on the rooftop. Rates include a limited breakfast, and there's free bike or luggage storage. Dorms NT$550, doubles NT$1540

Grand Hi-Lai Hotel 漢來大飯店; hànlái dàfàndiàn 266 Chenggong 1st Rd ☎07 216 1766, ⓦwww.grand-hilai.com.tw; KMRT R9 Central Park; map p.253. Located in Kaohsiung's third-tallest building,

this luxurious hotel offers rooms with Neoclassical decor and floors loaded with Chinese and Western objets d'art. There's also an attractive pool, and a gym and sauna. NT$6500

YANCHENG AND LOVE RIVER
Ambassador Hotel 國賓大飯店; guóbīn dàfàndiàn 202 Minsheng 2nd Rd ☎07 211 5211, ⓦambassador-hotels.com; KMRT 04 City Council; map p.253. Kaohsiung's first five-star, offering luxurious rooms with views of Love River. Discounts of up to forty percent can make this a good deal, especially given the location and facilities, although standard singles are a little small – and there are lots of tour groups here. Huge buffet breakfast included. NT$4000

City Suites 城市商旅; chéngshì shānglǚ 1 Dayi Street, Pier 2 ☎07 521 5116, ⓦcitysuites.com.tw; KMRT 02 Yanchengpu; map p.253. Part of the sleek nationwide chain, this Kaohsiung branch is located in the middle of trendy Pier 2 Arts District, and just a short walk from Love River. Rooms are contemporary, with all mod cons, and great value if you get discounted rates, but it can get overrun with tour groups. NT$2400

Hotel Kingdom 華王大飯店; huáwáng dàfàndiàn 42 Wufu 4th Rd ☎07 551 8211, ⓦwww.hotelkingdom.com.tw; KMRT 02 Yanchengpu; map p.253. Comfortable if slightly overpriced hotel with flat-screen TVs in all the rooms. Popular with tour groups, its location in the heart of the old pub district is excellent and conveniently close to Love River. NT$3000

EATING

Kaohsiung is well supplied with places to eat and drink, with new restaurants popping up all the time in trendy **Zuoying**, while traditional canteens and stalls continue to thrive in the city's older districts. As elsewhere, **night markets** provide the widest selection of cheap snacks and meals.

DOWNTOWN
Gan's Frozen Taro 甘家老店冷凍芋; gānjiā lǎodiàn lěngdòngyù 113 Zihciang 3rd; KMRT R8 Sanduo Shopping District; map p.253. Tiny dessert store on a section of Zihciang Rd crammed with enticing night-market stalls. Try the frozen taro (NT$45) – sweet relief on a hot day. No English. Daily except Weds 1pm–1am.

J Café at Urban Spotlight 城市光廊; chéngshì guāngláng Junction of Jhonghua and Wufu roads ☎07 272 1999; KMRT R9 Central Park; map p.253. Set in the trendy Urban Spotlight park at the southern end of Jhongshan Park, and currently owned by pop star Jay Chou, this is a great place to relax and people-watch. At weekends it tends to get busier, and features live music. Serves light Western-style meals (NT$220–280), cakes and teas and coffees (from NT$120). Mon–Thurs & Sun 10.30am–11pm, Fri & Sat 10.30am–midnight.

★**Kaohsiung Milk King** 高雄牛乳大王; gāoxióng

niúrǔ dàwáng 65 Jhonghua 3rd Rd ☎07 282 3636; KMRT 04 City Council; map p.253. Kaohsiung is renowned throughout Taiwan for papaya milk, popularized by this chain established in the 1960s. The canteen-style diner offers snacks and juices (NT$30–80) and the celebrated papaya drink for NT$65. English menu available. Daily 7am–2am.

Kaohsiung Pearl Barley King 高雄薏仁大王; gāoxióng yìrén dàwáng 455 Chenggong 1st Rd ☎07 211 2252; KMRT 04 City Council; map p.253. Fifty-year-old store that produces sweet mung bean desserts and barley drinks (NT$25–30) – traditional icy treats that are especially enjoyable in the tropical heat. Daily 10am–5pm.

Liuhe Road Night Market 六合路夜市; liùhélù yèshì Liuhe Rd between Jhongshan Rd and Zihli Rd; map p.253. The most famous night market in town, centrally located Liuhe bustles with a mixture of tourists and locals every night, year-round. Daily 5pm–midnight.

Old Capital City Dumplings 京成扁食; jīngchéng biǎnshi 11 Zili 1st Rd ☎07 286 0313; KMRT R11; map p.253. Traditional handmade pork or shrimp dumplings in soup broth, either with or without noodles. The sesame noodles are tasty and can be ordered as a vegetarian dish (ask for no pork), and there's a range of side dishes including tea eggs, tofu and seaweed. Daily 10am–1am.

★**Top Grade Vegetarian Noodle Shop** 上品齋素麵 坊; shàngpǐn zhāi sù miàn fāng 128 Qingnian 2nd Rd ☎07 215 2582; KMRT R9 Central Park; map p.253. Several noodle types including rice vermicelli and Hakka noodles feature (NT$60–90) at this excellent organic vegetarian restaurant. They also serve veggie dumplings. English menu. Mon–Sat 11am–2pm & 4.30–8pm.

YANCHENG AND HAMASEN

Aroma Mutton Pot 味味香羊肉爐; wèiwèixiāng yángròulú 100 Fuye Rd at Cisian 3rd Rd ☎07 551 8588; KMRT 02 Yanchengpu; map p.253. This popular canteen has been in business for over forty years and sells a combination of seafood and mutton hotpots (NT$120–200), as well as stir-fried dishes from NT$60. No English spoken. Daily 11am–2pm & 5pm–midnight.

ArtCo 典藏駁二餐廳; diǎncáng bóèr cāntīng C6 Dayi St ☎07 521 1936, ⓦartouch.com/food; KMRT 02 Yanchengpu; map p.253. Near the bike trail and outdoor sculpture park, this cavernous warehouse has been converted into an upscale restaurant with artworks on display. The Western-style menu includes Caesar salad with smoked salmon (NT$300) and crêpe with sautéed mushroom in brandy cream sauce (NT$250), while the drinks list offers coffee, tea, beer and wine. Daily 11.30am–10pm.

City of Steamed Glutinous Rice 米糕城; mǐgāo chéng 107 Daren Rd ☎07 533 3168; KMRT 02 Yanchengpu; map p.253. Cheap local diner that's over fifty years old, producing mouth-watering bowls of glutinous rice topped with pork or fish and cucumber (NT$30–50). No English spoken. Daily 9.30am–10.30pm.

Hamasen Black Marlin Fish Ball King 哈瑪星旗魚 丸大王; hāmǎxīng qíyúwán dàwáng 27 Gupo St (between Linhai Rd and Gushan St) ☎07 521 0948;

KMRT 01 Siziwan; map p.253. This celebrated food stall is located on the south side of the forecourt of Da Tian Temple in Hamasen. Locals reckon they serve the best fish-ball soup in the country – and it's a bargain at NT$50 per bowl. Daily 10.30am–8pm.

Tea and Art 古典玫瑰園; gǔdiǎn méiguī yuán British Consulate at Takao ☎07 5250 508; KMRT 01 Siziwan; map p.253. This sophisticated café and restaurant within the historic former British Consulate is a great place for a drink, and serves beer, decent cocktails and of course, English-style tea. The Consul Set meal (NT$590) consists of salad, soup with home-made bread, and a choice of grilled steak or pork knuckle with sauerkraut. Daily 9am–7pm.

ZUOYING

Andy's Pizza 安迪的披薩花園; āndí de pīsà huāyuán 273 Yucheng Rd, ☎07 557 2889; KMRT R14 Kaohsiung Arena; map p.257. Starting from a backyard operation near Chengching Lake, Andy's now has a full-blown restaurant in Zuoying and produces some of the best brick-oven pizzas in the city, with a great choice of toppings, including plentiful veggie options. Depending on size, pizzas cost NT$145–415. Tues 4.30–10pm, Wed–Sun 11.30am–10pm.

★**Conway's** 英國小館; yīngguó xiǎoguǎn 65-10 Xinzhuangzi Rd ☎07 343 0800; KMRT R15 Ecological District; map p.257. Conway's is the best place in town for a slap-up British meal, with a menu that includes fish and chips, home-made bangers and mash, ploughman's sandwiches, full English breakfasts and, of course, Sunday roasts. Indoor and outdoor seating. Mon & Wed–Sun noon–10.30pm, Tues 5–10.30pm.

Wakey Wakey Lakeview Café and Bar 蓮池潭威奇餐 廳; liánchí tán wēiqí canting Opposite 46 Xinzhuangzi Rd ☎07 588 5983; KMRT R15 Ecological District; map p.257. Lively waterside café-bar serving up international cuisine (mains NT$200) with prime views of the lake and wakeboarding cable. Daily happy hours, plus live music some evenings. Mon–Thurs noon–10.30pm, Fri noon–11pm, Sat 10am–midnight, Sun 10am–10.30pm.

DRINKING AND NIGHTLIFE

DOWNTOWN AND YANCHENG

Beerbee 啤酒瘋啤酒專賣; píjiǔfēng píjiǔ zhuānmài 200 Boai 1st Rd ☎07 322 0338; KMRT R12 Houyi; map p.253. Trendy and brightly lit craft-beer bar popular with young locals for its incredible selection of imported beers – over four hundred varieties are on offer. You can buy beers to take away, or enjoy your drink at the long bar or the outdoor tables. Daily except Tues 2pm–4am.

Black Dog Pub 黑狗酒吧; hēigǒu jiǔbā 142 Yunwen St ☎07 241 0270; KMRT R9 Central Park; map p.253. Popular with students and expats alike, this lively

bar (beers from NT$100) has a huge music collection and features live-music performances some nights. Also serves good food. Mon–Sat 8.30pm–2am.

Bottoms Up Saloon 236 Chenggong 1st Rd, at Cingnian 2nd Rd ☎07 269 3075; KMRT R9 Central Park; map p.253. Classically styled American-owned cocktail bar, doubling up as a sports bar with all the top events live on TV. The service, food and beer are excellent – think crab-cream-cheese dumplings and herbed T-bone pork chop. Try the signature martinis and superb mojitos (from NT$200). Daily 5.30pm–2am.

Brickyard 紅磚地窖; hóngzhuān dìjiào B1, 507 Jhongshan 2nd Rd ☎07 215 0024, ⓦbrickyardkaohsiung .com; KMRT R9 Central Park; map p.253. Basement bar and live-music venue, featuring everything from local rock and indie bands to open-mic nights and DJs spinning house and electronica. On Fri and Sat nights (plus other event nights) there's a cover charge (NT$300 for men, NT$150 for women, both including a drink). Mon & Sun 9pm–2am, Wed–Sat 9pm–4am

Lamp 3F, 42 Ziqiang 3rd Rd ☎07 269 6527; KMRT R8 Sanduo Shopping District; map p.253. Kaohsiung's swankiest club attracts a moneyed and up-for-it crowd with its state-of-the-art sound and lighting (including an LED wall), an international DJ line-up, and scantily clad dancers. Cover charge is NT$200 for women and NT$600 for men. Wed–Sat 10.30pm–4.30am, Sun 10pm–3.30am.

ZUOYING

★**Foster Hewitt's** 加楓酒吧; jiāfēng jiǔbā 30 Wenjhong Rd ☎07 555 0888; KMRT R14 Kaohsiung Arena; map p.257. Great little Canadian-run resto-bar with friendly service and a good range of beers, ciders (even Thatchers from the UK) and cocktails, plus excellent food – try the poutine or chicken wings. Daily 6pm–2am.

Lighthouse Bar & Grill 燈塔外觀; dēngtǎ wàiguān 239 Fuguo Rd, Zuoying, in between Yucheng and Minghua 1st roads ☎07 559 2614, ⓦthelighthouse.com.tw; KMRT R14 Kaohsiung Arena; map p.253. Expat favourite, with decent beer (from NT$100), live Premier League, themed food nights and daily drinks specials. Daily 6pm–2am.

SHOPPING

Kaohsiung is second only to Taipei as a place to **shop**, with the island's largest mall, plenty of department stores and a good choice of cheaper markets and gift shops. **Sanduo Road Commercial District** (三多商圈; sānduō shāngquān; KMRT R8 Sanduo Shopping District), in is Kaohsiung's principal **shopping zone**, containing Sogo, FE21 Mega and Shinkong Mitsukoshi department stores, while the alleys nearby are packed with clothes stores. North of Sanduo, **Xinjuejiang** (新堀江商場; xīnjuéjiāng shāngchǎng) is comparable to Taipei's Ximending, with narrow streets crammed with fashionable stalls, upmarket boutiques and coffee shops, and is the best place to check out local street fashions. Xinjuejiang is just south of Wufu 2nd Rd (KMRT R9 Central Park Station, exit 2) in the lanes between Wenheng 2nd Rd and Renjhih St. Stores in both Sanduo and Xinjuejiang generally open daily 11am–10pm.

Caves Books 敦煌書局; dūnhuáng shūjú 76 Wufu 4th Rd ☎07 561 5716, ⓦcavesbooks.com.tw; KMRT O2 Yanchengpu; map p.253. Well-stocked bookshop with plenty of English magazines and books. Daily 10.30am–9.30pm.

Dream Mall 夢時代購物中心; mèngshídài gòuwù zhōngxīn 789 Jhonghua 5th Rd ☎07 973 3888, ⓦwww.dream-mall.com.tw; LRT Lizihnei, or bus #15, #35, #36 or #70 from the city; map p.253. A shopping paradise, south of downtown, Dream Mall is the largest of its kind in East Asia and home to the giant Kaohsiung Eye (高雄之眼; gāoxióng zhīyǎn) Ferris wheel. Mon–Thurs 11am–10pm, Fri 11am–11.30pm, Sat 10.30am–10.30pm & Sun 10.30am–10pm.

Jade Market 高雄十全玉市場; gāoxióng shíquán yùshìchǎng 252 Shihcyuan Rd, at Zihli Rd ☎07 331 7199; KMRT R12 Houyi; map p.253. Vast hall crammed with jade, antiques, statues and jewellery. Make sure you bargain. Wed, Thurs & Sun 9am–4.30pm.

Sanfengjhong Traditional Covered Market 三鳳中街商圈; sānfèng zhōngjiē shāngquān Just north of Jianguo 3rd Rd, between Zihli Rd and Jhonghua Rd; KMRT R11 Kaohsiung Main Station; map p.253. This covered market, west of the train station, is crammed with stalls selling all sorts of traditional Chinese snacks and dried foods. Daily 9am–9pm.

Taroko Park Mall 大魯閣草衙道 dà lǔ gé cǎo yá dào 1-1 Zhongan Rd ☎07 796 9999, ⓦtarokopark. com.tw; KMRT R4A Caoya or red bus #6, #7A, #69A, #69B from the city; map p.253. In the south of town, near the airport, this is Kaohsiung's latest mall offering. It has shops galore, a movie theatre, rollerskating rink, fitness centre, go-karting and a few children's theme-park rides. Mon–Thurs 11am–10pm, Fri 11am–10.30pm, Sat 10.30am–10.30pm & Sun 10.30am–10pm.

DIRECTORY

Banks There are plenty of banks and ATMs in Kaohsiung, many located in 7-Elevens. HSBC has a branch at 693 Mingcheng 3rd Road, while Citibank is at 502 Jiouru 1st Rd, 111 Wufu 4th Rd and 38 Minzu 2nd Rd.

Hospital The Kaohsiung Medical University Chung-Ho Memorial Hospital (高雄醫學大學附設中和紀念醫院; gāoxióng yīxué dàxué fùshè zhōnghé jìniàn yīyuàn; ☎07 312 1101) at 100 Ziyou 1st Rd has outpatient clinics Mon–Fri 8.30am–11.30am & 1.30–4pm, Sat 8.30am–11.30am.

Internet access City Family is at the junction of Jhonghua 3rd Rd and Jianguo 3rd Rd (NT$20/hr).

Post The post office is conveniently located to the right of the train station exit (2-2 Jianguo 3rd Rd; daily 8am–5pm).

4

Foguangshan Monastery

佛光山寺; fóguāngshān sì • Xingtian Rd, Dashu District, 25km northeast of Kaohsiung • Mon–Fri 9am–7pm, Sat & Sun 9am–8pm; museums and galleries daily except Tues 9am–5pm • Free; guided tours (free) in English available if reserved in advance • ☎ 07 656 1921, ⊕ www.fgs.org.tw • Kaohsiung Bus operates a regular service here (40min) from their depot at 245 Nanhua St (junction with Jianguo 2nd Rd) in Kaohsiung

One of several wealthy Buddhist foundations established in Taiwan since the 1960s, **Foguangshan Monastery** makes an absorbing day-trip from Kaohsiung. A vast complex of grand temple architecture, giant statues and Buddhist art, the monastery is the home of the Foguangshan International Buddhist Order, founded in 1967 by **Master Hsing Yun**, an enigmatic monk from China who has spent his life travelling and teaching his unique brand of "Humanistic Buddhism". Having closed its doors to outsiders in 1997, Foguangshan reopened to the public following a request from then president, Chen Shui-bian in 2000. Today Foguangshan is part monastery, with several hundred nuns and monks, part educational complex, with over a thousand students at its on-site university, and part tourist attraction – with the completion of the enormous Buddha Memorial Centre in 2011, the monastery is now a major destination for domestic and overseas visitors. While visiting, you'll hear the word āmítuófó everywhere you go: this is another name for Buddha, and has become a catch-all for thank you, bless you or hello.

The Treasury Museum and Main Shrine

Starting at the **Non Duality Gate** at the front of the monastery, take a look inside the **Foguangshan Treasury Museum** on the right, packed with Buddhist art, carvings and cultural relics. From here climb straight up the hill towards the stunning **main shrine** or "Great Hero Hall" – it contains three 7.8m-high Buddha statutes, beautifully cast in bronze and surrounded on all sides by a staggering 14,800 smaller Buddha images lit by tiny lights and displayed within an intricate latticework of carved wood.

Great Buddha Land and the Buddha Memorial Centre

On the eastern edge of the complex in an area known as "**Great Buddha Land**", overlooking the Gaoping River, a 36m-high **statue of Amitabha Buddha** is the iconic symbol of the monastery, approached by a road lined with 480 *arhats*; however, this statue seems small when compared to the latest grandiose addition, a colossal temple and 50m-high statue of the Buddha as its centrepiece (it's over 100m tall including the base) in the **Buddha Memorial Centre**, 500m north. The hall houses the venerated **Buddha's tooth relic**, donated by a Tibetan monk in 1998. Don't come to this section expecting too much solitude and spirituality, though – busloads of visitors arrive here daily and there's even a (vegetarian) *Starbucks* in the main entrance hall.

Meinong

美濃; měinóng

Around 40km northeast of Kaohsiung, **MEINONG**, once a major tobacco-growing centre, is at the heart of **Hakka culture** in the south – ninety percent of its inhabitants claim Hakka ancestry and many still speak the traditional language. The town is littered with wonderful Qing dynasty courtyard houses, while the surrounding farmland offers an idyllic pastiche of rural Taiwan: this is the market garden of the south and narrow lanes, perfect for cycling, lead through rice paddies, banana and betel palms, past temples, farmhouses and old tobacco barns to a backdrop of swaying bamboo hills. Meinong is also celebrated for its tasty **Hakka food**, and has the

FROM TOP CONFUCIUS TEMPLE, TAINAN (P.239); BEACH, KENTING NATIONAL PARK (P.276) >

MEINONG ARTS AND CRAFTS

Famous for its **parasols**, the town of **Meinong** is also a traditional **pottery centre**. As well as browsing and purchasing, you can also try your hand at these local crafts in several workshops or shops. The larger tourist centres are great for a chance to eat, **shop** and paint parasols all in one location, but get packed on weekends and holidays – for more of a genuine painting experience try one of the smaller shops.

Hometown of Pottery 陶之鄉工作室; táozhī-xiāng gōngzuò shì 362-1 Zhongshan Rd Sec 1 ☏07 681 3486. Next door to *Meinong Traditional Hakka Restaurant* on the western edge of town, this pottery shop sells locally produced ceramics, and can also arrange DIY pottery sessions (NT$250). Mon–Fri 8am–6pm, Sat & Sun 9am–6pm.

Jinxing Blue Shirt Store 錦興行藍衫店; jīnxīng-háng lánshāndiàn 177 Yongan St ☏07 681 1191. Founded by award-winning master tailor Xie Jing Lai, who made traditional blue Hakka clothes until 2009, the shop is now run by his son. Everything is made by hand, and simple aprons cost from NT$500, and shirts or blouses NT$1000–1200. Daily 8am–7.30pm.

Meinong Folk Village 美濃民俗村; měinóng mínsú cūn 80 Lane 421, Zhongshan Rd Sec 2 ☏07 681 7508. Touristy but fun Hakka cultural centre designed as an old-style street, with a restaurant serving Hakka food, snack stalls, and of course plenty of shopping. You can paint mini umbrellas here for NT$100. Mon–Fri 8.30am–5pm, Sat & Sun 8am–6pm.

Meinong Prosperity Paper Umbrella Store 美濃廣德興紙傘店; měinóng guǎngdéxīng zhǐsǎndiàn 361 Zhongshan Rd Sec 1 ☏07 681 8921. On the west side of town, this friendly shop has beautifully crafted parasols costing NT$500–2000, or you can paint your own small one for NT$400. They also have a range of other wooden and rattan items for sale. Daily 9am–8pm.

---

additional appeal of producing exquisite oil-paper **parasols** (油纸伞; yóuzhǐsǎn), although the traditional Chinese craft only took off here in the 1920s. The town has become a popular tourist destination in recent years and can be overrun with visitors during weekends, so a weekday visit is advised.

A short walk south of the bus station, **Yongan Old Street** (永安街; yǒngān jiē) runs through the old town, lined by traditional courtyard houses. The street roughly follows the course of the Meinong River, once an important trade route, although here it's little more than a stream. At no. 178, **Lin Chun-Yu's House** (林春雨 林家夥房; línchūnyǔ línjiā huǒfáng) remains home to Meinong's richest family and is much bigger than it looks from the street. At the southern end of town, Yongan Old Street crosses **Dongmen Bridge**; off to the left you'll see the old **East Gate** (東門; dōngmén), a defensive work originally constructed in 1755 but rebuilt several times since. Northeast of the town centre, just beyond Zhongzheng Lake, lies the **Meinong Hakka Museum** (美濃客家文物館; měinóng kèjiā wénwùguǎn; Tues–Sun 9am–5pm; NT$40; ☏07 681 8338) at 49-3 Minzu Rd, housing an interesting collection of exhibits (with English labels), including a mock tobacco tower.

ARRIVAL AND GETTING AROUND   MEINONG

By bus Meinong is easily reached by bus from Kaohsiung (hourly; 1hr), and there are onward services to Liugui (hourly; 45min) and Baolai (3 daily; 1hr 35min).

By bike Given the quiet lanes, lack of hills, and signposted network of cycling trails, the best way to get around the local area is by bike. Basic bikes can be hired from a variety of places around town, including many of the homestays. You can pick up a map with cycling trails marked in English

from the Meinong Hakka Museum or any homestay. Across the car park from the Hakka Cultural Museum, the Meinong Agricultural Products Store (美濃農特產中心; měinóng nóngtèchǎn zhōngxīn; ☏07 681 8989) rents out bikes for NT$100/day. Grasshopper Adventures (see p.40) can arrange guided bike rides (on better bikes) through the area with Kaohsiung pick-up and drop-off.

ACCOMMODATION

Jhongjheng Lake B&B 中正湖民宿; zhōng-zhènghú mínsù 30 Fumei Shuangfeng St ☏07 681 2736. Out of town near Jhongjheng Lake, this homestay has a cheaper, older block and smarter rooms in the new

building at the back of the property (NT$2500). The friendly owners offer mangoes from their tree in the garden (in season). NT$1500

Renzi Homestay 人字山莊; rénzì shānzhuāng 66-5

Minquan Rd ☎07 682 2159. Comfortable rooms in a two-storey house in a tranquil area northeast of the centre. Only the more expensive doubles (NT$1350) are en suite. The owners speak some English, and are very knowledgeable guides; they'll also pick you up from the bus station. NT$1000

Shuangfeng Homestay 雙峰民宿; shuāngfēng mínsù 8 Shuangfeng St ☎07 682 0839. A 10min walk from the bus station, with a choice of simple dorm beds or en-suite doubles, plus free use of bikes. Dorms NT$400; doubles NT$1000

EATING

Local restaurants focus on **Hakka specialities**, most famously bǎntiáo (fried flat noodles), but the cuisine also includes hearty, often heavily salted pork, and super-fresh vegetable dishes such as Meinong water beans and lotus root. As well as the listings below, the Meinong Folk Village (see box opposite) has a restaurant serving authentic Hakka food.

Liu Mama 劉媽媽; liú māmā 9 Zhongshan Rd Sec 1 ☎07 681 8525. In the heart of town, this simple restaurant serves flat noodles (NT$40) and a host of other local delicacies, including – for the brave – pig intestines with ginger. There's a basic English menu on the wall. Daily 10am–2.30pm & 5–7.30pm.

Meinong Traditional Hakka Restaurant 美濃古老

文物客家菜; měinóng gǔlǎo wénwù kèjiācài 362-5 Zhongshan Rd ☎07 681 1156. On the west side of town, almost opposite Meinong Prosperity Paper Umbrella Store, this atmospheric restaurant is packed with antiques and serves up all of the local favourites, including flat noodles and excellent cold chicken with ginger. Daily 9am–2pm & 5–9pm.

Maolin National Scenic Area

茂林國家風景區; màolín guójiā fēngjǐngqū

Stretching over a sizeable expanse of the southern Taiwan hinterland, some 45km east of Kaohsiung, the **MAOLIN NATIONAL SCENIC AREA** offers an enticing combination of mountain scenery and aboriginal cultures. Sadly, the area was badly affected by **Typhoon Morakot** in 2009: 426 people in the tiny village of Sioulin lost their lives in a terrible mudslide, and the area is still in recovery. Virtually every concrete bridge in the area was destroyed (most have now been rebuilt in steel) and the famous **Duona Hot Springs** were lost, buried by mounds of debris. The **Scenic Area headquarters and visitor centre** at Maolin Village has been rebuilt, and it's still worth visiting the sections that remain open; the seldom-visited Rukai village of **Wutai** remains a highlight.

Heading into the far northern section of the Maolin National Scenic Area, picturesque **Provincial Highway 28** cuts through some gorgeous scenery (and prime mango-growing territory) on its way to the hot-springs town of **Baolai**. Several kilometres before you reach **Liugui** (六龜; liùguī), look out for the **18 Arhats Mountains** (十八羅漢山; shíbā luóhàn shān) on the left. These are a photogenic series of craggy, round-topped mountains nicknamed "Little Guilin" due to their resemblance to the world-famous karst mountains in southern China. Beyond Baolai, the **Southern Cross-Island Highway** (Provincial Highway 20) snakes its way east across the mountains, but is closed beyond Meishankou.

GETTING AROUND AND INFORMATION

MAOLIN NATIONAL SCENIC AREA

By bus The main access points of Maolin, Sandimen, Liugui and Baolai are served by buses. Kaohsiung Bus (高雄客運; gāoxióng kèyùn; ☎07 746 2141) at 245 Nanhua St in Kaohsiung has hourly buses to Liugui, as well as three daily buses to Baolai (7.20am, 1.20pm & 3.20pm; 3hr), the first of which heads as far as Meishankou, but no further along the Southern Cross-Island Highway. Pingdong city (屏東; píngdōng), a 20min train ride from Kaohsiung, is the starting point for buses to Maolin (6.50am, 11am & 5.05pm; 1hr 30min), Duona and Sandimen (hourly; 1hr). The bus station is about 100m to the left of the train station as you exit. If you come by bus,

hotels and homestays can usually offer pick-ups from the nearest bus station.

By car or scooter To get the most out of the region it is advantageous to have your own transport, most easily rented in Kaohsiung (see p.260).

Tourist information The most convenient visitor centres are in Maolin Village (☎07 680 1525) and in Baolai (☎07 688 1001). All of the centres are open daily 8am–5pm and have useful brochures and maps in English. Online information is available at ⓦwww.maolin-nsa.gov.tw.

Sandimen

三地門; sāndìmén

Twenty-five kilometres east of Kaohsiung is **SANDIMEN**, an aboriginal community nestled where the western plains meet the mountains, and the heartland of the Paiwan tribe (see p.401). Busloads of Taiwanese tourists come here to visit the rather commercial Indigenous People's Culture Park, but away from the crowds the little village itself is worth exploring for its collection of traditional slate houses, and there are some cafés and shops selling aboriginal goods. Sandimen is also the gateway to Highway 24, which winds its way into the mountains.

Sandimen Indigenous People's Culture Park

臺灣原住民族文化園區; táiwān yuánzhù mínzú wénhuà yuánqū • Across the river, 1.5km southeast of Sandimen village • Tues–Sun 8.30am–5pm; dance performances daily 10.30am & 2.30pm • NT$150 • ☎ 08 799 1219, ⊛ tacp.gov.tw

Touristy, and overrun with Taiwanese visitors on weekends and holidays, the **Sandimen Indigenous People's Culture Park** nonetheless offers a decent introduction to the island's principal indigenous groups, and is laid out amid beautiful scenery. The park is divided into several different zones, all connected by free trolleybuses, which features traditional housing (some of the houses are originals moved from other parts of Taiwan), a museum and daily dance performances at the Naluwan Theatre.

EATING	SANDIMEN

Shan Zhong Tian 山中天; shānzhōngtiān 10-1 Zhongzheng Road Sec 1 (Provincial Hwy 24) at the junction with Route 185 ☎ 08 799 3440. A justly popular place, set in an attractive wooden building with a large open terrace and serving aboriginal dishes including boar, river shrimps and bird's nest fern. Tues–Sun 9.30am–11pm.

Wutai

霧台村; wùtái cūn • Permits available on the spot from Sande Police Station at 175 Dafadawang Lane in Shenshan (daily 6am–5pm) • ☎ 08 799 2513

From Sandimen, the spectacular 19km stretch of **Provincial Highway 24** leads to the remote Rukai village of **WUTAI**. The area was devastated by Typhoon Morakot, and eight smaller communities beyond Wutai were evacuated; only Shenshan (神山; shénshān) and Wutai itself remain. However, it's well worth the effort to get here (an on-the-spot permit is required) – the road winds through some truly amazing scenery, with steep roadside drop-offs framed by **rushing waterfalls**. Wutai Village is a real treat, with Taiwan's most undiluted Rukai culture, stone-paved lanes and several friendly **homestays**.

ACCOMMODATION AND EATING	WUTAI

Both guesthouses listed below can provide pick-up from Sandimen as well as Rukai meals (if you reserve them several hours in advance); try the fresh, locally made **aiyu jelly**.

Dream House Guesthouse & Restaurant 夢想之家民宿餐廳; mèngxiǎng zhījiā mínsù cāntīng 38 Lane 5 ☎ 08 790 2312. Simple rooms and meals in Wutai Village; Dugu (Du Huei-lan), the owner, speaks some English. NT$1500

Salabo Leisure Village 撒拉伯休閒山莊; sālābó xiūxián shānzhuāng 14-6 Shenshan Lane, Shenshan Village ☎ 08 790 2277. Located in tiny Shenshan on the left-hand side of the road, just past the Km38 marker of Hwy 24 (about 2km before you reach Wutai), this guesthouse has simple doubles, quads (NT$2200) and six-person rooms (NT$2800). NT$1700

Maolin Recreation Area

茂林遊憩區; màolín yóuqìqū

The heart of the Maolin National Scenic Area, **Maolin Recreation Area** covers the region around County Route 132, 45km north and an hour's drive from Kaohsiung. In spite of extensive damage sustained during Typhoon Morakot, the area is slowly getting back on its feet, and Maolin remains a quiet haven of butterflies and waterfalls that makes a tranquil retreat from the rigours of urban Taiwan. The **visitor centre** is in the area's principal settlement, **Maolin Village** (茂林村; màolín cūn), a couple of kilometres into the park from the main entrance gate, accessed via the vast new Teldreka Bridge.

Purple Butterfly Valley

紫蝶幽谷; zǐdié yōugǔ

Over the road from Maolin Village is **Maolin Park** (茂林公園; màolín gōngyuán), in an area known as the **Purple Butterfly Valley** – so named because it is a major sanctuary and migration spot for several species of butterfly, four of which (genus Euploea) sport striking purple spotted wings. Thousands of butterflies descend on the park every **winter**, from November to April, clinging to vegetation and at times carpeting the entire valley. The most arresting time to see the butterflies is at daybreak, when the rising sun wakes them and their wings begin to flutter en masse.

Duona

多納; duōnà

Winding County Route 132 climbs the 15km from Maolin Village to the Rukai village of **DUONA**, one of the last bastions of the traditional Rukai slate-slab houses. This area was hammered by Typhoon Morakot in 2009, with the **Duona High Suspension Bridge** (多納高吊橋; duōnà gāodiàoqiáo) one of the few bridges to survive. The bridge is alarmingly high and yields sweeping views of the river valley. The village itself, about 6km past the bridge, no longer draws in the hot-spring crowds, but is hard to beat for travellers interested in a slice of Rukai life.

ACCOMMODATION AND EATING	MAOLIN RECREATION AREA

De En Gorge Hostel 得恩谷民宿; déēngǔ mínsù Luomusi Communications Rd ☎07 680 1540. Tucked away on a side road beyond Maolin Village, these grey stone cabins are currently the best place to stay in the valley, and offer a choice of plain dorms or en-suite doubles, plus camping (bring your own equipment). There's a canteen on site (with wi-fi) and the friendly Rukai and Bunun owners can also arrange local hikes. To get here, look for a right turn a kilometre into the park from Maolin village; turn off here, then continue across the bridge and turn left when the road forks 500m later – the hostel is signed (in Chinese) through a metal gateway to your left. Camping NT$250/person; dorms NT$500; doubles NT$2500

Fengshan Agricultural Activity Center 鳳山市農會 茂林會員活動中心; fèngshānshì nónghuì

màolín huìyuán huódòng zhōngxīn 16 Maolin Village ☎07 680 1115. In the same building as the Maolin Visitor Center, this place offers basic but clean hotel-style accommodation in twins, quads (NT$2000) and six-person rooms (NT$2500). There is also a restaurant on site serving Chinese meals using fresh local produce. NT$1000

Svongvong 手感烘焙; shǒugǎn hōngpéi Just across Dahjin Bridge, at the junction of Hwy 27 and county road 132 ☎0989 579 751, ⊕facebook.com/ Svongvong. Owned by the same people as *De En Gorge Hostel* (who also operate *Butterfly Café* in Maolin village), this light and airy bakery serves an interesting selection of tasty bread (NT$50–300), plus sells organic produce from the region, including the famed local red quinoa. Daily 9am–7pm.

Baolai

寶來; bǎolái

With the Southern Cross-Island Highway out of action and no public hot springs, post-Morakot, **BAOLAI** has lost some of its touristic raison d'être. Nonetheless, the village is now linked to Laonong and Liugui by a collection of steel bridges, and with the re-opening of **rafting** routes, Baolai is gearing itself up for visitors again. Whilst few of the resorts are willing to invest in rebuilding large outdoor-spring pools (most were swept into the river during Morakot), there are some great upscale offerings here, all of which have private **spring pools** in the rooms. The region also offers plenty of possible **cycling** routes through the challenging hills.

ACTIVITIES

Rafting Trips at Liugui can be arranged through most resorts; usually NT$700/2hr including transfers and insurance.

Cycling Baolai's terrain is well suited to mountain biking, and trail races occasionally take place in the rugged hills that engulf the village. Although some hotels have free bikes for

ACCOMMODATION

Fun Chen Resort Hotel 芳晨溫泉渡假村; fāngchén wēnquán dùjiàcūn 132 Zhongzheng Rd ☎ 07 688 1229, ⓦ phouse.com.tw. While hardly the grandest place on the strip, *Fun Chen* is a solid mid-range choice with cheap, slightly worn hotel-style rooms in the main block and more comfortable wooden riverside cabins (NT$1800) with large hot-spring baths. It's also one of the few places to re-invest in shared outdoor spring pools (just one hot and one cold pool), plus they have private spring enclosures (for six to ten people) with showers, seating and a partly open roof to enjoy the Baolai night skies (from NT$600). NT$1500

EATING

36 Café 咖啡愛玉; kāfēi aìyù 36 Zhongzheng Rd ☎ 07 688 1149. Just along the street from *Baolai Xiaochibu*, this small café specializes in *aiyu* jelly drinks and desserts, made from fig seeds (NT$50). Daily 9am–9pm.

Baolai Xiaochibu 寶來小吃部; bǎolái xiǎochībù

rent, these aren't well suited to trail-riding, so it's best to bring your own or one rented from Kaohsiung (see p.260), or arrange a guided ride through Blueskies Adventures (ⓦ blueskiesadventures.com.tw), or Grasshopper Adventures (ⓦ grasshopperadventures.com).

Villa 26 轉角; zhuǎnjiǎo èrshíliù 18-26 Lane 2 ☎ 07 688 1233, ⓦ corner26.com.tw. This upmarket resort has several room types, the best of which are the garden villas, which come with pleasing walled-garden spring pools, plus chic, compact rooms with all mod cons. To get here, turn up Lane 2 (which is almost opposite 7-Eleven on the main road in the village) and continue until the road rounds a bend, where you'll see the English sign. Prices include dinner and breakfast, both of which are served at a nearby restaurant. Half board NT$3299

34 Zhongzheng Rd ☎ 07 688 1125. On the left side as you enter the village from Laonong, this small, friendly place offers delicious local food, including honey plum pork ribs (NT$200). Mains NT$200–300; English menu available. Daily 10.30am–9pm.

Dapeng Bay National Scenic Area

大鵬灣國家風景區; dàpéngwān guójiā fēngjǐngqū • ⓦ dbnsa.gov.tw

Dapeng Bay National Scenic Area lies just south of the fishing town of **Donggang**, which boasts some of Taiwan's finest seafood and an extraordinary boat-burning festival. **Dapeng Bay** itself is a coastal lagoon which has been developed as a recreational and conservational area, with a 10km cycling trail and numerous wetland and mangrove boardwalks, as well as some watersports. However, most foreign visitors skip the bay in favour of the scenic area's main attraction, **Little Liuqiu Island**, Taiwan's only noteworthy coral island, which makes for a relaxing retreat from west-coast city life.

Donggang

東港; dōnggǎng

About an hour's bus ride south of Kaohsiung, **DONGGANG** is a frenetic fishing port traditionally known for its haul of highly prized **Pacific bluefin tuna** (黑鮪魚; hēiwěiyú), whose soft underbelly yields the finest cuts of **sashimi**. The town's **Bluefin Tuna Cultural Festival** (held every May and June) attracts thousands of domestic tourists, although how long this will last is a controversial issue – bluefin is an endangered species, with stocks at an all-time low. Donggang is also famous as the site of one of Taiwan's biggest **boat-burning** festivals (wángchuán jié), held every three years (see opposite).

Donglong Temple

東隆宮; dōnglóng gōng • 21-1 Donglong St

Framed with a majestic gold-plated archway, the **Donglong Temple** is the centre of Donggang religious life and attracts a continuous procession of worshippers

– particularly fishermen – who pray for safety from the storms that ravage the Taiwan Strait. The temple's most exalted deity is **Wen Hong**, a folk god based on a Chinese duke who drowned at sea and is part of Taiwan's vast pantheon of **Wang Ye protection deities** (see p.407).

Once every three years local devotees stage the dramatic **Donggang King Boat Festival** (東港王船節; dōnggǎng wángchuán jié; next ceremony Oct 2018). The climax of the festival is the spectacular **burning** of a large wooden vessel, filled with replicas of everyday items such as cars, clothing, houses and offerings of meat, in honour of Wen Hong. The festival is intended to rid the town of plague and demons, and in the week preceding the main event the Wang Ye boat is carried around the city, collecting disease and evil spirits, ready for the burning.

Donggang Fish Market

東港魚市場; dōnggǎng yúshìchǎng • Xinsheng 3rd Rd • Daily sunrise till around 8/9am

To fully appreciate the scale of the town's fish trade, visit the frenzied **Donggang Fish Market** along the waterfront, showpiece of the Bluefin Tuna Festival. You'll need to arrive early to see the boats unloading the fish (from 6am) and wholesale auctions, but the market continues for a few more hours, until all the fish has been sold.

Huaqiao Market

華僑市場; huáqiáo shìchǎng • Chaolong Rd • Daily 2–7pm • Sashimi from NT$100 for a small packet

Next to the Little Liuqiu Ferry Terminal (see p.273), **Huaqiao Market** opens in the afternoon and has a huge variety of fresh and dried seafood. There are also stalls selling cooked dishes, and some vendors will cook your freshly bought seafood for a small fee.

4

ARRIVAL AND INFORMATION | **DONGGANG**

By bus Regular buses from Kaohsiung (1hr) or Kenting (1hr 30min) drop passengers at the Pingdong Bus Company depot on Zhongshan Rd in the centre of town. Buy tickets at the counter inside the 7-Eleven. Share taxis and shuttle vans to both Kaohsiung (NT$150–200) and Kenting (NT$350) wait outside the ferry terminal on Chaolong Rd.
By ferry The Little Liuqiu ferry terminal is on Chaolong Rd: from the bus depot, walk northwest along Zhongshan Rd for about 1km until you reach Chaolong Rd (朝隆路; cháolóng lù), just before the big bridge over the Donggang River; turn left here and a short walk ahead on the right you'll see the ferry terminal, where boats depart for Little Liuqiu Island.
Information The best visitor centre in the region is at the entrance to the Dapeng Bay National Scenic Area (daily 9am–6pm; ☏ 08 861 4615); they have English language leaflets and maps, plus there's a café and leisure centre with kayaks and electric-bikes for hire.

ACCOMMODATION AND EATING

As well as tuna, Donggang is famous for two other "marine treasures": shrimp and **oilfish roe** (烏魚子; wūyúzi), the latter of which are baked into delicate cakes to be dipped in a garlic and radish sauce and can be sampled at Huaqiao Market (see above). For Western options, *McDonald's*, *Subway* and *Crown Café* are all within a couple of minutes' walk of the Pingdong bus terminal.

Sunrise Seafood Restaurant 東昇餐廳; dōngshēng cāntīng 66 Guangfu Rd Sec 2 ☏08 832 3112. One block north of Zhongshan Rd, this is one of the finest restaurants in town with exquisite seafood at reasonable prices. Those cynical about imminent bluefin tuna extinction (most of the diners here) will enjoy the tuna sashimi (NT$300/7 pieces), while the Sakura shrimp (櫻花蝦; yīnghuāxiā; NT$100/plate) is a delicious and less guilt-laden treat. Daily 11am–2.30pm & 5–9pm.
The Way Hostel 留下旅舍; liú xià lǚshě 24-1 Chuantuo Rd ☏08 833 6586, ⓦthewaytaiwan.com. This new hostel offers dorms and has one private double room, plus a bar serving cocktails and snacks. Free bike use. Dorms NT$450; doubles NT$1300

Little Liuqiu Island

小琉球; xiǎoliúqiú

The gem of the Dapeng Bay National Scenic Area, **Little Liuqiu Island** makes for a convenient, relaxing retreat from the din of the west-coast cities. Composed of **coral**, the

4km-long, 2km-wide boot-shaped island is covered with curious rock formations and caves, and offers endless sea views. With all of the coral around, it's unsurprising that there is also lots to see in the water itself, including green turtles. The island has suffered from its popularity in recent years, and while there is now a much wider choice of places to stay and eat, the trade-off is that the island heaves with Taiwanese visitors throughout the summer – balmy winter weekdays offer an altogether more pleasant experience.

Liuqiu is best explored by **scooter** or bicycle; most road signs feature English. Most of the sights are scattered alongside the **Island Ring Road**, a 13km loop from the main village, **Baisha** (白沙; báishā), where boats arrive from Donggang.

Vase Rock
花瓶石; huāpíng shí

Immediately north of Baisha, a small coral beach is the site of one of the island's most photographed landmarks, **Vase Rock** – a mushroom-shaped mound of eroded coral. It's worth a quick stop, but given the number of tourists, you're better off heading to one of the beaches elsewhere on the island.

Beauty Cave and Mountain Pig Ditch
美人洞; měiréndòng / 山豬溝; shānzhū gōu • NT$120 for combined ticket including these two sights and Black Ghost Cave

A kilometre southwest around the coast from Vase Rock (and connected by the Lingshan Temple Trail), **Beauty Cave** is actually a series of coral grottoes – a paved shoreline pathway cuts through them. Above the caves is a viewing platform.

Halfway down the west coast, **Mountain Pig Ditch** is a narrow labyrinth of coral cliffs choked by overhanging tree roots, so named because wild boars are once said to have roamed here. For a closer look at the cliffs, stroll along the raised wooden walkway that loops inland from the ring road. Well into the "ditch" are some small rock houses where locals sought shelter during a US bombing raid towards the end of World War II.

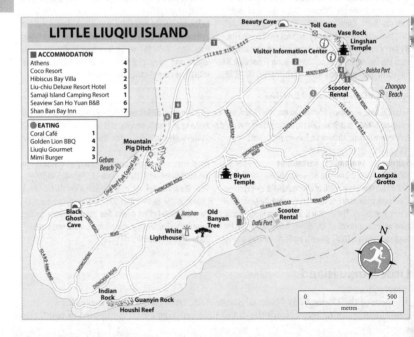

LITTLE LIUQIU ISLAND

ACCOMMODATION
Athens	4
Coco Resort	3
Hibiscus Bay Villa	2
Liu-chiu Deluxe Resort Hotel	5
Samaji Island Camping Resort	1
Seaview San Ho Yuan B&B	6
Shan Ban Bay Inn	7

EATING
Coral Café	1
Golden Lion BBQ	4
Liuqiu Gourmet	2
Mimi Burger	3

Geban Bay

蛤板灣; gébǎn wān

Half a kilometre south of Mountain Pig Ditch, **Geban Bay** is Liuqiu's prettiest **beach**, a gently curving stretch of white coral and sand backed by palm trees which can get packed on summer weekends. Swimming is possible here at high tide (although beware rip currents and sharp coral), and at low tide the intertidal zone is alive with small fish, crabs and brittle stars.

Black Ghost Cave

烏鬼洞; wūguǐdòng • NT$120 for combined ticket with Beauty Cave and Mountain Pig Ditch

At the far south of Liuqiu's west coast, **Black Ghost Cave** is a spectacular string of eroded seaside grottoes connected by a well-built pathway that offers sublime sea views. The caves' macabre name stems from a massacre by the Dutch of local cave-dwelling aborigines (at times referred to simply as "dark people") in retaliation for the slaying of some Dutch sailors.

Houshi Reef

厚石裙礁; hòushí qúnjiāo

Around the toe of the island, on Liuqiu's southeastern shore is a stretch of coral formations known as the **Houshi Reef**, which imaginative islanders liken to people and deities. From afar, **Indian Rock** does indeed look something like a head with lots of hair, and has been compared to the profile of politician Annette Lu.

White Lighthouse

白燈塔; báidēng tǎ

Near Houshi Reef, a road heads inland and uphill for 1km to Liuqiu's odd little **White Lighthouse**, just 10m high and built by the Japanese during the occupation period – it tops the mountain of Jianshan, but there are no views. On the way to the lighthouse you'll pass a short side-road that leads to the impressive **Old Banyan Tree** (老榕樹; lǎoróng shù), which seems to strangle the diminutive shrine upon which it dwells.

Zhongao Beach

中澳海灘; zhōngào hǎitān

If you're dying for a dip in the sea, **Zhongao Beach**, less than a kilometre southeast of Baisha, is one of the few stretches of sand that isn't fringed with razor-sharp coral. At night there are fine views of the lights of Kaohsiung from here.

ARRIVAL AND DEPARTURE
LITTLE LIUQIU ISLAND

By ferry Donggang's Little Liuqiu ferry terminal next to Huaqiao Market (see p.271) has frequent ferries to Liuqiu. Privately owned Taifu (☎08 833 5145) has seven daily departures to Liuqiu's main port at Baisha (白沙碼頭; báishā mǎtóu; 30min; NT$230 one-way, NT$410 return) at 7.30am, 9am, 10.30am, noon, 1.30pm, 3.30pm & 5pm; heading back, ferries depart at 8am, 10am, 11.30am, 1pm, 2.30pm, 4.30pm & 5.30pm. The slightly slower Liuqiu Township Ferry (☎08 833 7493; 40min; NT$200 one-way, NT$380 return) next door to Taifu has daily departures to Baisha at 8am, 11am, 2pm, 4.30pm & 6.45pm; returns are at 7am, 9.30am, 1pm, 3pm & 6pm. Bikes and scooters can be taken on ferries for NT$100.

GETTING AROUND AND INFORMATION

By scooter At the ferry terminal you're likely to be approached by touts renting petrol scooters (NT$300–350/day) and electric scooters (NT$400/day) which are vastly preferable to walking around the island in the summer heat. Although there are a few charging stations dotted around the island (including Baisha Harbour, Beauty Cave and Black Ghost Cave), the electric scooters run out of charge quickly, and at peak times charging stations are sometimes fully occupied. Sunny Alliance (daily 7am–5.30pm; ☎0988 735 226), just to the right as you come out of the ferry terminal, rents out electric and regular scooters. An international driving licence is usually required for petrol scooters; the island's petrol station is at Dafu Port (大福漁港; dàfú yúgǎng).

4

By bike Bicycles can be rented near the harbour in Baisha for NT$100–200/day – ask at scooter rental shops.

Tourist information The ferry terminals have small information desks where you can get Chinese maps and information, but for English maps and assistance, visit the main Little Liuqiu Visitor Information Center (daily 8am–5pm; ☎ 08 861 4615) above Vase Rock.

ACCOMMODATION

Liuqiu's tourism boom has seen new hotels popping up all over the island, many of them stylish villas aimed at the Kaohsiung summer weekend crowd, when prices are high and budget options are thinner on the ground. Some of the cheapest places to stay are in Baisha Port, and the nearby campsite at Samaji (see below).

★**Athens** 小琉球雅典民宿; xiǎoliúqiú yǎdiàn mínsù 298-4 Sanmin Rd, Baisha ☎ 08 861 3033, ⓦ athens.url.tw; map p.272. Justly popular modern Greek-style place facing Baisha harbour, with small, brightly painted en-suite rooms and flat-screen TVs. Great deals on weekdays. NT$1800

Coco Resort 椰林渡假村; yēlín dùjiàcūn 20–38 Minzu Rd ☎ 08 861 4368, ⓦ coco-resort.com.tw; map p.272. A 20min walk up the main road from Baisha Port, *Coco* boasts a tranquil location, with cosy white pre-fab bungalows shaded by palm trees in a former coconut plantation; the simple rooms are painted in bright colours with clean en-suite bathrooms. NT$2200

Hibiscus Bay Villa 芙蓉灣; fúróng wān 20–38 Minzu Rd ☎ 08 861 4368, ⓦ coco-resort.com.tw; map p.272. The owners of *Coco Resort* also manage this newer, more upmarket property, set just above its sister resort. Rooms here are more comfortable if somewhat garishly decorated, and the upper-floor doubles have balconies with fantastic views over Baisha to the ocean. NT$4600

Liu-chiu Deluxe Resort Hotel 白龍宮休閒渡假旅館; báilónggōng xiūxián dùjià lǚguǎn 272 Sanmin Rd, Baisha ☎ 08 861 2536; map p.272. Just to the right as you exit the ferry pier, the entrance to this place looks far from promising, and while it certainly isn't deluxe, the small, clean and pleasantly decorated rooms here have TVs and tiled floors. One of the best winter deals on the island. NT$1200

Samaji Island Camping Resort 沙馬基島露營渡假區; shāmǎjī dǎo lùyíng dùjiàqū Island Ring Rd, 3km west of Baisha ☎ 08 861 4880, ⓦ www.samaji.com.tw; map p.272. Set on a breezy, oceanside knoll, this was once one of the best places to stay on the island, but *Samaji* has seen better days. Though it still makes a great campsite, the cabins and grounds are in need of an overhaul and the pool no longer functions. Breakfast included. Camping NT$300/person; cabins NT$2000

Seaview San Ho Yuan B&B 海景三合院; hǎijǐng sānhéyuàn 53 Fuxing Rd ☎ 08 861 1318; map p.272. Fashioned in the style of a traditional Fujianese three-sided courtyard house (sānhéyuàn), this newly built property has a pleasant location on the west coast, and makes for an interesting and different stay on Liuqiu. Rooms are tastefully furnished, but the cheapest doubles are tiny; the four-person rooms (NT$4400) are substantially bigger. NT$2200

Shan Ban Bay Inn 杉板灣; shānbǎn wān 2 Duziping Rd, 2km south of Baisha ☎ 08 861 3300, ⓦ sbbay.com.tw; map p.272. One of the first of Liuqiu's newer upscale options, *Shan Ban* is located on the island's west coast. The property is set in pretty gardens where there's a pool, which is only open 4–10pm, but it's only a short walk to a swimming beach. Rooms in the main block are clean and comfortable but fairly simple for the price, while the superior villa rooms (NT$4200) offer a little more luxury. NT$3000

EATING

Seafood **restaurants** cram the streets around Baisha Harbour, but there are also cheap noodle and dumpling places, plus two 7-Elevens, one in Baisha, and the other on Zhongshan Rd near Biyun Temple in the centre of the island. Barbecuing is a popular summer eating option, and there are barbeque restaurants dotted around the coastline.

Coral Café 灰窯欠恙人文咖啡; huīyáo qiànyàng rénwén kāfēi 10 Minzu Rd ☎ 08 861 3576; map p.272. Chic little café, just above Baisha harbour, which serves the best coffee on the island (from NT$100). Drinks can be enjoyed at armchairs in the sleek interior, or on the small terrace with views over the harbour. Daily 10am–5pm.

Golden Lion BBQ 金獅子; jīn shīzi ☎ 08 861 3382; map p.272. This overwhelmingly popular BBQ restaurant opposite *Shanban Bay Inn* is easily recognized by the giant mock ship in the grounds. As with most of Liuqiu's BBQ places, you're provided with a variety of raw food (usually chicken, pork, fish, sweetcorn, mushrooms, peppers and other vegetables) which you can then cook at your table (adults NT$350, children NT$200). The restaurant is closed Nov–March; in summer, it's worth booking in advance to secure a table in time to enjoy the sunset. April–Oct daily 5.30–9pm.

Liuqiu Gourmet 小琉球美食家; xiǎoliúqiú měishíjiā Sanmin Rd, Baisha ☎ 08 861 2376; map p.272. This sweet little restaurant in Baisha harbour has been in business since 1950 and continues to turn out decent Taiwanese dishes, including fried rice with beef and green peppers, and delicious braised fish (NT$200), plus there's a

good range of juices and smoothies (NT$50–70), as well as refreshing shaved ice (NT$60–80). Daily 10am–8pm.
Mimi Burger 61-25 Zhongshan Rd ☎08 861 3009; map p.272. This trendy little diner on the edge of Baisha

prepares tasty burger-and-fries set meals (NT$95–120) and is popular with Kaohsiung's young weekend crowd. The restaurant has a rooftop seating area; the same owners also operate a hotel behind. Daily 11am–11pm.

County Route 199

Starting from the coastal town of Checheng, 20km north of Kenting, **County Route 199** cuts its way northeast through the low jungly hills of the Hengchun peninsula, passing pristine **highland scenery** and Paiwan tribal villages that remain largely untouched by Taiwanese tourism. Five kilometres from the west coast, the road passes through the small aboriginal village of **Sizhongxi** (四重溪 sìzhòngxī), whose **hot springs** make this a delightful place for an overnight stop (see box below).

Shimen Historic Battlefield

Around 5km east from Sizhongxi, the **Shimen Historic Battlefield** (石門古戰場; shímén gǔzhànchǎng) is where, in 1874, a defiant group of Paiwan tribesmen defended themselves against a 3600-strong, Samurai-led expeditionary force of Japanese seeking reprisal for the 1871 **Mudan Incident** (see p.390), commemorated by a stele. Just east of the battlefield on County Route 199, **Mudan** (牡丹; mǔdān) itself is an excellent place to try authentic Paiwan snacks, characterized by an astounding array of mountain vegetables. Mudan (shímén in Mandarin) has not been spoiled by tourism, but there are a few shops where you can buy **handmade Paiwan crafts**.

Shimen Reservoir and Xuhai

Northeast of Mudan, the road begins its steep ascent into the hills, offering fantastic views over the enormous **Shimen Reservoir** (石門水庫; shímén shuǐkù). Two-thirds of the way along its journey towards Shouka on Highway 9, an easterly branch of Route 199 sweeps down to the island's splendid southeastern seaboard at **Xuhai**, where there are

---

HOT-SPRING HOTELS AROUND SIZHONGXI

The indigenous village of **Sizhongxi** is home to a number of **hot-spring hotels**; there are several along County Route 199 as it runs through the village, but most of these are of the concrete-box variety, with spring water piped into tubs in the rooms. More attractive (and expensive) options can be found in the outlying hamlet of **Damei** (大梅; dàméi) – take the left-hand turn at a small sign at the far end of Sizhongxi. It's possible for non-guests to bathe at all of the springs listed below, for a fee.

Dashan Hot Spring Spa & Farm 大山溫泉農場; dàshān wēnquán nóngchǎng 60-1 Damei Rd ☎08 882 5725. This offbeat choice comes with a modest petting zoo with horses and deer. Its well-appointed cabins are clean and comfortable, and the outdoor public bathing pools (NT$200/person) are in a relaxed setting. Drive to the far side of Damei and turn left on the dirt road leading up the hill (marked with a sign in Chinese). After about 100m the road forks – take the left track and you'll soon get to the hotel car park. NT$2000
Fennel Resort 茴鄉戀戀溫泉會館; huíxiāng liànliàn wēnquán huìguǎn 1-16 Damei Rd

☎08 882 4900, ⊛www.fennel.com.tw. One of Sizhongxi's best spring resorts, *Fennel* has spotless doubles and plush wooden cabins. As well as outdoor communal springs with pools and jets, there's also a fish spa (NT$300). Doubles NT$2580, cabins NT$3600
The Mudan 牡丹風情; mǔdān fēngqíng 251-68 Damei Rd ☎08 882 3588, ⊛themudan.com. *The Mudan* has wonderful springs with a large selection of pools and shady pavilions (NT$300 non-guests). The spacious rooms are equally appealing and feature both indoor and outdoor springs. Room packages usually include dinner and breakfast. Half board NT$6000

small public hot springs. From Xuhai it's possible to continue south to Gangzi and then over the hills to Manzhou and back around to Kenting.

GETTING AROUND   COUNTY ROUTE 199

By bike, scooter or car You'll need your own transport to make the most of the area – indeed, with no public transport on this road, it remains delightfully underused. This loop (and using Route 199 to get from Kenting to Taitung) is a popular route for cyclists, but for the less energetic it's possible to cross over to the east coast by car or scooter from Sizhongxi in about 1hr 30min.

ACCOMMODATION AND EATING

There's a good choice of hot-spring **hotels** in and around Sizhongxi (see box, p.275); most of the upscale resorts have their own **restaurants**, but there are also a few simple places along the main road which turn out Chinese and aboriginal fare, plus a 7-Eleven. In addition, there are a couple of Paiwan restaurants in Mudan, but once you head up into the hills beyond, accommodation and dining choices are few and far between.

Xinxing Shancai Lecanting 新興山菜樂餐廳; xīnxīng shāncài lècāntīng Sizhongxi, opposite 7-Eleven on County Route 199 ☏ 08 882 3501. Friendly local restaurant serving an interesting array of aboriginal dishes including deep-fried bees and betel-nut flower salad, along with more regular offerings of boar with onion (NT$200), and river shrimps. Daily 11am–2pm & 5–8pm.

Kenting National Park

墾丁國家公園; kěndīng guójiā gōngyuán

Straddling Taiwan's southern tip and bounded by sea on three sides, **KENTING NATIONAL PARK** attracts millions of visitors each year, lured by its warm tropical climate and magnificent beaches. The park covers most of the **Hengchun peninsula**, which sits at the confluence of fault lines and tectonic plates. As a result, the peninsula has been pushed, pulled and twisted into a complex network of low-lying mountains, grassy meadows, steep cliffs, sand dunes and elaborate coral formations. Despite its remarkably varied natural scenery, most Taiwanese tourists cling to the amusement-park atmosphere of the main tourist area around **Kenting Town** and nearby **Nanwan**, leaving the rest of the park relatively quiet.

The park's **beaches** are definitely its biggest draw and, although those closest to Kenting Town and Nanwan are often crowded, it's not hard to find your own stretch of sand in a more secluded setting. Kenting's nightlife can be entertaining, and the main strip is busy on weekend evenings around the year, but is at its liveliest during the busy summer season and Spring Scream (see box, p.279). To avoid the crowds, visit midweek during the winter, when it'll be relatively peaceful and is often still warm enough to lounge on the beach.

Hengchun

恆春; héngchūn

The biggest town in the region, **HENGCHUN** is a busy little agricultural settlement which is gradually becoming more of a tourist hub as backpackers flee the high prices of Kenting itself.

As well as banks, hotels, hostels, cafés, and the region's little-used airport, Hengchun has several well-preserved sections of Qing dynasty city wall, most notably at the **East Gate** (東門; dōngmén). Hengchun also plays host to one of Taiwan's strangest festivals, the Hengchun Pole Climb, held during Ghost Month, which derives from a time when the town was one of Taiwan's wealthiest, and the rich sought a way to distribute offerings to the poor. Quite how they devised the idea that competing teams would race to climb up 12m-high greased poles to reach the goody stash remains a mystery,

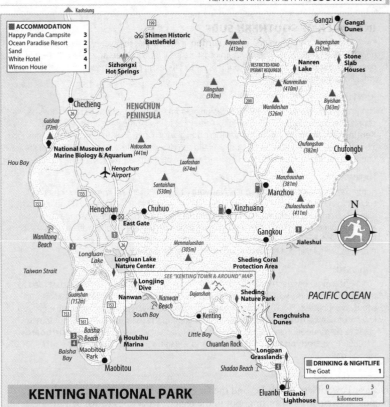

ACCOMMODATION
Happy Panda Campsite	3
Ocean Paradise Resort	2
Sand	5
White Hotel	4
Winson House	1

DRINKING & NIGHTLIFE
The Goat	1

KENTING NATIONAL PARK

but the spectacle is certainly entertaining. The festival attracts teams from all over the island, as well as local teams like the Hengchun Onion Warriors. You can see the pole festival site just north of the East Gate.

Chuhuo Special Scenic Area

出火特別景觀區; chūhuǒ tèbié jǐngguān qū • Free • 24hr

Less than a kilometre east of Hengchun on County Route 200, the **natural gas fires** at **Chuhuo Special Scenic Area** are a bizarre sight, caused by methane escaping through fissures in the mudstone. Most impressive at night during the dry season, the fires are nonetheless visible during the day (unless it's been raining hard). In spite of signs forbidding cooking and vendors, you can usually buy eggs and sweet potatoes to cook over the fires.

Nanwan

南灣; nánwān • Beach: 24hr • Free; parking NT$10/scooters, NT$40/car

The first beach area heading south from Hengchun on Provincial Highway 26 is **NANWAN**, about 6km northwest of Kenting Town. The main road runs through this busy strip of small hotels, cafés and **surf shops**, which overlook the golden sand and turquoise waters of the beach. Although views are somewhat blighted by the Maanshan

IN SEARCH OF SOUTHERN SURF

Kenting has become synonymous with **surfing** in the Taiwanese psyche, as the typically gentle beach breaks along the southern coast are ideal for beginners; the season generally peaks in the **summer** months, although operators here can also organize surf trips to Taitung, where it's best in winter.

KENTING

Though Kenting's main beach and Little Bay are seldom suitable for surfing, the town does have a couple of surf shops where you can pick up gear, chat to local surfers, and arrange lessons. **Kenting Surf Shop** (墾丁衝浪店; kěndīng chōnglàngdiàn; ☎08 885 6806, ⑩kentingsurfshop .com.tw) at 66 Kenting Road stocks surf gear and can also arrange lessons (3–4hr; NT$2000 for one-to-one instruction, or NT$1500/person in a group of two to four people).

NANWAN

Kenting's most popular surfing spot is **Nanwan**. The waves here are chronically soft and subject to close-outs, but they're good for beginners to practise their paddling and take-offs – and the handful of surf shops have **longboards** for rent and also offer lessons and accommodation. A-Fei is the best-known **surf school** in Nanwan; it offers private lessons for NT$2500 (3hr), or NT$1500 per person for groups of three or four. Their base of operations is the *A-Fei SurfHotel* at 264 Nanwan Road (☎08 889 6640, ⑩afei.com.tw).

JIALESHUI

For slightly more consistent surf (and a beautiful backdrop), drive around the coast road to the park's Pacific side, where the shallow bay and river mouth near **Jialeshui** can dish up some sweet barrels. The black-sand beach here is a nice place to camp, but there are also a few surf-oriented **hotels** and **hostels** about 200m up the road, just before the entrance gates to Jialeshui Geopark. *Winson House* at 244 Chashan Rd (see p.284) rents **surfboards** (NT$800/day), **bodyboards** (NT$500/day) and wetsuits (NT$100/day). **Lessons** are NT$2000 for one day.

Nuclear Power Plant visible beyond the far end of the beach, this remains the most popular watersports and surfing spot in the region, attracting crowds of Taiwanese holiday-makers year-round.

Kenting Town

墾丁; kěndīng

Undoubtedly the park's nerve centre, **KENTING TOWN** has by far the widest range of accommodation, dining and amenities, and during peak seasons it becomes a lively party town. The main drag, **Kenting Road** (墾丁路; kěndīng lù) is lined by hotels and cafés, and in the evenings **food stalls** serve a dizzying array of "little eats" and there are even a few **bars**, **clubs** and **discos** pumping out music. There are also myriad **souvenir stands** and shops, selling everything from bead necklaces to Kenting T-shirts and trendy surfwear.

Kenting Town beaches

Away from the frenetic tourist hubbub of the main street, the best bit of Kenting is the **beaches**. Kenting's beautiful 1.5km-long **Dawan Beach** (大灣海灘; dàwān hǎitān) is accessed by a number of tracks from Dawan Road, and can get busy at its eastern end and around the *Château Beach Resort* (technically the only area where you're allowed to swim), but elsewhere you can often have a whole strip of sand to yourself.

At the eastern end of town (and connected to *Caesar Park Hotel* by an under-road tunnel), the much smaller, but sheltered and pretty **Xiaowan Beach** (小灣海灘; xiǎowān hǎitān) offers good swimming and snorkelling (beware jet skis though), and one of Kenting's only real beach bars, *Relax* (see p.285).

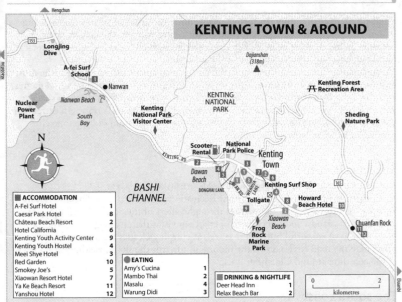

Frog Rock Marine Park

青蛙石海洋公園; qīngwāshí hǎiyáng gōngyuán • NT$30 • Parking NT$50/scooter, NT$100/car

The rocky headland separating Dawan and Xiaowan beaches on the west side of the bay is **Frog Rock Marine Park**, accessed via the lane to *Kenting Youth Activity Center*. A path leads the way around **Frog Rock** (which looks a bit like a giant frog) in around twenty to thirty minutes, hugging the coast over bizarre rock formations caused by the erosion of ancient lava flows. Frog Rock itself is off limits.

Kenting Forest Recreation Area

墾丁森林公園; kěndīng sēnlín gōngyuán • Daily 8am–5pm • Mon–Fri NT$100, Sat & Sun NT$150; parking NT$50/cars, NT$20/scooters (often not enforced)

The entrance to the park's main inland area is through the archway on the north side of the main intersection at Kenting Town's western edge. From the archway, a solitary road climbs northeast, with **Dajianshan** (大尖山; dàjiān shān; 318m) in view on the left. About 4.5km up the winding road, a car park signals the entrance to the **Kenting Forest Recreation Area**, a 435-hectare maze of **trails**, ranging from short nature walks to longer loops circuiting the entire area. The **visitor centre** is a ten-minute walk into the park from the ticket office and car park, and has drinks and snacks as well as

SPRING SCREAM

Kenting Town has become the site of one of Taiwan's biggest annual **rock festivals** – **Spring Scream** (春天吶喊; chūntiān nàhǎn; ⊕ springscream.com) – held every April since 1995. Popular with Taiwanese and expats alike, this three-day event showcases both international and home-grown talent and is consistently the country's biggest gathering of foreigners, with expats from all corners of the island converging on Kenting Town for days of unbridled indulgence. Book accommodation way in advance or prepare to crash on the beach. Expect to pay around NT$2500 for an all-event pass, or NT$1000 for single days. The venue changes, but all the most recent festivals have been held at the Eluanbi Lighthouse.

English-language literature. In spring and summer the area can swarm with visiting school groups, but the further from the visitor centre you get, the quieter trails become, giving the best chance of spotting **wildlife**, which includes Formosan rock monkeys, bamboo vipers, Sika deer and land crabs.

Comprised of eroded uplifted coral, the park is also renowned for its caves, the most impressive of which, **Fairy Cave**, leads visitors underground for several hundred metres. Near here the **Observation Tower** offers the chance to sit down for a drink or snack as you look out over the canopy to the ocean beyond. Near the area's northern extremity, **Valley of the Hanging Banyans** slices its way through a succession of limestone cliffs covered in hanging banyan tree roots.

Sheding Nature Park

社頂公園; shèdǐng gōngyuán • 24hr • Free • Parking NT$40/car, NT$10/scooter

A kilometre southeast of Kenting Forest Recreation Area, the diverse **Sheding Nature Park** also features a web of **hiking trails** through valleys of inland coral reef, limestone caves and grasslands, and offers more open ocean vistas than its neighbour. The park hosts legions of colourful **butterflies** as well as chirping cicadas for much of the year. From here the road circles down the mountain towards the shore, yielding clear views of the coastline around Chuanfan Rock.

The south coast

Southeast of Kenting, the coral-lined coast is interrupted by several pretty white-sand beaches, each of which has a collection of small hotels, cafés and amenities, offering a quieter alternative to staying in Kenting itself. Buses from Kaohsiung run along the strip as far as **Eluanbi**, Taiwan's southernmost point, making for convenient transport for those without their own wheels (see p.282).

Chuanfan Rock

船帆石; chuánfān shí

A few kilometres south of Kenting Town, **Chuanfan Rock** is a comparatively laidback cluster of hotels and restaurants looking out over an arresting stretch of coral-lined coast. A few hundred metres west of the hotel strip is a beach, while directly across from the main hotels is the village's namesake, a massive slab of eroded coral jutting from the water in a formation said to resemble a **Chinese junk sail** (chuánfān). The reef that encircles this tower of coral is home to an astonishing array of **tropical fish** and has become a popular **snorkelling** spot (you can rent equipment at the nearby hotels), although the jet skis that encroach on this area from the beach can make it a slightly unnerving pastime.

Shadao Beach

砂島海灘; shādǎo hǎitān

Heading southeast from Chuanfan Rock on the coast road you'll pass pristine **Shadao Beach**, composed almost entirely of sand from seashells, coral and marine microorganisms known as foraminifers. The beach is protected and off limits, but there is an adjacent exhibition hall with a **viewing platform**.

Eluanbi Park

鵝鑾鼻公園; éluánbí gōngyuán • Tues–Sun: April–Sept 6.30am–7.30pm; Oct–March 7am–5.30pm • NT$60; parking NT$10/scooter, NT$40/car

Seven kilometres southeast along the coast road from Kenting, **ELUANBI** (鵝鑾鼻; éluánbí) is Taiwan's southernmost village, and home to Eluanbi Park. The park's defining landmark is the **Eluanbi Lighthouse** (鵝鑾鼻燈塔; éluánbí dēngtǎ); first erected in 1882 and rebuilt in 1947 after being bombed by the US Air Force, the lighthouse is now one of Asia's brightest, and can be seen from up to twenty miles away. The views are well worth the short stroll up the hill. Continuing a few hundred metres uphill from the village, a road (signed in English) off to the right heads to Taiwan's southernmost point. A half-kilometre path through the jungle leads to a small viewing platform and monument marking the southern tip: from here it's less than 200km to the Batanes Islands, the most northerly outpost of the Philippines.

The east coast

From Eluanbi, Highway 26 curves sharply north, clinging to the **cliffs** and **dunes** along the park's Pacific shoreline. Along the way are numerous viewpoints where you can pull off the road and admire the scenery, while further to the north **Jialeshui** offers a host of outdoor activities. A few kilometres inland from Jialeshui, **Manzhou** is the biggest settlement in the area and the gateway to explore the remote northeastern corner of the national park, and the coastline at **Gangzi**, where there are more surf opportunities and Taiwan's biggest sand dunes. Heading north from Gangzi, a beautiful stretch of coastline leads past abandoned military bunkers all the way to Xuhai where you can connect with County Route 199 (see p.275).

Jialeshui

佳樂水; jiālèshuǐ • Geo Park: daily 7.30am–6pm • NT$80; parking NT$30/scooter, NT$50/car

The coastal road forks at **Gangkou** (港口; gǎngkǒu), with the left-hand branch heading inland towards Manzhou, while a right turn takes you past the beach, 1km to the entrance of **Jialeshui Geo Park**. The park is home to a string of **coral formations** which locals liken to an array of animal shapes – you can admire them on foot, along a 2km stretch of paved road, or on a free trolleybus (with nonstop Chinese-language commentary). Besides the Geo Park, the dramatic **beach** at Jialeshui is one of Taiwan's best **surf spots** (see box, p.278); there are a couple of cafés and hotels offering surf lessons just before the Geo Park entrance, while kayak rental (NT$250/kayak) and jeep rides (from NT$2600 for four) are available from the car park at the Gangkou bridge junction.

The west coast

Five kilometres north of Kenting, Route 153 branches off the main road to make a loop of the Hengchun peninsula's **west coast**, taking in viewpoints, beaches and Taiwan's best aquarium before rejoining the main Highway 26 at Checheng. Almost immediately after making the turn off, the road passes **Longluan Lake**, a popular birdwatching spot, and a couple of kilometres later it's worth making the short diversion to **Houbihu Yacht Harbour** (後壁湖遊艇港; hòubìhú yóutǐng gǎng). The harbour is pretty, but the real reason to visit is to savour the fresh sashimi and cooked seafood on offer at the crammed canteens in the **Hengchun Fishery Association Building** (恆春漁會大樓吃海鮮; héngchūn yúhuì dàlóu chīhǎixiān; daily 11am–8pm). Four kilometres south of Houbihu, **Maobitou Park** (貓鼻頭公園; máobítóu gōngyuán; daily 8am–5pm; free; parking NT$10/scooter, NT$40/car) is another patch of eroded coastal coral formations providing fabulous views across to Nanwan and Kenting Town.

Baisha Bay

白沙灣; báishā wān • Beach umbrellas and chairs NT$300/set

On the coastal Route 153, on the peninsula's southwestern tip, **Baisha Bay** looks and feels like the quintessential tropical beach, with glistening sands seeming to melt into the turquoise sea – **sunsets** here are truly outstanding. Baisha was used as a backdrop in the 2012 Ang Lee movie *Life of Pi*, a fact commemorated by a tacky replica boat with a model tiger inside. There are a few hotels and campsites, and in summers busloads of tourists crowd the beach, hiring umbrellas and chairs to protect against the fierce sun, while jet skis, banana boats and rings tear through the water; the beach is at its most pleasant on a winter weekday.

National Museum of Marine Biology and Aquarium

國立海洋生物博物館; guólì hǎiyáng shēngwù bówùguǎn • 2 Houwan Rd • July & Aug Mon–Fri 9am–6pm, Sat & Sun 8am–6pm; Sept–June daily 9am–5.30pm • NT$450; parking NT$50/car, NT$20/scooter • ☎08 882 5678, ⓦwww. nmmba.gov.tw

The major draw for tourists in the northwest corner of the national park is the futuristic **National Museum of Marine Biology and Aquarium**, just off Highway 26. This lavish facility is divided into several zones, and contains some enormous tanks, the largest of which holds over a million gallons of water and is home to a variety of marine species including stingrays and sharks. One of the highlights of the aquarium is the extensive tunnels which allow you to wander through the tanks as beluga whales swim above.

ARRIVAL AND DEPARTURE   KENTING NATIONAL PARK

By bus Kenting Express buses from Kaohsiung's Jianguo 2nd Rd run to Kenting around the clock (every 15–30min; 2–3hr), stopping at Fangliao, Checheng, Hengchun, Nanwan, Kenting Town, Chuanfan Rock, Shadao and Eluanbi. Buses also leave for Kenting from bus stop no.1 at Zuoying HSR Station; the big Kenting resort hotels have shuttle buses at stop no. 2. On the way back, you can normally hail Kaohsiung buses anywhere along the route,

but look for the nearest bus stop sign to be safe. Coming from Taitung, take a train to Fangliao (15 daily; 1hr 20min–2hr) and then catch one of the regular buses south to Kenting.
By taxi Share taxis operate from Zuoying HSR Station to Kenting, charging NT$400/person (or NT$2000 for the whole car). Return taxis can be found in Kenting and Hengchun, or you could ask your hotel.

GETTING AROUND

Although you can traverse much of the national park using **public transport**, the Hengchun peninsula is a region best explored with your own wheels, whether that means hiring a **car**, **scooter**, or **bike**.

By shuttle bus PT Bus runs shuttle buses from the Pingdong Bus hub in Hengchun to the park's major highlights every 30–40min (NT$20–50/section or NT$100/day-pass). The green line heads along Route 200 to Jialeshui; the blue line makes a loop around the west coast; the orange line runs from Xiaowan in Kenting, through the Hengchun hub, and then to the National Museum of Marine Biology and Aquarium; and an extension yellow line runs to Sizhongxi.
By bus Heading southeast towards Eluanbi, it's easiest to use the Kaohsiung–Kenting buses to hop along the coast: you should be able to pick up a ride anywhere between Nanwan

and Eluanbi every 30min (or less), around the clock.
By car or scooter It's easiest to rent a car in Kaohsiung, but there are plenty of places to rent scooters and motorbikes in Hengchun and Kenting Town. Most companies will insist that you have an international (or Taiwanese) driving licence. On the main National Park junction in Kenting Town, friendly Hartford Motor Rentals (哈特佛租車; hātèfó zūchē; ☎08 885 6802) has petrol scooters (NT$400), electric scooters (NT$600) and Yamaha 125cc motorbikes (NT$600) for rent. In Hengchun, Qiuzhang Betel Nut Store (秋莊檳榔; qiūzhuāng bīnláng; ☎08 888 0298) has decent scooters for hire.

DIVE KENTING

Kenting is better known for its surf than its **diving**, but the latter is fast improving thanks to better conservation and fishing regulations. Highlights include the Flower Garden and Maobitou sites, just offshore, with an incredible spread of soft corals, and Chuanfan Rock, where you can see blue spotted rays. **Boat dives** can access richer sites. One of the most professional setups is operated by Taiwan Dive (☎07 226 8854, ⓦtaiwandive.com), but they are based in Kaohsiung, so arrangements must be made in advance. Longjing Dive (☎08 888 0661, ⓦwww.longjing.com.tw) is another reputable operator, this one based at the turn-off for Baisha on highway 26; they charge NT$2500 for two shore dives.

Rates are typically NT$200/hr or NT$400/day for a 125cc scooter. There are petrol stations in Kenting, Hengchun, Checheng and Manzhou.

By bike A great way to explore the park is by bicycle. There are plenty of bike hire places along the strip in Kenting, which usually charge NT$100/2hr, and some hotels offer free use of bikes for guests. Grasshopper Adventures (see p.40) also runs fully supported multi-day rides through the region.

By taxi An expensive way to explore, taxis can be hired for NT$2000/half-day, most easily arranged through your hotel.

INFORMATION

Tourist information The Kenting National Park Visitor Center (daily 8am–5pm; ☎ 08 886 1321, ⊛ www.ktnp.gov .tw) at 596 Kenting Rd, a few kilometres northwest of Kenting Town, has useful maps and brochures, and English-speaking staff are always on hand. There are also interesting exhibits on aboriginal culture and the area's geology.

Banks Most 7-Elevens in Kenting Town have Chinatrust Commercial Bank ATMs.

ACCOMMODATION

Those looking for a quiet stay will find a smattering of **hotels** near pretty beaches on the **coastal road to Eluanbi** and Jialeshui, as well as on the **west coast** around Baisha. By far the greatest choice of rooms, however, is in **Kenting Town** itself – the tourist trade here lives and dies by its weekends and most places increase their rates substantially on Fri and Sat nights. **Rates** at the major resort hotels have soared in recent years (NT$6000/night is common), so to save money you'll need to try the smaller local places on the main street, or think about camping. Below are winter-time weekday rates – add up to fifty percent for peak times.

NANWAN

★A-Fei Surf Hotel 阿飛衝浪店; āfēi chōnglàng lǚdiàn 264 Nanwan Rd ☎ 09 889 6640, ⊛ afei.com.tw; map p.279. Owned by local surf legend A-Fei, this popular hotel has a range of tasteful Balinese-style rooms, plus dorm beds and a hip café-bar specializing in locally caught seafood. They also run a good surf school (see box, p.278). Similar rooms are available for rent in four other houses spread across Nanwan – see the website for details. Dorms NT$500; doubles NT$1200

KENTING TOWN

★Caesar Park Hotel 墾丁凱撒大飯店; kěndīng kǎisǎ dàfàndiàn 6 Kenting Rd ☎ 08 886 1888, ⊛ www.caesarpark.com.tw; map p.279. At the far eastern end of town, the *Caesar* is one of Kenting's most luxurious options. Superior and deluxe rooms all have balconies and tastefully understated decor, while the double-sized deluxe suites (NT$25000) come with expansive decks and opulent bathrooms. The pick of the lot is the four-person Bali villas (NT$70000), huge self-contained villas with gardens and pools and every conceivable amenity. Hotel facilities include a lovely pool looking out over Dajianshan, the elite Angsana Spa (operated by Banyan Tree), a kids' play area and some decent restaurants. NT$5000

Château Beach Resort 夏都沙灘酒店; xiàdū shātān jiǔdiàn 451 Kenting Rd ☎ 08 886 2345, ⊛ ktchateau.com.tw; map p.279. On the northwestern edge of Kenting Town, this five-star hotel enjoys a fantastic location in the middle of Dawan Beach. The resort encompasses a huge range of room types, several restaurants, plus multiple pools, a mini golf course, and a host of watersports, but its popularity with domestic and mainland Chinese groups sometimes make it feel more like an upmarket holiday camp than a refined beach resort. NT$4500

Hotel California 加州旅店; jiāzhōu lǚdiàn 40 Kenting Rd ☎ 08 886 1588; map p.279. Towards the eastern end of town, this laidback place is run by local surfer A-Liao (who can set you up with boards and gear) and offers simple but spacious doubles, quads and six-person rooms (three double beds). NT$1200

Kenting Youth Activity Center 救國團墾丁青年活動中心; jiùguótuán kěndīng qīngnián huódòng zhōngxīn 17 Kenting Rd ☎ 08 886 1221, ⊛ kenting.cyh.org.tw; map p.279. Although this China Youth Corps-run hotel caters mostly to student groups and Taiwanese families, its unique design and location make it an interesting option. Built in the layout of a traditional Fujian village, it features elaborate facades and ornate roofs as well as clean, modern twins, doubles and quads (two double beds; NT$4000). The extensive grounds offer sea views and lead into the Frog Rock Marine Park, all just a 10min walk from the centre of Kenting. NT$2500

Kenting Youth Hostel 墾丁淳青背包客棧; kěndīng chúnqīng bēibāo kèzhàn 2/F 243-1 Kenting Rd ☎ 08 886 1409, ⊛ ktyh.com.tw; map p.279. Near the western end of town, this cramped little hostel on the second floor has made the most of its space, and offers the cheapest night's sleep in town. Dorms NT$299

Meei Shye Hotel 美協渡假旅館; měixié dùjiǎ lǚguǎn 126 Kenting Rd ☎ 08 886 1176; map p.279. One of the cheapest hotels on the strip, with doubles for just NT$800 (weekdays), and rooms with balconies from NT$1000. Rooms lack style but are spotless and perfectly decent, with TVs and wooden floors. NT$800

4

Smokey Joe's 冒煙的喬雅客旅店; màoyān de qiáoyākè lǚdiàn 237-239 Kenting Rd ☏ 08 886 1272, ⊛ amy.com.tw; map p.279. The newest kid on the block, this mid-sized resort hotel in the heart of Kenting is part of the ever-growing *Smokey Joe's* restaurant chain, and offers clean, compact rooms set around a small pool. NT$3900

Xiaowan Resort Hotel 小灣旅店; xiǎowān lǚdiàn 82 Kenting Rd ☏ 08 886 1015, ⊛ uukt.idv.tw/inn /sw.htm; map p.279. Boutique-like mini-hotel, with each room sporting its own funky, contemporary design and colour scheme, embedded flat-screen TVs and compact but stylish bathrooms. Off-season rates are a steal at NT$1200 for the smallest doubles, but these can rise to over NT$3000 at peak times. NT$1500

CHUANFAN ROCK

★**Red Garden** 紅花園; hónghuāyuán 18 Lane 846, Chuanfan Rd ☏ 08 885 1001, ⊛ red-garden-resort.com; map p.279. Set just back from the main road through Chuanfan, this British-Taiwanese-owned garden hotel offers beautifully designed Balinese-style rooms with fittings from Indonesia. The better rooms have large sea-view balconies, and the garden is a great place to relax. NT$2400

Yanshou Hotel 岩手旅店; yánshǒu lǚdiàn 678 Chuanfan Rd ☏ 08 885 1360, ⊛ rockhand.okgo.tw; map p.279. Winning the award for craziest facade, with a remodelled exterior that resembles the mouth of a cave, this place also has some of the best-value rooms in Chuanfan. The cheapest ground-floor rooms are brightly coloured but don't have views, while those on higher floors have sleek contemporary design, funky sunken tubs and wooden floors, most with balconies overlooking the ocean (NT$2000). NT$1300

Ya Ke Beach Resort 亞哥之家; yǎgē zhījiā 690 Chuanfan Rd ☏ 08 885 1788, ⊛ www.yake.idv.tw; map p.279. Near the 7-Eleven, this small, friendly hotel offers stylish doubles, many with sea-view balconies (from NT$2280). They can also rent out basic snorkelling equipment. NT$2160

ELUANBI AND THE EAST COAST

Sand 沙點民宿; shādiǎn mínsù 230 Shadao Rd, ☏ 08 885 1107; map p.277. On the left-hand side of the road as you approach Eluanbi from Chuanfan Rock, this elegantly designed boutique hotel combines stone-slab minimalism with wonderful ocean vistas. As there are only nine rooms, reservations are recommended. NT$2800

Winson House 周文生衝浪教學會館; zhōuwénshēng chōnglàng jiāoxué huìguǎn 244 Chashan Rd, Jialeshui ☏ 08 880 1053, ⊛ tbay.com .tw; map p.277. Run by Winson, a friendly Taiwanese surfer, this former surf hostel has upgraded itself to something more like a boutique hotel, though dorm beds are still available. The doubles and quads are luxurious and offer fantastic ocean vistas. Also offers surf lessons (see box, p.278), equipment rental and simple meals. Dorms NT$600; doubles NT$2500

THE WEST COAST

Happy Panda Campsite 快樂熊貓樂園; kuàilè xióngmāo lèyuán Baisha Beach ☏ 08 886 7888, ⊛ happy-bs.com.tw; map p.277. On the site of a previously very low-key camping operation, *Happy Panda* is now the hub of the beach, with a range of pitches, plus a bar and a selection of snack stalls. They also have camping equipment for rent and even some expensive a/c tents (NT$2500). Camping pitches NT$500

★**Ocean Paradise Resort** 海境渡假民宿; hǎijìng dùjiā mínsù 2-6 Hongchai Rd (off Pingdong Route 153) ☏ 08 886 9638; map p.277. Fabulous hilltop hotel, great for a splurge if you can afford it, though you'll need wheels to get here. Rooms feature crisp blue-and-white decor, LCD TVs and sea-view balconies, and rates include breakfast and afternoon tea. NT$5800

White Hotel 白沙生活旅店; báishā shēnghuó lǚdiàn 28-8 Route 153, Baisha Beach ☏ 08 886 7168; map p.277. Across the road from the beach, this was the first hotel in Baisha and remains a decent choice. All rooms have sea-view balconies, and are simply decorated in plain white, with mock-wood flooring. There's also a tiny pool. NT$1800

EATING

While there are numerous **restaurants** in Hengchun and a few other places scattered around the national park area, by far and away the greatest choice of food is to be found in **Kenting Town**. A night market lines the main street year-round, and offers a huge range of cheap and tasty snacks, but Kenting is also a good place to enjoy some of the **Western goodies** you might have been missing during your Taiwan travels: there's good pizza, pasta and salads, and even a *McDonalds* and *Starbucks*. **Thai** restaurants are also popular, and dishes can be very tasty, if not always particularly authentic. There are **seafood** restaurants in town as well, but for the freshest (and cheapest) fish it's worth heading to the Hengchun Fishery Association Building on the west coast (see p.281).

Amy's Cucina 酒吧餐廳; jiǔbā cāntīng 131-1 Kenting Rd ☏ 08 886 1977, ⊛ amys-cucina.com; map p.279. This Kenting stalwart, a redbrick, Italian-style eatery, serves up some of the tastiest pizza and pasta in town. Reckon on NT$350–400/person for a full meal. Daily 11am–10pm.

Mambo Thai 曼波泰式料理; mànpō tàishì liàolǐ 46 Kenting Rd ☎ 08 886 2878; map p.279. A cut above the other Thai restaurants on the strip, and always busy, *Mambo Thai* has a cosy interior and a few outdoor seats. Eating here is comparatively expensive (around NT$300–500/person), but worth the money – standout dishes include steamed seabass with chilli and lime, and the green and red curries, plus there's Singha beer. Daily 11am–2.30pm & 5–10.30pm.

Masalu 瑪沙露; mǎshālù 21-3 Kenting Rd ☎ 08 886 1679; map p.279. Pleasant place, at the far eastern end of town, specializing in indigenous food. The menu includes classic dishes such as flying fish (NT$250), salted pork and fiddlehead fern, as well as more unusual offerings like wild pigeon. Meals can be accompanied by a bottle of millet wine (NT$600). Daily 10.30am–10pm.

★**Warung Didi** 迪迪小吃; dídí xiǎochī 26 Wenhua Lane ☎ 08 886 1835; map p.279. Probably the best restaurant in Kenting, *Warung Didi* is tucked away on a backstreet off Dawan Rd, but the location is no secret, and it's regularly packed out with diners feasting on a mix of Thai, Malay and Chinese dishes (mains NT$200–300). Daily noon–3pm & 5–11.30pm.

DRINKING & NIGHTLIFE

Spring Scream aside (see box, p.279), nightlife is focused on **Kenting Town**, where you'll find everything from blaring discos to quiet little hideaways. *Golden Beach* and *Langkawi*, both on the main strip, are popular with mainland Chinese visitors and feature tacky shows (and an NT$100 cover charge), while at the eastern end of town, **pop-up bars** serve cocktails from vans.

KENTING TOWN

Deer Head Inn 鹿角; lùjiǎo 29 Tonghai Lane ☎ 08 886 3336; map p.279. On a backstreet cutting between the main strip and Dawan Rd, this is easily Kenting's most sophisticated bar, with great cocktails (NT$300) and a good range of imported beers (NT$180) served in a softly lit interior. Opening hours can be somewhat erratic. Usually daily 8pm–1am.

Relax Beach Bar Xiaowan Beach; map p.279. Owned by *Caesar Park Hotel*, this chilled-out place sits on a wooden deck right on the beach – perfect for sunset drinks. There's live music nightly from 9pm. Daily 11am–11pm.

HENGCHUN

The Goat 山羊酒館; shānyáng jiǔguǎn 23-2 Hengnan Road ☎ 08 888 0183; map p.277. Though its location on busy Highway 26 in Hengchun isn't great, this is one of the best bars on the peninsula. Good food and drinks (Taiwan beer NT$140), friendly management and live music on Sat and Sun (8.30–10pm). Daily 5pm–1am.

4

The east coast

XIANGDE TEMPLE, TAROKO GORGE

5

The east coast

Nowhere shatters Taiwan's image as an industrial wasteland more definitively than its pristine east coast, cut off from the crowded west and north by the cloud-piercing central mountain ranges. The region is best known for the awe-inspiring Taroko Gorge, but also encompasses the magnificent Qingshui Cliffs and the picturesque East Coast and East Rift Valley National Scenic Areas. The main cities of Hualien and Taitung are slow-paced and tourist-friendly, while, off the coast of Taitung, lie two coral-fringed Pacific islands – Ludao (Green Island) and Lanyu (Orchid Island). The latter is home to the Tao people, the most isolated of Taiwan's indigenous tribes.

The region has Taiwan's densest concentration of **indigenous peoples**: nine officially recognized tribes are represented here, and they have managed to preserve many of their traditional beliefs, languages and practices. The stretch between the cities of Hualien and Taitung is the heartland of the Amis, and scattered throughout are villages of the Atayal, Bunun, Kavalan, Paiwan, Puyuma, Rukai, Sakizaya and Tao people (see p.399). Visiting the area during a festival period – the busiest of which is in July and August – gives a fascinating glimpse into a seldom-seen side of Taiwan.

Hualien

花蓮; huālián

The biggest city on the east coast, **HUALIEN** sits on a mountain-fringed plain 26km south of Taroko Gorge, making it an ideal base for expeditions to Taroko National Park. It is also a major producer of **marble**, and elegant stonework adorns temples, pavements, the airport and even the train station; Hualien also has an inexpensive stone market.

Zhongshan Road connects the train station area to downtown Hualien, home to most of the city's bars, restaurants and shops. The relatively large number of tourists passing through give Hualien a laidback, holiday-town atmosphere, with a growing number of pleasant teahouses and restaurants where you can try local specialities, as well as an increasing array of foreign food.

Note that some Hualien street signs still feature the old MPS2 pīnyīn system; Zhongshan Road is commonly labelled "Jung Shan Road", for example.

Ride east: cycling the coast and Rift Valley p.308
Taitung's secret surf spots p.311
Amis Folk Center p.312
Rafting the Xiuguluan p.316
The White Terror p.326
Green Island snorkelling and diving p.330
Orchid Island snorkelling and diving p.332
Tao traditions p.333
Meeting the Tao p.334
Lanyu's colourful festivals p.336

Highlights

❶ Taroko National Park Taiwan's most famous national park has something for everyone, from the spectacular Taroko Gorge to the awe-inspiring Qingshui Cliffs. **See p.298**

❷ East Coast National Scenic Area Hugging the island's isolated eastern coastline, this remote National Scenic Area has varied landscapes, sprawling beaches and intriguing offshore rock formations. **See p.306**

❸ East Rift Valley National Scenic Area Enchanting tropical valley packed with hot springs, indigenous culture and outdoor adventures including whitewater-rafting and paragliding. **See p.314**

❹ Ludao (Green Island) This ancient volcanic island attracts droves of tourists with its verdant coastal scenery, superb snorkelling and rare saltwater hot springs. **See p.325**

❺ Lanyu (Orchid Island) Home to the seafaring Tao indigenous tribe, whose traditional festivals are among Taiwan's most colourful and exotic. **See p.331**

HIGHLIGHTS ARE MARKED ON THE MAP ON P.290

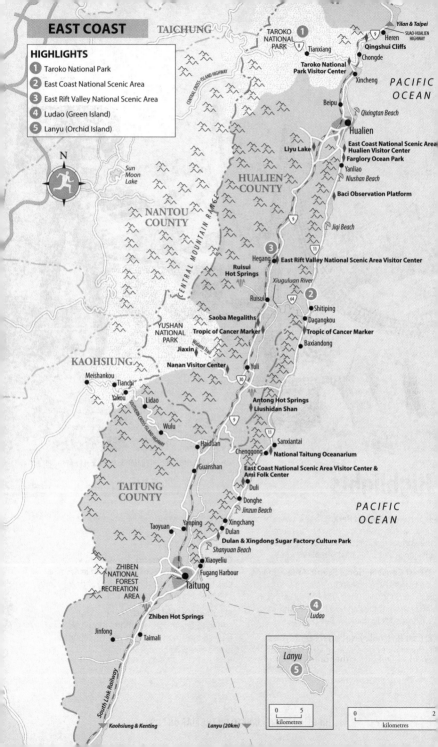

EAST COAST

TAICHUNG

HIGHLIGHTS

1 Taroko National Park
2 East Coast National Scenic Area
3 East Rift Valley National Scenic Area
4 Ludao (Green Island)
5 Lanyu (Orchid Island)

N

Sun Moon Lake

NANTOU COUNTY

YUSHAN NATIONAL PARK

KAOHSIUNG

Meishankou
Tianchi
Yakou
Lidao
Wulu
Haiduan
Guanshan

TAITUNG COUNTY

Taoyuan
Yanping

ZHIBEN NATIONAL FOREST RECREATION AREA

Zhiben Hot Springs

Jinfong
Taimali

TAROKO NATIONAL PARK
Tianxiang
Taroko National Park Visitor Center

1

8

Qingshui Cliffs
Chongde
Xincheng
Beipu

Yilan & Taipei
SUAO-HUALIEN HIGHWAY

9

Heren

PACIFIC OCEAN

Qixingtan Beach
Hualien

East Coast National Scenic Area Hualien Visitor Center
Farglory Ocean Park
Yanliao
Niushan Beach

Baci Observation Platform

Liyu Lake

HUALIEN COUNTY

9

Jiqi Beach

11

3 East Rift Valley National Scenic Area Visitor Center

Hegang
Ruisui Hot Springs

Xiuguluan River

Ruisui

64

2

Shitiping
Dagangkou

Saoba Megaliths
Tropic of Cancer Marker

Tropic of Cancer Marker
Baxiandong

Jiaxin

Wutai Trail

Nanan Visitor Center

Yuli

30

Antong Hot Springs
Liushidan Shan

9

11

Sanxiantai
Chenggong
National Taitung Oceanarium

East Coast National Scenic Area Visitor Center & Ami Folk Center

Duli

Donghe
Jinzun Beach

Xingchang
Dulan

Dulan & Xingdong Sugar Factory Culture Park

Shanyuan Beach

Xiaoyeliu
Fugang Harbour

Taitung

PACIFIC OCEAN

4

Ludao

5

Lanyu

CENTRAL MOUNTAIN RANGE

CENTRAL CROSS-ISLAND HIGHWAY

SOUTHERN CROSS-ISLAND HIGHWAY

South Link Railway

Kaohsiung & Kenting

Lanyu (20km)

0   5
kilometres

0   2
kilometres

Hualien is something of a frontier town: **Chinese settlers** from Danshui established the first village in 1851, but conflicts with various indigenous tribes resulted in the colony being abandoned twice; only in the 1890s did a permanent settlement take hold. The **Japanese** had a strong impact here, the region becoming an immigration zone for poor Japanese families during the occupation era, but Hualien remained a remote place for much of the twentieth century. Today Hualien is a city of 110,000, ethnically unique in having almost equal numbers of Hakka, Hoklo, mainlander and indigenous citizens (primarily Atayal and Amis).

Stone Art Street

石藝大街; shíyì dàjiē • 326 Chongqing Rd • Daily 2–10pm • Dance shows daily 7.30–8.30pm • Free

The best place to pick up locally produced marble is **Stone Art Street**, towards the southern end of Chongqing Road. The "street" is in fact a compound of market stalls selling cheap marble carvings and statues, fossilized coral and wood, and precious stone and jade jewellery. Touristy **dance shows** are performed here every evening by local Amis people.

Hualien Railway Cultural Park

花蓮鐵道文化園區; huālián tiědào wénhuà yuánqū • 71 Zhongshan Rd • Tues–Sat 8.30–noon & 1.30–5pm • Free • ☏ 03 833 8061

Once a shabby part of downtown, the southern end of Zhongshan Road is being transformed by the **Hualien Railway Cultural Park**, with a cluster of wooden Japanese-era buildings serving as galleries for exhibits about the original East Coast Line Railway. The venue was closed for building works at the time of writing, but is expected to open by the end of 2017. The exhibits (labelled in Chinese only) are nothing special, but the buildings have been beautifully restored: the best examples are the old police station on Chongqing Road next to the bus station, and the collection of timber administrative buildings at Fuding Road and Fujian Street, built in 1910, where you can still smell the rich scent of cedarwood.

Dongjingchan Temple

東淨禪寺; dōngjìng chánsì • 48 Wuquan St • Daily 4am–4.30pm

A tranquil Buddhist shrine, **Dongjingchan Temple** has a main hall containing three golden Buddha statues, several massive **geodes** (rocks with quartz cavities) and is plastered with local marble, making it unusually opulent. You must take off your shoes to go inside.

Sheng An Temple and Cihui Temple

勝安宮; shèngān gōng • **Sheng An Temple** 118 Cihui 3rd St • Daily 5.30am–10pm • Free • Turn right off Zhonghua Rd by the canal along Cihui (Tsz Huei) 1st St, then right at Sheng An 2nd St (marked by a large stele), then left along Cihui (Tsz Huei) 3rd St • **Cihui Temple** 慈惠堂; cíhuìtáng • 136 Cjhui 3rd St, next door to Sheng An Temple • Daily 5am–10pm • Free

Along Zhonghua Road are the two most important Taoist temples in Hualien. Both were consecrated in 1950 and are referred to by believers as the "Lourdes of Asia" for their power to heal the sick.

A modern, garish building, the **Sheng An Temple** is dedicated to the chief Taoist goddess **Queen Mother of the West** (wángmǔ niángniáng). It is significant because, in 1949, the goddess is supposed to have spoken on this spot through the body of a young man in a trance. Although dedicated to the same goddess as its neighbour, **Cihui Temple** belongs to another sect; here the deity is known as jīnmǔ niángniáng ("Golden Mother"). Cihui is the more alluring of the two temples by a long shot, and the main hall is impressively inlaid with marble.

5

Pine Garden

松園別館; sōngyuán biéguǎn • 65 Shuiyuan St, off Zhongmei Rd • Daily 9am–6pm, closed 2nd Tues of each month • NT$50

Overlooking the Meilun River, the **Pine Garden** is a former Japanese Navy command centre completed in 1944, just in time to host send-off parties for Japanese kamikaze pilots at the end of World War II. These days the main building serves as a series of temporary art galleries, while the **café** in the gardens outside is a tranquil place to contemplate the city and port below.

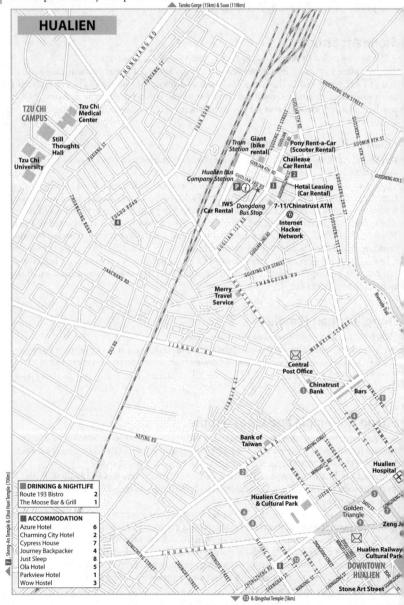

DRINKING & NIGHTLIFE
Route 193 Bistro	2
The Moose Bar & Grill	1

ACCOMMODATION
Azure Hotel	6
Charming City Hotel	2
Cypress House	7
Journey Backpacker	4
Just Sleep	8
Ola Hotel	5
Parkview Hotel	1
Wow Hostel	3

Cultural Center

花蓮縣文化局; huālián xiàn wénhuà jú • 6 Wenfu Rd • **City Library** Tues–Sun 9am–9pm • Free • **Hualien County Stone Sculpture Museum** 花蓮石雕博物館美術館; huālián shídiāo bówùguǎn • Daily 9am–5pm • NT$20 • ☎ 03 822 7121, ⓦ stone.hccc.gov.tw • **Museum of Fine Arts** 美術館; měishùguǎn • Tues–Sun 9am–5pm • Free • ☎ 03 822 7121, ⓦ www.hccc.gov.tw • Bus #105 (5 daily) from Hualien train station

Hualien's **Cultural Center** is a complex of buildings surrounded by a sculpture park, near the coast: facing Minquan Road is the **City Library** and, to the right, the **Hualien**

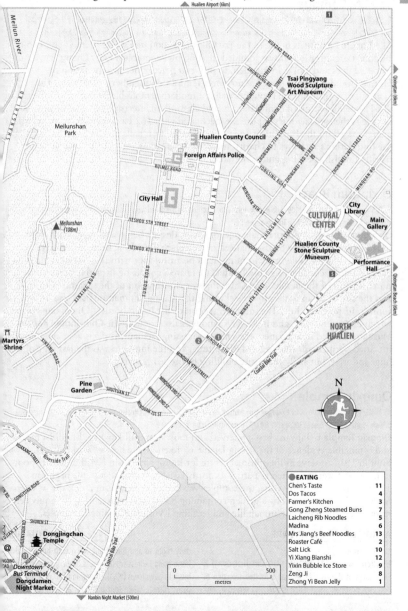

●EATING	
Chen's Taste	11
Dos Tacos	4
Farmer's Kitchen	3
Gong Zheng Steamed Buns	7
Laicheng Rib Noodles	5
Madina	6
Mrs Jiang's Beef Noodles	13
Roaster Café	2
Salt Lick	10
Yi Xiang Bianshi	12
Yixin Bubble Ice Store	9
Zeng Ji	8
Zhong Yi Bean Jelly	1

5

County Stone Sculpture Museum, containing a small but intriguing collection of contemporary and historical pieces of sculpture (labelled in Chinese only), with several impressive works on display outdoors in the museum's grounds. Also on site, the Museum of Fine Arts has a small but interesting collection of indigenous and, surprisingly, African arts.

Tzu Chi Campus

慈濟園區; cíjì yuánqū • 701 Zhyongyang Rd Sec 3 • ☎ 03 857 8600, ⓦ tzuchi.org • Still Thoughts Hall 靜思堂; jìngsī táng • Daily 9am–5pm • Free • Northwest of downtown and the train station, near junction of Zhongshan and Zhongyang roads

The Tzu Chi Campus is home to the Tzu Chi Foundation, the world's largest charitable Buddhist organization. It was founded in 1966 by Venerable Master Cheng Yen, a nun who still lives and works in Hualien, to put into practise her interpretation of Humanistic Buddhism; there are now over ten million members worldwide. The Campus's captivating Still Thoughts Hall is a modern temple-like structure completed in 2001, a combination of contemporary and classical architecture. Its most distinctive feature is the roof, with its triple eaves decorated with 362 bas-relief fēitiān, or celestial beings, based on the Buddhist sutras. Several exhibition halls on the first floor highlight the foundation's activities in charity, medicine, education and culture, and there are usually English-speaking guides on hand.

Qixingtan Beach

七星潭; qīxīngtán • Bus #105 (2 daily) from Hualien train station, via the downtown bus station and the Cultural Center; also accessible by bike on the Coastal Bike Trail (see opposite)

Qixingtan Beach is a popular hangout for locals, despite being a shingle beach right next to a major airforce base – chances are you'll see the odd fighter jet in flight. Though it's not suitable for swimming, it's a beautiful spot with the ever-changing hues of the ocean backed by huge mountains; there are a couple of attractive parks at the northern end of the beach. This is also the start/finish point of the Coastal Bike Trail, and the site of an annual festival celebrating the (eating of) mambo fish, also known as sunfish, in June and July. The southern section of the beach borders Qixingtan Village, which has several cafés and homestays, and was also home to the Chihsingtan Katsuo Museum, housed in a Japanese era *katsuo* processing factory. *Katsuo* is a Japanese word for dried, fermented, smoked and sliced tuna, and the museum was the last relic of this huge industry, but sadly the entire building burnt down in 2017.

Qingxiu Temple

慶修院; qìngxiūyùan • 345-1 Zhongxing Rd, 1km off Zhongyang Rd, southwest of Hualien near Jian (吉安; jían) • Tues–Sun 8.30am–5pm • NT$30 • Buses #303, #1131 & #1139 from Hualien train station

Qingxiu Temple is Taiwan's best-preserved and most beautiful Japanese Buddhist temple, and is tangible evidence of the strong Japanese presence here before World War II. It was built in 1917 to serve as the spiritual centre for immigrants from Kyushu, mostly poor farmers who were relocated as part of a controversial government scheme begun in 1909. Derelict for many years, the complex was skilfully restored in 2003: the wooden Main Hall is surrounded by a garden containing 88 statues, representing the equivalent number of "distresses" in human life and recalling Kyushu's 88 Shingon temples.

ARRIVAL AND DEPARTURE   **HUALIEN**

BY PLANE

Hualien Airport (花蓮機場; huālián jīchǎng) is 6km north of the city. As well as a limited selection of domestic destinations, Hualien is now also served by one

daily flight to and from Hong Kong with budget carrier Hong Kong Express (ⓦ hkexpress.com). There's an airport bus into downtown (via the *Astar* and *Parkview* hotels; 14 daily; 20min), while tour buses to Taroko also stop here twice a day. A taxi into the city costs around NT$250.

Destinations Hong Kong (1 daily; 1hr 50min); Kaohsiung (1 daily; 55min); Taichung (3 daily; 50min); Taipei (3–4 daily; 50min).

BY TRAIN

Hualien Train Station (花蓮火車站; huālián huǒchēzhàn) is a major stop on the Eastern Line, with regular express train services. The station is just over 2km northwest of downtown, with regular buses there. You can also hire bikes with panniers at the Giant shop outside the station.

Destinations Fulong (13 express daily; 1hr 25min–2hr 40min); Guangfu (19 daily; 30min–1hr); Luodong (44 express daily; 50min–1hr 40min); Ruisui (24 daily; 35min–1hr 40min); Taipei (47 express daily; 2hr–4hr 10min); Taitung (25 express daily; 1hr 30min–4hr); Yilan (43 express daily; 55min–1hr 45min); Zhiben (9 express daily; 1hr 40min–3hr 20min).

BY BUS

Hualien Bus Company runs one bus daily south to Taitung at 9.30am, while Dingdong has a service at 1.10pm. Both buses go via Baxiandong, Chenggong, Duli, Donghe and Dulan. Six other buses only go as far as Chenggong, while others travel through the Rift Valley and terminate at

Guangfu or Fuli (via Ruisui, Yuli and Antong); at any of these towns you can pick up onward buses to Taitung. Hualien Bus also has regular services northwest to Taroko Gorge between 6.30am and 3pm: buses stop at Xincheng Railway Station and at numerous points on the way to Tianxiang. Buses to Chongde (崇德; chóngdé) travel a short way along the coast road north, but the best way to go further to view the Qingshui Cliffs is to drive yourself or take a tour. Heading west, there's just one bus to Lishan (梨山; líshān) daily at 8.40am via Luoshao and Dayuling (大禹嶺; dàyǔlǐng), plus an extra service to Luoshao at 6.30am.

BUS STATIONS

Hualien has three principal bus stations: Hualien Bus Company services stop just outside the train station; Dingdong Bus Company has a stop a few shops down from the train station visitor centre; and some Hualien Bus Company services terminate in the smaller downtown bus station ("Old" or "Main" station) at the end of Zhongshan Rd. Taiwan tourist shuttle buses for Taroko also leave from outside the train station.

Destinations Baxiandong (10 daily; 2hr); Chenggong (10 daily; 2hr 45min); Dayuling (1 daily; 3hr 15min); Guangfu (frequent; 1hr 30min); Lishan (1 daily; 3hr 15min); Luoshao (2 daily; 2hr); Ruisui (hourly; 2hr); Taitung (2 daily; 4hr); Tianxiang (13 daily; 1hr 30min).

GETTING AROUND   HUALIEN

Hualien's downtown area is easily navigable on foot, but to get to outlying attractions – or between the train and bus stations and downtown – you'll need to either catch one of the many taxis, try the limited bus service, or rent a scooter, car or bike.

BY CAR AND SCOOTER

A good option is to take the train to Hualien and then hire a vehicle to explore Taroko, the East Rift Valley and East Coast – this gives you plenty of flexibility and the chance to get away from the crowds. There are several car and scooter rental outfits near the train station. Scooters generally cost NT$400/24hr, with cheaper rates for longer hire, while cars can be rented at discounted rates from NT$1700/day. Outlets generally open 8am–8pm, and you'll need an international licence and your passport.

CAR RENTAL

ChaiLease 41, Guolian 1st Rd ☎03 833 2755, ⊚rentalcar.com.tw.

Hotai Leasing 和運租車; héyùn zūchē 69 Guolian 1st Rd ☎03 831 5500, ⊚easyrent.com.tw.

IWS 138 Guolian 1st St ☎038 338 811, ⊚iws.com.tw.

SCOOTER RENTAL

Pony Rent-A-Car Group 小馬租車集團; xiǎomǎ zūchē jítuán) 21 Guolian 4th Rd ☎03 835 4888.

BY BIKE

The coastal plain around Hualien is mainly flat, making cycling a great way to get around, especially given the number of bike trails in the area. The Coastal Bike Trail runs from Nanbin Park in the south to Qixingtan Beach in the north (15.8km), and is a pleasant way to travel between the two places. If you'd prefer not to have to carry your luggage (or find your way around) you can join a bike tour (see box, p.308).

BIKE RENTAL

Giant 35 Guoxing First Street ☎038 336 761. Just across from the train station, Giant offers a variety of models. Prices start from NT$300/day for regular bikes, and NT$1200–1500 to hire a touring bike with panniers for three days.

BY TAXI

Taxis around the train station will offer to drive you on a short round-trip tour of Taroko Gorge: expect to pay NT$2000–2500 for a half day, NT$3000–4000 for a full day. One-way fares as far as Tianxiang are usually NT$1200. For journeys in the city, flagfall is NT$100.

5

INFORMATION AND TOURS

Tourist information The visitor centre (旅遊服務中心; lǚyóu fúwù zhōngxīn; daily 8am–8pm; ☎ 03 836 0634, ⓦtour-hualien.hl.gov.tw) in front of the train station is well stocked with English-language material and has helpful English-speakers. There is also a tourist office at the airport (daily 8am–6pm; ☎ 03 821 0625).

Tours Numerous small operators have set up in Hualien to cater for the growing outdoors market. Standard package-style tours of the East Coast, Taroko National Park and the East Rift Valley are provided by Merry Travel Service (8 Fuyang Rd; ☎03 846 6898), while more grassroots experiences are presented by foreign-owned companies such as Bamboo Trails, based in Chenggong (134 Qilin Rd; ☎089 851 835, ⓦbambootrails.com) and Hualien newcomer Island Life (☎0978 045 868, ⓦislandlifetaiwan.com).

ACTIVITIES

Kayaking, river tracing and rafting Ocean kayaking below the towering Qingshui Cliffs or on beautiful Liyu Lake, river tracing idyllic mountain streams and rafting trips down the Xiuguluan River (see box, p.316) are all highlights of the outdoor activities in Hualien's surrounding hinterlands – all best enjoyed in summer. Hualien Outdoors (☎0989 512 380, ⓦhualienoutdoors.org) organizes safe, professional adventure activities throughout the region

(minimum two people).

Whale-watching Summer is the season for whale-watching tours; Huadong (花東鯨世界; huādōng jīng shìjiè; ☎03 823 8000, ⓦhuadong.com.tw) is the main operator (April–Oct 5 daily 6am–3.30pm), but the visitor centre and many hotels can also offer information and bookings.

ACCOMMODATION

TRAIN STATION AREA

Charming City Hotel 花蓮香城大飯店; huālián xiāngchéng dàfàndiàn 19 Guoshing 2nd St ☎03 835 3355, ⓦwww.city-hotel.com.tw. Hualien's first boutique hotel remains a solid choice, with good service, stylish rooms and a blend of contemporary Asian and Art Deco themes. NT$1800

Wow Hostel 洄瀾窩青年旅舍; huílán wō qīngnián lǚshě 83 Goulian 1st Rd ☎03 833 0186, ⓦhualienwow.com. This new hostel is in a great location opposite the train station. The friendly owners encourage guests to mingle, and there's a huge choice of room types across the nine floors, including doubles and mixed dorms with – a little unexpectedly – just two beds in them. Breakfast is included, and snacks and drinks are available in the kitchen on an honesty payment system. There's also a café-bar downstairs, and you can book tours in English. Dorms NT$650, doubles NT$1799

DOWNTOWN

Azure Hotel 藍天麗池飯店; lántiān lìchí fàndiàn 590 Zhongzheng Rd ☎03 833 6686, ⓦazurehotel.com.tw. Elegant hotel, popular with well-heeled tourists. The compact rooms are stylishly furnished and have marble-clad bathrooms and great views of the city from the large French windows. NT$2390

Journey Backpacker 好室窩; hǎo shì wō 147 Fuguo ☎03 856 7010, ⓔjourneyhostel2013@gmail.com. A 10min walk behind the train station, this welcoming hostel is popular with backpackers from around the globe, while the laid-back bar attracts local expats. As well as beds in the two mixed dorms, there are a few private rooms. Dorms NT$400, doubles NT$1100

★**Just Sleep** 捷絲旅; jié sī lǚ 396 Zhongzheng Rd ☎03 890 0069, ⓦjustsleep.com.tw. Opened in 2014, this excellent chain hotel offers high-end comfort in a great central location and at surprisingly affordable prices. Rooms are sleek and modern, washing machines are available for free, and there's a library and vegetarian restaurant on site. NT$3400

NORTH OF THE MEILUN RIVER

Ola Hotel 洄瀾客棧; huílán kèzhàn 11 Haian Rd ☎03 822 7188, ⓦola.com.tw. Bright hotel overlooking a palm-fringed section of the seafront, though views of the ocean are obstructed somewhat by the cement-loading port in front. There's indigenous art in the lobby, plus a café, and free bikes for use on the nearby Coastal Bike Trail. NT$2100

Parkview Hotel 美侖大飯店; měilún dàfàndiàn 1–1 Linyuan ☎03 822 2111, ⓦparkview-hotel.com. Hualien's top luxury hotel, with a large pool, a spa, lavish buffets and landscaped gardens. There's a free shuttle bus from the airport, but otherwise it's a trek from downtown. NT$3200

ELSEWHERE

Cypress House 檜木居; guìmù jū 58 Cihui 1st St, Ji'an ☎03 854 6535, ⓦcypresshouse.com.tw. Reflecting the fact that the owners' main business is a cypress wood factory, the interior of this lovely property is almost entirely constructed of Taiwanese cypress; the whole place smells fantastic. There are free bikes, a spa (NT$1680) and a pleasant garden. The only downside is the location, which, while convenient for Cihui and Shengan temples, is quite a way from downtown. NT$2600

EATING

Hualien is known throughout Taiwan for máshŭ – cakes made of sticky, glutinous rice or millet, and stuffed with sweet fillings – and biǎnshí, a type of wonton or dumplings in soup, filled with pork and shrimp. Hualien's **Dongdamen Nightmarket** (東大門夜市; dōngdàmén yèshì) has been gentrified in recent years, but remains a great place for cheap eats, and occupies a full city block at the southern end of Zhongshan Rd. As well as all of the usual offerings, the night market also has a good selection of indigenous snacks and organic produce.

DOWNTOWN

Chen's Taste 陳記狀元粥舖; chénjì zhuàngyuán zhōupù 10 Xuanyuan Rd ☎03 833 3864. A congee specialist, housed in a gorgeous old Japanese-era wooden house with a tranquil dining room at the back. Various congees (chicken, fish, pork, vegetables) from NT$80, as well as smaller Cantonese snacks and teas. Daily 11am–9pm.

Dos Tacos 92 Fuxing St ☎03 831 1733. Expat favourite serving Hualien's best (and only) Mexican dishes. Famous for its tacos (NT$235–325), but also serves a host of other Mexican favourites including fajitas, nachos and quesadillas. Food is served until 9pm, but Dos Tacos is also a popular watering hole, offering a range of beers and cocktails. Tues–Sun 11am–2pm & 6–10.30pm.

★**Farmer's Kitchen** 有機蔬食; yǒujī shūshí 407 Zhongshan Rd ☎03 833 2810. Owned by a Malaysian woman, this fantastic farm-to-table vegetarian restaurant offers delicious organic Taiwanese and Western dishes in a pleasant setting. The farmer's breakfast (NT$168) makes for a hearty start to the day, whilst the eggplant-meatball linguine in marinara sauce (NT$168) is an enjoyable, healthy lunch or dinner. They also have sandwiches and fresh organic farm veggies for sale. Tues–Sun 8am–2pm & 5.30–8.30pm

★**Gong Zheng Steamed Buns** 公正包子店; gōngzhèng bāozi diàn 199–2 Zhongshan Rd ☎03 834 2933. Justly famous pork bun (bāozi) and dumpling place, with steamers piled high on tables and staff lined up making pork dumplings with super-human speed (NT$50 for ten). Expect long queues at meal times. Daily 6am–8pm.

Laicheng Rib Noodles 來成排骨麵; láichéng páigŭmiàn 544 Zhongzheng Rd ☎03 8323 121. No-fuss diner serving delicious bowls of noodles with a fried pork chop in soup, topped with green onions and leek (NT$60). Daily except Tues 10.30am–9.30pm.

Madina 瑪丁娜; mǎdīngnà 482 Heping Rd ☎03 833 4921. Quality Indian restaurant, with food prepared by the Pakistani owner and chef. The menu features classic Indian dishes including butter chicken (NT$200), a range of kormas and Indian breads. Daily 11am–2pm & 5–9pm.

Mrs Jiang's Beef Noodles 江太太牛肉麵店; jiāng tàitài niúròumiàn diàn 128 Zhongzheng Rd ☎03 832 0838. Made famous by visits of late president Chiang Ching-kuo, this traditional place with wooden tables

cooks up big bowls of sumptuous beef noodles (NT$130); the soup is spicy and delicious, though the meat might be a little fatty for some. Thurs–Tues 11am–2pm & 5–8.30pm.

Salt Lick 火車頭; huǒchē tóu 147 Zhongshan Rd ☎03 833 2592, ⊛lickbbq.com. An inviting place offering authentic American BBQ dishes cooked in a custom locomotive-shaped smoker by the American owners (who also operate Chicago, a pizza joint next door). Mains include pulled pork sandwiches (NT$235) and Kansas baby back ribs (NT$475 half-rack). Sides include chilli cheese fries (NT$175), gumbo (NT$125) and mashed potato with gravy (NT$85). Daily 11.30am–2.30pm & 5–10pm.

★**Yi Xiang Bianshi** 液香扁食店; yìxiāng biǎnshí diàn 42 Xinyi St ☎03 832 6761. The most famous biǎnshí shop in Hualien was established more than seventy years ago. Bowls of the tasty dumplings get dished out automatically when you sit down (NT$70). Daily except Weds 10am–8.30pm.

Yixin Bubble Ice Store 一心泡泡冰; yīxīn pàopàobīng 66 Zhonghua Rd ☎03 834 6179. Popular bubble-ice store serving interesting flavours including chestnut milk and green melon milk (both NT$170). Look for the penguin logo. Daily 11am–10pm.

Zeng Ji 曾記; zēng jì 142 Zhongshan Rd ☎03 834 5252. With bright-yellow stores all over town, Zeng Ji is probably the most popular muaji brand in town. The cakes here (from NT$15/piece, NT$100/bag) are always fresh and best eaten within two days. Try the ones with peanut or sesame fillings. Daily 9am–9.30pm.

NORTH OF THE MEILUN RIVER

Roaster Café 吉光片羽; jíguāng piànyǔ 38 Mingde 1st St ☎03 832 3738. This atmospheric coffee shop is set in a century-old Japanese wooden building which originally served as a teachers' dormitory. The menu features coffees from around the globe (NT$120), rooibos tea (NT$80) and cookies. Tues–Fri 1–6pm, Sat & Sun 10am–6pm.

Zhong Yi Bean Jelly 中一豆花; zhōngyī dòuhuā 2 Minquan 5th St ☎03 834 3302. Popular local place not far from the Astar Hotel, specializing in dòuhuā, a tasty soybean dessert mixed with syrup and peanuts (NT$35). It's especially delicious with lemon juice in the summer. Daily 10am–11pm.

5

DRINKING AND NIGHTLIFE

Hualien's nightlife remains fairly subdued, but there are a few places which can get lively on weekends.

Route 193 Bistro 美式小館; měishì xiǎoguǎn 129 Renai St ☎03 831 1022. This friendly, low-lit bar and bistro is popular with backpackers and locals alike. There's an extensive cocktail list (from NT$200), plus occasional live music. Daily 6pm–1am.

The Moose Bar & Grill 麋鹿餐酒館; mílù cān

jiǔguǎn 18-2 Mingli Rd ☎03 833 2003. Canadian-owned bar and grill with a decent range of craft beers (including Hualien Draft Beer NT$120), whiskeys (NT$100–900) and great steaks for when you get hungry. Food is served till 9pm. Daily 11.30am–2pm & 5.30–11pm.

DIRECTORY

Banks There are plenty of banks in Hualien; most 7-Elevens have Chinatrust ATMs inside.

Hospital The best-regarded hospital in Hualien is Tzu Chi Hospital (70 Zhongyang Rd, Sec 3; Mon–Fri 9am–noon and 2–5pm, Sat 9am–noon; ☎03 856 1825, ⓦapp.tzuchi.com.tw). Another option is Hualien Hospital (600 Zhongzheng Rd, near the *Azure Hotel*;

☎03 835 8141) which has walk-in clinics Mon–Fri 8.30am–noon.

Internet Most hotels offer free internet access: if you need to get online elsewhere, try Internet Hacker Network (24hr; NT$30/hr) at 439 Fujian Rd.

Post The main post office is at 408 Zhongshan Rd (Mon–Fri 8.30am–7pm, Sat 9am–noon).

Taroko National Park

太魯閣國家公園; tàilǔgé guójiā gōngyuán • ⓦtaroko.gov.tw

Framed by sheer ocean cliffs and majestic inland mountain peaks, **TAROKO NATIONAL PARK** is Taiwan's most diverse national park and one of the island's top tourist destinations. The narrow **Taroko Gorge** (太魯閣峽谷; tàilǔgé xiágǔ) is the main attraction for good reason: stretching some 20km, with marble walls that soar several hundred metres above the **Liwu River** (立霧溪; lìwù xī), the canyon offers some of Taiwan's most awe-inspiring scenery, from crystal-clear waterfalls to marble-cake cliffs. Most tour buses whip through Taroko Gorge to **Tianxiang** (the best place to stay and eat), briefly stopping at the main sights along **Provincial Highway 8** before speeding back to Hualien. But to really appreciate the national park you need to get **hiking**. Alongside the winding road through the canyon are several easy **trails**, providing superb vantage points for some of the most spectacular features and giving a greater sense of scale. Though the gorge is Taroko's claim to fame, it is only a small part of the park, which contains some of Taiwan's most challenging mountain climbs, including rugged **Qilai Ridge** and the revered **Nanhushan**. Another of the park's finest attractions are the **Qingshui Cliffs**, which plummet dramatically into the Pacific Ocean along the park's northeastern boundary and are accessible only by Highway 9 (the Suao–Hualien Highway).

The park is named after the **Truku (Taroko) indigenous tribe** (see p.403). The Truku, traditionally known for their hunting prowess and weaving skills, once populated many river valleys within the park's current boundaries, but few remain today. Most of those still living inside the park are located in Buluowan and the Bamboo Village.

Qingshui Cliffs

清水斷崖; qīngshuǐ duànyái • There are no buses between Suao and Hualien: rent a car or scooter in Hualien (1hr) or Xincheng (20min); the car park past the Km176 marker of the Suao–Hualien Highway (at the entrance of the Chongde Tunnel), has some of the best views of the cliffs; a hiking trail leads down to the shingle beach

The staggering **Qingshui Cliffs** are among the east coast's most awe-inspiring attractions. Spanning a 21km section of the coastline between the hamlets of Chongde (崇德; chóngdé) and Heren (和仁; hérén), these sheer cliffs plunge straight into the turquoise waters of the Pacific Ocean – from heights of almost a thousand metres at their tallest. The series of long **tunnels** carved straight through the cliffs is an engineering marvel, with each tunnel opening up to another invigorating view of more bluffs and sea. Note that the coastal highway has heavy traffic, with endless convoys of trucks that make it a hair-raising journey for motorcyclists and motorists alike: cycling is definitely not advised and it's wise to leave early in the morning so you can make the return trip before the traffic starts to pick up around 9am.

Buluowan

布洛灣; bùluòwān • 2km off Highway 8, 1.5km before Swallow Grotto, and accessed via a steep, curvy road; the Hualien bus runs twice a day to Buluowan (1hr 20min), and Taiwan Tour Bus operates nine buses daily (1hr); all services depart from Hualien train station

Once a cradle of Truku civilization, **BULUOWAN** is now a tiny tourist village devoted primarily to the preservation (and selling) of the tribe's **traditional arts**. The small community of Truku here makes a living producing handmade crafts, which are on display in the **Taroko Handicrafts Exhibition Room** (太魯閣手工藝展覽室; tàilǔgé shǒugōngyì zhǎnlǎnshì; daily 9am–4.30pm, closed first and third Mon of the month). This is a good place to see demonstrations of traditional loom, bamboo and rattan basket weaving. Buluowan also has an upscale accommodation option (see p.306).

Tianxiang

天祥; tiānxiáng • 19km west of the visitor centre • Served by frequent buses from Hualien and other stops within the park, and one daily bus from Lishan in the other direction

The tiny tourist village of **TIANXIANG** somehow manages to accommodate most of the overnight visitors to Taroko National Park while remaining remarkably free of tacky overdevelopment. There is little to do in Tianxiang itself, but it makes a convenient base for exploring the park's main trails. Everything is within easy walking distance of the **bus stop** – as well as the collection of small restaurants (which close at 6 or 7pm) on the edge of *Silks* car park, Tianxiang now has a 7-Eleven next to the post office.

Xiangde Temple

祥德寺; xiángdé sì • Near Tianxiang's eastern entrance • Daily 8am–5pm

On a hillside reached by the **Pudu Bridge** (普渡橋; pǔdù qiáo), **Xiangde Temple** is a Buddhist place of worship run by a handful of resident monks. Near the temple is a giant whitewashed statue of Guanyin and a graceful **pagoda** that visitors can climb for fine views of the surrounding valley.

Hiking trails in Taroko National Park

Most of the trails listed here can be reached by the bus from Hualien (ask the driver to stop in advance), and the trails west of Tianxiang can only be reached by once-daily Lishan buses or private transport; however, without your own vehicle you'll have to find onward transport once you've finished the hike – taxis congregate in certain places (Changchun Shrine, Shakadang Trail, Tianxiang), but you can't count on them, and in their absence, you'll either have to walk, hitch or wait for the next public bus

While the drive through Taroko Gorge is astounding, to experience it at its best you need to explore it on foot. There are at least half a dozen well-marked **trails** in the gorge itself, and countless more within the national park. Many of the most popular trails in the gorge are short and relatively flat, but even these are worthwhile, particularly if you aim for early morning or late afternoon when the bulk of visitors have left. Those looking for more of a challenge will be rewarded by the park's more extreme trails, notably the **Zhuilu Old Trail**, the **Dali-Datong Trail**, and further to the west, the mountain ascents of **Qilaishan** and **Nanhushan**, all of which require permits (see p.305).

Heavy seasonal rains and the resulting **landslips** result in frequent closures, and you should check online and with the visitor centre near the main entrance before heading out. The trails below are listed from east to west – the order in which you'll approach them if coming from the coast.

5

Shakadang Trail

砂卡礑步道; shākǎdàng bùdào • To reach the trailhead, walk west from the park headquarters, through the tunnel with a pedestrian walkway (870m) and descend the stairs on the right to the river's edge • Served by buses from Hualien (1hr 5min)

One of Taroko's easiest walks, the mostly flat **Shakadang Trail** hugs the bank of the bubbling Shakadang River, filled with translucent pools and time-worn boulders,

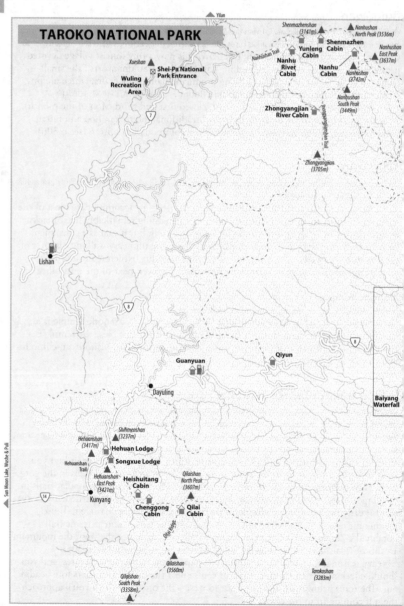

TAROKO NATIONAL PARK

and can get very busy, although numbers dwindle the further you get from the bridge. The path sticks to the river for 4.4km, passing a small Truku village at 1.5km that has been all but abandoned, although vendors selling sausages and bird's nest fern (an indigenous staple food) set up here in the daytime. The trail was officially closed from the 1.5km mark at the time of writing but once it reopens you can continue to the 4.4km point. Allow about three hours for the entire round trip.

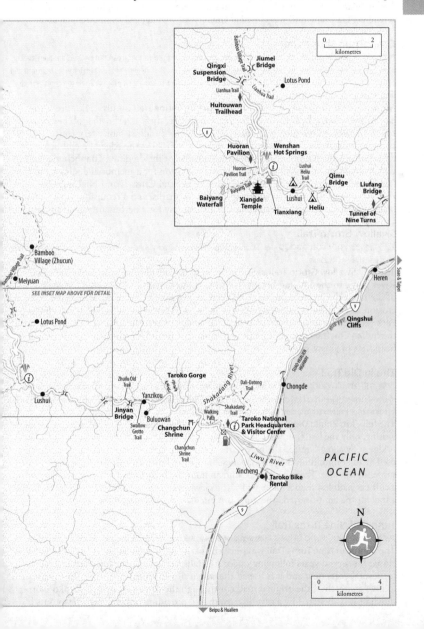

Dali-Datong Trail

大禮大同步道; dàlǐ dàtóng bùdào • Mountain Entry Permit required, obtainable from the police station next to the Taroko Visitor Center (with ID) • Trail can be broken overnight at Datong; Taroko Visitor Center can arrange accommodation and guides

After the Shakadang Trail's 4.4km point, you are technically on the **Dali-Datong Trail**, which leads to a pair of far-flung Truku villages and requires a permit. From this point the Dali-Datong climbs steeply, with many switchbacks, before reaching the dwindling Truku village of Datong, where you can stay overnight before looping back to the visitor centre via Dali. The trail was closed at the time of writing, but should reopen soon.

Changchun Shrine Trail

長春祠步道; chāngchūn cí bùdào • There are two possible starting points: the car park that overlooks the shrine itself, or from Highway 8 about 2.3km from the Taroko visitor centre; from the centre, the trail starts under an arch to the left of the main road, and if you go in this direction there is slightly less climbing involved; if you start your hike from the car park, you'll have to ascend the steep steps behind the shrine to complete the loop

More a scenic stroll than a hike, the **Changchun Shrine Trail** is only 1.4km from one end to the other. After crossing a suspension bridge, there is a short climb before you reach the ageing **Changuang Temple**, a Chan (Zen) Buddhist monastery with commanding views of the river. From here, the trail skirts the edge of a cliff before descending a steep flight of stone steps to the rear of the dignified **Changchun Shrine**, which straddles an elegant cascade – a fitting location for a memorial dedicated to the 226 workers who perished while building the Central Cross-Island Highway. The shrine is one of the park's most recognizable landmarks, and a requisite stop for all tour buses, whose passengers pile out throughout the day for a perfunctory photo shoot.

Swallow Grotto Trail

燕子口步道; yànzikǒu bùdào • The "Yanzihkou" stop – 1.4km inland along Highway 8 from the Buluowan turn-off • Served by buses from Hualien (1hr 25min)

The tiny **Swallow Grotto Trail** runs for 480m along the old roadway above the Liwu River gorge to the Jinheng Bridge. It's an easy but dramatic stroll along the steep sides of the river; the grottoes on the cliff face that give the trail its name are created by erosion as the groundwater seeps out of the rock. There's a small snack bar at **Jinheng Park** (靳珩公園; jìnhéng gōngyuán) near the bridge, where there's also a viewing point of the **Indian Chieftain's Rock** (a hunk of marble that resembles a human profile with a headdress of grassy vines).

Zhuilu Old Trail

錐麓古道; zhuīlù gǔdào • Mountain entry and National Park permits are required; hikers must list a Taiwanese national as an emergency contact (they will call and check) and pay a trail fee of NT$200/adult at the Zhuilu Old Road Toll Station, opposite the turnoff for Buluowan on Highway 8; hiking must commence between 7am and 10am

The full 7km **Zhuilu Old Trail** is part of the famed Hehuanshan Old Trail, but at the time of writing, only the last 3km was open, a route which begins at the vertiginous suspension bridge at Swallow Grotto. The hike starts with a steep thirty-minute climb, passing a cave used as an ammunition cache by Japanese troops, and then crosses the Badagang suspension bridge. From here it's around an hour to **Zhuilu Cliff**, a 500m traverse across on a cliff-cut path less than a metre wide. The views from here are astounding, but this is not a trail for the faint-hearted. The route isn't circular, so you descend the same way.

Tunnel of Nine Turns Trail

九曲洞步道; jiǔqūdòng bùdào • 4km west along Highway 8 from Swallow Grotto, on the left-hand side of the road

The **Tunnel of Nine Turns Trail** was once the park's most popular short **trail**, but has been closed for several years following major rockfalls; reconstruction has been in progress for several years now and it is hoped that the trail will reopen in 2018. The 1.9km path follows a stretch of the original road cut through the narrowest part of Taroko Gorge; much of it is sheltered by a cave-like overhang, providing unparalleled viewpoints of the smoothly **sculpted marble** with its ornate patterns and the precipitous canyon walls. The path can easily be walked in thirty minutes.

Lushui–Heliu Trail

綠水合流步道; lǜshuǐ héliú bùdào • Can be started from either Lushui or Heliu (2km from Tianxiang), both served by the Hualien bus

The mostly flat **Lushui–Heliu Trail** runs for 2km above a cliff overlooking the highway, offering clear views of the Liwu River; it takes thirty to forty minutes to complete. Just outside Lushui the trail winds through the remnants of an old **camphor forest**, with some ageing specimens of this valuable tree visible from the path. Both Heliu and Lushui have free public **campsites** (see p.306); Lushui also has a snack bar (daily 8.30am–5pm) where you can stock up on basic (overpriced) provisions.

Baiyang Waterfall Trail

白楊瀑布步道; báiyáng pùbù bùdào • To reach the trailhead, walk west along the main road from Tianxiang for 850m until you see a long tunnel on the left

A beautiful **trail** leads to the **Baiyang Waterfall**, which turns into a raging torrent during periods of heavy rain. At the time of writing, this trail was currently only open for the first kilometre: walk through the tunnel (380m; watch out for bats) and if it is open, carry on for another 2km, through a few shorter tunnels, to reach the waterfall – it's worth bringing a head-torch if you can. Cross the bridge leading to the **wooden platform** for direct views of the falls. Beyond here, the trail enters the **Shuiliandong** or Water Curtain Tunnels, so named because water drips from their roofs. The 921 Earthquake dangerously weakened the rocks around this tunnel, and the trail ends abruptly shortly after entering. From Tianxiang to the falls and back takes about two hours.

Wenshan Hot Spring Trail

文山溫泉步道; wénshān wēnquán bùdào • The springs are just off the main highway about 2.5km west of Tianxiang, on the right-hand side

Situated in the middle of the Dasha River, **Wenshan Hot Springs** is a magical spot offering the chance to bathe in soothing hot springs next to the river as you gaze up at the gorge. However, the short but steep trail down to the river is often closed due to hazardous conditions – ask at the visitor centre before heading up here.

Lianhua Trail

蓮花池步道; liánhuāchí bùdào • The Huitouwan Trailhead (迴頭灣登山口; huítóuwān dēngshānkǒu) marks the beginning of the Lianhua Trail, located by a hairpin bend behind the bus stop at Km163.4 on Highway 8, 5km west of Tianxiang

The **Lianhua Trail** is a little harder to reach than the others in the area, but is certainly worth the effort, although you should check its status with the visitor centre, as it was closed at the time of writing. You can walk to the **Huitouwan Trailhead** along the main highway from Tianxiang, but you'll have to pass through a handful of dark tunnels, so a torch is essential. The trail is exciting from the onset, as the beginning has been cut into the rocky face of a towering cliff overlooking the Dasha River, and there are sheer drop-offs all along this stretch. Carry on for about 1km, cross the **Qingxi Suspension Bridge** (清溪吊橋; qīngxī diàoqiáo; after 400m) and continue until you reach the **Jiumei Suspension Bridge** (九梅吊橋; jiǔméi diàoqiáo). Cross this bridge, turn right and start the steep ascent up the dirt path, where the earth has been secured by wooden planks embedded into the ground. The trail then follows a winding, grassy road up the hill for several hundred metres before flattening out for the final stretch to the Lotus Pond, which is covered in green algae – the walk is mainly notable for the **lush forests** along the way. From the Jiumei Bridge it's about a 7.4km (3hr) round-trip to the pond, so allow ample time to complete the return journey and still walk the 5km stretch of road back into Tianxiang before it gets dark. From the Jiumei Bridge it's also possible to hike along the river to the tiny

5

farming communities at Meiyuan (梅園; méiyuán or Plum Orchard) and Zhucun (竹村; zhúcūn or Bamboo Village) on the Meiyuan Trail (梅園步道; méiyuán bùdào), a 12.4km round-trip that will take between seven and eight hours.

Qilaishan

奇萊山; qíláishān · Trailhead is just inside Taroko National Park's southwestern entrance, on the road to Puli (Provincial Highway 14A), near Hehuanshan (合歡山; héhuānshān) · Mountain Entry and National Park permits required

The jagged saw-tooth protrusion known as **Qilaishan** is one of Taroko's most striking features and one of Taiwan's most challenging climbs. Narrow, craggy **Qilai Ridge** connects the main summit to several outstanding peaks, with steep drops on both sides, making it an exhilarating and sometimes dangerous climb. While the trail that runs over the ridgeline is well marked and in good condition, with no serious technical sections requiring the use of ropes, several climbers have fallen to their deaths over the years after losing their footing in thick mists, while typhoon-force winds have actually blown a few people off. In light of these risks, park officials are conservative in issuing the **permits** required to climb legally in this area, and the best strategy is to join a group (see opposite).

The main **trailhead** is near the **Hehuan Lodge** (合歡山莊; héhuān shānzhuāng; ☎049 280 2732), which offers information but does not provide accommodation. Instead, you can stay at **Huaxue Lodge** or the pricier **Songxue Lodge** (see p.214). Along the trail there are several **cabins** and most groups try to make it to the **Qilai Cabin** (奇萊山屋; qílái shānwū) for the first night so they can get an early start on the ridge and **Qilai North Peak** (奇萊被峰; qílái bèifēng), the highest on Qilaishan at 3607m. After negotiating the ridge, the majority of climbers return to *Qilai Cabin* for a second night before descending to the road on the third day. The safest time to climb here is in late **autumn**, when the summer typhoons have ceased and the weather is drier and less windy.

Nanhushan

南湖山; nánhúshān · Nanhushan can be reached from the north or south; north is more common as it begins closer to the peaks, via a trailhead just off Provincial Highway 7 between Yilan and Lishan · Mountain Entry and National Park permits required

Tucked away in Taroko's remote northwest corner is **Nanhushan**, Taiwan's fifth-tallest peak at 3742m and a favourite of Taiwanese climbers. Despite its reputation, it's very seldom scaled due to its isolation and inherent technical difficulties, although seasoned climbers are unlikely to find it overly challenging. As with the Qilai Ridge, the biggest obstacle here is the **harsh weather**, as Nanhushan is pelted with strong winds, rain or snow for an average of about two hundred days a year, making some key sections of the trail arduous. Winter is a popular time to climb Nanhushan, although only for experienced climbers; at the bare minimum, **crampons** are essential for the higher regions. Park officials are extremely cautious about issuing **permits** for Nanhushan, and as with Qilaishan, you are better off joining a group.

ARRIVAL AND DEPARTURE · TAROKO NATIONAL PARK

By bus Tianxiang is served by buses from Hualien (13 daily, 6.30am–3pm) and from Lishan (梨山; líshān) in the west (1 daily at 3pm, 3hr, continues to Hualien). There is a daily bus between Puli and Lishan (3hr 30min), but it's difficult to arrange onward transport in either direction. Though Hualien–Chongde (崇德; chóngdé) buses do travel a short way along the coast road to the north, the best way to see the Qingshui Cliffs is with your own transport or on a tour.

Destinations (from Tianxiang) Dayuling (1 daily at 10.20am; 1hr 35min); Hualien (13 daily; last bus 6pm; 1hr 30min); Lishan (1 daily at 10.20am; 2hr 35min); Luoshao (2 daily at 8am & 10.20am; 30min); Xincheng (13 daily; 30–40min).

By train Xincheng is the closest station to Taroko Gorge, and is served by train from Taipei (10 daily; 2hr–3hr 30min). Taxis congregate at the station and most of the Hualien–Taroko buses stop here.

GETTING AROUND

While Taroko National Park can easily be entered and traversed by public buses, to cross the park you'll need to plan your onward route carefully to ensure you make your connections. If you're relying on **public transport** it's definitely worth going to the visitor centre for maps and a bus timetable. For maximum flexibility, renting a **car**, **scooter** or **bike** in Hualien is recommended.

By bus The Hualien buses are the only public transport. From Hualien, stops include: Xincheng Railway Station (50min); Taroko Arch and the Visitor Centre (1hr); Shakadang Trail (1hr 5min); Buluowan (1hr 20min); Swallow Grotto (1hr 25min); and Lushui (1hr 25min) before arriving at Tianxiang (1hr 30min). Note that most buses don't stop at Buluowan.

By bike Cycling is a great way to explore the gorge, although you should stick to early mornings and late afternoons to avoid the worst of the traffic, wear a helmet, and be wary of rockfalls following heavy rain. If you don't have too much luggage it's fairly simple to ride up from Hualien into Taroko (see p.295), or alternatively you can rent bikes for NT$250/day from the bike shop at Xincheng (left out of the station; daily 7am–8pm; ☎03 861 0215). Silks Place in Tianxiang also rents bikes to guests ($150 for the first hour, then NT$100/hr).

INFORMATION

Park headquarters The Taroko National Park Headquarters and Visitor Center (太魯閣國家公園遊客中心; tàilǔgé guójiā gōngyuán yóukè zhōngxīn; daily 8.30am–4.45pm, closed second Mon and Lunar New Year's Eve; ☎03 862 1100, ⍾www.taroko.gov.tw) are located on the north side of the Liwu River, just across the bridge from Taroko Arch. All public buses stop here. Allow 45min by scooter or car from Hualien train station. As well as providing maps, leaflets, trail and transport advice, the centre can help to arrange guides and hiking permit applications. There are also a series of exhibition rooms detailing the geologic and cultural history of the region, plus a café and souvenir shop where you can buy English books on the park.

Visitor centres The Park has other visitor centres, though none as useful as the Headquarters. Buluowan Visitor Center (布洛灣遊客中心; bùluòwān yóukè zhōngxīn; daily 9am–4.30pm, closed second Mon of each month & Lunar New Year's Eve; ☎03 861 2528) has some interesting displays on traditional Taroko life. Tianxiang's Visitor Center (天祥遊客中心; tiānxiáng yóukè zhōngxīn; same opening hours as Buluowan Visitor Center; ☎03 861 2528) is seldom staffed with English-speakers.

Services Aside from the park headquarters and a few overpriced cafés within the gorge, there's little in the way of provisions in Taroko: best to stock up in Hualien, or at the 7-Eleven in Xincheng. There's a post office in Tianxiang, directly across the road from the bus stop (Mon–Fri 8.30am–noon & 1–3.30pm), which can handle international parcels. It has an ATM, but it doesn't accept foreign cards. Next door there's a new 7-Eleven, but it closes at 9pm, and often runs low on stock by the end of the day.

ACCOMMODATION

Most park accommodation is located in **Tianxiang**, but hotels tend to fill up quickly at weekends, public holidays or during the summer high season; be sure to book a room in advance. There are a few other options in and around the gorge, as well as a couple of camping grounds, provided you have your own tent.

TIANXIANG

Silks Place Taroko 太魯閣晶英酒店; tàilǔgé jīngyīng jiǔdiàn 18 Tianxiang ☎03 869 1155, ⍾www.silksplace-taroko.com.tw. The park's only five-star hotel, with spacious rooms, marble bathrooms, a gorgeous pool, spa, bar, nightly show and two pricey restaurants. The Gorge View ($11000) rooms are definitely worth the extra cash. NT$8000

Tianxiang Catholic Inn 天祥天主堂來賓宿舍; tiānxiáng tiānzhǔtáng láibīn sùshè 33 Tianxiang ☎03 869 1122. Taroko's only budget option, with clean fan and a/c (NT$1100) doubles – some with balconies overlooking the valley – and no-frills dorm beds, some with a/c. No breakfast. Dorms NT$300, doubles NT$700

Tianxiang Youth Activity Center 天祥青年活動中心; tiānxiáng qīngnián huódòng zhōngxīn 30 Tianxiang ☎03 869 1111, ⍾tienhsiang.cyh.org.tw. A good-value option, perched on the hill at the village's western edge, just past the Catholic Inn. The centre has a wide range of rooms, including spotless four-bed dorms and a mix of small and larger, more comfortable twins and doubles, many with views (NT$3300). Room rates include a Chinese-style breakfast, and the restaurant also serves lunch and dinner. Inside the hotel complex is a souvenir shop, a snack bar serving decent coffee and a handy coin-operated washing machine and dryer. Dorms NT$1000, doubles NT$2400

ELSEWHERE IN THE NATIONAL PARK

★Crossing the Rainbow Bridge 走過虹橋; zǒuguò hóngqiáo 210 Neighbourhood 3, Chongde

5

☎ 03 862 1328, ⓦ www.teyra.com.tw. If you don't mind not being in the gorge itself, try this lovely Truku-owned homestay, a 5min drive east from Taroko Visitor Centre, which offers tastefully furnished, comfortable and well-equipped rooms at affordable prices. Set in an attractive garden with café and views across the bridge and down the river valley, the only downside is the proximity to busy Highway 9. Free bike use. NT$2500

Heliu Campsite 合流營地; héliú yíngdì ☎ 03 869 1359. Located at the end of the 2km Lushui–Heliu Trail, this normally tranquil site has calming views of the Liwu River. It is equipped with clean cold-water showers, toilets and elevated wooden platforms for tents. Buses from Hualien can drop you off here (or at its sister campsite at Lushui), but you must let the driver know in advance. Pitches NT$200

★**Leader Village Taroko** 立德布洛灣山月村; lìdé bùluòwān shānyuècūn 231–1 Fushi Village (Highway 8 Km180) ☎ 03 861 0111, ⓦ leaderhotel .com. A magnificent location, 8km from the park entrance and 2km off the main highway in the mountains, this is a great option with standalone cabins, simply but beautifully finished in wood, and stylish bathrooms. There's a fine restaurant on site and a nightly cultural show (both included in the price). NT$4800

Liwu Hostel 立霧青年旅舍; lìwù qīngnián lǚshě 242–2, Xiulin ☎ 03 861 0769, ⓦ liwuhostel.wixsite .com. Next door to the *Liwu Hotel* and sharing the same building, this small HI-affiliated hostel has comfy communal areas, tidy rooms and small four- and six-bed dorms. Rooms at the front of the building overlook the road, those at the back on higher floors look across the river. Dorms NT$450

Liwu Hotel 立霧客棧; lìwù kèzhàn 242–2, Xiulin ☎ 03 861 0660, ⓦ liwu.hoseo.tw. On the main road through the tiny village of Xiulin, just a few hundred metres from the entrance to the gorge, this small hotel has friendly management and clean, simple rooms with flat-screen TVs. NT$1400

Lushui Campsite 綠水營地; lùshuǐ yíngdì ☎ 03 869 1359. A sister campsite to the *Heliu*, at the other end of the Lushui–Heliu Trail, this place is a bit more primitive, but it is free. Its shielded location makes it even more serene, although it's only about 2km from Tianxiang. Free

EATING

Tianxiang is pretty much the only place to eat inside the gorge, with a clutch of mediocre, overpriced **Chinese restaurants** located next to the bus station. At lunchtime, you simply fill up your plate at the buffet and the staff will weigh it and charge you accordingly. At dinner, you can order from the English menus. If you're stuck, the 7-Eleven (daily 7am–9pm) next to the post office is handy for ready meals.

Silks Place Taroko 太魯閣晶英酒店; tàilǔgé jīngyīng jiǔdiàn 18 Tianxiang ☎ 03 869 1155, ⓦ silksplace-taroko.com.tw. Being a luxury hotel, the dining is sophisticated at *Silks Place*'s in-house restaurants: a mountainous Western-style buffet at the *Wellesley* (lunch NT$715, dinner NT$880), or Chinese food at *Mei Yuan*. Both are technically only open to outsiders for lunch (and afternoon tea at the *Wellesley*; 2.30–4.30pm), but you could ask about dinner and they might let you in. Daily: Mei Yuan & Wellesley noon–2.30pm & 5.30–9.30pm; Wellesley only also 2.30–4.30pm.

Tianxiang Youth Activity Center 天祥青年活動中心; tiānxiáng qīngnián huódòng zhōngxīn 30 Tianxiang ☎ 03 869 1111. In the main restaurant, three bland but nourishing meals are served up daily (NT$150 for breakfast, NT$200 for lunch, NT$250 for dinner); or the more convivial open-sided snack bar, which dispenses microwaved pasta and pizza meals, and considerably better coffee. Daily: restaurant 7–8.30am, noon–1.30pm & 6–7.30pm; snack bar 12.30–2pm & 6.30–9.30pm.

East Coast National Scenic Area

東部海岸國家風景區; dōngbù hǎiàn guójiā fēngjǐngqū

The **East Coast National Scenic Area**, prime indigenous territory is scattered with idyllic fishing villages, rice paddies, herds of water buffalo and some of the best **surf breaks** in Taiwan. Buses ply the highway, and you can visit the main spots on public transport, but to make the most of the area, and particularly to hop between the coast and the Rift Valley, you'll need your own transport. If you're visiting in late summer and hope to witness some of the many indigenous **festivals** held each July and August, private transport is essential – indeed, one of the joys of coming at this time is whipping from one festival to another on a **scooter**, soaking up the boundless seascapes along the way.

5

Farglory Ocean Park

遠雄海洋公園; yuǎnxióng hǎiyáng gōngyuán • 20km south of Hualien along Highway 11 • Adults NT$890, children 13–17yrs NT$790, 7–12yrs NT$590, 3–6yrs and under 100cm tall NT$390 • ☎ 03 812 3199, ⓦ www.farglory-oceanpark.com.tw • Served by hourly buses from Hualien train station, or 20min by taxi

The village of **YANLIAO** (鹽寮; yánliáo) is home to **Farglory Ocean Park**, one of Taiwan's best-known theme parks. The park is divided into eight themed zones (including "Brighton by the Sea") and has a selection of mostly tame rides, best suited to younger kids, but there's also an aquarium with dolphins and seals, and of course, places to eat and shop.

Niushan Beach

牛山海岸; niúshān hǎiàn • 30km south of Hualien along Highway 11 • NT$50 entry to Niushan Huting • There are no direct bus services, so car or scooter is the best way to get here, although southbound coastal buses can take you to within a few km of the beach

Niushan Beach, an excellent day-trip from Hualien, is a secluded stretch of sand that comes to a dead end at rounded Cow Mountain. Unlike some of the other east-coast beaches, this one remains relatively undeveloped and is an ideal spot to relax and enjoy some solitude; just back from the beach is a simple campsite with a few cabins, plus *Huting Café* (see p.313). At times the swell is suitable for **surfing**, although experienced surfers are only likely to be challenged here during a tropical storm.

Jiqi Beach

磯崎海濱; jīqí hǎibīn • 40km south of Hualien • NT$100 entry to Jiqi Recreation Area; camping NT$1000 per pitch • Served by regular buses (40min) from outside Hualien train station

The water in the sheltered bay of **Jiqi Beach** is considerably calmer than that of many other east-coast beaches, making it a favoured **swimming** spot in the summer, when there are usually lifeguards on duty at the Jiqi Recreation Area section of the beach – but even strong swimmers should be wary of the currents offshore. The recreation area also has camping. A few kilometres north of the beach is **Baqi Observation Platform** (芭崎瞭望台; bāqí liàowàng tái), which commands a beautifully panoramic view of the south along the coast. There's also a pleasant café and souvenir store here (daily 9am–5pm) selling locally produced indigenous arts.

RIDE EAST: CYCLING THE COAST AND RIFT VALLEY

One of the world's largest bicycle manufacturers, Taiwan is blessed with rugged mountainous terrain and quality roads and is well-suited to **bike touring**, nowhere more so than the East Coast and East Rift Valley. The scenery is beautiful, but there are also plenty of attractions and beaches, plus relaxing hot springs to soothe aching muscles.

HIGHWAYS AND ROUTES

Highway 11 is more or less the only way down the coast, but in the Rift Valley, County Road 193 (which runs parallel to, and east of, the main Highway 9) is a better alternative for cyclists – its countryside is idyllic and there's less traffic. Several quiet county roads cross the Coastal Mountain Range, joining the two main highways, and reward the legwork up the hills with yet more spectacular landscapes, and hardly any vehicles.

PLANNING YOUR CYCLE TOUR

Making the journey either along the coast or through the valley, there are enough homestays, restaurants and stores to keep you in food and lodging, although it is worth booking accommodation in advance during the summer. The *Eastern Taiwan and Offshore Islands* map, available at visitor centres, should suffice for a general overview of the region, and you can pick up local cycling-path maps at visitor centres and Giant stores, though these are often in Chinese only. Hualien is a good place to hire bikes and book tours (see p.295).

Shitiping

石梯坪; shítīpíng • 30km south of Jiqi Beach, near the 66km marker of Highway 11 • There's a daily bus from Hualien

Shitiping is a 1km-long stretch of volcanic rock that has been eroded into terraces and other curious formations. The surrounding area is popular for **fishing**, and the **Shitiping Visitor Center** (石梯坪遊客服務中心; shítīpíng yóukè fúwù zhōngxīn; daily 9am–6pm; ☎03 878 1452) has exhibits on local marine life. From the visitor centre, a circular walkway allows visitors to inspect the rock formations more closely, and there are raised and covered wooden platforms for camping, plus a couple of seafood restaurants in the village.

Dagangkou

大港口; dàgǎngkǒu • South of Shitiping along Hualien Route 64

Just south of Shitiping is **Dagangkou**, which lies by the estuary of the Xiuguluan River. Here, the scenic Hualien Route 64, more commonly known as the **Ruigang Highway** (瑞港公路; ruìgǎng gōnglù), cuts across the coastal mountains, following the Xiuguluan River for 22.5km to Ruisui, the starting point for whitewater-rafting trips (see box, p.316). The road offers picturesque glimpses into the gorge below, but there is no bus service so it is only possible by private transport; however, it makes for an excellent scooter or bicycle ride.

Tropic of Cancer Monument

北迴歸線標誌; běihuíguīxiàn biāozhì

Down the coast, just south of Dagangkou, a towering **white monolith** shaped like a sundial marks the point where Highway 11 crosses the **Tropic of Cancer**. Very popular with mainland Chinese tourists, there are also souvenir and snack stores, toilets, and next to the monument itself, there's a map and list of countries crossed by the Tropic.

Baxiandong

八仙洞; bāxiāndòng • Visitor Center (八仙洞遊客服務中心; bāxiāndòng yóukè fúwù zhōngxīn) daily 8.30am–5pm • ☎089 881 418 • Buses from Hualien (10 daily; 2hr) and Taitung (1 daily; 2hr) stop just outside the car park (NT$50)

Baxiandong (Eight Immortals Cave) is worth a stop for its collection of more than a dozen **caves** eroded into the 150m-high coastal cliffs, but it is also one of Taiwan's most important archeological sites. In 1968, a number of **Stone Age artefacts** such as tools made of animal bones and stone were found in some of the caves, evidence of **Changpin Culture** (長濱文化; chángbīn wénhuà). Some of the artefacts date back thirty thousand years, placing the culture in the Palaeolithic period and making these hunter-gatherers the earliest people known to have inhabited Taiwan.

Today, most of the caves have been turned into Buddhist and Taoist shrines and filled with religious deities. Wooden walkways with steps leading up the cliff face link the caves, and from the highest ones there are outstanding sea views, although most of these have been off-limits to visitors for several years following path collapse. A venerable old nun (who speaks some English) is often on hand to show visitors around the lower caves, and will keenly point out the inverted shape of Taiwan formed by the cave outline when viewed from the back of the biggest cave. At the entrance is the **Baxiandong Visitor Center** (see above), which has some basic information in English about the caves and the artefacts they have yielded, plus a café.

Chenggong

成功; chénggōng • South of Sanxiantai, near the 117km marker of Highway 11 • Buses from Hualien (6 daily) and Taitung (2 daily)

The sizeable fishing town of **CHENGGONG** boasts one of Taiwan's liveliest **fish markets** and some of the freshest seafood on the island. Inhabited by a mix of Chinese, Amis, members of the officially unrecognized píngpǔ Siraya tribe (see p.400), Chenggong is the largest coastal settlement between Hualien and Taitung. Every afternoon at around

5

1 or 2pm, the local fishermen return to the town's Xingang Fishing Port to unload and sell the day's catch. These entertaining **auctions**, usually in full swing by 3pm, are a highlight of a visit, with betel-nut-chewing auctioneers rattling off prices in a maelstrom of Mandarin and Taiwanese, while weather-beaten fishmongers hack up the catch. One of the best times to visit is during the **swordfish** season in October and November, when scores of the pointy-nosed fish are put on auction each day. Next to the fishing dock is a small market with a variety of local fish specialities, the most famous of which are the delicious dried tuna fish shavings (cháiyú). Highway 11 runs along the outskirts of Chenggong; you'll find a few restaurants here, and there are more options in the town centre, east of the highway.

Sanxiantai

三仙台; sānxiāntái • 3km north of Chenggong, accessed by signed side roads from Highway 11 • Sanxiantai Visitor Center (三仙台遊客服務中心; sānxiāntái yóukè fúwù zhōngxīn) daily 8.30am–5pm • Car park NT$50 • ☎ 089 854 097

Just south of Baxiandong, the main highway crosses a flat plain, passing by several unusual rock formations along the coastline. By far the most famous of these is the **Sanxiantai**, a series of small islets crowned with three rocky outcroppings, named after a trio of legendary Taoist sages. The highway's turn-off leads to a car park and a lengthy **footbridge** with eight arches spanning the shallow water that separates the islets from the mainland. Though the bridge tends to be packed with tour groups on weekends and during the summer, it's worth crossing it to reach the **boardwalks** that skirt the islets, leaving the crowds behind. Beside the car park is the **Sanxiantai Visitor Center**, which has English-language exhibits on local geology and marine life. The bridge was closed for repairs at the time of writing, but is scheduled to reopen in 2018. There's also a bike path which runs the first 3km of the route to Chenggong.

Donghe

東河; dōnghé • 7km south of Duli • Served by buses from Hualien, Taitung and Chenggong

Don't be surprised if you see long queues of tourists in the otherwise sleepy Amis village of **DONGHE**; it has become justifiably famous island-wide for its delicious *baozi* (see p.313). The village is also a top-notch **surf** destination (see box opposite), with beaches at Donghe itself and nearby at **Jinzun Recreation Area** (金樽休憩區; jīnzūn xiūqìqū), a couple of kilometres south of the village where there's also a tranquil café overlooking the waves at the 136.5km mark on Highway 11.

Dulan

都蘭; dūlán • 14km south of Donghe • Frequent buses come here from Taitung train station (50min)

DULAN is one of the largest Amis settlements on the coast, and is a centre for the revival and reinterpretation of indigenous music and arts. It's also a burgeoning **surf** destination – although **Dulan Beach** is a pleasant spot for just lounging – and there are some good B&Bs, which make it the perfect place to stay a few nights. At *Cape Paradise* (see p.314), there's a good range of **watersports** on offer, or if you're more into land-based challenges, try the steep five-to-6-hour **hike** up Dulan Mountain – ask for details at your hotel.

Xindong Sugar Factory Culture Park

新東糖廠文化園區; xīndōng tángchǎng wénhuà yuánqū • 61 Dulan Village • Park Wed–Sun 10am–5pm; galleries opening hours variable, though you'll usually find at least some open • Free • ☎ 089 531 212

Dulan's primary attraction is the **Xindong Sugar Factory Culture Park**, formerly the **Dulan Sugar Factory** (都蘭紅糖文化藝術館; dūlán hóngtáng wénhuà yìshùguǎn), a 1930s sugar plant converted into a popular art centre. Lining the car park, old warehouse buildings now serve as **workshop-galleries**, and hold some unique and beautiful, if expensive, pieces. There are also a couple of cafés and bars here, notably *Highway 11* (see p.314).

Shanyuan Beach

杉原灣; shānyuán wān • North of Taitung, near the Km158 marker of Highway 11 • Buses heading north from Taitung, or bound for Dulan, can drop you here

With over a kilometre of palm-fringed golden sands backed by towering mountains, **Shanyuan Beach** is one of the east coast's most picturesque. Sadly, since 2003 the beach has been at the heart of a dispute concerning a mammoth hotel project, which was built without a full environmental impact assessment. Local environmental and indigenous rights groups are now pushing for the structure to be torn down, while the developers continue to bide their time. During the course of the construction, access to the beach was restricted, but at the time of writing it was easy to get to the sand from the hotel car park, where there are pay-showers.

Xiaoyeliu

小野柳; xiǎoyěliǔ • 6km south of Shanyuan Beach • Daily 8.30am–5pm • Free

Marking the southernmost point of the East Coast National Scenic Area is **Xiaoyeliu**, a smaller version of the fanciful geological marvel Yehliu (see p.128) in northern Taiwan. Xiaoyeliu is known for its surreal coastal **rock formations**, composed of a rare mix of sandstone and shale that is easily eroded by wind and waves, but it also offers a very attractive accommodation alternative to the hotels of Taitung – one of Taiwan's most charming **campsites**, perched on a grassy plateau overlooking the sea (see p.313). Behind the visitor centre are walkways leading to the rock formations, which have been given names such as "tofu rock", "mushroom rock" and "honeycomb rock". By the car park is a shelter that houses souvenir stalls and snack shops selling instant noodles and drinks.

TAITUNG'S SECRET SURF SPOTS

Taiwan's strongest and most consistent **surf** can be found along the 50km stretch of coastline north of Taitung. Most of the best spots are shielded from the road by small villages, keeping them the closely guarded secrets of a hardcore handful of expat and local surfers living in Taitung. It's best to arrange your own transport so you can explore the coast at your leisure. If you're an experienced surfer and are here in winter or just before a typhoon, you won't want to miss the **Donghe River-mouth** – the turn-off is just north of town.

• **Chenggong** (成功; chénggōng) Just north of Chenggong, on the back road to Sanxiantai, you can access a reef break known as "The Point", which churns out barrel after barrel on windy days; only suitable for experienced surfers.

• **Donghe** (東河; dōnghé) Several surfer-friendly hostels here. Though there are rocks on either side of the estuary, if there's groundswell from a tropical storm, you should get some lovely river-mouth barrels.

• **Jinzun** (金樽; jīnzūn) For some pure beach action, head south another 3km until you reach the popular Jinzun Beach: 3km of fine dark sand with some rideable waves close to shore. Be careful of paddling too far out, as the seabed drops off sharply, and there is a formidable riptide.

• **Xingchang** (興昌; xīngchāng) A couple of kilometres north of Dulan, Xingchang offers the area's top summer breaks. Just past the village, when the coastal road starts to veer eastwards, you'll see a statue of a giant custard apple by the road – the first right after this leads to the shore. At the northern end is reef, while the southern end is mostly sandy. Another kilometre or so north, near the Km141.5 marker, is a narrow lane leading down to the shore, where you'll find two howling breaks: one left and one right (be prepared to kick out early, as there are lots of rocks close to shore); if you reach Longchang Village (隆昌; lóngchāng), then you've gone too far north.

• **Dulan** (都蘭; dūlán) This is the closest option to Taitung, and the easiest for novice surfers. To get to this sandy beach, which has small but consistent waves, cross the bridge just north of Dulan and turn east on the third lane to your right. There's plenty of accommodation in the village and around (see p.313).

5

GETTING AROUND   EAST COAST NATIONAL SCENIC AREA

Most people tour the East Coast using either **car**, **scooter** or **bike**, making staying anywhere along the coast an option. Broadly speaking, Hualien is a good base from which to explore the northern section; Chenggong, Dulan and Donghe, and perhaps Taitung or Zhiben, make good bases for the southern section.

By bus Dingdong and Hualien Bus Company both run one bus a day from Hualien to Taitung along the coast, at 9.30am and 1.10pm respectively, via Baxiandong, Chenggong, Duli, Donghe and Dulan. Regular services head south to Jiqi (1hr), and eight other buses only go as far as Chenggong.

By car and scooter Cars and scooters can easily be rented in both Hualien and Taitung, but for foreigners without a Taiwanese licence, scooters are most easily sourced in Hualien. Decent English maps of the whole region are available from visitor centres and the main sights are signed in English.

By bike Bikes with panniers can be rented at Giant in Hualien (see p.295) or Taitung (see p.323) and dropped off in either location. For day-rides you can hire bikes from several of the train stations along the East Rift Valley line. For those who want to tour the coast or valley but don't want to carry their luggage, bike specialists Grasshopper Adventures (☎0970 782 393, ⊛grasshopperadventures .com) operate regular tours in the region.

By taxi Though it's more expensive than driving yourself, you can hire a taxi for a day-trip along the coast from Hualien for around NT$3000–4000, and there are also taxis for rent in some of the bigger towns along the way.

INFORMATION

Tourist information Twelve kilometres south of Chenggong, near the 129km marker of Highway 11 not far from Duli (都歷; dūlì), is the East Coast National Scenic Area Headquarters and Visitor Center (都歷處本部遊客 中心; dūlì chù běnbù yóukè fúwù zhōngxīn; daily 8.30am–5pm; ☎089 841 520), where staff can provide a broad overview of the east coast's main attractions.

ACCOMMODATION

YANLIAO, NIUSHAN AND JIQI

Farglory Hotel 遠雄達飯店; yuǎnxióng fàndiàn 3km north of Yanliao Village ☎03 812 3900, ⊛www .farglory-hotel.com.tw. Convenient if you're planning to visit Farglory Ocean Park, but also expensive and garish, albeit very comfortable and with every amenity imaginable. The cheaper rooms look out over the Rift Valley, while sea-view rooms are more expensive. NT$5280

Half Moon Bay B&B 半月灣小築; bànyuèwān xiǎozhù Jiqi ☎03 871 1159, ⊛halfmoonbay.com.tw /index_eng.htm. This tiny B&B is owned by a Taipei retiree, and has just five rooms looking over a garden which opens straight out onto a rugged stretch of beach. The bottom three rooms are all en suite and have sofa-beds as well as a double, while the two smaller rooms upstairs in the main section of the house share communal bathrooms. Breakfast is included, but no other meals are served – the nearest restaurant is several kilometres away, so you'll need your own transport. NT$2800

Hemingway Homestay 海明蔚民宿; hǎimíngwèi mínsù Highway 11, Km11 marker, Yanliao ☎03 867 1088, ⊛wayocean.com. A range of comfortable rooms spread over two buildings, set in a pleasant oceanside garden. Rooms in the new building are more modern and upscale and include some lovely suites, while the older wooden building has cheaper, cosier rooms, most of which have sea views. NT$2400

CHENGGONG

Bayview Hotel 看得到海民宿; kàndédàohǎi mínsù 131 Qilin Rd, Chenggong ☎0921 231 463. Owned by a Taitung surfer and his family, this sweet little place offers just five rooms, ranging from small doubles to a four-person penthouse (NT$4000) with large balcony and fantastic ocean views. There are surfboards for hire and a scooter for guest use – it's a 5min drive to Chenggong. Oh, and the author of this chapter lives next door. NT$2000

★**Villa** 擁月星宿; yōngyuè xīngsù Highway 11, 5km south of Chenggong ☎089 841 639. A tasteful resort set in spacious gardens, right on the ocean. Rooms

---

AMIS FOLK CENTER

The East Coast National Scenic Area Headquarters and Visitor Center headquarters includes the sprawling **Amis Folk Center** (阿美族民俗中心; āměizú mínsù zhōngxīn; Tues–Sun 8.30am–5pm), an open-air **museum** with reconstructions of historic Amis buildings and daily **dance performances** (Tues–Sat 11am & 2pm, Sun 2pm & 3.30pm). The centre, managed by Taitung County's Aborigine Social Welfare Commission, also has a variety of traditional Amis **handicrafts** for sale. In summer, there are sometimes open-air **music performances and festivals** here which attracts an interesting mix of tourists, local families and Taipei hipsters.

are divided between a modern new block of twin/doubles and a series of solid wooden cabins, the best of which face the ocean and have large verandas. The upper section of the resort has a pleasant café (one complimentary drink for guests) with magical tropical views across the palm-laden coastal plains to the mountains beyond. The restaurant can arrange lunch and dinner (if ordered in advance). NT$2900

DONGHE
Low Pressure 熱帶低氣壓民宿; rèdài dīqìyā mínsù 99 South Donghe Rd ☎089 896 738, ⓦeasttaiwan-surf.com. A comfortable, modern guesthouse targeted at surfers, with a range of bright, well-equipped rooms. As well as doubles and twins, they also have four-bed dorms. Across the road, the same owners operate a trendy surf café (see p.314). Taitung pick-ups from NT$1000 and surf lessons from NT$1500. Dorms NT$500, doubles NT$2500

DULAN
Happy House 聚樂山莊; jùlè shānzhuāng 30–6 Xinshe ☎089 530 0368. Very comfortable B&B set in a large garden in the coastal foothills behind Dulan. The owners are friendly and the spacious rooms enjoy excellent sea views. It's quite difficult to find, so best call for a pick-up. NT$2400
Piao Yang 飄洋; piāo yáng 196-2, Neighbourhood 27 ☎089 831 310. Comfortable and tastefully styled B&B set in the quieter backstreets behind the main road. There's no restaurant, but breakfast is included at a nearby café. NT$2800

Taitung Sea Art Hostel 台東海之藝民宿; táidōng hǎizhīyì mínsù 71 Neighbourhood 13, Lane 5 ☎0935 061 578, ⓦtaitung-sea-art-hostel.webs.com. Tucked up in the lushly forested hills back from the ocean, this lovely old Taiwanese house offers just three simple, cosy fan rooms, all beautifully decorated by the artist owners. Getting there is half the adventure and is best done in daylight – snakes are common on the road on summer evenings. There are signposts (twelve in total, all in Chinese and featuring animals shown on their website), but the hostel can also arrange pick-ups from Dulan or Taitung. Minimum two-night stay. NT$1000
Wagaligong 哇軋力共; wayàligòng 89 Dulan Village ☎089 530 373, ⓦwagaligongtaiwan.com. A comfortable South African-owned surf hostel right in the centre of town with a choice of doubles or single-sex dorms, all sharing communal bathrooms. Downstairs is a popular bar and café serving burgers and pizza. One of the owners is a keen surfer and the hostel can provide surf board and SUP board rental and instruction. Dorms NT$500, doubles NT$1200

XIAOYELIU
Xiaoyeliu Campsite 小野柳露營區; xiǎoyěliǔ lùyíng qū ☎089 281 530. With elevated wooden platforms, some with roofs and attached barbecue pits, and toilet and hot shower facilities (NT$20/15min), this breezy campsite is vastly underused most of the year. You need to bring your own tent, and can register and pay at the Xiaoyeliu Visitor Center (小野柳遊客服務中心; xiǎoyěliǔ yóukè fúwù zhōngxīn; daily 9am–5pm), next to the car park. The rate doubles on Fri & Sat. NT$500

EATING
Many of the dining options along the east coast have unreliable **opening hours**, particularly those in remote areas. During winter, some places will close early if there are no customers, and in surf spots you may find a café closed because the owners are out surfing. The opening hours below are as listed by the establishment, but call ahead to avoid disappointment.

YANLIAO, NIUSHAN AND JIQI
Huting Café 牛山呼庭; niúshān hūtíng Niushan Beach ☎03 860 1400. A friendly and peaceful beach café serving a tasty selection of set meals including curry rice (NT$280), tea and coffee (from NT$150). Daily 10am–6pm.
Longxia Haixian Canting 鹽寮龍蝦海鮮餐廳; yánliáo lóngxiā hǎixiān cāntīng Yanliao ☎03 867 1128. Popular for its first-rate seafood (priced by weight) including clams, shrimps and lobster chosen from the tanks outside the restaurant, the clean, bright interior also enjoys good sea views. Expect to pay NT$300–500/person in a group. Mon–Thurs 10am–2.30pm & 4.30–9.30pm, Sat & Sun 10am–9.30pm

CHENGGONG
Penghu Restaurant 澎湖餐廳纏; pénghú cāntīng Chenggong ☎089 852 780. Popular seafood restaurant on the main road through Chenggong. They also serve meat dishes including tasty duck rolls. Daily 11am–2pm & 5–8pm.
Sister's Cupcake 3km south of Chenggong on Highway 11 ☎089 853 211. Owned and run by two Amis sisters, this is a great place to stop and re-fuel on a ride down the coast. As well as cupcakes, they offer all kinds of sweet goodies including brownies, lemon meringue pie and banana choco pie (NT$80), as well as good coffee and tea. Mon–Fri 1–8pm, Sat 3.30–8pm & Sun 10am–6pm.

DONGHE
Donghe is famed for *baozi* (東河包子; dōnghé bāozi), exquisite steamed buns with a range of tasty fillings including peanut, sesame, juicy pork and vegetables.

5

Chanji Donghe Baozi 記東河包子; chánjī dōnghé bāozi Donghe ☎089 896 168. The most popular shop for *baozi* is on the highway and claims to be the original, but the real deal is here, on the main old street through town, a block inland. With bigger and tastier fillings than its competitors, and outdoor seating under an old banyan tree, this is the best place to try this local delicacy. Choices include peanut, red beans, sesame, pork, vegetables and kimchi; there's also cold tea and coffee. Daily 8am–5.30pm.

Low Pressure 熱帶低氣壓民宿; rèdài dīqìyā mínsù 99 South Donghe Rd ☎089 896 738, ⓦeasttaiwan-surf.com. Trendy surf café serving great hamburgers, fish burgers and Taiwanese dishes (mains around NT$250). Meals can be eaten in the funky interior or out on the deck. Soft drinks (including refreshing local lemon juice), beers and cocktails are also on offer. Daily 8am–9pm.

DULAN

Cape Paradise 海角咖啡; hǎi jiǎo kāfēi Turn right off main road between Dulan Crap and the CPC petrol station, and follow signs for another 2km ☎0913 275 661, ⓦcapeparadise.tw. This remote spot is mainly a base for kayaking, sailing, surfing and windsurfing, but also has a pool and café with a menu featuring Spanish dishes including *paella*, (NT$750 for two people), *patatas bravas* (NT$100) and casserole (NT$250), plus fruit juices, coffee and sangria (NT$300/jug). Daily 11am–7pm.

Dulan Café 都蘭糖廠61號; dūlán tángchǎng 61 hào Dulan Sugar Factory car park ☎089 530 330. At the heart of Dulan's arts revival, this trendy café-bar is housed in an attractive old building in the sugar factory car park. Recently renovated in elegant Japanese style, the café serves interesting Taiwanese dishes including swordfish dumplings (NT$180 for four pieces), plus quality coffee (NT$100). Daily 9am–9pm.

★**Dulan Crap** 法式創意料理; fàshì chuàngyì liàolǐ 445-5 Neighbourhood 43; a kilometre north of town on highway 11 ☎0926 836 816. Owned and run by a French–Taiwanese couple, this is easily the best French restaurant in eastern Taiwan. The menu features enticing starters such as fried goat's cheese with avocado, tomato, red onion and balsamic vinaigrette (NT$150), while mains (NT$270–560) include duck, lamb, steak, mahi-mahi and stews. Be sure to save some room for dessert: the chocolate almond terrine with raspberry coulis and the crème brûlée are both excellent. The restaurant's two dining halls are packed with antiques from France, and the walls display art by local painters. Thurs 6–9pm, Fri–Sun noon–2pm & 6–9pm.

Dulan Indian 印度咖哩; yìndù gālí 431-2 Neighbourhood 42 ☎089 530 484. Set in the hills just behind Dulan, this restaurant serves reasonably authentic Indian dishes in a lovely little wooden dining room. Set meals include chicken tandoori (NT$260) and are served with a tasty soup. There's a variety of breads including *roti* and *naan*, and for dessert there's ice cream and chai. The place is a bit tricky to find – look for the sign on Highway 11. Wed–Sun 10am–6pm.

Marino's Kitchen 馬利諾廚房; mǎlìnuò chúfáng Highway 11, just north of Dulan ☎089 531 848. Owned by former radio chat-show host David Marino and his Taiwanese wife, this place made a name for itself with its delicious, freshly baked bread (NT$220–420 per loaf), but also sells home-made pasta and sauces. Next door, *Dulan Dinner* is run by their daughters, and serves pasta and pizza. Daily 9.30am–6.30pm.

Moonlight Inn 月光小棧; yuèguāng xiǎozhàn 20, Neighbourhood 46 ☎089 530 012. Housed in a Japanese-style building that was originally a forestry administrative centre, this café enjoys a magnificent location on the hillside overlooking the coast. They serve tea, coffee (from NT$100) and a limited selection of light snacks, and the place has become a popular destination since it was used as a location in the film *The Moon Also Rises*, which won best female lead and best screenplay at the 2004 Golden Horse Awards (Taiwan's Oscars). Follow the signs from Highway 11 to Dulan site, after which you should see signs for *Moonlight Inn*. Mon & Thurs–Sun 10.30am–5.30pm.

DRINKING

Highway 11 台11工作室tái; 11 gōngzuò shì Dulan Sugar Factory, Dulan ☎0978 092 087. Owned by a long-term expat, this small bar tucked into the side of the sugar factory is the outlet for locally produced Highway 11 craft beers, which include IPA (NT$150), lemon wheat ale and even tangerine and vanilla. There's sometimes live music at the outdoor stage on Sat. Wed–Sat noon–midnight, Sun noon–5pm.

East Rift Valley National Scenic Area

花東縱谷國家風景區; huādōng zònggǔ guójiā fēngjǐngqū

The **East Rift Valley National Scenic Area**, a lush swathe of rice paddies and hot springs is nestled between the Coastal Mountain Range and the eastern fringe of the central ranges. Provincial Highway 9 heads southwest from Hualien, cutting through the East

Rift Valley National Scenic Area. To its east, parallel to it, County Road 193 offers a more intimate and slower-paced look at the countryside, passing through fruit orchards and indigenous villages, and is a favourite with cyclists. **Whitewater-rafting** on the Xiuguluan River is also a popular East Rift Valley pastime, while the area also provides access to **Yushan National Park** and the **Southern Cross-Island Highway** (although this remained closed at the time of writing).

Liyu Lake

鯉魚潭; lǐyú tán • 15km southwest of Hualien city • Hourly buses from Hualien train station (30min)

At the very northern end of the Rift Valley, the picturesque **Liyu Lake** offers a pleasant escape from Hualien. A 5km walking and cycling path encircles the lake, with information boards in English detailing the life cycle of the fireflies which can be seen here between March and May. **Bikes** can be hired from the café next to the information centre, and **kayaks** are for rent at the lakeside. A network of **hiking trails** runs through the jungly hills that surround the lake, and there are cafés and shops along Highway 9, which follows the lake's western edge. As well as a few small-scale B&Bs, there is also a campsite a kilometre south of the lake.

Ruisui Hot Springs

瑞穗溫泉; ruìsuì wēnquán • 4km northwest of Ruisui train station • Frequent trains from Hualien and Taitung along the East Rift Valley line; hourly buses from Hualien

Ruisui Hot Springs, a short taxi-ride from Ruisi station, were developed as a resort by the Japanese in 1919. The carbonated, yellow-tinted, iron-rich spring water has an average temperature of 48°C and is effective in treating rheumatism and some skin rashes, while some Taiwanese also believe that if women bathe regularly in the water it will increase their chances of bearing a male child.

Saoba Megaliths

掃叭石柱; sāobā shízhù • 2km south of the Ruisui train station • Buses running along Highway 9 can drop you here, or you could hire a taxi from Ruisui train station

The **Saoba Megaliths** stand alongside Highway 9, nestled into the tea-growing hills of Wuhe (舞鶴; wǔhè). The pair of 2m-high stone columns are thought by archeologists to be remnants of the Beinan civilization that thrived in the valley some five thousand years ago. According to local legend, they are the incarnations of incestuous twins who tried to escape the wrath of their tribe and were turned to stone.

Nearby, a white monolith that's shaped like a sundial denotes the point where the valley road crosses the **Tropic of Cancer**; there is also an identical marker along the coast road.

Yuli and around

玉里; yùlǐ • All trains through the East Rift Valley stop at Yuli station • The Giant store at 47 Heping Rd (daily 8am–9.30pm; ☎ 03 888 5669), a short walk from the train station, rents out bicycles and electric bikes (NT$150–500) and can give advice (in Chinese only) on bike trails

A major stop on the Hualien-Taitung train line, **YULI** is the jumping off point for nearby Antong Hot Springs, the stunning Walami Trail and Liushidanshan, home to fields of daylilies which paint the landscape a golden yellow in summertime. Aside from these nearby attractions, the town itself has shops and some decent places to eat, but not much else to detain visitors. There are a few bike trails around the town, which are more popular for families on weekends than dedicated cyclists.

RAFTING THE XIUGULUAN

The **Xiuguluan River** (秀姑巒溪; xiùgūluán xī) is Taiwan's premier whitewater-rafting spot and a wet and wild trip down it can be the highlight of a visit to the East Rift Valley. Running 104km from its source near Xiuguluan Mountain to the Pacific estuary at Dagangkou, it's eastern Taiwan's longest river, and the main 24km rafting route can be an exciting run for amateurs after prolonged rains or a typhoon. But the best bit is definitely the scenery – the river cuts through a **deep gorge** in the coastal mountains and is surrounded by steep vertical cliffs and badlands in many places, with your raft providing an unparalleled perspective on the immensity of it all. Though the **rafting season** depends mostly on the level of rainfall, it generally runs from early April to late October, with May and June offering the most exciting conditions.

Trips start from the town of **Ruisui** (瑞穗; ruìsuì) at 8 or 9am, and depending on the water level usually take three to four hours, including a lunch break at the Amis village of **Qimei** (七美; qíměi); by the end you'll be soaking wet. Though most travel agents and hostels in Hualien can arrange rafting trips, including return transport, equipment rental and lunch, for about NT$1000 per person, they usually only charge about NT$750 if you have your own transport to and from Ruisui. It's also possible to arrange trips in Ruisui itself, at the **Ruisui Rafting Service Center** (瑞穗泛舟服務中心; ruìsuì fànzhōu fúwù zhōngxīn; 215 Zhongshan Rd Sec 3; daily 8.30am–5pm; ☎ 03 887 5400), a 4km taxi or bike ride from the train station. At the centre are several private rafting operators; however, unless you're with a group of six or more people it can be time consuming to arrange a trip here, as individual travellers may have to wait to join a group.

Antong Hot Springs

安通溫泉; āntōng wēnquán • 8km southeast of Yuli station (Antong station is now closed) • A taxi from Yuli station costs NT$300; buses from Hualien stop on Highway 9, a short walk from the springs

The **Antong Hot Springs** were discovered by loggers in 1904 in the Antong Creek. The clear, hydrogen sulphide-laden springs well up in the stream at temperatures ranging from 60 to 66°C and can be enjoyed at the small resorts in the valley. There is a cycle path along the old rail line near here, but a relaxing soak at the springs is the main attraction.

Liushidanshan

六十石山; liùshí shíshān • 20km southeast of Yuli station • A half-day taxi tour costs from NT$1500, or you can hire a bike from the Giant store at 47 Heping Rd in Yuli (☎ 03 888 5669), but it's a steep ride

Beautiful at any time of year, the foothills of the Coastal Mountain Range around **Liushidanshan** (Sixty Stone Mountain) are cloaked in a carpet of yellow **daylilies** during August and September each year. During the daylily bloom, the narrow access roads can be clogged with sightseers, and, though the spectacle is certainly worth seeing, you'll have a much quieter experience at other times of year. The daylilies themselves are prized for their medicinal qualities, and can be purchased dried from farm stores in the East Rift Valley.

Nanan

南安; nánān • Highway 30 (just past the 294km marker of Highway 9, south from Yuli) • Nanan Visitor Center (南安遊客中心; nánān yóukè zhōngxīn) daily 8.30am–4.30pm, closed second Tues each month • ☎ 03 888 7560 • Taxis charge NT$400 for the 30min journey from Yuli station to the Nanan Visitor Center

Scenic Highway 9 winds its way down to the eastern entrance of **Yushan National Park** (玉山國家公園; yùshān guójiā gōngyuán; ⊛ysnp.gov.tw) where **NANAN**, a peaceful, little-visited fringe of the park, makes a worthwhile detour for those with private transport. About 8km from the turn-off along the western extension of Highway 30 is the **Nanan Visitor Center**. Around 2km on, the **Nanan Waterfall** (南安瀑布; nánān pùbù) is a thin but impressive seven-storey cascade.

The Walami Trail

瓦拉米古道; wǎlāmǐ gǔdào • Trailhead located 4km beyond the Nanan Waterfall, at the end of the road • Mountain and National Park permits are required for the full trail with an overnight stop (apply between seven days and two months in advance at

Ⓦmountain.ysnp.gov.tw), but you can walk as far as Jiaxin without a permit, or can secure an express day-trip permit all the way to Walami by visiting Nanan Visitor Center before 9am

A stunning hike along the wild Lakulaku River, the **Walami Trail** is 14km long, with 400m of ascent, and requires permits. It's typically completed as an overnight trip, spending the night at the solar-powered, 24-bed *Walami Cabin* at the end of the trail (reservations can be made when applying for your permit). If you're in good shape and are prepared to walk quickly without too many breaks, consider getting an express on-the-spot day return permit, but you should make sure that you set off early, especially in winter when it can be dark by 5pm – it's an eight-to-ten-hour round trip. Another option is to hike the first 4km of the trail without a permit. This takes you beyond the magnificent **Shanfeng Waterfall** (山風瀑布; shānfēng pùbù) and on to **Jiaxin** (佳心; jiāxīn), which has fine views of the valley to the east and a basic but free campsite with showers and toilets. The return hike to Jiaxin takes about half a day.

Wulu

霧鹿; wùlù • Off the Southern Cross-Island Highway, near its eastern entrance via Highway 20 (around 30km south of Yuli) • Two buses trundle up to Wulu (1hr 30min) from Taitung each day at 6.20am and 1.10pm

A tiny Bunun village, **Wulu** is known chiefly for its hot-springs hotel, and for the **Tianlong Suspension Bridge** (天龍吊橋; tiānlóng diàoqiáo), which crosses the Wulu Gorge (霧鹿峽谷; wùlù xiágǔ) at a dizzying height behind the hotel. Wulu is a stop on the **Southern Cross-Island Highway** (南橫公路; nánhéng gōnglù), a thrilling stretch of road which reaches 2700m above sea level on its traverse across the southern Central Mountain Range, although the full route across to the west coast has remained closed since it was damaged by Typhoon Morakot in 2009.

Bunun Tribe Cultural Park

布農部落文化園區; bùnóng bùluò wénhuà yuánqū • Taoyuan, near the southern end of the East Rift Valley, 18km north of Taitung, via a small road that heads west • Daily 8am–5pm; daily show at 10.30am & 2pm, if there are more than thirty guests • NT$100 • ☏089 561 211 • No public transport

The idyllic **Bunun** village of **TAOYUAN** (桃源; táoyuán) offers a genuine glimpse of the tribe's culture and heritage. The village is a relaxing retreat overlooking a tributary of the Beinan River, and at weekends the tribe puts on one of the most authentic indigenous song and dance shows in Taiwan at the **Bunun Tribe Cultural Park**. The park contains over a hundred pieces of locally made sculpture and a spacious **craft workshop** where you can watch traditional handicrafts being made.

GETTING AROUND & INFORMATION	EAST RIFT VALLEY

While the train can shuttle you quickly between destinations, and slower buses also serve the main towns, the best way to explore the East Rift Valley is with your own transport, whether that's a car, scooter or bike.

By train Hualien–Taitung trains pass through the valley, with useful stops including Guangfu (13 daily; 30min–1hr), Ruisui (16 daily; 40min–1hr 20min) and Yuli (for Antong and Nanan; 19 daily; 45min–2hr).

By bus Most services along the East Rift Valley from Hualien terminate in Guangfu, but there are a few buses as far as Fuli (NT$335) via Ruisui (NT$199), Yuli (NT$269) and Antong (NT$286) – at any of these towns you can pick up onward buses to Taitung.

By taxi You can hire a taxi for a day-trip into the valley from Hualien for around NT$3000–4000, and there are also taxis in some of the bigger towns along the way.

By car and scooter Cars and bikes can easily be rented in both Hualien and Taitung, but for foreigners scooters are more easily sourced in Hualien.

By bike Several of the train stations along the way (including Yuli) have bike rental stores. Decent English maps of the whole region are available from visitor centres, and the main sights are signposted in English.

Tourist information The East Rift Valley Visitor Center (168 Xinghe Rd Sec 2; daily 8.30am–5.30pm; ☏03 887 5306, Ⓦerv-nsa.gov.tw) is based in Hegang Village, 4km north of Ruisui.

5

ACCOMMODATION

RUISUI

★**Butterfly Valley Resort** 蝴蝶谷溫泉渡假村; húdié gǔ wēnquán dùjiàcūn 161 Guangdong Rd, Fuyuan Village ☎03 881 2377, ☻bvr.com.tw. Twelve kilometres north of Ruisui, nestled in a valley which holds Taiwan's largest remaining camphor forest, this eco-resort is one of the most upmarket places to stay in the East Rift Valley. It has tasteful rooms and villas, with prices to match. The resort is set amid wonderful tropical foliage, complete with high-end hot springs, and there are numerous nature trails offering butterfly viewing, a waterfall and an impressive display of insects under glass. Non-guests can pay NT$100 to access the resort's hiking trails, and a further NT$250 to use the hot springs. NT$9000

Hongye Hot Springs Hotel 紅葉溫泉旅社; hóngyè wēnquán lǚshè 188 Hongye Village ☎03 887 2176, ☻188hy.com. A Japanese-developed hot-spring resort, the attractive *Hongye* has a choice of Western-style or tatami-matted rooms, with flat-screen TVs and stone hot-spring tubs. The clear, odourless alkaline water is also pumped into private bathhouses (NT$200 for non-guests). NT$1800

Hoya Hot Spring Resort 虎爺溫泉會館; hǔyé wēnquán huìguǎn 23 Xiangbei Rd ☎03 887 5505, ☻hoya-spa.com.tw. *Hoya* has the best spring pools in Ruisui and a choice of rooms: the cheapest rooms are small wooden cabins next to the springs, while across the road are more expensive, bland but comfortable rooms (from NT$2200) in a modern building. The best rooms are new wooden cabins set around a pond next to the main building (NT$2700). NT$1800

SAOBA MEGALITHS

Saobading Homestay 掃叭頂民宿; sǎobādǐng mínsù 211 Wuhe Village ☎0910 552 019. Not far from the stones off Highway 9 at the Km276.8 mark, this amiable homestay offers good-value, well-equipped neat double rooms. Also renowned for its food, with dishes including "Hitting the Wall" dumplings (zhuàngqiáng shuǐjiǎo). NT$1600

YULI AND AROUND

Antong Hot Spring Hotel 安通溫泉大飯店; āntōng wēnquán dàfàndiàn 36 Wenquan Rd, Antong ☎03 888 6108, ☻an-tong.com.tw. The original and still the best springs in Antong, with attractive outdoor springs and comfortable, renovated rooms in a variety of sizes. NT$2200

ANTONG

Yu Hot Spring 玉溫泉; yù wēnquán 58–8 Wenquan Rd, Antong ☎03 888 8588. Clean, simple rooms with TVs and half-decent hot springs just across the road from the more famous Antong Hot Springs. NT$1800

WULU

Chief Spa Hotel 天龍飯店; tiānlóng fàndiàn ☎089 935 075, ☻chiefspa.com.tw. A comfortable, if isolated place to stay, with good views from many of the rooms. There's a small outdoor spa, and the rooms have spring-fed baths. NT$2700

EATING

RUISUI

Zhu Cun 竹村; zhúcūn Zhongshan Rd ☎03 887 6083. Straight across from the train station on the right-hand side before the traffic lights, this pleasant little Japanese diner serves asparagus and shrimp hand rolls (NT$60), plus decent sashimi (NT$200). Daily 10.30am–1.30pm & 5.30–8.30pm.

YULI AND AROUND

Koukovagia 咕咕發芽; gūgū fāyá 58 Datong Rd, Yuli ☎03 888 9088. Surprisingly chic café on the outskirts of Yuli serving sandwiches (NT$120–140), salads, (NT$90–120), pizzas (NT$150–350), waffles (NT$150–220) and great coffee (NT$120–140). Daily except Tues 11am–9pm.

Our Café 我們的咖啡屋; wǒmen de kāfēiwū 62 Heping Rd, Yuli ☎0919 289 979. Trendy café set in an old Japanese building, 5min walk from the train station. The café features interesting driftwood furniture and serves local teas such as Wuhe honey-scented tea (NT$120), coffee (NT$100–150) and beer (NT$150) as well as light snacks including waffles (NT$85). Daily 2pm–midnight.

WULU

Wulu Sichuan Restaurant 霧鹿川菜馆; wùlù chuāncài guǎn 7 Tianlong Bridge Rd. Near the *Chief Spa*, as its name suggests, this simple restaurant serves spicy Sichuan dishes and also sells basic snacks and drinks. Set meals for two cost NT$420. Daily noon–9pm.

Taitung and around

台東; táidōng

Stretched across an open plain between lush mountains and the ocean, **TAITUNG** is the gateway to Taiwan's rugged southeast coast and the dreamy Pacific islands of **Ludao** and

Lanyu. With a population of 110,000 – including significant numbers of the Amis, Bunun, Rukai, Paiwan, Puyuma and Tao tribes – it has the laidback feel of a place half its size. Just to the south are the immensely popular **Zhiben Hot Springs**, with a range of resorts to suit most budgets, and the adjacent Zhiben Forest Recreation Area, which offers some leisurely hiking options. Given the proximity of Zhiben, Dulan and Green Island, many travellers head straight out of Taitung from the train station, but it's certainly worth taking the time to visit the excellent **National Museum of Prehistory**, and for those with time on their hands there are a couple of attractive parks within the city.

Tiehua Art Village

鐵花村; tiěhuācūn • Between Xinsheng Rd and Liyu Park • Market daily except Tues 4–10pm; live music Wed–Sat 8–10pm & Sun 7.30–9pm

Close to both Liyu Park and the shopping and restaurants of Xinsheng Road, **Tiehua Art Village** has become something of a cultural hub. Set on the disused tracks to Taitung's old train station, the "village" was developed into a cultural space in 2010 and hosts a small arts and crafts market; it also features a variety of live music acts several evenings a week.

Liyushan Park

鯉魚山公園; lǐyúshān gōngyuán • A short walk northwest of the old train station

Liyushan Park is crisscrossed with concrete walking paths, some with steps leading up to the spine of the 75m-high Liyushan itself. A path along the backbone of the hill leads to several lookout points offering 360-degree panoramas of the city, and is an ideal place to catch Taitung's cooling afternoon breezes. Within the park, the imposing **Longfong Temple** (龍鳳寶玉塔; lóngfèng bǎoyùtǎ) is a Buddhist sanctuary popular with worshippers and early morning t'ai chi practitioners, and has a pagoda which you can climb.

Seaside Park

海濱公園; hǎibīn gōngyuán • 2km east of the old train station, walkable from downtown

Covering Taitung's southeastern flank is the sprawling **Seaside Park**, with commanding views of the coastline. The park is filled with indigenous sculptures and woodcarvings, and is sliced by the 20km **cycle path** that loops around peaceful **Pipa Lake** (琵琶湖; pípá hú) and links up with the adjacent **Black Forest Park** (台東森林公園; táidōng sēnlín gōngyuán; NT$30) before making a circuit of downtown Taitung.

National Museum of Prehistory

國立台灣史前文化博物館; guólì táiwān shǐqián wénhuà bówùguǎn • Tues–Sun 9am–5pm, last entry 4.30pm • NT$80 • ⓦ www.nmp.gov.tw • Take a train to Kangle (康樂; kānglè; 5 daily; 5–10min) and walk (5min); alternatively there are 3 buses daily (7am, 11am & 3.30pm; 20min) from the old train station to the museum, or you could take a taxi

Located 8km west of the city centre, the **National Museum of Prehistory** is one of Taiwan's best museums. Created primarily to house the fascinating hoard of Neolithic artefacts dug up from the Beinan Culture Park around 7km away, the museum also provides a thorough introduction to Taiwan's rich prehistory, and information on all its major archeological sites, via two permanent exhibitions: the **Natural History of Taiwan** and **Taiwan's Prehistory**.

Large, futuristic halls combine contemporary design and technology with a fascinating collection of exhibits, models and dioramas to present each section in English and Chinese. The first exhibition explains the geological and ecological development of the island over millions of years, while the second takes a chronological journey from the first known humans in Taiwan to the early Iron Age. The exquisite **jade** ornaments and

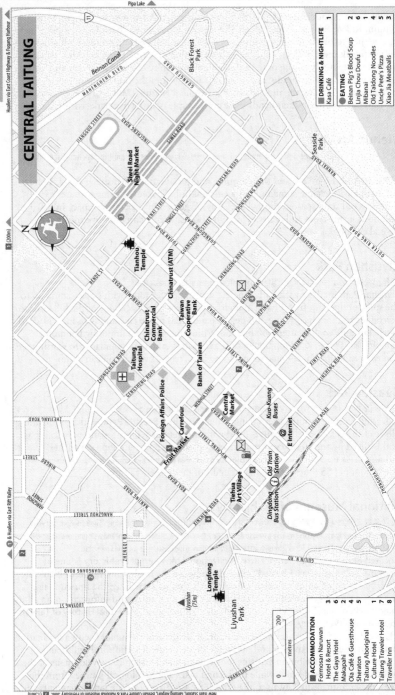

CENTRAL TAITUNG

Pipa Lake

Beinan Canal

Black Forest Park

Siwei Road Night Market

Tianhou Temple

Chinatrust (ATM)

Chinatrust Commercial Bank

Taiwan Cooperative Bank

Taitung Hospital

Bank of Taiwan

Foreign Affairs Police

Carrefour

Central Market

Fruit Market

Kuo-Kuang Buses

E Internet

Old Train Station

Dingdong Bus Station

Tiehua Art Village

Longfong Temple

Liyushan (75m)

Liyushan Park

Seaside Park

New Train Station, Taitung Airport, Beinan Culture Park & National Museum of Prehistory (1.5km)

Hualien via East Coast Highway & Fugang Harbour

Hualien via East Rift Valley

■ ACCOMMODATION	
Formosan Naruwan Hotel & Resort	3
The Gaya Hotel	6
Makapahi	2
Oia Café & Guesthouse	4
Sheraton	5
Taitung Aboriginal Culture Hotel	1
Taitung Traveler Hotel	7
Traveller Inn	8

■ DRINKING & NIGHTLIFE	
Kasa Café	1

● EATING	
Beinan Pig's Blood Soup	2
Linjia Chou Doufu	6
Miibanai	1
Old Taidong Noodles	4
Uncle Pete's Pizza	5
Xiao Jia Meatballs	3

0   200   metres

pottery taken from the Beinan site have their own exhibition areas, but the most startling finds are the distinctive **stone coffins** and moon-shaped **stone pillars**, the latter reminiscent of the stone circles of northwest Europe. The museum also has an exhibition on the **Indigenous Peoples of Taiwan**, charting the development of Taiwan's indigenous tribes and how they may relate to the island's prehistoric peoples.

Beinan Cultural Park

卑南文化公園; bēinán wénhuà gōngyuán • Park and visitor centre Tues–Sun 9am–5pm • NT$30 • The park is at the back of the New Station in the northern suburbs of Taitung; follow the road round (right as you exit) and under the bridge (10min); taxis from Taitung charge NT$250

Once the location of a flourishing Neolithic community, **Beinan Cultural Park** is a major archeological site with a series of landscaped open spaces and an exhibition hall managed by the Museum of Prehistory. The Japanese began working here in the 1940s, but most excavation was carried out in the 1990s, and today it's the largest and most productive archeological site in Taiwan, having yielded more than twenty thousand artefacts (mostly pottery) and 1600 slate coffins. The park's informative **visitor centre** contains a sunken area displaying the **coffins** and an exhibition dedicated to the people who once lived here, between 1500 and 300 BC. The local Puyuma people call themselves "Beinan", but some anthropologists think it's the Paiwan or the Amis that are more likely to be related to the prehistoric Beinan culture.

Elsewhere in the park, the two-level **observation deck** offers fine views over the area, while the **stone pillar** or standing stone is the only ancient artefact still in its original location – archeologists think this may have marked the centre of the village.

Zhiben Hot Springs

知本溫泉; zhībĕn wēnquán • Renting a car or scooter will give you much more flexibility, but it's also fairly easy to reach Zhiben from Taitung by buses operated by Dingdong (15 daily; 40min) or train (14 daily; 10–20min), although you will need to take a bus or taxi from the train station which is 6km from the resort area; there are also trains from Kaohsiung (15 daily; 2–3hr), which go via Fangliao

Zhiben Hot Springs, nestled in a long river valley about 20km southwest of Taitung, are among the most famous in Taiwan. A few kilometres inland from Zhiben Village, the hot spring area was developed into a resort by the Japanese in the early twentieth century, and the **sulphur carbonate waters** are believed to be effective in treating everything from arthritis to intestinal disorders.

All of the natural springs have been tapped and are pumped into the proliferation of hotels that line the valley entrance, popular with both Japanese and mainland Chinese visitors. As you enter the valley you're likely to be greeted by a welcoming party of indigenous people on scooters, entreating you to stay at their hot-springs hotels. Most of these places are near the highway turn-off, an overdeveloped area of faceless high-rises and you'll do better going to the far end of the valley, near the entrance to the serene Zhiben National Forest Recreation Area, where there are several more attractive options. If you don't plan to stay overnight, it's possible to soak in some of the hotels' **public pools** for a nominal fee – *Ayawan* and *Royal Chihpen* both offer access to their pools. Hotel springs are usually open from 9 or 10am until 10 or 11pm, but during quiet times they may empty many of the pools for cleaning.

Zhiben National Forest Recreation Area

知本森林遊樂區; zhībĕn sēnlín yóulèqū • 320 Longcyuan Rd • Jan–June & Sept–Dec 7am–5pm; July & Aug 8am–6pm • NT$80

At the end of the main Longquan Road – which cuts straight through the valley – is the tranquil **Zhiben National Forest Recreation Area**, a haven of attractive scenery with several walking paths. Badly damaged by Typhoon Morakot, the park has gradually

5

recovered, and now all of the trails are open. The ticket office is accessed across a large red bridge, and has English-language park maps. From here it's a ten-minute stroll up to the visitor centre, which has some interesting displays on the local ecology. From the visitor centre a network of trails covers the park, the most challenging of which is the **Banyan Shaded Trail** (榕蔭步道; róngyīn bùdào), which as the name suggests, is sheltered by old-growth forest, including seventeen 100-year-old banyans, and you can often see **Taiwanese macaques** leaping from tree to tree. At the top, a ten-minute diversion will take you to the park's highest point, the Ocean Viewing Platform.

ARRIVAL AND DEPARTURE

TAITUNG AND AROUND

BY PLANE

Taitung Airport (台東機場; táidōng jīchǎng; ⓦ www.tta.gov.tw) is about 7km northeast of the city centre and has daily flights to Taipei Songshan, as well as flights on nineteen-seater aircraft to Ludao and Lanyu with Daily Air (ⓣ 089 362 676, ⓦ www.dailyair.com.tw), although these are often cancelled in winter. The airport bus to the old train station downtown operates from the terminal (7.10am–9pm; NT$26); taxis will charge at least NT$200.
Destinations Lanyu (8 daily; 30min); Ludao (5 daily; 20min); Taipei Songshan (5 daily; 1hr).

BY TRAIN

Taitung train station, known as the "new train station" (新火車站; xīn huǒchēzhàn), is about 6km northeast of the city centre; the old station (舊火車站; jiù huǒchēzhàn) in the centre is no longer in use. Buses run irregularly from the bus station just outside the new train station (turn right as you exit) to the Dingdong Bus Station downtown (15min), passing all the cheap hotels on Zhongshan Rd. There are express train services to Hualien and Taipei, some of which stop at towns in the East Rift Valley including Yuli and Ruisui. There are also express trains daily to Kaohsiung (2hr 10min) via Fangliao. To get to Kenting, take the train to Fangliao and catch one of the regular buses south from Kaohsiung.
Destinations Fangliao (15 daily; 1–2hr); Hualien (19 express daily; 1hr 25min–3hr 30min); Kaohsiung (15 express daily; 2hr 10–3hr 15min); Pingdong (14 express daily; 1hr 45min–2hr 45min); Ruisui (15 express daily; 1–2hr); Taipei (13 express daily; 3hr 30min–5hr 45min); Yuli (19 express daily; 40min–1hr 30min).

BY BUS

Dingdong Bus Station (鼎東客運站; dǐngdōng kèyùn zhàn; Coastal ⓣ 089 333 443; Inland ⓣ 089 333 443) at 371 Tiehua Rd has regular services to destinations along coastal Provincial Highway 11 and inland Provincial Highway 9. There is only one daily service along the coast to Hualien (6.10am), while there are regular buses to Chenggong (1hr), from where it's possible to catch one of the several Chenggong–Hualien buses for the remainder of the journey. Dingdong also has hourly buses along the East Rift Valley, with destinations including Luye, Chishang, and Fuli. Some of these buses also pass the new train station, and there are also a couple of services to Lidao (6.20am & 1.10pm), which make a stop at Wulu (NT$200); this is currently the furthest you can get on the Southern Cross-Island Highway. Dingdong also runs fifteen buses daily to Zhiben Hot Springs (6am–9pm) and the Forest Recreation Area beyond from here. Kuo Kuang (國光; guóguāng) buses to Kaohsiung (daily 7am, 12.30pm, 5.30pm & 11.30pm; 4hr) via Fangliao leave from bus stop #8 outside the Dingdong Station.
Destinations Chenggong (22 daily; 1hr 30min); Fangliao (4 daily; 3hr); Hualien (1 daily; 3hr); Kaohsiung (4 daily; 4hr); Lidao (2 daily; 2hr); Wulu (2 daily; 1hr 45min); Zhiben (15 daily; 40min).

GETTING AROUND

Taitung's downtown area is eminently walkable, and its bus service is very limited. The easiest way to get around Taitung is either on foot, by taking taxis (which are plentiful), or hiring a bike.

By car and scooter It's tough for foreigners to rent scooters in Taitung without an Alien Resident Certificate and local licence, but there are a few places worth trying – Taidong Luyou Tong (台東旅遊通; táidōng lǚyóu tōng; ⓣ 089 221 058) at 88 Guotai St, near the new train station charges NT$300/day for 125cc scooters. It's easier to rent cars (with an international driving licence) at the airport or from Car Plus (243 Xinzhang Rd; ⓣ 089 227 979; daily 8.30am–8.30pm), near the train station.

By taxi Taxis from the new station to the old station, or to anywhere in the downtown area, usually cost NT$250 – drivers generally prefer to charge a flat rate rather than use the meter, but for trips within the city you can insist on the latter. The meter starts at NT$100 and goes up in increments of NT$5, rarely topping NT$150 for most journeys. Taxis from the new train station to Fugang Harbour (富岡漁港; fùgǎng yúgǎng) for the Lanyu/Ludao ferries charge NT$300.

By bike Renting a bike is a viable option for getting around the city (and beyond). Several hotels offer them to guests for free, and there's a Giant rental store (daily except Thurs 9am–6pm; ☎089 235 879) near the train station;

the store was operating out of a kiosk in front of the station at the time of writing, but is set to move to Xinzhang Rd.

INFORMATION

Tourist information There are convenient visitor information centres inside the new train station (Mon–Fri 8.30am–5pm, Sat & Sun 8.30am–6pm; ☎089 238 231), at the airport (daily 8.30am–5.30pm; ☎ 089 362 476) and in the old train station downtown (daily 9am–5pm; ☎089 357 131). They all have an assortment of English-language brochures and maps of the area, including the offshore islands, sights along the east coast, and cycling trails.

Services The best place to exchange foreign currency is the Bank of Taiwan (台灣銀行; táiwān yínháng) at 313 Zhongshan Rd, which also has an ATM that recognizes most international cards. Many of the 7-Elevens have Chinatrust Commercial Bank ATMs. The main post office (Mon–Fri 8am–5.30pm) is at the junction of Datong and Xinsheng roads, and there's another branch on Zhongshan Rd, near Xinyi Rd.

ACCOMMODATION

TAITUNG

Formosan Naruwan Hotel & Resort 娜路灣大酒店; nàlùwān dàjiǔdiàn 66 Lianhang Rd ☎089 239 666, ⓦnaruwan-hotel.com.tw; map p.320. Located in the city's northwest, a short taxi ride from the airport and new station, this five-star hotel has lavish, airy rooms with all the usual amenities. Included in the complex are restaurants, a nightclub, a shopping area, a spa, and a saltwater swimming pool. NT$4500

The Gaya Hotel 169 Xinsheng Rd ☎089 611 888, ⓦwww.gaya-hotels.com; map p.320. Another smart new addition to Taitung's hotel selection, *Gaya* is in a great location close to shops and restaurants on Xinsheng Rd. Rooms are subtly styled and feature all mod cons, plus there are a couple of restaurants and a lap pool on the roof. NT$5390

★**Makapahi** 台東伊亞咖啡民宿; táidōng yīyà kāfēi mínsù 517 Gengsheng Rd ☎089 342 394, ⓦmakabahi.idv.tw; map p.320. This unique, indigenous-themed hotel is a bit of a trek from downtown, but thoroughly worth the journey. The exterior is boldly painted with indigenous murals, and each room is styled to reflect one of the different eastern tribes. Handmade indigenous crafts and clothes are for sale in the lobby, plus there's a small garden area at the back and free bike hire. NT$1800

Oia Café & Guesthouse 台東伊亞咖啡民宿; táidōng yīyà kāfēi mínsù 11 Alley 62, Lane 76, Zhengqi N Rd ☎089 333 010, ⓦoiacafe.com; map p.320. Seven rooms in a modern two-storey house with a vaguely Mediterranean theme (red-tile bathrooms, small balconies and wrought-iron beds); the café serves great coffee, tea, beef stew and chicken curry (from N$150). Free bike use. NT$1600

★**Sheraton** 桂田喜來登酒店; guìtián xǐláidēng jiǔdiàn 316 Zhengqi Rd ☎089 328 858, ⓦwww .sheraton-taitung.com; map p.320. Taitung's first international five-star hotel opened in late 2014 and offers a great central location and all of the trimmings you'd expect: elegant rooms with all mod cons, two restaurants,

a gym and 25m indoor pool, and an atmospheric rooftop café. NT$5390

Taitung Aboriginal Culture Hotel 原住民文化會館; yuánzhùmín wénhuà huìguǎn 10 Zhongshan Rd ☎089 340 605; map p.320. Run by friendly local tribal groups, this hotel makes up with ambience for its slightly inconvenient location about 1km north of the city centre. NT$2700

Taitung Traveler Hotel 台東旅行家商務會館; táidōng lǚxíngjiā shāngwù huìguǎn 42 Anqing St ☎089 326 456, ⓦtravelerhotel.com.tw; map p.320. Solid budget option in the heart of town, close to the bus stations, with small but comfortable doubles and Japanese-style rooms; rates rise significantly on weekends and holidays. Free bike use. NT$1180

Traveller Inn 旅人驛站; lǚrén yìzhàn 414 Zhongshan Rd, at Xinsheng Rd ☎089 353 300, ⓦwww .traveller-inn.com; map p.320. With an exterior painted like a street map, it's difficult to miss this new place. The property is divided into two parts, a hotel and a hostel, both of which are modern, clean and well run. The traffic theme continues indoors, where hotel rooms are marked as bus stops and walls are decorated with murals of famous sights along the east coast and Rift Valley. The ten-bed dorms are single sex. Dorms NT$500, doubles NT$1800

ZHIBEN

Ayawan ㄚ一ㄚ旺; aya wàng 136 Longquan Rd ☎089 515 827. A sprawling place below the main road, two-thirds of the way up to the national park, offering extensive springs and charming, if slightly shabby, rooms looking over the valley, with some camping available. Camping NT$600 per tent plus NT$200 per person, doubles NT$2500

Hotel Royal Chihpen 知本老爺大酒店; zhīběn lǎoyé dàjiǔdiàn 23 Lane 113, Longquan Rd ☎089 510 666, ⓦhotelroyal.com.tw. Zhiben's poshest hotel, with 183 rooms equipped with hot-spring tubs. Occupying the side of a hill just off the main Longquan Rd, the complex includes a swimming pool, recreation area,

5

putting greens, an archery range and an outdoor stage where touristy Puyuma dance performances are held nightly. Non-guests can soak in the enticing bathing pools for as long as they want for NT$350. NT$8580

Hoya Hot Springs Resort & Spa 知本富野渡假村; zhīběn fùyě dùjiǎcūn 16 Longquan Rd ☎089 510 510, ⓦwww.hoyaresort.com.tw. Stylish option close to the main strip of hotels and overpriced restaurants, with sleek, modern rooms and an attractive spa (private rooms NT$900/hr). NT$3300

Ming Chuan Hotel 名泉旅遊山莊; míngquán lǚyóu shānzhuāng 267 Lane 2, Longquan Rd ☎089 513 996. A cheap and cheerful option, on the hill directly across from the Forest Recreation Area entrance. Facilities are basic but clean, with a small outdoor bathing pool, and some of the motel-style rooms and private cabins look out onto the valley's best scenery, including a spectacular waterfall. Price includes breakfast. NT$1500

EATING

Every Sunday night, Taitung's lively **Siwei Rd Night Market** (四維路夜市; sìwéilù yèshì) sets up between Zhonghua and Guangfu roads. One of the most popular treats, but not one for the finicky, is pigs' blood soup (豬血湯; zhūxiě tāng), a thick broth filled with diced cubes of congealed pig's blood. Taitung is also known for its amazing variety of **fruit**, most famously the **custard apple** (釋迦; shìjiā). The best place to find it is along "**Fruit Market**" (水果市場; shuǐguǒ shìchǎng), the long stretch of Zhengqi Rd between Zhongshan and Boai roads. As well as the Western options listed below, Taitung has two *McDonald's* branches (on Xinsheng Rd and at the southern end of Zhonghua Rd) and a *Starbucks* on Boai Rd.

TAITUNG

Beinan Pig's Blood Soup 卑南豬血湯; bēinán zhūxiětāng 117 Chuanguang Rd ☎089 324 472; map p.320. No-frills place famous in the area for pig's blood soup (NT$40), a concoction that tastes a lot better than it sounds. No English spoken. Tues–Sun 10am–6pm.

★**Linjia Chou Doufu** 林家臭豆腐; línjiā chòudòufú 130 Zhengqi Rd, between Fujian and Guangdong roads ☎089 334 637; map p.320. This tiny shop is legendary with locals, as much for its eccentric owner as for its unique stinky tofu (NT$50 for small portion, NT$100 for large), which is made from green beans rather than the usual soya. Mon–Fri 2–9.30pm, Sat & Sun noon–10.30pm.

Mibanai 米巴奈; mǐbānài 470 Chuanguang Rd, at Renai Rd ☎089 220 336; map p.320. Touristy indigenous restaurant, and ostensibly Amis-themed (the staff wear traditional dress), this place is aimed squarely at groups, but it's not bad; the betel-nut salad (NT$250), corn-wrapped in bacon (NT$50) and salty wood-fired pork (NT$280) are delicious. Daily 11am–2pm & 5–9pm.

★**Old Taidong Noodles** 老台東米台目; lǎotáidōng mǐtáimù 151 Datong Rd ☎089 348 952; map p.320. Beloved noodle shop, open since 1955, which remains so popular that it has recently upgraded from the original tiny store next to *Linjia Chou Doufu* to a vast, modern restaurant around the corner. The big bowls of aromatic soup noodles with tea eggs for just NT$45 are still just as popular, though the setting is now far more refined. No English spoken. Daily 11am–10pm.

Uncle Pete's Pizza 披薩阿伯; pīsà ā bó 167 Linhai Rd Sec 1 ☎0952 179 165; map p.320. Quirky little place serving some of the best pizza in Taiwan; the owner sometimes plays the banjo while customers dine. Pizzas cost NT$250–350 and can be requested with two different flavours – one per half. Mon & Wed–Fri 5–9pm, Sat & Sun 11.30am–2pm & 5–9pm.

Xiao Jia Meatballs 蕭家肉圓; xiāojiā ròuyuán 177 Zhonghua Rd Sec 1, at Siwei Rd ☎089 327 316; map p.320. Small shop that opens in the afternoons only, selling the local version of *bah-oân* – meatballs of delicately fried glutinous rice with a pork filling (NT$40/bowl). Daily 2–5.30pm.

ZHIBEN

Datoumu Restaurant 大頭目野食館; dàtóumù yěshí guǎn 45 Longquan Rd ☎089 510 280. The best restaurant in town, often busy with groups dining and, less appealingly, singing karaoke. Friendly staff are decked out in tribal costumes, and the menu includes some tasty indigenous dishes, featuring boar, betel-nut flower and bird's nest fern. Main dishes NT$200–300. Daily 4–11.30pm.

Houqu Chufang 猴區廚房; hóuqū chúfáng 268 Longquan Rd ☎089 516 011. Set in a lovely location just a stone's throw from the Forest Recreation Area, this sweet little place serves simple dishes such as fried rice, plus regional specialities including wild vegetables (NT$150) and hot-spring eggs. Mon, Tues, Thurs, Fri & Sun 10am–5.30pm, Sat 10am–8pm.

DRINKING

TAITUNG

Kasa Café 102 Heping St ☎0970 927 291; map p.320. The most appealing place in Taitung's centre for a quiet drink, furnished with thick wooden tables and chairs, laidback *Kasa* serves coffee, beers (NT$100–150) and cocktails (from NT$170), as well as appealing snacks including barbecue ribs and nachos (NT$160). Daily 7pm–2am.

Ludao (Green Island)

5

綠島;lǜdǎo

A verdant Pacific gem about 33km east of Taitung, **LUDAO** flourishes with tropical vegetation inland and a jaw-dropping abundance of colourful **marine life** amid the nourishing coral that skirts its shoreline. Its beauty and relative accessibility – a fifteen-minute flight or fifty-minute ferry ride from Taitung – have made it an immensely popular tourist destination, with a holiday atmosphere starkly at odds with its recent history as Taiwan's principal place of exile for political prisoners. Site of the notorious **Ludao Lodge**, where tens of thousands were held without proper trials and routinely tortured during the **White Terror** period (see box, p.326), the island is now equally well known for some of Taiwan's finest **snorkelling** and **diving**. It also boasts the atmospheric **Zhaori Hot Springs**, one of only a handful of natural **saltwater hot springs** in the world.

Given its small size – an 18km surfaced road loops round it – Ludao can easily be explored by scooter, car or bike, and some Taiwanese opt to fly in for a day-trip before returning to Taitung for the night. There are accommodation and dining options dotted in all of the villages around the coast, but the greatest concentration is in the tourist centre of **Nanliao Village** (南寮村; nánliáocūn); boats and flights arrive and depart nearby. Ludao gets very crowded during the **summer holidays**, and especially at

0   1
kilometre

Loumen Rocks

Zhongliao Bay

Ludao Lighthouse

Chaikou Diving Area

Green island Human Rights Culture Park

New Life Correctional Centre

Niutou Hill

Zhongliao Village

Gongguan Village

Human Rights Memorial Monument

Ludao Lodge

Ludao Airport

Ludao Prison

Sika Deer Ecological Park

Guanyin Cave

Ludao Visitor Center

Youzihu

7-Eleven

Nanliao Village

Little Great Wall

Family Mart

Scooter Rental

Sleeping Beauty Rock

Haishenping Bay

Nanliao Harbour

Ameishan (176m)

Pekingese Dog Rock

Shilang Diving Area

Huashaoshan (281m)

Gaoshan Historic Trail

Gaoshan Mountain Trail

EATING
Blue Coral	
Island Homestay	1
Chi Tang You Yu	2
Fisherman	4
Mei Er Mei	5
Monica	3
Mr Hot Dog	6

ACCOMMODATION
Blue Coral Island Homestay	1
Blue Safari Dive Centre	3
Green Ocean Castle	4
Jack's Inn	2
Kaihsing Hotel	7
Shuang Far Hotel	5
Sea Home Hotel	6
Ziping Camping Area	8

Gui Bay

Mati Bridge

Baishawei Beach

N

DRINKING & NIGHTLIFE
| Rudi Bar | 1 |
| Sun Bar | 2 |

Zhaori Hot Springs

Dabaisha Beach

Fanchuanbi Prairie

LUDAO (GREEN ISLAND)

5

weekends, when tourist numbers easily dwarf the island's summer population of around three thousand. In contrast, during the **winter** months, there is a sharp decline in the number of visitors and transport links, and ferries and flights are prone to last-minute cancellations due to stormy weather. If you come during this time, you're likely to have the island mostly to yourself, but it can often be blustery and rainy, and many tourist facilities are closed.

Brief history

Archeological evidence suggests that humans inhabited Ludao as long ago as 1000 BC. According to local myth, it was known as *Sanasai*, and the Amis, Kavalan and Ketagalan tribes believe their ancestors used it as a land bridge for migration. The first **Han Chinese** immigrants arrived in the early 1800s and named it *Huoshaodao* (火 燒島; huǒshāodǎo) or "Fire-burned Island", in reference to the fires that locals would light to help guide fishing boats to shore (the island's highest point, at 281m, is still named Huoshaoshan). In the early 1930s, the occupying Japanese built processing plants for dried fish, which was shipped to Japan. By the 1970s, the raising of **Sika deer**, prized commercially for their antlers, had become a boom industry, and at one point there were more deer than people. This industry has been in decline on Ludao since the mid-1980s, but there are still plenty to be seen, and today they are something of a tourist attraction.

Ludao Lighthouse

綠島燈塔; lǔdǎo dēngtǎ

A good place to start (or end) a circuit of the island is the 33m-tall **Ludao Lighthouse** on the island's northwest corner, one of Ludao's most prominent landmarks. Accessible via a side road from Zhongliao Village (中寮村; zhōngliáo cūn), it's an especially dramatic place to watch the sunset. It was built in 1938, a year after the US cruise liner SS *President Hoover* ran aground on an offshore reef, prompting villagers to stage a valiant rescue effort. In gratitude, the US Government financed the construction of the lighthouse, which sustained serious damage during World War II a few years later.

Green Island Human Rights Culture Park

綠島人權文化園區; lǔdǎo rénquán wénhuà yuánqū • Daily 8am–5.30pm • Free • ☏ 089 671 285 • Round-island bus service stops here

To the east of Gongguan Village are two former prisons and the oceanside **Green**

THE WHITE TERROR

In the minds of many Taiwanese, especially the elderly, Ludao's natural beauty is overshadowed by its brutal past as the primary place of imprisonment, torture and execution during the country's **White Terror** (白色恐怖; báisè kǒngbù). Although in the late 1940s and early 1950s it was mostly targeted at those suspected of being **Communist spies** for the mainland, eventually students, intellectuals and professionals accused of criticizing the government were rounded up, tortured and interrogated before being imprisoned or executed. During this time, more than ninety thousand people were arrested in Taiwan and at least half were put to death. From 1951 until the end of martial law in 1987, more than twenty thousand political prisoners were shipped to Ludao, where they were held in the notorious Green Island Reform and Re-education Prison or **Ludao Lodge**, just east of Gongguan Village. Here, inmates were confined to damp underground bunkers and routinely tortured. Some were held for more than thirty years before being freed, and an estimated one thousand were executed here. The prison, dubbed "**Oasis Villa**" in Chinese in the 1970s (in extreme irony) is now part of the Green Island Human Rights Culture Park (see above).

Island Human Rights Culture Park, which looks out over impressive General Rock, and has walls inscribed with the names of those who were persecuted during the White Terror. The words on the graceful stele of the **Human Rights Monument** (人權紀念碑; rénquán jìniàn bēi) are by writer Bo Yang, who spent twelve years in prison here: "During that era, how many mothers have cried through the night for their children imprisoned here?"

Across the road, the former prison now known as **Ludao Lodge** (綠島山莊; lǜdǎo shānzhuāng), was built in 1972 to house an influx of inmates following the 1970 Taoyuan Prison Uprising. The prison buildings offer an eerie insight into life in the prison; you might well find that touring the cells, particularly the padded ones, is a disturbing experience.

A little further east, the **New Life Correctional Center** houses an exhibition centre recounting the history of the site through films and displays, detailing the daily lives of prisoners with the use of scarily real-looking mannequins. Continuing along the road past the prison takes you up a hill from where there are captivating **views** over the prison to the ocean.

Guanyin Cave

觀音洞; guānyīn dòng • Round-island bus service stops here

Near the island's northeast corner is **Guanyin Cave**, a water-eroded limestone opening containing several stalactites and stalagmites: one of the latter is said to resemble Guanyin, the goddess of mercy, and is wrapped accordingly in a flaming red robe. Legend has it that during the Qing dynasty a fisherman in peril was led safely to shore near here by a mysterious light emanating from the cliffs. The area was then searched by locals, who found the stalagmite and likened it to Guanyin sitting on a lotus.

Youzihu

柚子湖; yòuzihú

South of Guanyin Cave, a steep, winding road leads down to the left to an extraordinary stretch of wave-beaten coral coastline, surrounded by towering crags. The sheltered, sandy area just inland is an abandoned indigenous settlement known as **Youzihu** (Pomelo Lake) where several derelict **old dwellings** are slowly succumbing to the encroaching vegetation. The area is one of the island's most atmospheric and, largely hidden from view of the main road, it escapes the student-driven scooter armadas that race round the island.

Xiao Changcheng Trail

小長城步道; xiǎochángchéng bùdào • Round-island bus service stops here

About halfway down the east coast the **Xiao Changcheng Trail** (or Little Great Wall Trail) is a short path that follows the spine of a hill to a lookout point, and indeed bearing some resemblance to a stretch of the Great Wall winding towards a guard tower. It's a quick walk to the lookout point, from where there are truly majestic views of the shoreline to both north and south. Jutting out of Haishenping Bay (海參坪; hǎishēnpíng) to the south are two giant **rock formations** named Sleeping Beauty Rock and Pekingese Dog Rock (哈巴狗與睡美人岩; hābāgǒu yǔ shuìmĕirén yán).

Guoshan trails

Just below Huoshaoshan (火燒山; huǒshāoshān), the now-extinct volcano whose eruption created the island, two **trails** lead from the Nanliao Service Road down to the

5

southeastern corner of the island. Coming from Nanliao, the first you'll come to is the **Guoshan Historic Trail** (過山古道; guòshān gūdào), a short but quiet walk of less than 2km which rejoins the coastal road at Km11. The second hike, the **Guoshan Mountain Trail** (過山步道; guòshān bùdào) is a similar length but begins a little further south and is a bit more exhilarating, skirting the eastern flank of 281m Huoshaoshan, and passing through typhoon-damaged forests before emerging onto the coastal road at Km13, near the campsite and hot springs. Note that the mountaintop has a military radar installation and is strictly off-limits.

Zhaori Hot Springs

朝日溫泉; zhāorì wēnquán • Daily: May–Sept 5am–2am; Oct–April 6am–midnight • NT$200 • ☎ 089 671 133 • Round-island bus service stops here

Near Ludao's southern tip are the **Zhaori Hot Springs**. The saltwater hot springs are created by a rare phenomenon: the tide carries seawater into coral crevices, where it's funnelled deep underground, heated geothermally and pressurized back to the earth's surface. They have been harnessed into three circular **seawater bathing pools**, each with different temperatures that allow you to adjust gradually to the hottest one: the range is typically 30–43°C, and once you get too hot you can clamber into the sea to cool down. During the scorching-hot summer, the pools are open until 2am, allowing you to come for a late-night dip, as the waves crash against the surrounding tidal flats.

As the oceanside pools are very exposed to the elements, they are often closed during rough seas, but there are a selection of tiled pools and gushing water jets just inland, where you'll also find changing rooms and a simple café and shop.

ARRIVAL AND DEPARTURE | **LUDAO (GREEN ISLAND)**

BY PLANE

Flying from Taitung is more expensive than taking the ferry and, in clear weather, flights offer spectacular views of both the Taiwan coastline and the island emerging from the deep blue of the Pacific. Ludao Airport (綠島機場; lǜdǎo jīchǎng; ☎ 089 671 261) is less than 1km north of Nanliao Village. There are three flights per day from Taitung (7.20am, 1pm & 4.40pm), and three leaving Ludao (8.10am, 1.50pm & 5.30pm; 15min) with Daily Air (☎ 089 362 485, ⓦ www.dailyair .com.tw). Taitung Airport is easily reached from the centre of Taitung or from Taitung train station. You can reserve a seat over the phone, or buy a ticket at the Daily Air offices at any of the three airports. Be aware that schedules change and flights are often delayed or cancelled, especially in winter.

BY FERRY

Most visitors arrive in Ludao by boat from Fugang (富岡; fùgǎng), a few kilometres north of Taitung, accessible by taxi or Dingdong Bus (make sure the driver knows you're getting off at Fugang). Ferries dock at Nanliao Harbour (南寮漁港; nánliáo yúgǎng), about 1km south of Nanliao village. Boats (50min–1hr; NT$900 return) make the journey between two and six times per day in the summer, with more services on weekends and

holidays. In the winter, there is usually only one ferry in either direction per day. Crossings are notoriously rough, especially in winter, when many passengers end up using the sick bags provided. You can buy seasickness tablets at the store next to the Fugang ferry terminal, and at shops in Nanliao.

FERRY TICKETS

On weekdays you can usually just turn up and secure a ticket on the next boat, but on weekends and holidays it's essential to have a reservation, and given the variable schedules it's always best to call in advance (Chinese only) or ask your hotel in Taitung to do it for you. At Fugang, several companies sell tickets including: Farnlin (凱旋客輪; kǎixuán kèlún; ☎ 089 281 047); Golden Star (金星客輪; jīnxīng kèlún; ☎ 089 281 477); and Uranus (天王星號; tiānwáng xīnghào ☎ 089 281 617).

ON A TOUR

You can arrange package tours to Ludao from travel agents in Taitung and further afield, as well as from touts at the Nanliao ferry terminal. These usually include accommodation, ferry tickets, scooter rental and snorkelling trips and start from around NT$4000/person (based on a minimum of two people sharing a room).

GETTING AROUND

By scooter The easiest way to get around Green Island is on a scooter. However, following a fatal accident in 2013, scooter rental outfits have tightened up regulations and often only rent to foreigners with a Taiwanese licence; it's worth enquiring at your hotel. Scooters cost around NT$300/24hr. Electric scooters can be rented without a licence and cost NT$600/day; bring your passport.

By car Cars and vans can generally be rented easily (with an international licence) and start at NT$1500/day. Although vehicles are often in poor condition, they should be sufficient to get you around the coastal loop a few times. There's only one petrol station on the island, 200m north along the coastal road from the harbour.

By bike Although it's hilly and sometimes windy, the 18km coastal road is well-suited to cycling, and bikes can be rented from a variety of places in Nanliao Village, including *Green Island Bay Resort* near the ferry terminal (NT$300/day), and there's also a free bike service at the visitor centre. The free bikes are available from 8.30am, but they get rented out quickly in summer and must be returned to the visitor centre by 4pm – you'll also need a copy of your passport.

By bus A bus service makes a circuit of the island (April–Oct 13 daily 8.30am–5pm; Nov–March, 9 daily 8am–5pm), starting in Nanliao Village and stopping at all major attractions. Note that the service isn't always entirely reliable though – check at the visitor centre or call ☎ 089 671 272 to check bus times if you will be relying on the service. There are thirteen bus stops around the island. Tickets cost NT$100, which covers unlimited use for one day.

INFORMATION AND SERVICES

Tourist information The helpful Ludao Visitor Center (綠島遊客服務中心; lǜdǎo yóukè fúwù zhōngxīn; daily 8.30am–5pm; ☎ 089 672 026), across the road from the airport and just north of Nanliao Village, has maps and some English-language information, plus free bike use. There's also an exhibition hall with displays on the island's ecology. The staff can help to arrange snorkelling and diving trips and also make reservations for the campsite near the island's southern tip (see p.330), although this was closed indefinitely at the time of writing.

Services The main post office in Nanliao has an ATM, but this doesn't accept foreign cards. The island's only convenience stores are to be found in Nanliao.

ACCOMMODATION

Accommodation on Green Island is mostly expensive for what you get, but in the winter substantial discounts can be negotiated. The bulk of **accommodation** is concentrated in **Nanliao Village**, which teems with Taiwanese tourists all summer, especially at weekends, when most hotels are fully booked. A more relaxed alternative to Nanliao is **Gongguan Village** (公館村; gōngguǎn cūn), in the north of the island, where there are a handful of small hotels near one of the top snorkelling and diving spots. Note that standard check-out on Green Island is 10am.

NANLIAO VILLAGE

Kaihsing Hotel 凱薪飯店; kǎixīn fàndiàn 102–12 Nanliao Village ☎ 089 672 033, ⊛ kaihsing.okgo.tw; map p.325. Ludao's biggest and busiest hotel, catering mostly to domestic tour groups; rooms are comfortable and modern, with wooden floors and bright colours, although a/c units are often noisy. **NT$2300**

Shuang Far Hotel 雙發渡假飯店; shuāngfā dùjiǎ fàndiàn 146 Nanliao Village ☎ 073 425961; map p.325. Often fully booked, *Shuang Far* has a good location in the centre of Nanliao, and offers bright, spotlessly clean rooms, some with sea views. **NT$1600**

Sea Home Hotel 海洋之家渡假村; hǎiyáng zhījiǎ dùjiǎcūn 39 Nanliao Village ☎ 089 672 515, ⊛ ocean-resort.com.tw; map p.325. Large hotel with immaculate, breezy rooms, some with sea views. It's a little pricey and the management is reluctant to offer discounts in summer, but in winter sizeable discounts can be had. Breakfast included. **NT$2520**

GONGGUAN VILLAGE

Blue Coral Island Homestay 藍色珊瑚島民宿; lánsè shānhú dǎo mínsù 1 Gongguan Village ☎ 0920 572 356; map p.325. Above an ice cream parlour, this small place has clean, comfortable rooms with a/c and TV. The friendly owners will usually let singles stay in a double room for half of the price making it one of the best deals on the island for solo travellers. **NT$2000**

Blue Safari Dive Centre 籃莎潛水中心; lánshā qiánshuǐ zhōngxīn 72 Gongguan Village ☎ 089 671 888, ⊛ blue-safari.com.tw; map p.325. A dive centre with dorms and simple doubles. As well as organizing diving and snorkelling trips, the centre also has bikes and scooters for hire. Staff speak English. Dorms **NT$600**, doubles **NT$1960**

Jack's Inn 傑克會館; jiékè huìguǎn Coastal Rd, just before Gongguan Village ☎ 089 671 018, ⊛ ck79.okgo.tw; map p.325. Clean and attractive rooms with fridge, TV and wood floors, set in a pleasant garden just west of Gongguan Village. **NT$3200**

5

GREEN ISLAND SNORKELLING AND DIVING

Snorkelling is a highlight of Green Island, ringed as it is by remarkably intact coral that teems with tropical fish. The sheer diversity of marine life here easily rivals many better-known snorkelling areas in Southeast Asia, making it a real treat if you can manage to avoid the summer weekend crowds. If you plan to snorkel, it's recommended that you bring your own kit: mask, snorkel and neoprene booties (to protect your feet from sharp coral) should be sufficient. At times **jellyfish** can be a problem, in which case you can easily **rent a wetsuit** from one of the many snorkelling and diving operators in Nanliao and Gongguan villages.

DIVING AND SNORKELLING SITES

The best-known snorkelling spots are **Chaikou** and **Shilang** (石朗潛水區; shíláng qiánshuǐ qū), both of which have gentle currents. The stretch of reef near **Dabaisha Beach** (大白沙潛水區; dàbáishā qiánshuǐ qū) in the southwest also has excellent snorkelling and a pathway out to the drop-off, but as currents here are less predictable it's better suited to strong swimmers and scuba divers.

OPERATORS

Unless you're a weak swimmer or are uncomfortable in the ocean, it's best to avoid the **organized snorkelling trips** arranged by local operators. Such outings will usually entail a group of several dozen people, clad in life vests and linked together by a rope. Professional diving operators on the island include: **Blue Safari Diving Center** (籃莎潛水中心; lánshā qiánshuǐ zhōngxīn; ☏089 671 888, ⓦblue-safari.com.tw) at 72 Gongguan Village; and **Cool Diving** (庫達潛水; kùdá qiánshuǐ; ☏0911 736 739, ⓦkudaokgo.com) at 52-1 Zhongliao Village. **Taiwan Dive** (☏07 226 8854, ⓦtaiwandive.com), which operates from Kaohsiung, can also arrange dive trips to the island, and runs winter trips to dive with **hammerhead sharks** here.

ELSEWHERE ON THE ISLAND

Green Ocean Castle 綠海城堡; lǜhǎi chéngbǎo 52-1 Zhongliao Village ☏089 672 797, ⓦwww .ilovegoc.com.tw; map p.325. Clean, bright rooms set in a Greek-style building in the small village of Zhongliao, less than 1km east of the visitor centre. They have also opened a new wing, which houses *Cool Diving Resort*, with equally good rooms and dorms, plus a dive centre. Dorms **NT$1000**, doubles **NT$3000**

Ziping Camping Area 紫坪露營區; zǐpíng lùyíng qū ☏089 671 133; map p.325. This shady campsite is wonderfully located near the island's southern tip, close to the hot springs and lovely Baisha beach. However, it was damaged by Typhoon Nepartak in 2016 and at the time of writing was still closed – when it reopens, the easiest way to book your pitch is usually through the tourist office.

EATING

Both Nanliao and Gongguan villages are filled with **seafood** restaurants, although some cater mainly to large tour groups, making it difficult for independent travellers to order specific items.

NANLIAO VILLAGE

Chi Tang You Yu 池塘有魚; chítáng yǒuyú 150 Nanliao Village ☏089 672 683; map p.325. This long-established restaurant serves up tasty seafood and has a relaxing seafront patio on the first floor. Popular dishes include sashimi (NT$250) and garlic octopus (suàn xiang zhāngyú). Daily 8am–2.30pm & 5.30–8.30pm.

Fisherman 釣魚人餐廳; diàoyúrén cāntīng Nanliao Village ☏089 671 022; map p.325. Popular restaurant serving delicious seafood and venison as well as Chinese classics including *gongbao jiding* (NT$200). In good weather, they open the back of the restaurant up and there are a few tables looking out to the ocean. Daily 11am–2.30pm & 5–8.30pm.

Mei Er Mei 美而美; měiérměi 103–1 Nanliao Village; map p.325. A great spot for a light breakfast of egg pancakes (dàn bǐng). The breezy upstairs balcony has splendid sea views. Daily 6am–11am.

Mr Hot Dog 哈狗店; hāgǒu diàn 103 Nanliao Village ☏089 671 711; map p.325. This trendy café-bar has a brightly painted interior and comfy outdoor seating. The menu features burritos (NT$180–200), spaghetti, pizza and salads. Also popular for drinks: happy hour runs noon–2pm and 6–8pm. Daily 10.30am–1am.

Monica 海景精典餐旅; hǎijǐng jīngdiǎncānlǚ 126 Nanliao Village ☏089 671 057; map p.325. With a warm and sophisticated interior, this place serves Chinese food, including Green Island specialities. Dishes include stir-fried venison with scallion (NT$250), and sashimi (NT$100–200). Daily 9am–2.30pm & 5–9pm.

GONGGUAN VILLAGE
Blue Coral Island Homestay 藍色珊瑚島; lánsè shānhúdǎo 1 Gongguan Village ☎0920 572 356; map p.325. Friendly café serving an interesting selection of ice creams (NT$30 per scoop) and juices, focusing on local fruits; the custard apple ice cream is delicious. There are also rooms for rent upstairs (see p.329). Daily 9am–5pm, later in summer.

DRINKING

Green Island's lively summer bar scene centres on **Nanliao**, where several bars are spread across the main street, but there are also open-air **barbecue restaurants** dotted around the island, including the northwest end of Gongguan Village – in season, these are popular drinking spots for the university crowd, but tend to be closed in winter.

NANLIAO VILLAGE
Rudi Bar 鹿出沒注意; lù chūmò zhùyì 111–2 Nanliao Village ☎089 672 008; map p.325. Popular bar run by Sonic, a friendly guy from Taipei. As well as the standard Jinpai (NT$100), the drinks list includes a range of flavoured beers, including pink grapefruit and lychee (NT$150). Daily 11am–2pm & 6pm–late.

Sun Bar 森吧; sēn bā 142 Nanliao Village ☎0955 836 600; map p.325. Opened in 2017 by a young Taipei emigre, this bar has quickly gathered a local following, and is a good place to meet divers and travellers. *Sun Bar* is also one of the only places on the island to feature live music (on summer weekends) and does a good line in Belgian beers (NT$190), plus simple snacks. Daily 6pm–late.

Lanyu (Orchid Island)

蘭嶼; lányǔ

Jutting sharply out of the sea some 91km southeast of Taitung, **LANYU** is one of Taiwan's most picturesque destinations. This volcanic island consists of a green-velvet mountain surrounded by a flat, narrow coastal plain, which stretches into some of the most unspoilt **coral reef** in Asia. In addition to its astounding natural allure, Lanyu is the sole

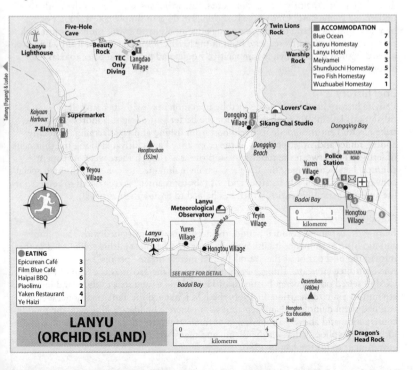

5

ORCHID ISLAND SNORKELLING AND DIVING

The combination of untainted coral reef and the Japan Current, which brings in all manner of tropical marine life, makes Lanyu an ideal place for **snorkelling** and **diving**, and even in summer you can usually have an entire section of reef all to yourself. One distinctive aspect of Lanyu's coral is that it is home to an abundance of amazingly beautiful **sea snakes**, which are easy to spot even when snorkelling. The most common snake is the banded sea krait, which sports zebra-like black-and-white stripes, and though they are venomous, they tend to keep their distance and are seldom aggressive.

DIVING AND SNORKELLING SITES

Though superb snorkelling can be had all around the island, and there are over twenty dive sites in the coastal waters, the two spots that are easiest to access and which consistently have the greatest variety of fish are on the **northern shore**, between Twin Lions Rock and Langdao Village.

OPERATORS

Most hotels in Hongtou can arrange **snorkelling trips**, but it's not necessary to participate in these if you have rented your own transport, and snorkels and masks can be rented for NT$100 per day. The island's most professional dive outfit is **Tec Only Diving** (☏089 732 151 or ☏0939 612 030, ⦿www.lanyuscuba.com) based in Langdao.

domain of Taiwan's purest indigenous tribe: the seafaring **Tao** or "Dawu" (see p.402), whose isolation has allowed them to preserve much of their traditional heritage. Much of the island's appeal is its sheer simplicity: apart from a budding seasonal tourism business, there is no industry on the island and it remains blessedly free of development. There are few tourist sites per se – the main attractions are the rich tropical scenery, the Tao villages with their signature **semi-subterranean houses** and some of the world's most underrated **snorkelling**. One of the best things to do is to simply take a scooter or bicycle round the island (37km), stopping at your leisure to swim, snorkel or just soak up the captivating coastal scenery. Even in the height of summer, when nearby Ludao is choked with tourists, Lanyu is comparatively quiet and peaceful, a place to relax and absorb its timeless rhythms.

Brief history

Lanyu's history has long been defined by its remoteness, with its native Tao inhabitants left mostly to themselves for the better part of eight hundred years. The tribe has for centuries made its livelihood from **fishing** and taro farming, gradually adding millet and sweet potatoes to the crops they have cultivated along the thin belts of fertile land between the mountains and the sea. Though there were infrequent conflicts between villages, the tribe as a whole maintained its cohesion through social conventions, particularly its strict code of **taboos**: many of these related to respect for life and protection of nature, which has helped to ensure their survival.

Outside influence

During the **Japanese** colonial period, the occupiers were intrigued with Tao culture and did little to influence it, although an error by a Japanese anthropologist led to the misnaming of the tribe as the "**Yami**" (which merely means "people") – a name that stuck until recent years. Things began to change for the Tao after the Kuomintang (KMT) seized power, when boatloads of Han Chinese were sent to the island in an attempt to Sinicize the tribe. In 1966, the KMT banned the Tao's traditional **homes** and had them demolished and replaced with concrete buildings. However, the shoddy construction and above-ground design of these structures made them vulnerable to the formidable typhoons that hit the island, and many were destroyed, forcing the government to lift the ban in 1980.

The future

Modernization is taking its toll, with Lanyu's Tao population dwindling fast as young men leave the island in search of greater economic prospects. Another threat, and one that has catapulted Lanyu into the international news headlines over the years, is the presence of 98,000 barrels of low-level **nuclear waste** that the Taiwan Power Company has stored on the island's southern tip since 1982. Following deterioration, storage facilities have been reinforced, but in spite of Taipower's lease on the site expiring in 2014, the government's promises to remove the waste have yet to materialize. In 2016, Tao Foundation chief executive Sinan Mavivo presented draft legislation demanding removal of the radioactive waste from the island within two years and a NT$10 billion (US$316 million) budget to restore local ecology, residents' health, and to assist with development, but it remains unclear if the bill will be enacted – the issue remains highly contentious and "No nukes" signs can be seen all over the island.

Hongtou and around

紅頭; hóngtóu

Lanyu's west coast is the island's most populated area, and holds its three biggest settlements: **HONGTOU** and smaller **Yuren** (漁人村; yúrén cūn) lie 1km apart, and between them form the island's de facto tourist centre, with several hotels and places to eat; less than 10km north of here, **Yeyou** (椰油村; yéyóu cūn) is a larger village, but with little in the way of food or lodging. Just north of Yeyou, **Kaiyuan Harbour** is where boats arrive, and is also where you'll find the island's only petrol station and 7-Eleven, plus a small strip of newer accommodation and eating options.

The island's southwest coast offers wonderful ocean views out to the rugged outcrop of **Little Lanyu** (小蘭嶼; xiǎolányǔ), 3km offshore, and one of the Tao's main fishing grounds. On the island's southern tip, **Dragon's Head Rock** (龍頭岩; lóngtóu yán) is an impressive rock formation which – for once – does actually resemble its name without visitors having to use too much imagination.

Lanyu Meteorological Observatory

蘭嶼氣象觀測站; lányǔ qìxiàng guāncèzhàn • Mon–Fri 8am–12.30pm & 1.30–5.30pm • Free • No bus service

One of the most exciting things to do in Lanyu is to take a ride over the winding **mountain road** (5.7km) that connects the villages of Hongtou and Yeyin. Each bend offers a new perspective on the coastline far below. At one of its highest points is a small car park where you can leave your scooter or car to make the steep fifteen-minute climb up the side road to the **Lanyu Meteorological Observatory**. The observatory

---

TAO TRADITIONS

The **Tao** have been more successful than any other Taiwanese indigenous group in preserving their old ways of life, and time-honoured customs are routinely observed. A few villages still have the traditional stone **semi-underground dwellings** (地下屋; dìxiàwū). These sunken houses, fortified with low walls of wood or stone and covered with asphalt roofs (traditionally thatch), still withstand the test of the typhoons that rip through the Pacific each year. Close to many homes are covered **sitting platforms**, where villagers while away balmy afternoons chatting, playing cards, chewing betel nut – and, for the men, often drinking copious amounts of alcohol. Some elderly men still wear traditional **loincloths**, although the number is rapidly diminishing. The rite of handing down massive **silver helmets** from father to son is also observed, although the younger generation is losing interest in this custom and the art of silversmithing is in danger of dying out. One conventional practice that looks set to stay is the building of handmade **wooden canoes**, intricately carved and colourfully painted vessels.

5

commands astounding views of Dongqing Bay to the east, with truly spectacular sunrises, and one of the Japanese-era buildings here still has American bullet holes from World War II.

Yeyin

野銀部落; yěyín bùluò • The round-island bus service stops here

On the opposite side of the mountain road from Hongtou, intriguing **Yeyin** (aka **Ivalino**) is the only community on the island where many Tao still live in traditional **semi-underground homes**. Coming from Hongtou on the mountain road, the village is strikingly photogenic, and offers the chance to see the traditional houses and boats up close, but you should be wary of taking photographs of people, their boats or houses without their permission (see box below).

Dongqing Bay and around

東清灣; dōngqīng wān • A few kilometres north of Yeyin • The round-island bus service stops here

A few kilometres north of Yeyin, dazzling **Dongqing Bay** has a shingle and grey-sand beach, and offers some of Lanyu's safest swimming. Nearby is **Dongqing** itself (東清; dōngqīng), which has some inviting homestays and cafés, and an intriguing art studio. In front of the village, along the waterfront, is Lanyu's largest collection of traditional wooden canoes, each exquisitely carved and painted in red and white. North of the village the road climbs uphill, and near the top of the hill a trail to the right leads down to a viewing pavilion overlooking a natural rock arch. Slightly further uphill, a wooden pathway heads up to a viewpoint with magnificent vistas along the coast, although at the time of writing the path was badly damaged.

Sikang Chai Studio

希岡菜工作室; xīgāngcài gōngzuōshì • 23 Dongqing Village • Usually open afternoons only; if the studio is locked up, ask in the village for the owner, Sikang Chai • ☏ 089 732 793

The **Sikang Chai Studio**, inside a weather-beaten waterfront shack adorned with a motley array of ornaments, has a curious selection of Tao-influenced **woodcarvings** and sculpture, many with maritime themes. The owner, a Tao fisherman-cum-artist who renders his Chinese name as "Sikang Chai", should be happy to show you around his shop, which is closed most mornings while he's out fishing.

The north coast

About halfway along the rocky north coast lies **Langdao** (朗島; lǎngdǎo), an idyllic Tao community with a few semi-underground houses and handmade wooden canoes visible on the beach. It's also home to the island's best diving outfit, Tec Only (see box, p.332).

MEETING THE TAO

After hundreds of years of isolation, in the past century the **Tao** have been scrutinized, subjugated and persecuted by outsiders, and are now a source of fascination for Taiwanese and international visitors. In spite of all of this, people remain warm, friendly, and open to meeting strangers. That said, wandering around the villages taking photos of everything that comes into your viewfinder, exploring the underground houses (even if they seem uninhabited), sitting in traditional boats, or covertly photographing people should all be avoided. If you really want to meet (and photograph) the Tao and their possessions, the best way is with the assistance of local **guides**, who can be booked through many hotels and homestays (approximately NT$1000 for a group of four for a 2hr exploration, including a visit to an underground home). Without a guide, people may well invite you in to their houses, but communication can be difficult as many older Tao don't speak Chinese.

Continuing on to the north coast of the island, the road passes distinctive stone configurations: **Warship Rock** (軍艦岩; jūnjiàn yán), **Twin Lions Rock** (雙獅岩; shuāngshī yán) and **Beauty Rock** (玉女岩; yùnǚ yán). Just past Beauty Rock is the **Five-Hole Cave** (五孔洞; wǔkǒngdòng), a series of five grottoes eroded into petrified coral. The Tao once called these grottoes the "Home of Evil Spirits" and forbade women and children to come here.

ARRIVAL AND INFORMATION   LANYU (ORCHID ISLAND)

Lanyu is even more prone to flight and ferry **delays** and cancellations than Ludao, especially in winter, when weather and choppy seas make schedules a fluid concept: factor in plenty of extra time in case you get stuck.

By plane Lanyu Airport 蘭嶼機場; lányǔ jīchǎng (☎089 732 220) is about 2km north of Hongtou, the island's main commercial hub. The airport is served by eight flights per day from Taitung (30min; NT$1428) with Daily Air (☎089 732 278, ⓦwww.dailyair.com.tw), although these are frequently cancelled in winter. In summer, on arrival you're likely to be greeted by touts offering you accommodation and scooter rental.

By ferry Touts also greet arrivals at Kaiyuan harbour (開元港; kāiyuán gǎng), several kilometres north of Hongtou, near the village of Yeyou. There are scooters for rent here, plus a few places to stay, and the island's only petrol station and 7-Eleven. Boat schedules from Fugang to Lanyu are notoriously subject to change, but generally speaking there are two services daily in summer (2hr 30min–3hr; NT$1200), dropping to one-to-two weekly in

winter. In summer, there is also a service (once or twice daily) from Houbihu Marina, near Kenting (2hr 30min; NT$1200), as well as a boat from Lanyu to Ludao (2hr; NT$920).

Tourist information The best maps and leaflets about the island are available from visitor centres in Taitung, but there is a small kiosk at the airport with basic information. Aside from this, your guesthouse will likely be your best source of information, and may be able to provide a basic map, as well as organize guides and local tours.

Services The post office in Hongtou (Mon–Fri 8am–noon & 12.30–4pm, Sat 9am–noon) has an ATM, but this doesn't accept international cards. While Hongtou is the island's commercial hub, the best-stocked shops, namely the only 7-Eleven, and a supermarket, are located at Kaiyuan harbour.

GETTING AROUND

By scooter and bike Scooters can be hired at the airport and ferry harbour for NT$500/day. In Hongtou there's a rental shop along-side the main road, just below *Lanyu Hotel*. Make sure there's enough fuel in the tank to get you to the island's only petrol station, next to the harbour. A few bicycles are also available for rent here, a pleasant way to tour around the mostly flat, 37km paved road that loops round the island.

By car If you're visiting in winter or during a rainy spell, you might consider the more comfortable option of renting a car

(NT$2000/day) or van (NT$2500/day); ask at your hotel.

By bus There are no taxis, but a bus makes four daily circuits round the island (7.30am, 9.30am, 1.10pm & 2.30pm; day-pass NT$125), starting from the Lanyu Township Office near Kaiyuan harbour. The bus stops at all villages – and basically anywhere you like, so long as you ask the driver in advance. If you want to flag it down you'll need to make your intentions fairly obvious. Many villagers depend on it, and it's a great way to rub elbows with the locals.

ACCOMMODATION

HONGTOU AND YUREN

Blue Ocean 藍海屋渡假村; lánhǎi wū dùjiàcūn 1–8 Hongtou Village ☎0988 331 116, ⓦboh.com.tw; map p.331. Taiwanese-run dive centre with attractive but pricey wooden cabins across the road, mainly aimed at diving groups. Cabins come in a variety of bed configurations, but all have flat-screen TVs, fridges, and modern bathrooms. NT$4200

★**Lanyu Homestay** 蘭嶼民宿; lányǔ mínsù Hongtou ☎089 731 601; map p.331. Directly across the main road from the hospital, and within a few minutes' walk of several restaurants and small shops, this friendly and homely guesthouse offers half a dozen double and

quad rooms, plus a large, bright six-person dormitory. Free pick-up from the airport or ferry, and they can also arrange snorkelling and night eco-tours. Dorms NT$400, doubles NT$1600

Lanyu Hotel 蘭嶼別館; lányǔ biéguǎn 45 Hongtou ☎089 731 611; map p.331. Faded concrete box catering mostly to Taiwanese tour groups, but just about acceptable if everything else is full. Guests can order breakfast (NT$100), lunch (NT$220) and dinner (NT$220) in advance. NT$1200

Shunduochi Homestay 薰多琦海景休閒民宿; xūnduōqí hǎijǐng xiūxián mínsù ☎089 732 555; map p.331. Owned by a Taipei emigre, this cute

5

LANYU'S COLOURFUL FESTIVALS

Every year, Lanyu's villages are swept up in traditional **festivals**, considered by many to be the most colourful and exotic in Taiwan, and certainly the most profound and vivid expressions of the enduring Tao identity. The three major events are listed below.

The **Flying-Fish Festival** (蘭嶼飛魚季; lányǔ fēiyújì) takes place every spring – usually in March – just before the flying-fish (fēiyú) season begins. It is essentially a coming-of-age ceremony for young Tao males that also is viewed as the harbinger of a plentiful summer flying-fish catch. During the festival, young men dressed in loincloths, steel helmets and breastplates chant for the return of the flying fish before they paddle out to sea in their canoes. The flying fish is an important figure in Tao mythology, and historically it was felt that the more flying fish a young man could catch, the greater his merit to a would-be bride.

The **Millet Harvest Festival**, usually held in mid-June, is a vibrant extravaganza, the highlights of which are an ancient dance performed by the men and the surreal **hair dance** of long-haired Tao women. The latter entails the synchronized, dervish-like whirling of long locks of hair by women in a circle, and is an unforgettable sight.

Boat-launching festivals are much harder to track down, as they are only held when a village has finished building a handmade canoe, and the completion dates for these are always very rough estimates (but are usually in the warmer months). However, if your visit coincides with the launch of a new canoe, you're in for a real treat. The ornate vessels are built through a painstaking process of binding 27 separate pieces of wood together without a single nail, which typically takes two to three years. Once a canoe has been built, intricately carved and painted in red, white and black, villagers hold a monumental **feast** in preparation for the ceremonial launch. Once everyone has finished eating, the canoes are carried down to the sea, where the men perform an elaborate dance in the water before paddling out into the open ocean.

---

little homestay, halfway between Hongtou and Yuren, is easy to spot thanks to its bright-pink facade painted with butterflies. The clean, bright, compact rooms are each decorated in a different colour, and are decent value. NT$1800

YEYIN AND DONGQING

Meiyamei 美亞美; měiyà měi Dongqing Village ☎089 732 949; map p.331. On the main coastal road through Dongqing, this vibrantly painted hotel has small, clean doubles and four-person dorms, and there's also an attractive café-diner downstairs. Dorms NT$550, doubles NT$1800

ELSEWHERE ON THE ISLAND

Two Fish Homestay 兩雙魚民宿; liǎng shuāngyú mínsù Kaiyuan Harbour ☎089 732 210; map p.331. Sleek new place above 7-Eleven at Kaiyuan harbour, with modern, tastefully decorated rooms. The location by the roadside isn't pretty, but it is handy for the ferry and shops, plus there are a couple of restaurants nearby. Advance booking rates are steep, but walk-in guests might be able to secure a room for NT$2000. NT$3800

Wuzhuabei Homestay 五爪貝民宿; wǔzhuābèi mínsù ☎0921 207 124; map p.331. This friendly place opposite Langdao harbour has small but clean and pleasant doubles, and some larger four- and six-person sea-view rooms (NT$2800–3200). NT$1800

EATING

Several simple **restaurants** can be found in Hongtou, Yuren and Dongqing, where you can sample traditional Tao dishes and fresh seafood or simply usher in a summer evening with a cold beer. Dongqing also hosts a weekend **night market** which opens late afternoon, where you can buy cheap grilled fish, barbecued pork and other snacks.

HONGTOU AND YUREN

★ **Epicurean Café** 無餓不坐; wúèbúzuò 77 Yuren Village ☎089 731 623; map p.331. One of the island's best restaurants, this place is perched above the main road in Yuren. Downstairs, the cosy restaurant and bar is decked out in driftwood and one of the tables is cut in the shape of the island, while upstairs the roof deck has low seating and ocean views. An interesting menu offers tasty local set

meals, plus some international dishes including a decent Thai curry; they also serve coffee, beer and cocktails. The Tao Village set meals (NT$350) offer a choice of flying fish, mutton or pork, served with yam and vegetables. Local handicrafts are for sale. Daily except Weds 11am–1.30pm & 6–8.30pm; bar till 11.30pm.

Film Blue Café 海很藍影像咖啡; hǎihěnlán yǐngxiàng kāfēi Hongtou Village ☎0983 092 327;

map p.331. Trendy little café kiosk with shaded outdoor seating in the centre of Hongtou. The English menu includes brownies (NT$120), sandwiches, coffee (NT$70–80), beers and cocktails. April–Oct daily 11am–2pm & 7–11pm.

Haipai BBQ 海派露天炭烤; hǎipài lùtiān tànkǎo 23–1 Yuren Village ☎ 0938 831 200; map p.331. One of a few barbecue places on the southern edge of Hongtou, in a great location looking out over the sea. DIY barbecues cost NT$350 per person and includes pork, chicken, fish and vegetables. April–Oct daily 5.30–10.30pm.

Piaolimu 漂流木; piāoliúmù 24–2 Yuren Village ☎ 089 732 668; map p.331. Inviting little café on the main road through Yuren, with a host of interesting dishes including flying fish in tomato sauce (NT$330), and cream of Lanyu sweet-potato soup, as well as coffee (NT$80). Also has wi-fi. April–Oct 10am–2pm & 5–8pm.

Yaken Restaurant 茶坊; yaken cháfāng 38 Hongtou Village just across from the post office ☎ 089 731 635; map p.331. Friendly and cosy little café, popular with locals and visitors alike. A brightly painted interior and sea views make this a great place to start the day – they offer a range of tasty breakfast meals (until 11am) including scrambled eggs and bacon (NT$80) and pancakes (NT$25–60). The menu also includes simple lunch set meals, such as rosemary chicken leg with rice (NT$180), plus milkshakes, tea and coffee. Daily 7am–4pm.

DONGQING

Ye Haizi 野海子 yě hǎizi kāfēi Dongqing ☎ 0932 732 841; map p.331. Festooned with driftwood, this tiny little café has an interesting menu focusing on local products – main dishes include Lanyu pumpkin with coconut milk (NT$250), cured pork with fried rice (NT$180) as well as the mandatory flying fish set meal (NT$280). They also serve Alishan coffee (NT$110). Tues–Sun 11am–8pm.

The Taiwan Strait Islands

WAIAN, XI ISLAND, PENGHU

The Taiwan Strait Islands

Sprinkled across the windswept channel that separates Taiwan from the People's Republic of China, the Taiwan Strait Islands hold endless fascination for travellers and Chinese-history buffs alike. Closest to the main island of Taiwan, the Penghu archipelago is littered with ruins from the Dutch colonial period and successive Chinese regimes. It boasts some of Asia's most magnificent golden-sand beaches and unspoilt coral reefs.

Kinmen and the **Matsu Islands**, huddled just off the mainland Chinese coast, were once among the world's most forbidding Cold War flashpoints but are now becoming the main bridges for closer ties between Taiwan and the People's Republic of China. Kinmen, an island of extensive tunnels and imposing military installations, boasts especially well-preserved Ming dynasty structures and villages of hybrid Chinese-European houses.

The Penghu Islands

澎湖群島; pénghú qúndǎo

The windswept **PENGHU ISLANDS** are considered national treasures by the Taiwanese, who gush over their rich history, striking landscapes and fine-sand **beaches**. Situated in the south of the strait, the sprawling archipelago stretches some 60km north to south and 40km east to west, and encompasses 64 islands, of which just twenty are inhabited. The major population centres are on the main islands of **Penghu** (whose principal town of **Magong** is the entry and exit point for most tourists), **Baisha** and **Xi**, large landmasses that comprise the island-chain's heart. To the north and south are the **North Sea Islands** and the **South Sea Islands**, accessible by ferries from Baisha and Penghu.

The strong winds that buffet the Penghu Islands during winter have exposed magnificent **basalt mesas** that rise sharply from the sea. These astonishing, temple-like columns are a major draw in themselves, but the islands are also havens for **watersports** such as windsurfing, kitesurfing, sailing, sea-kayaking, fishing and snorkelling. There are also intriguing **historic sites** scattered throughout the chain, and unusual local snacks to try such as dried squid, brown sugar cakes and cactus ice cream. You'll need at least a week to see everything.

Brief history

The first settlements in the Penghu archipelago were not formed until the early twelfth century. In 1281, shortly after conquering China and founding the Yuan dynasty, the **Mongols** set up an official garrison to govern the islands. During the late Ming period of the sixteenth century, Penghu's population began to rise dramatically as droves of **Fujianese** fled the political and military upheaval on the mainland. The **Dutch** set up a temporary base in 1604, but the Ming government expelled them under threat of force. After failing to seize other outposts in the South China Sea, the Dutch returned in 1622, reoccupied the main island of Penghu and built a fort near Magong. In response, Ming forces attacked in 1624 and, after eight months of fighting, the Dutch signed a treaty that allowed them to build outposts on the main island of Taiwan in exchange for leaving Penghu.

Top 5 Phenghu beaches p.343
Penghu watersports p.345

Roaring in the wind p.358
Getting an edge on the enemy p.361

BASALT COLUMNS, PENGHU

Highlights

❶ **Magong** The capital of the Penghu Islands is a laidback town with plenty of sights, including the atmospheric Tianhou Temple, plus a host of snack food specialities. **See p.345**

❷ **Pengnan beaches** Stroll along tranquil Shili, or enjoy watersports at beautiful Shanshui, two of Taiwan's most alluring beaches. See **p.350**

❸ **North Sea Islands** Snorkel in the turquoise waters surrounding Xianjiao and Mudou islets. See **p.352**

❹ **Wangan Island** Spend the night on this tiny islet, the annual nesting site of the endangered green sea turtle. See p.354

❺ **Tongpan's basalt columns** Penghu's volcanic past is most impressively evidenced on Tongpan Island. See **p.355**

❻ **Kinmen** Just a few kilometres from China, this former battleground features extensive tunnels, war museums, ancestral halls and unique hybrid architecture. **See p.356**

❼ **Beigan** Stroll secluded beaches, sample superb seafood and stay the night in Qinbi Village. **See p.380**

❽ **Dongyin** The most dramatic scenery in the Matsu Islands, with sheer cliffs plunging to the sea, capped by the lonely Dongyong Lighthouse. See p.381

HIGHLIGHTS ARE MARKED ON THE MAPS ON P.342 & P.344

TAIWAN STRAIT ISLANDS

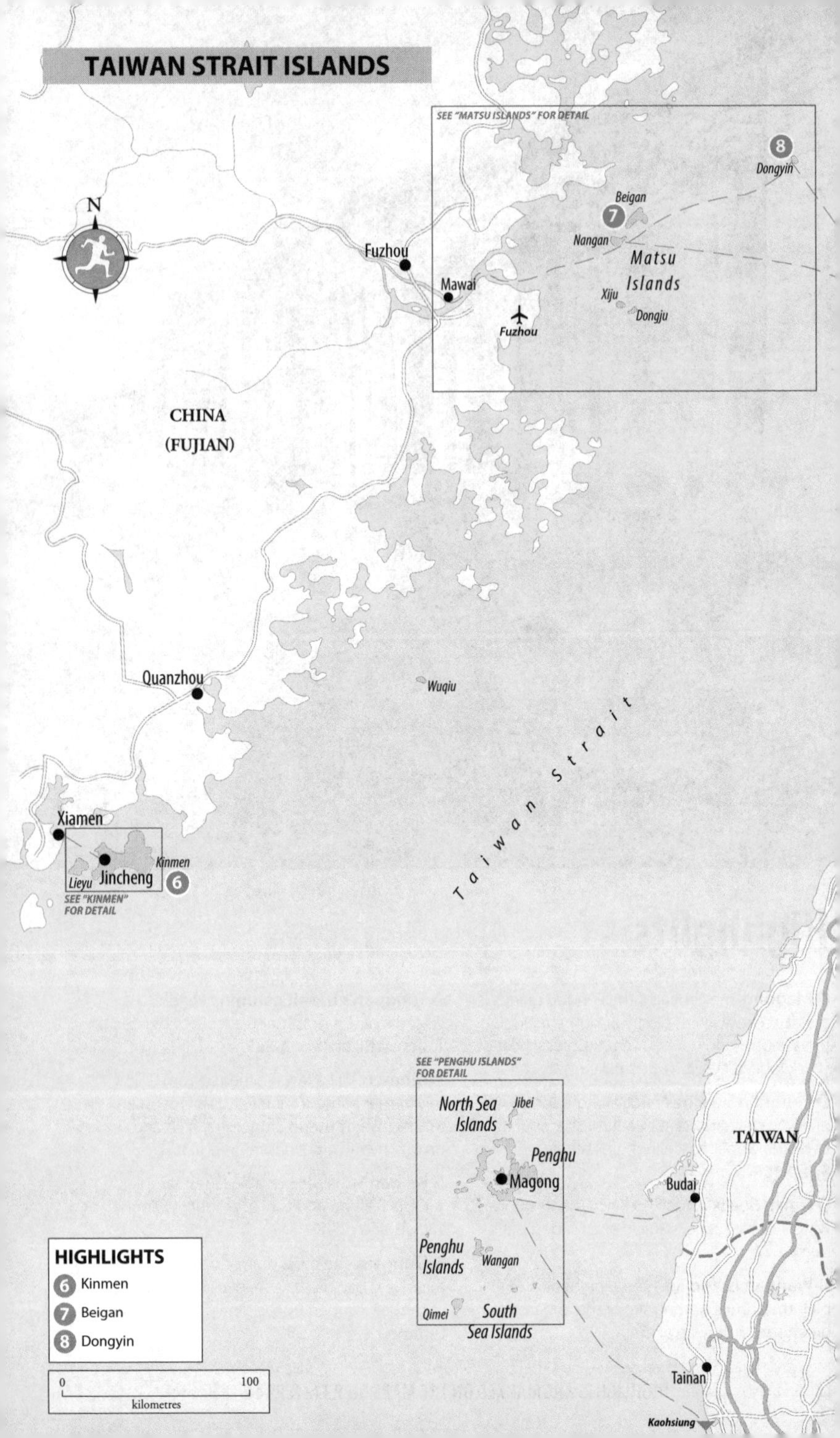

N

SEE "MATSU ISLANDS" FOR DETAIL

Fuzhou

Mawai

✈ Fuzhou

Dongyin 8

Beigan
7
Nangan

*Matsu
Islands*

Xiju

Dongju

CHINA
(FUJIAN)

Quanzhou

Wuqiu

Xiamen

Lieyu Jincheng
SEE "KINMEN"
FOR DETAIL

Kinmen
6

T a i w a n   S t r a i t

SEE "PENGHU ISLANDS"
FOR DETAIL

*North Sea
Islands*   *Jibei*

Penghu

Magong

Budai

TAIWAN

*Penghu
Islands*   *Wangan*

Qimei   *South
Sea Islands*

Tainan

HIGHLIGHTS

6 Kinmen

7 Beigan

8 Dongyin

0 ⊢————————⊣ 100
kilometres

Kaohsiung ▽

In 1661, when Ming loyalist commander **Koxinga** was en route to Taiwan (see box, p.240), he used Penghu as a base, and a garrison was later established here. But his family's rule over the islands was short-lived: Qing-dynasty admiral **Shi Lang** seized Penghu in a naval battle in 1683. The Qing ceded the islands to **Japan** in the 1895 Sino-Japanese Treaty of Shimonoseki. In 1945, the archipelago again fell into Chinese hands, when the **Nationalists** seized it during their retreat from the mainland, placing it under martial law.

Following democratic reforms in the 1980s, Taiwanese began to visit, and the archipelago was officially designated a **National Scenic Area** in 1995. Though development of Penghu has been decidedly low-key until recently, the local government has pushed to attract more international and mainland Chinese tourists. Plans for Penghu to be the next big Chinese gambling haven were scuppered in a 2016 vote, and with any luck the island chain will realize its potential as an eco-destination rather than becoming another Macau.

ARRIVAL AND DEPARTURE

THE PENGHU ISLANDS

BY PLANE

In the busy March–Oct season, Magong can be reached by air daily from Taipei, Taichung, Chiayi, Tainan and Kaohsiung. Flights take 30–50min and prices range from around NT$1200 to NT$2000. There are also flights from Kaohsiung to the biggest of the South Sea Islands – Qimei and Wangan – with Daily Air, and from Kinmen, with Uni Air. In winter, flights are cut back dramatically.

> ### TOP 5 PHENHU BEACHES
> **Shanshui** See p.350
> **Shili** See p.350
> **Peng Peng** See p.352
> **Banli** See p.379
> **Tanghoudao** See p.379

AIRLINES

Magong: Far East Asia Travel 📞06 922 8801; Mandarin Airlines 📞06 922 8692; Uni Air 📞06 922 8986; Wangan: Daily Air 📞06 999 1009.

Destinations from Magong Chiayi (1 daily; 30min); Kaohsiung (17 daily; 40min); Kinmen (5 weekly; 40min); Qimei (1 daily; 15min); Taichung (5 daily; 35–40min); Tainan (4 daily; 30min); Taipei (10 daily; 50–55min).

Destinations from Qimei Kaohsiung (2 daily; 40min); Magong (1 daily; 20min).

Destinations from Wangan Kaohsiung (3 weekly; 45min).

BY FERRY

Ferries are considerably cheaper than flying and are convenient, with several fast services daily from Budai (布袋; bùdài) during the summer months, while Kaohsiung is served by larger, slower boats year-round. To book tickets, bring your passport. If you speak Chinese, you can call ahead to make a reservation and pay on arrival, or you can also book tickets at convenience stores.

FERRIES FROM BUDAI

All Star (滿天星; mǎntiānxīng; 📞05 347 0948 in Budai, 📞06 926 9721 in Penghu), First Today Ferry (今一之星; jīnyīzhīxīng; 📞05 347 6210 in Budai, 📞06 926 0666 in Penghu), Pescadores Ferry (📞05 347 2366 in Budai, 📞06 926 8199 in Penghu) and Taiqi Zhixing (📞06 926 1125 in Budai, 📞05 347 5501) each operate at least one fast ferry service daily (1hr 30min) between Budai and Magong from the beginning of April to the end of Sept. Most services leave Budai at 10am or 10.30am and return at 4.30pm (with more services in the peak summer months). Ferries typically cost NT$1000/1950 one-way/return, although discounted tickets are sometimes offered for as little as NT$750 one-way. Pescadores also offers services from Budai to Qimei (1hr 40min; NT$1000).

Getting to Budai Budai is connected to Chiayi by bus from Chiayi Transport Co Bus Station (嘉義客運總站; jiāyì kèyùn zǒngzhàn) at 503 Zhongshan Rd. Buses leave at 8am to connect with ferries and stop at the High-Speed Rail Station 20–30min later. Heading back, buses usually meet ferries at Budai, with the last bus to Chiayi city (NT$128) at 6.30pm.

FERRIES FROM KAOHSIUNG

Taiwanline Taihua Ferry (台華輪; táihuá lún) runs four to five weekly services from Kaohsiung to Magong (4–5hr; NT$860; 📞07 561 5313) and from Magong back to Kaohsiung (4–5hr; NT$819; 📞06 926 4087). Although the sailing time is longer than from Budai, the Taihua Ferry is larger, so the ride is far smoother and operates year-round.

GETTING AROUND

For transport purposes, the archipelago is divided into three parts: the main islands of **Penghu**, **Baisha** and **Xi**, connected by bridges and best explored by scooter or car; the **North Sea Islands**, reached by ferry from either the North Sea Visitor Center or Qitou Visitor Center (both on Baisha); and the **South Sea Islands**, served by ferry from South Sea Visitor Center in Magong. **Inter-island transport** is set up primarily for tour bus groups; getting to the outlying islands on your own requires a little more perseverance, but once there, scooters (and electric scooters) are available for rent and are your best bet for exploring.

By car and petrol scooter Hiring a scooter or car is definitely the way to go to explore the main island group, and will allow you to escape the tour groups and explore quiet beaches at leisure. You should be able to rent a

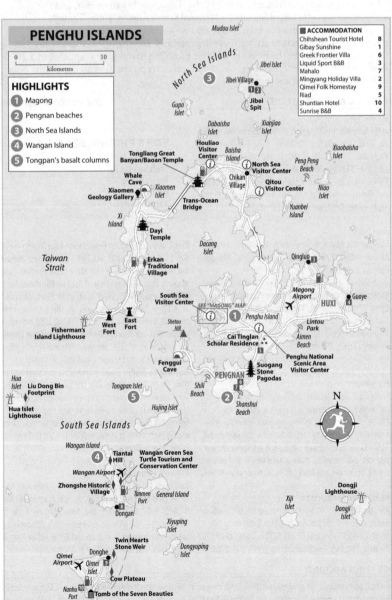

PENGHU ISLANDS

0 _____ 10
kilometres

HIGHLIGHTS

1 Magong
2 Pengnan beaches
3 North Sea Islands
4 Wangan Island
5 Tongpan's basalt columns

█ **ACCOMMODATION**

Chihshean Tourist Hotel	8
Gibay Sunshine	1
Greek Frontier Villa	6
Liquid Sport B&B	3
Mahalo	7
Mingyang Holiday Villa	2
Qimei Folk Homestay	9
Riad	5
Shuntian Hotel	10
Sunrise B&B	4

Mudou Islet

North Sea Islands

Jibei Islet

Jibei Village
Jibei Spit

Gupo Islet

Dabaisha Islet

Xianjiao Islet

Xiaobaisha Islet

Houliao Visitor Center
Tongliang Great Banyan/Baoan Temple
Baisha Island
Peng Peng Beach
Niao Islet
North Sea Visitor Center
Qitou Visitor Center
Chikan Village

Whale Cave
Xiaomen Islet
Xiaomen Geology Gallery
Trans-Ocean Bridge
Yuanbei Islet

Xi Island

Dayi Temple

Dacang Islet

Erkan Traditional Village

Taiwan Strait

Qingluo

Magong Airport
HUXI
Guoye

South Sea Visitor Center
SEE "MAGONG" MAP
Magong Island
Lintou Park

West Fort
East Fort
Shetou Hill
Cai Tinglan Scholar Residence
Aimen Beach

Fisherman's Island Lighthouse

Fenggui Cave
Suogang Stone Pagodas
Penghu National Scenic Area Visitor Center
PENGNAN

Hua Islet
Liu Dong Bin Footprint
Tongpan Islet
Shili Beach
Shanshui Beach

Hua Islet Lighthouse

Hujing Islet

South Sea Islands

Wangan Island

Tiantai Hill
Wangan Green Sea Turtle Tourism and Conservation Center

Wangan Airport

Zhongshe Historic Village
Tanmen Port
General Island

Dongji Lighthouse

Dongan

Xiyuping Islet

Xiji Islet
Dongji Islet

Twin Hearts Stone Weir
Donghe
Dongyuping Islet

Qimei Airport
Qimei Islet

Cow Plateau

Nanhu Port
Tomb of the Seven Beauties

N

PENGHU WATERPORTS

Powerful winter winds make Penghu – the archipelago as a whole but Penghu Island specifically – one of the world's premier **windsurfing** and **kitesurfing** venues, though there's also good old-fashioned **surfing** too. **Guanyinting Recreation Park** (see p.347) has equipment for rent and lessons, or contact the recommended operators listed below.

Liquid Sport 22-3, Qingluo Village ☎0911 267 321, ⊛liquidsportpenghu.com. In a new location close to the action in Qingluo Village, this is one of Penghu's top watersports organizations. They rent out kayaks (NT$400/day), SUP boards (NT$500/day) and full windsurfing equipment ($1500/day). Beginner windsurfing lessons, including all equipment, cost NT$1500/2hr, or NT$1000/hr for more experienced riders. They also have rooms for rent (see p.351).

Mahalo Surfing Shanshui Beach ☎06 995 2893, ⊛mahalosurfing.com. Based in Shanshui, Greg Nolan's surf hotel (see p.350) rents out boards and offers lessons (NT$1200/3hr lesson).

Poseidon Waterpsorts Club 52-7 Shili Village ☎06 995 0178. A few minutes' scooter ride from Shili Beach, Poseidon offers a range of watersports packages including wakeboarding and snorkelling trips (NT$800), as well as SUP rental (NT$800).

Sunrise B&B Guoye Village ☎0956 065 509, ⊛sunrisebb.idv.tw. Jan and Karen Hou of *Sunrise B&B* (see p.351) provide kitesurf (NT$2500/day), windsurf (NT2000/day), and SUP rental (NT$1000/day). They also provide one-on-one kitesurfing lessons which cost NT$5000/2hr including equipment. Guests at the B&B get NT$1000 discount for lessons.

vehicle with an international driver's licence, though some places will only rent out a vehicle to holders of a Taiwanese driving licence and an ARC (see p.27). Shang Zheng Travel Company (☎06 927 0791) at 36 Linhai Rd in Magong will accept your passport for scooter and car rentals. Plenty of other rental shops can be found in central Magong while the *Sunrise B&B* in Guoye (see p.351) has cars and scooters for hire. Scooters generally cost from NT$300/day, while small cars start at NT$1500/day.

By electric scooter Another option – and one which doesn't require a licence – is to hire an electric scooter; there are recharging points at many car parks. These vehicles are less powerful than petrol-powered ones, but more environmentally friendly and totally adequate for

getting around.

By bus The islands have limited public transport, with hourly bus services (NT$19–93) operating along two routes from Magong. One heads to Fenggui Cave on the Pengnan peninsula, while the other route ambles its way across to West Fort on Xi Island. Note that these services are principally aimed at locals, and don't always run to schedule.

By taxi While taxis are useful for short trips between the airport and Magong (NT$200), or around the town (NT$100–150), they work out expensive for longer trips. A full-day tour of the main islands is likely to cost around NT$3500. They can be hailed on the street or ask your hotel to call one for you.

Magong

馬公; mǎgōng

Penghu Island (澎湖本島; pénghú běndǎo) is home to the archipelago's biggest town, **MAGONG**, which is also the major transport hub with an abundance of hotels, restaurants and **historic monuments**. The downtown area itself is easy to navigate on foot and you can duck into the narrow lanes that traverse the old centre without fear of getting lost.

Tianhou Temple

天后宮; tiānhòu gōng • Hui An Rd • Daily 7am–5pm

Set in the city's oldest quarter, the **Tianhou Temple** is Magong's most important historic and religious site. The name "Magong" derives from the Chinese nickname for the temple, dedicated to **Mazu**. Originally a small shrine, said to have been erected by **Fujianese fishermen** at the end of the sixteenth century, the earliest surviving remnant is a **stone stele** eviction notice to the Dutch by the Ming court dated 1604. This stele, unearthed in 1919, bears the weathered inscription of Ming general **Shen You-rong**'s demand that the Dutch "red-haired barbarians" leave the island, and is displayed in a chamber at the rear right-hand side of the temple. The temple itself has undergone numerous renovations.

6

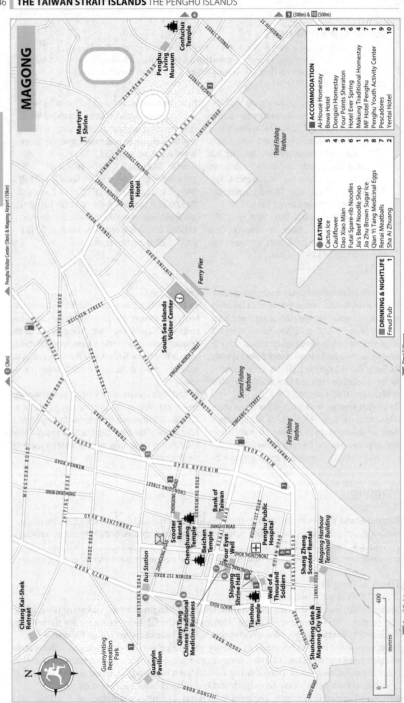

MAGONG

▲ Penghu Visitor Center (5km) & Magong Airport (10km)
▲ ⑪ (2km)
▲ ⑨ (300m) & ⑩ (500m)

Confucius Temple

Penghu Living Museum

Martyrs' Shrine

Sheraton Hotel

Third Fishing Harbour

Ferry Pier

South Sea Islands Visitor Center

Second Fishing Harbour

First Fishing Harbour

Chiang Kai-Shek Retreat

Guanyinting Recreation Park

Bus Station

Scooter Rental

Chenghuang Temple

Beichen Temple

Bank of Taiwan

Penghu Public Hospital

Four Eyes Well

Shigong Shrine Hall

Well of a Thousand Soldiers

Shang Zheng Scooter Rental

Magong Harbour Terminal Building

Guanyin Pavilion

Qianyi Tang Chinese Traditional Medicine Business

Tianhou Temple

Shuncheng Gate & Magong City Wall

● EATING	
Cactus Ice	5
Cauliflower	4
Dao Xiao Mian	9
Futai Spare-rib Noodles	6
Jia's Beef Noodle Shop	1
Jia Zhu Brown Sugar Ice	8
Qian Yi Tang Medicinal Eggs	7
Renai Meatballs	3
Sha Ai Zhuang	2

■ ACCOMMODATION	
Ai-House Homestay	5
Bowa Hotel	8
Dongxin Homestay	2
Four Points Sheraton	3
Hotel Ever Spring	6
Makung Traditional Homestay	4
MF Hotel Penghu	1
Penghu Youth Activity Center	7
Pescadores	9
Yental Hotel	10

■ DRINKING & NIGHTLIFE	
Freud Pub	1

N

0   400   metres

Chinese artistry coupled with Japanese influence present the elegant yet simple fusion of styles that makes this one of Taiwan's most visually captivating temples.

Zhongyang Street

中央街;zhōngyāng jiē

Magong's oldest thoroughfare, pedestrian-only **Zhongyang Street** is now a busy hive of craft shops and guesthouses. At the head of the street is a tiny square containing the **Four Eyes Well** (四眼井; sìyǎnjǐng), said to have been dug as in the fifteenth century. Locals believe there is a "Well Mother God" inside, and many come here to pray every month. On the square behind the well is the **Qianyi Tang Chinese Traditional Medicine Shop** (乾益堂藥行; qiányìtáng yàoháng), a historic building, filled with aromatic medicinal herbs, which has been running since 1918.

6

Guanyin Pavilion

觀音亭;guānyīntíng • Jieshou Rd • Daily 5am–8pm

A short walk northwest of Zhongyang Street is the **Guanyin Pavilion**, a small but graceful temple dedicated to Guanyin, the Bodhisattva associated with compassion, dating from 1696. Although the temple structure itself has been levelled twice during respective wars with the French and the Japanese, the **old bell** inside is original.

Guanyinting Recreation Park

觀音亭親水遊憩區;guānyīntíng qīnshuǐ yóuqìqū

The western edge of downtown Magong meets the ocean in the form of the expansive **Guanyinting Recreation Park**. The park looks out over a bay that is a world class **windsurfing** spot, and windsurf equipment and lessons can be arranged at the park's watersports centre. **Bike routes** also run through the park; there is a bike rental station at the Guanyin Temple entrance.

Penghu Living Museum

澎湖生活博物館;pénghú shēnghuó bówùguǎn • 327 Xinsheng Rd • Daily except Thurs 9am–5pm • NT$80 • ☏ 06 921 0405, Ⓦ www.phlm.nat.gov.tw • You can walk here in around 20min from the ferry pier, or take a taxi for NT$120

On the newer, eastern edge of town, the vast multi-storey **Penghu Living Museum** is a fascinating celebration of the Penghu archipelago's unique history and culture. Inside you'll find multimedia exhibits and videos, a huge scale model of Wangan Village and displays on early migrations to Penghu from China, folk belief, everyday life and the modern history of the islands. Labels are in English, but some of the explanations are in Chinese only.

Confucius Temple

孔廟;kǒngmiào • Daily 10am–5pm, courtyard open 24hr

Next to the Penghu Living Museum, the austere **Confucius Temple** originally housed the **Wenshi School**, built by the Qing in 1766 as Penghu's only centre of higher learning; the school was converted into a Confucius temple during the Japanese occupation. Access to the main **courtyard** is via a pathway to the right of the temple.

ARRIVAL AND INFORMATION | **MAGONG**

By plane Flights (see p.343) arrive at Magong Airport (馬公機場; mǎgōng jīchǎng ☏ 06 922 8188), about 8km east of Magong itself. There is an irregular airport bus (daily 7am–7pm; 30min; NT$23) with some journeys going via Penghu Visitor Center, but the service isn't timed with arrivals from major cities – most buses run in the morning. Some hotels include an airport pick-up service in their rates; otherwise, take a taxi, which should cost about NT$200 to the town centre.

By ferry Next to the main ferry pier is the Magong Harbor Passenger Terminal (馬公港務大樓; mǎgōng gǎngwù dàlóu), where you can buy return tickets for ferries (see p.343) to mainland Taiwan.

Destinations Budai (April–Sept 4 daily; 1hr 30min); Kaohsiung (4–5 weekly; 4–5hr).

Tourist information While there is a small visitor

6

information centre at the airport (open for flight arrivals; ☎ 06 922 8115), the best information can be sourced from the Penghu Visitor Center (澎湖遊客中心; pénghú yóukè zhōngxīn; daily 8am–5.30pm; ☎ 06 921 6521, ⓦ www.penghu-nsa.gov.tw) at 171 Guanghua St, halfway between the airport and Magong; if you have transport (taxis charge around NT$150 from the ferry pier) this is an excellent place to visit before you head out to the islands. In addition to maps and information, there are interesting exhibits on Penghu culture, geology and marine life, but

English-speakers are not always on hand. The closest visitor information desk (daily: April–Sept 6.30am–9.30pm; Oct–March 7am–5pm) to the main ferry pier is inside the South Sea Islands Visitor Center.

Services Magong is the only place in the Penghu Islands with banking services, but many ATMs do not accept foreign cards, so bring plenty of cash with you. The Bank of Taiwan at 24 Renai Rd is your best bet for foreign cards; it also has the only foreign-currency exchange desk.

ACCOMMODATION

Thanks to government incentives, the Penghu Islands are experiencing something of an **accommodation boom**, with more than a hundred and fifty homestays opened and several new five-star hotels built since 2008 – most of these are in or around Magong, many just a short walk from the pier. Still, rooms can become scarce during the June–Aug school break, when **reservations** are recommended. Note that few hotels have signs in English or pīnyīn, so look out for the relevant Chinese characters.

Ai-House Homestay 澎湖愛鄉民宿; pénghú àixiāng mínsù 14 Zhengyi St (near Tianhou Temple) ☎ 06 927 9296; map p.346. Friendly homestay in a great location, with basic but clean rooms – some en suite (NT$1600), some with shared bathrooms – plus a pleasant balcony overlooking the temple. Some English spoken. NT$1200

Bowa Hotel 寶華大飯店; bǎohuá dàfàndiàn 2 Zhongzheng Rd ☎ 06 927 4881, ⓦ bowahotel.com .tw; map p.346. The pick of the older hotels in town, offering good discounts on weeknights. Rooms are bland but modern with large flatscreen TVs. The pricey sea-view rooms (NT$3100) are considerably more comfortable. NT$1820

Dongxin Homestay 東信民宿; dōngxìn mínsù 12 Zhongxing Rd ☎ 06 927 9123; map p.346. Though it's hardly anything special, this small budget hotel with Japanese-style rooms offers some of the cheapest private accommodation in Penghu. Popular with Taiwanese students, especially in summertime, so make sure you book ahead. No wi-fi. NT1000

Four Points Sheraton 澎湖福朋喜來登酒店; pēnghú fúpéng xǐláidēng jiǔdiàn 197 Xindian Rd ☎ 06 926 6288, four-ⓦ points.starwood hotels.com; map p.346. The first international five-star hotel in Penghu, Four Points opened its doors in 2015 and is everything you'd hope it would be, at this price. The 331 rooms have balconies with views of the harbour or city, and there are a host of amenities and facilities, including an infinity pool, gym, spa, sauna and steam room, plus three dining options and a subterranean bar. Free airport shuttle. Breakfast included. NT$5415

Hotel Ever Spring 長春大飯店; chāngchūn dàfàndiàn 6 Zhongzheng Rd ☎ 06 927 3336, ⓦ www.everspring-hotel.com.tw; map p.346. One of downtown's more upmarket options, featuring bright, attractive rooms with breakfast included. Pricier rooms

have harbour views (NT$4000). NT$2400

★**Makung Traditional Homestay** 邂逅老街民宿; xièhòu lǎojiē mínsù 8, Lane 1, Zhongyang St ☎ 06 926 6161; map p.346. This immaculate homestay has wonderful rooms with traditional tiled floors, wood furnishings, fridges and TVs. The owners are friendly and some rooms have balconies overlooking the Shigong Shrine. NT$2300

★**MF Hotel Penghu** 和田大飯店; hétián dàfàndiàn 2 Minquan Rd ☎ 06 926 3936, ⓦ mhoteltw.com; map p.346. This small but stylish boutique hotel offers a variety of rooms with chic, minimalist furnishings, LCD TVs and English-speaking staff, plus a spa and restaurant on site. NT$2900

Penghu Youth Activity Center 澎湖青年活動中心; pénghú qīngnián huódòng zhōngxīn 11 Jieshou Rd ☎ 06 927 1124, ⓦ penghu.cyh.org.tw; map p.346 Located near the waterfront, this comfortable hotel, run by China Youth Corp, has fifteen spacious en-suite doubles with TVs, plus a variety of larger rooms catering to different-sized groups. Prices are cut almost by half Nov–Jan. The location is perfect if you're planning to wind- or kitesurf. NT$2300

Pescadores 百世多麗花園酒店; bǎishì duōlì huāyuán jiǔdiàn 420 Xindian Rd ☎ 06 921 9399, ⓦ pescadoresresort.com.tw; map p.346. The original resort-style hotel in Penghu can be lots of fun: plush rooms with opulent furnishings and sunken marble baths, plus there's a pool and a gym. Good deals offered online. NT$4100

Yentai Hotel 元泰大飯店; yuántài dàfàndiàn 477 Xindian Rd ☎ 06 921 1111, ⓦ yentai-hotel.com.tw; map p.346. A large luxury hotel on Magong's outskirts, slightly reminiscent of a posh mainland China hotel. Rooms are beautifully decorated with polished wooden floors and contemporary takes on traditional Chinese furniture. NT$3850

EATING

Magong is renowned for its **culinary specialities**, ranging from fresh seafood and dried squid to signature noodle dishes, brown-sugar cake (黑糖糕; hēitánggāo), peanut candy (花生糖; huāshēngtáng), seaweed cake (海苔酥; hǎitāisū), and even cactus (仙人掌; xiānrénzhǎn) juice and ice cream, sold in shops all over town. There are a number of small outdoor **night markets** where you can sample cheap local food, while upmarket **seafood restaurants** specialize in several-course meals for large parties. Among the seafood delights that Penghu is most famous for are steamed grouper, raw lobster, abalone and "five-flavour" balloonfish (河豚; cìhétún).

Cactus Ice 掌上明珠; zhǎngshàng míngzhū 39 Minzu Rd ☎06 927 2323; map p.346. This bright and lively little ice-cream café is popular with students for its cactus ice and ice cream (NT$60/cone). Daily 1–10pm.

★**Cauliflower** 花菜干餐廳; huācàigān cāntīng 4-2 Xindian Rd ☎06 921 3695; map p.346. On the outskirts of town, this wonderful little restaurant is worth the journey for its traditional Penghu cuisine, served in an old coral-and-brick house, decked out with period furniture and old movie posters. The restaurant's namesake dish, sun-dried cauliflower, is served stir-fried with green onion and pork julienne. Mains cost NT$250–350. Daily 11am–2pm & 5–10pm.

★**Dao Xiao Mian** 刀削麵; dāoxiāomiàn 30 Zhongshan Rd; map p.346 Penghu's most famous noodle joint has no name; it's a tiny, unassuming place identified by its main dish, dāoxiāo miàn ("knife-cut noodles"), shaved out in thick, wide slabs and fried with pork and bean sprouts (NT$65/plate). Daily except Weds 9.30am–4.30pm.

Futai Spare-rib Noodles 福台排骨麵; fútáipáigǔ miàn 30 Minzu Rd at Gongming Rd ☎06 927 3397; map p.346. Another popular no-frills noodle place, this one specializes in delicious spaghetti-like noodles topped with fragrant chunks of pork off the bone (from NT$90/ bowl). Daily 3.30–10.30pm.

Jia's Beef Noodle Shop 賈老闆紅燒牛肉麵專賣店; jiǎlǎobǎn hóngshāo niúròumiàn zhuānmàidiàn Siwei Rd, outside National Penghu Institute of Technology ☎06 927 9737; map p.346. Students queue at this no-fuss place for the spicy, Sichuan-style braised beef noodles, a fragrant dish with chilli sauce and large chunks of meat (from NT$70). Daily 11am–2pm & 5–9pm.

★**Jia Zhu Brown Sugar Ice** 家竹黑砂糖冰; jiāzhú hēishātáng bīng 27 Fuguo Rd ☎06 927 6722; map p.346. Magong's best-known ice-dessert shop continues to serve up its speciality eight-flavour delight, with all the "little treasures" made by hand on site – think taro balls, red and green beans, fresh mango. Choose six toppings with brown-sugar sauce on top (NT$50). Daily 10am–11pm.

Qian Yi Tang Medicinal Eggs 乾益堂藥膳蛋; qiányìtáng yàoshàndàn 42 Zhongyang St; map p.346. Just in front of the Traditional Medicine Shop, this stall's main product is a lot tastier than it sounds, with eggs (NT$13) and tofu (NT$15/two pieces) boiled in a rich, aromatic broth. It also sells refreshing cactus juice (NT$40). Daily 8am–8pm.

Renai Meatballs 仁愛小吃; rénài xiǎochī 73-1 Renai Rd; map p.346. This tiny place is famous for its Taiwanese meatballs, wrapped in a glutinous coating (NT$34 for two), and is usually packed. Daily 3–9pm.

★**Sha Ai Zhuang** 傻愛莊; shǎài zhuāng 14 Xinsheng Rd ☎06 926 3693; map p.346. This atmospheric restaurant and teahouse, decorated with local crafts, is set in a renovated house that once belonged to Penghu's first county chief. The menu features items such as spiced chicken with chilli (NT$230) and baked potato with pine nuts (NT$200). There are also freshly squeezed juices (from NT$120) and cocktails (from NT$180). Daily 11am–3pm & 5–11pm.

DRINKING

Freud Pub 弗洛伊得酒吧; fúluòyīde jiǔbā 2-1 Xinsheng Rd ☎06 926 4166; map p.346. One of Magong's longest-running bars, with by far its most extensive drinks list, including a huge selection of whiskies/ white liquors and a range of imported bottled beers (NT$110–160). Taiwan Beer is just NT$90, basic cocktails start from NT$150, and the house special "Absolutely Drunk" (NT$300) – mixed with five different spirits – would suit the thirstiest of frat parties. Daily 6pm–2.30am.

Pengnan

澎南地區; péngnán dìqū

Winding south and then west from Magong along a narrow peninsula, the area of Penghu Island known as **PENGNAN** is packed with historic sites as well as some of the archipelago's finest scenery and most accessible beaches, plus a decent selection of places to stay and eat.

6

Cai Tinglan Scholar Residence
蔡廷蘭進士第; càitínglán jìnshìdì

The **Cai Tinglan Scholar Residence** is the ruined house of Penghu's only jìnshì, a scholar possessing the highest degree of attainment in Imperial China's examination system – during the Qing dynasty. Built in 1846, the house is a popular sight despite its dilapidated state, thanks to the fame (in Taiwan at least) of its original owner.

Suogang Stone Pagodas
鎮港子午寶塔; suǒgǎng zǐwǔ bǎotǎ • Halfway down the Pengnan peninsula's east coast

The small fishing village of **Suogang** is the site of the **Suogang Stone Pagodas**, a pair of 11m-high pyramid-shaped towers. The pagodas are believed to drive away evil spirits and provide protection during natural disasters, and are located a few hundred metres apart; one is called the "north tower" and the other the "south tower".

The beaches
On Pengnan's southern coast, **Shanshui Beach** (山水沙灘; shānshuǐ shātān) offers fine golden sand, clear water and a gentle break that is suitable for surfing in winter. There are also plenty of places to stay nearby, plus a few cafés and surf shops in Shanshui itself, although this means it gets very busy at times.

Halfway along the narrowest stretch of the Pengnan peninsula, the shimmering crescent of **Shili Beach** (蒔裡沙灘; shílǐ shātān) is one of the prettiest strips of sand in the entire archipelago. Adjoining a small village, the beach offers good paddling and swimming at high tide.

Fenggui Cave
風櫃洞; fēngguì dòng

On the westernmost tip of the Pengnan peninsula, **Fenggui Cave** is actually a blowhole, a wave-carved hole into the columnar basalt rock through which water rushes at high tide, creating a spectacular plume.

Shetou Hill
蛇頭山; shétóu shān

North of Fenggui Cave, **Shetou Hill** is the site of Penghu's first Western-style fort, built by the Dutch in 1622. A few remnants are all that remain of this once heavily fortified point, but these are far overshadowed by the splendid views across the bay to Magong.

ACCOMMODATION   **PENGNAN**

Greek Frontier Villa 希臘邊境; xīlà biānjìng Route 26, Shanshui ☎ 06 995 0625, ⓦ penghu.in; map p.344. Greek villa-style hotels are hardly original in Taiwan, but this small place delivers spacious, comfortable, nicely styled rooms with TVs and fridges. There's a small garden and a tiny plunge pool, and the property is walking distance from Shanshui Beach. NT$3420

Mahalo 山水衝浪民宿; shānshuǐ chōnglàng mínsù Shanshui Beach ☎ 06 995 2893, ⓦ mahalosurfing.com; map p.344. Relaxed surf hotel and café just back from the beach in Shanshui. Rooms are

light, modern and well furnished, and the owner, Greg Nolan, can arrange surf hire and lessons (see box, p.345). NT$2200

Riad 北非花園旅店; běifēi huāyuán lǚdiàn Route 201, 400m south of Route 204 junction ☎ 06 921 0612, ⓦ penghu.in; map p.344. Owned by the same corporation as *Greek Frontier Villa*, here the style is North African – and though the theme is hardly authentic, the rooms are well presented and furnished. They offer free airport transfers, but the location is still only convenient if you have your own transport. NT$3420

Huxi
湖西; húxī

The central and eastern sections of Penghu Island comprise an area known as **HUXI**, a broad swath of flat land fringed by beautiful beaches and filled with farmland and parks – indeed, **Lintou Park** (林投公園; líntóu gōngyuán) is the only place in the archipelago where trees grow in abundance. Near the region's centre, the township of Huxi itself has basic amenities and services, including a few restaurants and convenience stores. The east coast is lined by a string of attractive coral and sand beaches.

Aimen Beach

隘門沙灘; àimén shātān · Accessed via a short road on the east coast, which branches to the south from Highway 204

Beautiful **Aimen Beach** has a bay that is ideal for swimming and a variety of watersports, and there are toilet, shower and barbecue facilities. At the edge of the beach is a **granite stele** with an inscription commemorating the landing here in 1895 of the Japanese navy.

ACCOMMODATION   **HUXI**

★**Liquid Sport B&B** 澎湖民宿愛玩水; pénghú mínsù ài wánshuǐ 22–3, Qingluo Village ☎0911 267 321, ⓦliquidsportpenghu.com; map p.344. This attractive B&B, in Qingluo on Penghu's northeast coast, opened in 2015 and lies within a few minutes' scooter ride of both choppy and flat ocean waters. There are a range of rooms (sea-view and family rooms from NT$2000), but all are modern with balconies. Tasty Taiwanese or Italian meals are served and, in the winter wind- and kitesurfing season, watersports packages including accommodation

make for a good deal (see box, p.345). NT$1300
★**Sunrise B&B** 菓葉觀日樓; guǒyè guānrì lóu Guoye Village ☎0956 065 509, ⓦsunrisebb.idv .tw; map p.344. This lovely B&B, set on the harbour, offers clean, bright and comfortably furnished rooms. The friendly owners, Jan and his daughter Karen, both speak excellent English and can arrange kitesurfing and windsurfing packages (see box, p.345), and also rent out snorkels and SUP boards, as well as scooters and cars. A tasty breakfast is included in the price. NT$1800

Baisha Island

白沙島; báishā dǎo

Directly north of Penghu Island, and connected by two short bridges, is the island of **BAISHA** where Qitou Village (岐頭村; qítóu cūn) is the jumping-off point for the appealing North Sea Island group.

The enormous roots of the extraordinary **Tongliang Great Banyan** (通梁古榕; tōngliáng gǔróng; daily 5.30am–7pm) form a magnificent canopy that stretches some 660m above and beyond the entrance to the **Baoan Temple** (保安宮; bǎoāngōng). More than 300 years old, the sprawling tree is one of Asia's biggest temple-bound banyans and far overshadows the temple itself. The shops nearby are famed for their "**purple ice**" treats (仙人掌冰; xiānrénzhǎn bīng) made from cactus fruit.

Xi Island

西嶼; xīyǔ

Linked to Baisha Island by the impressive 2.5km Trans-Ocean Bridge (澎湖跨海大橋; pénghú kuàhǎi dàqiáo), **XI ISLAND**, the main island group's most westerly extremity, has enough natural and historic attractions to keep you busy for a full day.

Xiaomen

小門嶼; xiǎoményǔ

On the tiny islet of **Xiaomen**, you'll find the **Whale Cave** (鯨魚洞; jīngyúdòng), a basalt cliff whose underbelly has been worn by waves into a noteworthy arch – prompting imaginative locals to liken the formation to a beached whale. At the entrance to Whale Cave path, the **Xiaomen Geology Gallery** (小門地質館; xiǎomén dìzhì guǎn; daily 8am–5.30pm; free; ☎06 998 2988) has exhibits on the islet's predominant geological features. The route from the car park to the gallery is lined with stalls selling local specialities including cactus juice (NT$50), ice cream and fried squid.

Erkan Traditional Village

二崁聚落; èrkǎn jùluò • Halfway down the east coast of Xi Island

Erkan Traditional Village is a picturesque compound of old houses with basalt foundations and coral walls, the oldest dating back to 1690. Although many of the buildings on the edge of the village are in a state of disrepair, plenty in the centre have been renovated (and are inhabited), while others have been converted into shops and food stalls.

West Fort

西嶼西台; xīyǔ xītái • 278 Waian Village on the island's southern coast • Daily: summer 7am–7pm; winter 8am–5.30pm • NT$25

The sunken Qing dynasty **West Fort** offers a glimpse of Penghu's military past. Dug into the clifftop, the fort is barely visible from afar, but up close reveals itself to be a walled enclosure containing a series of tunnels and raised gun emplacements, which still sport impressive artillery. Completed in 1887, the angled, rampart-like walls were made of a mixture of mud, black-sugar water and glutinous rice.

Fisherman's Island Lighthouse

西嶼燈塔; xīyǔ dēngtǎ • Tues–Sun 9am–5pm • Free

On Xi Island's southwestern extremity, the **Fisherman's Island Lighthouse** was originally constructed in 1779, but the seven-storey structure was rebuilt in its current Western style in 1875, designed by British civil engineer David M. Henderson. Set within a military compound, the lighthouse is now dwarfed by a radar tower, but there are fantastic views out to sea, particularly at sunset – you can see the dangerous shoals that the lighthouse warns against.

The North Sea Islands

北海遊憩系統; běihǎi yóuqì xìtǒng

The smattering of tiny islets in the north of the archipelago, known collectively as the **NORTH SEA ISLANDS**, have broad appeal, with white-sand beaches, basalt formations and some of Taiwan's top snorkelling spots. If you join a group boat tour, a snorkel and mask are often included in the price, but if you plan to explore independently you're best off bringing your own gear.

ARRIVAL AND DEPARTURE   THE NORTH SEA ISLANDS

BY FERRY

In the busy summer season, the islands are well served by boat tours and ferries from Baisha, but most of these services dry up in the windy winter. There are separate departure points on Baisha for the two different North Sea island groups. Boats for Jibei and points north (including Mudou and Gupo) leave from the North Sea Visitor Center (北海遊客中心; běihǎi yóukè zhōngxīn; daily 8am–5.30pm; ☎06 993 3082), on the waterfront near Chikan Village (赤崁村; chìkǎn cūn), while boats to Yuanbei Island, Peng Peng Beach and Niao Island depart from the Qitou Visitor Center (歧頭遊客中心; qítóu yóukè zhōngxīn; daily 8am–5.30pm; ☎06 993

1527). The North Sea Visitor Center is bigger and better stocked, but you can get maps and boat information at either.

Frequencies and prices Most sailings are effectively package day-trips, offering multi-stop tours, usually including lunch, snorkel and scooter rental. Prices for these tours start at NT$1000 for the most basic trip with snorkelling; higher prices come in for other watersports such as jet-skiing and sea-kayaking. There are also a few scheduled ferry services out to some of the bigger islands, including Jibei and Niao Island. The range of options and schedules can be confusing, and few of the operators speak English, so try the information desks first in the visitor centres (see above).

Jibei

吉貝嶼; jíbèiyǔ • A few kilometres west of the ferry pier • Return ferry tickets (15min each way) from the North Sea Visitor Center on Baisha to Jibei cost NT$300–350; the spit is easily accessible by electric scooter, which can be rented from the ferry pier (NT$200) – rental is included with many day-trip packages • The small Jibei Visitor Center (吉貝遊客中心; jíbèi yóukè zhōngxīn; daily 8am–5.30pm; ☎06 991 1487) is next to the ferry pier

The largest and most popular islet, **Jibei** (吉貝嶼; jíbèiyǔ) is covered in golden-sand beaches and is home to the spectacular **Jibei Spit** (吉貝沙嘴; jíbèi shāzuǐ), a mini-peninsula of sand that stretches out into the teal-blue waters for almost 1.5km. Fortunately, most tourists tend to congregate on the beach to the right of the ferry pier – where watersports activity is concentrated – leaving the spit itself refreshingly devoid of people.

ACCOMMODATION AND EATING	JIBEI

Jibei is not cheap for **accommodation** in summer, but the homestays that remain open in winter offer discounts of up to fifty percent. The section of Jibei Village to the right as you leave the ferry pier has several small **restaurants** with reasonably priced Chinese dishes as well as local seafood specialities.

Gibay Sunshine 香榭民宿; xiāngxiè mínsù 188-2 Jibei Village ☎06 991 1555, ⓦgibay-sunshine.com; map p.344. Clean, simple en-suite rooms with TVs, set around a central atrium, in a brightly painted concrete block on the way between the ferry pier and the spit. NT$2100

Mingyang Holiday Villa 名楊山莊; míngyáng shānzhuāng 182-8 Jibei Village ☎06 991 1188, ⓦmingyangcottage.idv.st; map p.344. Decor from a different millennium, but good value, cosy and inviting nonetheless. The best rooms have balconies and sea views (NT$3200), and the owner rents out scooters. NT1700

Peng Peng Beach

澎澎灘; péngpéng tān • No scheduled ferries here: you have to join one of the multi-islet boat tours

Idyllic **Peng Peng Beach** is actually a stretch of glistening offshore **sandbars** between Yuanbei Island and nearby Niao Island. The water here is remarkably clear, making it prime **snorkelling** territory. Boats moor offshore and you wade or swim to the beach, while the area is also becoming popular with sea kayakers, who paddle over from Baisha or Huxi. In summer, about three-quarters of the beach is off limits to visitors in order to protect nesting terns, leaving only the northeast tip open for tourist activity.

Xianjiao Island

險礁嶼; xiǎnjiāoyǔ • No scheduled ferries here: you have to join one of the multi-islet boat tours

Surrounded by spectacular **coral reef** and rich in marine life, **Xianjiao Island** is another favoured snorkelling, diving and watersports spot. In addition, the blinding **white-sand beaches** here are probably the archipelago's most stunning, and good for swimming.

Mudou and Gupo islets

The archipelago's northernmost islet, 7km north of Jibei, tiny **Mudou** (目斗嶼; mùdǒuyǔ) is dominated by a towering 40m-high lighthouse built in 1921. It's a remarkably photogenic spot, but thanks to heavy storms in recent years the nearby reefs that once proved so enticing have been severely damaged. Local operators now visit **Gupo Islet** (姑婆嶼; gūpóyǔ) instead, another basalt outcrop ringed by stunning coral gardens and an anchovy breeding ground; it's also known for the huge laver (edible seaweed) beds on the north side.

The South Sea Islands

南海遊憩系統; nánhǎi yóuqì xìtōng

Dozens of landmasses comprise the **SOUTH SEA ISLANDS**, but only five are regularly accessible by public or private ferries. While there are some notable historic sites on these islands, the overwhelming focus of most is on the natural environment, particularly the curious **basalt formations** that decorate their fringes.

ARRIVAL AND DEPARTURE	SOUTH SEA ISLANDS

By ferry Services to these islands leave from the South Sea Visitor Center (南海遊客中心; nánhǎi yóukè zhōngxīn; daily: April–Sept 6.30am–9.30pm; Oct– March 7am–5pm; ☎06 926 4738), at 25 Xinying Rd in

Magong. The ferry for Wangan departs daily at 9.30am (45min; NT$275); it then heads to Qimei (NT$440 from Magong). The boat leaves Qimei at 1.30pm to arrive at Wangan at 2.15pm; it then leaves Wangan at 2.30pm for arrival in Magong at 3.20pm. There are only two services per day to Tongpan (7.30am & 4.30pm; 15min; NT$120 return) and Hujing (9.30am & 3.30pm; 20min; NT$120).

On a tour Also departing from the South Sea Visitor Center, private operators offer a variety of tours; weather permitting, these sail daily to Tongpan, Hujing, Wangan and Qimei for around NT$850–950, leaving at 7.30–8.30am and returning mid-afternoon. The boats make very short stops at each island. For NT$550 you can visit the first three islands only.

Wangan

望安島; wàngān dǎo

The archipelago's fourth-largest island, **WANGAN**, is one of the highlights of a visit to the Penghu Islands, with secluded beaches, one of Taiwan's best-preserved traditional fishing villages and the chain's only nesting sites for the endangered **green sea turtle**.

Zhongshe Historic Village

中社古厝; zhōngshè gǔcuò • On the island's west side

Written records of the captivating **Zhongshe Historic Village** date back some two hundred years, but locals claim it was first established about three hundred years ago. Although there is a small, ageing population, most of the houses are abandoned, their tiled roofs and coral walls collapsed. The upside of this neglect is that the village has retained its original dynastic layout, giving it a timeless aura.

Tiantai Hill

天台山; tiāntáishān • Just north of Zhongshe Historic Village

The 53m-high **Tiantai Hill** is an excellent spot for a panoramic view of the island. On top of the hill is "God's Footprint" (仙腳印; xiānjiǎoyìn) where, according to legend, the footprint of **Lu Dong Bin** – one of the most renowned of China's "Eight Immortals" – is said to be embedded. According to the tale, the footprint was left after Lu stopped to relieve himself while walking through the Taiwan Strait.

Wangan Green Sea Turtle Tourism and Conservation Center

望安綠蠵龜觀光保育中心; wàngān lùxīguī guānguāng bǎoyù zhōngxīn • About 1km north of Wangan's ferry pier • March–Oct daily 9am–5.30pm; Nov–Feb 10.30am–3.30pm • NT$50 • ☎ 06 999 7368

The **Wangan Green Sea Turtle Tourism and Conservation Center** features exhibits on all marine turtles endemic to the region. Wangan's beaches are the only nesting sites in Penghu where green sea turtles return regularly to lay eggs, and the centre is mostly geared towards educating visitors about the importance of not disturbing them. The turtles usually mate in March and April and typically crawl onto Wangan's **southwestern beaches** in May and June to lay eggs. If you're visiting during this time, or even later in the summer, there's a chance you could see them. However, access to these beaches is restricted during this period – ask at the centre.

ARRIVAL AND DEPARTURE
WANGAN

By boat Multi-island boat tours starting from the South Sea Visitor Center call here for up to 2hr as part of their circuits (see above), but to really gain an appreciation of the island, it's best to stay overnight.

By plane It's possible to fly between Wangan Airport (望安機場; wàngān jīchǎng; ☎ 06 999 1806) and Kaohsiung. Daily Air (see p.343) offers flights (3 weekly; 45min; around NT$2000) in a small propeller-driven plane.

GETTING AROUND

By scooter The sights are spread out, so renting a scooter from the ferry pier is the best way to get around (NT$200/2hr or NT$400/day, including a full tank of fuel).

No driving licence required.
By tour bus You can board a bus at the ferry pier for a dizzying tour (NT$150) in Mandarin and Taiwanese.

ACCOMMODATION

Chihshean Tourist Hotel 致仙屋海景民宿; zhìxiānwū hǎijǐng mínsù 24 Dongan Village ☎06 999 1946; map p.344. A great place to stay, with spotless, pinewood rooms in a variety of sizes from doubles up (all en-suite with TVs). NT$1200

Qimei

七美嶼; qīměiyǔ

One of the best-known islets, **QIMEI** (also "Cimei"), has some of the area's most stunning scenery, with **steep cliffs** plunging down to craggy coastlines. Despite its relative isolation, it gets swamped with domestic tourists in summer and the giant tour buses and legions of scooter-revving students greatly disrupt the tranquillity.

Tomb of the Seven Beauties

七美人塚; qīměirén zhǒng • On Qimei's southeast coast • Daily 8am–5pm • NT$60

Qimei means "Seven Beauties" and relates to a legend about seven Ming dynasty maidens who were attacked by Japanese pirates while doing laundry at a well. Rather than surrender their chastity they jumped to their deaths inside the well, which was later filled and covered with a tomb in their honour. Shortly afterwards, seven trees began to grow around the site. The **Tomb of the Seven Beauties** commemorates this story and is a mandatory stop for Taiwanese tourists, making it worth a visit just to observe some of the rituals that take place here.

Twin Hearts Stone Weir

雙心石滬; shuāngxīn shíhù

Located at the base of a cliff on Qimei's northeast corner is the **Twin Hearts Stone Weir**, a traditional **fish trap** made of stones piled into the shape of two large hearts. Although the archipelago is covered in stone weirs, this one is the most famous and now sees far more tourists trampling over it than fish.

ARRIVAL AND DEPARTURE   QIMEI

By boat Multi-island ferry tours starting from the South Sea Visitor Center (see p.353) make Qimei their last port of call before returning to Magong, usually allowing passengers a measly 1hr 30min to look around. If you want to soak up the scenery you'll need to spend the night at one of the hotels near the ferry pier.

By plane Daily Air operates flights (NT$1800 one-way) on propeller-driven aircraft from Kaohsiung to Qimei Airport (七美機場; qīměi jīchǎng; ☎06 9971 256) in summer. They also fly to and from Magong.
Destinations Kaohsiung (2 daily; 40min); Magong (2 daily; 20min).

GETTING AROUND

By scooter Renting a scooter at the ferry pier is the best way to get around (NT$200/2hr or NT$400/day, including a full tank of fuel). No driving licence required.

By tour bus Bus tours (NT$150) depart from the ferry pier and are aimed at Taiwanese tourists, but you can join in if you speak Mandarin or Taiwanese.

ACCOMMODATION AND EATING

Qimei Folk Homestay 七美風情民宿; qīměi fēngqíng mínsù 5 Donghu Village ☎06 997 1271; map p.344. The best accommodation on Qimei has shared dorm beds and comfy doubles. Dorms NT$300, doubles NT$1200
Shuntian Hotel 順天旅社; shùntiān lǚshè 18 Nangang Village ☎06 997 1888; map p.344. A cheap option, close to the pier, with doubles and eight-bed dorms. The reasonable Qimei Fishing Village Restaurant (七美漁村餐廳; qīměi yúcūn cāntīng) is on the hotel's first floor. Dorms NT$300, doubles NT$800

Tongpan

桶盤嶼; tǒngpányǔ • About 15min south of Magong by boat

The tiny inhabited islet of **TONGPAN** is best known for the vertical cliffs of symmetrical **basalt columns** that surround it. Most boats stop here for no more than 45 minutes, but you can still see some of the islet's finest columns in this time. **Fuhai Temple** (福海宫; fúhǎigōng), located near the pier, is dedicated primarily to the pestilence god Wen Wang Ye and is the archipelago's most popular shrine.

Hujing

虎井嶼; hǔjǐngyǔ • With boat tours usually stopping here for less than an hour, you might want to rent one of the scooters lined up near the pier (NT$200) to make the most of your time

Just southeast of Tongpan is **Hujing**, known for its towering mesas of **basalt columns** but with the added interest of **Japanese military tunnels** from World War II. The most visually striking – and accessible – of the columns line the road that leads up the hill to the west. You can also follow the road to the right of the pier to reach **Xishan Park** (西山公園; xīshān gōngyuán), home to a line-up of imposing basalt columns to the left of the road. If you look closely, you can see the openings of tunnels dug by Japanese soldiers. At the top of the hill is a viewpoint looking out over the sea and a few tunnel entrances concealed in concrete buildings.

The Kinmen archipelago

金門; jīnmén

Of the fifteen islands in the **KINMEN ARCHIPELAGO**, twelve are under Taiwanese administration and three under mainland Chinese control. Only the two biggest – **Kinmen** and **Lieyu** – are inhabited by civilians and open to visitors. Huddled just over 2km off the mainland Chinese coast, and once the front line in the struggle between Mao Zedong's Communists and Chiang Kai-shek's Nationalists, these neighbouring islands are among Taiwan's most fascinating travel destinations, with a wealth of historic, cultural and culinary delights rolled into one of the most heavily fortified places on earth.

Kinmen Island

金門島; jīnmén dǎo

Kinmen Island is shaped like a dumbbell, spanning only 3km from north to south at its centre. Most visitors make the main commercial hub of **Jincheng** their first base, but there are plenty of enticing homestays across the island. By renting a scooter, car or bicycle, you could probably take in most of the main attractions in four or five days: double that if you're relying on public buses.

In 1995, much of the island became Taiwan's sixth **national park**, the only one dedicated to the preservation of historic monuments and battlefield memorials. Many once important **military sites** have been decommissioned and are now open to the public, giving insights into the grim reality that has only recently begun to brighten for Kinmen's hardy residents, and providing a new source of revenue for locals – tourism. For the most part, Kinmen's **beaches** remain underdeveloped and many in the north are littered with rusting iron spikes, but there are some attractive stretches of sand in the south of the island.

Brief history

Though archeological evidence suggests that Kinmen was inhabited as long as 6500 years ago, it was not until 317 AD that the first traceable ancestors of contemporary **Kinmen clans** moved to the island to escape turmoil in central China. The island remained a backwater until the Tang dynasty, when the ancestors of twelve clans, led by **Chen Yuan**, arrived to breed and raise horses in 803. Horse breeding met with limited success, and much of Kinmen's development over the next few centuries consisted in the establishment of **oyster farms**. Over the following centuries, the island became a popular hiding place for Chinese and Japanese **pirates**. In the 1640s, the Ming loyalist

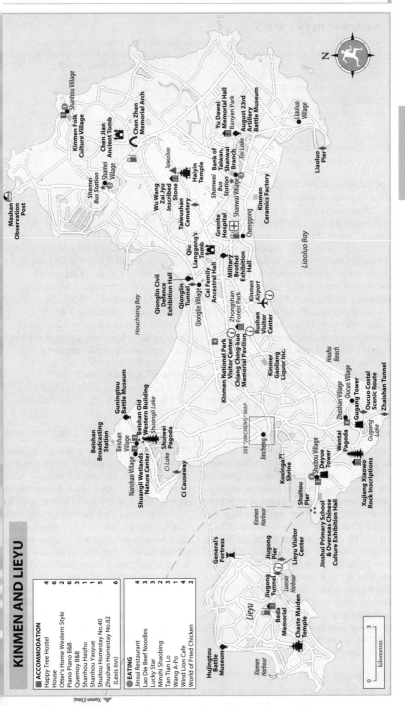

KINMEN AND LIEYU

■ **ACCOMMODATION**

Happy Tree Hostel	4
House	6
Otter's Home Western Style	2
Piano Piano B&B	6
Quemoy B&B	3
Shanhou Haizhu	1
Shanhou Yaoyue	1
Shuitou Homestay No.40	5
Zhushan Homestay No.82	
(Lexis Inn)	6

● **EATING**

Jinsui Restaurant	4
Lao Die Beef Noodles	3
Lucky Star	3
Minshi Shaobing	2
Tan Tian Lo	1
Wang A-Po	1
Wind Lion Cafe	4
World of Fried Chicken	2

6

> ## ROARING IN THE WIND
>
> Kinmen is home to an impressive concentration of **historic structures**, from Ming-dynasty memorial arches to Qing-inspired burial mounds. Scattered all over the island are Kinmen's signature folk icons, notably the intriguing granite **wind-lion god statues** (風獅爺; fēngshīyé). For centuries they have watched over the island's villages and are believed to protect them from the ravages of heavy winds and storms. Touching the lion's head is said to cure certain ailments and restore good health, while touching its genitalia will, ostensibly, bring male heirs.

general **Koxinga** occupied the island while preparing his navy to fight against the Qing forces that had overrun China.

The modern era: wealth, occupation and war

After the **Opium War** in 1842, when the nearby city of Xiamen became one of China's five **treaty ports**, many Kinmen residents began travelling to Southeast Asia via Xiamen to do business, in the process amassing considerable wealth, which they used to build lavish, European-inspired houses back home. But when the Sino-Japanese War broke out in 1937, **Japanese forces** immediately seized the island and occupied it for eight years, bringing to an end its most prosperous period. In 1949, Kinmen bore the brunt of another invasion force, this time from Chiang Kai-shek's retreating **Nationalist army**, which used the island as the front line in its preparations to recover mainland China from Mao Zedong's Communists. On August 23, 1958, the Communists launched a brutal **artillery attack** on Kinmen, subjecting it to 44 consecutive days of shelling. Moreover, mines were laid throughout the island and the assault continued intermittently for the next twenty years. Since the lifting of **martial law** in 1987, Kinmen has undergone a small-scale renaissance, with promising economic ties to mainland China being forged, setting the stage for a new period of growth and development. In 2014 the islands were officially declared **free of landmines**, following nearly a decade of clearance. However, some locals remain sceptical – twelve mines were found near Beishan in September 2014 – and advise sticking to paths and roads.

ARRIVAL AND DEPARTURE   KINMEN ISLAND

FROM MAINLAND TAIWAN

By plane Aside from very occasional holiday services, essentially there are now no boats between Kinmen and Taiwan. To get to Kinmen from the Taiwanese mainland you must fly. There are daily flights throughout the year from five west-coast cities and five weekly from Magong on Penghu. Return tickets typically cost between NT$3200 and NT$3500, with one-way fares starting from NT$2000. Mandarin Airlines (☎ 082 324 280) flies from Taichung and Taipei, FAT (☎ 082 320 666) flies from Kaohsiung, Taichung and Taipei, and Uni Air (☎ 082 372 725) flies to Kinmen from all five west-coast cities. Kinmen Airport (金門機場; jīnmén jīchǎng) is located just over 4km from the centre of Jincheng.

Destinations Chiayi (1–2 daily; 50min); Kaohsiung (7–10 daily; 1hr); Taichung (9–14 daily; 55min); Tainan (3 daily; 50min); Taipei (14–23 daily; 55min).

FROM CHINA

By ferry Foreigners can now take a ferry from Xiamen

(厦门; xiàmén) in Fujian, China. Coming from China to Taiwan is relatively straightforward, but going the other way most travellers will need a Chinese visa, which cannot be acquired directly in Taiwan. All Xiamen ferries arrive at Kinmen's Shuitou Pier (水頭碼頭; shuǐtóu mǎtóu), where you'll find a visitor information centre (daily 8.30am–5pm; ☎ 082 322 124) that usually has English-speakers and renminbi (Chinese currency) exchange counters, but no ATMs. Ferries depart Shuitou for two different ports in Xiamen hourly between 8am and 5.30pm and cost NT$725. Coming from China the fare is RMB185. In Xiamen, there are two ferry terminals: Wutong Port (五通碼頭; wǔtōng mǎtóu) is around 30min from Kinmen and just 15min by taxi from Xiamen Airport (shuttle buses connect the port with downtown), while ferries also run to the more central Dongdu International Ferry Terminal (东渡国际油轮码头; dōngdù guójì yóulún mǎtóu) in around 1hr. Moving on, and assuming you have a Chinese visa, it's possible to take the ferry to Xiamen, an express bus from

Xiamen to Fuzhou and then another ferry to Matsu (see p.374), from where you can fly or take a ferry back to Taiwan main island.

Destination Xiamen (hourly; 30min–1hr);

INFORMATION AND SERVICES

Tourist information The most convenient visitor centre is at the airport (daily 8am–6pm; ☏ 082 329 354) which has an array of English maps and brochures on Kinmen's main attractions. You won't learn much more at the Kinmen National Park Visitor Center (金門國家公園遊客中心; jīnmén guójiā gōngyuán yóukè zhōngxīn; daily 8.30am–5pm; ☏ 082 313 100), in the centre of the island at Zhongshan Forest Park (see p.368).

Banks Although there are ATMs scattered across the island, many will not accept international cards (MasterCard is your best bet). The most reliable one on Kinmen is the 24hr ATM at Jincheng's main Bank of Taiwan branch at 162 Minquan Rd (Mon–Fri 9am–3.30pm), which is also the only place on the island where you can change foreign currency and traveller's cheques.

Internet For internet access outside of your hotel, try Network Xing Qiu at 4, Alley 161 Zhongxing Rd, Jincheng (Mon–Fri 4pm–midnight, Sat & Sun 8am–midnight; $20/hr).

Post The Kinmen Post Office at 4 Minsheng Rd (Mon–Fri 7.30am–5pm, Sat 8–11.30am) is across the street from the main bus station in Jincheng.

GETTING AROUND

By scooter The most convenient way to get around the island is by scooter (NT$400/day), provided you can produce a valid international drivers licence; renters are fairly strict about enforcing this rule. Try KM Fun Scooter Rentals (金豐租車; jīnfēng zūchē; Mon–Thurs & Sun 8.30am–5.30pm, Fri & Sat 8.30am–6.30pm; ☏ 082 371 888) at 359-1 Poyu Rd Sec 1 in Jincheng. They also have a branch in the airport next to the 7-11 (daily 7.30am–6.30pm; ☏ 082 335 333), and offer free luggage transfer to your hotel if you collect from the airport. As well as regular petrol scooters, KM Fun also offer electric scooter rental (NT$800/day), which only requires showing your ID – a useful option if you don't have an international licence.

By car Cars can be rented with any national driving licence, and cost from NT$1500/day. At the airport try Guan Cheng Car Rental (daily 8am–5.30pm; ☏ 082 323 390, ☏ 323390. com), or in Jincheng head for San De Rental Cars (三德租車; sānde zūchē) at 7–3 Minsu Rd (☏ 082 328 610, ☏ 3car.com.tw). The latter also have an office at 128 Yu Village, Shanwai (☏ 082 330 505), which will usually deliver the car to you and can offer free airport transfer on your return. They can also arrange scooter rental. Many hotels can assist with car rentals.

By bike Kinmen has a new automated bike rental system, K Bike (☏ kbike.com.tw), with 24 locations on Kinmen and two on Lieyu, and bikes can be returned to any location, providing there is space. Bikes cost NT$10/30min, with a NT$250 maximum daily charge; you'll need a Mastercard credit card and international phone number to rent the bike. K Bike rental can also be paid for using an EasyCard (see box, p.25). For a better quality bike, visit the Giant store near the bus station at 31 Minsu Rd in Jincheng (daily 8am–7.30pm; ☏ 082 326 626) which charges NT$300/day for a decent mountain bike. Kinmen National Park (金門國家公園; jīnmén guójiā gōngyuán) provides free bikes at Shuangli Wetlands Nature Center (see p.367) and Zhongshan Forest Park (see p.368) during opening hours; you must return the bike the same day and will need to show photo ID.

By bus Travelling the island by public bus is possible but painfully slow and it requires careful planning to get to the main sights. Jincheng Bus Station (金城車站; jīnchéng chēzhàn) at Minsheng and Chubu East roads has regular bus services to Shanwai and Shamei, the next-biggest villages and near several worthwhile attractions; services start at 6am and end at 8pm, and fares are set at a flat rate of NT$12 for any destination.

On a tour Kinmen's system of tour buses (☏ www.taiwantrip.com.tw) offers half-day passes for NT$250, one-day passes for NT$400 and two-day passes for NT$700. Short stops at sights along the way are programmed into the schedule, although each route tends to operate just one service a day. There are four main loop routes: A (Shuitou and Zhaishan; 8.30am; 3hr 40min) and B (Guningtou; 2.05pm; 3hr 15min) run from Jincheng Bus Station, while C (Mashan & Shanhou; 8.30am; 3hr 45min) and D (Banyan Park; 1.30pm; 3hr 45min) run from Shanwai.

Jincheng
金城; jīnchéng

The core of **JINCHENG**, Kinmen's only major town, is a labyrinth of narrow lanes and alleys, twisting their way through a hotchpotch of curious old houses and an incredible assortment of tiny temples and shrines. Most of the best-known attractions are situated around Juguang Road and quaint Mofan Street (模範街; mófàn jiē), both of which have some superb little restaurants and teahouses.

Qiu Liang-gong's Maternal Chastity Arch

邱良功母節孝坊; qiūliánggōng mǔjié xiàofāng

Framing the main intersection of Juguang Road, **Qiu Liang-gong's Maternal Chastity Arch** is the largest surviving monumental archway in Taiwan. **Qiu Liang-gong**, a Kinmen native who rose through the Qing military ranks to become commander-in-chief of the navy stationed in China's Zhejiang province, ordered the imposing, intricately carved arch built in 1812 as a tribute to his mother's devotion to his father – she refused to remarry during the 28 years between her husband's death and hers.

Qing Dynasty Military Headquarters

清金門鎮總兵署; qīngjīnménzhèn zǒngbīngshǔ • Daily 9am–10pm • Free • Visitor Information Center ☎ 082 371 717

Halfway along the northern side of Juguang Road is a small square that ends with the **Qing Dynasty Military Headquarters**, a large complex of traditional Chinese halls dating to 1682. The compound now serves as a history museum for the island, focusing on the Qing period and particularly this building's role in its military past (with English labels), including eerie subterranean prison cells. There's also a **visitor information centre**, usually with English-speakers.

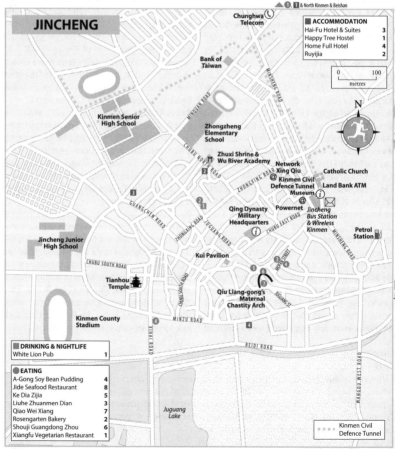

GETTING AN EDGE ON THE ENEMY

By far the most unique of Kinmen souvenirs – and the most telling of its recent history – is the amazing range of cutlery forged and fashioned from melted-down **artillery shells** left over from mainland attacks. More than 970,000 shells pounded Kinmen over a twenty-year period, and industrious locals have learnt how to make a living from designing knives, meat cleavers, axes and even swords from the seemingly endless supply of spent casings.

Although you'll find the cutlery for sale in shops all over Jincheng, usually starting at about NT$900 for a basic knife or meat cleaver, the creations at **Maestro Wu's Steel Knives** (金合利 鋼刀; jīn hé lì gāng dāo) are considered the finest. Founder Wu Chao, son of an iron caster who learned tool-making techniques in Xiamen during the Qing dynasty, carried on the family tradition with Allied bomb shells in World War II, then continued during the years of mainland bombardment, transforming the exploded casings into magnificent instruments (after 1958 he used mostly propaganda shells that only partly broke up).

His business continues to thrive under third-generation Wu Tseng-dong, who draws on Japanese designs. There are outlets all over Kinmen, but the flagship showroom at 50–54 Poyu Rd Sec 1 offers the chance to see the knife-making process in action, as well as to buy the finished product. Other branches include 51 Wujiang Street, just outside the Qing Dynasty Military Headquarters on a small square off Juguang Road (☎ 082 373 977) and a **store** at 21 Mofan Street (☎ 082 311 168). Expect to pay from NT$500 for penknives and up to NT$2200 for the best cleavers.

Kinmen Civil Defence Tunnel Museum

金城民防坑道; jīnchéng mínfáng kēngdào · Just above the bus station on the east side of town · Daily 10am–9.30pm; guided tours (40min) depart hourly 10.30am–8.30pm, though only the 1.30 & 8.30pm are guaranteed – other tours need a minimum of five people · Free

The **Kinmen Civil Defence Tunnel Museum** gives an overview of the island's "combat villages" and the tunnel dug under Jincheng in 1978. At 1285m, it's the longest on Kinmen that you can walk through (by guided tour only) and the most evocative of the island's military past. You emerge at Kinmen Senior High School on the northwest side of town, although there are a couple of emergency exits along the way; the return leg is overland. The museum also contains a visitor information centre.

Juguang Tower

莒光樓; jǔguānglóu · Daily 8am–10pm · Free · Buses #3 and #6 stop just outside the tower

On Jincheng's southeastern fringe the 16m-high **Juguang Tower** was built in 1953 in the style of a classical Chinese palace tower to honour Nationalist soldiers. On the first floor is yet another **visitor information centre**, as well as bilingual displays introducing the key themes in Kinmen's history and culture. On the second floor is a particularly enlightening exhibit on Jincheng's City Gods, while the third and final storey offers more Kinmen history, as well as fine views of Juguang Lake, the outskirts of Jincheng and the hazy towers of Xiamen beyond.

ARRIVAL AND DEPARTURE JINCHENG

By plane Flights from the Taiwan mainland land at Kinmen airport, 4km from Jincheng. There are plenty of taxis which can take you to the centre of Jincheng for about NT$200. Alternatively, take bus #3 (16 daily 6.50am–6.20pm; 25min; NT$12 one-way), but note that it also runs in the opposite direction to the village of Shanwai, so make sure Jincheng or Shuitou is displayed on the front.

By ferry Taxis between Shuitou Pier and Jincheng charge NT$300; bus #7 is NT$12.

ACCOMMODATION

Kinmen's conventional **hotel** accommodation is concentrated in Jincheng's commercial district. While this is the most convenient place to stay, the hotels here lack character and for a bit more charm it's worth opting for one of the growing number of family-run **homestays** (☺ guesthouse.kmnp.gov.tw) around the island.

Hai-Fu Hotel & Suites 海福商務飯店; hǎifú shāngwù fàndiàn 85 Minquan Rd, Jincheng ☎ 082 322 538, ⓦ haifu.com.tw; map p.360. One of Jincheng's higher-end options, offering plush, contemporary-style rooms with cable TV and clean modern bathrooms. Prices include breakfast, and the friendly hotel staff will pick you up at the airport or ferry pier (NT$150) if you make arrangements in advance. NT$1980

Happy Tree Hostel 幸福樹宿; xìngfú shùsù 613 Huandao North Rd, Sec 2, Jinning Township ☎ 0928 700 031, ⓦ happytree211.pixnet.net; map p.360. This small backpacker hostel is located 3km outside of Jincheng, on bus route #2, #5 and #5A. There are two four-bed dorms, plus two doubles. Facilities include a kitchen and communal washing machine, and there's a TV room with books and maps. The friendly owner speaks a bit of English

and can help arrange car/scooter rental and island tours. Reductions on dorm beds if you stay two or more nights. Dorms NT$700, doubles NT$1500

Home Full Hotel 宏福大飯店; hóngfú dàfàndiàn 169 Minzu Rd, Jincheng ☎ 082 326 768, ⓦ hongfu-hotel.com; map p.360. Conveniently located close to Juguang Rd, this place has attractive modern rooms, but those overlooking busy Minzu Rd can be noisy – ask for a room away from the traffic. NT$2000

Ruyijia 如一家; rúyījiā 35-1 Zhupu North Rd ☎ 082 322 167, ⓔ kinmen.rujia@gmail.com; map p.360. Well located in the heart of the old centre, the *Ruyijia* has clean, modern rooms decorated with silhouettes of European architecture. There's a free coffee bar for guests in the lobby. NT$1580

EATING

Jincheng is packed with delightful places to eat – the area between central Juguang Rd and Mofan St is teeming with **food stalls** and tiny **restaurants**. Among Kinmen's most famous **specialities** are the handmade thin noodles (miànxiàn) that can be seen drying on racks all over town, and guǎngdōng zhōu, a local approximation of Cantonese congee. Street-side shops sell locally made "tribute candies" (gòngtáng), including the popular **peanut candy** made from a mix of malt and peanuts grown on the island.

A-Gong Soy Bean Pudding 阿公的豆花; āgōng de dòuhuā 15 Mofan St ☎ 082 325 870; map p.360. Huge bowls of shaved ice (tsua bing) with six toppings, as well as creamy soybean pudding (dòuhuā); they also do Japanese-style octopus balls. All dishes are a bargain at NT$40. Tues–Sun 10am–8pm.

Jide Seafood Restaurant 記德海鮮餐廳; jìdé hǎixiān cāntīng 253 Minzu Rd ☎ 082 324 461; map p.360. Family restaurant favoured by locals for its fresh seafood but with a wide selection of dishes, from fried rice and noodles to indigenous staples and well-known Chinese recipes with a Kinmen twist. Dishes start from about NT$150. Daily 11am–2pm & 5–11.30pm.

Ke Dia Zijia 蚵嗲之家; kēdiā zhījiā 59 Juguang Rd Sec 1 ☎ 082 322 210; map p.360. Just behind Qiu Lianggong's arch is this immensely popular snack stall, which sells everything from deep-fried oyster fritters (NT$30) to scrumptious sweet balls filled with pastes made of green bean, red bean and peanuts (NT$15). Daily except Thurs 2.30–7pm.

Liuhe Zhuanmen Dian 六合專門店; liùhé zhuānméndiàn 22–24 Mofan St ☎ 082 312 606; map p.360. Sophisticated modern hotpot restaurant set in a traditional redbrick building, which serves pricey but excellent two-person hotpots for NT$1390. Less elaborate one-person pots start from NT$360. Hotpot items include Australian beef, New Zealand lamb, local seafood and seasonal veggies. Daily 11.30am–2.30pm & 5.30–9.30pm.

★**Qiao Wei Xiang** 巧味香小吃店; qiǎowèixiāng xiǎochīdiàn 39 Juguang Rd Sec 1 ☎ 082 327 652;

map p.360. The best place in Jincheng to try handmade glass noodles, served in big, steaming bowls of soup with fresh oysters (ké cài miàn xiàn). It's conveniently located, clean and offers bowls of the noodle (NT$80) without the chopped pig intestine that crops up in most of the town's other miàn xiàn diners. Daily 7am–1.30pm &4–7pm.

Rosengarten Bakery 玫瑰園烘焙坊; méiguīyuán hōngbèifāng 120 Juguang Rd Sec 1 ☎ 0984 257 757; map p.360. Located next to the Wu Temple in the heart of Jincheng, this takeaway bakery was opened in 2016 by a group of young Kinmen college graduates and quickly gained a loyal following. The breads come in a variety of flavors such as chocolate and walnut (NT$45), raisin and cranberry, pumpkin and even azuki bean, and are baked with local gāoliáng (sorghum liquor). Burgers (NT$60–75) and Western-style brunch are also available. Come early in the day for the best selection. Daily except Tues 10am–8pm.

Shouji Guangdong Zhou 壽記粥糜; shòujì zhōumí 50 Juguang Rd Sec 1 ☎ 082 327 878; map p.360. Kinmen's most famous breakfast spot, specializing in the local version of Cantonese congee, served in huge bowls (NT$80) and usually eaten with fried bread sticks (yóutiáo). The family-run establishment has been in business for almost ninety years, and the owners are proud of their congee-making heritage, which began when some of their clan emigrated to southern Guangdong province. Daily 8am–11.30pm.

Xiangfu Vegetarian Restaurant 祥富素食館;

xiángfù sùshíguǎn 23 Huandao North Rd ☏082 311 276; map p.360. Located just across the street from the Cultural Center, this restaurant is one of Jincheng's best value vegetarian options. The menu includes plenty of

fresh vegetables, as well as tofu, rice, and noodles (with a great chilli sauce), plus there's free barley tea. Most dishes cost NT$60–$80. Mon–Fri 11am–2pm & 5.30–8.30pm, Sat 11am–2pm.

DRINKING

It can be as if Jincheng is under curfew come evening, but a few places sometimes get lively – usually after several Kinmen gāoliáng (sorghum liquor) cocktails have been consumed.

White Lion Pub 白獅子; bái shīzi 7, Alley 110, Juguang Rd ☏082 312 062, ☏whitelion@mind-ltd. com; map p.360. This Canadian-owned pub is Jincheng's only real bar. There's a good selection of imported beers

(including Hoegarden NT$150), and interesting cocktails – try the Kinmen mudslide (NT$180). There's a pool table, and outside seats in the public square. Tues–Sun 7pm–midnight.

Shuitou and around

水頭; shuǐtóu • Around 3km southwest of Jincheng along the road leading to Shuitou pier • Bus #7 and Tour Bus A from Jincheng stop just outside the village

The enchanting village of **SHUITOU** is filled with traditional southern Fujianese houses and Kinmen's best-preserved yánglóu, the European-Fujianese hybrid homes that have become a hallmark of the island. Ever since moneyed Shuitou émigrés began returning to the village in the 1920s and 30s and started building elaborate houses inspired by the colonial architecture of Malaysia and Singapore, Kinmen residents have had a saying: "Just because you're as rich as a Shuitou person doesn't mean you can build a house as beautiful as a Shuitou house." A leisurely stroll (English signs and maps dot the village) affords a close-up view of some of their painstakingly detailed ornamentation. Even the tour buses and numerous homestays haven't yet managed to spoil the place.

Jinshui Primary School

金水學校; jīnshuǐ xuéxiào • South of the main road next to a small car park • Daily 8.30am–5pm • Free

Shuitou's **Jinshui Primary School** is a handsome yánglóu structure completed in 1932. No longer a functioning school, today it contains a series of bilingual exhibits highlighting Kinmen emigration, the subsequent remittance arrangements and the development of local school systems. Most of the predominantly male immigrants went to Singapore and Malaysia in several waves starting in the 1860s, migrations that generated huge cashflows back to Kinmen, funded elaborate construction projects and even fed cultural changes.

Deyue Tower

得月樓; déyuè lóu • Daily 8.30am–5pm • Free

Shuitou's best-known landmark is the 11m-high **Deyue Tower**, built in the 1930s by businessman Huang Huei-huang to protect his estate from burglary. Essentially a glorified gun emplacement, the four-storey tower has no staircase, with each floor connected to the next by a removable wooden ladder. You can't go inside the tower, but the "false house" (another deterrent) and stately **Huang Residence** next door have been turned into a series of absorbing display rooms, this time focussing specifically on the culture of Chinese immigrants to Indonesia and Malaysia.

Overseas Chinese Culture Exhibition Hall

僑鄉文化展示館; qiáoxiāng wénhuà zhǎnshìguǎn • Next to the Deyue Tower • Daily 8.30am–5pm • Free

Next door to Deyue Tower, a European-style house contains the **Overseas Chinese Culture Exhibition Hall** with exhibits charting the cultural impact of the overseas Chinese, from architecture and fashion, to language and cuisine.

Youtang Villa
西堂別業; yŏutáng biéyè

Shuitou's largest traditional swallowtail house is the **Youtang Villa**, built in 1766 by Huang Jun, the head of the village's founding Huang clan and still privately owned. A prominent part of traditional architecture, swallowtail roofs (燕尾; yànwěi) consist of an ornate ridgeline which curl up into the air at the end to resemble the tail of a swallow, and are common throughout Taiwan, but especially prevalent in Kinmen. The villa fronts the small sun- and moon-shaped **fishponds**, north of Deyue Tower. Though it's acceptable to look at the building from the outside, the owner doesn't appreciate people peeking in, and there are aggressive dogs within the compound, so park officials recommend keeping your distance.

Wentai Pagoda
文台寶塔; wéntái bǎotǎ · Southeast of Shuitou, signposted down a narrow lane off the main road to Zhushan · Free · Bus #6 & Tour Bus A from Jincheng

Built in 1387, the serene **Wentai Pagoda** is one of Taiwan's oldest surviving relics. The only one of Kinmen's three ancient stone towers still in existence, the granite structure sits atop an enormous boulder, cutting a solitary figure above the surrounding trees and car park below. It may well have been a marker for heavenly worship, as characters carved on the northeast side of its third level state: "The star of literature shines high in the sky." Underneath these characters is a time-worn relief of **Wenchang Dijun** – known as the god of literature – kicking a vessel said to resemble the Big Dipper. Kinmen historians, however, reckon that the pagoda's main function was as a navigational marker for ships plying the nearby shallows.

Xujiang Xiaowo Rock Inscriptions
虛江嘯臥碣群; xūjiāng xiàowò jiéqún · Next to the Wentai Pagoda

Overlooking the sea on Kinmen's southwest coast, the **Xujiang Xiaowo Rock Inscriptions** were carved into the rock face in honour of **Ming general Xujiang**, who was said to enjoy the sea views from this spot. The characters read: "Xujiang shouts while lying here."

Zhaishan Tunnels
翟山坑道; zháishān kēngdào · Just southeast of Wentai Pagoda · Daily 8.30am–5pm · Free; November concert NT$200 · Bus #6 & Tour Bus A from Jincheng stop just outside Gugang Lake and the tunnels

The man-made **Zhaishan Tunnels**, completed in 1966, are unique: a wide, cave-like passage that runs down to a cavernous, U-shaped water tunnel, with both ends filtering into the sea (now blocked by gates). This arrangement could safely shelter up to 42 **supply boats** during intensive artillery attacks, becoming a crucial lifeline for the island. You can wander to the end and back, although there's not much more to do except wonder at the effort that went into such a thing.

However, one day in November every year, the tunnel is brought to life by a remarkable **concert** with musicians performing on a floating platform that moves through the main tunnel and produces an impressive reverberated sound. To attend, you'll need to contact the tourist office in Jincheng well in advance, as tickets sell out within minutes of being released – indeed, there is talk of adding more performances to accommodate the overwhelming demand.

Oucuo Coastal Scenic Route
歐厝濱海景觀道路; ōucuò bīnhǎi jǐngguān dàolù · Stretches 2.4km from Zhaishan to Oucuo · Bus #6 & Tour Bus A from Jincheng stop just outside Gugang Lake and the tunnels, and there's a K Bike station outside the tunnel entrance

Beaches in the north are still littered with rusting spikes, but there is a very pleasant string of beaches on the coast from the Zhaishan tunnels to near the airport. The **Oucuo Coastal Scenic Route** takes you from Zhaishan past beautiful beaches where you

6

can dig for clams and swim. Continuing a couple of kilometres further east along the main road from Oucuo (歐厝濱海景觀道路; ōucuò) will bring you to Houhu Beach, part of the Houhu Coast Park (後湖海濱公園; hòuhú hǎibīn gōngyuán), where there are showers and picnic areas. At the time of writing, the visitor center and performance stage were still under construction.

ACCOMMODATION   SHUITOU AND AROUND

SHUITOU

Shuitou Homestay No. 40 水頭40號民宿; shuǐtóu 40hào mínsù 40 Shuitou Village ☎0932 517 669, ⓦfamilyinn.idv.tw; map p.357. A characterful option in a traditional house offering cosy, softly lit rooms, all with wood beams and terracotta-tiled floors. Handy for the ferry to Lieyu. NT$2000

ZHUSHAN

★**Official House** 珠山大夫第; zhūshān dàfū dì 41 Zhushan Village ☎0963 166 171; map p.357. Built by a wealthy merchant during the Qing dynasty, this friendly place has six cosy rooms and bags of character. Many traditional Kinmen houses have a secret hiding hole to stow valuables – at this homestay the friendly owner will hide a "treasure" in your room and, if you find it, it's yours

to keep. NT$2000

Piano Piano B&B 慢漫民宿; mànmàn mínsù 75 Zhushan Village ☎0988 182 832, ⓦwww.pianopiano. com.tw; map p.357. Very classy homestay in a traditional-style house with antique beds, tiled floors, Tiffany lamps and a peaceful courtyard, as well as a soporific roof deck. NT$2000

Zhushan Homestay No. 82 (Lexis Inn) 珠山82號民宿 (來喜樓); zhūshān 82hào mínsù (láixǐ lóu) 82 Zhushan Village ☎0932 838 966; map p.357. This handsome two-storey yánglóu was built in 1928 by a Chinese merchant who earned his fortune in the Philippines; the renovated interiors are classical Chinese (though the bathrooms are modern), with rosewood beds, attractive common areas and a tranquil balcony for chilling out. NT$2000

EATING

SHUITOU

Jinsui Restaurant 金水食堂; jīnshuǐ shítáng 48 Shuitou Village ☎082 373 919; map p.357. Housed in a restored traditional building close to Deyue Tower, this restaurant has an English menu featuring a host of local specialities including fish with fruit vinegar (NT$250), braised pork with steamed taro (NT$250) and seaweed soup with fresh oysters (NT$70). There's local art on the walls and, on occasion, a Taiwanese band performs traditional music on the second floor. The restaurant is open for lunch and dinner, but only for advance bookings,

so make sure you call ahead.

Wind Lion Café 風獅爺文物坊; fēngshīyé wénwùfāng 42 Shuitou Village ☎082 321 600; map p.357. Located in the old, pink, two-storey Huang Residence, set in a courtyard next to the Deyue Tower, this quiet and peaceful café serves a range of coffees including with Gaoliang 58 proof – a sort of Kinmen Irish coffee – for a mere NT$80, smoothies (NT$150), handmade cookies (NT$120) and waffles (NT$150). The owner is a local artist; his work, including miniature ceramic wind-lion statues is on sale from NT$500 upwards. Daily 8.30am–5.30pm.

Beishan and around

北山; běishān • Buses #10 and #11 stop at the village bus shelter, which has a handy map inside

With many of its traditional homes restored and still inhabited, **BEISHAN** is well worth a quick look. To the north of the village, the **Beishan Broadcasting Station** (北山播音站; běishān bòyīnzhàn; 30min broadcasts at 9am & 10am, then hourly from 1–4pm) is a huge wall of 48 speakers which used to blast out propaganda to China, less than 2km away. These days the speakers play tunes by Teresa Teng, a 1970s pop icon revered on both sides of the Straits.

Guningtou Battle Museum

古寧頭戰史館; gǔníngtóu zhànshǐguǎn • Daily 8.30am–5pm • Free • Buses #9, #10, #11 & Tour Bus B stop in a car park near the museum entrance

Once brutally scarred by war, Kinmen's **northwestern tip** has made a remarkable recovery in the last twenty years, although look closer and you'll still see signs of destruction. The area's best-known attraction is the fort-like **Guningtou Battle Museum**, located near the beachfront that was the site of a pivotal Nationalist victory during the Chinese civil war. After a series of crushing defeats and retreats, it was here, in October

1949, that Chiang Kai-shek's troops finally stopped Mao's Communists, and ensured the KMT's survival; after three days of savage fighting, a ragtag invasion force of more than ten thousand Communist soldiers was routed, with just nine hundred remaining soldiers surrendering on the beach. In total, more than fifteen thousand soldiers from both sides were killed. The museum's collection consists primarily of a dozen enormous **oil paintings** depicting the battle's defining moments, in graphic (and predictably biased) detail – you are unlikely to see mainland Chinese tourists at this museum.

Beishan Old Western Building

北山古洋樓; běishān gǔyánglóu

Near the centre of the village, the **Beishan Old Western Building** is a bullet-hole-riddled *yánglóu* that has become a symbol of the Nationalist victory at Guningtou. Seized early in the conflict by the Communists, who turned it into a **command post**, it was eventually recaptured by the Nationalists after a series of vicious battles. Although there's little to see here but a few crumbling old walls, it's an important point of pilgrimage for patriotic Taiwanese.

Shuiwei Pagoda

水尾塔; shuǐwěitǎ • Beside the road between Beishan and Nanshan villages • Free • Tour Bus B passes the pagoda

The **Shuiwei Pagoda** is a quadrilateral granite tower erected in 1695 upon the recommendation of a geomancer who predicted it would help stem **flooding**. The pagoda faces **Shuangli Lake**, on the left-hand side of the road as you head towards **Nanshan** (南山; nánshān). Opposite, about 100m up the small lane leading to the national park's administrative centre, is one of Kinmen's most celebrated **wind-lion god statues**.

Shuangli Wetlands Nature Center

雙鯉溼地自然中心; shuānglǐ shīdì zìrán zhōngxīn • Daily 8.30am–5pm • Free • Buses #10 and #11 stop near here; you can rent basic, small bikes (for free) at the center to explore the area

Overlooking Shuangli Lake, the **Shuangli Wetlands Nature Center** is a two-storey facility with exhibits (some in English) on local flora and fauna, with particular emphasis on some of the two hundred and fifty species of **migratory bird** that stop at Shuangli and Ci lakes throughout the year. The best time for birdwatching is from November to March. Nearby **Ci Lake** (慈湖; cíhú) – which until 1950 connected the villages to the sea – is Kinmen's best all-round birdwatching spot. On its western edge, the **Ci Causeway** is the best place to see the now rusting rows of anti-amphibious landing spikes that once lined all the beaches of Kinmen. There's also a café at the centre with viewing windows out to the wetlands.

ACCOMMODATION	**BEISHAN AND AROUND**

★Otter's Home Western Style 湖畔江南; húpàn jiāngnán 23–3 Beishan Village ☎ 0939 725 883; map p.357. Great option in a restored *yanglou* building which was used as a KMT retreat command post during the 1949 Communist bombardment of Beishan. Rooms are small and simple, but common areas are full of traditional Chinese furniture, plus there's a delightful second-floor balcony overlooking the water and surrounding hamlets. The knowledgeable owner can arrange scooter rentals and transfers to and from the airport. NT$1800

Quemoy B&B 北山洋玩藝洋樓民宿; běishān yángwán yìyánglóu mínsù 171 Beishan Village ☎ 082 320 879; map p.357. Built in 1920 by a local trader who made his fortune in the Philippines, this two storey yanglou has simple but attractively decorated doubles. Like many other Western-style houses in Kinmen, it has bullet holes on the outside and original woodcarvings and paintings inside. The second floor has a pool table, and the owners sometime screen films here. There is also a small café where guests can purchase tea, coffee, and cookies. NT$2000

Qionglin and around

瓊林村; qiónglíncūn • Bus #1A, #2 or Tour Bus D from Shanwai

Northeast of Zhongshan Forest Park is the strategically significant village of **QIONGLIN**, renowned equally for its extensive network of tunnels and its ancestral homes (瓊林祠堂;

qiónglín cítáng). These crumbling Chinese homes (usually open during daylight hours) were predominantly inhabited by the scholarly **Cai clan**, the grandest of which is the **Cai Family Ancestral Hall** (蔡氏祠堂; càishì cítáng), its ancient interior embellished with intricate woodcarvings and large lanterns looming from the ceiling. The hall is in the heart of the village, 200m south of the main road.

Qionglin Civil Defence Exhibition Hall

瓊林民防館; qiónglín mínfángguǎn • Daily 8.30am–5pm • Free

6

Entering Qionglin from the north, the main square fronts the old Farmers' Association Hall, spruced up and converted into the **Qionglin Civil Defence Exhibition Hall**, a remarkable record of Kinmen's organization of "combat villages" and the incredible paranoia and restrictions that governed local lives until 1992: no swimming, no kites, no radios, a nightly curfew and restricted travel included. Exhibits are labelled in English.

Qionglin Tunnel

瓊林坑道; qiónglín kēngdào • Daily 8am–noon & 1.30–5.30pm • NT$10

Due to the village's strategic location, **Qionglin Tunnel** was hacked out by villagers in the 1970s. The shallow, narrow passage enabled villagers to move between buildings unseen and also offered some protection from artillery bombardments. The tunnel winds under the houses for several hundred metres, and just as you think it's never going to end, you emerge at the northern end of the village, opposite an impressive wind-lion god standing guard.

Military Brothel Exhibition Hall

特约茶室展示館; tèyuē cháshì zhǎnshìguǎn • Daily 8.30am–5pm • Tour Bus D from Shanwai

The **Military Brothel Exhibition Hall**, a former "special engagement teahouse", offers a fascinating insight into the military "service" industry. The teahouse was run by Unit 831, the team tasked with managing Taiwan's eleven military brothels. Regulations stipulated a maximum stay of thirty minutes, that no weapons could be brought inside, and that no "official business" was to be discussed. The teahouse was the backdrop to the 2014 Taiwanese movie *Paradise in Service*, set in 1969. There's also a pleasant café on site.

Zhongshan Forest Park

中山紀念林; zhōngshān jìniàn lín • Kinmen National Park Visitor Center and Rushan Visitor Center both daily 8.30am–5pm • Bus #1 from Jincheng and Tour Bus B from Shanwai stop outside Kinmen National Park Visitor Center

In the centre of the island, the **Zhongshan Forest Park** is a peaceful evergreen forest lined with paved pathways that are great for short nature walks and bike rides. Access is via the **Kinmen National Park Visitor Center** (see p.359) at the northern end, which has free bike hire, a small bike museum and camping facilities (free with your own tent), or the **Rushan Visitor Center** (乳山遊客中心; rǔshān yóukè zhōngxīn) at the south, which contains displays on the park's flora and fauna.

Chiang Ching-kuo Memorial Pavilion

蔣經國紀念館; jiǎngjīngguó jìniànguǎn • Zhongshan Forest Park • Daily 8.30am–5pm • Free

Within Zhongshan Park, the **Chiang Ching-kuo Memorial Pavilion** commemorates the son of Chiang Kai-shek, who commanded troops on Kinmen and eventually succeeded his father as president. Inside the pavilion is a bust of the younger Chiang, as well as displays of items from his wardrobe and personal **grooming kit**, including such essentials as razors, a comb, hair cream and a bottle of his favourite cologne. Exhibition halls on either side chronicle Chiang's life, and his involvement with Kinmen in English and Chinese, although this is predictably flattering stuff.

Kinmen Gaoliang Liquor Inc

金門酒廠; jīnmén jiǔchǎng · 1 Taoyuan Rd · Shop daily 8am–5.30pm · Free; group tours (Chinese only) available if booked in advance · ☎ 082 325 628, ⓦ kkl.com.tw

Kinmen's most famous product is its fiery **Kinmen gaoliang liquor**, made here from local sorghum (gāoliáng) since 1953 and most commonly available in 38- or 58-proof incarnations. Shops all over Jincheng sell the liquor in ornate ceramic bottles, but you can also visit the shiny headquarters of **Kinmen Gaoliang Liquor Inc**. Guided **tours** of the distillery and small museum are available, but usually only in Chinese; at the **shop**, you can buy and taste the various liquors. A huge gāoliáng bottle on the main road marks the entrance.

Shanwai and around

山外; shānwài

Kinmen's second-largest settlement, **SHANWAI** (often referred to as Jinhu township), is mostly populated with young soldiers. It is useful for tourists principally as a transport hub, with a **bus station** in the centre offering services to nearby attractions. There's a small visitor centre in the bus station and plenty of taxis outside. Just east of Shanwai is **Tai Lake** (太湖; tàihú), a recreation area favoured by locals and an important breeding ground for cormorants and ospreys.

August 23 Artillery Battle Museum

八二三戰史館; bāèrsān zhànshǐguǎn · Daily 8.30am–5pm · Free · Tour Bus D from Shanwai

On Tai Lake's northeastern side, **Banyan Park** (榕園; róng yuán) contains several historic attractions, notably the **August 23 Artillery Battle Museum**, which chronicles the crippling battle that began on the eve of August 23, 1958, when Communist forces launched an artillery attack against Kinmen and Lieyu that lasted 44 days, firing almost 475,000 shells and destroying 2649 buildings. The museum provides an excellent overview of the bombardment and its aftermath, including fascinating exhibits about the prolonged **propaganda war** between the two sides. Most of the displays have English captions, and there is a variety of black-and-white photos and video footage from the period.

EATING   **SHANWAI AND AROUND**

Shanwai has numerous **cafés and restaurants**, and there are plenty of **bakeries and teashops** along the main road near the bus station and 7-Eleven.

Lao Die Beef Noodles 老爹牛肉麵; lǎo diē niúròu miàn 26 Wude Xin Zhuang ☎ 082 334 504; map p.357. Locals drive all the way from Jincheng just to eat at this award-winning little beef noodle joint. As well as the signature beef noodles (NT$110), the beef dumplings (NT$70 for ten) are also tasty. Daily except Fri 11am–2.30pm & 5–8pm.

Lucky Star 滿天星; mǎntiānxīng 47 Fuxing Rd ☎ 082 333 316; map p.357. Inviting restaurant owned by an avid cyclist and swimmer. The menu offers a wide range of simple Chinese and Western dishes including egg flower soup (NT$50), pork noodles (NT$80) and black pepper steak (NT$200). Daily 11am–2pm & 5.30–8pm.

Tan Tian Lo 談天樓; tántiānlóu 3 Fuxing Rd ☎ 082 332 766; map p.357. Running for more than fifty years, this clean, local favourite serves superb savoury and sweet sesame dumplings with shaved ice (NT$60–80). Daily except Weds 10.30am–7pm.

Taiwushan

太武山; tàiwǔshān

The hilly terrain north of Shanwei gives rise to **Taiwushan**, or Taiwu Mountain, which at 253m is Kinmen's highest peak. It is home to a military base, but is also a popular walking area, with a paved, pedestrian-only 3.5km road, the **Taiwushan Footpath** (太武山步道; tàiwǔshān bùdào), leading towards the mountaintop. There are also several worthwhile historic attractions, not least the enormous **Taiwushan Cemetery** (太武山公墓; tàiwǔshān gōngmù) at the mountain's foot, filled with thousands of headstones of Nationalist soldiers.

6

Wu Wang Zai Ju Inscribed Stone

毋忘在莒勒石; wúwàngzài jǔlèshí

Just over 1km up the Taiwushan Footpath is the famous **Wu Wang Zai Ju Inscribed Stone**, a massive, smooth-faced outcrop inscribed with the four characters of Chiang Kai-shek's oft-recited rallying cry to reclaim the Chinese mainland. The slogan, which literally means "Forget Not the Time in Chu", refers to the ancient military achievement of **General Tian Dan**, who retreated to the territory of Chu to regroup and train his troops before recovering their former territory of Qi during the Zhou dynasty. Chiang ordered the characters inscribed in the stone in 1952, exhorting civilians and soldiers alike to be inspired by Tian Dan's historic example.

Haiyin Temple

海印寺; hǎiyìnsì

Further up the footpath, close to the summit of Taiwushan, is **Haiyin Temple**, which was originally built during the Song dynasty between 1265 and 1274. At first it was a Taoist shrine, but during Ming-dynasty renovations the Taoist statuary was replaced with Buddhist images. The original temple was destroyed during the August 23 Artillery Battle in 1958 and then rebuilt as the current version. From the temple you can continue to follow the footpath as it descends to Taiwushan's northeast base or retrace your steps to the entrance near the cemetery.

Northeast Kinmen

The village of **Shamei** (沙美; shāměi), in the northeastern section of Kinmen Island, is primarily a transportation hub but does offer easy access to a number of interesting sites. The village of **Shanhou**, meanwhile, is a tranquil, traditional place, home to some fabulous homestays and close to the charming **Kinmen Folk Cultural Village**.

Mashan Observation Post

馬山觀測站; mǎshān guāncèzhàn • About 3km north of Shamei • Daily 8.30am–5pm • Free • Tour Bus C leaves from Shanwai

Mashan Observation Post, right on the island's northeastern tip, is a once-heavily fortified station from which Taiwanese troops still keep tabs on the mainland. Near the entrance is a mocked-up radio operator's station, and from here a 174m-long tunnel leads to a concrete bunker that offers clear views of some inhabited mainland Chinese islands less than 2km away. Inside the bunker, high-powered binoculars afford close-up views of the islands.

Kinmen Folk Culture Village

金門民俗文化村; jīnmén mínsú wénhuàcūn • 5km southeast of the Mashan Observation Post • Daily: village 24hr, shops 8.30am–5pm • Free • Buses #25 and #31 from Shamei, and Tour Bus C from Shanwai stop at the entrance gate

The **Kinmen Folk Culture Village** is a spectacularly photogenic compound of well-preserved southern Fujian-style houses on the edge of **SHANHOU** (山后; shānhòu) village. The compound contains sixteen traditional houses and gardens, plus the **Wang Ancestral Hall** (王氏宗祠; wángshì zōngcí) and the **Haizhu Hall** (海珠堂; hǎizhūtáng), a traditional private school, all aligned in perfect symmetry and accessible via a neatly organized network of narrow lanes. It was built by members of the wealthy **Wang clan**, overseas merchants who made their fortunes in Japan. The entire complex took more than twenty years to build and was completed in 1900.

Most of the family homes are still privately owned, although some have been converted into shops and cafés and a couple of others are open to the public. The **Wang Ancestral Hall** (the main building at the front to the right) has displays, labelled in English, that shed light on the history of the village and Wang family, while the **Marriage Custom Exhibition Hall** behind it offers basic displays on Chinese marriage customs and more Wang memorabilia.

ACCOMMODATION

Shanhou Haizhu 山后海珠; shānhòu hǎizhū 65 Shanhou Village ☎082 355 380 or ☎0935 001 434, ⊛sunho65.myweb.hinet.net; map p.357. A lovely, traditional homestay with clean, comfy rooms, a large courtyard garden, a coffee bar and a selection of board games for guests' use. <u>NT$1500</u>

★**Shanhou Yaoyue** 山后邀月; shānhòu yāoyuè 45 Shanhou Village ☎0929 121 008; map p.357.

Fabulous, modern interpretation of a traditional Fujianese-style compound, with five guest rooms surrounding the main hall of a family home. The building is new, though the antique-styled tiled floors and Chinese calligraphy look very authentic. Rooms include a small living area w ith flatscreen TV, modern bathrooms and cosy bedrooms with Chinese dressers. The helpful owners speak good English and can help arrange scooter and car rental. <u>NT$1600</u>

6

EATING

Minshi Shaobing 閩式燒餅; mǐnshì shāobǐng 48 Bohai Rd, Shamei Village ☎082 352 922; map p.357. This humble place has been open for forty years and is famed for its crumbly, tasty pork (NT$15) and sweet shāobǐng flatbread (NT$15), turning out over a thousand pieces a day. Daily 7am–4pm.

★**Wang A-Po** 王阿婆小吃店; wáng ā-pó xiǎochīdiàn 64 Shanhou Village ☎082 352 388; map p.357. This small, simple snack shop is famed throughout Kinmen for its delicious oyster omelettes

(NT$70) and oyster noodles (NT$70). Daily 8am–5pm.

World of Fried Chicken 世界炸雞; shìjiè zhájī 19 Houxing St, Shamei Village ☎0911 883 022; map p.357. Popular with locals and military personnel, this place is festooned with ammo boxes and old artillery shells, and has camo-covered tables. Go for fried chicken (NT$60) or barbecue your own outside; french fries NT$30. In summer, they also offer missile-shaped big ice (NT$50). Daily: Jun–Oct 11am–8pm; Nov–May 3–8pm.

Lieyu (Little Kinmen)

烈嶼; lièyǔ

Commonly known as "Xiao Jinmen" (Little Kinmen), **LIEYU** – the small island just west of Kinmen – was relentlessly shelled by the PRC for decades and today it reflects Kinmen at its most surreal. The island's regeneration has produced swathes of bucolic wheatfields and largely rebuilt traditional villages, yet the **military** remains firmly entrenched here – sometimes metres from the tourists. It's well worth exploring by bike, as the island's most appealing asset is the blissfully traffic-free, 18km-long cycle path that sets off just above the visitor centre before circling the coast. As you head north from Jiugong pier on the bike trail, the first attraction you'll encounter is the **General's Fortress** (將軍堡; jiāngjūnbǎo), an abandoned command outpost situated on a lonely stretch of golden-sand beach.

Jiugong Tunnel

九宮坑道; jiǔgōng kēngdào • Daily 8.30am–5.30pm • Free

A pathway connects the Lieyu Visitor Center with the entrance to the **Jiugong Tunnel**, commonly referred to as the "Siwei Tunnel". Blasted into solid granite in the 1960s to transport and shelter personnel and rations, it was hacked out in a double-T configuration, with four exits to the sea and five connecting tunnels leading to piers. You can walk through the main, cavern-like tunnel (790m) to **Luocuo Harbour** (羅厝漁港; luócuò yúgǎng) on the other side, from where you could make your way back to the visitor centre overland, although it's quicker to return via the tunnel.

Hujingtou Battle Museum

湖井頭戰史館; hújǐngtóu zhànshǐguǎn • Daily 8.30am–5.30pm • Free

On the island's northwestern corner, the **Hujingtou Battle Museum** is essentially a lookout post, with unparalleled views of the mainland Chinese city of **Xiamen**. The museum itself (English labels) commemorates the local Lieyu Regiment and its role in the defence of tiny Dadan and Erhan islets, and also has videos of current special forces training (mainly bare-chested exercises on the beach). There are also high-powered binoculars which give you a close-up view of Xiamen's ever-expanding skyline.

ARRIVAL AND INFORMATION

By ferry Ferries leave regularly from Shuitou Pier to Jiugong Pier on Lieyu's southeast coast (daily every 30min 7am–7.30pm, then at 8, 9 & 10pm; 15min; NT$60). Bus #7 runs from Jincheng to Shuitou Pier (the Lieyu ferry is along the pier behind the large China ferry terminal).

Tourist information Upon arrival at Jiugong Pier you can get detailed maps of the island at the Lieyu Visitor Center (烈嶼遊客中心; lièyǔ yóukè zhōngxīn; daily 8.30am–5pm; ☎082 364 401) which has a small display area in Chinese, a coffee shop and a souvenir stand.

GETTING AROUND

By bike and scooter You can rent a K Bike at one of their two docks on Lieyu, or bring your scooter on the ferry from Shuitou (an extra NT$100). It's also possible to borrow bikes for free on arrival: the stand (daily 8am–noon &

1–5pm; bring ID/passport) is near the Lieyu Visitor Center entrance.

By bus Buses do run across the island (NT$12–15) but are not very practical for sightseeing.

The Matsu Islands

馬祖列島; mǎzǔ lièdǎo

Poised tantalizingly close to the coast of mainland China's Fujian province, the **MATSU ISLANDS** are second only to Kinmen in their proximity to the PRC – a fact that explains the heavy military presence on most of them. The archipelago is geographically, historically and culturally distinct from mainland Taiwan. Its inhabitants' ancestors originally migrated from **northern Fujian**, and here more than anywhere else their traditional ways of life are preserved. In addition to upholding their fishing heritage, most of the islanders speak the **Minbei dialect** (commonly referred to in English as the "Fuzhou" dialect) – it's markedly different from the "Minnan" (southern Fujian) dialect that's predominantly spoken throughout Taiwan.

Although the archipelago comprises nineteen islands and islets, only six of them are accessible to tourists, each with a distinct flavour and appeal. While the main island and tourist centre, **Nangan**, has the greatest variety of attractions, less crowded **Beigan** has the best beaches and examples of northern Fujianese architecture. Hilly **Dongyin** and **Xiyin** – which are connected by a causeway – feature the most striking topography, and the sister islands of **Dongju** and **Xiju** are brimming with historic landmarks. Note that, while the entire archipelago is named "Matsu", locals and Taiwanese tourists routinely refer to the biggest, most visited island of Nangan as "Matsu" as well (according to legend, the Chinese goddess **Mazu**'s dead body washed ashore on one of its beaches).

In fair weather, most of the islands can be reached via **ferries** originating at Nangan, but you should allow at least a week if you want to visit them all – and given the distance required to travel here from mainland Taiwan, it makes sense to take your time and soak up the atmosphere of each one.

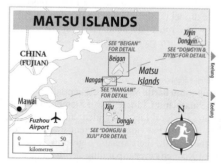

MATSU ISLANDS

CHINA
(FUJIAN)

Mawai

Fuzhou
Airport

0   50
kilometres

Xiyin
Dongyin
SEE "DONGYIN &
XIYIN" FOR DETAIL

SEE "BEIGAN"
FOR DETAIL
Beigan

Matsu
Islands

Nangan
SEE "NANGAN"
FOR DETAIL

Xiju

Dongju
SEE "DONGJU &
XIJU" FOR DETAIL

Keelung   Keelung

N

The **best period to visit** is from late April to September, as warm weather and clear visibility allow for regular flights and ferry services. This is also the best time to see Matsu's eerie "blue tears" – bewitching luminescent blue algae which laps the coastline in April, May and June. The islands are often shrouded in thick fog from March to early May and battered by heavy winds in winter, making air and sea connections highly erratic and visits far less enjoyable at these times.

Brief history

The Matsu Islands were first settled in the mid-1300s, when **fishermen** from China's Fujian province used them for shelter during stormy weather and eventually set up permanent bases. The heaviest migration took place in the 1600s, when boatloads of mostly northern-Fujianese refugees began arriving in the wake of the **Manchu invasions** from northeast China. Throughout much of the Qing dynasty, the islands were plagued by **piracy**, with periodic raids forcing many settlers at least temporarily to abandon their homes.

Matsu in the middle

Unlike the rest of Taiwan, the Matsu Islands were never colonized by the Japanese and they remained sleepy fishing outposts until 1949, when the retreating **Nationalists** seized them (along with Kinmen) and, over the following decades, built numerous military installations and an astounding 256 tunnels to fend off advances by mainland Communists. In August 1954, the Nationalist government sent 15,000 troops to Matsu, instigating an artillery bombardment by the Communists. The shelling continued steadily until 1956, when the **US** supplied the Nationalists with sophisticated weaponry that effectively countered the Communist offensive. In August 1958, however, the Communists resumed their artillery attack on the island and threatened to **invade**. The US responded by deploying its **Seventh Fleet** to the Taiwan Strait, providing naval aircraft that enabled the Nationalists to establish control of the region's airspace. In October 1958, Communist Party Chairman **Mao Zedong** proposed a deal: if US warships stayed away from the mainland coastline, the Communists would only bomb the strait islands on odd-numbered days. The offer was rejected at first, but two years later the Americans and Taiwanese agreed and the alternate-day shelling continued until 1978.

Matsu as stepping stone to China

Martial law wasn't lifted on Matsu until 1992, but since then the military presence has been gradually scaled back and local businesses have increasingly turned towards **tourism**. In recognition of the islands' unique history and culture, the archipelago was designated the **Matsu National Scenic Area** in 1999. In 2001 Matsu (and Kinmen) received an economic boost with the implementation of the **Three Small Links** agreement, which allows local residents to engage in limited direct travel and trade with mainland China. Since then regulations have further relaxed to allow foreign travellers to use Matsu as a transit point between Taiwan and China.

ARRIVAL AND DEPARTURE
THE MATSU ISLANDS

FROM TAIWAN

BY PLANE

There are regular flights from Taipei (Songshan) to Nangan and Beigan, as well as one daily flight from Taichung to Nangan. All of these flights are operated by Uni Air (Nangan ☎ 0836 26522; ⊚ uniair.com.tw). During the March–May foggy season, flights are often delayed or cancelled.

BY BOAT

The overnight ferry is a fun if time-consuming way to get to the islands, and is the only means of transport to Dongyin and Xiyin. The waters of the Taiwan Strait can be rough, but the ferry's large size minimizes seasickness. There is one ferry to Matsu (daily except Tues), departing from the northern port of Keelung (see p.132) at 10pm; on odd days (Mon, Wed, Fri, Sun) it sails first to Nangan, arriving at

around 7am (9hr), before departing for Dongyin at 9.30am. It arrives Dongyin at 11.30am and then leaves for Keelung, arriving back around 6pm. On even days (Thurs & Sat; none on Tues) the order is reversed, and the boat stops at Dongyin first before heading on to Nangan. It's worth noting, however, that in winter and during the March–May foggy season this ferry is sometimes cancelled, so it's only a reliable means of transport June–Sept.

Ferry companies Services are operated by Shinhwa Navigation (新華航業公司; xīnhuá hángyè gōngsī; 2/F, 16 Guangxi St in Keelung; ☎ 02 2424 6868) on the ship *Taima Zhixing*. Their offices are on the second floor of the West Passenger Terminal in Keelung. To get there, turn left as you exit the Keelung train station and walk straight for a few hundred metres.

Tickets and reservations It's best to reserve your ticket

6

at least one day in advance, but same-day purchases are possible (8–9pm only). You'll need to show your passport when reserving and paying for your ticket (2nd class NT$1050, six-bed dorm NT$1575, double from NT$1680/person), as well as before you board the boat. During summer, reservations can be made by phone sixty days in advance (Keelung ☎ 02 2424 6868, Nangan ☎ 0836 26655, Dongyin ☎ 0836 77555, but all only in Chinese). On Nangan you can buy tickets at the port, while on Dongyin you can buy your ticket at 7–8am for that day or 2–5pm for the following day, before departure from Zhongzhu Port.

FROM CHINA

By boat Ferries (1hr 30min) between Fuzhou (福州; fúzhōu) in China and Nangan are now open to foreigners (some use this as a cheap shortcut between Taiwan and the mainland for visa runs). Leaving Fuzhou's Mawei Port (马尾; mǎwěi), ferries depart at 9.15am, arriving in Nangan at 11.15am. Ferries usually depart from Nangan at 2pm to arrive at Mawei at 4pm. You can buy tickets at the pier daily noon–1.30pm (NT$1300 one-way, NT$2400 return) or through an agent such as Sanlin (☎ 0836 23868).

GETTING AROUND

Once on the Matsu Islands, getting around by taxi, scooter, car or even bike is fairly straightforward (see individual island accounts), but getting to some of the outlying islands can be more difficult, particularly in winter or bad weather.

By ferry Unfortunately, it isn't possible to hop directly from one island to another, as all local ferries originate from Nangan's Fuao Port. This means you'll have to return to Nangan after visiting each island to catch a ferry to another one. The only exception is that most of the ferries from Nangan to Dongju call at nearby Xiju along the way, so it's possible to alight at Xiju and then catch an onward ferry later to Dongju. Ferry direction rotates monthly, meaning one month it will run Nangan–Dongju–Xiju, and the following month Nangan–Xiju–Dongju. While there are usually daily ferries from Nangan to the other islands from June to August, weather permitting, at other times of year schedules can be cut back considerably. For local ferry information, check individual island accounts.

By helicopter A spectacular if expensive way to get between the islands is the winter helicopter service (Oct–March). Daily flights leave Nangan at 12.40pm bound for Dongyin (NT$3000) and Dongju (NT$2000). Minimum four passengers; call ☎ 0836 25350 for more information.

INFORMATION

Money It's a good idea to bring enough cash for your entire stay in the Matsu Islands, as there is only one bank with an ATM that accepts international credit cards, just north of Jieshou on Nangan (see p.377).

Nangan

南竿; nángān

As the largest of the Matsu Islands and their administrative and cultural centre, **NANGAN** captures the vast majority of the area's tourist traffic. There's a wide range of sights here, from former **military installations** that have been opened to the public to restored **traditional stone houses** and one of Taiwan's most famous distilleries. It's also a place of legend, where the earthly body of the goddess **Mazu** is reputed to have washed ashore.

The sights on Nangan are spread out, so it's best to visit all the attractions in each area while working your way round the island in order to avoid backtracking. Starting from **Fuao Village** (福澳村; fúào cūn), for example, a convenient **circuit** would be to head southwest on the main road before making a clockwise loop around Nangan's sight-filled western half, and then moving to the east.

Zhenge Daidan Memorial Park

枕戈待旦紀念公園; zhěngē dàidàn jìniàn gōngyuán

Once dedicated to Chiang Kai-shek, the pleasant **Zhenge Daidan Memorial Park** lies along the road on a hilltop southwest of Fuao. Just across the main road is the rather forlorn-looking symbol of the unfulfilled aspirations of the KMT, the **Fushan Illuminated Wall** (福山照壁; fúshān zhàobì). The imposing whitewashed wall is emblazoned with four giant red characters that comprise an old idiom meaning "sleep with one's sword ready", and were inscribed on the orders of the Generalissimo himself during a 1958 inspection of Nangan. There's also a pleasant café over the road, *Zhenge Daidan Ocean View* (see p.378).

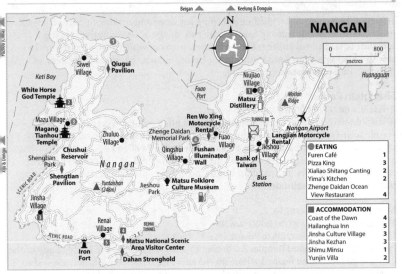

6

Matsu Folklore Culture Museum

民俗文物館; mínsú wénwùguǎn • Tues–Sun 9am–5pm • NT$40

Just outside of Qingshui (清水; qīngshuǐ), the multistorey **Matsu Folklore Culture Museum** gives a good introduction to the Matsu Islands. The prehistoric exhibits on the first floor include bones, pottery and early artefacts; explanations are in Chinese and English, but the mock-up traditional house and other exhibits on the upper floors are only labelled in Chinese.

Beihai Tunnel

北海坑道; běihǎi kēngdào • Daily 8.30am–5pm • Free; NT$150 boat ride; NT$300 kayak rental

Nangan's major decommissioned **military sites** are located towards the island's most southerly point near **Renai Village** (仁愛村; rénàicūn), and are now promoted as tourist attractions. East of the village, the 700m-long **Beihai Tunnel** was built as a shelter for military vessels and ammunition. You can walk through it at low tide, or rent a boat or kayak at the site.

Dahan Stronghold

大漢據點; dàhàn jùdiǎn • Daily 8am–5pm • Free

On Nangan's southern extremity, a few hundred metres beyond Beihai Tunnel, is the **Dahan Stronghold**, a decommissioned labyrinth of underground fortifications, completed in 1976, that lead through a granite hill to some abandoned gun emplacements overlooking the ocean. It's worth the short walk for the sea views alone.

Iron Fort

鐵堡; tiěbǎo • 24hr • Free

On a small islet just off the coast to the east of Jinsha, the **Iron Fort** contains an armoury, gun emplacement, toilets, and even a doghouse, all excavated from the rocky outcrop and barely visible from the outside, were it not for the tell-tale bridge that leads to the fort.

Jinsha

津沙; jīnshā

The scenic **coastal road** that runs between Renai and Mazu villages on Nangan is an attraction in its own right, yielding sweeping sea views and making for a superb walk or scooter ride. About halfway between the two villages is lovely **Jinsha**, a living museum of traditional **Fujianese stone houses**, many of which have been restored to their original grandeur. Jinsha surrounds a beautiful rocky bay and boasts some of Nangan's finest **homestays** (see p.377).

Shengtian Park

勝天公園; shèngtiān gōngyuán

A few kilometres beyond Jinsha, **Shengtian Park** offers some of Nangan's loveliest seaside scenery. In the middle of the park, next to the **Chushui Reservoir** (儲水澳水庫; chúshuǐào shuǐkù), is the tastefully designed **Shengtian Pavilion** (勝天亭; shèngtiān tíng), a Song dynasty-style structure built by the military in 1990. With its graceful flying eaves and natural hues, the pavilion blends in with the surroundings and is a relaxing place to enjoy some solitude.

Magang Tianhou Temple

馬港天后宮; mǎgǎng tiānhòu gōng · Daily 24hr

On Nangan's west coast, **Mazu Village** (馬祖村; mǎzǔcūn) is home to the nationally famous **Magang Tianhou Temple**. According to one local legend, the earthly body of the Chinese goddess **Mazu** washed ashore on the adjacent beach. The villagers are said to have recovered Mazu's body and buried it in the **stone coffin** embedded in the temple floor directly in front of the altar. Some locals say it now holds only the clothes recovered from Mazu's body, while others maintain it actually contains the remains of Mazu's drowned father. Regardless of the coffin's contents, one thing everyone agrees on is that it's the only part of the temple with historic significance: while the building itself was first constructed at the end of the Qing dynasty on the site of a much smaller shrine, it has been renovated and expanded several times since. Despite this, locals claim the coffin is still lying in its original location.

A huge, 30m-high **statue** of Mazu was built on the hill west of the temple in 2009, and combined with the site's historic import, makes this a requisite stop for Taiwanese tourists and worshippers alike.

White Horse God Temple

白馬文武大王廟; báimǎ wénwǔ dàwángmiào · Just north of Mazu Village, on the road that leads to Siwei (四維; sìwéi) · Daily 24hr

The tiny **White Horse God Temple** is devoted to two Qing dynasty generals whose bodies floated ashore at nearby Keti Bay in the late 1800s. Villagers buried the bodies and, shortly after they were interred, one of the generals reputedly instructed the villagers through a spirit medium to build a temple in his honour. Locals believe that the temple deity now provides protection for boats in the bay, as a mysterious warning light is said to flash across the water every time a storm is approaching.

Yuntaishan

雲台山; yúntáishān · Daily 24hr

At 248m, **Yuntaishan** is the island's highest point and a favoured place to watch the sun set. From the top there are unparalleled views of Nangan and nearby islands and, accordingly, there is an active **military observation post** bristling with soldiers. Tourists are welcome to photograph the scenery to the north, but turning your camera towards the guard station isn't recommended.

Matsu Distillery

馬祖酒廠; mǎzǔ jiǔchǎng · Mon–Fri 8.30–11.30am & 1–5pm, Sat & Sun 3–5pm · Free · ☎ 0836 22820

At Nangan's northeast corner is the **Matsu Distillery**, a fitting place to cap off a long day of sightseeing. Here you can sample some of Matsu's fiery **gaoliang sorghum liquor** as well as the milder lǎojiǔ, a traditional rice spirit. Although there is no actual distillery tour, samples are usually provided in the exhibition room and shop inside.

Tunnel 88

八八坑; bābā kēng · Daily 8–11.30am & 2.30–5pm · Free

Next to the Matsu Distillery lies **Tunnel 88**, a former air-raid shelter completed in 1974 and named in honour of Chiang Kai-shek's 88th birthday. The entrance is lined with giant decorative jars, and the 273m-long tunnel is now used for the fermentation and storage of strong-smelling spirits from the distillery next door.

6

ARRIVAL AND INFORMATION   NANGAN

By plane Nangan Airport (南竿機場; nángān jīchǎng) is at Nangan's eastern end; you'll find plenty of taxis awaiting passengers, and there are also hourly buses for the short ride to Jieshou (NT$15).

Destinations Taichung (1 daily; 1hr 5min); Taipei (6 daily; 50min).

By boat Nangan's Fuao Port (福澳港; fúàogǎng) is the ferry hub of the Matsu Islands. There are hourly buses to Jieshou, which is just 2km away (NT$15).

Destinations Beigan (hourly in summer; 15min); Dongju (3 daily; 50min); Dongyin (every other month Tues, Thurs, Sat & Mon; 2hr); Xiju (3 daily; 50min).

Tourist information The Matsu National Scenic Area

Visitor Center (馬祖國家風景區管理處; mǎzǔ guójiā fēngjǐngqū guǎnlǐchù; daily: Jun–Sept 8am–6pm, Oct–May 8am–5.30pm; ☎0836 25630, ⓦ www.matsu-nsa.gov.tw) is in Renai Village in the south of the island; it's off to the left before the entrance to the Beihai Tunnel complex, about a 15min scooter ride from either the airport or ferry pier. The centre has some English pamphlets and maps and can dispense basic travel information in English.

Banks The Bank of Taiwan, 257 Jieshou Village, is the only bank on the Matsu Islands that accepts foreign cards; it's on the steep hill that heads northwest out of the settlement. You can also change money here.

GETTING AROUND

By taxi Taxis have meters (starting fare NT$100, then NT$5 every 250m), but also have a fixed-rate schedule to main destinations: from the airport to Fuao Port is NT$100, while to Matsu Village it's NT$200. Taxis are also an option for sightseeing, with whirlwind island tours starting at about NT$500/hr, or NT$1500/half-day.

By car and scooter If you want to stay at one of the interesting homestays in the island's villages, your best option is to rent a car or scooter. Scooter rentals are widely available for about NT$500 a day (NT$300/half-day), and cars cost from NT$1500. Some companies insist on an international driving licence for overseas visitors. At the ferry terminal, try Nongyu Techan (農漁特產中心;

nóngyú tèchǎn zhōngxīn; ☎0836 25228). Near the airport, at 72 Jieshou Village, Langjian Motorcycle Rental (良健機車行; liángjiàn jīchēháng; ☎0836 22577) is a reliable option.

By bus Nangan has two bus lines: one that hugs the coast (via the distillery and Siwei); and the mountain line (via the distillery, Jinsha and Renai), both originating at Jieshou (介壽; jièshòu) bus station. Tickets are NT$15 per trip, or NT$50 for a day-pass. Some of these services also stop at the airport. Buses run roughly every hour between 6.10am and 5.55pm – pick up a schedule from the visitor centre if you plan to get around by bus.

ACCOMMODATION

Although there are about a dozen villages on Nangan, most of the attractive accommodation options are concentrated in only a few of them. If you arrive by ferry, there are a handful of fairly run-down old **hotels** in Fuao Village, a few minutes' walk from the pier. These establishments charge a premium due to their proximity to the port, and you'll do better at one of the atmospheric **homestays** in either Jinsha, Niujiao or Renai.

MAZU

Yunjin Villa 雲津客棧; yúnjīn kèzhàn 103-2 Mazu Village ☎0836 26228, ⓔ matsutea.bnb@gmail.com. Opened in 2017 by Matsu's only tea-growers, this boutique-style hotel offers fresh, bright rooms, all with balconies overlooking the ocean or forested hills. The owners also sell tea from the hotel, and can arrange short tours to their farm (from NT$300). <u>**NT$2600**</u>

JINSHA

★**Jinsha Culture Village** 津沙文化村; jīnshā wénhuàcūn 70 Jinsha Village ☎0836 26190, ⓦ hotel.matsu.idv.tw/jinsha. By far the best deal on Nangan, featuring several rooms in beautifully restored traditional houses scattered throughout idyllic Jinsha. The office and excellent restaurant are tucked into an alley – turn left at the far end of the village and you'll see it to the left. If you don't mind climbing steps, ask for the rooms on the hilltop to the right as you enter Jinsha – all have aromatic wooden interiors, some command sweeping bay views, and one has an attached balcony. NT$1600

Jinsha Kezhan 津沙客棧; jīnshā kèzhàn 12 Jinsha Village ⓣ0836 23020, ⓦbnb.matsu.idv.tw/jinsha. Clean, simple, modern wooden rooms in an attractive 100-year-old stone property, with clean, communal bathrooms. Room 201 has a private balcony. Dorm beds are available in another property close by. The owners speak some English. Dorms NT$800, doubles NT$2000

NIUJIAO

Shimu Minsu 拾木民宿; shímù mínsù 124 Niujiao Village ⓣ0978 215 898, ⓦblog.roodo.com/wood. The simple, all-wooden rooms here are a little on the dark side, but this is offset by the beautiful bay views from the first-floor patio. To get here, take the path to the right of *Yima's*

Kitchen, past the water tank and up the steps; take a left towards a snorkel mural and then a right at no. 109, where you'll see the guesthouse. Make sure you call to confirm your arrival time – the rate includes free transport from the ferry pier or airport. NT$1000

RENAI

Coast of the Dawn 日光海岸; rìguāng hǎiàn 6 Renai Village ⓣ0836 26666, ⓔcoasthotel.liu@gmail. com. Along the main road to the east of Renai Village, one of Nangan's swankiest abodes features modern, chic rooms overlooking the Beihai Tunnel entrance and the coastline beyond. The price include breakfast, and afternoon tea is served on request. NT$3900

Hailanghua Inn 海浪花客棧; hǎilànghuā kèzhàn 64 Renai Village ⓣ0836 22568. Dated, eighteen-room hotel, immediately to the south of the village's Tianhou Shrine, with six good-value, sea-view rooms, plus scooter rental. NT$1500

EATING

Nangan is an outstanding place for eating, with inexpensive restaurants in many villages offering authentic **northern Fujian cuisine**, including "red sauce" (hongzao) made from excess yeast used in lǎojiǔ production and used to seal in the natural juices of pork or fish. Another popular local speciality dish, Buddha's hand clams (chǎofó shǒu), are so named because the prongs on their shells are thought to resemble the fingers of the Buddha.

MAZU

Pizza King 比薩大王; bǐsà dàwáng 66 Mazu Village ⓣ0836 25859. This cosy restaurant offers a good range of local specialities including *mazu hanbao* (local style hamburger; NT$200 for 4), *hongzao manyu* (hongzao eel; NT$200), and *laojiu mianxian* (rice wine noodles; NT$120). True to its name, there are also a range of pizzas on the menu (from NT$320). Daily 10am–2pm & 5–8pm.

NIUJIAO

Xialiao Shitang Canting 蝦寮食堂; xiāliáo shítáng 110-1 Niujiao Village ⓣ0836 23452. In the same building as adjoining *Yima's Kitchen*, this former fisherman's hangout has reinvented itself as a Mazu specialty restaurant, including Buddha's hand clams. They also serve beer and have an attractive outdoor seating area with pleasant views. Daily 11.30am–2pm & 4.30–10.30pm.

Yima's Kitchen 依嬤的店; yīmā de diàn 72-1 Niujiao Village ⓣ0836 26125. At the bottom of the village, this trendy restaurant housed in a traditional stone building focuses on traditional northern Fujian dishes, with red-marinaded seafood taking centre stage, and dishes including deep-fried eel with rice wine sauce (NT$300). Their set meal for one costs NT$380 and includes eel,

shrimp, pork and Buddha's hand clams – a great introduction to local cuisine. Daily 11am–2pm & 5–8.30pm.

FUAO

Zhenge Daidan Ocean View Restaurant 枕戈待旦海景餐廳; zhěngēdàidàn hǎijǐng cāntīng 139 Fu'ao Village ⓣ0905 889 609. Opened in 2017, this place is worth visiting for the views alone, but the food, prepared by the original chef from *Yima's Kitchen* in Niujiao, is also excellent. The menu includes local favourites such as Buddha hand clams and pork dumplings and noodles (NT$350), both made with a flour base that contains fish, which adds a unique depth of flavour. Daily 11am–2pm & 5–9pm.

SIWEI

Furen Café 夫人咖啡館; fūrén kāfēiguǎn 40-1 Siwei Village ⓣ0836 25138, ⓦfuren.com.tw. This lovely little café overlooking the coast serves an interesting range of dishes including fried rice and noodles (NT$250), and even paella (NT$250), which can be rounded off with a cup of Vietnamese-style coffee with condensed milk (NT$150). There's a pleasant patio with ocean views and they also have a few rooms for rent upstairs. Daily 10am–10pm.

Beigan

北竿; běigān

Five kilometres northeast of Nangan, the archipelago's second-largest island, **BEIGAN** has charming villages and superb scenery, including several **secluded beaches** with dramatic mountain backdrops. The small, functional settlement of **Tangqi** (塘岐; tángqí) once boasted the Matsu Islands' only airport and was the nerve centre for tourism, but since the 2003 opening of Nangan Airport it has become sleepy even by comparison, with its bucolic neighbour to the south. Although some tourists still fly to Beigan from Taipei, many arrive at Baisha port by ferry from Nangan and spend a night in a rustic village homestay.

Banli Beach

坂里沙灘; bǎnlǐ shātān

Starting from Baisha Port and heading northeast, the first stretch of sand you'll encounter is beautiful **Banli Beach**, at the edge of Banli Village, where there are shower and toilet facilities. At the southwest end of the beach is a tiny **Tianhou Temple** (天后宮; tiānhòugōng), dedicated to Mazu.

Tanghoudao Beach

塘后道沙灘; tánghòudào shātān

Heading east from Tangqi, which has hotels, restaurants and food shops but little in the way of tourist attractions, continue along the main road, past the airport, until you reach **Tanghoudao Beach**, a long spit of sand that forms a natural causeway between Tangqi and Houao to the east.

Houao and the War & Peace Memorial Park

戰爭和平紀念公園; zhànzhēng hépíng jìniàn gōngyuán • Exhibition Center daily 8.30–noon & 1.30–5.30pm (Nov–April till 5pm) • Free

Houao (后澳; hòuào) is a small fishing community with some beautifully restored stone-slab houses. It's a nice place for a stroll, especially around dusk, when elderly villagers typically come out to socialize. Behind the village, up the steep road heading southeast, the **War & Peace Memorial Park** is built around a handful of decommissioned army outposts, designed to commemorate Beigan's recent military history. The centrepiece is the **War & Peace Memorial Park Exhibition Center** (戰爭和平紀念公園主題館; zhànzhēng hépíng jìniàn gōngyuán zhǔtíguǎn), which chronicles the troubled modern history of the islands, from 1949 to the present, through films and exhibits.

Qiaozai and Daqiu Island

橋仔; qiáozǎi / 大坵; dàqiū • Boats leave for Daqiu in the morning and take 15min (NT$300) – you need to show ID

Nestled in the island's northwest corner is the village of **Qiaozai**, so named because of the many small bridges ("qiao" means "bridge") that span the gullies carrying runoff from nearby **Leishan** (雷山; léishān). While most villages in Matsu were settled by northern Fujianese, Qiaozai is unique in that it was founded by fishermen from the southern part of the province. Once Beigan's biggest, most affluent village, these days it's not much more than a laidback fishing settlement, although it is noted for having more **temples** than any other village in the Matsu Islands.

Qiaozai is also the departure point for boats to **Daqiu Island**, once a military stronghold, but now populated by a sizeable and incredibly tame herd of sika deer. It takes about an hour to wander around the island's network of paths – there are no roads.

Qinbi

芹壁; qínbì • Kayak rental (summertime only) from Qinbi NT$100/40min

To the west of Qiaozai along the main road is the unmistakable village of **Qinbi**, with terrace upon terrace of two-storey **stone houses** tumbling down a hillside to the sea – arguably the archipelago's most picturesque community. Spending a night in one of Qinbi's rustic **homestays** (see opposite) is highly recommended, but even if you don't stay here it's definitely worth a stroll through its narrow lanes and up its steep steps. A short swim across the shallow water to **Turtle Islet** (龜島; guīdǎo) – a granite outcrop in the middle of the bay – yields unrivalled views of the village as well as of the sea to the north.

Bishan

壁山; bìshān

For a bird's-eye view of Beigan's eastern half, nearby **Bishan** – at 298m, the Matsu Islands' highest hill – is the place to go. Near the top is an **observation point** looking out over Tangqi and Houao villages, as well as the airport, making it a perfect place to watch the small planes undertaking their precarious landings. You can drive a scooter up the road or walk to the top along the challenging, stone-stepped path that starts behind Tangqi.

ARRIVAL AND INFORMATION
BEIGAN

By plane The main advantage of arriving by air from Taipei (see p.373) is that Beigan Airport (北竿機場; běigān jīchǎng) is located next to Tangqi and is a very short walk from the town's main hotels.

Destination Taipei (3 daily; 50min).

By ferry Beigan's Baisha Port (白沙港; báishāgǎng) is easy to reach by passenger ferry from Nangan's Fuao Port.

In summer these leave every hour (daily 7am–5pm; 20min; NT$160 one-way; ☏ 0836 22193).

Tourist information Along the road from Baisha Port to Tangqi, just behind Banli Beach, is the Beigan Visitor Center (北竿遊客中心; běigān yóukè zhōngxīn; daily 8am–5pm; ꙮ bit.ly/BeiganVisitor), which also has a pleasant coffee shop.

GETTING AROUND

By scooter You can rent scooters in Baisha and Tangqi for NT$500/day. A scooter is the most convenient means for sightseeing and is particularly useful if you wish to stay in one of the restored stone-house hotels, as they are on the island's north side, separated from Tangqi by a steep hill.

By taxi If you manage to catch a taxi from the ferry pier it should cost about NT$200 to get to Tangqi, where most of

Beigan's hotels and restaurants are located. Taxis also run 2hr tours of the island for about NT$1000.

By bus Beigan's one bus makes an hourly circuit of the island, starting at Tangqi and stopping at Shangcun, Banli Reservoir, Banli Village, Baisha, Qinbi and Qiaozai. Rides cost NT$15/journey.

ACCOMMODATION

Your choice of accommodation is limited to the uninspiring but convenient **hotels** in Tangqi, one of the traditional **stone-house homestays** in Banli Village, or captivating Qinbi on Beigan's north side. You might also consider *Just Coffee* (see opposite) in Qinbi.

TANGQI

Beihai'an Hotel 北海岸飯店; běihǎiàn fàndiàn 240 Tangqi Village ☏ 0836 55036, ꙮ north-coast. myweb.hinet.net; map p.379. Features modern rooms, most of which are Japanese style with raised wooden platforms, roll-up beds and flatscreen TVs. Some rooms

have sea views, though others are windowless. NT$1750

Taijiang Hotel 台江大飯店; táijiāng dàfàndiàn 200 Tangqi Village ☏ 0836 55256; map p.379. While the *Taijiang* has seen better days, its prices include breakfast and a pick-up from the ferry pier. Spacious rooms have TV, tiled floors and adequate but old-fashioned decor. Each floor has a shared sea-view balcony. NT$1600

QINBI

★**Qinbi Holiday Village** 芹壁休閒渡假村; qínbì xiūxián dùjiàcūn 49 Qinbi Village ☎0836 55456; map p.379. One of Taiwan's most distinctive accommodation options, perched on a terrace in the midst of the village. Rooms occupy restored old stone houses – rustic but clean – with comfy beds and traditional windows that frame splendid views of the ocean. Rates are good value mid-week and during the off-season; individual travellers can get single rooms for NT$1200. NT$1400

Qinbi Mediterranean B&B 芹壁地中海民宿; qínbì dìzhōnghǎi mínsù 68 Qinbi Village ☎0836 56612; map p.379. Unlike the *Qinbi Holiday Village*, the collection of buildings that make up this B&B look rustic, with stone walls and wood floors, but the rooms are actually modern. The B&B also offers pick-ups from the airport or ferry pier. Make enquiries at the adjoining *Chin-Bi Village Café*. NT$2300

BANLI

Banli Dazhai Homestay 坂里大宅特色民宿; bǎnlǐ dàzhái tèsè mínsù 48 Banli Village ☎0836 55663, ⓦbanli.8898.tw; map p.379. Lovely little budget homestay set in a Qing dynasty house close to the beach. Stone-walled rooms come in a variety of sizes, including singles (NT$900), and have mosquito-netted (hard) beds and communal bathrooms. The friendly staff speak some English and can arrange transfers and motorbike hire. NT$1400

EATING

Beigan is an excellent place to try fresh **seafood** at reasonable prices. The island is most famous for its **fish noodles** (yúmiàn), made from corn starch and pressed fish such as eel and drum.

TANGQI

A-Po's Fish Noodles 阿婆魚麵; āpó yúmiàn 115 Zhongshan Rd ☎0836 56539; map p.379. To see noodles being handmade and dried in the sun, pop into this unassuming little shop, which is run by a friendly elderly woman who is happy to give demonstrations. You can also buy a bag of the uncooked noodles here for NT$100 to take out. Daily 11am–2pm & 5–7pm.

Hong Xing Ping Seafood Restaurant 鴻星平海鮮樓; hóngxīngpíng hǎixiānlóu 242 Zhongzheng Rd ☎0836 55426; map p.379. Crowded at lunchtime with Taiwanese tourists making day-trips from Nangan, this is the best place in Tangqi to try a bowl of hot fish noodles. Daily 10.30am–1pm & 5–7pm.

Meihua Canyin 梅花餐飲; méihuā cānyǐn 272 Zhongshan Rd ☎0836 55518; map p.379. Just across the street from the airport exit, this Spartan canteen caters to local soldiers with cheap noodle and rice dishes starting from NT$50. The friendly owner is from Qiaozai and can arrange boats from there to Daqiu Island. Daily 10.30am–9pm.

QINBI

Just Coffee 家適咖啡; jiāshì kāfēi 56 Qinbi Village ☎0836 55669; map p.379. Another lovely little café in Qinbi, *Just Coffee* is, in fact, more than just coffee: as well as serving drinks (NT$100–150) on the tiny patio and in the cosy bar, they also have rooms for rent in a building across the street. Daily 11.30am–7pm.

★**Qin Wo Coffee Bakery** 芹沃咖啡烘培館; qínwò kāfēi hōngpéi guǎn 43-1 Qinbi Village ☎0836 56099; map p.379. Attractive new café serving an enticing array of freshly baked breads (NT$100–200), coffee and tea (NT$100–180), plus a range of meals including calzone (NT$350) and seafood curry (NT$380). You can sit in the cosy wood and stone interior, or out on the terrace which enjoys sweeping views of the coastline and Turtle Islet. Daily except Weds 10am–9pm.

Dongyin and Xiyin

東引; dōngyǐn / 西引; xīyǐn

Matsu's most visually compelling islands are **DONGYIN** and **XIYIN**, two hilly tracts of land connected by a causeway at the archipelago's northernmost point. Characterized by sheer **granite cliffs** that plunge dramatically to the sea, the scenery here is sublime – especially on the larger island of Dongyin, where most of the sights and all of the tourist amenities are located. Dongyin also has some standout historic sites, such as the solitary **Dongyong Lighthouse** that dominates the island's far eastern tip. Due to their isolation, the islands get comparatively few tourists and locals tend to go well out of their way to make them comfortable – although both islands are still heavily **militarized**, even the soldiers are exceedingly friendly.

DONGYIN & XIYIN

0   2
kilometres

■ ACCOMMODATION
Lao Yue Hotel   2
Mingjian Star Hotel   1
Xinhua Hotel   2

Xiyin

Dongyin

Martyred
Maiden Cliff

Kai-shek
Bridge   Zhongliu   Thread of
Zhongzhu Port Village Dongyin   Sky
                      Visitor Center
                                    Dongyong
             Lehua   Lighthouse
             Village
                         Andong
N   Tunnel

BEIHAI
TUNNEL
                Taiwan Strait

● EATING
Maiweideng   1
Zhen Shan Mei   2

Andong Tunnel

安東坑道; āndōng kēngdào • About 1km east of Dongyin's visitor centre • Daily 8am–6pm (Oct–May till 5.30pm) • Free

The extensive **Andong Tunnel** cuts through the heart of a hill before ending up at vertical **cliffs** on Dongyin's southern coast.

The 640m-long tunnel, which once housed soldiers and military equipment, contains old barracks, ammunition depots and even a pen where pigs were raised to feed the troops.

Walking to the cliffs and back again should take about an hour.

Thread of Sky

一線天; yíxiàntiān • 6km northeast of Andong Tunnel along the main road, Dongyin • Daily 24hr • Free

The so-called **Thread of Sky** is one of Dongyin's most celebrated examples of eroded coastline, a vertical, narrow crevice between two sharply angled cliff faces that yields only a fragmentary glimpse of the sea beyond. Listening to the waves crashing against the rocks here is obligatory for Taiwanese tourists: the four-character **inscription** on the cliff means "hearing waves at the crevice of heaven".

Dongyong Lighthouse

東湧燈塔; dōngyǒng dēngtǎ • East coast, Dongyin • Daily 24hr • Free

Crowning the island's far eastern tip is the highlight of a visit to Dongyin – the **Dongyong Lighthouse**, built by British engineers in 1902. A path leads up to the lighthouse, and you can wander around the former residential buildings to the rear.

Martyred Maiden Cliff

烈女義坑; liènǚ yìkēng • East coast, Dongyin • Daily 24hr • Free

Just around the coast from Dongyin's eastern extremity, **Martyred Maiden Cliff** (or **Suicide Cliff**) is another evocative section of coastline. According to legend, a young woman leapt to her death here during the Qing dynasty to escape from pirates. You can walk out to the edge of this sea-eroded cliff, which plunges more than 100m to the rocks below – a guardrail is in place to prevent falls.

ARRIVAL AND INFORMATION   DONGYIN AND XIYIN

By ferry The easiest way to get here from mainland Taiwan is on the Keelung ferry (see p.373), which stops at Zhongzhu Harbour (中柱港; zhōngzhùgǎng) on Dongyin every day except Tues. If you want to get here from Nangan, your only option is to take the Keelung ferry at 9.30am on Mon, Wed, Fri or Sun; buy tickets on the day (7–8.30am) at Nangan's Fuao Harbour. Tickets cost NT$350, and the boat usually arrives at around 11.30am.

By helicopter In winter you also have the indulgent option of taking a helicopter from Nangan (see p.374).

Tourist information The Dongyin Visitor Center (東引遊客中心; dōngyín yóukè zhōngxīn; daily 8am–6pm, Oct–May till 5.30pm; ☎0836 77267) at 160–1 Lehua Village has interesting English-captioned exhibits on the islands' attractions.

GETTING AROUND

There is no **public transport** on the islands, so you're best off renting a scooter or hiring a taxi; walking is a possibility, but Dongyin is several kilometres in width and it would take the better part of a day to see the main sights on foot.

By scooter There are no scooter rentals at Zhongzhu Harbour, but it's possible to rent them for NT$500 from hotels in the nearby village of Zhongliu on the hill that rises from the harbour, a short walk or taxi ride from the pier.

By taxi Taxis can be hired from the ferry ports or through your hotel for NT$2000/half-day or NT$3500/day.

ACCOMMODATION

All of the islands' **accommodation** is centred in the villages of Lehua and Zhongliu on Dongyin, and consists of standard but affordable hotels whose management will often book onward ferry tickets for you without charging commission.

DONGYIN

Lao Yue Hotel 老爺大飯店; lǎoyé dàfàndiàn 29 Lehua Village ☎0836 77168; map opposite. Small, clean rooms with TVs, some with views over the harbour. Breakfast included. NT$1800

Mingjian Star Hotel 明建星大飯店; míngjiànxīng dàfàndiàn 66 Zhongliu Village ☎0836 77180; map opposite. The Mingjian Star has decent rooms, some with sea views (NT$1800). NT$1600

Xinhua Hotel 昕華飯店; xīnhuá fàndiàn 46 Lehua Village ☎0836 77600; map opposite. A short walk from the ferry pier, near the post office, this place offers great value. Rooms on higher floors (NT$1700) and those with sea views (NT$2000) are more expensive. NT$1500

EATING

The best **eating** places, all on Dongyin, are down-to-earth, and serve up mostly northern Chinese specialities.

DONGYIN

Maiweideng 麥味登早餐; màiwèidēng zǎocān 123 Lehua Village ☎0836 77255; map opposite. Dongyin's most popular breakfast stop, *Maiweideng* has morning goodies ranging from Taiwanese pancakes and Western-style sandwiches to hot soybean milk. Daily 5am–10.30am.

Zhen Shan Mei 珍膳美餐廳; zhēnshànměi cāntīng 93 Lehua Village ☎0836 77289; map opposite. The friendly owner of this ramshackle canteen serves up delicious fish dumplings and noodles. Daily 10am–2pm & 4–9pm.

Dongju and Xiju

At the southernmost point of the Matsu Islands lie **DONGJU** and **XIJU**. Originally called "East Dog" and "West Dog" (Dongquan and Xiquan) for their resemblance to the animal when viewed from the sea, their modern names, which mean "East Chu" and "West Chu", were symbolic of Chiang's ambitions to reclaim the mainland (see p.370). Outside of the busy summer months, both islands – easily accessible by **ferry** from Nangan – are laidback, with ample accommodation and restaurants.

ARRIVAL AND DEPARTURE

DONGJU AND XIJU

By ferry In good weather, and especially during the busy summer tourist season, there are ferries daily from Nangan's Fuao Port at 7am, 11am & 2.30pm (NT$200); on odd months (Jan, March, May and so on) to Xiju first (50min) then Dongju (another 15min), and even months to Dongju first then Xiju (same times). Boats then return to Nangan. There are also four daily sailings just between Dongju and Xiju (NT$80): 7.30am, 10am, 2pm and 5.10pm (Xiju–Dongju); and 7.35am, 10.05am, 2.05pm and 5.15pm (Dongju–Xiju).

By helicopter In winter you can take a helicopter from Nangan (see p.374).

Dongju

東莒; dōngjǔ

The larger of the two islands, **DONGJU** can be covered on foot in several hours. With few trees, however, it gets scorching hot in summer, so it's easier to rent a scooter (see above). **Daping Village** (大坪村; dàpíng cūn) is where most of the island's hotels and restaurants are to be found. Atop a small hill at the island's northeast tip, **Dongju Lighthouse** (東莒島燈塔; dōngjǔdǎo dēngtǎ) was built by the British in 1872 to help with the navigation of ships trading with China in the wake of the Opium Wars. Dongju is famous for its "three treasures", watermelon, tofu and clams, the latter of which is celebrated with a **festival** in the first two weeks of August.

6

ACCOMMODATION
Chuanlao Homestay	3
Friendship Hotel	1
Haijing Holiday Village	1
Haishang Renjia Minsu	2
Hongjing Hostel	3

●**EATING**
Guanhailou	1
Huamei Meishi	2
Zhao Cha	2

Fuzheng Beach (福正海灘; fúzhèng hǎitān), in the middle of Dongju's north coast, just beyond the visitor centre, is a popular place for Taiwanese to collect mussels and **limpets** at low tide – the latter are recognizable by their distinctive oval-shaped shells. The village here also has a selection of homestays.

Dapu

大埔; dàpǔ • On Dongju's south coast

The village of **Dapu** is an abandoned fishing settlement that has been completely restored. While it lacks the character of some of the archipelago's inhabited communities – the **stone buildings** here essentially comprise an open-air museum – the village's location on an isolated, rocky promontory is quite a setting, particularly when viewed from a distance. Further south, at Dongju's southern tip, you'll find the **Dapu Stone Inscription** (大埔石刻; dàpǔ shíkè), a rare tablet with a 41-character engraving commemorating the capture of pirates by a Ming-dynasty general in 1617. Below the pavilion built around the tablet is a set of **steps** leading gently to the sea. This spot, another prime shellfish-gathering area, is a favourite place to watch the sunset.

GETTING AROUND AND INFORMATION   DONGJU

Mengao Port (猛沃港; měngwògǎng), where the **ferry** arrives (see p.383), is about 1km from Daping Village, so you could walk there or take a taxi (NT$50). Some hotels have a pick-up service for guests with reservations.

By scooter Scooters can be rented at Baihe Homestay, 31 Daping Village (☎0836 88018; NT$300/500 for a half-day/ full day; no identification required).
Tourist information A good place to start a tour of Dongju is the Juguang Visitor Center (莒光遊客中心; jǔguāng yóukè zhōngxīn; daily 8am–6pm, Nov– May till 5.30pm), 1 Fuzheng Village, a 15min walk northeast of Daping. Here you can pick up an English map of Dongju and Xiju, and there are English-captioned exhibits on local culture and flora and fauna.

ACCOMMODATION

Most of Dongju's accommodation is in Daping, but there are a few newer places to stay in Fuzheng Village.

DAPING

Chuanlao Homestay 船老大民宿; chuánlǎodà mínsù 72 Daping Village ☎0836 88022; map above. Big, comfortable doubles in a modern building; rooms on the second and third floors have balconies. The welcoming owners offer free ferry transfers and can arrange scooter rental. No English spoken. **NT$1400**

Hongjing Hostel 鴻景山莊; hóngjǐng shānzhuāng 5 Daping Village ☎0836 88033; map above. In the north of Daping Village, this modern building has clean, airy rooms and some of the island's comfiest beds. **NT$1400**

FUZHENG

Haishang Renjia Minsu 海上人家民宿; hǎishàng rénjiā mínsù 38-1 Fuzheng Village ☎0935 648 716, ⓦoceanhome.okgo.tw; map above. This budget option enjoys a great location at the end of Fuzheng Village and has a lovely patio and outdoor sitting area. The owner is very friendly and will arrange free ferry transfers. The rooms are passable, but nothing to write home about, with bunk dorms and simple doubles. There's also a clean common area and kitchen, plus laundry facilities. **NT$1600**

EATING

Huamei Meishi 華美美食; huáměi měishí 28 Daping Village ☎0836 88388; map p.382. This popular snack shop serves green-onion pancakes (NT$60), tofu (NT$30), and noodles (NT$70). Daily 6.30am–7pm.

Zhao Cha 找茶; zhǎochá 30 Daping Village ☎0836 88009; map opposite. A beach-themed teahouse, *Zhao Cha* has comfy blue wicker chairs on which to enjoy a grass-jelly tea or refreshing watermelon juice (drinks NT$30–60). Daily 9am–8.30pm.

Xiju

西莒;xījǔ

The smallest of the Matsu Islands, **XIJU** today is but a shadow of its former self, its once bustling **Qingfan Port** (青帆港; qīngfángǎng) now serving a slow trickle of tourists. Xiju has long been a pivotal **command post** and has absorbed more than its share of artillery fire from mainland China. The island's heyday was during the **Korean War**, when spies from the Western Enterprise Co – a CIA front – were stationed here, ushering in Western goods and decadence. Qingfan Village (青帆村; qīnfáncūn) was flooded with bars, ballrooms and brothels, earning it the nickname "**Little Hong Kong**". It continues to be of immense strategic importance and a strong military presence remains – you'll need to sign in with the army before visiting.

The best thing to do is take a **walk** around the island, which can easily be covered in a few hours. On its northeast corner is **Caipuwo** (菜埔沃; càipǔwò), a beach that was once the favoured place for villagers to gather **laver** (edible seaweed).

ARRIVAL AND GETTING AROUND   XIJU

Ferries from Nangan and Dongju (see p.383) arrive at **Qingfan Port**, a few minutes' walk from Qingfan Village.

By scooter Scooters from Qingfan Village can be rented (NT$300/500 for a half-day/full day).

On a tour Hotel owners can arrange island tours for NT$500/hr.

ACCOMMODATION

Most of the **hotels** are located in Tianwo (田沃; tiānwò), over the hill to the northeast of Qingfan. If you bring your own gear, it's possible to **camp** on Sheshan Beach on the west of the island where there are free toilets, showers and charging points.

Friendship Hotel 友誼山莊; yǒuyí shānzhuāng 48 Tianwo Village ☎0836 88028; map opposite. The nicest place to stay in Tianwo has bright, clean rooms with tiled floors, some with sea views. The friendly owner speaks a little English and can arrange ferry transfers. NT$1400

Haijing Holiday Village 海景渡假村; hǎijīng dùjiàcūn 68-3 Tianwo Village ☎0836 88125; map opposite. A decent budget choice with basic rooms and a kitchen/dining area on the first floor. In spite of the hotel's name (which means sea view), only two rooms on the second floor have ocean views. NT$1000

EATING

Guanhailou 觀海樓餐廳; guānhǎilóu cāntīng 40 Qingfan Village ☎0836 88188; map opposite. The ramshackle entrance to this place looks far from promising, but the second floor has a clean, if characterless dining hall, popular with soldiers for its range of decent lunchboxes (NT$110) and seafood noodles (NT$100). Daily 10am–2pm & 5–7pm.

6

RELIEF AT GUNINGTOU BATTLE MUSEUM

Contexts

History

Taiwan has an exceptionally short recorded history by Asian standards, starting with the arrival of the Dutch in 1624. Though the Taiwanese have a long tradition of rebellion and resistance, they've rarely been masters of their own fate – what ex-president Lee Teng-hui calls the "Taiwanese Sadness"; in addition to the Dutch, the island has been occupied by the Spanish, mainland Chinese, Japanese and, briefly, the French.

Early history

Humans have inhabited Taiwan for thousands of years, arriving in a series of migrations from mainland Asia; the simple bone, horn and stone implements found on the east coast and dating from 30,000 to 50,000 years ago represent the **Changpin Culture**, Taiwan's first, while **Tsochen Man**, who lived between 20,000 and 30,000 years ago, is the earliest remains of a human found in Taiwan. The **Shisanhang** people were the last of these prehistoric cultures and the only one to possess iron-smelting capabilities, flourishing from 200 to 1500 AD. By this time the indigenous tribes recognized today were well established, having been in Taiwan for at least four thousand years, and the first temporary **Chinese settlements** were starting to emerge, with small groups of fishermen and pirates thought to have arrived sometime in the sixteenth century. Though vague references are made to the island in Chinese sources from the Sui dynasty (581–618 AD), and an official party on their way to the Ryukyu Islands made a brief landing in 1292, it was regarded as a wild, uninhabitable place and largely ignored by mainland China.

The Dutch

The **Dutch East India Company** had established a base in Indonesia in 1619, and occupied **Penghu** in 1622. In 1624 the Chinese attacked and, in the subsequent truce, agreed that the Dutch could have Taiwan if they abandoned Penghu (though whether this means the Ming dynasty regarded Taiwan as part of its territory is still debated).

THE BEAUTIFUL ISLAND

Portuguese sailors, passing Taiwan on their way to Japan in the sixteenth century, named it **Ihla Formosa**, "the beautiful island". In the West, Taiwan was referred to as Formosa until the 1950s, and the name is still used by companies, hotels and museums today. The origin of the Chinese word **Taiwan** is less clear, though Ming-dynasty negotiators used the name in their treaty with the Dutch in 1624. It seems likely that it stems from the aboriginal word "Taiyan", which meant alien, or from early Chinese references to the island as "Dayuan", pronounced "Dai Wan" in Fujianese. Since 1949 its official name has been the "**Republic of China**", but locals rarely use this in practice.

50,000–30,000 BC	1500–300 BC	200–1500 AD	1500–1600
Changpin Culture is first evidence of human habitation on Taiwan.	Beinan Culture.	Shisanhang Culture.	Chinese fishermen settle on the west coast of Taiwan.

WHO ARE THE TAIWANESE?

Around 98 percent of Taiwanese citizens today claim descent from Han Chinese immigrants from mainland China. Over eighty percent of immigrants came from Quanzhou and Zhangzhou prefectures in Fujian province: the descendants of these people form the Taiwanese or **Hoklo** (hō-ló in Taiwanese) majority today, around seventy percent of the country. Taiwan's smaller **Hakka** (kèjiārén) population hails from Guangdong province, migrating in the early eighteenth century, and now forming fifteen percent of the population. Taiwan's "**mainlanders**" (wàishēngrén) came with Chiang Kai-shek in 1949, political migrants from the eastern provinces of Zhejiang and Jiangsu, but including people from almost every major region in China – they now represent around thirteen percent. Though Taiwan's **indigenous population** (yuánzhùmín) is officially just two percent of the total, it's worth remembering that very few Chinese women crossed the Taiwan Strait in the early years of colonization, and that in reality most Hoklo Chinese have some aboriginal blood – as this will almost certainly be on the mother's side it's rarely recognized. Some studies suggest that up to sixty percent of Taiwanese have aboriginal genes.

The Dutch made a base at **Anping** (near Tainan), where they found a small group of Chinese settlers, and well-established indigenous tribes. As Dutch rule spread across the island, many of the latter were converted to Christianity, but relations were often hostile: in 1629 the aborigines at Madou massacred some Dutch soldiers, resulting in a brutal punitive campaign between 1635 and 1636 which brought much of the southern plains under Dutch control. Farming was developed on a large scale for the first time, but the greatest Dutch legacy was **Chinese immigration**: the Dutch needed Chinese labour and settlers to build a successful colony, offering land (to rent, not to buy) to farmers who made the voyage across the Taiwan Strait. When the Dutch arrived in 1624, they estimated only one thousand to 1500 Chinese were living on the island, but 38 years later the figure had increased to over fifty thousand. These farmers had to pay a five to ten percent levy on profits, a head tax and sales tax on commodities like butter and alcohol. These high taxes and resentment of Dutch authority led to a series of **rebellions**, notably in 1652, when a plot by local leader **Guo Huai-yi** was exposed before he had time to properly organize his force of sixteen thousand, and at least four thousand were killed by an army of Dutch and aboriginal warriors.

The Spanish

Spain had carved out a profitable colony in the Philippines in the 1560s, and the Spanish were eager to expand their trade with Japan; Taiwan seemed perfectly located midway along the sea routes, and in 1626 they occupied **Heping Island** near modern-day Keelung and built Fort San Salvador. In 1628 a second base at **Tamsui** was established, Fort Santo Domingo, but the Spanish had a fairly miserable time in Taiwan. The local aborigines proved impossible to subdue, the wet tropical climate was debilitating and profits from deer hides and the sulphur trade meagre. In the 1630s the Dutch launched a series of violent assaults on the Spanish forts, and with Japan now closed to foreign trade the whole venture seemed pointless. In 1638 Tamsui was abandoned and in 1642 the Dutch occupied Heping Island, forcing the Spanish back to Manila.

1622	1624	1626	1642
The Dutch occupy Penghu.	The Ming dynasty agrees to give the Dutch Taiwan in return for Penghu; Fort Zeelandia is established.	The Spanish establish a base on Heping Island.	The Spanish leave Taiwan after defeat by the Dutch.

The Zheng dynasty

In 1661 Chinese general **Zheng Chenggong**, also known as Koxinga, attacked the Dutch capital at Tainan with 25,000 men as part of a strategic retreat from mainland China. He'd been fighting a civil war on behalf of the Ming dynasty, which had been toppled by the Manchurian Qing dynasty in 1644 (see box, p.240). After a nine-month siege, he secured the Dutch surrender in February 1662, kicking them off the island and establishing an independent Chinese state that included Penghu (known as the "Kingdom of Tungning" or dōngníng wángguó).

Koxinga died later that year, but his son, **Zheng Jing**, ruled until 1681. Tainan was developed as an imperial capital, Dutch land was privatized and Chinese-style taxation, administration, education and finance were introduced. The Chinese population continued to expand, reaching around 100,000 in the 1680s, but after Zheng Jing's death, fighting between his sons, **Zheng Kezang** and **Zheng Keshuang**, weakened the kingdom. In 1683 the Qing regime in China decided to bring the Zhengs to heel. **Admiral Shi Lang** led the Qing navy to a devastating victory in Penghu, and by the time he reached Tainan, Keshuang, who had won the leadership struggle with his brother, had no stomach for a fight. The Zheng kingdom was handed over without further bloodshed, the "King" being pensioned off to a small palace in Beijing.

The Qing era

At first, Qing Emperor Kangxi wanted to force Taiwan's Chinese inhabitants back to the mainland and abandon the island. Shi Lang managed to persuade him that it was worth keeping, primarily as a defensive measure, but also to develop its potentially rich resources, and in 1684 Taiwan was officially admitted into the **Chinese empire** as a prefecture of Fujian province. Taiwan, or at least the part of it inhabited by Chinese farmers, was ruled by the Qing for another 212 years.

Early Qing rule

From the start, the Qing administration segregated the aboriginal and Chinese sectors of the island, banning interracial marriages and limiting contact. Despite travel restrictions, illegal immigration flourished. The growing Taiwanese population became resentful of corrupt officials, who typically served three to five years in a place they considered the end of the earth and ripe for plunder. Morale within the relative tiny militia kept on the island was low and it's no surprise there were 159 major incidents of civil disturbance during the Qing era, several of them serious rebellions against imperial authority.

Rebellion

Rebellion in the early years of Qing rule was motivated primarily by political factors, while economic grievances became more important in the nineteenth century. In the most serious cases, troops from the mainland were required for the Qing to regain control, an expensive undertaking that exasperated the emperors. In the **Zhu Yi-gui Rebellion** of 1721, when Zhu (a duck farmer) managed to occupy Tainan and declare himself king, a mainland army only restored order six months later. Taiwan's most serious insurgency was the **Lin Shuangwen Rebellion** of 1786–88, when Lin's "Heaven

1661–62	1683	1721	1786–88
Chinese Ming dynasty general Koxinga expels the Dutch.	China's Qing dynasty defeats Koxinga's grandson in Taiwan and occupies the island.	Zhu Yi-gui Rebellion.	Lin Shuangwen Rebellion.

and Earth Society" mobilized tens of thousands in an attempt to overthrow the government and reinstate the Ming dynasty – Lin ruled Taiwan for over a year, and was finally defeated by a combination of mainland, Hakka and aboriginal troops.

Between 1780 and 1860 Taiwan underwent an **agricultural revolution** as more land was cultivated for rice and sugar cane, but tensions grew between the now increasingly large immigrant communities – the Qing era saw hundreds of bitter fights and brawls between Chinese settlers, some of them, like those in Taipei and Keelung in the 1850s, resulting in scores dead.

The nineteenth century: Taiwan opens up

In the nineteenth century the Qing dynasty was weakened by a series of external crises, all of which affected Taiwan. In 1841 the British shelled Keelung during the **First Opium War**, and in 1860 the **Treaty of Beijing** forced China to open its ports to foreign trade: in Taiwan, only Anping and Danshui were included, but in the 1860s the list was expanded to include the deeper harbours at Keelung and Takao (now Kaohsiung). These ports subsequently attracted a mix of missionaries such as **George Mackay** (see box, p.109), and merchants and officials, many of them British – the latter administered customs and represented the other Western nations, including the US from 1875. In 1868 the Qing monopoly on **camphor** was abolished, and this, along with a huge upsurge in **sugar** and **tea production** (the latter encouraged by entrepreneurial Englishman **John Dodd**), created a boom in exports in the 1870s, dominated by the foreign *hongs* or trading companies.

The Mudan Incident

The **Japanese**, modernizing incredibly fast after the Meiji Restoration in 1868, were eager to match the West in every way, including imperialist ambition. Taiwan, as one of the closest territories to Japan, was a natural target. In 1871 a ship from the Japanese-held Ryukyu Islands ran aground near the southern tip of Taiwan. The 66 survivors stumbled on the **Paiwan** village of **Mudan**; traditional accounts suggest the sailors were mistaken as enemies and 54 sailors were beheaded in the melee that followed. After the survivors finally returned to Japan, their government spent the next three years demanding the Qing regime take action – the Qing claimed that the Paiwan were beyond their jurisdiction. In 1874 the Japanese took matters into their own hands, sending a punitive force to Taiwan, resulting in a series of bloody encounters and **massacres** in several Paiwan villages. The Qing government deployed an army to Taiwan from the mainland, but war was narrowly avoided: instead the Chinese paid the Japanese compensation for the dead men and expenses for the operation. The attack shocked the Qing into a review of their Taiwan policy, with Imperial Commissioner **Shen Baozhen** initiating a building programme of forts around the island (1874–75), reversing the immigration policy to boost the Chinese population and proposing the establishment of Taipei.

The Sino-French War and provincial status

In 1884 Taiwan became involved in another war, this time a conflict between China and France over Vietnam. French troops raided the Tamsui area, and managed to occupy Keelung for over six months. The general credited with holding them back was

1860	1874	1884–85	1885
The Treaty of Beijing opens up Anping and Tamsui to foreign trade.	The Mudan Incident results in a brief Japanese invasion of Taiwan.	Taiwan attacked by the French during the Sino-French War.	Taiwan becomes a province of China; Liu Mingchuan is first governor.

Liu Mingchuan, regarded as hero in Taiwan and more recently in China, where he's buried in Hefei and is one of only a handful of Qing officials rehabilitated by the Communist Party. After the war, in 1885, Taiwan was finally given **provincial status**, and Liu was appointed its first governor. Liu began the modernization of the island in earnest, building rail lines, developing coal mines and improving infrastructure. However, he was less successful in pacifying the mountain tribes and, after forty military missions and heavy Chinese casualties, Taiwan's wild hinterland remained virtually independent. After he was replaced in 1891 by Shao You-lian, attempts to modernize were stymied and momentum was lost.

The Sino-Japanese War and the Taiwan Republic

In 1894 China became embroiled in a war with Japan over the sovereignty of Korea. Though none of the fighting took place near Taiwan, China's defeat in 1895 led to the **Treaty of Shimonoseki**, a humbling agreement in which the Qing regime agreed to hand over Taiwan and Penghu to the Japanese. Shocked by the abandonment of the island, a group of wealthy and educated Chinese in Taiwan pressed the recently appointed governor, **Tang Jing-song**, into declaring an independent **Taiwan Republic** on May 15, 1895. Tang was made president and a cabinet was appointed; the new nation even had a flag and stamps printed. Japan had no intention of letting its first colony slip away that easily however, and landed a force of twelve thousand men on the north of the island on May 29. Lacking the stomach for a fight, the regime collapsed almost immediately, Tang fleeing back to the mainland ten days after his inauguration. After overcoming the Republic's army with relative ease, the Japanese marched into Taipei on June 7, beginning the period of **Japanese occupation**.

The Japanese occupation

The **Japanese** ruled Taiwan for fifty years, a period of colonial exploitation but also of unparalleled economic development: by the time the KMT took control in 1945, Taiwan was a model economy, far more modernized than China. In recent years the period has been undergoing a thorough reassessment: under Chiang Kai-shek (as in China today), children were taught that Japan was a wicked, imperialist power, but many older Taiwanese compare the Japanese favourably with what they see as the equally alien and cruel KMT regime. Though it's certainly true that Japanese rule could be beneficial and even enlightened, especially in the 1920s and early 1930s, Taiwan was developed primarily to benefit Japan – it's also the case that the initial occupation was fiercely resisted, and violently imposed.

The Japanese invasion and Taiwanese resistance

The Japanese army took five months to suppress formal resistance to their occupation (Tainan surrendered on October 21), a violent campaign in which fourteen thousand Taiwanese died, but it took another seven years before they mopped up smaller bands of guerrillas or "bandits". Resistance was fiercest in Yunlin and Chiayi, and for the first time Chinese fought with aborigines in numbers.

In 1898 the appointment of **Governor Kodama Gentaro** and his chief administrator **Goto Shinpei** signalled a change in tactic and the imposition of "bandit laws" (which

1895	1895–1945	1930	1944–45
Treaty of Shimonoseki: China cedes Taiwan to Japan; Taiwan Republic proclaimed but lasts less than a month.	The Japanese rule Taiwan.	The Wushe Incident: Seediq uprising crushed by the Japanese.	Heavy US bombing destroys Keelung and Kaohsiung harbours during World War II.

expanded the definition of what included banditry, made relatives of rebels equally guilty and imposed severe punishment for all those accused) – 32,000 Taiwanese were punished under this authoritarian piece of legislation. With the massacre of famed rebel leader **Lin Shao Mao** and his army in 1902, guerrilla resistance was effectively wiped out. During the 1920s there was a series of attempts to petition the colonial government for a Taiwanese assembly, without success, and the **Taiwan Cultural Association**, formed in 1921, organized large-scale events to encourage a sense of identity in the face of continued Japanization. The Japanese increasingly cracked down on left-wing movements after 1931, and after full-scale war broke out in China in 1937, all popular organizations were banned.

Economic development

Kodama and Goto instituted an ambitious programme of **economic development**, building factories, harbours, rail lines, highways and bridges, as well as introducing medical schools and hospitals. They also established a central **Bank of Taiwan** in 1899, stabilizing the currency, and encouraged the development of rice and sugar exports to Japan – the European *hongs* were gradually forced out. Kodama was governor until 1906, but development continued: the appointment of **Den Kenjiro** in 1919, Taiwan's first civilian governor-general, ushered in a period of relatively enlightened colonial government that lasted until 1936, when militarism started to dominate Japanese politics.

The Wushe Incident and aboriginal resistance

The Japanese were the first rulers of Taiwan to undertake a comprehensive study of the mountain-dwelling aborigines, but also to demand their complete subjugation – in order to exploit Taiwan's rich **lumber** and **camphor** resources, they had to control the mountains. After a series of military campaigns (1911–14), when Bunun and Atayal areas were especially hard hit, policemen were stationed in every village and a school system established, making Japanese compulsory for all aboriginal children. Such policies angered tribal leaders, and in October 1930 a misunderstanding at a wedding provided the spark for an **Atayal** uprising led by **Chief Mona Rudao** at **Wushe** in central Taiwan. The local school – which was holding a sports day – was attacked, the Atayal warriors slaughtering 132 Japanese men, women and children (and two Chinese by mistake). Japanese reaction was swift: an army of 2700 was sent, along with trackers from rival Atayal clans, to hunt down the rebels, a campaign which took fifty days, involved aerial bombing and poison gas and left around 644 Atayal dead – Chief Mona Rudao, along with almost three hundred other warriors, opted to hang himself rather than surrender. In the aftermath most of the local villages were wiped out, the Japanese offering bounties to other Atayal warriors to mop up resistance, leading to further massacres of those who surrendered.

World War II

War between China and Japan from July 1937 meant that Japanization in Taiwan was intensified, traditional Chinese customs banned and Chinese writing suppressed. To feed the Japanese war machine, Taiwan was transformed into a giant military-industrial base, a policy that created an economic boom. While fighting in China continued,

1945	1947	1949
Taiwan is returned to China at the conclusion of World War II; Kuomintang under Chiang Kai-shek assumes control.	2-28 Incident: Forty years of martial law known as "White Terror" begins.	Communists defeat the Kuomintang in China; Chiang Kai-shek flees to Taiwan, establishing the Republic of China.

TAKASAGO VOLUNTEERS

In 1974 the discovery of a man in the Indonesian jungle, described as "the last Japanese soldier from World War II" made headlines around the world. In fact, the soldier was an **Amis tribesman** from Taiwan called Suniyon, who had joined the **Takasago Volunteers** in 1943. Recruitment of indigenous tribesmen into the Imperial Army was largely covered up after the war, but between four thousand and eight thousand men are thought to have fought and almost half were killed. After the Wushe Incident, the Japanese regarded aboriginal warriors as excellent fighters, and ironically many volunteers came from the Atayal region, devastated by the Japanese. After the war many of them were enshrined with Shinto ritual at the Yasukuni Shrine in Tokyo (along with over 27,000 other Taiwanese) without family consent, and many Taiwanese aborigines still visit Japan to protest.

Japan attacked the US at **Pearl Harbor** in 1941, marking the official start of **World War II** in Asia.

Initially the war left Taiwan physically untouched, but between 1942 and 1944, an estimated six thousand Taiwanese volunteered to fight for the Japanese, including 1800 members of the aboriginal **Takasago Volunteers** (see box above). In 1944 a further 22,000 Taiwanese were conscripted and by the war's end an estimated 200,000 personnel were involved in war-related activities, including over seven hundred "**comfort women**" forced to serve as sex slaves. In total, around thirty thousand Taiwanese died. The island was also home to fifteen **Allied Prisoner of War camps**, including the notorious **Kinkaseki** (see box, p.136). Heavy US bombing destroyed Keelung and Kaohsiung harbours and many other parts of the island between 1944 and 1945, but when the Japanese surrendered in August 1945, Taiwan was still occupied – the last governor, Ando Rikichi, committed suicide soon after.

Return of mainland rule and the 2-28 Incident

According to the terms of the **1943 Cairo Declaration** agreed (but not signed) by Franklin Roosevelt, Winston Churchill and Chiang Kai-shek, Taiwan was returned to China after Japan's surrender in 1945, though the mainland had changed dramatically since it handed the island to Japan in 1895. The Qing dynasty had been overthrown by revolutionaries led by **Sun Yat-sen**, creating the **Republic of China** in 1911 and the Chinese Nationalist Party in 1912, commonly known as the **Kuomintang** (KMT). The KMT held power in China, on and off, for the next twenty years, and from the 1920s was led by **Generalissimo Chiang Kai-shek**. The party had been involved in a fierce civil war with the rival Communist forces of Mao Zedong since 1927, only briefly put on hold during the struggle with the Japanese, and when **Chen Yi** was appointed the Chinese governor of Taiwan in 1945, he promptly began stripping Taiwan of all its industrial wealth in order to bolster the KMT's renewed campaign against the Communists. Methods were often brutal and the Taiwanese quickly came to resent the brusque and corrupt officials sent to replace the Japanese. Meanwhile, the 480,000 Japanese inhabitants of Taiwan, many of whom had been born on the island, were told to leave by April 1946 – the KMT confiscated all Japanese real estate and property left behind.

1951	1954	1958	1960–70
Japan officially gives up sovereignty over Taiwan in the Treaty of San Francisco but does not specify who will take over.	China mounts major attacks on Kinmen and Matsu – they are repulsed.	China bombards Matsu and Kinmen for 44 days.	Taiwan becomes the world's fastest-growing economy, averaging 9.7 percent GNP growth a year.

THE CHIANG DYNASTY

Chiang Kai-shek and his descendants have had a greater impact on modern Taiwan than any other family. Chiang ruled the island for 26 years, though it's his activities in China pre-1949 that appear most colourful to outsiders and the focus of most biographies. Born in Zhejiang province in 1887 and trained as a soldier, he worked his way up to the position of general and then leader of the KMT in the 1920s, in part due to his wife's (**Soong Mei-ling** aka Madam Chiang) connections and links to the Shanghai mob. By the time of his flight to Taiwan in 1949, his position as Generalissimo was unchallenged. After his death in 1975 and a brief but fruitless attempt at influencing politics, Madam Chiang moved to the US, dying in New York in 2004 at the age of 106. Chiang's only son **Chiang Ching-kuo** (by his first wife – he had no children with Mei-ling) was president between 1978 and his own death in 1988. Ching-kuo married Russian-born **Faina Epatcheva Vahaleva** (1916–2004, known as Chiang Fang-liang) in 1935, but their three sons died shortly after Ching-kuo and only their daughter Chiang Hsiao-chang is still alive, living in the US. In the early 1990s, Chiang Kai-shek's adopted son **Chiang Wei-kuo** briefly mounted a political challenge to Lee Teng-hui, but the Chiang family was falling out of favour and he died in 1997. That wasn't the end of the Chiangs however. Ching-kuo also had two illegitimate sons: one of them, **John Chiang** (born 1942) who used his mother's family name Chang until March 2005, is now the family's unofficial political heir in Taiwan, serving as a member of the Legislative Yuan since 2002. Meanwhile, **Demos Chiang** (born 1976) a grandson of Chiang Ching-kuo, has become a bit of a celebrity in Taiwan, dating actresses and starting a successful brand-marketing company (DEM Inc).

The 2-28 Incident

The **2-28 Incident** began in Taipei on February 27, 1947, when a local vendor selling smuggled cigarettes was roughed up by KMT government officials – in the ensuing fracas a bystander was shot and killed. The next day, a large crowd gathered outside the local police station to protest, and fearing attack, the police opened fire, killing more civilians. Protests, strikes, riots and school closures spread across the island until March 8, when reinforcements from the mainland arrived to restore order in a bloody crackdown that took at least 28,000 lives (estimates vary wildly) and initiated forty years of martial law known as "White Terror". During this period, all discussion of the massacre was banned, and today it's still the source of heated debate among Taiwanese, especially the elderly, many of whom regard the KMT as murderers. No one has ever been charged over the incident, though Chen Yi was recalled to China in disgrace, and Chiang later had him executed.

The Republic of China: the Kuomintang and martial law

In 1949 the Communists finally defeated Chiang's Nationalist forces, and the remnants of his army retreated across the Taiwan Strait – almost two million "mainlanders" arriving in Taiwan to establish the last outpost of the **Republic of China**. Chiang Kai-shek became president in 1950, a post he held until his death in 1975. During martial law, opposition parties and the Taiwanese language were banned, mainlanders dominated positions of authority and Chiang had statues of himself built in every town. Although the economy began to flourish in the late 1970s (see box opposite), resources in the early part of KMT rule were primarily

1971	1975	1978	
Taiwan withdraws from the United Nations in protest at the admission of the People's Republic of China.	Chiang Kai-shek dies; Yen Chia-ken becomes president.	Chiang Ching-Kuo becomes president. USA switches recognition of the "official" China to the	People's Republic – most of the world follows suit; Taiwan becomes isolated politically.

earmarked for defence and stockpiled for an eventual invasion of China. In reality, Taiwan's independence, as today, was made possible solely by **US support**. The conflict against Communism in Korea and later Vietnam ensured that US administrations backed Chiang's anti-communist KMT as an important ally – President Truman sent the Seventh Fleet to patrol the Taiwan Strait in the 1950s and stationed troops in Taiwan, but despite a vicious Communist assault on **Kinmen** and **Matsu** in 1954 (which was repulsed by Taiwanese troops), and the heavy bombardments of 1958, major conflict was avoided. In 1951 Japan signed the **Treaty of San Francisco** with the Allies, formally ending World War II and officially giving up sovereignty over Taiwan, but without specifying whom to – a fudge which provides plenty of bitter debate today. Independence activists want the date of the treaty – September 8 – to become **Taiwan's Independence Day**.

Withdrawal from the United Nations

Taiwan became increasingly isolated in the 1970s. Mao Zedong's People's Republic of China (PRC) was finally admitted to the United Nations in 1971, but rather than share a seat, Chiang's Republic of China **withdrew**, a move which was to have serious implications in the years to follow. In 1972 President Nixon made his historic visit to China, and in December 1978 the unthinkable happened – President Carter switched US recognition to the PRC, severing formal relations with Taiwan. Much of the world has since followed suit. Though the **Taiwan Relations Act** (1979) ensured the US would still supply the island with weapons, US troops left and with the reconquest of China now impossible, the KMT began to commit more resources to infrastructure and economic development, creating one of the world's most dynamic economies.

THE TAIWAN MIRACLE

Perhaps the greatest achievement of KMT rule was economic reform, laying the foundations of what became known as the **Taiwan Miracle** – the rise from developing nation status to one of the top twenty largest economies in the world in the early twenty-first century. **Land reform** in the 1950s was a crucial first step, resulting in the opening up of new land to farmers and increased agricultural yields and incomes. From 1951 to 1964, the US supplied Taiwan with around US$1.5 billion in non-military aid, much of this channelled to infrastructure projects and investment in the **textile industry**, Taiwan's first big export success story.

Education was another factor, with the KMT building new schools and universities in the 1950s. In the 1960s, the government initiated an aggressive export-oriented strategy: liberalizing the financial system and setting up a stock market, increasing manufacturing and creating export-processing zones (Kaohsiung was the first in Asia). Between 1960 and 1970 Taiwan became the world's fastest-growing economy, averaging 9.7 percent GNP growth a year. In the 1980s, Taiwan began to produce high-quality electronics, especially **semiconductors** and **computers**, and though it has few recognizable domestic brands (Acer and BenQ the obvious exceptions), chances are that your PC or laptop contains components made by Taiwanese companies – however, all of their production factories are now in mainland China where Taiwan is the largest investor. Today the service sector accounts for around two thirds of GDP, while agriculture accounts for just 1.86 percent and industry around thirty percent.

1979		1986	1987
Taiwan Relations Act ensures that the US will still support Taiwan (and supply the island with weapons).	The Kaohsiung Incident increases support for democratic reform.	The Tangwai movement establishes the Democratic Progressive Party (DPP).	President Chiang lifts martial law.

Democracy

After Chiang Kai-shek's death in 1975, the now largely forgotten **Yen Chia-ken** became president, but in 1978 Chiang's son, **Chiang Ching-Kuo** took over and ruled till his own demise in 1988. Chiang Ching-kuo was a complex figure, presiding over a period of unprecedented economic growth and eventual political liberalization in Taiwan, while remaining dedicated to KMT hegemony and the goal of reunifying China.

Opposition to one-party rule and KMT corruption (dubbed "**Black Gold**" because of notorious links with local mafia) grew in the 1970s. The **Tangwai** (dǎngwài), or "outside the party" movement, involved students and academics at first, almost all of them Taiwanese; members started by contesting local elections, but government oppression led to the 1979 **Kaohsiung Incident**, now regarded as a landmark in Taiwan's democracy movement (see box, p.255), and the trial of the "Kaohsiung Eight" which garnered much public sympathy. Between 1980 and 1985 however, progress was limited: the Chiang regime continued to crack down on dissent, though informal opposition grew. In September 1986 the leaders of the Tangwai movement illegally established the **Democratic Progressive Party** (DPP). In response, President Chiang lifted martial law in July 1987 and press restrictions were removed in January 1988. Much of this was due to US pressure, but with growing opposition inside Taiwan, Chiang seems to have genuinely accepted the need for change.

KMT chairman **Lee Teng-hui** became Taiwan's first native-born president in 1988, ushering in a period of reform and the end of formal hostilities with China in 1991. **Student demonstrations** in Taipei in 1990 (now known as the **Wild Lily Movement**) led to more democratic concessions, and though the DPP made gains in the Legislative Yuan, Taiwan's **first free presidential election** in 1996 was won by KMT incumbent Lee. This despite intimidation from China, which tested missiles close to the island to mark its disapproval of Lee's growing independence sympathies. Though now retired from government, Lee remains an enigmatic and active figure, despised by many in China and even Taiwan – once a KMT loyalist, he's now the spiritual father of the independence movement and an outspoken critic of China.

In 2000, in a landmark election, the KMT lost power for the first time in almost fifty years: **Chen Shui-bian** of the DPP, a lawyer by training who earned his political stripes defending dissidents after the Kaohsiung Incident, became president with 39.3 percent of the vote, beating independent and ex-KMT member James Soong (36.84 percent) and KMT candidate Lien Chan (23.1 percent). The peaceful change of regime was vindication of how far Taiwan had come – the world's first Chinese democracy, while a little rough around the edges, was largely created by the Taiwanese themselves in a dramatic rebuttal to pundits who claimed democracy was alien to "Asian Values".

Taiwan today: the struggle for political identity

Since the election of 2000 Taiwan's **struggle for political identity** has become the primary issue of the day. While ordinary Taiwanese and especially the youth have continued to develop a very recognizable identity in terms of music, pop culture, food, fashion and art, Taiwan's status in the world remains unclear, its **relationship with China** its most challenging problem. The China debate reflects a very real and passionate **divide** across Taiwanese society, although you're unlikely to see much expression of this

1988	1990	1996	1999
Chiang Ching-Kuo dies; Lee Teng-hui becomes Taiwan's first native-born president.	Wild Lily Movement (student demonstrations) in Taipei lead to more democratic concessions.	Taiwan's first free presidential election is won by KMT incumbent Lee Teng-hui.	The 921 Earthquake kills 2455 people.

ONE CHINA AND THE "STATUS QUO"

Taiwan's existence depends largely on the concept of "**One China**", but what does this actually mean? Taiwanese officials (mostly KMT) claim that there is "one China controlled by two governments". The Communist Party in China believes there is one China controlled by one government (them), and that this includes the actual territory of Taiwan, its "**renegade province**". This poses a thorny problem for the international community: no nation wants to upset China, but at the same time it would be extremely hypocritical for the West to turn its back on a flourishing democracy. The solution since the 1950s has been to focus on semantics: that only one country can call itself China. As long as Taiwan calls itself the "**Republic of China**", nations can simply refuse to recognize it by invoking the One China policy.

It seems like a good compromise: Taiwan goes unrecognized in much of the world, its athletes at the Olympics compete under the embarrassing designation "**Chinese Taipei**", and it has no representation at the UN, but it remains de facto independent. Even better, China has indicated it is content to maintain this status quo, and therefore the de facto independence of Taiwan (though of course this would never be admitted publicly), as long as Taiwan keeps the door open for eventual reunification.

If Taiwan were to abandon the concept of it being an alternative China, drop the "Republic of China" moniker and become the "Republic of Taiwan" instead, China would threaten to invade, and the world would have to choose between upsetting an up-and-coming superpower or turning its collective back on a new democracy. Not surprisingly, the international community is focused on maintaining the status quo at all costs.

Up to the 1970s, most nations tended to recognize Taiwan (aka the "Republic of China") as the real China. Though the **Communists** took control of mainland China in 1949, Chiang Kai-shek and the KMT maintained the belief that they were the legitimate government of all China, a claim that looked increasingly delusional by the 1970s. After the People's Republic of China joined the UN in 1971 and Taiwan withdrew, the situation changed; following the example of the US in 1978, most nations began to switch official recognition to the PRC.

Only a tiny rump remains. Today, in its official guise as the Republic of China, and bolstered by considerable sums of financial aid, Taiwan is recognized as the "real" China by only **19 states** (as of December 2017), plus Vatican City: Belize, Burkina Faso, Dominican Republic, El Salvador, Guatemala, Haiti, Honduras, Kiribati, Marshall Islands, Nauru, Nicaragua, Palau, Paraguay, St Kitts and Nevis, St Lucia, St Vincent and the Grenadines, Solomon Islands, Swaziland and Tuvalu.

on the streets. Around 75 percent of Taiwanese remain in favour of what's called the "**status quo**" (see box above), while ten percent favour reunification and fifteen percent formal independence. Given this, most politicians support the status quo position, masking a fundamental division between many KMT and DPP supporters: the real issue remains **unification** versus **formal independence**.

Taiwan's highly adversarial political parties are drawn into two informal alliances, broadly reflecting their positions on China: the **pan-green** (which has no relation to the Green parties of the West), including the DPP, pro-independence Taiwan Solidarity Union and the minor Taiwan Independence Party; and the **pan-blue coalition**, comprising the KMT, the People First Party, led by James Soong, and the marginal New Party. Many pan-blues believe that Taiwan ought to be, at some stage, united with the mainland, while independence-minded pan-green members want a truly sovereign nation and membership of the UN.

2000	2004	2008	
Chen Shui-bian of the DPP becomes president, ending KMT rule.	Chen Shui-bian wins re-election by just thirty thousand votes, following an assassination attempt.	Ma Ying-jeou of the KMT wins the presidential election.	Wild Strawberries Movement in support of Taiwanese nationalism.

The return of the KMT

In 2004 Chen Shui-bian won re-election by just thirty thousand votes (50.3 percent), after an **assassination attempt** that many opposition members believe was staged. Chen's presidency hit rock-bottom in 2006, after corruption allegations involving his close aides as well as family members led to widespread calls for his resignation – in 2009 Chen himself was given a life sentence for corruption (reduced to twenty years in 2010). He attempted suicide in 2013 (unsuccessfully), and was released on medical parole in 2015.

In 2008, the popular ex-mayor of Taipei, **Ma Ying-jeou** (born 1950) of the KMT, won the presidential election in a landslide. Ma is one of Taiwan's most accomplished politicians, earning a doctorate in law at Harvard Law School and spending time at firms in the US before returning to work for President Chiang Ching-kuo in the 1980s. Unlike Chen Shui-bian (and most other Taiwanese politicians), he speaks fluent English.

The DPP regroups

Protests by DPP supporters dogged Ma's premiership from the beginning, starting with the **Wild Strawberries Movement** against the suppression of displays of Taiwan's national flag and the playing of Taiwanese songs during mainland official Chen Yunlin's visit to the island in 2008. The government's response to **Typhoon Morakot**, which caused widespread devastation in 2009, with 461 people dead (192 others are still "missing") and around NT$110 billion in damages, came under severe criticism. Despite this, Ma **won re-election in 2012** with 51.6 percent of the vote (defeating the DPP's Tsai Ing-wen, Taiwan's first female presidential candidate).

Though Ma has certainly eased tensions with China (Taiwan and the Chinese mainland resumed direct sea, air and mail links in late 2008, ushering in a major boom in mainland tourism), DPP supporters believe he has gone too far (Ma has said that his goal is to lead Taiwan to "eventual unification"). In 2014 the **Sunflower Student Movement** organized more protests against the passing of Ma's signature **Cross-Strait Service Trade Agreement** between Taiwan and China (signed in 2013 but still not ratified by the Taiwanese legislature at the time of writing), designed to liberalize trade and services between the two countries.

After a crushing defeat in the **2014 local elections** (the KMT's worst result since 1949, including the sensational victory of Independent candidate Ko Wen-je over KMT insider Sean Lien for Taipei mayor), Ma resigned his position as KMT chairman. In 2016, the DPP regained the presidency, when **Tsai Ing-wen** defeated Eric Chu of the KMT with 56 percent of the vote; the DPP also secured a majority in the Legislative Yuan. Unlike some of her more independent-minded colleagues, Tsai is more moderate, and maintaining the status quo is the centerpiece of party policy. She also supports same-sex marriage, which is expected to become legal in Taiwan by 2019. Also in 2016, Taiwan made world news when US President-elect Donald Trump spoke to Tsai by phone – the first direct conversation between the leaders of Taiwan and the US in 37 years.

2009	2012	2014	2016
Ex president Chen Shui-bian is given a life sentence for corruption (reduced in 2010). Typhoon Morakot is the worst storm to hit Taiwan in fifty years.	Ma Ying-jeou re-elected president with 51.6 percent of the vote.	Sunflower Student Movement protests against the KMT.	DPP's Tsai Ing-wen elected president in landslide victory.

Taiwan's indigenous peoples

More commonly known as aborigines, or yuánzhùmín ("original inhabitants") in Chinese, Taiwan's indigenous peoples represent just two percent of the island's 23 million people. Things have improved over the last few years, but Taiwan's indigenous population still suffers discrimination and remains very much at the bottom of the country's economic and social ladders.

Taiwan's indigenous tribes form part of the **Austronesian** cultural and linguistic family. The **origins** of Taiwan's aborigines are still fiercely debated, though most agree that they are descendants of Neolithic peoples who have inhabited the island for thousands of years. The most radical theory, and the one currently in favour in Taiwan, claims that the island is in fact **the homeland of all Austronesian people** – that migrations from Taiwan would eventually, over thousands of years, colonize the entire Pacific. The formation of the **Alliance of Taiwan Aborigines** in 1984 marked the formal beginning of the indigenous political movement, and a cabinet-level **Council of Indigenous Peoples** was established in 1996 to oversee aboriginal affairs. In 2001 the Ministry of Education added **aboriginal classes** to the schools language curriculum (in aboriginal areas), but in practice lesson time is limited and the incentives to learn poor. In 2005 the **Indigenous Television Network**, a 24-hour cable TV station (with programmes in Mandarin and aboriginal languages) dedicated to aboriginal news, documentaries and entertainment was launched, one of the requirements of the Aboriginal Education Law (2000). In 2016, President Tsai Ing-wen gave the indigenous community an official apology "for the four centuries of pain and mistreatment you have endured".

One of the key differences between the aboriginal population and the Chinese today is religion: thanks to an aggressive missionary effort, the indigenous population is now almost completely **Christian** (mostly Presbyterian); a proliferation of churches and a Christian graveyard are easy ways to tell if you are in an aboriginal village.

The tribes

As of December 2017, there were sixteen **official indigenous tribes** in Taiwan: the Amis, Atayal, Bunun, Kevalan, Hla'alu, Kanakanavu, Paiwan, Puyuma, Rukai, Saisiyat, Sakizaya, Sediq, Tao, Thao, Truku (Taroko) and Tsou. Being recognized as an official tribe brings public recognition and government subsidies for community projects, but the process has been highly controversial and is based largely on simplistic classifications established by Japanese anthropologists in the 1920s.

During the Qing era, aborigines were classified as either shēng fān, "raw" or uncivilized barbarians who inhabited the mountains, or shóu fān, "cooked" or civilized tribes who lived on the plains and generally paid taxes. Although most aborigines primarily associated themselves with their village and locale, in the 1920s the Japanese grouped the shēng fān into nine core "mountain" tribes. The plains aborigines were referred to collectively as píngpǔ: until very recently these people were considered totally assimilated by the Han Chinese and even today many Taiwanese will tell you that there are no píngpǔ left on the island – quite untrue. The reason for this is that most píngpǔ tribes have yet to gain official recognition as distinct ethnic groups, partly because they have ceased to speak tribal languages and maintain limited cultural traditions. This has been changing: in addition to the acknowledgement of píngpǔ tribes (like the Kevalan), those regarded as subgroups of larger "mountain" tribes are becoming recognized as distinct communities (the Thao were once considered part of the Tsou, the Truku part of the Atayal). The **Ketagalan**, **Makatau** and **Pazeh**, supposedly extinct píngpǔ tribes, are currently pushing for official recognition. Depending on how you classify them, there are at least seven officially unrecognized píngpǔ tribes: Babuza, Hoanya, Ketagalan (which includes the Basay, Luilang and Trobiawan clans), Papora, Pazeh, Siraya (including the Makatau), and Taokas (Dougai).

The sixteen official tribes are usually distinguished by traditional dress, rituals and exotic customs such as headhunting that have long died out, and though you will see bright costumes, singing and dancing at festivals, little of this has much bearing on contemporary aboriginal life.

Amis

The **Amis** (阿美族; āměizú) are Taiwan's **largest tribe** with around 200,000 members, concentrated along the east coast between Hualien and Taitung. The **Harvest Festival**, known as *Ilisin*, is the most important Amis event, usually taking place in July or August and marking New Year: each village holds its own celebration, lasting from one to seven days. Although Taitung city contains the largest concentration of Amis people, there are numerous Amis villages along the east coast and East Rift Valley, notably **Dulan** (see p.310). Its annual **Art Festival** (October) acts as a magnet for traditional performers. The Amis are particularly well known for their **musical** traditions, producing Mandopop star Van Fan and alternative rocker Chang Chen-yue – more familiar to Western audiences, New Age dance project Enigma sampled an Amis performance group singing the traditional "Song of Joy" (without their permission) on their 1993 single "**Return to Innocence**", which was later used to promote the 1996 Atlanta Olympics. The Amis singers sued the group and reached an out-of-court settlement in 1998.

Atayal

The **Atayal** (泰雅; tàiyǎ) is the third largest tribe (86,000) and the most widely spread, inhabiting the mountainous northern half of Taiwan. Despite their geographical dispersion, the Atayal have offered the most resistance to colonization over the years, gaining a reputation as fierce fighters after the 1930 Wushe Incident (see p.392). In 1999 the Atayal began opposing the creation of the **Makao National Park** as it threatened local land rights, with vociferous Independent Legislator **May Chin** (a former actress), whose mother was Atayal, one of those against it. The Atayal are best known in Taiwan however, for their quality **weaving** and the tradition of **facial tattoos**, particularly on women: the practice was banned by the Japanese in 1913 and died out in the 1920s – the few remaining elders with tattoos live in the **Taian** area. Other important Atayal centres are **Fuxing**, **Smangus**, **Wulai**, **Baling** and **Wushe**.

Bunun

The **Bunun** (布農; bùnóng) occupy the central mountains of Taiwan and are another widely dispersed tribe of around fifty thousand, divided into six clans. High mountain dwellers with a reputation for being formidable hunters and skilled guides, the Bunun were the last tribe to be suppressed by the Japanese. Their most important celebration is the **Ear-shooting Festival** held in April or May, traditionally a test of archery skills designed to mark the coming of age of men in the tribe and to pray for a good millet harvest – traditionally hunted animals (usually deer) are used as target practice. The Bunun are also known for the haunting **Pasibutbut**, eight-octave harmonies that sound a bit like humming, first recorded by the Japanese in 1943.

The Bunun have also been active players in the campaign for aboriginal rights: the **Bunun Culture and Education Foundation** was established in 1995 in **Yenping**, Taitung county, while in 1987 the destruction of ancient Bunun graves by a hotel contractor in **Dongpu** sparked the "Return Our Land" campaign – since the 1970s the village has also clashed with Yushan National Park over water and land rights. **Luona** in Nantou county and **Haiduan** (Taitung county) are also large Bunun communities, but the village of **Hongye** is the best known in Taiwan: this was the home of a Little League baseball team whose defeat of a side from Wakayama (Japan) in 1968 thrilled the nation (though the Japanese team were not the world champions as is still sometimes claimed). As with many other tribes, one of the most visibly recognizable Bunun in Taiwan is a popular singer, **Wang Hong-en**, though another tribe member, **Topas Tamapima**, became a noted writer in the 1980s, and his novel *The Last Hunter* is highly acclaimed.

Hla'alua

The **Hla'alua** (拉阿魯哇; lā ā lǔwa), or Saaroa, became Taiwan's fifteenth indigenous tribe in 2016, previously considered part of the southern Tsou. The tribe's main villages are Taoyuan and Gaojhong near Taoyuan, Kaoshiung County, with a total population of around five hundred.

Kanakanavu

The **Kanakanavu** (卡那卡那富; kǎnàkǎnàfù) became Taiwan's sixteenth indigenous tribe in 2016 – like the Hla'alua, they were previously considered "southern Tsou", and can be found in the villages of Manga and Takanua in Kaoshiung County (around 520 people in total).

Kavalan

The 1100 **Kavalan** (噶瑪蘭族; gámǎlánzú) became Taiwan's eleventh indigenous tribe in 2002 (the first píngpǔ tribe to be given such status), after a ten-year campaign and the strong support of former premier Yu Shyi-kun. Originally from Yilan county, where legend has it they drove the Atayal into the mountains, most Kavalan migrated south along the east coast in the nineteenth century and developed cultural ties with the Amis. Today their largest settlement is **Xinshe** near Fongbin in Hualien county.

Paiwan

The **Paiwan** (排灣; páiwān; 96,000), inhabiting the far south of Taiwan in Pingdong and Taitung counties, have managed to retain a strong cultural and linguistic identity. The Paiwan call themselves the "descendants of the paipushe snake" and the snake, associated with their ancestors, is a common symbol among the tribe and eating it is banned. Major Paiwan settlements include **Sandimen**, **Taiwu** and **Mudan**, but their villages are also spread throughout the Hengchun peninsula and Kenting National Park – many still use slate or **slab-stone houses**. The most important Paiwan **festival** is **Masaru**, which is an end-of-year celebration rather than a harvest festival, taking place in individual villages between July and November. The Paiwan are renowned **woodcarvers** but have also produced some talented writers: **Chen Ying-hsiung**'s collection of short stories *Traces of Dreams in Foreign Lands* (1971), is considered Taiwan's first piece of aboriginal literature, while blind poet **Monaneng** has been publishing since 1984. Writer **Sakinu Ahronglong**, whose *Mountain Pig, Flying Fox, Sakinu* was a big hit in Taiwan, also starred in a film adaptation of his book *The Sage Hunter* in 2005, which won plaudits in the US. Other Paiwan celebrities include the rock band **Power Station**, famous Asia-wide in the late 1990s, and female pop singer **Dai Ai-ling**.

Puyuma

Inhabiting the plains around Taitung city, the 11,000 **Puyuma** (卑南族; known as **Beinan** or bēinánzú in Chinese, after the district in which most of them live), are traditionally divided into two main subgroups with different origin myths: the **Nanwang** group are "born from bamboo" while the **Zhiben** group are "born from stone". The tribe is further divided into eight villages, traditionally independent and ruled by a chief – villages often fought among each other, the Puyuma developing a tradition for Spartan-like training of young men in community halls known as **parakwan**. The tribe's most important festival, the **Mangamangaya**, or "Monkey Ritual", grew out of this warrior tradition, marking the coming of age of male teenagers and involving wrestling and hunting monkeys – today the monkeys are made of straw. Puyuma singer **A-mei** (Chang Hui-mei or just MEI) has become one of the island's most successful pop stars, while **Samingad** is almost as famous for singing in Puyuma as well as Mandarin.

Rukai

The 13,000-strong **Rukai** (魯凱族; lǔkǎizú) tribe is loosely divided into three groups: **Taitung** (east), **Wutai** (west) and those inhabiting the **Maolin National Scenic Area**. The tribe, like the Paiwan, is noted for its striking slate houses in villages such as **Duona** – the Rukai also traditionally cook food on stone slabs. In 1990 the **Return to Kochapongan Movement** was established to rebuild traditional stone houses in an abandoned mountain village (with no roads), evolving into a symbol of the Rukai's determination to maintain their culture (events are now held at **Kochapongan**, also known as Old Haocha, twice a year).

Saisiyat

The **Saisiyat** (賽夏; sàixià), numbering around 5300, are based in the **Lion's Head Mountain** region and comprise a Northern Branch (**Wufong**) and a Southern Branch (**Nanzhuang** and **Shitan** in Miaoli), each with its own dialect. Given the size of the tribe and its proximity to larger Atayal and Hakka populations, the struggle to maintain Saisiyat culture is particularly hard. The "**Ritual of the Short Black People**", held by both clans every ten years, with a smaller version every two, has become their most powerful expression of identity. The ceremony commemorates a legendary tribe of black pygmies, called *taai*, or "short people", who once lived in harmony with the Saisiyat. Things changed after some of the *taai* sexually molested Saisiyat women – the whole tribe was exterminated. The ritual is meant to appease their spirits, many anthropologists suggesting the story might be based on true events, and that the *taai* may represent peoples who inhabited Taiwan before the aborigines.

Sakizaya

The **Sakizaya** (撒奇萊雅族; saqílàiyǎzú) were once considered part of the Amis, but became the thirteenth officially recognized tribe in January 2007. The tribe has around 335 registered members, having been long absorbed by the Amis tribe after a devastating military campaign against the Qing in 1878. Estimated actual tribe numbers range from 5000 to 10,000.

Sediq

The **Sediq** (also Seediq; 賽德克族; sàidékèzú), once considered part of the Atayal, were officially recognized as Taiwan's fourteenth indigenous group in 2008 with around 10,000 members (living primarily in Nantou and Hualien counties).

Tao

The 3000 **Tao** or **Dawu** (達悟族; dáwùzú; previously known as the Yami) retain the strongest identity of any tribe in Taiwan, mainly because of their relative isolation. The only seagoing tribe, they inhabit **Lanyu** (Orchid Island) off the southeast coast, their language more closely related to that of the Philippines than to the aboriginal languages of mainland Taiwan. The most iconic expression of that identity is the Tao wooden canoe, hand-carved and richly decorated but serving a mostly ceremonial purpose today. The Tao's traditional dress is also very distinctive, the men wearing loincloths and striking steel helmets, generally worn now only at celebrations like the **Flying Fish Festival** in March/April. The Tao's traditional underground houses, protection against the fierce Pacific weather, are also becoming rare.

  It's not as tranquil as it seems on Orchid Island, however; in 1982 the state-owned Taiwan Power Company (Taipower) duped the Tao into building a **nuclear waste**

storage site on Lanyu in return for more jobs (they were told it was a fish canning factory). The Tao have campaigned long, and so far unsuccessfully, to have the waste removed, with as yet no success – instead, the company has provided some NT$1.7 billion in compensation and many younger Tao have simply given up (the company also provides free electricity and financial assistance for medical treatment).

Thao

Sun Moon Lake is the ancestral home of the Thao (邵族; shàozú), **Taiwan's smallest aboriginal tribe**, with around 648 members. One of the most important Thao legends tells that a chief known as Paidabo stumbled upon Sun Moon Lake after an exhausting chase of a large **white deer** – Paidabo was so impressed he ordered the whole tribe, originally located near Alishan, to move here, and today you'll see symbols of the white deer everywhere. Many fear the Thao will become completely assimilated by the Chinese, with only a handful of "pure" Thao still living and fluent in the Thao language. However, the destruction wrought by the 921 Earthquake (see box, p.180) led to a re-examination of government policy and a greater focus on preserving Thao culture: in 2000 Lalu Island was renamed to reflect Thao tradition, and its sacred shores protected (only Thao are allowed on the island), while in 2001 the Thao became Taiwan's tenth official aboriginal tribe (previously they had been regarded as a subgroup of the Tsou).

The most popular Thao festival is the **Harvest** or **Moon Festival** held Lunar August 1–15, marking the start of the Thao new year. On the last day of Lunar July, in the Sun Moon Lake village of Itashao, local Thao pound huge wooden pestles on stone mortars to call the tribe together – the thumping sound created, or **pestle music**, is one of the festival's chief attractions.

Truku

In 2004, after an eight-year campaign, the 24,000 **Truku** (太魯閣族; tàilǔgézú; also sometimes romanized as Taroko) were officially recognized as the twelfth indigenous ethnic group in Taiwan, though not without controversy. The Truku were formerly part of the Sediq subgroup of the Atayal tribe, and the seven thousand Sediq from Nantou that remain are unhappy at what they feel is an unnecessary split. As the name suggests, the tribe once inhabited the area around **Taroko Gorge** (Taroko means "lookout on a hillside") though the largest settlements today lie outside the national park at Sioulin, Wanrong and Jhousi in Hualien county. The tribe is most noted for suffering one of the worst abuses of **land rights** in Taiwan; between 1973 and 1995 **Asia Cement** leased land from the tribe, but when the lease expired, it said it had documents proving all claim to it had been surrendered. The tribe denied this, and because the company had done little for the community, wanted it removed. Even after the Council of Indigenous Peoples found in favour of the Truku in 2012, Asia Cement refused to budge and nothing has been done by the government since – the local Land Reclamation Committee continues its protests.

Tsou

The Tsou (鄒; zōu) homeland is centred on the Alishan National Scenic Area, where around 6000 people claim Tsou ancestry. There are only two Tsou **hosas** (also called *dashe*), which means "major village": Dabang and Tefuye, both in Alishan. Each *hosa* has a hereditary chief or *peogsi* who still has limited authority over the villagers. Only these villages contain a **kuba**, the traditional, male-only meeting house which lies at the centre of all Tsou festivals and rituals. Other villages have smaller structures known as **hufu** that have similar functions but are less important.

By far the most interesting Tsou festival to watch, the **Mayasvi Festival** is hosted annually in rotation by Tefuye and Dabang villages in February: traditionally a celebration of warriors returning from battle, the rituals give thanks to the god of war and god of heaven.

Religion in Taiwan

Religious belief is apparent everywhere you look in Taiwan: in addition to literally thousands of temples, almost every home and store has a shrine, taxi drivers hang icons inside their cars, and small altars laden with offerings or braziers burning "ghost money" stand on pavements outside shops and offices. Popular religious practice, often described as "folk religion", is usually lumped together with Taoism to distinguish it from the clearly identifiable Buddhist and Confucian traditions, and while it's true that Taoist concepts are important, popular "folk religion" is really a blend of ancient animist beliefs with all three traditions. As a result, Taiwan has a broad pantheon of gods and goddesses that include Buddhist and Taoist deities, as well as famous historical figures.

The beliefs outlined below are subscribed to by the vast majority of Taiwanese, but there are many other faiths practised on the island. Since the 1950s there has been a **Buddhist revival** in Taiwan, with several monasteries advancing a purer form of teaching and practice, and strict adherents (there are around four million) dismissing the Buddhist deities in older folk temples as childish superstition. **Christianity** is the next most popular, with over one million believers (mostly Protestant), followed by **I-kuan Tao** (yīguàn dào) with around 900,000 followers, a mixture of various religions, but with a fundamentally Chinese character and roots in late Qing-dynasty China. It's now primarily a Taiwanese faith after suppression on the mainland. There are also around sixty thousand Taiwanese **Muslims** (mostly of the Chinese Hui ethnic group).

Core beliefs

Ancestor worship lies at the heart of Taiwanese (and traditional Chinese) belief, based on the hazy boundary between the human and spirit worlds. Worship of ancestors, by offering incense, food or spirit money at family or clan shrines, is imperative to ensure a peaceful afterlife. After death, everyone is said to pass through a series of supernatural courts (where a period in hell might be prescribed for wrongdoing). The deceased then become either **ancestral spirits** or **"hungry ghosts"**, uncared for by their families and destined to haunt the living (these are the unfortunates appeased in "Ghost Month"). If worshipping certain individuals over the years proves particularly efficacious, these eventually become elevated to the status of **god** (Mazu and Guan Di are the best examples), joining the vast pantheon of folk and Taoist deities. Gods live in an alternative reality, with an administration modelled on the old imperial bureaucracy, with their own courts and a strict system of hierarchy. The supreme deity is the **Jade Emperor** or the Lord of Heaven. Worship of **gods** is slightly different from that of ancestors as the latter (and ghosts) are spirits that must be appeased or looked after, while gods are worshipped in exchange for protection, specific types of help or general good fortune (usually in the form of wealth). Note that although almost all Taiwanese subscribe to the concept of ghostly afterlife, people describing themselves as Buddhists will normally believe in reincarnation.

Confucianism

More philosophy than religion, **Confucianism** is associated with **Kong Zi** (kǒngzǐ; 551–479 BC), known as "Confucius" in the West, a real scholar and teacher who lived during the Warring States period in modern Shandong, China. Confucius taught that if people behaved according to a strict code of moral and social values, society would be transformed and happiness achieved – discussion of gods and spiritualism is unimportant, though Confucian temples were created later in order to commemorate the great sage and perform important rituals. His sayings, collected in the *Analects*, along with the five ancient Confucian Classics, became the basis for Chinese imperial examinations until the end of the Qing dynasty, and the emphasis on virtuous rulers, strict hierarchy and education has influenced Chinese thought ever since. Confucianism, along with its temples, was completely abandoned in mainland China after 1949, but thrives in Taiwan, and the official 79th descendant of Confucius (born in 1975), **Kung Tsui-chang** (kǒng chuícháng) is the "Sacrificial Official to Confucius" in Taipei and Senior Advisor to Taiwan's president.

Taoism

Taoism (or "Daoism"; dàojiào), stems from the philosophy laid out in the *Tao Te Ching*, attributed to quasi-historical monk **Lao Zi** (lǎozǐ; a contemporary of Confucius), and the later teachings of **Zhuang Zi** (zhuāngzǐ). "Tao" means "the way" and, in contrast to the humanistic ethos of Confucianism, Taoism emphasizes man's need to connect with the natural universe in order to lead a fulfilling life, replacing greed with harmony in nature.

Contemplative, spiritual and abstruse, **philosophical Taoism** is often differentiated from the more superstitious **religious Taoism**: the latter is closer to the "folk religion" practised in most of Taiwan, with its vast pantheon of gods and goddesses. Taoist thought is closely linked to practices such as fēngshuǐ, and the concepts of yīn and yáng, as well as many common daily rituals.

Buddhism

Buddhism (fójiào) is essentially a way of life, based on the teachings of Indian prince Siddhartha Gautama (563–483 BC), who attained enlightenment in 528 BC and was thereafter known as the Buddha or "enlightened one". The **Four Noble Truths** stand at the core of his teachings: the truth about *duhkha* (usually translated as "suffering"); the truth of how suffering in life arises; the truth that giving up desire will eliminate suffering; and that the eightfold path is a practical way to achieve this goal. **Enlightenment** (or *nirvana*) means to escape the endless cycle of rebirth and therefore suffering. A few hundred years after Buddha's death, his followers divided into two schools: **Theravada** (which thrives in Sri Lanka and Southeast Asia) and **Mahayana**, the interpretation most prevalent in northeast Asia and Taiwan today. Mahayana Buddhism, and particularly the form that developed in China (where it mixed with Taoist and Confucian thought), differs primarily in its belief that there are multiple Buddhas (that the historical Buddha, known as **Sakyamuni**, is just one of a series of past and future enlightened ones); and that there are **Bodhisattvas**, enlightened beings who have chosen continued rebirth in order to end the suffering of others (**Guanyin** is the most common in Taiwan; see p.407).

Buddhism in Taiwan

Taiwan is one of the world's great strongholds of Buddhism. The two main forms practised today are **Pure Land** and the meditative **Chan** (or Zen), though most Buddhist organizations on the island tend to blend aspects of the two. Buddhist **monasteries** developed in Taiwan during the Japanese occupation, and since the 1960s have blossomed, giving the island one of the highest monastic populations in Asia. As Taiwan has grown richer, it's become a pioneer for what's known as **Humanistic Buddhism** and its attempt to accommodate modern capitalism: accepting that becoming a monk isn't practical for most people, the emphasis is on blending daily life with Buddhist tenets, and particularly on performing charity and good works.

Other than Sakyamuni, the most common Buddhas represented in Taiwan are **Amitabha** (the Buddha of Boundless Light, who oversees the "Pure Land", a paradise attainable by prayer recitation), and the **Medicine Buddha** (yàoshīfó in Chinese), a past Buddha famed for his healing abilities and usually portrayed holding a medicine ball or pagoda. The three are often arranged together in temples as a trinity, with Sakyamuni in the middle. The **Maitreya Buddha**, known as mílèfó in Chinese, is portrayed as a fat, happy monk, an image that commemorates a past incarnation as a quasi-historical Chinese monk. Though he's still technically a Bodhisattva, mílèfó is expected to return as the next future Buddha, and is worshipped as such.

The Taoist pantheon

Most Taiwanese worship a mixture of Taoist and Buddhist **deities**, though this blurring of faiths would be considered wholly Taoist or "folk religion" by strict Buddhists today. The following is an introduction to the most common gods, though there are literally hundreds, often within the same temple. The relevant festival days (usually described as "birthdays" in English) for each one are outlined in Basics (see p.36).

Mazu

Mazu (媽祖; mázǔ), also known as the Queen of Heaven (天后; tiānhòu), is the most important deity in Taiwan. Regarded as the **goddess of the sea**, it's not hard to work out why she became so important in Taiwan, an island nation that was in large part dependent on fishing and immigration by sea in its early history. Like many deities in Taiwan, Mazu has historical roots in Fujian province, the ancestral home of most Taiwanese. Her popularity can also be explained by her perceived ability to grant the wishes of her believers, most evident in the tremendous wealth of Mazu temples, and their attraction of celebrities, politicians and huge donations. The historical Mazu was a woman called **Lin Mo-niang**, who was born around 960 AD on Meizhou Island off the Fujian coast. As a teenager, she's said to have been taught the mysteries of the Tao by a priest, and thereafter began a life of selfless charity, guiding ships into harbour and saving seafarers from drowning. This culminated in the dramatic rescue of her father or brothers while in a trance (some stories say her father was lost after Lin was disturbed mid-trance). She died at the age of 28, and was later deified, being awarded the title "Queen of Heaven" in the Qing dynasty.

Statues of Mazu are usually identifiable by her mortarboard-like headdress, fronted with beads. She is usually flanked by statues of "**Ears That Hear on the Wind**" (shùnfēngěr) and "**Thousand-Mile Eyes**" (qiānlǐyǎn), two demons who fell in love with her (she never married), and whom she converted to the Tao, now serving as trusted guardians with special powers indicated by their names.

"SPIRIT DIVISION" AND THE MAZU HIERARCHY

Given the importance of the "Goddess of the Sea", it's no surprise that **Mazu's birthday** is one of Taiwan's most exuberant and intense festivals, while the hugely important **Dajia Mazu Pilgrimage** (see box, p.187) has its roots in the practice of "spirit division". This is essentially a system of hierarchy, where "mother" temples, containing ancient or revered Mazu deities, provide new statues or relics to smaller "branch" temples (the system also applies to other deities). Traditionally these subsidiary temples return their deities to the mother temple every year at the time of Mazu's birthday, to enhance their spiritual power. The highest-ranking temple is undoubtedly the shrine on **Meizhou Island** in Fujian, but the problems start when trying to identify Taiwan's most senior place of worship: almost every major temple claims it's the "first" or "oldest" and many hold precious deities from Meizhou. Rivalries are fierce and disputes can become very heated. Today, the most popular contenders are in Beigang (see p.216), Dajia (see box, p.187), Xingang and the Tainan area (see p.236).

Guanyin

Though a Buddhist Bodhisattva, **Guanyin** (觀音; guānyīn) is worshipped in Taoist temples throughout Taiwan, and even where she's the main deity in a nominally Buddhist temple, practice tends to follow popular Taoism rather than orthodox Buddhism. Guanyin was originally worshipped as a male Indian Bodhisattva called Avalokitesvara, who represented the ideal of compassion, able to relieve suffering and grant children: the deity began to be depicted as a female during the twelfth century in China, and she's now known as the **goddess of mercy**. She's normally depicted as an elegant lady, robed in white and, being associated with **vegetarianism**, her image also adorns many vegetarian restaurants.

Wang Ye

Wang Ye (王爺; wángyé) gods are incredibly popular throughout Taiwan, but particularly in the south where they equal Mazu in importance. The name Wang Ye, or "pestilence gods", is an umbrella term for around 360 different deities: there are reckoned to be around 106 to 132 individual family names for each (Chi, Chu, Fan, Li, Su, Wen and Wu are the most common), and they are thought to have originally been diseased spirits, now honoured in an attempt to ward off plague and disease. The tradition migrated to Taiwan from Fujian and is linked to the practice of burning "spirit ships", or wángchuán: model boats loaded with Wang Ye gods, set alight, and launched into the ocean in an attempt to expel disease/bad luck. Taiwan's chief Wang Ye temple is in **Nankunshen** (see p.250), north of Tainan – pestilence gods rarely appear in temples on their own, and are usually represented in groups of three, five or seven.

Guan Di

Red-faced **Guan Di** (關帝; guāndì, or just guāngōng), is one of the most admired deities in Taiwan, with over three hundred temples and numerous shrines in homes and shops. He's usually described as the **god of war**, but this is misleading. He was originally more like a patron of chivalrous warriors, and is today worshipped by executives, police, restaurant owners, rebels and criminal gangs, as well as being revered as a god of wealth and literature by the public in general. His appeal derives from being one of the most respected characters in the Chinese classic the *Romance of the Three Kingdoms*, loosely based on the historical events of the Three Kingdoms period (206–220 AD). Known then as **Guan Yu**, the general was one of the **three oath brothers** (the main characters in the saga), and noted for his extreme bravery and loyalty. Apart from the red face, he's usually depicted with a long, flowing beard and a Chinese halberd in his hands. Buddhists claim Guan Di was taught Buddhism by a great master on the night of his death, and as a result swore to protect the *dharma* (Buddhist teachings) – he's often seen in Buddhist temples where he's known as qíelán.

Earth God

The **Earth God**, known as *Tudi Gong* (土地公; tǔdìgōng, or fúdé zhèngshén in Chinese), is traditionally one of the most important in the Chinese pantheon, though as Taiwan has modernized his popularity has waned. His main task in the Jade Emperor's administration is to keep a register of births and deaths and govern the local area in his charge, usually a village or parts of a town (towns traditionally had five Earth God shrines for north, south, east, west and central districts), though he's more associated with agriculture and probably evolved from ancient harvest rituals. In his secondary role as a god of wealth, shopkeepers erect temporary altars on the roadside to make offerings to him twice a month. Earth God shrines are usually very small but ubiquitous, found literally all over the island. He's normally represented by a statue of a cheerful old man, dressed in yellow robes with a long white beard and a stick in his right hand. Tucked away under his altar is usually an effigy of the **Tiger God**, thought to be his servant and ridden by the Earth God on his spiritual "inspection tours" of the locale.

City God

Every major city in Taiwan has a **City God** (城隍; chénghuáng), which protects the inhabitants and, like the Earth God, acts as a registrar of all births and deaths in the area. He also keeps account of the citizens' moral behaviour, and it's his report after death which will determine punishment in the courts of the underworld – it's usual to find a giant abacus somewhere in his temple, as well as graphic images of hell. Though the City God tradition is thought to have evolved from nature worship, and his role is the same in every city, each deity tends to double as an incarnation of a famous local figure, meaning his birthday is celebrated on different days. In Taiwan, many City God temples are branches of mainland counterparts, usually in Fujian.

In temples, the City God usually appears flanked by a large entourage of smaller statues, representing officials in his administration; there are military and civilian branches, the latter with six departments. The most famous officials, and prominent at festivals, are **General Xie** (bāyé) and **General Fan** (qīyé), charged with capturing evil spirits.

Wenchang Dijun

Known as the **god of literature** or culture, **Wenchang Dijun** (文昌帝君; wénchāng dìjūn) is portrayed today as a particularly honest court official; legend has it that the Jade Emperor made him head of all officials on Earth, including all appointments through examinations. With the imperial system long gone, today he's popular with students (and their parents) preparing for school and university exams. Wenchang Dijun is one of **five culture gods** or wǔ wénchāng: kuí xīngjūn, zhūyī, guāndì and lǚ dòngbīn, one of the Eight Immortals.

Qingshui Zushi

A quasi-historical figure, popular in North Taiwan, **Qingshui Zushi** (清水祖師; qīngshuǐ zūshī) is another deity who originated in Fujian. There are several legends concerning his life: some portray him as a Fujianese monk, while others claim he was Chen Zhao-ying, born in Kaifeng during the Song dynasty (960–1128). Awarded a local government post in recognition of his wisdom and munificence, he later established a shrine at Qingshui rock near Anxi in Fujian where he spent his retirement – after his death people began to worship him as the "Divine Progenitor of Qingshui" and he became one of the guardian gods of the county ("Zushi" is an honorific title meaning "ancestor and teacher of the people"). His most famous temple is in Sanxia (see p.114), outside Taipei.

Baosheng Dadi

Baosheng Dadi (保生大帝; bǎoshēng dàdì) or the "Great Emperor Who Preserves Life" is known as a god of medicine or healing, and is another deity based on a historical figure. Wu Tao was born in Tong'an (Xiamen) in Fujian, in 979 AD, and led a selfless life helping and curing sick people. Villagers began to worship Wu after his death in 1037, claiming that this was very efficacious in times of epidemic, and he soon became part of a popular Fujianese cult that was brought to Taiwan in the seventeenth century – his formal title was awarded by an emperor in the Ming dynasty. Today there are over two hundred temples dedicated to him island-wide.

Jade Emperor

The **Jade Emperor** (玉皇; yùhuáng), or "Heavenly Grandfather" (天公; tiāngōng), is the chief Taoist deity (though not the most revered), and the head of the celestial government that was thought to mirror that of imperial China. Traditionally, he could only be worshipped by the living emperor and was symbolized by a tablet rather than an image (as in Tainan; see p.238). In Taiwan today he's been absorbed into the pantheon of folk deities, with important temples in Daxi and Taichung. Often depicted sitting on a throne, his face obscured by strings of pearls hanging from his hat (a bit like Mazu), he usually holds a piece of jade in his hands as a symbol of authority.

Queen Mother of the West

The highest ranking female deity, the **Queen Mother of the West** (西王母; xīwángmǔ) is often portrayed as the **Jade Emperor's wife** and known by a confusing number of alternate names in Chinese; *Wangmu Niangniang* (王母娘娘; wángmǔ niángniáng), Golden Mother (金母; jīnmǔ) and *Laomu* (老母; lǎomǔ) among them. She's said to live in the Kunlun Mountains in China's far west, and guards the "Peaches of Immortality" which only ripen every 3600 years – eating at the banquet she holds in honour of this event confers immortality. She's regarded as a particularly liberated female figure in the male-dominated pantheon, and is subsequently popular with women; she's also a protector against epidemics and a symbol of longevity. Hualien is the centre of her cult in Taiwan (see p.291).

Birth Goddess

The **Birth Goddess** (注生娘娘; zhùshēng niángniáng) is a popular subsidiary deity in many temples, worshipped primarily by pregnant women, or those hoping to get pregnant. She's also thought to be able to determine the sex of a child and protect mothers during pregnancy and the birth itself, as well as being a guardian of children up to the age of 16. At many shrines she is flanked by the **Twelve Maternal Ancestors**, lesser deities who are thought to help the Birth Goddess deliver children, one for each month of the year. Legend suggests she's based on a historical figure from the Tang dynasty, but there's little evidence to back this up. In many respects she's similar to the deity **Lady Linshui** (臨水夫人; línshuǐ fūrén), also guardian of children and childbirth.

Matchmaker

The Old Man Under the Moon (月下老人; yuèxià lǎorén), better known as the **Matchmaker** (媒人; méirén), is the Chinese version of Cupid and one of the more fashionable of the minor deities in Taiwan today. Like a modern dating agency, he uses a list supplied by Lady Linshui to match ideal partners at birth, tying them together by an invisible red thread. Fate ought to bring these couples together later in life, but just to make sure, offerings are made to the Matchmaker (he's usually represented by an old man with a long white beard); single men and women buy "matrimonial thread" from the temple, keeping it close to them until their predetermined partner is found.

Dizang Wang

Dizang Wang (地藏王; dìzàngwáng), otherwise known as the Buddhist Bodhisattva Ksitigarbha, is misleadingly called the **King of Hell** in English. Though portrayed as a monk in Chinese tradition, legend has it that Dizang Wang was originally a girl, heartbroken at the death of her mother who had been disrespectful of Buddhist teachings and had gone to hell. Through intense prayer and meditation her daughter managed to assume enough merit to ensure her mother's release, but in the process glimpsed all the suffering in the underworld and vowed to empty hell before becoming a Buddha. Though from the Buddhist pantheon, Dizang Wang is now portrayed as a man and worshipped in many Taoist temples (see Chiayi, p.215).

Temples

Most folk or **Taoist temples** (miào or gōng) in Taiwan feature south-Fujianese architecture dating from the Qing dynasty, which is when most of them were established. Such temples are always built according to the principles of fēngshuǐ, a geomantic practice concerned with the balancing of qì, or cosmic energy, in the natural world. Note that the temple establishment date rarely refers to the building you'll see today: early shrines were built solely from wood, and in addition to damage caused by Taiwan's harsh typhoon- and earthquake-prone environment, it's typical for temple followers to rebuild them every few generations. As a simple rule, the more paintings or visual decoration inside the temple, as opposed to calligraphy, the older it is; Qing-dynasty Taiwan was mostly illiterate. Note that in this guide, directions (right and left), are provided assuming the reader is facing the temple: in Chinese it's normal to describe the sides of the temple as if looking outwards, from the point of view of god or goddess inside.

Exterior

Taiwanese temples tend to have similar gable-and-hip-style **roof** structures, often with double eaves, and usually decorated with colourful dragons and jiǎnnián figures (literally "cut and stick"), made from pieces of coloured glass. Older temples usually have koji figures outside and inside the temple: these are hand-sculpted pottery figurines, usually making up vivid tableaux from Chinese legends – the craft is traditionally Chiayi-based (see p.216). **Stone lions** (shíshī) guard the temple entrance: the left is female, the right male, primarily decorative symbols of nobility and royalty. Always **enter** at the side entrance to the right of the main gate, and exit on the other side. The right side is more important in fēngshuǐ terms (being yáng), and is usually adorned with paintings or images of **dragons** (lóng), while **tigers** (hǔ) appear on the opposite (yīn) side. Dragons are immensely powerful creatures in Chinese mythology, emblems of the emperor and symbols of fertility.

Interior

Most temples are laid out as a series of halls and courtyards: the main gate, or **entrance hall**, leads to a **front hall** or a small courtyard facing the **main hall** in which the chief deity is enshrined. There is sometimes a **rear hall** beyond this, and often numerous shrines tucked away all over the site. Every temple has at least two **Door Gods** (ménshén) painted on the main doors, usually selected from a group of around twenty different historical figures. The most common are Tang-dynasty generals Qin Shu-bao and Yu-chi Jing-de, whose protection of the emperor against an evil dragon spirit was so effective even their painted images seemed to scare it away. The ceilings above the entrance hall are usually incredibly elaborate. Known as **algal wells**, they are supposed to trick demons into thinking the temple is underwater, and therefore impermeable to fire. Though they serve as enigmatic decoration today, the paintings inside temples once had a dual purpose – they can be hard to decipher without a guide, but the images are loaded with practical advice ranging from what to wear inside and how to pray, to when to have children.

The chief deity is worshipped at the main **altar**, usually represented by several statues (in some temples there are numerous images of the same god). Different **statues** can represent different incarnations of the god, and can have different uses: the oldest, most venerated effigy rarely leaves the protected casing of the altar, but others will be used for festivals and inspection tours (when the god "inspects" the local area as part of a boisterous parade). Towards the back or sides of the temple you're likely to see towers of tiny lights, known as guāngmíng: believers pay the temple to have their name inscribed under one of these lights for a set period, in the hope their generosity will be rewarded by the chief deity.

Buddhist and Confucian temples

Traditional **Buddhist temples** (sì) are similarly designed, but usually feature statues of the **Four Heavenly Kings** (風調雨順; fēngtiáo yǔshùn) at the entrance, protecting the main images of Buddha inside and depictions of the eighteen *arhats* (luóhàn) along the walls: these are Buddhist saints respected for their great wisdom and power. Newer

Buddhist temples in Taiwan tend to be less gaudy than Taoist or popular shrines, and often form a part of monasteries or nunneries. **Confucian temples** (kǒngmiào) have a fairly standardized layout of halls and courtyards based on the original in China, the most notable difference to Taoist temples being the absence of deities – Confucius is commemorated with a **tablet**. The best example of a Confucian temple is in Datong, Taipei (see p.68).

Rituals

The most common form of bàibài (worship) in Taoist (or "folk religion") temples is to make a series of bows before the image of the deity, hands together before the chest – usually, **incense sticks** (xiāng) are held, the smoke symbolizing prayers floating to heaven. Believers ask for the deity's help for a specific problem, or just general good fortune, and it's also normal to give thanks to the deity for previous help. You'll often see people buying bundles of incense at the temple entrance, before making a circuit of all the main shrines and deities inside. Once bàibài is complete, incense is placed in the large **censer**, usually facing the main hall. In addition, the tables in front of the main altars are often covered in **offerings**, usually food (especially types of fruit, which often have symbolic meaning), incense and **joss money** or "gold paper" (jīnzhǐ), all intended to help convey the sincerity and loyalty of the worshipper. In order to pass into the spiritual realm, the money must be burnt – you'll see people throwing piles of it into the large chimney-like furnaces that stand in courtyards or outside the temple.

Various forms of **divination** or fortune-telling are practised in traditional Taiwanese folk religion, and you're likely to see several versions of this in temples. The most common is the use of zhǐjiǎo (pronounced buǎ-buēi in Taiwanese) or **throwing blocks**, also known as "moon blocks" on account of their crescent shape. Worshippers use these to ascertain the gods' answer to a specific question. If one lands flat-side up and the other the opposite, this is taken to be positive – this needs to happen three times in a row for the believer to be sure the deity is in agreement. If any other combination comes up before the third positive, the believer must start all over again. If both blocks fall round-side up, this is taken as a negative, while both landing round-side down is the "laughing" response, meaning that you must rephrase the question.

Drawing lots (chōuqiān) is also popular. These are the thin bamboo strips lodged into a cylindrical container, each marked with a number. This corresponds to a piece of paper (usually contained in numbered drawers nearby) that contains an obscure saying or poem, a piece of ancient wisdom that usually requires an expert to interpret. Temples are also the best place to see **spirit mediums** or jītóng (dáng-gī in Taiwanese), men who become possessed by a deity while in a trance (they usually specialize in just one), and thus can deliver far more effective oracles or responses to petitioners' queries. These men usually work in temples, but are not attached to them, being independent and free to work wherever they choose.

Arts and culture

Taiwanese culture is rooted in millennia of Chinese tradition, art and philosophy, but much of what is considered "Taiwanese" today emerged relatively recently, during the Japanese occupation. The Taiwanese contemporary arts scene is a dynamic blend of Western, Japanese, indigenous, Fujianese and northern Chinese influences, much of it tied to the search for a separate identity, at its most intense since the 1980s.

Visual arts

Generally recognized as the "father of modern Taiwanese art", **Kinichiro Ishikawa** (1871–1945) was one of many Japanese painters who came to Taiwan to paint and teach. In the 1920s and 30s, artists such as **Chen Cheng-po** (1895–1947) and **Yang San-lang** (1907–95), who had been pupils of Ishikawa and studied European oil painting in Japan, particularly French Impressionism, created the first **Nativist** movement, characterized by the depiction of typically Taiwanese images and scenes. Chen grew up in Chiayi, and his work captures the essence of rural south Taiwan and its languid street life: the oil painting *Streets of Chiayi* (1926) was the first by a Taiwanese painter to be exhibited at the Imperial Art Expo in Japan. Yang's contrast of light and colour is heavily reminiscent of Monet, his natural landscapes and scenes containing a nostalgic, plaintive quality.

Modern art

After World War II, there was renewed interest in traditional Chinese painting, but by the 1960s disillusionment with conservative styles had precipitated a move towards abstract Western art; **Lee Chun-shan** (1911–84) and **Liu Kuo-sung** (b.1932) were the most important and innovative painters of the period. Lee was an avant-garde pioneer, maintaining a reclusive existence in Changhua.

In the 1970s, **Nativism** (also known this time as the "Native Soil Movement") was revived, partly as a rejection of the Western-inspired art of the 1960s. **Hung Tung** (1920–87) became one of its most celebrated exponents, noted for his use of vivid colours and imaginative interpretation of Buddhist themes, Chinese myth and traditional historical drama. The movement also incorporated sculptors such as **Ju Ming** (see p.128) and his teacher **Yu Yu Yang**, who had studied in Japan.

The 1980s was a transitional period in art terms, mirroring the political upheavals that led to the ending of martial law in 1987. The most significant figures were **Yang Mao-lin** and **Wu Tien-chang**, both of whom dealt with social and political issues in their work. Wu became famous for his *Portraits of the Emperors* (completed in 1990), large caricatures of Mao Zedong, Deng Xiaoping, Chiang Kai-shek and Chiang Ching-kuo, but turned to photography in the 1990s and now uses digital imagery to blend flat and 3D graphics. Yang's *Made in Taiwan* series is a more subtle approach to Taiwanese history, blending a diversity of images such as aboriginal peoples, references to the Dutch period, and domestic fruits and vegetables.

Contemporary art

In the 1990s, influenced by Postmodernism and the growth in art galleries and museums, art in Taiwan blossomed in several different directions: the Nativist movement continued to evolve, and multimedia, particularly photography, video and installation art became more mainstream. **Lee Ming-sheng** is one of the most influential proponents of a mixed media approach, while **Chen Chieh-jen's** work has been exhibited all over the world, best known for his shocking photographic images such as *A Way Going to an Insane City* (1999). In 2014, the *Huffington Post* dubbed Taiwan "a rising power in the art world" thanks to the thought-provoking work of artists such Pei-Shih Tu, Li-Ren Chang, Chi-Yu Wu and Chao-Tsai Chiu.

Taiwan also has a strong tradition of **art photography**: Chang Tsai, Deng Nan-guang and Lee Ming-diao are known as the "Three Swordsmen of Taiwanese Photography", their work documenting the island's development in the postwar period – Tsai is particularly lauded for his portraits of folk festivals and aboriginal people.

Music

Traditional Chinese music was brought to Taiwan with immigrants from the mainland, most audibly in the form of **folk music** played at celebrations, festivals and temples, but in recent years there has been a revival of the more complex traditions of Chinese **classical music**, particularly nánguǎn. **Contemporary** pop, rock and hip-hop are also important elements of modern Taiwanese identity.

Traditional music

Traditional Chinese music comes in many different styles, but in Taiwan it's usual to divide the whole field into two groups: běiguǎn ("northern music"), a fast-tempo music that commonly accompanies operas and traditional puppet shows, and nánguǎn, which originated in Fujian and has a more delicate and soothing sound, traditionally far more popular in Taiwan. The **Han-Tang Yuefu Music Ensemble** (漢唐樂府; hàntáng yuèfǔ) is a Taiwanese cultural icon, founded in 1983 by famous performer Chen Mei-o to preserve nánguǎn.

In addition, there are several professional Chinese music orchestras in Taiwan: the **Kaohsiung City Chinese Orchestra** (高雄市國樂團; gāoxióngshì guóyuètuán); the **National Chinese Orchestra** (國家國樂團; guójiā guóyuètuán), based at the National Theater in Taipei; and the **Taipei Chinese Orchestra** (臺北市立國樂團; táiběi shìlì guóyuètuán), based at Zhongshan Hall in Taipei.

Contemporary music

Taiwan is home to some of the biggest **Mandopop** (Mandarin Chinese pop music) stars in the world. The undisputed queen of Chinese pop was (and some would say still is), **Teresa Teng** (dèng lìjūn) whose tragic early death in 1995 was mourned throughout Asia. Often compared to Karen Carpenter, she influenced a generation of singers, and dominated pop music in the region throughout the 1970s and 1980s. **Jay Chou** has been the undisputed king of Taiwan and Chinese pop since 2001 (even gracing the cover of *Time* magazine), while Chang Hui-mei, aka **A-Mei**, remains one of Asia's favourite female singers. There's plenty of other stars however, as the island has a seemingly endless production line of singers/models/actresses, epitomized by cutesy **Jolin Tsai**, the "little queen of pop".

Though pop certainly dominates, Taiwan also has a vibrant **rock** scene and a growing **hip-hop** culture. A small but well-attended network of live venues supports an eclectic **indie rock** and **alternative music** scene, with Mayday, 1976, Sodagreen and Tizzy Bac leading players. **Rock festivals** have become an important part of the scene in recent years: the largest are Ho Hai Yan in Fulong, Spring Scream in Kenting (see box, p.279), and the Formoz Festival in Taipei. The **Golden Melody Awards** are Taiwan's version of the Grammies or Brit Awards, held every June.

Dance

Taiwan's **modern dance** groups are world class, noted for their creative fusion of Western and Chinese traditions. **Liu Feng-shueh** is credited with bringing modern

U-THEATRE

Laoquan Mountain, shrouded in lush vegetation south of Taipei, is the home of esoteric drum and performance troupe **U-Theatre** (優人神鼓; yōurén shéngǔ; ☎ 02 2938 8188, ⓦ www .utheatre.org.tw), one of Taiwan's most famous and reclusive artistic groups. Not a conventional theatre troupe, the group is lauded internationally for its traditional **drumming** performances, often combined with powerful movement and dance, as well as traditional gongs and singing. Established in 1988 by Taiwan's most famous actress at the time, **Liu Ruo-yu**, U-Theatre comprises a group of ascetic performers who take their training very seriously. They spend up to two years creating new performances, often with a premiere at their outdoor mountain theatre, where the performers meet each day to practise martial arts, drumming and meditation. A U-Theatre production can be an incredibly powerful, hypnotic experience.

dance to Taiwan in the 1960s, creating the **Neoclassic Dance Company** (新古典舞團; xīngǔdiǎn wǔtuán) in 1976, and still choreographing shows today. The best-known group internationally is **Cloud Gate Dance Theatre** (雲門舞集; yúnmén wǔjí), another Taiwanese cultural treasure. Established in 1973 by **Lin Hwai-min**, who studied in New York under Martha Graham, one of America's most famous dancers, the troupe fuses classical Asian traditions such as t'ai chi with modern dance – the result is hauntingly beautiful. One of the best known of the newer companies is the **Taipei Dance Circle** (光環舞集舞蹈團; guānghuán wǔjí wǔdàotuán), established in 1984 by Liou Shaw-lu (a Cloud Gate founder who died in 2014) and his wife Yang Wan-rung.

Opera

Traditional Chinese opera is thriving in Taiwan. The most famous form is **Beijing Opera** (performed in Mandarin), though **Taiwanese Opera** (performed in Taiwanese) is just as popular. **Hakka Opera**, which is based on traditional tea-farming folk songs and originally developed in China's Jiangxi province, has made a comeback in Taiwan in recent years, while the more obscure **Kun Opera** (from Jiangsu province), best known for the mammoth opera *Peony Pavilion*, and **Beiguan Opera** styles are also performed on the island.

Opera is actually a mix of acrobatics, music, singing, stylized movements and dialogue, still performed on outdoor stages at festivals or in front of temples, as well as in formal indoor theatres. In either case you won't need to understand Chinese to appreciate what's going on, since most operas are visually stunning, elaborately costumed affairs.

Opera basics

The following primarily applies to Beijing Opera, though other styles more or less follow the same principles. Traditionally, operas have four types of lead characters. The shēng (male lead), who can be old, young or a soldier; the dàn (female); the jīng, usually a male character with a painted face; and the chǒu (male clown). The **painted face** of the jīng characters each has a meaning: red symbolizes loyalty; black signifies bravery or determination; white means treacherous or sly; and blue or green signifies a violent temper. **Clothing** is similarly colour-coded: yellow robes are worn by the imperial family, red by high officials, black by the short-tempered, brown by the elderly and green by the virtuous.

Sets are very basic: the same table and chairs are normally used throughout, operas relying on the ability of the actors and a strong imagination. **Props** are also used simply and symbolically (a single oar can represent a boat). Live **music** is an important part of any production, the action complemented by traditional instruments such as the sānxián, a three-stringed lute; the pípá, a four-stringed lute; the dòngxiāo, a flute; and the suǒnà, a trumpet-shaped bamboo horn.

Opera companies

The **Guoguang Opera Company** (國光劇團; guóguāng jùtuán; ☎02 2938 3567, ⓦwww .ncfta.gov.tw/guoguangopera_71.html) is the foremost exponent of Beijing Opera in Taiwan and regularly performs in Taipei, though it often tours smaller villages or suburbs during festivals and holidays. Tainan-based **Ming Hwa Yuan Arts & Cultural Group** (明華園戲劇總團; mínghuáyuán xìjù zǒngtuán; ☎02 2772 9398, ⓦwww.twopera. com) was established in 1929 by opera star Chen Ming-chi, and is now the most respected name in Taiwanese Opera, still run by the Chen family. The **Holo Taiwanese Opera Troupe** (河洛歌仔戲團; héluò gēzǎixìtuán; ☎02 2581 3029) is primarily known in Taiwan for its acclaimed work on television, but it also performs on stage all over the world. The **Rom-shing Hakka Teapicker Opera Troupe** (榮興客家採茶劇團, róngxīng kèjiā cǎichá jùtuán; ☎037 725 099) is one of the best Hakka Opera companies, usually performing outdoors in small venues, festivals and temples across the island.

Film

Taiwan has a strong tradition of **film-making** dating back to the Japanese occupation, but these days the local movie industry knocks out little more than a dozen popular and high-quality art-house films per year; revenues are minuscule (just two percent of the domestic box office) compared to output from nearby Hong Kong, and light years away from the far more popular Hollywood-produced blockbusters. Taiwanese movie stars often double as pop singers, frequently working on both sides of the Taiwan Strait. Their profile beyond the Chinese-speaking world is limited, though respected actress **Sylvia Chang** has appeared in films such as *Red Violin* (1998) and **Shu Qi** appeared in Hollywood action flick *The Transporter* in 2002 and *New York, I Love You* in 2009. Singer **Jay Chou** has also popped up in Hollywood, appearing in *The Green Hornet* (2011) and *Now You See Me 2* (2016). Taiwanese **directors** are generally better known internationally, **Ang Lee** being the most famous.

The **Golden Horse Film Awards**, held annually in November or December, is Taiwan's version of the Oscars, honouring film throughout the Chinese-speaking world, but often dominated by Hong Kong movies and actors.

The New Taiwanese cinema

Between the 1950s and early 1980s, Taiwan's domestic film industry was dominated by romantic melodramas and martial arts epics. In 1982 the movie *In Our Time* broke with tradition by depicting gritty social change in Taiwan over three generations, and is generally regarded as the birth of the **New Wave Movement**. **Hou Hsiao-hsien** and **Edward Yang** (both born in mainland China) are the best known of what is sometimes called the first generation of Taiwanese directors. Hou was one of three directors of the ground-breaking *Sandwich Man* (1983), a dramatization of three short stories written by Huang Chun-ming, examining the disintegration of Taiwanese rural life in the 1950s and 60s; this theme, with particular focus on adolescent male characters, dominated Hou's subsequent movies. His most famous film is *City of Sadness* (1989), which was the first to allude to the 2-28 Incident (see p.394). *The Puppet Master* (1993), which followed the life of Li Tien-lu, a master puppeteer, and *Café Lumière* (2003), a tribute to Japanese film-maker Ozu Yasujiro, were both well received by critics. *Three Times* (2005), which blends three stories set in three different time periods and sees a return to familiar Hou themes, was nominated for the Palme d'Or at Cannes. His latest movie, *The Assassin* (starring Shu Qi; 2015), saw Hou turn to the martial arts genre; it won him "best director" at Cannes and at the Golden Horse Film Awards.

In contrast, Yang tended to focus on female characters, the newly emerging middle class and urban society. He's best known for *Taipei Story* (1985) and especially *Yi Yi* (2000), a three-hour epic depicting a troubled year in the life of a Taipei family that won him the Best Director award at Cannes (Yang died in 2007).

The Second New Wave

The most famous of the "**second generation**" of New Taiwanese cinema directors is undoubtedly **Ang Lee**, Oscar-winning director of *Crouching Tiger, Hidden Dragon* (2000), *Brokeback Mountain* (2005) and *Life of Pi* (2012). In 2007 *Lust, Caution* earned him a second Golden Lion (*Brokeback Mountain* was his first). He's respected locally for his immensely entertaining *Wedding Banquet* (1993), which highlighted the dilemmas facing gay Chinese men, and *Eat Drink Man Woman* (1994) set in contemporary Taipei.

Often considered part of the New Taiwanese film movement, despite being born and raised in Kuching, Malaysia, **Tsai Ming-liang** settled in Taipei in 1977 and has become one of the country's most acclaimed directors. A successful TV film-maker, Tsai made his jump to the big screen in 1992 with *Rebels of the Neon God*, the story of a high-school dropout who becomes involved with organized crime. Tsai's films are highly stylized and thought-provoking, though the lack of dialogue, confusing plots and focus on dysfunctional families, inebriation and delinquency make them hard to watch and strictly art-house material. *Vive l'Amour* (1994) won the Golden Lion, while *Goodbye, Dragon Inn* (2003) and the sexually explicit *Wayward Cloud* (2005) were received less kindly by critics. His Taiwanese-French drama *Stray Dogs* (2013) won the Grand Jury Prize at the 70th Venice International Film Festival.

Chiayi-born **Sylvia Chang** is sometimes regarded as part of this group (though she's also been acting for over thirty years), and is one of Taiwan's few female Chinese directors. Chang's *20, 30, 40* (2004) is an entertaining portrayal of the lives of three women in modern Taipei, while *Murmur of the Hearts* (2015) was a financially successful romantic drama. She is also the star of the cross-cultural comedy *American Fusion* (2005).

The Seventh Graders

The New Wave directors, while critically acclaimed overseas, were gradually seen as elitist and obscure in Taiwan, turning audiences away from even mainstream domestic movies. The hopes of Taiwan's film industry now rest with the island's younger directors. Referred to as the "**seventh-grade generation**" (a reference to the 1980s, the seventh decade after the 1911 Revolution), many were still university students when they started making movies. **Chen Yin-jung** scored a big hit in 2004 with *Formula 17*, a frank and humorous exploration of gay life in Taipei, following up with the less well received *Young Dudes* in 2012. **Leon Dai**'s *Twenty-Something Taipei* (2002) also focused on youth, sex and modern Taipei, with the director going on to sweep the 2009 Golden Horse Awards for his *No Puedo Vivir Sin Ti* ("*Cannot Live Without You*"). He's since been more prolific as an actor in Chinese-language movies.

Since 2010 Taiwanese movies have continued to earn critical, if not financial acclaim: *Monga* (2010), directed and co-written by Doze Niu, depicted gangster life in 1980s Taipei, while *Warriors of the Rainbow: Seediq Bale* (2011), a lavish production dramatizing the Wushe Incident (see p.392), is the most evocative depiction of aboriginal life yet made. **Chao Te-Yin** (aka "Midi Z") is a Myanmar-born Taiwanese film director who has garnered critical acclaim for *Ice Poison* (2014) and *The Road to Mandalay* (2016). Another notable recent success story is Taiwanese American film director **Justin Lin** – born in Taipei – best known for his work on the *The Fast and the Furious* movies (2006–2013) and *Star Trek Beyond* (2016).

Books

Taiwan has a rich literary tradition that dates back over a century, and a dynamic contemporary scene which is a fusion of all the island's multicultural elements. The problem is that very little of this is translated into English, in part a reflection of Taiwan's low profile on the international stage. Seminal figures such as Lai He (regarded as the father of Taiwanese literature), and Hakka pioneer Chung Li-ho, as well as modern writers such as Li Ang (one of Taiwan's top female authors), are rarely translated.

In other areas, apart from a fairly dry ensemble of books analyzing Taiwan's economic success, there's a dearth of material on the island, though you'll find plenty on Chinese culture in general. Expats have started writing guides to fill the gaps, usually published by local houses, and those interested in **Buddhism** will find a voluminous amount of English-language material knocked out by the island's premier monasteries.

FICTION

Chang Ta-chun *Wild Kids*. Two novellas (in one book) from the 1990s popular literature icon, exposing the frustrations of Taiwanese youth and the darker side of Taipei in the 1980s. Chang's unpretentious style, with dashes of black humour, works well in translation.

Chu T'ien-wen *Notes of a Desolate Man*. A thoughtful study of a Taiwanese gay man reflecting on his life and loves as his friend lies dying of AIDS in the 1990s, by turns erotic, morose and humorous. Chu is one of Taiwan's best contemporary female writers.

Hsiao Li-hung *A Thousand Moons on a Thousand Rivers*. A captivating tale of love, betrayal and complex family relationships in a traditional south Taiwan town in the 1970s, from one of Taiwan's pre-eminent female writers.

Huang Chun-ming *The Taste of Apples*. Collection of nine compelling short stories, portraying the poverty and disintegration of traditional Taiwanese rural life in the face of rampant modernization. Penned by the doyen of the Nativist movement in the 1970s.

Indigenous Writers of Taiwan *An Anthology of Stories, Essays and Poems*. The first collection of indigenous literature in English, with contributions from writers such as Topas Tamapima (*The Last Hunter*), Sakinu (*Wind Walker*) and Moaneng (*Five Poems*), providing an enlightening perspective on the state of aboriginal culture in modern Taiwan.

Li Ang *The Butcher's Wife and Other Stories*. This short novel from Taiwan's best-known female writer shocked the island in 1983 with its powerful critique of traditional Chinese society and fearless portrayal of superstition, violence and abuse of women. Her haunting novel of loss, *The Lost Garden* (translated in 2015) is also worth seeking out.

Li Qiao *Wintry Night*. Vivid historical saga, following the lives of the Peng family from the 1890s to the end of World War II, Hakka settlers battling the elements, corrupt officials, aboriginal tribes and the Japanese.

Pai Hsien-yung *Crystal Boys* and *Taipei People*. *Crystal Boys* is still regarded as a ground-breaking classic, a tragic love story and evocative depiction of Taiwan's gay community in the repressive 1960s and 1970s. *Taipei People* is a fascinating collection of short stories, examining life in the post-1949 capital.

Shawna Yang Ryan *Green Island*. The latest novel from the Hawaii-based Taiwanese-American author involved extensive research in Taiwan. The plot follows the fate of a family through the decades of "White Terror" after the February 28 Incident of 1947.

Wang Chen-ho *Rose, Rose I Love You*. One of Taiwan's most outrageous comic novels, this irreverent satire follows the citizens of Hualien as they prepare for a boatload of US soldiers on R&R. The result is hilarious, though Wang's subtle word plays are difficult to appreciate in translation.

Wang Wen-hsing *Family Catastrophe*. The publication of this Modernist classic caused a sensation in 1972, with its subtle but powerful depiction of the unravelling of a traditional Chinese family.

Wu Zhuoliu *Asia's Orphan*. Wu was one of Taiwan's leading literary figures in the 1940s and 1950s; this masterpiece spans the entire period of Japanese occupation, an allegory of colonial rule and Taiwan's disillusion with Chinese nationalism.

HISTORY AND POLITICS

Macabe Keliher *Out of China* and *Small Sea Travel Diaries*. This Taipei-based writer has knocked out a decent translation of Chinese official Yu Yonghe's diary of his trip to Taiwan in 1697, a fascinating account of the island at the time. *Out of China* is an easy-to-read companion volume, enhancing the journal with history, anecdote and useful background.

George Mackay *From Far Formosa*. Part autobiography, part history of the island, Mackay's original work of 1896 has been republished in Taipei. The Canadian missionary's observations are a fascinating insight into 1880s Taiwan, as well as the often chauvinistic attitudes dominant in the West at that time.

Jonathan Manthorpe *Forbidden Nation: A History of Taiwan*. A well-written and comprehensive history of the island.

Denny Roy *Taiwan A Political History*. Roy's crisp history of Taiwan is a good introduction, though its primary focus is political events post-1949.

Jay Taylor *The Generalissimo's Son*: *Chiang Ching-kuo and the Revolutions in China and Taiwan*. Long-overdue study of Chiang Kai-shek's son and successor, one of Taiwan's most complex figures who oversaw its transition from martial law to nascent democracy.

Shih-shan Henry Tsai *Lee Teng-hui and Taiwan's Quest for Identity*. Biography of former President Lee Teng-hui, the primary figure in the island's political transformation over the past two decades.

RELIGION

Mark Caltonhill *Private Prayers and Public Parades*. Accessible introduction to Taiwan's eclectic religious practices, especially focusing on its Taoist and folk traditions and customs. The author is an English long-time resident of Taiwan.

Dharma Master Cheng Yen *Still Thoughts I & II*. These books contain a series of thought-provoking quotations derived from the numerous speeches and talks of Taiwan's senior female Buddhist master, the founder of the Tzu Chi Foundation.

Confucius *The Analects*. Modern translation of this classic collection of Confucius's sayings, compiled by his pupils after his death in 479 BC and still one of the most important texts in Chinese philosophy.

Venerable Master Hsing Yun *Humanistic Buddhism*: *A Blueprint for Life*. The founder of Foguangshan Monastery is one of Taiwan's most prolific Buddhist writers and teachers of Chan Buddhism. This book outlines the principles of Humanistic Buddhism and how it can be applied to daily life.

Lao Zi *Tao Te Ching*. The collection of laconic, esoteric sayings that provides the philosophical basis for Taoism, attributed to the sixth-century-BC Chinese mystic.

Chan Master Sheng Yen *Zen Wisdom* and *Hoofprint of the Ox*. The founder of Dharma Drum Mountain monastery has written numerous books on Chan (or Zen) Buddhism and these two works are the best introductions. *Zen Wisdom* is structured as a series of questions and answers, while *Hoofprint* follows a more traditional essay-type structure.

MISCELLANEOUS

Cathy Erway *The Food of Taiwan: Recipes from the Beautiful Island*. Finally, a decent book on Taiwanese food, from steamed pork buns to oyster noodle soup, with one hundred recipes from Taiwanese-American author Erway.

Menno Goedhart *The Real Taiwan and the Dutch*. Part history, part travel guide and written by the former long-time Dutch envoy to Taiwan, this book provides a readable and fascinating insight into areas of the island rarely visited by foreigners, and especially its aboriginal and Dutch heritage.

Richard Saunders *Taipei Day Trips 1 and 2*. Written by another long-term English expat, these two books are handy for anyone contemplating an extended stay in the Taipei area, especially for those interested in hiking. Usually on sale in local bookshops, along with his comprehensive guide to Yangmingshan.

Yeh Yueh-yu and Darrell Davis *Taiwan Film Directors*: *A Treasure Island*. Insightful study of Taiwan's New Cinema via four of its most famous directors: Hou Hsiao-hsien, Ang Lee, Edward Yang and Tsai Ming-liang.

Language

The official language of Taiwan is the same as China, Mandarin Chinese, commonly referred to as guóyǔ ("national language") on the island and pǔtōnghuà ("common speech") across the Taiwan Strait. Though there are some differences in word use, pronunciation and slang, Chinese spoken on the mainland is indistinguishable from that used in Taiwan. The major divergence comes with written Chinese: Taiwan (like Hong Kong) uses traditional characters, while China follows the simplified system devised in the 1950s.

Mandarin Chinese is a relative newcomer to the island however: before 1945 very few people ever spoke the language in Taiwan. Although everyone learns Mandarin these days, **Taiwanese** (táiyǔ) was once the dominant tongue, and is still widely spoken as a first language. In much of south Taiwan you'll hear nothing else, though even here everyone but the very elderly will be able to understand Mandarin (though they'll try, optimistically, to converse with you in Taiwanese if they can). Taiwanese is a form of **Fujianese** (mǐnnán yǔ), which originated in southern Fujian province in China and is similar to the Hokkien spoken by other Fujianese communities in Southeast Asia. Part of the same Sino-Tibetan family and usually described as a dialect of Chinese on the mainland, Taiwanese is in fact a totally different language, with its own dialects, seven tones, unique vocabulary and distinct philology. In the nineteenth century, missionaries developed a written form of Taiwanese known as péh-ōe-jī, using Roman letters, but otherwise Taiwanese can be written with the same Chinese characters as Mandarin. **Hakka** (kèjiāhuà) is still spoken in Taiwan (see box, p.158), though along with numerous **aboriginal languages** on the island, it faces an uphill struggle for survival. Given Taiwan's history and current economic and cultural ties with the country, it's no surprise many Taiwanese can also speak **Japanese** quite well. The following section focuses exclusively on **Mandarin Chinese**.

Pronunciation and pīnyīn

The main distinguishing characteristic of Chinese languages is that they are **tonal**: each word must be pronounced not only with the right sound, but also the right tone. Mandarin has four tones, and in order to be understood it's vital to get these as accurate as possible. The **pīnyīn system**, a way of writing Chinese using the Roman alphabet, is the best way to learn the correct tones, represented by **accents** above each syllable.

In China, where pīnyīn is taught in schools, the system is widely used, but most Taiwanese have never seen or used pīnyīn. Schools on the island still use zhùyīn or **bopomofo** to teach children pronunciation, a system of symbols that looks much the same as characters. As a result, Chinese characters on street signs, buildings or in restaurants are rarely translated. Where pīnyīn is used, Taiwan's notorious penchant for using a hotchpotch of different systems often adds to the confusion. Mainland China uses hànyǔ pīnyīn, favoured throughout most of the world by Chinese-speakers and students. Since 2008, this system is finally being introduced throughout Taiwan (replacing tōngyòng pīnyīn, created in Taiwan in 1998 and favoured by the former DPP government), though it's still only used extensively in Taipei, Taichung and Hsinchu. These two systems have largely replaced nineteenth-century **Wade Giles** and **MPS2** (another Taiwanese script used in the 1980s), though you might still see vestiges of these in places – the names of Taiwan's major cities retain their basic Wade-Giles forms (for example "Kaohsiung" would be "Gāoxióng" in hànyǔ pīnyīn). The Chinese terms in this section have been given in both characters and hànyǔ pīnyīn, to reflect the predominant global trend. In the main body text the approach has been to use the system most visible in each locale: hànyǔ is now considered the default, in line with government policy.

The tones

First or "High" tone (usually described as flat or level) is represented by a (ˉ) added to the vowel: ā ē ī ō ū ǖ.

Second or rising tone (as when expressing surprise) is represented by an acute accent (ˊ): á é í ó ú ǘ.

Third or "falling-rising" tone is represented by (ˇ): ǎ ě ǐ ǒ ǔ ǚ.

Fourth or falling tone is represented by a grave accent (ˋ): à è ì ò ù ǜ.

The so-called "fifth tone" or **neutral tone** is just represented by a normal vowel without any accent mark. In practice however, you'll need to take some lessons (or at least listen to a native speaker) if you're serious about coming to grips with spoken Chinese.

Useful words and expressions

Note that all the words below are Mandarin Chinese terms, expressed in Chinese characters, hànyǔ pīnyīn and the English equivalent.

BASICS

Hello	你好	nǐ hǎo
Good morning	早!	zǎo!
Thank you	謝謝	xiè xiè
You're welcome	不客氣	búkèqì
Sorry	對不起	duìbúqǐ
No problem	沒關係	méi guānxì
Goodbye	再見	zài jiàn
I	我	wǒ
You	你	nǐ
He	他	tā
She	她	tā
We	我們	wǒmén
You (plural)	你們	nǐmén
They	他們	tāmén
Mr	先生	xiānshēng
Mrs	太太	tàitài
Miss	小姐	xiǎo jiě
Toilet (men)	男廁所	nán cèsuǒ
Toilet (women)	女廁所	nǔ cèsuǒ

USEFUL PHRASES

I want	我要	wǒ yào
I don't want	我不要	wǒ bú yào
Have	有	yǒu
Have not	沒有	méiyǒu
I don't speak Chinese	我不會說中文	wǒ bú huì shuō zhōngwén
Can you speak English?	你會說英語嗎?	nǐ huì shuō yīngyǔ mā?
Please speak slowly	請慢慢說	qǐng màn màn shuō
I understand	我聽得懂	wǒ tīngdedǒng
I don't understand	我聽不懂	wǒ tīngbùdǒng

What does this mean?	這是甚麼意思?	zhè shì shènme yìsī?
What's your name?	你叫什麼名字?	nǐ jiào shénme míngzì?
My name is…	我的名字是	wǒ de míngzì shì…

COUNTRIES

What country are you from?	你是哪國家的人?	nǐ shì nǎ guójiā de rén?
Australia	澳洲	àozhōu
Canada	加拿大	jiānádà
China	中國	zhōngguó
England	英國	yīngguó
Hong Kong	香港	xiānggǎng
Ireland	愛爾蘭	àiěrlán
Japan	日本	rì běn
Macau	澳門	àomén
Malaysia	馬來西亞	mǎlái xīyǎ
New Zealand	紐西蘭	niǔxīlán
Scotland	蘇格蘭	sūgélán
Singapore	新加坡	xīnjiāpō
South Africa	南非	nánfēi
Taiwan	台灣	táiwān
United States	美國	měiguó
Wales	威爾士	wēiěrshì

NUMBERS

Zero	零	líng
One	一	yī
Two	二/兩	èr/liǎng
Three	三	sān
Four	四	sì
Five	五	wǔ
Six	六	liù
Seven	七	qī
Eight	八	bā
Nine	九	jiǔ
Ten	十	shí
Eleven	十一	shíyī
Twelve	十二	shíèr
Twenty	二十	èrshí
Twenty-one	二十一	èrshíyī
One hundred	一百	yībǎi
Two hundred	二百	èrbǎi
One thousand	一千	yīqiān
Ten thousand	一萬	yīwàn
One hundred thousand	十萬	shíwàn
One million	一百萬	yībǎiwàn
One hundred million	一億	yīyì
One billion	十億	shíyì

TIME

Now	現在	xiànzài
Today	今天	jīntiān
Morning	早上	zǎoshàng
Afternoon	下午	xiàwǔ
Evening	晚上	wǎnshàng

Tomorrow	明天	míngtiān
Yesterday	昨天	zuótiān
Week/month/year	星期/月/年	xīngqī/yuè/nián
Monday	星期一	xīngqī yī
Tuesday	星期二	xīngqī èr
Wednesday	星期三	xīngqī sān
Thursday	星期四	xīngqī sì
Friday	星期五	xīngqī wǔ
Saturday	星期六	xīngqī liù
Sunday	星期天	xīngqī tiān
What's the time?	幾點了?	jǐ diǎn le?
6 o'clock	六點	liù diǎn
6.20	六點二十	liù diǎn èrshí
6.30	六點半	liù diǎn bàn

GETTING AROUND

Map	地圖	dìtú
I want to go to...	我要去...	wǒ yào qù...
When does it leave?	幾點開車?	jǐ diǎn kāi chē?
When does it arrive?	幾點到?	jǐ diǎn dào?
How long does the journey take?	旅途需要多久?	lǚ tú xū yào duō jiǔ?
Airport	飛機場	fēijīchǎng
Dock/pier	碼頭	mǎtóu
Taxi	計程車	jì chéng chē

DIRECTIONS

Where is...?	...在那裡?	...zài nǎ lǐ?
Go straight on	直走	zhí zǒu
Turn right	轉右	zhuǎn yòu
Turn left	轉左	zhuǎn zuǒ
North	北	běi
South	南	nán
East	東	dōng
West	西	xī
Road	路	lù
Street	街	jiē
Section	段	dùan
Number 12	十二號	shí èr hào
Lane	巷	xiàng
Alley	弄	nòng

BY TRAIN

Train	火車	huǒchē
Train station	火車站	huǒchē zhàn
Left luggage office	寄存處	jìcúnchù
Ticket office	售票處	shòupiàochù
Ticket	票	piào
Taiwan High-Speed Rail	台灣高速鐵路	táiwān gāosù tiělù
Platform	站台	zhàntái
Underground/subway	捷運	jiéyùn

BY BUS

| Bus | 公車 | gōngchē |
| Bus station | 公車站 | gōngchē zhàn |

Regional bus station	客運站	kèyùn zhàn
When is the next bus?	下一班車幾點開?	xià yí bān chē jǐ diǎn kāi?
Does this bus go to…?	這輛車到…嗎?	zhè liàng chē dào…ma?
Please tell me where to get off	請告訴我在哪裡下車	qǐng gàosù wǒ zài nǎlǐ xià chē

BY CAR/SCOOTER

Car	汽車	qìchē
Bicycle	腳踏車	jiǎotàchē
Motor scooter	摩托車	mótuōchē
I want to rent…	我想租	wǒ xiǎngzū
How much is it per hour/day?	一小時/一天多少錢?	yí xiǎo shí/yí tiān, duō shǎo qián?

PLACES

Beach	海濱	hǎibīn
Bookshop	書店	shūdiàn
Buddhist temple	寺	sì
Cave	洞	dòng
Church	教堂	jiāotáng
City	市	shì
Farm	農場	nóngchǎng
Harbour/port	港	gǎng
Hot spring	溫泉	wēnquán
Island	島	dǎo
Lake	湖	hú
Laundry	洗衣店	xǐyīdiàn
Library	圖書館	túshūguǎn
Lighthouse	燈塔	dēngtǎ
Market	市場	shìchǎng
Mountain	山	shān
Museum	博物館	bówùguǎn
Park	公園	gōngyuán
River	河	hé
Stadium	體育場	tǐyùchǎng
Temple	廟	miào
Waterfall	瀑布	pùbù

ACCOMMODATION

Hotel	飯店/旅館	fàndiàn/ lǚguǎn
Homestay	民宿	mínsù
How much for a room?	一晚多少?	yī wǎn duō shǎo?
Can I have a look at the room?	能不能看一下?	néng bù néng kàn yí xià?
Single room	單人房	dānrénfáng
Twin room	雙人房	shuāngrénfáng
Passport	護照	hùzhào
Key	鑰匙	yàochí

SHOPPING AND MONEY

How much is it?	多少錢?	duōshǎo qián?
It's too expensive	太貴了	tài guì le
Do you accept credit cards?	可不可以用信用卡?	kěbúkěyǐ yòngxìnyòngkǎ
NT$1	一塊	yí kuài
US$1	一塊美金	yí kuài měijīn
£1	一個英磅	yí gè yīngbàng

Change money	換錢	huàn qián
Chinatrust Commercial Bank	中國信託銀行	zhōngguó xìntuō yín háng
Bank	銀行	yínháng
ATM	提款機	tíkuǎnjī

COMMUNICATIONS

Post office	郵局	yóujú
Envelope	信封	xìnfēng
Stamp	郵票	yóupiào
Airmail	航空信	hángkōng xìn
Telephone	電話	diànhuà
Reverse charges/collect call	對方付錢電話	duìfāngfùqián diànhuà
Fax	傳真	chuánzhēn
Telephone card	電話卡	diànhuàkǎ
Internet café	網吧	wǎngbā

HEALTH

Hospital	醫院	yīyuàn
Pharmacy	藥店	yàodiàn
Medicine	藥	yào
Chinese Medicine	中藥	zhōng yào
Diarrhoea	腹瀉	fùxiè
Vomit	嘔吐	ǒutù
Fever	發燒	fāshāo
I'm ill	我生病了	wǒ shēngbìng le
I've got flu	我感冒了	wǒ gǎnmào le
I'm (not) allergic to…	我(不)對過敏…	wǒ (bù) duì… guòmǐn
Antibiotics	抗生素	kàngshēngsù
Condom	避孕套	bìyùntào
Mosquito coil	蚊香	wénxiāng

FOOD AND DRINK

GENERAL

Beerhouse	啤酒屋	píjiǔ wū
Bill/cheque	買單	mǎidān
Chopsticks	筷子	kuàizi
Ice	冰	bīng
Knife and fork	刀叉	dāochā
Lunchbox	便當	biàndàng
Market	市場	shìchǎng
Menu	菜單	càidān
Night market	夜市	yèshì
Restaurant	餐廳	cāntīng
Snacks ("little eats")	小吃	xiǎo chī
Spoon	勺子	sháozi
Supermarket	超級市場	chāojí shìchǎng
Taiwan buffet/self-service	自助餐	zìzhù cān**caféteria**
Take-away	帶走	dàizǒu
Teahouse	茶館	cháguǎn
How much is that?	多少錢?	duōshǎo qián?
I'm a vegetarian	我是吃素的	wǒ shì chīsù de
I don't eat (meat)	我不吃 (肉)	wǒ bù chī (ròu)
I would like	我想要	wǒ xiǎng yào
Not spicy	不辣	bùlà

DRINKS

Aiyu jelly drink	愛玉凍飲	àiyù dòngyǐn
Beer	啤酒	píjiǔ
Coffee	咖啡	kāfēi
Fruit juice	果汁	guǒzhī
Gaoliang	高粱酒	gāoliáng jiǔ
Milk	牛奶	niúnǎi
Papaya milk	木瓜牛奶	mùguā niúnǎi
Red wine	紅酒	hóng jiǔ
Rice wine	米酒	mǐjiǔ
Shaohsing wine	紹興酒	shàoxīng jiǔ
Starfruit juice	楊桃汁	yángtáozhī
Sugar cane juice	甘蔗汁	gānzhèzhī
Taiwan Beer	台灣啤酒	táiwān píjiǔ
Tea	茶	chá
Baozhong tea	包種茶	bāozhǒng chá
Black tea	紅茶	hóng chá
Bubble tea	泡沫紅茶	pàomò hóng chá
Dongding oolong	凍頂烏龍	dòngdǐng wūlóng
Fruit tea	水果茶	shuǐguǒ chá
Green tea	綠茶	lǜ chá
Iron Guanyin tea	鐵觀音茶	tiěguānyīn chá
Jasmine tea	茉莉花茶	mòlìhuā chá
Oolong tea	烏龍茶	wūlóng chá
Oriental Beauty tea	東方美人茶	dōngfāng měirén chá
Pearl milk tea	珍珠奶茶	zhēnzhū nǎichá
White wine	白酒	bái jiǔ
Wine	酒	jiǔ
Yoghurt	酸奶	suānnǎi

STAPLE FOODS, MEAT AND VEGETABLES

Beef	牛肉	niúròu
Bread	麵包	miànbāo
Chicken	雞	jī
Chilli	辣椒	làjiāo
Crab	螃蟹	pángxiè
Duck	鴨子	yāzi
Eel	鰻魚	mán yú
Egg	雞蛋	jīdàn
Fish	魚	yú
Garlic	蒜	suàn
Ginger	薑	jiāng
Green bean	綠豆	lǜ dòu
Lamb	羊肉	yángròu
MSG	味精	wèijīng
Mushroom	香菇	xiānggū
Noodles	麵	miàn
Oyster	蠔	háo
Pork	豬肉	zhūròu
Prawn/shrimp	蝦	xiā
Red bean	紅豆	hóngdòu
Rice (uncooked)	米	mǐ
Rice (steamed)	白飯	bāifàn

Rice (fried)	炒飯	chǎofàn
Salt	鹽	yán
Soup	湯	tāng
Soy sauce	醬油	jiàngyóu
Squid	魷魚	yóuyú
Sugar	糖	táng
Tofu	豆腐	dòufǔ
Vegetables	菜	cài

FRUIT

Fruit	水果	shuǐguǒ
Apple	蘋果	pīngguǒ
Banana	香蕉	xiāngjiāo
Cherry	櫻桃	yīngtáo
Coconut	椰子	yēzi
Durian	榴蓮	liúlián
Grape	葡萄	pútáo
Guava	芭樂	bālè
Honeydew melon	哈密瓜	hāmìguā
Kiwi fruit	奇異果	qíyìguǒ
Longan	龍眼	lóngyǎn
Lychee	荔枝	lìzhī
Mango	芒果	mángguǒ
Orange (tangerine)	橘子	júzi
Papaya	木瓜	mùguā
Peach	桃子	táozi
Pear	梨子	lízi
Persimmon	柿子	shìzi
Pineapple	鳳梨	fènglí
Plum	李子	lǐzi
Pomelo	柚子	yòuzi
Watermelon	西瓜	xīguā

BREAKFAST

Clay oven roll	燒餅	shāobǐng
Congee	稀飯	xīfàn
Dough fritter	油條	yóutiáo
Egg pancake	蛋餅	dànbǐng
Soybean milk	豆漿	dòujiāng
Spring onion pancake	蔥油餅	cōngyóubǐng
Steamed bread	饅頭	mántóu
Steamed bun	包子	bāozi

EVERYDAY DISHES/SNACKS

Baked sweet potatoes	烤蕃薯	kǎo fānshǔ
Beef noodles	牛肉麵	niúròu miàn
Boiled dumplings	水餃	shuǐjiǎo
Braised pork rice	滷肉飯	lǔròufàn
Fish balls	魚丸	yúwán
Fried dumplings	鍋貼	guōtiē
Fuzhou beef pepper pies	福州牛肉胡椒餅	fúzhōu niúròu hújiāo bǐng
Hot and sour soup	酸辣湯	suānlàtāng
Knife-cut noodles	刀削麵	dāoxiāo miàn

Lu wei	蘆薈	lú huì
Oyster omelette	蚵仔煎	é a jiān
Rice dumplings	粽子	zòngzi
Rice noodles	米粉	mǐfěn
Sanbei	三杯	sānbēi
Sesame paste noodles	麻醬麵	májiàng miàn
Shaved ice (dessert)	刨冰 (礤冰)	bàobīng (tsuàbīng in Taiwanese)
Soybean pudding	豆花	dòuhuā
Spring roll	潤餅	rùnbǐng
Steamed dumplings	小籠包	xiǎolóng bāo
Steamed meat buns	肉包子	ròubāozi
Steamed vegetable buns	素菜包子	sùcài bāozi
Stinky tofu	臭豆腐	chòu dòufǔ
Tea eggs	茶葉蛋	cháyè dàn

LOCAL SPECIALITIES

Brown-sugar cake (Penghu)	黑糖糕	hēitánggāo
Coffin bread (Tainan)	棺材板	guāncáibǎn
Danzi noodles (Tainan)	擔仔麵	dān zǐ miàn
Deep-fried meat cakes	竹塹餅	zhúqiàn bǐng(Hsinchu)
Dumplings in soup (Hualien)	扁食	biǎnshí
Green bean cakes (Keelung)	綠豆沙餅	lùdòushā bǐng
"Little pastry wrapped in big pastry" (Taipei)	大餅包小餅	dà bǐng bāo xiǎo bǐng
Mashu (Hualien)	麻薯	máshǔ
Meatballs (Changhua/Hsinchu)	貢丸	gòngwán
Milkfish (south Taiwan)	虱目魚	shīmù yú
Ox-tongue cake (Lugang)	牛舌餅	niúshé bǐng
Phoenix-eye cakes (Lugang)	鳳眼糕	fèngyǎngāo
Rice dumplings (Shihmen)	肉粽	ròuzòng
Rice powder tea (Lugang)	麵茶	miàn chá
Shrimp monkeys (Lugang)	蝦猴	xiāhóu
Shrimp rolls (Tainan)	蝦捲	xiājuǎn
Square cookies (Chiayi)	方塊酥	fāngkuàisū
Suncakes (Taichung)	太陽餅	tàiyáng bǐng
Taro balls (Jiufen)	芋丸	yùwán
Turkey rice (Chiayi)	火雞肉飯	huǒjīròu fàn
Wah gwei (Tainan)	碗粿	wah gwei (Taiwanese)

HAKKA SPECIALITIES

Bamboo shoots	竹筍	zhúsǔn
Ban tiao	板條	bǎntiáo
Braised stuffed tofu	釀豆腐	niàng dóufù
Fried pork intestines with ginger	生薑炒豬腸	shēngjiāng chǎozhūcháng
Hakka mashu	客家蔴薯	kèjiā máshǔ
Lei cha (cereal tea)	擂茶	léichá
Wild lotus	蓮	lián

ABORIGINAL SPECIALITIES

Bamboo rice	竹筒飯	zhútǒngfàn
Betel nut chicken	檳榔雞	bīnlángjī
Millet wine	小米酒	xiǎo mǐjiǔ
Mountain pig (boar)	山豬	shānzhū

REGIONAL CHINESE CUISINE

Beijing duck	北京烤鴨	běijīng kǎoyā
Buddha jumps over the wall (Fujianese)	佛跳牆	fótiàoqiáng
Chicken with peanuts (Sichuan)	宮保雞丁	gōngbǎo jīdīng
Dim sum (Cantonese)	點心	diǎnxīn
Drunken chicken (Shanghai)	醉雞	zuìjī
Hotpot (Sichuan)	火鍋	huóguō
Mapo doufu (Shanghai)	麻婆豆腐	mápó dòufù
Songren yumi (Shanghai)	鬆軟玉米	sōngrén yùmǐ
Yellow croaker (Shanghai)	黃魚	huángyú

JAPANESE CUISINE

Japanese curry rice	日本咖哩飯	rìběn kālǐfàn
Ramen	拉麵	lāmiàn
Sashimi	生魚片	shēngyúpiàn
Shabu shabu	涮涮鍋	shuànshuàn guō
Sushi	壽司	shòusī
Teppanyaki	鐵板燒	tiěbǎnshāo

Glossary

Aborigines 原住民 (yuánzhùmín) Common English name for Taiwan's indigenous population.

Amitofu 阿彌陀佛 (āmítuófó) Greeting used by Buddhist monks, a reference to Buddha.

ARC Alien Resident Certificate.

Arhat Buddhist saint.

Austronesian Cultural and linguistic family that stretches across the Asia-Pacific region, and includes Taiwan's indigenous population.

Betel nut Seed of the betel palm, also known as areca nut, and used extensively in Taiwan as a stimulant, chewed but not swallowed.

Betel nut beauty 檳榔西施 (bīnláng xīshī) Used to describe the scantily dressed young women who sell betel nut from glass booths along roadsides island-wide. Xīshī was a legendary beauty in ancient China.

Black Gold Term used to describe the KMT's links with local mafia and endemic corruption during the martial law period.

Bodhisattva Buddhist who has attained enlightenment, but who has chosen not to leave the cycle of birth and death (samsara) until all other beings are enlightened. Worshipped as a god or goddess.

Camphor Tree containing camphor crystals that produce aromatic oil. Used for its scent, as an embalming fluid and in medicines, especially in the nineteenth century.

Daizi 袋子 (dàizi) Bag. Supermarkets and convenience stores will ask if you want to buy one (you don't get them for free in environment-friendly Taiwan).

Dalu 大陸 (dàlù) Common term for mainland China, formally known as zhōngguó.

Democratic Progressive Party (DPP) 民主進步黨 (mínzhǔ jìnbù dǎng) Taiwan's first opposition party when it was established in 1986, winning the presidency under Chen Shui-bian in 2000 and 2004 (see p.396) and again under Tsai Ing-wen in 2016 (see p.398).

Executive Yuan The prime minister's cabinet.

Fo 佛 (fó) Buddha.

Formosa Name given to Taiwan by Portuguese sailors in the sixteenth century, and used in the West to describe the island until the 1950s.

Fujian Southeastern province in China, ancestral home of seventy percent of Taiwan's population.

Fuxing 復興 (fùxīng) "Revival". Common street name.

Hakka 客家人 (kèjiā ren) Chinese ethnic group and language.

Han Chinese Used to describe all the Chinese ethnic groups (including Taiwanese, Hakka and mainlanders), as distinct from Taiwan's Austronesian indigenous population.

Hanyu Pinyin 漢語拼音 (hànyǔ pīnyīn) System of transliterating Chinese script into roman characters favoured by mainland China and Taiwan's KMT.

Heping 和平 (hépíng) "Peace". Common street name.

Hoklo See under "Taiwanese".

Homestay 民宿 (mínsù) Private hotel, usually supplying bed and breakfast and often located in a family home.

Jianguo 建國 (jiànguó). "National founding" or "to found a nation". Common street name.

KTV Karaoke TV. Usually refers to lavish karaoke centres with private rooms, drinks and food.

Kuomintang (KMT) 國民黨 (guómíndǎng) Chinese Nationalist Party, established in 1912 in China, and led by Chiang Kai-shek from the 1920s. Defeated by Mao Zedong's Communist Party in China's civil war, and based in Taiwan from 1949 where it held power until 2000, and from 2008 to 2016 (see p.398).

Legislative Yuan Taiwan's parliament.

Mainlanders 外省人 (wàishěngrén) Term used to describe the Chinese who fled to Taiwan from the mainland in the wake of the Communist victory in 1949. Resented by younger generations who feel the term suggests they are less Taiwanese.

Mandarin Chinese English name for the official language of China and Taiwan, where it's called pǔtōnghuà ("common speech") and guóyǔ ("national language") respectively. Originally based on the Beijing dialect (spoken by "mandarins", or imperial government officials).

Mandopop Slang for Mandarin Chinese pop music. Cantopop refers to music from Hong Kong (Cantonese language).

Meiguoren 美國人 (měiguórén) American, but often applied to all foreigners in Taiwan.

Ming dynasty Imperial family which overthrew the Mongolian Yuan dynasty and ruled China from 1368 to 1644, when China was seized by the Manchurian Qing dynasty.

Minquan 民權 (mínquán) Second of Sun Yat-sen's "Three Principles of the People", meaning "people power" or democracy. Common street name.

Minsheng 民生 (mínshēng) Third of Sun Yat-sen's "Three Principles of the People", meaning "the people's welfare" or "government for the people", and equated with socialism in China. Common street name.

Minzu 民族 (mínzú) First of Sun Yat-sen's "Three Principles of the People", loosely translated as "nationalism", or freedom from imperial domination. Common street name.

Oolong 烏龍 (wūlóng) Type of semi-fermented tea, as opposed to black tea (fully fermented) and green tea (unfermented).

Pingpu 平埔 (píngpǔ) Umbrella term used to describe the indigenous peoples who traditionally lived on the plains rather than the mountains.

PRC 中華人民共和國 (zhōnghuá rénmín gònghéguó) People's Republic of China. Official name for mainland China.

Qing dynasty Last imperial family to rule China (1644–1911), a Manchurian dynasty that overthrew the Ming and was in turn replaced by Sun Yat-sen's Nationalist Party.

Renai 仁愛 (rénài) "Beneficence". Common street name.

Republic of China (ROC) 中華民國 (zhōnghuá mínguó). Taiwan's official name.

Sakyamuni Name given to the historical Buddha.

Shophouse Chinese-style house, long and narrow, with a store in the front and living quarters at the back.

Stele Freestanding stone tablet carved with Chinese characters.

Sutra Sacred Buddhist text.

Taiwanese Commonly used to describe the ethnically Fujianese Chinese in Taiwan, and the language they speak. The term "Hoklo" is preferred officially, as technically all citizens on the island are Taiwanese.

Takasago Former Japanese colonial name for Taiwan, meaning "the country of high mountains".

Tongyong Pinyin 通用拼音 (tōngyòng pīnyīn) System of transliterating Chinese script into roman characters favoured by Taiwan's former DPP government, devised by a Taiwanese professor in 1998.

Wade Giles Antiquated system of transliterating Chinese script into roman characters, formerly used in Taiwan and still the preferred method of writing names for many of its citizens.

Waiguoren 外國人 (wàiguórén) Foreigner (literally "someone outside their own country"). Foreigners are also sometimes called laowai (老外; lǎowài), literally "old foreigner".

Xinsheng 新生 (xīnshēng) "New life" or "new born". Common street name.

Xinyi 信義 (xìnyì) "Honesty". Common street name.

Zhongshan 中山 (zhōngshān) Chinese name for Sun Yat-sen. Common street name.

Zhongxiao 忠孝 (zhōngxiào) "Loyalty and filial piety". Common street name.

Zhongzheng 中正 (zhōngzhèng) Chinese name for Chiang Kai-shek. Common street name.

Small print and index

HELP US UPDATE

We've gone to a lot of effort to ensure that the fourth edition of **The Rough Guide to Taiwan** is accurate and up-to-date. However, things change – places get "discovered", opening hours are notoriously fickle, restaurants and rooms raise prices or lower standards. If you feel we've got it wrong or left something out, we'd like to know, and if you can remember the address, the price, the hours, the phone number, so much the better.

Please send your comments with the subject line "**Rough Guide Taiwan Update**" to mail@roughguides.com. We'll credit all contributions and send a copy of the next edition (or any other Rough Guide if you prefer) for the very best emails.

A ROUGH GUIDE TO ROUGH GUIDES

Published in 1982, the first Rough Guide – to Greece – was a student scheme that became a publishing phenomenon. Mark Ellingham, a recent graduate in English from Bristol University, had been travelling in Greece the previous summer and couldn't find the right guidebook. With a small group of friends he wrote his own guide, combining a contemporary, journalistic style with a thoroughly practical approach to travellers' needs.

The immediate success of the book spawned a series that rapidly covered dozens of destinations. And, in addition to impecunious backpackers, Rough Guides soon acquired a much broader readership that relished the guides' wit and inquisitiveness as much as their enthusiastic, critical approach and value-for-money ethos. These days, Rough Guides include recommendations from budget to luxury and cover more than 120 destinations around the globe, from Amsterdam to Zanzibar, all regularly updated by our team of roaming writers.

Browse all our latest guides, read inspirational features and book your trip at **roughguides.com**.

Rough Guide credits

Editor: Helen Abramson
Layout: Pradeep Thapliyal
Cartography: Carte and Katie Bennett

Picture editor: Aude Vauconsant
Managing editors: Andy Turner and Rachel Lawrence
Cover photo research: Sarah Stewart-Richardson

Publishing information

This fourth edition published July 2018 by
Rough Guides Ltd

Distribution
UK, Ireland and Europe
Apa Publications (UK) Ltd; sales@roughguides.com
United States and Canada
Ingram Publisher Services; ips@ingramcontent.com
Australia and New Zealand
Woodslane; info@woodslane.com.au
Southeast Asia
Apa Publications (SN) Pte; sales@roughguides.com
Worldwide
Apa Publications (UK) Ltd; sales@roughguides.com
Special sales, content licensing and co-publishing
Rough Guides can be purchased in bulk quantities
at discounted prices. We can create special editions,
personalized jackets and corporate imprints tailored to
your needs. sales@roughguides.com
roughguides.com
Printed in Poland

440pp includes index
A catalogue record for this book is available from the
British Library
ISBN: 78-0-24130-882-0
The publishers and authors have done their best to
ensure the accuracy and currency of all the information in
The Rough Guide to Taiwan, however, they can accept
no responsibility for any loss, injury, or inconvenience
sustained by any traveller as a result of information or
advice contained in the guide.

Readers' updates

Thanks to all the readers who have taken the time to write in with comments and suggestions (and apologies if we've
inadvertently omitted or misspelt anyone's name):

Alain Bracchi, Neil Silver and Kaihsu Tai.

Photo credits

All photos © Rough Guides, except the following:
(Key: t-top; c-centre; b-bottom; l-left; r-right)

1 Getty Images
2 Getty Images
4 Shutterstock
7 iStock (t); Getty Images (b)
8 Shutterstock
9 Alamy
10 Shutterstock
11 Shutterstock (t & c)
12 Shutterstock
13 iStock (t); Alamy (c)
14 iStock (tl); Getty Images (tr); Shutterstock (c)
15 Shutterstock (t); Getty Images (c); iStock (b)
16 iStock (t); Shutterstock (cl); Getty Images (cr & b)
17 Getty (t); iStock (c); Getty Images (b)
18 Shutterstock (tl); Robert Harding (tr); Alamy (b)
19 Shutterstock (t & c); iStock (b)
20 iStock
22 iStock
52/53 Shutterstock
55 iStock
81 iStock (t); SuperStock(b)

111 Shutterstock (t)
120/121 Shutterstock
123 Shutterstock
147 iStock (b)
172/173 Shutterstock
175 Getty Images
189 iStock (t)
211 Getty Images (t)
230/231 Shutterstock
243 Getty Images (t); Shutterstock (b)
265 Getty Images (t & b)
286/287 Getty Images
289 Robert Harding
307 Shutterstock (t & b)
338/339 Getty Images
341 Shutterstock
365 Shutterstock (b)

Cover: *Taxi on street with chinese characters, Taipei* LOOK
Die Bildagentur der Fotografen GmbH / Alamy Stock Photo

ABOUT THE AUTHORS

Thomas Bird Being raised in the rain-soaked suburbs of South Wales was reason enough to get on one's bike and see what the world had in store. Armed with a master's degree in Chinese Studies and a cycling proficiency certificate, Thomas Bird did just that. He has since been wandering so long he can no longer remember how long, though thankfully his vivid memories of his recent Taiwan sojourn remain intact. You can follow his journey at www.thomasbird.info.

Simon Foster was born in London and grew up in rural Yorkshire. Family trips first kindled his wanderlust, and after graduating in geography from University College London, he set off to seek what he had been studying. SImon started work as an adventure-tour leader in the Middle East in 1997, and was then posted to India and China. Lengthy emails home evolved into travel writing, and since 1999 he has contributed to a variety of international guidebooks and magazines, and completed his first solo work in 2008. Simon and his wife moved to Taiwan in 2003, founded a travel company, Bamboo Trails (bambootrails.com) in 2009, and now lead and operate adventure tours all over Asia. Time not on tour is divided between their home on Taiwan's wild Pacific east coast, and exploring more of the island with their two daughters and dog.

Stephen Keeling spent seven years as a financial journalist and editor in Hong Kong, Singapore and Shanghai before moving to Taipei, where he lived for three years and co-authored the first Rough Guide to Taiwan. Since then he has worked on numerous books for Rough Guides, including the Philippines, USA, Colombia, Brazil, Mexico and Canada. Stephen lives in New York City.

Martin Zatko has been in a near constant state of motion since 2002. In his more productive periods, he has written or contributed to over thirty Rough Guides, including those to Korea, China, Japan, Vietnam, Myanmar, Turkey, Morocco, Fiji and Greece. It's East Asia where he feels most at home, with Taiwan providing a particularly perfect balance of Asian calm and chaos.

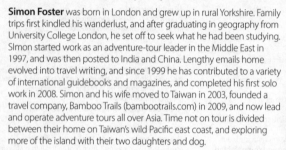

Acknowledgements

Thomas Bird The good people of Taiwan were charming and helpful during my travels, and it is to them I dedicate my chapter of the book. I would like to raise a glass of *pijiu* to the following fine souls: Harvey Thomlinson, Bruce Humes, Mike Bossick, David Sivell, Sarah Griffiths, James and Claudia Loughran, Gareth Phillips, Jon Heeter and The Beijing Dead, Yan Qing Qing, Yu Miao, Wu Tiao Ren, Li Zhengde, Chen Jin, the artists of Songzhuang, Post Magazine, the people at Old Heaven Books, the family Wu and the family Bird.

Simon Foster Thanks to: Bradley Goldhorn and Emily Milanak for their valued input on a host of locations around the country. Mandy Rose Chung for her recommendations on the East Coast and Matsu, and also for her assistance with the Chinese translations. Mark Roche for his expertise on high-mountain areas and permit regulations. Tot, Molly and Sasha for spending time on the road exploring the island with me. My mum, Christine,

as always, for poring through the text, questioning my grammar, and spotting little mistakes I would otherwise have missed. Fellow author Stephen Keeling and all of the staff at Rough Guides for their patience and painstaking attention to detail. The Taiwan Tourist Bureau and the super helpful staff at visitor centres across the island. The people of Taiwan for all of their help, support and smiles.

Martin Zatko would like to thank various entities, both human and non-human, for their assistance during his time in Taiwan. Firstly, to *xiaolongbao* (fried dough-sticks and soybean milk) for their very existence. Secondly, to various 7-Elevens for providing less-refined sustenance in times of need (the times in question often being between 1am and 4am). And finally, to certain human beings, including Andy Turner for commissioning the project, Helen Abramson for her typically fine editing, and Yu Shan Lin for the company in Taipei and Beitou.

Index

Maps are marked in grey

Map symbols

The symbols below are used on maps throughout the book

---	Chapter boundary	👥	Toilet	🏯	Pagoda	▲	Mountain peak
	Motorway	P	Parking	☪	Mosque		Mountain range
	Main road	@	Internet access		Chinese temple		Rocks
	Minor road	ⓘ	Visitor center		Buddhist temple	☾	Sand dune
	Pedestrian road	✚	Hospital	🏛	Monument		Cave
---	Path	✉	Post office		Viewpoint		Mountain lodge
	Steps		Petrol station	☀	Lighthouse		Fort
	Wall		Spring		Tower		Banyan tree
	Ferry	✂	Battlefield	☖	Campsite		Building
	Railway	◆	Point of interest		Picnic area		Church
	High speed railway	∩	Arch		Distillery		Stadium
•	Cable car	🐘	Zoo		Observatory		Market
✈	International Airport	⊠	Gate		Diving		Beach
✕	Domestic Airport	⋮	Ruin		Surf area		Park
★	Bus stop	☉	Statue		Waterfall	✝	Christian cemetery
Ⓜ	Metro station	⊓	Shrine	♀	Museum		

Listings key

- ■ Accommodation
- ● Eating
- ■ Drinking/nightlife
- ● Shopping